Übersicht der Einheitssätze der Reichsbahntarife.

Drucksache Nr. 2 (1926).

Der Reichsverkehrsminister.
E_I 12 Nr. 8134

Berlin, den 10. Dezember 1926.

Dem Reichseisenbahnrat lasse ich hierunter eine Übersicht der den deutschen Reichsbahntarifen zugrundeliegenden Einheitssätze der Beförderungsgebühren für Personen und Güter zur gefälligen Kenntnis zugehen.

Dr. Krohne.

An
den Reichseisenbahnrat.

A. Personen- und Gepäcktarif

(einschließlich Verkehrssteuer).

Ia. Fahrpreise für Personenzüge und zuschlagfreie Eilzüge.

1. Klasse	10,8 Pf.	für 1 Personenkilometer.
2. "	7,5 "	
3. "	5,0 "	
4. "	3,3 "	

Ib. Schnellzugzuschläge.

Zone I (für 1 bis 75 km): in 1. Klasse 2,00 *RM*; in 2. Klasse 1,00 *RM*; in 3. Klasse 0,50 *RM*
" II (" 76 " 150 "): " 1. " 4,00 " ; " 2. " 2,00 " ; " 3. " 1,00 "
" III (über 150 "): " 1. " 6,00 " ; " 2. " 3,00 " ; " 3. " 1.50 "

Bei der Benutzung von F-Dzügen werden die doppelten Schnellzugszuschläge erhoben.

II. Hunde.

Für die Beförderung von Hunden wird der halbe Preis 3. Klasse für Eil- und Personenzüge erhoben.

III. Gepäck.

Die Gepäckfracht wird nach dem auf volle 10 kg aufgerundeten Gewicht und der nachstehenden Preistafel berechnet. Keine weitere Abrundung. Mindestfracht 0,20 *RM* Mindestgewicht 10 kg.

km	Gepäckfracht für 10 kg *RM*	km	Gepäckfracht für 10 kg *RM*	km	Gepäckfracht für 10 kg *RM*
1—25	0,20	247—275	1,20	606— 663	2,20
26—48	0,30	276—305	1,30	664— 720	2,30
49—69	0,40	306—334	1,40	721— 799	2,40
70—92	0,50	335—368	1,50	800— 930	2,50
93—117	0,60	369—402	1,60	931—1152	2,60
118—140	0,70	403—436	1,70	1153—1347	2,70
141—166	0,80	437—475	1,80	1348—1569	2,80
167—192	0,90	476—516	1,90	1570—1750	2.90
193—217	1,00	517—557	2,00		
218—246	1,10	558—605	2,10		

IV. Expreßgut.

Die Expreßgutfracht wird nach dem auf volle 10 kg (bei Sendungen bis zu 5 kg auf volle 5 kg) aufgerundeten Gewicht und der nachstehenden Preistafel berechnet.

Die Fracht wird auf volle 0,10 RM in der Weise abgerundet, daß Beträge unter 5 Pf. gar nicht, Beträge von 5 Pf. ab für 0,10 RM gerechnet werden.

Mindestgewicht 5 kg. **Mindestfracht 0,40 RM**

km	Expreßgutfracht für 10 kg RM	km	Expreßgutfracht für 10 kg RM	km	Expreßgutfracht für 10 kg RM
1—16	0,2	236—257	1,4	575—612	2,6
17—34	0,3	258—279	1,5	613—656	2,7
35—54	0,4	280—305	1,6	657—710	2,8
55—72	0,5	306—330	1,7	711—769	2,9
73—89	0,6	331—355	1,8	770—842	3,0
90—108	0,7	356—381	1,9	843—958	3,1
109—130	0,8	382—412	2,0	959—1152	3,2
131—150	0,9	413—441	2,1	1153—1319	3,3
151—169	1,0	442—470	2,2	1320—1486	3,4
170—189	1,1	471—499	2,3	1487—1652	3,5
190—213	1,2	500—540	2,4	1653—1750	3,6
214—235	1,3	541—574	2,5		

V. Leichen.

Für die Beförderung

mit Personenzügen . . . . . 0,50 RM } für das Tarifkilometer
„ Eil- oder Schnellzügen 0,80 „ }

in beiden Fällen unter Zuschlag einer Abfertigungsgebühr von 7,50 RM für den Wagen.

B. Gütertarif.

a) Normaltarif.

1. Die Frachtsätze sind nach folgenden — die Verkehrssteuer von 7 v. H. mitenthaltenden — Einheitssätzen berechnet.

Entfernung km	Stückgut allgem. I	Stückgut ermäßigte Stückgutklasse II	Wagenladungen Haupt- (15 t) Klasse A	B	C	D	E	F
A. Abfertigungsgebühren für 100 kg in Reichspfennig.								
Alle Entfernungen	32	32	20	20	18	14	12	10
B. Streckensätze für das Tonnenkilometer in Reichspfennig.								
1—100	17,1	13,4	11,5	9,6	7,8	6,2	3,7	2,7
101—200 (Anstoß)	15,4	12,0	10,3	8,6	7,1	5,5	3,4	2,5
201—300 "	13,7	10,8	9,3	7,7	6,2	5,0	2,9	2,1
301—400 "	11,9	9,4	8,0	6,7	5,4	4,4	2,6	1,9
401—500 "	10,3	8,0	6,9	5,8	4,7	3,7	2,2	1,6
501—600 "	8,6	6,7	5,8	4,8	3,9	3,1	1,9	1,4
601—700 "	6,8	5,4	4,6	3,8	3,1	2,5	1,4	1,0
701—800 "	5,1	4,0	3,4	2,9	2,4	1,8	1,1	0,8
801—900 "	3,4	2,7	2,3	1,9	1,5	1,3	0,8	0,6
über 900 "	1,8	1,3	1,2	1,0	0,8	0,6	0,4	0,3

2. Bruchpfennig, die sich bei Ermittlung der Frachtsätze in Reichspfennig nach den unter Ziffer 1 angegebenen Einheitssätzen ergeben, werden von 0,5 ab aufwärts abgerundet, im übrigen außer Betracht gelassen.

3. Die Frachtsätze für die Neben- (10 und 5 t) Klassen der Wagenladungen werden durch Erhöhung der abgerundeten Frachtsätze für die entsprechenden Hauptklassen gebildet, und zwar:

A 10	um 10%	der Hauptklasse A	abgerundet wie unter Ziffer 1 angegeben.
A 5	" 20%	der Hauptklasse A	
B 10	" 10%	der Hauptklasse B	
B 5	" 20%	der Hauptklasse B	
C 10	" 15%	der Hauptklasse C	
C 5	" 30%	der Hauptklasse C	
D 10	" 20%	der Hauptklasse D	
D 5	" 40%	der Hauptklasse D	
E 10	" 25%	der Hauptklasse E	
E 5	" 50%	der Hauptklasse E	
F 10	" 30%	der Hauptklasse F	

4. Für Eilgut werden im Stückgutverkehr bei der allgemeinen Eilgutklasse (Ie) die doppelten, bei der ermäßigten Eilgutklasse (IIe) die einfachen Frachtsätze der Stückgutklasse I angewendet. Im Wagenladungsverkehr wird die Fracht berechnet:

   a) für die Güter der allgemeinen Eilgutklasse (Ie) nach der Tarifklasse A, A10 oder A5 für das doppelte Gewicht,

   b) für die Güter der ermäßigten Eilgutklasse (IIe) nach dem einfachen Gewicht und den gewöhnlichen Frachtgutsätzen.

5. Bei beschleunigtem Eilgut werden der Frachtberechnung für die Güter aller Tarifklassen zugrundegelegt:

   a) im Stückgutverkehr: die Frachtsätze der allgemeinen Eilgutklasse (Ie) für das $1^1/_2$ fache Gewicht;

   b) im Wagenladungsverkehr: die Frachtsätze der Wagenladungsklasse A, A10 oder A5 für das Dreifache des für Frachtgut zu berechnenden Gewichts.

Anmerkung. Die näheren Bestimmungen über die Frachtberechnung sowie die Übersicht über die den ermäßigten Stückgutklassen II und IIe und den Wagenladungsklassen B bis F angehörenden Güter sind aus dem deutschen Eisenbahngütertarif Teil I Abteilung B zu ersehen. Alle dort in der Gütereinteilung nicht genannten Erzeugnisse gehören im Stückgutverkehr den Klassen I, im Wagenladungsverkehr der Klasse A an.

b) Einheitssätze einiger verkehrswichtiger Ausnahmetarife.

1	2	3	4	5
Ausnahmetarife Nr.	Streckensatz km	für 1 tkm Reichspfennig	Abfertigungsgebühr für 100 kg Reichspfennig	Bemerkungen (Geltungsbereich, Ursprung u. a.)
1. Stammholz usw. Beschlagenes Holz	1—100	5,1	11	Allgemein.
	101—200	4,5 (Anstoß)		
	201—300	4,1 "		
	301—400	3,6 "		
	401—500	3,0 "		
	501—600	2,6 "		
	601—700	2,0 "		
	701—800	1,5 "		
	801—900	1,0 "		
	über 900	0,5 "		

1	2	3	4	5
Ausnahmetarife Nr.	Streckensatz km	für 1 tkm Reichspfennig	Abfertigungsgebühr für 100 kg Reichspfennig	Bemerkungen (Geltungsbereich, Ursprung u. a.)
1b. Schnittholz usw., Daub- usw. Holz	1—100	5,6	13	Allgemein.
	101—200	5,0 (Anstoß)		
	201—300	4,6 „		
	301—400	4,0 „		
	401—500	3,3 „		
	501—600	2,8 „		
	601—700	2,3 „		
	701—800	1,6 „		
	801—900	1,2 „		
	über 900	0,6 „		
5. A. Steine aus Naturgestein, Schlackenpflastersteine, Kies, Hochofenschlacken, Scherben usw. zum Wege-, Bahn- u. Wasserbau	1—50	2,6	8,0	Zu A—C Allgemein. Zu D zwischen allen Stationen der R.B.D. Dresden.
	51—100	1,6 (Anstoß)		
	101—200	1,4 „		
	ab 201	Klasse F—30%		
B. Kies usw. zur Herstellung ortsfester Betonbauten auf der Baustelle				
C. Grenz-, Nummer- u. Vermessungssteine				
D. Sandsteinhorzeln				
5a. Steine, rohe; Pflastersteine (ausgenommen solche mit rechtwinkligen Kopf- und gleichmäßigen Seitenflächen); Packlage- (Stick-) steine, Steinschrotten, Steinschlag u. Schotter zum Wege-, Bahn- u. Wasserbau	wie A.-T. 5c		wie A.-T. 5c	Von Stationen an und östlich der Linie Cammin (Pom.) — Stettin — Cüstrin — Frankfurt (Oder) — Cottbus — Horka — Kohlfurt — Breslau — Brieg — Neisse — Ziegenhals Hbf. (mit Ausnahme der Stationen Deutsch Wette, Neisse, Ziegenhals Hbf.) sowie von bestimmten Stationen der Reichsbahndirektionen Breslau, Dresden und Halle nach Stationen an und östlich der Linie Rostock — Pritzwalk — Neustadt (Dosse) — Rathenow — Brandenburg — Belzig — Jüterbog — Falkenberg b. Torgau — Cottbus — Horka — Kohlfurt — Breslau — Brieg — Neisse — Ziegenhals Hbf. und einigen Privatbahnen.

1	2	3	4	5
Ausnahmetarife Nr.	Streckensatz km	für 1 tkm Reichspfennig	Abfertigungsgebühr für 100 kg Reichspfennig	Bemerkungen (Geltungsbereich, Ursprung u. a.)
5c. Steingrus u. Steinsplitt, ungemahlen u. ungewaschen, Steinschutt u. Abraum aus Steinbrüchen, ungereinigt, zur Herstellung ortsfester Betonbauten auf der Baustelle usw.	1—50 51—100 101—200 ab 201	2,2 1,8 (Anstoß) 1,2 „ Klasse F—35%	7,0	Allgemein. Unterstützung der Steinindustrie durch Erleichterung der Abbeförderung des lästigen Abfalls.
6. A. Steinkohlen, Steinkohlenbriketts, Steinkohlenkoks, B. Braunkohlen Braunkohlenbriketts Braunkohlenkoks C. Gaskoks	1—350 351—400 401—500 501—600 601—704 übrige Entfernungen	3,0 1,1 (Anstoß) 0,7 „ 0,3 „ 0,2 „ 1,4*) „ **)	11	Zu A und B; von den deutschen Kohlengewinnungsstätten und Wasserumschlagstellen allgemein. Zu C allgemein.
7. I A. Eisenerz usw. an Eisen und Stahl erzeugende Hochöfen usw. B. Eisenerz usw. an Bleihüttenwerke C. Schwefelkiesabbrände zur Entzinkung II. Blechwaren, alte an Entemaillierungs-, Entzinkungs- und Entzinnungsanstalten	1—100 101—190 über 190	2,5 2,2 (Anstoß) 1,4 „	10,0	Allgemein mit Ausnahme einiger Privatbahnen nach allen Stationen, die für diese Betriebe als Empfangsstationen in Betracht kommen. (Erleichterung des Erzbezuges.) Soweit die Frachtsätze der Klasse F niedriger sind, werden diese berechnet.
8. Seefische, frische usw. von Stationen des Küstengebiets	a) Stückgut 1—150 151—200 201—300 ab 301 km Zuschlag von 30% zu den Sätzen der Wagenlad. Kl. B 5	 regelr. Frachten 1,4 (Anstoß) 0,7 „		Von Stationen mit Seefischerei nach allen deutschen Stationen.

*) Anstoß des Vorkriegssatzes, so daß von 704 km ab die Frachtsätze des Vorkriegstarifs gelten.

**) Ohne Verkehrssteuer, da diese für Kohlen nicht erhoben wird.

1	2	3	4	5
Ausnahmetarife Nr.	Streckensatz km	für 1 tkm Reichspfennig	Abfertigungsgebühr für 100 kg Reichspfennig	Bemerkungen (Geltungsbereich, Ursprung u. a.)
	b) Wagenladungen			
	1. Hauptklasse			
	1—150	regelr. Frachten		
	151—200	3,0 (Anstoß)		
	201—300	1,4 „		
	301—500	0,7 „		
	über 500 halbe Frachtsätze der Kl. B			
	2. Nebenklassen			
	10 t-Klasse	Hauptkl. + 10%		
	5 t-Klasse	„ + 20%		
11. Düngemittel				
A. der Klasse D, z. B. phosphorsaures Ammoniak u. phosphorsaurer Kaliammonsalpeter u. andere.	zu A Klasse E, E 10, E 5 ungekürzt			Bei Verwendung zum Düngen im Deutschen Reich: allgemein.
B. der Klasse E, a) hochprozentige Kalisalze und bestimmte Mischungen mit diesen,	zu Ba Klasse E, E 10, E 5 gekürzt um 20%			
b) bestimmte Stickstoffdüngemittel (z. B. schwefelsaures Ammoniak, Kali-Kalk-Salpeter) und andere Düngemittel	zu Bb gekürzt um 30%			
C. der Klasse F, a) Stalldünger usw., Phosphate, Schlamm, Schlick usw.	zu Ca Klasse F, F 10 u. E5 gekürzt um 20%			
b) geringere Kalisalze, Kainit, Kieserit usw.	zu Cb gekürzt um 30%			
c) Düngekalk	zu Cc „ „ 35%			
d) Mischkalkmergel	zu Cd „ „ 40%			
e) Gips, Höhlendünger, Kalkasche u. Staubkalk, Kalkschlamm, gemahlener Kalkstein u. Marmor, Mergel usw.	zu Ce „ „ 45%			

C. Tiertarif.

a) Vorbemerkung.

Der Frachtberechnung für lebende Tiere wird eine Normalklasse (Stückklasse S 3 für Schweine über 75 kg) zugrundegelegt. Die Normalklasse ist in Stufen eingeteilt, derart, daß je eine Stufe einem Stück entspricht. Die übrigen vier Tierklassen sind zur Normalklasse S 3 in folgendes ziffernmäßiges Verhältnis gebracht:

Verhältnis der Klasse S 3

zu S 1 (Pferde, Maultiere, Ponies über 1 Jahr alt, Elefanten, Kamele usw.) . . . . = 1:8

zu S 2 (Pferde, Maultiere, Ponies bis zu einem Jahr, sowie sonstiges Großvieh (Rinder usw.), soweit nicht zu Klasse S 1 gehörig) . . . . = 1:3

zu S 4 (Schweine, das Stück über 35 bis zu 75 kg schwer, Kälber bis zu 6 Monaten, Schafe, Ziegen, Hunde) . . . . = 1:$^1/_2$

zu S 5 (Ferkel, Lämmer, Zicklein, sonstige kleine Tiere (ausgen. Geflügel), das Stück nicht über 35 kg schwer) . . . . = 1:$^1/_5$

Für Geflügel, das in der Regel in mehrbödigen Wagen befördert wird, sind besondere Ladungsklassen (L 1 bis L 7) eingerichtet, die ebenfalls in ein bestimmtes Verhältnis zur Normalklasse S 3 gebracht worden sind.

Es gilt für Sendungen in einem Wagen mit:

1	Boden	die	Fracht	für	20	Stück	der	Klasse	S 3
2	„	„	„	„	40	„	„	„	S 3
3	„	„	„	„	45	„	„	„	S 3
4	„	„	„	„	50	„	„	„	S 3
5	„	„	„	„	55	„	„	„	S 3
6	„	„	„	„	60	„	„	„	S 3
7	„	„	„	„	65	„	„	„	S 3

Zu den Streckensätzen wird eine Abfertigungsgebühr von 20 Rpf. für das Stück der Normalklasse S 3 oder für die Stufe hinzugerechnet.

Die Grundsätze für die Frachtberechnung und die sonstigen Tarifbestimmungen sind aus Abschnitt B des deutschen Eisenbahntiertarifs Teil I und dem Anhang zum Reichsbahntiertarif (Tierfrachtzeiger) zu ersehen.

b) 1. Einheitssätze für das km für 1 Stück der Normalklasse S3 in Rpf.

Stufe (= Stück)	1	2	3	4	5	6	7	8	9	10	11	12	13	14	15	16	17	18	19	20	21	22	23	24
km	Pf.	Pf.	Pf.	Pf.	Pf.	Pf.	Pf.	Pf.	Pf.	Pf.	Pf.	Pf.	Pf.	Pf.	Pf.	Pf.	Pf.	Pf.	Pf.	Pf.	Pf.	Pf.	Pf.	Pf.
1— 100	2,42	2,38	2,33	2,29	2,24	2,20	2,15	2,11	2,06	2,02	1,97	1,93	1,88	1,84	1,79	1,75	1,70	1,66	1,61	1,57	1,52	1,48	1,43	1,39
	(Abstufungen von je 0,045 Pf. für die Stufen 1—40)																							
101— 200	1,98	1,94	1,91	1,88	1,84	1,80	1,76	1,73	1,69	1,66	1,62	1,58	1,55	1,51	1,48	1,44	1,40	1,37	1,33	1,30	1,26	1,22	1,19	1,15
	(Abstufungen von je 0,036 Pf. für die Stufen 1—40)																							
201— 300	1,87	1,83	1,80	1,76	1,73	1,69	1,65	1,62	1,58	1,55	1,51	1,47	1,44	1,40	1,37	1,33	1,29	1,26	1,22	1,19	1,15	1,11	1,08	1,04
	(Abstufungen von je 0,036 Pf. für die Stufen 1—40)																							
301— 400	1,55	1,52	1,49	1,47	1,44	1,41	1,38	1,35	1,33	1,30	1,27	1,24	1,21	1,19	1,16	1,13	1,10	1,07	1,05	1,02	0,99	0,96	0,93	0,91
	(Abstufungen von je 0,028 Pf. für die Stufen 1—40)																							
401— 500	1,23	1,21	1,19	1,17	1,15	1,13	1,11	1,09	1,07	1,05	1,03	1,01	0,99	0,97	0,95	0,93	0,91	0,89	0,87	0,85	0,83	0,81	0,79	0,77
	(Abstufungen von je 0,02 Pf. für die Stufen 1—40)																							
501— 600	1,03	1,02	1,00	0,99	0,97	0,96	9,94	0,93	0,91	0,90	0,88	0,87	0,85	0,84	0,82	0,81	0,79	078	0,76	0,75	0,73	0,72	0,70	0,69
	(Abstufungen von je 0,015 Pf. für die Stufen 1—40)																							
601— 700	0,88	0,87	0,85	0,84	0,82	0,81	0,79	0,78	0,76	0,75	0,73	0,72	0,70	0,69	0,67	0,66	0,64	0,63	0,61	0,60	0,58	0,57	0,55	0,54
	(Abstufungen von je 0,015 Pf. für die Stufen 1—40)																							
701— 800	0,70	0,69	0,68	0,66	0,65	0,64	0,63	0,62	0,60	0,59	0,58	0,57	0,56	0,54	0,53	0,52	0,51	0,50	0,48	0,47	0,46	0,45	0,44	0,42
	(Abstufungen von je 0,012 Pf. für die Stufen 1—40)																							
801— 900	0,40	0,39	0,39	0,38	0,37	0,37	0,36	0,35	0,34	0,34	0,33	0,32	0,32	0,31	0,30	0,30	0,29	0,28	0,27	0,27	0,26	0,25	0,25	0,24
	(Abstufungen von je 0,007 Pf. für die Stufen 1—40)																							
901—1000	0,20	0,20	0,19	0,19	0,19	0,19	0,18	0,18	0,18	0,17	0,17	0,17	0,16	0,16	0,16	0,16	0,15	0,15	0,15	0,14	0,14	0,14	0,13	0,13
	(Abstufungen von je 0,003 Pf. für die Stufen 1—40)																							

Stufe (= Stück)	25	26	27	28	29	30	31	32	33	34	35	36	37	38	39	40	41.—80. Stufe in Abstufungen von bis	für die Stufe	Von der 81. Stufe ab Anstoß für die Stufe
	Pf.	Pf.	Pf.	Pf.	Pf.	Pf.	Pf.	Pf.	Pf.	Pf.	Pf.	Pf.	Pf.	Pf.	Pf.	Pf.	Pf.	Pf.	Pf.
km																			
1— 100	1,34	1,30	1,25	1,21	1,16	1,12	1,07	1,03	0,98	0,94	0,89	0,85	0,80	0,76	0,71	0,67	0,652—0,145	0,013	0,110
	(Abstufungen von je 0,045 Pf. für die Stufen 1—40)																		
101— 200	1,12	1,08	1,04	1,01	0,97	0,94	0,90	0,86	0,83	0,79	0,76	0,72	0,68	0,65	0,61	0,58	0,564—0,096	0,012	0,090
	(Abstufungen von je 0,036 Pf. für die Stufen 1—40)																		
201— 300	1,01	0,97	0,93	0,90	0,86	0,83	0,79	0,75	0,72	0,68	0,65	0,61	0,57	0,54	0,50	0,47	0,456—0,066	0,010	0,066
	(Abstufungen von je 0,036 Pf. für die Stufen 1—40)																		
301— 400	0,88	0,85	0,82	0,79	0,77	0,74	0,71	0,68	0,65	0,63	0,60	0,57	0,54	0,51	0,49	0,46	0,448—0,058	0,010	0,058
	(Abstufungen von je 0,028 Pf. für die Stufen 1—40)																		
401— 500	0,75	0,73	0,71	0,69	0,67	0,65	0,63	0,61	0,59	0,57	0,55	0,53	0,51	0,49	0,47	0,45	0,440 - 0,050	0,010	0,050
	(Abstufungen von je 0,02 Pf. für die Stufen 1—40)																		
501— 600	0,67	0,66	0,64	0,63	0,61	0,60	0,58	0,57	0,55	0,54	0,52	0,51	0,49	0,48	0,46	0,45	0,435—0,045	0,010	0,045
	(Abstufungen von je 0,015 Pf. für die Stufen 1—40)																		
601— 700	0,52	0,51	0,49	0,48	0,46	0,45	0,43	0,42	0,40	0,39	0,37	0,36	0,34	0,33	0,31	0,30	0,289—0,035	0,0065	0,035
	(Abstufungen von je 0,015 Pf. für die Stufen 1—40)																		
701— 800	0,41	0,40	0,39	0,38	0,36	0,35	0,34	0,33	0,32	0,30	0,29	0,28	0,27	0,26	0,24	0,23	0,227—0,032	0,005	0,032
	(Abstufungen von je 0,012 Pf. für die Stufen 1—40)																		
801— 900	0,23	0,23	0,22	0,21	0,20	0,20	0,19	0,18	0,18	0,17	0,16	0,16	0,15	0,14	0,13	0,13	0,124—0,007	0,003	0,007
	(Abstufungen von je 0,007 Pf. für die Stufen 1—40)																		
901—1000	0,13	0,13	0,12	0,12	0,12	0,11	0,11	0,11	0,10	0,10	0,10	0,10	0,09	0,09	0,09	0,08	0,081—0,003	0,002	0,002
	(Abstufungen von je 0,003 Pf. für die Stufen 1—40)																		

2. Abfertigungsgebühr: 20 Rpf. für jede Stufe.

www.ingramcontent.com/pod-product-compliance
Lightning Source LLC
LaVergne TN
LVHW081342011026
849161LV00013BB/2987

CONTEMPORARY INTERNATIONAL LAW of CIVILIZED PEOPLES

GENERAL PART

Bust of Martens frontispiece courtesy of Vitalii Semenovich Ivanenko, St. Petersburg University Law Faculty. Sculpted by Alexander Mikhailovich Taratynov (1956-), Moscow.

CONTEMPORARY INTERNATIONAL LAW of CIVILIZED PEOPLES

GENERAL PART

Suum cuique

F.F. MARTENS

Professor of St. Petersburg University and Member, Institute of International Law

Edited and Translated by

WILLIAM E. BUTLER

John Edward Fowler Distinguished Professor of Law, Dickinson Law, Pennsylvania State University
Emeritus Professor of Comparative Law, University College London
Foreign Member, National Academy of Sciences of Ukraine, and National Academy of Legal Sciences of Ukraine

TALBOT PUBLISHING

Clark, New Jersey

ISBN 9781616196608

TALBOT PUBLISHING
AN IMPRINT OF
The Lawbook Exchange, Ltd.
33 Terminal Avenue
Clark, New Jersey 07066-1323

Please see our website for a selection of our other publications and fine facsimile reprints of classic works of legal history www.lawbookexchange.com

Library of Congress Cataloging-in-Publication Data

Names: Martens, Fedor Fedorovich, 1845-1909, author. | Butler, William Elliott, 1939- editor, translator.
Title: Contemporary international law of civilized peoples : general part / Friedrich Fromhold Martens, Professor of St. Petersburg University and Member, Institute of International Law ; edited and translated by William Elliott Butler, John Edward Fowler Distinguished Professor of Law, Dickinson Law, Pennsylvania State University Emeritus Professor of Comparative Law, University College London Foreign Member, National Academy of Sciences of Ukraine, and National Academy of Legal Sciences of Ukraine.
Other titles: Sovremennoe mezhdunarodnoe pravo t͡sivilizovannykh narodov. English
Description: Clark, New Jersey : Talbot Publishing, an imprint of The Lawbook Exchange, Ltd., [2021] | Includes bibliographical references and index. | Summary: "The first English translation of a historic Russian treatise on international law that was originally published in 1882/1883"-- Provided by publisher.
Identifiers: LCCN 2021045372 | ISBN 9781616196608 (hardcover)
Subjects: LCSH: International law.
Classification: LCC KZ2951.A3 S6813 2021 | DDC 341--dc23/eng/20211020
LC record available at https://lccn.loc.gov/2021045372

TABLE OF CONTENTS

Editorial Preface to English Translation xxiv

Biographical Sketch of F. F. Martens xxviii
William E. Butler
Vitalii S. Ivanenko

Abbreviations lviii

Preface to Fifth Edition lix

Preface to First Edition lix

Introduction

I. Grounds of International Law

§1. Subject-matter of science of international law. Different view on significance of this science. Deniers of international law. Romanists. Real school. Theoretical unfoundedness of their views. Practice of international agreements. International economic interests. Emigration. Spiritual interests. Interests of justice. Congresses and conferences. Right of war. "Political equilibrium". Conclusion. 1

§2. Special legal objections against positive international law. Absence of coercive force. Opinion of Jhering. Unfoundedness thereof. Absence of legislative power. Opinion of Bluntschli. International laws as result of agreement of States. Shortcoming of court. Arbitration. War and laws thereof. Highest source of international law – idea of truth and justice 6

II. Definition of Concept of International Law

§3. Diversity of definitions and reasons thereof – difficulty of any scientific definition, youth of science of international law. Incorrect designation of this science: *jus gentium*. Contemporary name thereof. Our definition. Development thereof and conclusions therefrom. Elements of international interaction: common religious faiths, intellectual and moral aspirations, identical tribal origin, economic interests and trade relations, commonality of political interests. Awareness by peoples of their needs is a measure of the development of international turnover and degree of culture and civilization of State 12

§4. Actors in international relations. States. Link of international life with State life. Supreme purpose of State may be achieved only in international interaction. Division of international law into public international law and private international criminal law 16

§5. Social classes and private individuals – their role in international relations. Meaning of social interests in international life. Relations between society and State determine character of international relations 17

III. History of International Relations and Law

§6. Task. Significance of ideas in history of international law. Internal existence and structure of States. Law of progressive development of international relations is expressed by principle of respect for human individual. Recognition of human individual in Antiquity – in Middle Ages – in recent time 19

§7. Division into periods. Three periods of international relations as expression of ideas dominant in various epochs. First period: dominance of physical force. Peoples of ancient East, Greeks, and Romans. War is law of feudalism. Birth of new principles in Middle Ages. Second period: idea of political equilibrium. Congress of Westphalia. Significance of 1789 French Revolution. Third period: principle of nationality – development of trade and economic relations. 1856 Peace Treaty of Paris. Idea of law as guiding principle of future international relations. 20

First Period
From Antiquity to Peace of Westphalia

A. Ancient Times

§8. General Description. Did ancient peoples know international law? Their isolation. Opposite facts. Wars. Colonization. Hospitality. General conclusion. 25

§9. International relations of the East. Theocratic and caste structure. India. Brahmins. Influence of caste on international relations. Laws of Manu. Status of foreigners. Treaties. Trade relations. Hospitality. Embassies. War – Persians, Jews, Phoenicians, Egypt 28

§10. Greece. Favorable conditions for development of international relations. Equality of citizens and slavery. Barbarians. Internal structure of municipia. Inborn separateness of Greeks. Common vital and cultural interests of Greek peoples. Dorian conquest. Athens. Sparta. Hellenes. Significance of Delphic Oracle and Olympic games. Greek education. Trade and crafts. Resettlers and surrounding peoples. Aversion to sailing. Piracy. Treaties σvμβoλα – isopoly. Hospitality – *proxenes*. Greek colonies – their significance. Was international law known to the ancient Greeks? Amphyctonia. System of political equilibrium. Conclusion 30

§11. Rome. Comparison with Greece. Rome – representative of flagrant force. Roman *jus civile*. Mitigation under its influence of international relations. Two periods 40

§12. Epoch of republican government. Struggle of plebians against patricians. Result thereof. Description of international relations of Romans. Conquests. Policy of Rome with respect to Italian peoples. Law of municipia. Roman provinces 42

§13. Treaties of Romans – *foedera aequa* – *foedera non aequa*. Roman law 44

§14. Attitude of Romans to foreigners. *Jus hospitii*. Patronage. Praetor peregrinos. Wars and conquests as instrument of coming together with other peoples. Trade relations. Wars against pirates. Roman colonies 45

§15. Period of Roman Empire. General description. Unification of conquered territories. Role of emperors. International relations. Did the Romans know international law? *Jus feciale*. Envoys. *Recuperatores*. *Jus gentium*. Origin, essence, and role thereof in development of Roman law. What is *jus gentium*? 47

B. Middle Ages

§16. Grounds of international orders in Middle Ages and beginning of contemporary international law. Fall of western Roman Empire. Causes. Barbarians. Byzantine Empire. Description of ancient Germans. Respect for physical force. Idea of the individual. Christianity. Role of Roman curia 51

§17. Attitude of Barbarians to subjugated peoples. Franks. Empire of Charlemagne 54

§18. Consequences of division of Carolingian monarchy: dispersion and localization of supreme State power. France, Italy, Germania. Feudal order – description thereof. Feudal aristocracy, free and enserfed. Decline of governmental power. Right of private warfare. Kulak law. Alliances of private individuals. Description of international relations. War and robberies. Foreigners. *Droit d'aubaine*. Coastal law. Atrocities and treachery during war 56

§19. General social and political conditions of life of peoples of Middle Ages as source of European international law. Character of feudal aristocracy. Cosmopolitanism thereof. Knighthood. Trade and industrial estate. Communes. Rights Thereof. Unions of cities. Hansa. Peasant estate. Roman Catholic Church and popes. Role of popes as international arbitrators. Church assemblies. God's peace. Private individuals and societies. Royal power in France, Germany, and England 59

§20. Decline of feudalism and rise of royal power: influence of these facts on change of international relations of Middle Ages. Crusades. Legists. Alliance of kings with city communes. Distinctive features of political system and international role of France – England – Germany – Italy – Spain. Epoch of Renaissance; inventions; introduction of standing forces; discoveries 63

Second Period From Peace of Westphalia to 1815 Congress of Vienna

A. International Relations from Peace of Westphalia to First French Revolution

§21. Reformation. Thirty Years War. Peace of Westphalia. Major provisions of Westphalian Treaty. Its significance for international relations 67

§22. State and social orders in seventeenth and eighteenth centuries. Royal absolutism. Nobility, clergy, middle estate, and agricultural class. International relations. Dynastic interests and Machiavellianism. Principles of law and morality. Status of France. Louis XIV. War for Belgian succession and Aachen Peace (1668). War against Holland. Nijmegen Treaty (1678). *Chambres de reunion.* Seizure of Luxembourg and Strasbourg. William of Orange and political equilibrium. War against Germany. Ryswick Treaty of 1697. 1698 Treaty at The Hague on the division of Spanish possessions. Testament of Charles II. War for Spanish succession. 1713 Treaty of Utrecht. Change of political relations of States 70

§23. Character of initial relations of Russia with western powers: England – Austria—Hansa –Prussia –Netherlands – France – Sweden. 1721 Peace of Nystadt. 76

§24. Rise of Prussia. Pragmatic Sanction. First Silesian war and peace in Breslau of 1742. Second Silesian war and Dresden peace (1745). War for Austrian succession. 1748 Peace of Aachen. Alliance of Elizaveta Petrovna with Maria-Theresa. 1756 Versailles Treaty of Alliance between Austria and France. Seven Years War.

Accession to Russian throne of Peter III and peace of Russia with Prussia. Hubertsburg Peace Treaty and peace in Paris of 1763 82

§25. Partition of Poland. Conditions under which first Partition of Poland occurred in 1772. Kuchuk-Kainardzhii Treaty of 1774. Dispute over Bavarian succession. Mediation of Russia and France and 1779 Teschen peace. War of North American colonies against England and formation in 1776 of North American states. 1783 Peace of Versailles between France and England 85

B. On International Relations from the 1789 French Revolution to the 1815 Congress of Vienna

§26. International status of France at end of eighteenth century as one of causes of 1789 French Revolution. International significance of French Revolution. First coalition of 1793. Attitude of Catherine II to revolution. 1795 Basel peace of France with Prussia. 1797 Peace in Campo Formio between France and Austria. Second coalition 89

§27. Victories of Suvorov in Italy. Refusal by Paul I of alliance with Austria in 1799. Principles of political system of Alexander I set out in Instruction to Russian ambassador in Vienna on 10 September 1801. 1801 Lunéville peace. 1802 Amiens peace between France and England. Adoption by Napoleon of title of Emperor in 1804 and change of his international policy. Third coalition of 1805. Peace of Pressburg 1805. Confederation of the Rhine. Continental system and "system of starvation". 1807 Peace in Tilsit. 1808 Congress of Erfurt. War between France and Russia, on one side, and Austria on the other. 1809 Treaty of Schoenbrun (Vienna). War of 1812. 1813 Treaty of Kalisz. Transfer of allied army beyond Rhine. Treaty in Chaumont. Occupation of Paris. First Paris peace treaty. Flight of Napoleon from Island of Elba and Declaration of European powers of 13 March 1815. One hundred days. Waterloo. Second Paris peace 91

§28. Character of international relations in second period. Eliciting of basic rights of States as subjects of international law. Rights of envoys. International law of sea: Declaration of Armed Neutrality of 28 February 1780. Second Armed Neutrality of 1801. Prisoners of war, sick, and wounded warriors. Idea of political equilibrium. What does it consist of? Its legal unfoundedness. International significance of first French Revolution and empire of Napoleon I 96

Third Period
From Congress of Vienna to Present Time

A. International Relations from 1815 Congress of Vienna to 1856 Paris Peace

§29. Congress of Vienna. Three kinds of view revealed at congress. Views of Metternich – Talleyrand – Stein and Emperor Alexander I. Ideas of 1815 Holy Alliance. Dispute over Duchy of Warsaw and Kingdom of Saxony. Act of Congress of Vienna. Its provisions on territorial possessions, freedom of navigation on rivers, trade in negroes, and rank of diplomatic agents 99

§30. Description of international relations after 1815. Mood of European peoples. Reaction. Aspirations of social classes are reflected in international social relations – in religious domain – in sphere of intellectual and spiritual interests – economic activity. Awareness of common national origin 103

31. Pentarchy. Interference in internal affairs of States. 1818 Aachen Congress. Carlsbad and Vienna conferences of 1819. Congresses in Troppau in 1820, Laibach in 1821, and Verona in 1822. England and principle of non-interference. Uprising of Greeks in 1821. 1826 Petersburg Protocol. 1827 London Convention. 1827 Battle of Navarino. Russo-Turkish war. 1829 Peace of Adrianople. Independence of Greece. 1830 French revolution. Separation of Belgium from Holland. 1831 London treaty. 1848 French revolution. People's movements in other European States. War between Denmark and German alliance. 1850 Treaty of Berlin. Expulsion of Pious IX and occupation of Rome by French forces to benefit of pope 105

B. International Relations from 1856 Paris Peace to Present Time

§32. Eastern war 1853-1856. 1856 Paris Peace treaty. Limitation of sovereign rights of Russia, repealed by1871 London convention. Declaration of 4(16) April 1856. Formation of Italian kingdom. 1859 Peace in Villa Franco and Zurich. Garibaldi. 1860 Turin Convention. Occupation of Rome in 1870. Unification of Germany. Austro-Russian-Danish war. 1864 Treaty of Vienna. 1866 Austro-Prussian war. Peace in Nikolsburg and Prague. Article V of Prague treaty. Negotiations on Luxembourg. 1867 London conference. Rupture between France and Prussia in 1870. Occasions for this. Versailles Preliminaries and Frankfurt final peace treaty of 1871. Formation of German empire. 1874 Brussels conference. 1875 Herzogovina uprising leads to war of 1877-1878 between Russia and Turkey. San Stefano preliminary treaty on peace. 1878 Berlin Congress. Provisions of

Berlin treaty. Internecine war in America of 1861. 1866 Mexican expedition 108

§33. International relations in third period. Development of principles of contemporary positive international law. Congresses and conferences. Special and general treaties. Principle of nationality. Definition of Mancini. Opposition of nationality to historical State. Legal and practical unfoundedness of views of nationalists 115

IV. Development of Science of International Law

§34. Connection of development of science of international law with history of international relations. Three periods of this development and characteristic distinctive features thereof. Their correlation with three periods of history of international relations 118

A. Period of Domination of Natural Law

§35. Hugo Grotius and his predecessors: Francisco Suarez and Alberico Gentili. Grotius' work *De jure belli ac pacis*. Basic principles of international law; their abstract character. System. Influence of Grotius' book on life contemporary to him. Abstract orientation in science of international law. Pufendorf – Hobbes – Spinoza – Thomasius. Principles of positive law in work of Wolff. Division of international law adopted by him. Fiction of world State. Shortcomings of theory of Wolff and Vattel 120

B. Period of Predominance of Positivist Orientation

§36. Zouche. Distinction established by him between jus gentium and international law. View on *jus feciale*. Rachel. Evidence in favor of autonomous character of international law. Common interest – basis of international relations and law. Mixing of international law with jus gentium. Promulgation of treaties and diplomatic negotiations. Collections of international treaties. Development thereof. Mably. Johann Jacob Moser. Unscientific nature of his works. System thereof. Bynkershoek – his scientific method 126

C. Period of Combination of Philosophical Principles with Elements of Positive International Law

§37. Georg-Friedrich von Martens – progenitor of new orientation – method and system thereof – mixing of philosophical international law with natural law – excessive partiality to facts. Shortcoming of scientific critique of English and American critics. Wheaton. His definition of positive international law. Unfoundedness of his method. Phillimore. Merits of his work "Commentaries on International Law". Division. View on Roman law. Shortcomings 130

§38. Literature of international law in Germany. Philosophy of international law: Kant – Fichte – Hegel. Their followers: Fillati, Gelschner, L. von Stein. Philosophical elaboration of international law. Oppenheim. Heffter. Merits of his textbook and shortcomings of system. Bluntschli. Literature of international law in Italy. Defenders of national principle: Mancini, Pierantoni, Luigi Palma, and others. Opponents thereof: Mamiani and Padeletti. French literature. Funck-Brentano and Sorel. Calvo. Russian literature: works of Kachenovskii – Stoianov – Kapustin – Bialecki. 134

V. Task and Purpose of Science of Contemporary International Law

§39. Wherein lies the task of the science of contemporary international law on the basis of the study of the history of international relations and development of the science of international law? Purpose of scientific elaboration of international law. Sovereignty of States and idea of international interaction. Positive legal norms and personal views. Critique from standpoint of idea of law. Recognition of legal principle at 1818 Congress in Aachen 138

VI. Basic Features of System

§40. Requirements of scientific system. System of international law is system of vital international relations. Systematica borrowed from Roman law. Our system 140

VII. Space of Operation of International Law

§41. Contemporary international law has force for States of European civilization. Non-applicability thereof to Muslim and non-educated peoples. Natural law. Objections against exclusion of Turkey from international alliance; unfoundedness thereof. Is international law based solely on Christian principles? View of Bluntschli. John Stuart Mill 141

VIII. Relations of International Law to Other Legal and Political Sciences

§42. Organic link of science of international law with other parts of jurisprudence: I) civil and criminal law; II) social law; III) State law; IV) international law and policy: correct correlation thereof; V) diplomacy 143

IX. Sources of International Law

§43. Awareness of States on need for international legal order is basis of international law. External expression of this awareness. I. International customs – their practical and legal significance – process of formation. II. International treaties. Division thereof. Examples. Binding nature. III. Diplomatic treaties and acts. IV. National laws and governmental regulations. V. Judicial practice. Prize courts. Collections of their decisions. Mixed international courts in Egypt. VI. History and science of international law. 145

X. Codification of Principles of International Law

§44. Possibility of codification of international law. Codification experiments. Bentham. Kachenovskii. Parodo. Domin-Petruschevecz. Lieber. Bluntschli. Dudley Field. Objections. Task of codification. Usefulness and necessity. Performance of task. Institute of International Law in Ghent. Codification works thereof 149

GENERAL PART
CHAPTER 1
LAW OF INTERNATIONAL INTERACTION

I. Concept and Definition of Law of International Interaction

§45. Can international law be built on the sovereignty of States? What is international interaction? Definition of law of international interaction. Necessity of international interaction arises from purpose of State. International interaction does not destroy individuality of peoples. Free alliance of States. Ideal order of international relations 157

II. Development of Idea of International Interaction

§46. Why did societies of States not exist in Antiquity and Middle Ages? Conditions of development of international interaction in contemporary life. Significance of economic interests. International interaction as results of European culture and civilization. Conclusions. Example: initial relations of Russia with western States 159

III. Basic Principles of Law of International Interaction

§47. Tasks and purposes of international interaction. Basic principles arising of law of international interaction 161

IV. Basic Tasks of International Interaction

§48. Three main kinds of interests satisfied by international interaction. Tasks of international interaction: A. In domain of mutual State relations. a) in sphere of legislation. Examples: 1865 Italian Civil Code – English parliamentary acts of naturalization and conclusion of 1870 cartel conventions – Swiss legislation from 1848 – Russian law of 10 February 1864 and Statute on Civil Procedure. Attempts at international legislation. b) in sphere of administration. International administrative institutions. Rhine Navigation Commission. Danube European Commission, and others. International administration. c) in domain of judicial power. Mutual assistance of States in sphere of civil and criminal justice 162

§49. B. In domain of social interests. Recognition of legally existing societies in foreign State. Right to their international protection. Churches. Scientific-literary societies, trade companies, and others 168

§50. C. In domain of relations of individual subjects. Respect for the individual and rights of foreigners. Material assistance to foreigners under treaties and *de facto* 169

V. Organization of International Interaction

§51. Necessity of organization of international interaction. Absence of organized international power. Drafts of organization of international union in form of State. A. Projects for perpetual peace. Christian republic of Henry IV. Project of Abbot Saint-Pierre. Jean-Jacques Rousseau. Bentham. Kant. Fallati, Malinovskii, Zubov. B. Projects emanating from real data. a) Universal monarchy. b) Projects on principle of representation. Sartorius. Poirer. Two projects of Lorimer. Bluntschli. Project of one reigning sovereign. c) Structure of international relations on basis of political equilibrium. d) Pentarchy. Projects for organization of international court. Inconsistency 170

VI. Organs of International Interaction: Congresses and Conferences

§52. a) Concept of congress and conference: they in essence are organs of international interaction and not individual States. Definition. b) Distinction between congresses and conferences – with respect to identity of representatives – subject-matter of discussion – purposes. c) Clerical work. 1) Procedure for convocation. 2) Participating States. 3) Representation. 4) Subject-matter of meetings. 5) Procedure for meetings. 6) Adoption of decisions. 7) Performance of decisions 176

Chapter 2
Subjects of International Law and International Relations

I. General Remarks

§53. States – sole subjects of international law. Role and status of monarchs, diplomatic agents, societies, and private individuals in international relations 182

II. The State as International Person

§54. In what sense is the State a person? Definition of State. Significance of internal orders and might of States. Nomadic tribes – social groups – Eastern States – nations. Death of State 182

III. Division of States

§55. International independence and classification of States. Simple and complex or combined States. Union of States. Combinations of States: personal and real. Union State. Semi-Independent States. Significant of these forms for positive international law 184

A. Simple States

§56. Distinctive features of simple States. Colonies – accessioned regions. Russia and Poland – mutual status thereof 185

B. Complex States

a) Union of States

§57. Definition. Peculiarities of union of States – international cultural significance thereof. 1815 German Union. Contemporary structure of Germany 187

b) Combined States

§58. α) Personal combination – Grounds and indicia thereof – Examples – β) Real combination – Indicia – Austria and Hungary – Norway and Sweden – View on Grand Duchy of Finland. 191

§59. γ) Union State. Conditions making State a union. Swiss union. North American United States. United States of Venezuela. Brazilian United States. Argentine Republic 194

§60. δ) Semi-independent States – How is their existence to be explained? – Indicia – Forms of semi-independence – Termination thereof – Egypt – Bulgarian principality – Eastern Rumelia 197

§61. Barbarian possessions: Tunisia, Tripoli, and Algiers – Samos Islands – Syria – San Marino – Republic Andorra – Principality of Monaco – Khiva Khanate – Nomadic princes in English India – Indian tribes on the territory of the North-American United States 204

§62. States formerly semi-independent – Romania – Serbia – Ionian Islands – Krakow Republic – Addition: on Montenegro – Provisions of Berlin Treaty – View of Bluntschli. 208

IV. Conditions of Existence of States as International Persons

§63. Basic conditions. Historical development of State. Essential changes to which States are subjected in their development and legal consequences 212

A. Recognition of New States

§64. Necessity of recognition – in event of separation of part of State – creation of one State from several regions – adoption of new title. Examples. Conditions of recognition. Opinion of Phillimore. Forms of recognition. Freedom of recognition. Examples. Conditional and unconditional recognition. Legal consequences and moral significance 213

B. Influence of Internal State Coups d'État

§65. State coups d'état or transformations do not change international legal status of State. London Protocol of 19 February 1831. Examples. Exceptions. Influence of internecine strife and usurpation. Historical facts 216

C. Significance of Territorial Changes of State

§66. Important significance of territory. Influence of changes thereof on legal relations of States. Types of changes 218

§67. 1) State territory is lost. Accession. Examples. Instances of Death of State cited by Heffter and Phillimore. Legal consequences of accession. Succession to rights and duties. Obligations and treaties. *Public domaine*. Treasury ownership. Instances from recent history 219

§68. 2) State territory is reduced. Influence of this fact on international obligations of State. Examples. Causes of reduction of territory. Internecine war. Interference of neutral powers. Conditions of recognition of independence of regions which rose up. 1875 Message of President Grant. Attitude of Washington Government to 1849 uprising in Hungary. Instances from files of State Archive of

1811. Legal consequences of separation of art of territory: succession to personal and local obligations 221

§69. 3) State territory is increased. Consequences. Unconditional and conditional accession of the possessions of others. Examples of conditional accessions. Duration of bindingness of conditions of accession and consequences of violation thereof 224

V. International Attributes of State

§70. Definition, a) Sovereignty. Volume thereof in international relations. Necessity thereof. b) Dispositive legal capacity. Legal capacity of States coincides with dispositive legal capacity. Semi-Independent States. International Responsibility Thereof. Instances from practice: c) Equality of rights. Withdrawal thereof from concept on international community and practical significance thereof. Words of Sumner. Opinion of Funck-Brentano, Sorel, and Lorimer. Actual inequality of States. "Great Powers". Freedom of internal administration 225

§71. Rank and titles of States – recognition thereof. Examples. Arguments and the Role of the Popes. Bull of Julius II (1504). Contemporary Law. Religious titles. Royal honors. Titles of emperors and kings: unfounded opinion of Bluntschli. Semi-independent States. Mutual relations and maritime salutes. Agreements on rank. Changes of form of government 228

VI. Basic International Rights of States

§72. Concept. Distinction between acquired and basic rights. May a State renounce basic rights and under what conditions? What are these rights? 231

§73. 1. Right of self-preservation. Source thereof. Of what does it consist? Means of self-preservation. Conditions of use thereof. Examples. Adoption of measures of self-preservation outside territory. Subject-matter of defense. Action. Limitation of rights of self-preservation by treaties 232

§74. 2. Right of territoriality. Of what does it consist? Conclusions. 234

§75. 3. Right of independence. Implementation thereof in internal administration and international relations. 235

§76. On interference. What is called interference? Motives of interference. 236

1. Interference in internal affairs. View of contempory writers: a) interference in relations between civilized peoples. Collective inter-

ference. Exceptional instances of application thereof. b) instances of its application in civilized relations. Legality of interference from standpoint of natural law 236

2. Interference in external relations. Occasions. Duties of non-interference. When is interference in external affairs legal? Distinction from interference in internal affairs 238

§77. 3. Claims of North American United States to direct the international relations of America. Facts. Critique. Monroe Doctrine. Content thereof. Conclusion 238

§78. 4. Right to respect and honor. Desecration of flag, arms, title. Examples. Respect for representatives of State. Duty to not commit dishonorable actions 240

§79. 5. Right of international communication. Necessity thereof. Implementation thereof in relations between formed States. Unfounded conclusions of Heffter. Relations of civilized States with uncivilized. 241

6. Right of coercion 242

VII. Sovereigns as Subjects of Rights in International Relations

§80. Opinion of writers. International status of sovereigns and presidents of republics. Rights of monarchs. Ordinary relations between monarchs. Different status of presidents of republics 243

§81. a) Right of representation. Grounds of this right *de facto* and *de jure*. Constitutional rights of sovereigns. Who should be considered a sovereign? Representatives of uprising party and usurpers. Recognition on part of people. Examples. Non-reigning sovereigns: their international status. Facts. Honorary and other rights of sovereigns 244

§82. b) Right of exterritoriality. Fiction. True meaning thereof. Conditions. Incognito sovereigns. Consequences of exterritoriality 247

1. Non-subordination of monarch to police instructions. Freedom from taxes and assessments. 248

2. Criminal non-jurisdiction. Practical meaning thereof. Opinion of Bynkershoek. Analysis. 248

3. Civil non-jurisdiction. View of old writers. New judicial practice. Suits against sovereigns as monarchs. Suits against sovereign or government as private individuals. Suits brought by sovereigns. Conclusion. View of Holtzendorff. Limiting interpretation of princi-

ple of civil non-jurisdiction of sovereigns. Instances of their uncontested jurisdiction. Practical grounds of broad application of non-jurisdiction. Ex-sovereigns 248

VIII. International Status of Members of Family and Suite of Sovereign

§83. Grounds of failure by members of family and suite of sovereign to use international rights. Relations of persons of suite to their sovereign. Opinion of Phillimore. Unfoundedness thereof 253

IX. Social Classes as Subjects of Rights in Domain of International Communication

§84. Rights which might belong to societies in international relations. Religious societies. Nations. Basic rights of legal societies and rights of territorial authorities with respect thereto 255

X. Private Individuals as Subjects of Rights in Domain of International Communication

A. Human Rights in International Relations

§85. Protection and respect for the individual. "*L'air fait libre*". Russia: 1820 Case of Negro Ivanov. Struggle against slavery 256

a) Struggle against trade by Europeans. European States and Algiers. Russia on the Black Sea and in Central Asia. 258

b) Abolition of trade in negroes. History. Declaration of 27 January (7 February) 1815. Two systems of struggle – England – Russia. Treaty of 1841. Trade in slaves at present time 259

c) Trade in coolies. – 1866 Chinese law 263

§86. 1) Right to existence. 2) Right to development of spiritual forces. 3) Right of communication. Emigration. Sanction of international law 263

B. On Rights of States with Respect to Subjects and Foreigners

§87. a) With respect to subjects. 1) Subordination to fatherland law abroad. 2) Recourse to foreign authorities. 3) Right of recall. 4) Protection of subjects. Denial of justice. Commercial enterprises. 1848 Despatch of Palmerston. b) With respect to foreigners. 1) Admission of foreigners to State. 2) Subordination to territorial orders. Russia and England: affair of the Jew Levinson 1881. Exceptions.

3) Non-violation of local law. Political emigrants. Local duties. 4) Free exit 264

Chapter 3
State Territory and International Routes

I. On State Territory in General

§88. Definition of territory. International ownership. *Dominium eminens*. Right of Taking Possession (Occupation). United States 270

II. Boundaries of Territory

§89. Importance of determination of boundaries. 1) Natural boundaries: sea, rivers, mountains, steppe, and sand-bars. Conclusion. 2) Artificial or treaty boundaries. Application: social boundaries 271

III. On Means of Acquisition of Territorial Possessions

§90. 1) Initial means: a) Increment. b) Limitation. c) Taking possession. History. Conditions. Opinion of Bluntschli on limits of taking possession. Examples 275

§91. 2) Derivative means: a) Purchase. b) Voluntary cession. c) Conquest. Conditions. On international plebiscite. Choice (Option). Examples 280

IV. On Means of Alienation and Loss of Territory

§92. Coerced cession. Voluntary refusal 284

§93. Addition: status of Cyprus, Bosnia and Herzogovina, Kiao-chu and Port Arthur 284

V. Limitations of Right of Territoriality

§94. Rent, fief, and mortgage. International duties (servitudes) – natural and treaty. Negative and positive servitudes. Subjects, subject-matter, origin. Interpretation 288

§95. a) Negative international duties. Examples 290

§96. b) Positive international duties. Examples 292

VI. On the High Seas

§97. Freedom of high seas. Substantiation. Previous views. Contemporary views. Baltic Sea. Mramor and Black, Adriatic, Narrow-Seas, Azov, Kara Sea. Closed seas: Dead and Caspian 295

§98. Consequences of principle of freedom of high seas 298

VII. On the Coastal or Territorial Sea

§99. Definition. Justification of authority of State. Boundary. Old claims. Bynkershoek. Contemporary setting of this question 299

§100. On the territorial sea in the strict sense. Bay of Klek. Gulfs of Finland and Riga. King's Chambers. Power of coastal State 302

VII. On Straits

§101. Contemporary theory and practice. Difference between straits from viewpoint of freedom of the sea. Sound Strait. Bosphorus and Dardanelles 304

VIII. On Rivers

§102. Territorial and international rivers. 1815 Act of Vienna. 1856 Treaty of Paris. European Danube Commission 305

Chapter 4
International Treaties

I. On International Treaties

§103. General principles. Substantiation of binding nature of treaties. Conclusions 307

II. Conditions of Conclusion and Legal Force of Treaties

A. Subjective Conditions

§104. Independence of States. Empowered persons and compliance with law 310

§105. Ratification. Definition, conditions, and operation of ratification 311

§106. Refusal of ratification. Opinion of writers. Resolution of question from standpoint of prerogatives of supreme power. Powers to ratify. Instances when ratification was not necessary 312

§107. When refusal to ratify is legal. Consent of chambers. 1867 Convention between Denmark and United States. Consequences of confirmation of treaty without consent of chambers, non-confirmation by one party, performance before ratification 314

§108. Operation of ratification. Unfoundedness of generally-recognized principle. Examples of refusals to confirm treaties 316

§109. Freedom of will of contracting parties. Significance of mistake, fraud, and coercion. Facts. Mutuality of expression of will 318

B. Objective Conditions

§110. Subject-matter of treaties. Conditions of validity of content thereof. Examples 320

III. On Participation of Third Powers in Treaties

§111. Forms of participation of third States in treaty. 1) Good services. 2) Mediation. 3) Accession. 4) Attack. 5) Interference 321

IV. On External Form of International Treaties

§112. Binding nature of form. Force of Declaration. Treaty in form of letters. Form of treaties and conventions. Oral treaties. Example 323

V. Types of International Treaties

§113. Classification of treaties. Hugo Grotius. Heffter. Bluntschli. Division into treaties and conventions. Real and personal treaties. Division of treaties into social and political. Increase in number of treaties. View of Montague Bernard – Treaties of alliance in former times 325

VI. Performance of International Treaties

§114. Good faith performance. Consent of parties. Provision of London Conference of 5(17) January 1871. Means and forms of performance. Promulgation. Secret agreements 328

VII. International Means of Securing Treaties

§115. Chief means. 1) Oath. 2) Hostages. 3) Pawn and pledge. 4) Suretyship (guarantee). Types of guarantee by content and form. Operation of suretyship. Termination 329

VIII. On Interpretation of International Treaties

§116. Applicability of principles of civil law. Interpretation of words and content 334

IX. Termination of Operation and Binding Nature of International Treaties

§117. Legal termination of force of treaty. Fixed-term treaties. Peace treaties. John Stuart Mill. Revision. "*Clausula rebus sic stantibus*". 1855 Concordat with Austria 335

X. Addition: International Obligations from Permitted and Impermissable Actions

§118. Contribution of Heffter. I. Obligations *quasi ex contractu*. Example. II. Obligations *ex delicto*. Responsibility of State for actions of sovereign, officials, and private individuals. Crimes against international law 337

Index 341

Editorial Preface to English Translation

It is remarkable and regrettable that the single most significant Russian treatise on public international law should have taken 140 years to achieve its first English translation since its initial appearance at St. Petersburg in 1882. Carl Bergbohm (1849-1927) produced a German translation within a year after the first volume of the Russian text appeared,[1] followed shortly by the French version prepared by Alfred Leo (1838-).[2] A Spanish edition appeared ca. 1894 with the translator unmentioned but a preface and notes by Joaquin Fernandez Prida (1863-1942),[3] two Japanese language versions in 1900 and 1908 respectively, each edition in two volumes translated by Shingo Nakamura (1870-1939),[4] reportedly a Chinese language translation, and a Persian edition which may be in essence a concise summary of probably the French-language text.[5]

The Russian language original went through five editions as follows, each edition in two volumes published at St. Petersburg:

First edition: 1882-1883
Second edition: 1887-1888
Third edition: 1895-1896
Fourth edition: 1898-1900
Fifth edition: 1904-1905

The volumes are conceptualized and divided into the "General Part" and the "Special Part". The section numbering and pagination between the two parts is not sequential as between them, but in the Russian versions they share a common rudimentary Index. They were never published in the same year; the title page designates them as volumes I and II. Unlike many multi-volume Russian legal treatises, one rarely encounters mixed sets. When he did revise the volumes, Martens was careful to complete the revision, if never within the same year, at least within a year or so of one another.

No foreign language version exists of the final version of the Martens treatise, and no one has attempted a version of Martens which incorporates

[1] F. F. Martens, *Völkerrecht: Das internationale Recht der Civilisirten Nationen,* transl. Carl Bergbohm (Berlin, Weidmannsche Buchhandlung, 1883-1886). 2 vols.

[2] F. F. Martens, *Traité de droit international*, transl. Alfred Leo (Paris, A. Chevalier-Marescq et Cie, 1883-1887). 3 vols.

[3] F. F. Martens, *Tratado de derecho internacional*, preface and notes by Joaquín Fernández Prida (Madrid, La Espana Moderna, [c. 1894]). 3 vols. + appendix.

[4] See F. F. Martens, *Kokusaihō / Furīdorihhi Fon Marutensu* (Tokyo, 1908). The Japanese translation was made from the Bergbohm German version. I am indebted to Professor Nobuyoshi Fujinami for details on the Japanese versions.

[5] See Moshen Nikbin, "On the Origins of the Earliest Lecture on International Law in Persia", *Jus Gentium: Journal of International Legal History*, V (2020), pp. 179-183.

passages from earlier volumes that were omitted in later editions. This English edition accomplishes both.

There have been at least two reprint editions of the treatise converted into modern orthography, at Moscow in 1996 and 2008.[6] Both have been substantially abridged. The original volumes are available online. In addition to the "normal" edition, students at St. Petersburg University and the Imperial School of Jurisprudence took careful notes of the Martens lectures and published these transcripts in a student lithographed version at modest cost.[7]

A word is in order on the editorial policies and practices followed when preparing this translation:

Text. The translation is based on the fifth edition but with the interpolation of materials which appeared in earlier versions and were omitted from the last Russian edition. In his Preface to the fifth edition, Martens cautioned that it differs from all earlier European and Asian versions of the treatise. While, of course, these changes include revisions, changes, and emendations from one edition to the next, in editions two to five §§58 and 60-62 were omitted, each of which dealt with some aspect of statehood and, by implication, with the concept of a "civilized people" or "nation". In the Russian language editions after the first, even though the said sections were omitted, the numbering was left intact, meaning that the reader was

[6] F. F. Martens, Современное международное право цивилизованных народов [Contemporary International Law of Civilized Peoples], ed. Lev Nikitich Shestakov (Moscow,1996). 2 vols. 3000 ptd.; Martens, Современное международное право цивилизованных народов [Contemporary International Law of Civilized Peoples], ed. Vladimir Alekseevich Tomsinov (Moscow, 2008). 2 vols. 1000 ptd.

[7] See F. F. Martens, Курс международного права [Course of International Law], comp. A. Il'in and A. Zamiatin (1883-1884). 661 p.; Martens, Лекции по международного права цивилизованных народов: курс II-го класса Императорского училища правоведения [Lectures on the International Law of Civilized Nations: Course of the II Class of the Imperial School of Jurisprudence], comp. A. Miakinin (undated; ca. 18?). 475 p. Both are held by the Harvard Law School Library. Also see Martens, Конспект международного права, составленный по курсу профессора Санкт-Петербургского университета Ф. Ф. Мартенса 1880-1881 гг. [Synopsis of International Law Compiled for the Course of Professor of St. Petersburg University F. F. Martens 1880-1881] (Spb., 1881). 157 p. (lithographed manuscript); Martens, Курс международного права. Лекции, читанные профессором Мартенсом в Санкт-Петербургском университете в 1878/79 академ. году [Course of International Law. Lectures Read by Professor Martens at the St. Petersburg University in 1878/79 Academic Year] (Spb., 1879). 428 p. (lithographed manuscript); Martens, Международное право [International Law] (Spb., 1875). 208 p. (lithographed); Martens, Международное право. Особенная часть. Лекции проф. С.-Петербургского университета Ф. Мартенса [International Law. Special Part. Lectures of Professor of St. Petersburg University, F. Martens] (Spb., 1882). 720 p. (lithographed manuscript); Martens, Международное право. Курс лекций, читанных в 1-м классе Императорского Училища правоведения [International Law. Course of Lectures read in the I Class of the Imperial School of Jurisprudence in 188/9] (Spb., 1889). 312 p. (lithographed manuscript).

aware of the omission but left wondering what had been said that was no longer relevant or appropriate. And the mystery is more intriguing because the missing passages addressed matters of public international law central to the title of the book. These passages have been restored in this English translation.[8]

Wherever possible, the first mention of an individual is accompanied by additional basic biographical data giving the full name and years of birth and death. The data is set off in square brackets in the text or footnotes to indicate that it did not appear in the original text. In nearly all instances we have succeeded in identifying the persons involved.

Where Russian names or words are transliterated, the Library of Congress system of transliteration is used or adapted in simplified form. French, German, and other foreign language materials in the Latin alphabet require no transliteration and are given as in the original.

Terminology. The title of the Martens treatise poses two conundrums for a translator in the twenty-first century. First is the term "civilized", which is no longer politically correct even though the word and concept are ensconced in the Statute of the International Court of Justice (Article 38). Martens explains his use of the concept in the treatise and, as a man of his time and generation, it is important to his perception of international law.

Second is the term translated in this volume as "people" (народ) but often rendered as "nation" (нация), including at times by the present writer. That, of course, begs the question that bedevils political scientists and international relations specialists: when does a people become a nation? In some English usages the terms overlap and have been known to be used as synonyms. The Bergbohm translation used the German "nation"; the French and Spanish versions avoided the issue at least in the title of the book by eliminating the word altogether. Having considered the work as a whole, the term "people" was determined to be most appropriate and that practice has been followed.

A third term, frequently used by Martens and central to his understanding of the international system, is общение. Its dictionary meaning is "communion", which has strong religious overtones for the western reader that are not intended by the author. In some contexts that rendering seems appropriate, but most often it is translated as "community" and very occasionally as "interaction".

A fourth expression which appears in the General Part but is central to the Special Part is the concept of international управление, here translated as "administration", but where appropriate, also as "governing" or a variant thereof.

[8] W. E. Butler, "The Martens Treatise: Missing Passages", *Jus Gentium: Journal of International Legal History*, IV (2019), pp. 633-653.

Another term that appears with some frequency is оборот, translated as "turnover"; it is a comprehensive term that encompasses commercial and non-commercial relations, tangibles and intangibles.

Footnotes. The Russian editions number the footnotes anew on each page. That approach enabled the author to revise each edition without re-setting and renumbering the footnotes and will have facilitated the preparation of each revision and reduced setting costs. One result of that approach, however, is inconsistencies in citation form and duplication of content. Cross references are impossible. The present edition follows the opposite approach: footnotes are numbered consecutively in each segment or chapter of the book. In most instances additional data is supplied: forenames or full names of the authors or editors; publication data, fuller titles when appropriate, and in a few cases the editor has introduced a new footnote set entirely in square brackets with initials indicated. Misprints have been corrected without indication; some anonymous works have been identified whose authors were unknown to Martens. When, however, it has been impossible to determine which version of a work Martens referred to, his original version of the footnote has been retained and only reliable information added.

Citations have not been checked for accuracy, however. Pagination, volume numbers, and the like have not been verified against the original. Any errors remain with Martens.

During the late eighteenth and throughout the nineteenth centuries there were three distinguished international lawyers bearing the surname Martens: Georg Friedrich von Martens (1756-1821); Baron Karl, or Charles, de Martens (1790-1863), nephew of Georg; and Fedor Fedorovich (Friedrich Fromholz) von Martens (1845-1909), unrelated to both so far as we know. They are often confused with one another. They each produced standard treatises on the law of nations and important treaty collections. Georg Friedrich and Karl were based in Germany; Fedor was Estonian born and based in Russia. A fictional relationship among the three was memorialized in the best-selling novel by Nobel-nominee, Jaan Kross (1920-2007).[9] To minimize confusion, in this volume they are respectively identified by their initials or, when necessary, their full forenames are given.

[9] J. Kross, *Professor Martens' Departure*, transl. Anselm Hollo (New York, 1994), reviewed: *American Journal of International Law*, LXXXVIII (1994), pp. 863-864 (W. E. Butler). Martens passed away on 7(20) June 1909 while en route from his Lifliand estate to St. Petersburg at the age of 64.

Biographical Sketch of F. F. Martens

William E. Butler
Vitalii S. Ivanenko

The best-known public international lawyer of Imperial Russia, Fedor Fedorovich Martens (1845-1909), was born at Pärnu (Pernov) of unknown parentage in present-day Estonia and victim at Valka Station, Livonian Province (now Estonia), of a heart attack. Diplomat, legal advisor to the Ministry of Foreign Affairs, Professor of International Law at St. Petersburg University (successor to Ignatii Ioakinfovich Ivanovskii (1807-1886) in this position), international arbitrator, member of the State Council of Russia, corresponding member of the Russian Academy of Sciences, honorary member of a number of foreign academies, recipient of honorary doctorates at American, British, and continental universities, and confidant of rulers throughout Europe (including Austria-Hungary, England, France, and Germany), Martens achieved remarkable stature in an international community where stature among colleagues mattered.[1]

Life and Career

The considerable body of materials on the early life, origins, parents, date of birth, and marriage, religious preference, change of name, and other personal details contains much that is inconsistent, inaccurate, or ambiguous. The widely propagated view is that Martens was born on 15 August 1845 into the family of a junior deacon or sexton of the Evangelical Lutheran faith. On 25 September 1879 he married Catherina Ture, the daughter of Senator Nikolai Andreevich Ture (1834-1905),[2] of St. Petersburg, converted to the Russian Orthodox Church pursuant to the laws of that time,[3]

[1] On the life and career of Martens, see V. V. Pustogarov, *Our Martens: F. F. Martens, International Lawyer and Architect of Peace*, ed. & transl. W. E. Butler (2000); V. S. Ivanenko, Санкт-Петербургская школа международного права [St. Petersburg School of International Law] (2019), I, pp. 150-202; W. E. Butler and V. S. Ivanenko, "F. F. Martens: Russian Scholar, Diploma, and Arbitrator", *Jus Gentium: Journal of International Legal History*, IV (2019), pp. 145-178.

[2] Senator Ture (or Tur) shared much in common with his son-in-law, F. F. Martens. Tur also graduated as a candidate of laws from St. Petersburg University and then visited the Universities of Berlin and the École de droit in Paris. He served in the Ruling Senate from 1 January 1893. See N. A. Murzanov, Словарь русских сенаторов 1711-1917 гг. Материалы для биографий [Dictionary of Russian Senators 1711-1917: Materials for Biographies] (Spb., 2011), p. 441.

[3] Archival documents disclose that Martens never converted to the Russian Orthodox faith; he remained a Lutheran for all of his life, and a Lutheran cross embellishes his gravestone. On some Russian documents, including his application to St. Petersburg University

and took the name Fedor Fedorovich Martens. Archival documents suggest some adjustments are in order with respect to these standard accounts.

One such document is an extract from the metric marriage book of the Baden Evangelical-Protestant Congregation, which records: On 30 December 1879, Friedrich Fromgold Martens, an Imperial Russian privy councilor, residing in St. Petersburg, born in Pernov, Livonia, on 10 August 1845, son of the deceased Friedrich Wilhelm Martens and Teresa Wilhelmina, born Knast, of Evangelical faith, bachelor, and Ekaterina Louisa Maria Ture, of Evangelical faith, spinster, born in St. Petersburg on 27 July 1861, daughter of Nikolai Edouard Ture and of Ekaterina Wilhelmina von Shneider, were duly married.[4]

Several observations are in order. As to the birth date on the metric marriage document, Martens in many other places, including his personal diaries which repose in the Archive of Foreign Policy of Russia (AVPR), recorded his birth date as 15 August 1845.[5] The same date is recorded in the biographical dictionary of St. Petersburg professors, the data for which he will have supplied personally or verified. We therefore have variant dates which he supplied, although the month is consistent. On the other hand, an Estonian lawyer reported in 1975 that after exhaustive searching of all church registries in Pernov, he was unable to locate any birth registration for the Martens parents.[6] Such registration was obligatory in those times and served as the basis for a metric certificate or for christening a child.[7] That opens the possibility that Martens never precisely knew his birth date in the absence of official records and relied on family tradition for this information.

As to parentage, the most detailed account is recorded in the historical novel by Jaan Kross (1920-2007).[8] According to Kross, Martens was

and his graduation diploma, the name "Fromhold" is listed as his forename. In his activities abroad, including his publications, "Friedrich", or a variation thereof, is always given as the forename.

4 ЦГИА СПб., f. 536, opis 6, file 4813, l. 5-5obverse. The genuineness of the extract is confirmed by a notary in Baden-Baden and the Imperial Russian Mission attached to the Baden court.

5 AVPR, opis 787, file 9, ed. khr. 1-7; cited in Pustogarov, note 1 above, p. 8.

6 L. Lesment, «Новые сведения из жизни Ф. Ф. Мартенса» [New Information from the Life of F. F. Martens], Советское право [Soviet Law], no. 5 (1975), pp. 358-370.

7 Pustogarov reported that the Martens metric certificate was not to be found in his personal file or other materials in the AVPR. See Pustogarov, note 1 above, p. 10.

8 Jaan Kross, *Professor Martensi Ärasõit* (Tallinn, 1984), translated into Russian as Kross, Уход профессора Мартенса [The Departure of Professor Martens] (Moscow, 1989); published in English as Kross, *Professor Martens' Departure*, transl. Anselm Hollo (1994). The English translation, published separately in London and New York, is Kross's best-known work abroad; there were translations into other languages. Kross' nomination for

the last of nine children born to Fredrich Wilhelm Martens (1795-1850), for many years the sexton of the Lutheran Church in Audre. In 1844 F. W. Martens was dismissed from this position and moved to Pernov, where he purchased a house on Gartenstrasse 10 and engaged in tailoring.[9] His mother died in 1854. Kross related that Fedor Fedorovich had brothers: Heinrich, who became a cobbler in Riga; August, who graduated from university and became a medical doctor on the Island of Madeira; Johannes, who found employment at a local sawmill; Julius, who studied pharmacy in St. Petersburg and later founded a factory for the production of hygiene products. According to the novel, Fedor Fedorovich was sent to Julius in St. Petersburg. He himself wrote to contemporaries: "He was not of the nobility or wealthy by birth, and the fairy of protectionism did not practice sorcery at his modest cradle".[10]

As to marriage, Martens was not married on 25 September 1879, but on 30 December, as the metric certificate officially attests. The certificate was issued in Baden-Baden on 10 January 1880. On the other hand, Pustogarov reported 18 December 1879, for which there seems to be no empirical evidence unless the difference arises from the difference in Julian and Gregorian calendars.[11] The metric certification from Baden-Baden also confirms that, whenever Martens may have converted to the Russian Orthodox faith, it was not at the time of his marriage, nor did he change his name on that occasion.[12]

As to the various versions of his name, in his personal life Martens used several versions of his forenames: on his marriage certificate (1867) and on the birth and baptismal certificates of his son Nikolai (1880) and daughter Edith (1886), all issued by the Evangelical Lutheran Church in

the Nobel Prize in Literature was unsuccessful. A lawyer by training whose historical fiction was known to be based on scrupulous investigation of the factual background, Kross was acting docent at the Chair of Public International Law in 1945-1946 at Tartu University. See Pustogarov, note 1 above, p. 8.

[9] A memorial plaque has been placed on the house in Pärnu in commemoration of F. F. Martens. Martens, according to Lesment, later purchased his father's house and routinely spent the summers there. Lesment, note 6 above. Pustogarov observed that the Martens diaries held in the AVPR contain not a single word about his parents, brothers, childhood, or adolescence, although some passages relate to his wife and children or relatives of his wife. In the diary left by his son, Nikolai, references are made to his mother, but nothing on the relatives of his father. See note 6 above, p. 12.

[10] Cited in L. Sidorenko, «Главный судья христианского мира» [Chief Judge of the Christian World], Санкт-Петербургские ведомости [St. Petersburg Gazette], 8 May 2012.

[11] Pustogarov, note 1 above, p. 10.

[12] This would suggest that Pustogarov was incorrect in these details. See note 1 above, pp. 10-11.

Baden-Baden or in St. Petersburg, Martens specified his name as "Friedrich Fromgold von Martens". In official materials Martens preferred "Friedrich", "Fromgold", "Fedor", "Fromgold Fedorovich"; his application in the name of the Rector of St. Petersburg University for admission contained the names "Fridrikh" and "Fromgold Fedorovich"; in 1867 his kandidat diploma described him as "Fromgold Fridrikhof, son of Martens"; in 1869 his magister diploma read "Fromgold Fridrikhovich Martens"; and only after the issuance in 1873 of the diploma of doctor did he use "Fedor Fedorovich Martens". He named himself and signed this name in the official sphere – the University, the Ministry of Foreign Affairs, and so on. Abroad, Martens was called in German and English "Friedrich von Martens", and in French, Frédéric de Martens.

As to nationality, it is disputed as to whether Martens is of Baltic-German stock and/or native Estonian. Continental European doctrinal writings have on numerous occasions described Martens as "German";[13] Russian writings tend to describe him as Baltic-German; Kross made a detailed argument in favor of his Estonian roots. The debate continues.

It is uncontested that at the age of nine, in 1854, with the assistance of his teacher in a local school, Lutheran Pärnu clergy, and possibly his older brother, he was sent to St. Petersburg and in January 1855 was placed in an orphan home attached to the St. Peter's German Evangelical Lutheran Church. It was proposed that he become in time a junior deacon of the church. Distinction in his school studies led to Martens being transferred to the St. Peter's Chief School (German Gymnasium), where he graduated in 1863.[14]

The German school was of a high standard, but strict. Martens distinguished himself in his studies by diligence, talent, well-prepared lessons, and model behavior; he found himself attracted to poetry, history, and foreign languages. The teachers and director of the School predicted a future in the fields of history or philology. But Martens chose instead to enroll at the Law Faculty of St. Petersburg University. He applied to the Law Faculty of St. Petersburg University on 31 August 1863 and was enrolled on 10 October 1863.[15] A petition to the Rector of the University seeking exemption from tuition fees was granted, following the usual bureaucratic correspondence between the Rector, Administration of the Petersburg Educational

[13] See the appreciation by H. Wehberg, "Dr. Friedrich v. Martens und die Haager Friedenskonferenzen", *Zeitschrift für internationales Recht*, XX, no. 4 (1910). Other German sources have described Martens as a "Russian international lawyer of Baltic-German origin". See *Brockhaus Enzyklopedie* (1971), XII, p. 190.

[14] Биографический словарь профессоров и преподавателей Императорского С.-Петербургского университета за истекшие четверть века его существования. 1869-1894 [Biographical Dictionary of Professors and Lecturers of the Imperial St. Petersburg University for the Past Quarter Century of its Existence. 1869-1894)] (Spb., 1896), II, p. 6.

[15] ЦГИА СПб., f. 14, opis 5, file 2549, l. 1.

District, and the Ministry, with a request for the views of the Director of the German Gymnasium attended by Martens.[16]

Initially attracted by the philosophy of criminal law. Martens accidentally came across materials on public international law and produced a graduation diploma thesis "On Relations Between Russia and the Ottoman Empire in the Reign of Empress Catherine II". The thesis was well received, and in August 1867 Martens graduated with the degree of candidate of laws.[17] Martens' talent and abilities came to the attention of the Dean of the Law Faculty, Professor I. I. Ivanovskii, who simultaneously was the Head of the Chair of International Law.[18] When Martens approached Ivanovskii as Dean about remaining at the University to prepare for a career in the professoriate, preferring his favorite subject – criminal law – at the time, the Dean vigorously objected: "No better to remain at the Chair of International Law. Then we will have our own Martens".[19] As time was to prove, the phrase, whosoever first uttered it, was appropriate, for he came to rival, if not surpass, his continental colleagues and occupy a worthy place in the world of international law exceeded by no other Russian international lawyer.[20] In

16 Ibid., ll. 6-8, 11.

17 The diploma was issued to Martens on 11 September 1867. The diploma recited that Martens was 22 years of age, of the guild estate in Pernovo [Estonia], Evangelical Lutheran by profession of faith, enrolled on 10 October 1863, and listed all subjects studied with the grades received, His candidate dissertation was mentioned without specifying the topic. The diploma is preserved in the Central State Historical Archive of St. Petersburg: ЦГИА Спб., fond 14, opis 5, file 2549, l. 21.

18 See V. S. Ivanenko, "Ignatii Ivanovskii: First Head of the Chair of International Law at St. Petersburg University", *Jus Gentium: Journal of International Legal History*, IV (2019), pp. 77-94.

19 Quoted from M. A. von Taube, Ф. Ф. Мартенс. 1845-1909 (Некролог) [F. F. Martens. 1845-1909 (Obituary)] (Spb., 1909), pp. 3-4. Also see note 3 above, II, p. 7. This anecdote floated about over the years, being attributed to Ivanovskii, to Prince Aleksandr Mikhailovich Gorchakov (1798-1883), who hired Martens for the Ministry of Foreign Affairs, and others. Ivanovskii was referring to the well-known German international lawyers Georg F. Martens and Charles de Martens, as noted above, and the anecdote influenced the title of the biography of Martens by Pustogarov and the English translation thereof by Butler. See V. V. Pustogarov, Федор Федорович Мартенс: Юрист, Дипломат [Fedor Fedorovich Martens: Iurist, Diplomat] (2d ed., 1999); Pustogarov, note 1 above.

20 Kross makes excellent narrative use of the incident. Upon learning of Martens' inclination to pursue the criminal law, Ivanovskii advised: "*Criminal* law? But why? No, I don't agree with that. It's true that we have lost Spasovich, but we'll appoint Tagantsev his successor … You were born for a career in international law … No more buts … Go for the chair in international law. Any other choice would indicate such a lack of knowledge on your part that I wouldn't be able to support you. But in my own department I'll support you with all my heart. What's more. I predict that if you choose international law, Russia will gain its own Martens, and the world will once again have a Martens – this time, a

the event, Martens took his Dean's advice, remained at the Chair of International Law to prepare himself for a career in the professoriate, and served for 34 years in that capacity. In parallel, he took up a position as from 6 January 1869 in the Ministry of Foreign Affairs, where he retained a position for more than four decades.

Martens' preparations for his magister dissertation are instructive. He chose a topic virtually unresearched in Russia: the inviolability of private ownership during wartime. His command of foreign languages was an advantage, and he collected materials from German, English, Italian, French, and medieval Latin sources. As he completed chapters, he read them out in the evenings to Professor Ivanovskii and on the basis of their discussions prepared a final variant of each chapter. In the course of a year of diligent labor he assembled and mastered a substantial body of factual, normative, and doctrinal materials and submitted to the Faculty of Law a dissertation amounting to 464 printed pages. This he defended on 5 October 1869 – a Sunday – in a public session of professors of the Law Faculty and was awarded the degree of magister of international law (the actual diploma was presented to him the following day, 6 October 1869, in a formal ceremony).

The magister dissertation was so topical and so theoretically proficient, and its author so obviously a talented and serious researcher, that the Learned Council adopted a decision to publish the dissertation at University expense.[21] In October 1869 at the recommendation of the Law Faculty Martens was sent abroad, as was customary in those days for individuals preparing for a professorial career, at the expense of the Ministry of the Enlightenment in order to hear lectures by foreign professors, work in the libraries of Vienna, Heidelberg, Leipzig, Berlin, Paris, and elsewhere, thereby gaining a first-hand familiarity with the doctrine and practice of international law in Europe.[22]

As Martens himself later recalled, Professor Lorenz von Stein (1815-1890), at the University of Vienna, and Professor Johann Caspar Bluntschli (1808-1881), of Heidelberg University, left the strongest impressions on him. The time abroad greatly influenced Martens' scientific views and laid the foundations for enduring relations with foreign colleagues, especially in Europe, Martens being among the few Russian international lawyers who remained close to, and contributed to, the European doctrines and practice of international law.

Although his trip abroad was to be for eighteen months, within a year of his absence St. Petersburg University sent Martens an official letter requesting that he return from his travels in order to become the Head of the Chair of International Law after Ivanovskii was not re-elected to that position for

Russian!". Kross, note 8 above, pp. 59-60.

21 F. F. Martens, О праве частной собственности во время войны [On the Right of Private Ownership During War] (Spb., 1869). viii, 453 p.

22 Note 14 above, II, p. 7.

a new 5-year period. Martens returned and in January 1871 was confirmed in the title of docent and at the age of 25 occupied the Chair of International law,[23] remaining in that position for 32 years, until 1903. Immediately after taking up the post, Martens began to deliver the lectures in the basic course on public international law, which in turn became the foundation for his celebrated treatise on the subject. He also commenced work on a doctoral dissertation for the degree of doctor of international law. Two years later, in 1873, Martens submitted a doctoral dissertation on consuls and consular jurisdiction in the East, at the age of 28 defended the dissertation,[24] received the degree of doctor of international law, and was appointed professor *extraordinarius* at the Chair of International Law. The following year Martens' dissertation was published at Berlin in a German translation,[25] which confirmed his reputation among foreign colleagues. Three years later, in 1876, Martens at the age of 31 became a professor *ordinarius* and remained in his position until his departure from the University in 1903.

Martens held other teaching appointments together with his position at St. Petersburg University and the Ministry of Foreign Affairs: at the Imperial Aleksandrov Lycée,[26] from 1866 to 1905; from autumn 1886 to the end of his life, at the Imperial School of Jurisprudence.[27]

Scholarly and Lecturing Activity in International Law

Turning first to Martens' magister dissertation on private ownership in time of war, this was the first study of its kind. Martens himself wrote in his preface: "So far the question of the inviolability of enemy private ownership was more the subject-matter of practical and political consideration in the parliaments and chambers of commerce of England, France, and Germany than the subject-matter of a detailed scientific study.[28] In this his first scholarly work Martens already had turned to a consideration of the reasons for and nature of inter-State conflicts. Having regard to the international realities of his day, Martens acknowledged the inevitability of armed conflicts between States, but believed their character and results change as human

23 ЦГИА Спб., fond 14, opis 1-1, file 6958 (1870).

24 Martens, О консулах и консульской юрисдикции на Востоке [On Consuls and Consular Jurisdiction in the East] (Spb., 1873). 599 p. The defense was held on a Sunday, 18 March 1873, at 13:00 hours; the official opponents were Professors Aleksandr Dmitrievich Gradovskii (1841-1889) and Ivan Efimovich Andreevskii (1831-1891).

25 Martens, *Das Consularwesen und die Consularjurisdiction im Orient*, transl. H. Skerst (Berlin, 1874). [vi], 594 p.

26 ЦГИА Спб., fond 11, opis 1, file 3784.

27 ЦГИА Спб., fond 355, opis 1, file 3943.

28 Martens, note 21 above, p. vii.

culture and civilization develop. He expressed his own conviction that as peoples become aware of their own advantage and self-improvement, "mutual conflicts which represent the most actual brake on human development should be reduced proportionately" (pp. 54-55).

Martens allotted an important role to law in the prevention and humanizing of military conflicts. "Any war", he suggested, "will only be proper and consistent with the condition for the development of international life when it satisfies the requirements of international law" (p. 95).

The basic premise of Martens' magister dissertation was demonstrating the unlawfulness and inadmissibility of the seizure by belligerents of enemy private ownership because war is not against private individuals, but States; therefore, reprisals are admissible only against State ownership.

An important merit of Martens' work is that he went beyond the framework of this declared topic and for the first time in Russian international-legal literature considered a broad range of problems connected with the behavior of belligerents. Therefore, Martens by right may be considered the founder of the Russian science of international humanitarian law applicable during armed conflicts. As Danevskii noted eight years after the publication of Martens' book, devoting seven full pages to analysis and commentary, Martens' work

> by virtue of the talent and erudition of the author, partly also by fulfillment, may compete with similar works of western scholars and, in some respect, even exceed them … Martens' monograph, in our view, is the most talented of Russian works and unusually rich in historical information. It is read with true satisfaction and should be a manual for those studying international law in Russia, especially the law of war.[29]

Having become docent at the Chair, Martens on 28 January 1871 gave his first lecture to the students. This was the address of a 24-year old young lecturer whose content would program and determine the future of his position also as a scholar, diplomat, and international arbitrator. In his lecture he attempted a scientific substantiation of the relatively young science of international law, gave a critical and severe evaluation of the state of international relations, science, and practice of international law, and set out his vision of the basic orientations of their further development. The entire content and pathos of the lecture was presented in an optimistic spirit, with faith in human reason, and the great potential opportunities for the science and practice of international law.[30]

[29] V. P. Danevskii, Очерк новейшей литературы по международному праву [Survey of Recent Literature on International Law] (Spb., 1876), pp. 232, 236-237.

[30] For details, see Martens, «О задачах современного международного права: Вступительная лекция, читанная 28-го января 1871 года в Ст.-Петербургском университете» [On the Tasks of Contemporary International Law: Inaugural Lecture Delivered 28 January 1871 at St. Petersburg University], Журнал Министерства народного просвещения [Journal of the Ministry of Public Enlightenment], no. 6 (1871),

Martens declared himself to be an opponent of the then dominant school of natural law and a proponent of legal positivism, then gathering impetus. International law should rely on the study of positivist legal material. Only history and actual reality may provide firm foundation for international-legal structures: "A change in the conditions of international life", he said, must result in a change of law, and therefore only a study of the conditions of international life at a particular time, and of its historical development, can elucidate the true international legal consciousness". However, in his view, the science of international law "up to now has not investigated the elements and phenomena of real life, has not even attempted to study the internal laws of the community of States and international relations ...", and therefore the time had come to turn to the study of the laws of historical development of peoples in their international life.

Martens attached significance in principle to the link between the development of international law and the history of international relations, and also to the study of concrete legal material. He was convinced that only history may serve as a firm foundation for scientific conceptions. As is evident, this was an initiative of Martens for the creation of a new theory of international law meeting the realities of contemporary international relations. The science of international law, he suggested, should substantiate the defense of the individual. Martens was the first in Russia to place the degree of civilization of the State and the development of international law in close connection with the development of the individual, with the recognition and defense thereof and his rights on the part of State authorities.

Having critically analyzed the state of inter-State relations, the degree of compliance by States with norms of international law in peacetime and in wartime, Martens severely condemned war as a barbaric means of settling international disputes which should not triumph over peaceful legal means.[31] Having in his first lecture claimed a renewal of the Russian science of international law, Martens should have suggested research at the theoretical level, breadth of generalization of factual material, and fundamental character of the research would noticeably exceed the standard of his predecessors and raise the general progress of the science of law in Russia to the level of achievements of the world science of international law.

This task Martens fulfilled. His legacy of legal scholarship is expressed in capital treatises, which enhanced his reputation as a jurist and diplomat throughout the world; many were devoted to individual topical issues of international law and politics, accompanied by innumerable contributions to periodical and serial publications. The apotheosis of Martens' contributions to international legal doctrine, however, was the present two-volume

pp. 251-268; by decision of the Ministry, the lecture was published as a separate pamphlet (Spb., 1871). 17 p.

[31] Ibid., pp. 257-262.

treatise on the contemporary international law of civilized nations and his fifteen volume collection of treaties of Russia with foreign States.

The present two-volume treatise (called a "course" in Russian) was the first autonomous manual that fully treated international law in Russia: it became one of the best courses in legal literature, original in content and system, based on completely new facts of international and Russian diplomatic history.[32] The treatise was epochal – it changed the position in the study and understanding of international law by 180 degrees. Until then the teaching of international law in Russian universities had been based principally on the works of foreigners.

Martens' treatise filled this gap in Russian jurisprudence with interest: it was one of the best-known and basic textbooks until the revolutionary events of 1917 to 1920 in Russian higher educational institutions.[33] The treatise became one of the best-known in the world, where it was perceived not only as a textbook, but as an encyclopedic publication in which original views and positions were reflected of one of the most authoritative scholars and diplomats on major aspects of international relations and international law. During Martens' lifetime, the treatise was revised four times, translated and published abroad in the German, French, Spanish, Serbian, Persian, Chinese, and Japanese languages and was widely consulted, which cannot be said of any doctrinal work by Russian jurists either before or after Martens.

Martens achieved in this treatise the methodological approach that he had set out in his inaugural lecture: to place research of international law on a stable foundation of the socio-political development of States, on the materials the history of their international relations, and contemporary State practice. The treatise was distinguished by its well-foundedness, realism, satiation with historical and normative material, including the materials of "Russian international policy according to the sources of our archives". Martens was convinced that "underlying international law are factual, real, living relations".

It is evident from the treatise here considered that Martens adhered to the positivist orientation developing at that time in the science of international law. International law, in Martens view, was the "aggregate of legal norms determining the conditions for the achievement by nations of their vital purposes in the sphere of mutual relations".

[32] Grabar described Martens' treatise as "Original in its system and for the first time illuminating norms of law by examples from the diplomatic history of Russia". See Vladimir Emmanuilovich Grabar, *The History of International Law in Russia, 1647-1917: A Bio-Biographical Study*, transl. W. E. Butler (1990), p. 380.

[33] Several generations of law students read it, as did future State officials of the Imperial, Soviet, and post-Soviet Russia, and under the guidance of professors of St. Petersburg (Leningrad) university, so too did future political leaders of Russia: Emperor Nicholas II, V. I. Lenin, A. F. Kerenskii, V. V. Putin, D. A. Medvedev, and many others.

Martens thus entered the history of the science of law at the end of the nineteenth and early twentieth centuries as the author of the two most original theories concerning the essence and functioning of international law: the theory of the international community and the theory of international administration. Underlying Martens' doctrinal positions were four basic propositions:

(1) nations and States by virtue of objective factors of their development aspire to and enter into communion with one another;

(2) the community of interests of nations and their international communion generated international law;

(3) the level of freedom of the individual is determined by the extent of the participation of States in international communion;

(4) international communion requires international administration and "international administrative law".

At the base of all his international-legal theory Martens placed the idea of international communion. In his view, international communion did not exist either in ancient times or in the Middle Ages because peoples of that period were not conscious of the need for mutual assistance and a general law; such consciousness was generated only in contemporary international thought. But he, as already noted, confined international communion and international law only to the peoples of "European civilization", excluding such communion and law with non-Christian peoples; with them European States are in communion on the basis of norms of "natural law", without clarifying what he understood by this. Thus, Martens' material progressive contribution to the development of international law was not in tune with his failure to recognize the international legal personality of so-called "uncivilized peoples".

Martens substantiated his position as follows: the progress of international law depends upon the development of the free individual and free State institutions. Only the State in which the individual has received recognition of his rights may become a member of a properly organized international community. Therefore, Martens limited the operation of international law to States of European civilization – the relations of States of Europe and North America. Martens rejected the possibility of compliance arising with any guarantees of international treaties in Antiquity and the Middle Ages and carried over this possibly only to the era contemporary to him. It is clear that this approach excluded any possibility of applying civilized treaty guarantees in relations with non-European nations contemporary to him. These guarantees Martens divided into simple and complex. Simple guarantees, he believed, arise when a civilized third State gives surety for the performance of a treaty, and complex guarantees exist as mutual or collective guarantees of States.

The essence of the theory of international community Martens saw in the following: States exist and develop, objectively entering into communion with one another on various issues:

> The international community is a free union of States in order to achieve by common actions the full development of their powers and satisfy their reasonable requirements. The aggregate of legal norms determining the effectuation of the idea of international communion comprises the law of the international community; that is, international law.

Martens logically derived the theory of international administration from the theory of the international community. The idea of international administration as the meaning and property of inter-State relations of States was first substantiated by Martens in the aforesaid doctoral dissertation on consuls and consular jurisdiction, the purpose of which he defined as an "investigation of the laws of international administration". Martens believed:

> The real grounds for international activity of States or international administration lies in the inadequacy of the forces and means for an individual nation to achieve its vital aim. By international administration we understand the free activity of a State in the domain of international communion in view of the achievement by them of their vital aims within the limits placed by international law.

Martens reasoned as follows. States are members of a single international community, but each of them preserves its autonomy and independence. The international community itself has a certain order; it is based on certain legal principles.

In order to regulate the international community, international administration is necessary and, respectively, agencies of international administration. All States in the international community are represented by agencies for the expression of their will, by means of which they administer both political and social relations existing between nations. These agencies he called international administrators.

Martens distinguished two aspects in international administration: (1) administration of the foreign relations of a State with the assistance of legislative, administrative, and judicial power; (2) administration of international relations by the joint efforts of States (through an administrative association of sovereign States).

In developing the theory of international administration, Martens devoted the second volume of his treatise to this question. Martens included within the system of international administration all activity of the State transcending the limits of one country and effectuated in the international sphere – all "international activity of State power". He wrote: "The aggregate of legal conditions and norms determining the international activity of a State is the law of international administration or international administrative law". Only States are subjects of the law of international administration. The object of the law of international administration is the "aggregate of all vital relations between States, social groups, and private individuals which requires assistance, patronage, or the defense of State power".

Martens was convinced that the

progressive development of mankind inevitably will lead to the ever greater intensive communion of States and thereby to the strengthening and improvement of international administration … the gradual work of international law with regard to the creation of a legal order in the world community which responds to the achievements of human civilization and the gradual development of international administration which seals the peaceful cooperation of nations – that is the path towards establishing perpetual peace on Earth, a path complex, not rapid, but the sole true and real path.

David Borisovich Levin (1903-1990) characterized Martens' theory of the law of international administration as "one of the most original theories concerning the essence of international law in Russian literature of the end of the nineteenth and early twentieth centuries.[34]

As a legal positivist, Martens, nonetheless, did not confine himself to merely one statement of legal norms and institutions. He sought, on one hand, by means of historical study to discover laws and developmental trends of the said norms and institutions and, on the other, by means of an analysis of contemporary international relations and actions of States to determine their significance and role in ensuring international communion and international administration. Inter-State relations Martens considered should be studied not in isolation, but in their natural linkage with the legal institutions of individual States and diversities such as the economic and spiritual interests of a society.

The undoubted service of Martens was his new conception of the system and science of international law. He for the first time drew a boundary between them. Martens built his scientific system on the idea of an international community:

> Underlying the scientific system of contemporary international law should be the idea of an international community, according to which each autonomous state is an organic part of a single whole and linked with other States of the community of interests and rights.

With regard to the system of the science of international law, Martens wrote:

> The system in which we set out the science of international law differs materially from others existing in the rich Western European literature … In continuation of eleven years of our lecturing activity this system was and remains, in our extreme understanding, that procedure which best corresponds to the essence and degree of the development of contemporary international relations.

Martens pointed out that the majority of legal scholars structure the system of international law as a continuation of ancient 'roman law, which in

[34] D. B. Levin, Наука международного права в России в конце XIX и начале XX в. [Science of International Law in Russia at the End of the XIX and Beginning of the XX Centuries] (Moscow, 1982), p. 12.

essence was civil law, and considered such an approach to be unscientific. An understanding of the peculiarities and law of the development of international law required an analysis of those real relations which linked States as member of the international community and their constant communion.

Martens rejected the division dominant in scholarship of his time of international law into the "law of war" and "law of peace". A completely different approach underlay Martens' system – the idea of international community and international administration "in the sphere of spiritual, physical, and economic interests of peoples" and "in the domain of the legal interests of subjects and peoples". According to Grabar, the system proposed by Martens "was confirmed in Russian literature and influenced some foreign writers".[35]

As followed from the treatise, Martens considered international law to be a unified complex of public-law and private-law principles and norms and determined the basic fundamental methodological principles for investigating the correlation of public international law and private international law. From the idea of an international community upheld by him, Martens derived the legal duty of each State and even directly a court to recognize "on the territory of the entire international community" any "law which arose on the basis of the laws of any State". He asserted: "Each State must be autonomous within its territory, but it does not follow that it had the right to use its autonomy to violate the legal interests or rights of private individuals acquired on another's territory".

Martens opposed conceptions which based law on force. If law is protected by force, this does not mean that force underlies law. He believed in the progressive development of international law and its inevitable triumph in international relations. Having structured his international-legal theory on a careful study of historical and contemporary international events, he came to the following important conclusion:

> For every jurist and public figure who elicits for himself a reasonable purpose for international relations and properly grasps the tasks and purposes of States, the dominant principle of the future may be only one – the idea of law in the broadest sense of this word. Neither the idea of enslavement nor the idea of an inclination toward physical force, nor the idea of political equilibrium, nor, finally, the principle of nationality can be deemed to be the guiding principles for a properly structured international life. The guiding principle thereof – is the idea of law.

Martens' ideas that the interference of some States in the internal affairs of other States was admissible only if there is on its face a legal ground for the immediate declaration of war" was quite progressive for that period, and he considered that "other exceptions cannot be from the standpoint of law".[36]

35 Grabar, note 32 above, p. 482.

36 Martens, «Начало невмешательства гр. Л. Камаровского» [Principle of Non-

As regards the issue of international legal personality, Martens substantiated the conception of parallel subjects of international law, according to which "independent peoples or States of European civilization are direct subjects of international law and actors in the domain of the international community", and juridical and natural persons "conduct their international turnover under the control, patronage, and even responsibility of State authority in which they are subjects … throughout the entire spatial operation of international law".

Martens' scientific views also determined his practical actions as a jurist and diplomat. Martens was a realist: unlike other pacifists and humanists, he believed the idea of eliminating war in the near future and even in the remote future was utopian. The sole resolution of this problem, in his view, meeting the humane ideas of law was to limit the terrors of war by certain norms recognized by all peoples and States.

Martens placed the human being in the center of international life. Therefore, one may call him rightfully one of the creators of an orientation such as the international defense of human rights. Martens was inspired by a high degree of humanism in its scholarly writings, placing the individual above all; he saw in the protection thereof the ultimate purpose of international law.

Martens asserted that throughout the history of peoples one law passes – "respect for the human individual". The inviolability of life, honor, and dignity is deemed to be the right of each person not because this is protected by a criminal law, but because every person has the inalienable right to life, honor and dignity. Martens considered respect for human rights as the measure of a State being civilized and of international relations.

Martens placed in Russian international legal doctrine also the conceptualized foundations of international criminal law, having determined that this right "consists of the aggregate of legal norms determining the conditions for international legal assistance of States to one another when they effectuate their chastisement activity in the domain of the international community" (II, p. 348).

Martens made a significant contribution to the development of the international defense of human rights which, regrettably, remains little noticed by present-day specialists. Martens humanity inspired him to place the individual above all else. No doubt Martens idealized the position with respect to the recognition and protection of human rights in that period. In his words, all education States contemporary to him recognized for man, as such, "certain basic rights which are inextricably linked with the human personality". The individual is under the defense of international law and has rights in international relations. This thesis Martens elaborated as follows:

interference of Count L. Kamarovskii], Журнал гражданского и уголовного права [Journal of Civil and Criminal Law], no. 3 (1875), pp. 253-259.

> All contemporary civilized States are agreed that man is a person, that is, a subject of certain inalienable rights which should be respected in their mutual relations. Therefore, each person, irrespective of his subjecthood or nationality, finds at present the protection of his person and ownership in all the space of operation of international law. The protection of a person is the ultimate purpose of the State and the purpose of international relations (II, p. 248).

Martens drew up a digest of basic human rights in which he included:

(1) the right to existence and the development of the natural person (this is a right to the acquisition of the means necessary for the support of life by his physical labor, trade turnover, engaging in trades or by other legal means; for this every person enjoys a perfected freedom within the limits established by a law);

(2) the right to the development of one's spiritual and intellectual abilities and powers (this is the right to enjoy by all means which a country provides for the education thereof and satisfaction of aesthetic aspirations, such as: school, library, museums, and so on);

(3) the right to communication and free movement within the limits of the international union of States (this is the right not to be attached to land and concrete territory of residence, the right to emigration as an inalienable human right).

Making the content of this digest of human rights even more concrete, Martens wrote:

> From the aforesaid rights recognized for every person in international relations arise other inalienable human rights: the right to inviolability of the person, life, honor, health, the right to possess ownership, to enter into obligations, the right to the conclusion of a family union, and so on (II, p. 348).

The inviolability of life, honor, and dignity, Martens noted, are recognized as the right of every person not because this is protected by a criminal law, but because every person as an individual has by his nature an inalienable right to the said inviolability.

It would be no exaggeration to suggest that Martens himself was aware of the clear unreality of his assertion concerning international recognition for every person of the rights he enumerated. He was a realist, and in advancing the desirable for the real and aspiring to approximate the triumph of the recognition and defense of the said desired rights, he was guided by a general thesis previously formulated by him: the defense of human rights is a common purpose and the ultimate aim of States and the international community. The following passage addressed to the governments of States is evidence of this:

> If States actually considered these rights to inhere in the human individual and were sanctioned by the international community, then many instances of conflicts of legislation and mutual squabbling of States, explicable only by the excessive exaggeration which governments give to a territorial law or simply to their own discretions, would be eliminated (II, p. 348).

Having regard to the foregoing, one may rightly call Martens one of the founders of the international defense of human rights, or of international humanitarian law.

One cannot fail to note the significant contribution of Martens to the science of private international law, the need for which at the time was affected by the intensive development from the mid-nineteenth century of various forms of international communion and cooperation of Russia with the participation of private individuals: trade, communicative, cultural, and others.[37] When evaluating Martens' contribution to the development of private international law, one must bear in mind that this part of jurisprudence during the period here considered was only beginning to be formed, legal science had made the first steps towards a theoretical contemplation of legal relations in this sphere of the international communion of private individuals, and therefore generalizing ideas, proposals, constructions, and terminological formulas were so important for the newly developing legal sphere of international cooperation. Martens did make a material contribution to the development of fundamental provisions of private international law; the commencement of the systematic investigation of this part of the law and its extensive academic study in Russia are rightly linked with his name. Moreover, Martens himself provided occasion for this view: in 1883 he stated in the preface to volume two of his treatise: "international private and criminal law are set out in this volume for the first time in the Russian language".

Questions of private international law were also reflected in the "General Part" of volume one, consisting of four chapters, which included his remarkable law of the international community (including its organization and organs), and also the participants of international relations and subjects of international law. In connection with the consideration of the last Martens included within the ambit of the study "rights of private individuals in the domain of international relations". Relegating private international law to the sphere of "international administration in the domain of legal interests of subjects and peoples", Martens at the same time considered this also as the "law in force of each civilized State", an "essential addition to the civil law of each civilized State" (I, p. 183). In this sense, he wrote, "there is an organic part of the territorial civil law of a country, and the application by a court, in a concrete instance, of foreign laws will not by on its part an excess of power, but merely the strict performance of its duties" (II, p. 282).

The Special Part of this treatise contains an extensive chapter entitled "Private International Law". Bearing in mind that Martens' treatise was the most in demand during the prerevolutionary period, this chapter played a large role in the teaching of private international law at Russian law faculties. Martens pointed in this chapter to, in his view, three material charac-

[37] For details, see T. M. Iablochkov, «Значение Ф. Ф, Мартенса в науке частного международного права» [Significance of F. F. Martens in the Science of Private International Law], Юридические записки Демидовского юридического лицея [Legal Notes of Demidov Juridical Lycée], I (Iaroslavl, 1910), pp. 465-481.

teristic peculiarities of private international law: the civil-law nature of the relations being regulated; the presence of an international element in such relations, and such relations being in the sphere of the international administration of legal interests of subjects and peoples.

Martens proceeded from the idea of States being legally linked by basic principles of private international law elaborated in the process of international communion, by which he understood the "free union of States in order to achieve by common actions the full development of their forces and satisfaction of their various requirements". Lazar Adol'fovich Lunts (1892-1979) noted in this connection: "the idea of a sovereign State being bound by certain basic principles of private international law elaborated in international communion has material theoretical and practical interest".[38]

Consequently, in adhering to the idea of an international community, Martens believe that the sole true and positive ground on which private international law might be realized is an international community, and, proceeding from this, might only resole the confusing and complex issues of the relations of private individuals of private individuals from various States, especially "questions of the application of the laws of various States". The following characteristics of private international law arise from the doctrinal positions formulated by Martens and structures on the idea of an international community:

(1) States, in allowing private-law relations between their own and foreign subjects, thereby recognize the binding nature of the norms regulating these relations;

(2) the legal duty of States to recognize any law on the territory of the entire international community arose on the basis of the laws of any State;

(3) private international law is law in force for each civilized State;

(4) the recognition of rights arising under the operation of laws of other States is the legal duty of all States which are subjects of international law;

(5) every court, being obliged to apply the law of its own State, at the same time bears the legal duty to recognize the law of other States based on a law;

(6) the purpose of every court is to protect existing private rights;

(7) in each instance where there is a possibility or requirement of a choice between territorial and foreign laws, a court should determine which law, native or foreign, will be applied: "a court does not exceed the boundaries of power belonging to it if it will adhere in the administration of justice to the principles of private international law" (II, p. 281);

(8) if the laws of individual States do not contain principles of private international law or do not eliminate misunderstandings arising in the practice of their application, it is necessary to apply a general international agreement with regard to these questions or to conclude a new agreement;

38 L. A. Lunts, Международное частное право. Общая часть [Private International Law. General Part] (Moscow, 1973), p. 150.

(9) private international law ceased to operate when it violates the public policy of a country.

The position of Martens relative to the terminological aspects of private international law also was unique: he sharply criticized all international lawyers for the extensive use in "contemporary international law" of the terms of Roman private law.

Martens formulated his own definition of private international law: "the aggregate of legal norms determining the application to a particular legal relation of an interested person in the domain of international turnover of the law [*jus*] or law [*lex*] of the fatherland or foreign state" (II, p. 267). He believed that private international law is "a necessary addition to the civil law of every civilized State" which fully responded to the state of international legal regulation of private-law relations of his time. Civil-law relations including a foreign element Martens called "international civil relations".[39]

Martens' contribution to the codification of private international law was significant. He actively participated as a delegate of Russia to the Hague conferences in 1893, 1894, 1900, and 1904 on private international law convened by the Government of The Netherlands to determine the basic principles of private international law. He was the "first delegate"; that is, the head of the delegations of Russia to these Hague conferences and always elected a vice-president of the conferences. Tikhon Mikhailovich Iablochkov (1880-1926) wrote:

> Every time that the Dutch Government send its program of the conference to work out questions of private international law, the Russian Government appointed and attached to the Ministry of Foreign Affairs a meeting from representatives of various departments to consider this program; the chairman of these meetings was Martens. The opinions of these meetings concerned basically the instructions to be given by the Russian Government to delegates at conferences. One of these delegates always was Martens himself, who thus might directly influence the attitude of the Russian legislator to the agreements drafted at the conferences … At these conferences Martens was always elected one of the vice-presidents of the conference.[40]

As Lunts noted, Martens in practice, as an official, sometimes was forced to deviate from his doctrinal principles. In constructing the role of certain principles of private international law in the organization of the international community this became especially clear when these principles are ignored in practice. Thus, Martens as a representative of the Government at the Third 1900 Hague Conference on the codification of private international law opposed the application to the form of marriage one of the most

[39] Boguslavskii expressed the view that "F. F. Martens proceeded above all from the international-legal conception of private international law". See M. M. Boguslavskii, Международное частное право [Private International Law] (7th ed.; Moscow, 2016), p. 9.

[40] Iablochkov, note 46 above, p. 6.

generally-recognized conflicts principles, according to which the form of an act is determined according to the law of the place where it is performed. Not willing to recognize the marriage of Russian subjects performed abroad in civil form without complying with religious rites, the Government of Russia refused to accede to the Hague Convention in which the said principle was applied to the form of a marriage. The Imperial Government did not consent to the application of a national law of those marrying to the form of a marriage because this might lead to allowing civil marriages of foreigners in Russia. The position of the Russian Government on this question, submitted by Martens to the 1900 Hague Conference and subsequent Hague conferences, showed to what practical consequences a departure from certain generally-accepted organizing principles of private international law would lead which in theory were developed and energetically upheld by Martens himself.[41]

Martens' difficult situation as a scholar and as a State official at international conferences was well-expressed by Iablochkov: "A difficult task fell to Martens of combining in one person the scholar and the diplomat. Therein lies the tragedy of his life and justification of his theories not being upheld". Continuing, he observed: "As a theoretician, Martens was a convinced adept of the principle *locus regit actum*; as a politician, Martens was ready to view the law through the prism of 'public policy', which cannot be violated by any international agreements".[42]

The services of Martens to private international law were significant also because this part of the law in the period here considered was only beginning to develop. Therefore, it is no surprise that not all the tenets of his doctrinal positions were perceived positively: there were sharply critical judgments, including among his students.[43] Nonetheless, Martens was among the pioneers in the theoretical consideration of complex private international legal relations (which today remain controversial, often irreconcilable, and serious theoretical passions are stirred); therefore, without avoiding certain contradictions in his views, he attracted the attention of the scientific world to conflicts problems in the world of private law and

[41] See Lunts, note 38 above, p. 149.

[42] Iablochkov, note 37 above, pp. 278, 281.

[43] One of the most authoritative of his students, B. E. Nolde, criticized Martens' positions. Nolde wrote that Martens was not so "great a scholar in this domain of international law. In his person Russian science, in comparison with Malyshev, took a step backward". His idea of an international community was "completely senseless in connection with structuring conflict norms, because it merely stated the undisputed fact that conflicts of legislation of various countries arise by virtue of the existence of links between these countries". B. E. Nolde, «М. И. Брун (1860-1916) и наука международного частного права в России» [M. I. Brun (1860-1916) and the Science of Private International Law in Russia], Вестник гражданского права [Herald of Civil Law], no. 3-5 (1917), pp. 23-24.

generated additional interest among scholars in pursuing more detailed research.[44]

Martens' services were as significant as a historian and publicist with regard to the history of international law and universal history. His legacy in the field of history is enormous and much under-studied. He was an active full member of the Russian Imperial Historical Society and a member of its Council. Martens was elected to the authoritative French society on diplomatic history, was a founding member of the international colonial institute in Brussels, joined the American Ethnological Society of New York, and others. Martens left a large number of articles on international law and politics published in numerous journals and newspapers in Russia and abroad.[45]

Martens was not an idol of students, being overloaded in his professional life – scholar, diplomat, international arbitrator, and consultant. His manner did not encourage this either – pedantic, reserved, business-like. But one fact is noteworthy: when in 1896 his twenty-fifth anniversary as a pedagogue was honored in celebrations at the University (which honored him not only as a pedagogue and scholar, but also as a politician, diplomatic, and publicist), the students carried him from the auditorium on their shoulders.

Martens respected colleague, Viacheslav Mikhailovich Gribovskii (1867-1924), who although a specialist in State law also taught courses on international law during his career, wrote:

> Fedor Fedorovich, scholar, politician, diplomat, and publicist; his multi-facetedness and the depth of his education are astonishing; foreign languages he knows to perfection; in his works he not only is a learned thinker, but also a convinced champion of the good, truth, and beauty; his literary talent argues with the talent of a quiet researcher; his works are read as *belles lettres*, his treatise on the international law of civilized peoples is nothing other than a majestic epic of the past and present life of European States. There is no educated person in Russia or in Europe who does not know the name of 'our Martens'.[46]

International-Legal Practitioner

Martens was an effective lecturer partly because of his successful diplomatic career, which he pursued simultaneously with his academic activities. From his initial appointment in 1869, he remained with the Ministry

[44] Taube wrote of his teacher, Martens: "The significance of his life and activity lie in the fact, practically speaking, that he planted and inculcated … the science of international law in us …". Taube, note 19 above, p. 16.

[45] A full list has never been undertaken; Martens often wrote anonymously or under pseudonyms, particularly to the editors of newspapers.

[46] V. Gribovskii, «Юбилей профессора Ф. Ф. Мартенса» [Jubilee of Professor F. F. Martens], Вестник права [Herald of Law], no. 2 (1896), pp. 44-45.

throughout his lifetime,[47] acting as an advisor on international legal issues for all ministers of foreign affairs: A. M. Gorchakov, Nikolai Karlovich Giers (1820-1895), Aleksei Borisovich Lobanov-Rostovskii (1824-1896), Nikolai Pavlovich Shishkin (1830-1902), Mikhail Nikolaevich Murav'ev (1796-1866), Vladimir Nikolaevich Lamzdorf (1844-1907), and Aleksandr Petrovich Izvolskii (1856-1919). In 1879 he was appointed an official with special portfolio attached to the State Chancellor, Gorchakov. He became in 1881 a permanent member of the Council of the Ministry of Foreign Affairs (consisting of six heads of departments within the Ministry, plus Martens).[48]

It happened that Martens was able to first implement his scholarly plans and doctrinal views in his monumental collection of treaties and conventions.[49] On 5 December 1873 on the basis of a Report by Gorchakov concerning the need to systematize and analyze the international obligations of the Russian Empire, Emperor Alexander II (1818-1881) assigned Martens to collect, systematize, and publish a collection of all international treaties of Russia, giving him free access to all State archives of the Russian Empire. Within a year the first volume appeared. The commencement date of the series was 1648, the year when the treaties of Westphalia were concluded and what is regarded by many as the date of the formal entry of Russia into the concert of European powers. The series was published in the French and Russian languages, in parallel texts.[50]

Martens worked on the treaty series as a compiler, systematizer, commentator, and chief editor for the remainder of his life. Fifteen volumes saw the light of day; at the time of his death he was laboring on the sixteenth, devoted to Russian relations with the Ottoman Empire. His introductory commentaries and annotations are remarkable examples of international-legal scholarship, likewise in parallel French and Russian texts. No serious work on Russian diplomacy addressing the period covered fails to mention

[47] Martens appears to have been the first of many international lawyers at St. Petersburg and other universities to hold significant administrative and diplomatic posts in the Ministry of Foreign Affairs, among them: M. A. Taube, B. E. Nolde, Andrei Nikolaevich Mandelstam (1869-1949), Eval'd Karlovich Simson (1869-19?), Aleksandr Mikhailovich Gorovtsev (1878-1933).

[48] This highest consultative organ attached to the Ministry of Foreign Affairs was created in 1832.

[49] Martens, Собрание трактатов и конвенций, заключенных Россиею с иностранными державами [Collection of Treaties and Conventions Concluded by Russia with Foreign Powers] (Spb., 1874-1909). 15 vols.

[50] For background, see W. E. Butler, "Treaty Collections in Eighteenth-Century Russia: Encounters with European Experience", *Russia and the Law of Nations* (2009), pp. 259-267. Martens had the advantage of drawing upon the labors of predecessors, including Gerhard Friedrich Müller (1705-1783), Nikolai Nikolaevich Bantysh-Kamenskii (1737-1814), Count Nikolai Petrovich Rumiantsev (1754-1826).

the Martens collection;[51] the French text made the series accessible to foreign scholarship, and the Russian Ministry of Foreign Affairs, at whose expense the series was published, routinely sent copies of volumes to foreign embassies in St. Petersburg or to foreign offices abroad.

In 1888 Martens was a delegate of the Russian Government to the International Congress on Maritime and Commercial Law in Brussels. The following year he acted as the plenipotentiary of Russia to a diplomatic conference in Brussels which adopted the Brussels Conference Act of 1890 putting an end to the worldwide slave trade; States assumed the obligation to introduce criminal legislation punishing slavery. Martens made substantial contributions to drafting and seeking agreement for the draft Convention, for which Belgium bestowed its highest orders. Queen Victoria (1819-1901) in England and King Leopold II (1835-1909) in Belgium sent notes of special thanks to Emperor Nicholas II (1868-1918) for appointing Martens as the Russian plenipotentiary to the Conference and complimenting his outstanding role as a conciliator of the positions of the delegates and being the author of a large portion of the provisions of the Convention.[52]

During the 1870s, Martens began to undertake major assignments from his Ministry. He gained great authority in Russia and in the world generally. His performance of often delicate assignments brought him into contact with the heads of States and governments, ministers of foreign affairs, and other leaders. But "stardom" came to Martens without doubt at the 1899 First Hague Peace Conference, convoked by the Netherlands at the initiative of Russia and laying the foundation for established legal norms for waging war, disarmament, and the peaceful settlement of disputes. Martens actually wrote the draft program of the Conference.[53] They called him the "spirit" of the Conference. He was elected chairman of the Third Commission for drafting the Convention on the laws and customs of warfare. The basis of the Convention was a draft prepared by him for the 1874 Brussels Conference. But there were many difficulties in agreeing it. One of the "deadend" problems was a dispute over the occupation regime. A group of small countries headed by Belgium demanded the unlimited right of the population in the event of occupation to resist, refusing to sign the Convention already prepared and threatening to leave the Conference.

A way out was found thanks to the "genius of Martens" – the expression of the prominent Swiss jurist active in the International Red Cross, Jacques

[51] Grabar said that the treaty collection alone would have been sufficient to perpetuate Martens' name. Grabar, note 32 above, p. 382.

[52] Note 10 above, p. 9.

[53] The Swiss international lawyer, H. Wehberg, wrote of Martens: "He created the practically realizable program for the First Hague Peace Conference and spoke at the Conference with all the power of his personality". See F. Eliashevich and H. Wehberg, «Ф. Мартенс и Гаагские конференции мира» [F. Martens and the Hague Peace Conferences], Журнал Министерства юстиции [Journal of the Ministry of Justice], no. 2 (1911), p. 332.

Pictet (1914-2012).[54] Martens proposed to include in the preamble of the Convention the following provision:

> Until a more complete code of the laws of war is issued, the High Contracting Parties think it right to declare that in cases not included in the Regulations adopted by them, populations and belligerents remain under the protection and empire of the principles of international law, as they result from the usages established between civilized nations, from the laws of humanity and the requirements of the public conscience [1899 Convention].

The Conference delegates received Martens' proposal with applause. The Convention was adopted unanimously.[55]

Martens formulation went into history and exists in international law as the "Martens clause", continuing to play an important role in the humanizing of the methods and means of waging war. The essence of the clause is that it encompasses all situation which at a certain moment are not regulated by international law. It is noteworthy that in a somewhat renewed form the Martens Clause was included in contemporary international conventions on military humanitarian law: Article 1(2), 1977 Additional Protocol to the 1949 Geneva Conventions. All this confirms the special role Martens played in the development of international military humanitarian law; that is, the international law applicable during wartime.

Among Martens' services are his proposal at the Conference to introduce a new international-legal institution – international commissions of inquiry. In a Report to the Conference, Martens summarized the experience of a number of national commissions and substantiated the advisability and advantages of this means for the peaceful settlement of international disputes. His proposal was incorporated into the Convention on the Pacific Settlement of International Disputes; section III is devoted to commissions of inquiry and regulates the procedure for their creation, competence, composition, and work procedure, the duty of States in dispute with respect to the commission, and the content and character of the final conclusion of the commission with regard to the specific dispute. The leading role of Martens in this is recognized in Russia and abroad.[56]

An opportunity soon presented itself to test this new means for settling international disputes. An International Commission of Inquiry was created to consider the 1904 Dogger Bank Incident (the representative of Russia was the former student and successor of Martens as Head of the Chair of

[54] Jean Pictet, Развитие и принципы международного гуманитарного права [Development and Principles of International Humanitarian Law] (Moscow, 1994), p. 78.

[55] See V. S. Ivanenko (comp.), 100-летие инициативы России: От Первой конференции мира 1899 г. к Третьей конференции мира 1999 г.: Сборник материалов [Centenary of the Initiative of Russia: From the First 1899 Hague Peace Conference to the Third 1999 Peace Conference: Collection of Materials] (Spb., 1999), p. 68.

[56] See, for example, Wehberg, note 13 above.

International Law at St. Petersburg University, M. A. Taube);[57] material additions were made to the 1899 Convention as a result of the experience with the commission of inquiry at the 1907 Hague Peace Conference.

Also worthy of note was the leading role of Martens in elaborating in detail the institution of international arbitration commissions and their practical realization and popularization.[58] The procedural rules which he drew up for resolving international disputes were accepted by the 1899 Convention on the pacific settlement of disputes (Section IV: "On an International Arbitration Court"), and then, after his death, by the 1920 Statute of the Permanent Court of International Justice and the 1945 Statute on the International Court of Justice.

Martens became widely known as an international arbitrator through his successful resolution of complex inter-State disputes (England and France concerning fishing off Newfoundland in 1891); United States and England on catching fur seals in the Bering Sea in 1893; England and the Netherlands concerning the arrest by Dutch authorities of the *Costa Rica Packet* in 1897; England and Venezuela concerning the boundary between Venezuela and British Guiana near the Orinoco River, in 1899;[59] the first two disputes in the Permanent Court of International Arbitration: between the United States and Mexico concerning the "Pious Fund", in 1902; and between England, Germany, Italy, and Venezuela regarding violations of the rights of citizens, in 1905; and others.

[57] The Dogger Bank Incident involved the shelling on 21/22 October 1904 by a Russian squadron commanded by Rear Admiral Zinovii Petrovich Rozhestvenskii (1848-1909) en route to the Far East to take part in the Russo-Japanese War of English fishing boats mistaken for Japanese naval ships. One English ship was sunk, five were damaged, three Englishmen were killed, and five wounded. Anglo-Russian relations deteriorated; it was decided to create an International Commission of Inquiry, the Commission sat for two months, and concluded: no traces of Japanese naval vessels were discovered, but the danger of an attack was real. Russia acknowledged fault and paid 65,000 pounds sterling as compensation to the fishermen.

[58] See F. F. Martens, "International Arbitration and the Peace Conference at The Hague", *North American Review*, CLXIX (1899), pp. 604-624. Also see S. A. Malinin, «Реализация и развитие идеи Ф. Ф. Мартенса о согласительной процедуре в современном международном праве» [Realization and Development of the Idea of F. F. Martens on a Conciliation Procedure in Contemporary International Law], Российский ежегодник международного права 2000: специальный выпуск [Russian Yearbook of International Law 2000: Special Issue] (Spb., 2000), pp. 75-80.

[59] The roots of this dispute dated back to the sixteenth century. Martens, in his capacity as chairman of the tribunal, proposed a set of procedural rules which was accepted by other members of the tribunal. This is regarded as an early, if not the first, example in international practice when a case was considered on the basis of procedural rules composed by the chairman and approved by all members of the tribunal.

Martens' role as arbitrator led to him be called in the United States "the chief arbitrator of the Christian world".[60] Thomas Erskine Holland (1835-1926), the personal lawyer of the King of England, wrote of Martens: "He was in such great demand as an arbitrator in international disputes that as a joke he was called the Lord Chancellor of Europe".[61]

Martens viewed the Hague conference solely "as governmental attempts to organize and order mutual relations of peoples to the benefit of peace and a better mutual society", but did not believe that "any international conference will succeed in creating perpetual peace and lead to disarmament". Nonetheless, the "Hague Conferences", suggested Pustogarov, "are a monument to an outstanding jurist, F. F. Martens, a monument the more noteworthy in that they in our days continue to serve people".[62]

The last conferences in which Martens participated were: the 1904 Hague conference on private international law; the 1905 Portsmouth conference in the United States to conclude a peace treaty between Russia and Japan; the 1906 Geneva conference on the protection of sick and wounded warriors, and the 1907 Second Hague peace conference. In addition, from 1884 until the end of his life Martens took an active part in the conferences of the International Committee of the Red Cross as the plenipotentiary of the Government of Russia. He became a member in 1886 of the Chief Administration of the Russian Red Cross Society and represented it in international measures of the Red Cross.

At the first international Red Cross conference after the 1899 Hague Peace Conference, held in May 1902 at St. Petersburg, Martens presented a Report entitled: "Red Cross Societies. Reference Bureau for Rendering Assistance to Prisoners of War Provided by the Hague Convention on the Laws and Customs of Land Warfare". When the Russo-Japanese War broke out, a commission was created in the Ministry of Foreign Affairs of Russia to draft provisions on prisoners of war; the representatives of several ministries (war, navy, internal affairs, and finances) and the Chief Administration of the Russian Red Cross were represented. Martens was appointed Chairman of the Commission. The Commission drafted a Provisional Statute on Prisoners of War of the Russo-Japanese War, confirmed by the Emperor on 13 May 1904, on the basis of which a Central Reference Bureau on Prisoners of War was created and attached to the Chief Administration of the Russian Red Cross; Martens was confirmed as the leader. The Reference Bureau became the first such type of institution. It carried out colossal work

[60] See Pustogarov, note 1 above, pp. 177-183; Судебно-юридическая газета [Judicial-Legal Newspaper], no. 103 (12 September 2011).

[61] T. E. Holland, "Frederick de Martens", *Journal of the Society of Comparative Legislation*, no. 10 (1909), p. 10.

[62] Pustogarov, note 1 above, pp. 242, 268.

to establish and render assistance to Russian and Japanese prisoners of war respectively on the territories of Russia and Japan.[63]

Martens devoted considerable time to various internal Russian interdepartmental commissions and meetings, especially with regard to preparing and coordinating draft laws on the procedure the admission to and leaving subjecthood (citizenship), the boundaries of the territorial sea, and participation in the name of the Ministry of Foreign Affairs of a Supreme Prize Court during the Russo-Japanese War. Martens also prepared a draft Consular Statute of the Russian Empire, reworked by a commission under this direction and entered into force in 1893.

Martens was among the initiators and organizers of the founding of the Russian Society of International Law, the first in that country. The Society was opened in 1880 in St. Petersburg under the patronage and with the support of a well-known political figure, and philanthropist, Prince Petr Georgievich Oldenberg (1812-1881). Martens was elected secretary of the Society. On 22 May 1880 Emperor Alexander II confirmed the Charter of the Society, mostly drafted by Martens, and on 31 May the solemn inauguration of the Society took place in the palace of Prince Oldenberg.[64]

Martens was an active member of the Institute of International Law. On the basis of Reports by Martens the Institute adopted resolutions on the Suez Canal (1879), the regulation of proceedings in consular courts in the Orient (1881-1882), the slave trade (1885), navigation on international rivers (1887), and an international bureau for the publication of treaties (1885). Jointly with Bluntschli, Martens drafted within the framework of the Institute of International Law a manual on the laws of land warfare,[65] many provisions of which comprise the basis of the 1899 and 1907 Hague conventions and today are an important component of contemporary international humanitarian law.

The diplomatic and peace-keeping activity of Martens inspired colleagues to propose his candidacy for the Nobel Peace Prize. Martens was nominated eight times for the Nobel Peace Prize (1901-1908), each time without success. Politics interfered. It has been suggested that European countries were apprehensive that Russia, by relying on the opinions of an authoritative professor who had become a Nobel laureate, might more ac-

[63] See E. A. Bukhe (comp.), Военнопленные: Обзор деятельности Центрального справочного бюро о военнопленных во время Русско-японской войны [Prisoners of War: Survey of Activity of Central Reference Bureau on Prisoners of War During the Russo-Japanese War] (Spb., 1907). [xvi], 152 p. The volume was prepared under the direction of F. F. Martens.

[64] For details, see W. E. Butler and V. S. Ivanenko, "On the Russian Society of International Law", *Jus Gentium*, II (2017), pp. 189-199.

[65] Законы сухопутной войны. Краткое руководство, изданне Институтом международного права [Laws of Land Warfare. Concise Manual published by the Institute of International Law] (Spb., 1881), p. 3.

tively seek to expand its influence in the world; perhaps, but it must also be noted that most, if not all, of those submitting the nominations were western European colleagues, not other Russians.

The last great diplomatic matter for Martens was the preparation for the Second Hague Peace Conference in 1907. At the time, serious international difficulties were aggravated by the rivalry between England and Germany. The British Government proposed additionally to include on the agenda of the forthcoming Conference a point about the limitation of military expenditures by States. This was intended to show the public that Germany had unleashed an arms race, especially by its extensive program of naval expenditures. Moreover, the resolution of several major legal issues deferred at the 1899 First Hague Peace Conference was anticipated: the inviolability of private ownership in naval warfare, the binding nature of awards of an international arbitration court, and others.

Under these conditions, the Russian Ministry of Foreign Affairs decided to undertake diplomatic soundings relating to the program of the forthcoming Conference. The choice fell on Martens, and in early 1907 he commenced a notable diplomatic tour about the European capitals for the purpose of eliciting the positions of the governments of these countries. Martens conducted negotiations in Berlin with Emperor Wilhelm II and the State-secretary of the German Ministry of Foreign Affairs, Wilhelm Freiherr von Schön (1851-1933); in Paris with President Armand Fallières (1841-1931); in London, with King Edward VII (1841-1910), Prime Minister Henry Campbell-Bannerman (1836-1908), and Foreign Secretary, Edward Grey (1862-1933); in The Hague, with all the royal family; in Rome, with King Victor Emmanuel III (1869-1947) and Prime Minister Giovanni Giolitti (1842-1928); in Vienna, with Emperor Franz-Joseph I (1830-1916), and the Minister of Foreign Affairs, Alois Lexa von Ährenthal (1854-1912). For the first time in Russia, an international lawyer was assigned to perform such a politically delicate diplomatic mission.

The authority of Martens in the world was high and irreproachable. One example. As a Dutch specialist noted, Martens through the United States Ambassador to Russia, Andrew Dickson White (1832-1918) suggested to the American philanthropist Andrew Carnegie (1835-1919) that he might invest a large sum of money that served the cause of international peace. Martens advised to appropriate the money to build a Peace Palace in The Hague and even indicated a specific site for the construction.[66] Thanks to Martens' efforts, the Government of The Netherlands provided a land plot

[66] A. Eyffinger, *The Hague International Center of Justice and Peace* (2003), pp. 27-37; Eyffinger, «От оговорки Мартенса до Международного уголовного суда (Гаагская традиция в международном гуманитарном праве)» [From the Martens Clause to the International Criminal Court (Hague Tradition in International Humanitarian Law)], Российский ежегодник международного права 2004. Специальный выпуск [Russian Yearbook of International Law 2004. Special Issue] (Spb., 2005), p. 95.

to build the Palace of seven hectares in the center of The Hague, and Carnegie provided the necessary funds.

The building of the Peace Palace proposed by Martens was built and solemnly opened in 1913, after his death; but today the Peace Palace serves the cause of peace, being the site of the International Court of Justice, the Permanent Court of International Arbitration, the Hague Academy of International Law, and one of the major libraries in the world on international law. Thus, the capital of The Netherlands thanks to the suggestion and authority of Martens over time has been transformed into the international capital of justice in which, in addition to the aforesaid bodies, the International Criminal Court and the International Tribunal for Crimes on the Territory of the Former Yugoslavia operate.

On 2 November 2005, the President of Russia, Vladimir Vladimirovich Putin, visited the Peace Palace and the International Court of Justice. The President of the Court, Shi Jiuyong, in his welcoming address noted: "Professor Martens illuminated an era, played a noteworthy role in the peace movement. His dream for a "temple of peace" inspired the creators of the Peace Palace. A proponent of the idea of the supremacy of international law, Martens was convinced that flagrant force can never triumph over law and "not extinguish our aspirations for right and justice".[67]

President Putin, also a graduate of the Chair of International Law at St. Petersburg University, in his reply noted the outstanding role of Martens:

> With special feeling I would wish to note the motivating role of Fedor Fedorovich Martens which you mentioned, Mr. President. To a great extent, thanks to his insistence and brilliant mind, the initiative of Russia to hold the I Peace Conference in 1899 was successfully realized. It happened in The Hague, for always having determined this city to be the capital of international justice.[68]

Martens collected numerous honors. In 1907 he was elected a Corresponding Member of the Russian Academy of Sciences. He was a member and Vice President of the Institute of International Law in Ghent, Belgium; a member of the Belgian Royal Academy, a doctor of laws *honoris causa* of Yale, Cambridge, Oxford, and Edinburgh universities, and an honorary member of the Berlin and Dublin law societies. Upon the proposal of the King of Belgium and with the consent of Emperor Alexander III (1845-1894), by edict of the King, Martens became a life member of the State Council of the Congo for his outstanding role as a conciliator of the positions of the delegates to the 1899-1900 Brussels Conference and for drafting the Act of the Conference which established a prohibition against trade in Negroes in the basin of the Congo River.

[67] Московский журнал международного права [Moscow Journal of International Law], no. 1 (2006), p. 5.

[68] Russian text available at www.kremlin.ru/events/president/transcripts

The University of Vienna in 1883 invited Martens to take the Chair of International Law, among the most prestigious in Europe. But Martens declined to accept this invitation and remained in Russia.[69] Sixteen high Russian and foreign orders were conferred on Martens for international diplomatic and scholarly activity to the benefit of peace and the international community.

An undoubted service of Martens was that he left a rich heritage in the form of a galaxy of young international lawyers, both scholars and practitioners. Almost every year, students regularly defended dissertations and remained at the chair to prepare for a learned degree and the professoriate. Many became international lawyers and achieved varying degrees of reputation in Russia and abroad. But they all made their contribution to the further development of the St. Petersburg School of international law; regrettably because of the Soviet revolution many have been undeservedly forgotten.

Martens was the first to create a scientific school of international law which rightly carried his name. Martens' students pursued various paths. Some engaged in the history and theory of international law (Aleksandr L'vovich Baikov (1865-1943), A. M. Gorovtsev, E. K. Simson, M. A. Taube); other devoted themselves to studies basically of conflicts problems in private international law (A. N. Mandelstam, Aleksandr Aleksandrovich Pilenko (1873-1956), Lev Adamovich Shalland (1868-1919); yet others combined the study of international law and State law (Sergei Aleksandrovich Korf (1876-1924), B. E. Nolde); and others took up State service (Dmitrii Petrovich Nikol'skii (1855-1915). The most multi-faceted scholar was Nolde; his scholarly interests encompassed not only international and public law, but also private law, the history of diplomacy, a number of other problems of international law, but also many issues of State law.

Under Martens as head of the Chair, specialist courses on international law began to appear; their numbers grew as the numbers of his students increased – docents and professors.

Martens retired from St. Petersburg University in 1903. In the competition to fill his Chair, Baron von Taube emerged victorious, but according to the regularly published surveys of teaching at the University, Martens apparently continued to lecture until 1906 together with Taube in the course on international law. His work at the Ministry and at the School of Jurisprudence Martens continued until his death.

Martens is buried at the Volkov Lutheran cemetery in St. Petersburg. Over time the gravesite deteriorated and in the 1990s was severely damaged by vandals. Efforts undertaken by the Chair of International Law of St. Petersburg University and philanthropic sources in Russia led on 23/24 Octo-

[69] Отчет о состоянии Императорского С.-Петербургского университета и деятельности его ученого сословия за 1883 год, читанный на Акте 8 февраля 1884 года [Report on the State of Imperial St. Petersburg University and Activity of its Academic Estate for 1883, Delivered at the Act of 8 February 1884] (Spb., 1884), p. 19.

ber 2019 to the dedication of its complete restoration or, rather, replacement with a suitable gravestone bearing a classical Lutheran cross. A bronze bust of Martens was placed in the Law Faculty of St. Petersburg University in 2002. A similar bust was given by the Government of the Russian Federation to the Peace Palace in The Hague, where it reposes together with the remarkable jasper "Russian Vase" presented by Emperor Nicholas II to the Peace Palace in 1913; the Vase bears his initials and the State emblem of the Russian Empire.

ABBREVIATIONS

p.(p.)page(s)

Spb.St. Petersburg

vol(s).volume(s)

PREFACE TO FIFTH EDITION

The present fifth edition of volume one of my Course of International Law is significantly augmented by new facts from international life and the science of international law.

In this respect the present edition materially differs from the translations of my Course into the major European and Asian languages which have appeared at the present time.

F. Martens
St. Petersburg
December 1903

PREFACE TO FIRST EDITION

From the very time when by the powerful will of Peter the Great, Russia was introduced into the family of western European civilized peoples, she to the present minute has not ceased to take direct participation in international life and in its development. But the role of Russia was not confined to merely participation. No, as the Russian people moved forward on the path of the development of a civil society and its domestic system, Russia acts in the field of international relations as a great and mighty power which especially keenly relates to all questions moved to the forefront by the aspirations of European peoples for stability of the international order in forms needed for the comprehensive internal, social, and cultural development thereof. The great intelligence of Empress Catherine II found in an alliance of "armed neutrality" created by her the best means for protection of the legal rights of powerless neutral peoples. By the magnanimous initiative of the Tsar-Liberator, the Brussels Conference was convened in 1874 to determine the binding customs and laws of war with a view to mitigation of its calamities and sufferings. But it is remarkable if Russia as a Great Power takes a very active role in the resolution of international question and, on the other hand, the science of international law firmly takes root in Russian soil. Russian literature on international law, as a matter of fact, does not exist at all, and there is not a single systematic manual on this science by a Russian scholar. The need for such a manual which would make it possible to orient oneself in international questions arising every day is felt not only by jurists, but also by all educated Russian people interested in foreign policy and following the development of the general cultural life of civilized peoples.

With a view to filling this gap we publish the present work, the two volumes of which encompass the entire domain of international law in peacetime and during war.

With regard to this first volume allow us to say several words. The system in which we set out the science of international law differs materially from other scientific systems in the rich western European literature on international law. How well-founded it is may be judged only upon the appearance of the second volume. At present, we allow ourselves only to note that in the course of eleven years of lecturing activity this system was and remains, at least in our understanding, the order that best corresponds to the essence and degree of development of contemporary international relations.

The history of international relations, which elicits the thought underlying this entire work, occupies a leading place in this system. This thought may be expressed concisely as follows: the degree of the development of social interests and internal system of a State determines the measure of its participation in international life.

Indeed, the study of the history of international relations in general and the participation therein of Russia in particular led us to the unshakeable conviction that the internal life and order of a State reveal their fatal effect on its international relations and policy. International relations always are a mirror precisely reflecting the internal state of State societies during a certain epoch of their existence, and likewise the principles which underlie their social and political systems. The more governments are aware of their duties with respect to all their subjects, the more they treat them with respect for their rights and legal interests, the more stable is the internal State order and the better is the peaceful and lawful flow of international life ensured. Therefore, it is necessary only to determine the strength of the internal State order and the degree of social development of a particular people in order to determine, in addition to its external physical power, the degree of its influence and significance in international relations. The amount of political power of a State at various moments of its existence may, at first glance, remain completely unchanged, but the internal and real power of the State itself and its international influence will be positively different if the link is disturbed between its general social interests and the interests of other peoples and the fundamentals of its internal order and power become rickety.

We are deeply convinced that all significant international relations and all the power of international law are based on the community of social cultural, and legal interests combining civilized peoples. We have made an attempt to identify this link between the social life of peoples and their mutual external relations throughout the entire history of international relations, beginning with Antiquity and down to the present time, and we have concluded that if the human individual in a State is recognized as such to be a source of civil and political rights, the international life represents a high degree of the development of order and law. On the contrary, in a State in which the human individual enjoys no rights, where it is lawless and oppresses, international relations cannot develop, cannot be established on stable grounds. The distinctiveness of a people in the sense of cultural originality may develop and strengthen only in international relations on condition of mutual respect and the friendly aspiration of peoples to achieve common cultural ideals.

These are the principal ideas and conclusions of the present work. They are based not on predetermined notions, but on the study in good faith of the history of international relations according to the sources of our archives. Many facts relating to the diplomatic relations of Russia are published here for the first time.

For the thoughts and propositions uttered in this book we support with all the power of our personal convictions and the entire aggregate of positive facts cited by us.

Easter Sunday, 1882

Introduction

I. Grounds of International Law

§1. The subject-matter of the science of international law is the aggregate of vital relations existing between peoples. These relations are generated by the various interests and aspirations of peoples as a whole and the individual members thereof, the subjects of various States, for the satisfaction by means of international exchange of their physical and spiritual needs. Consequently, the science of international law has international life as its grounds and serves as an expression of the legal community of civilized peoples. Under the contemporary development of international relations, it should obviously be of great practical interest and vital importance.[1]

Not all jurists, however, are agreed on the significance of the science of international law. Whereas such a remarkable publicist as Lorenz von Stein [(1815-1890)] relegated it to the highest domain of the legal and political sciences, other representatives of jurisprudence and primarily legal practitioners do not find it possible to even consider international law to be a branch of law, or – as [Adolf] Lasson [(1832-1917)] – prove that the sole subject-matter thereof is the use of flagrant physical force in international relations.[2]

This negative view of the science of international law is to be explained by reasons of a dual nature: first, the character of legal education in the West of Europe which has dominated until recently; second, the newest realist orientation of historical science, especially jurisprudence.

In western Europe, and particularly in German universities, the study of Roman law and the Pandects until recently has constituted the almost exclusive subject-matter of the education of jurists. This overwhelming dominance of Roman law not only slowed the development of other

[1] Compare Robert Joseph Phillimore, *Commentaries upon International Law* (3d ed.; London, 1879), I, p. 3: "To move, and live, and have its being in the great community of nations, is as much the normal condition of a single nation, as to live in a social state is the normal condition of a single man". James Kent, *Kent's Commentary on International Law*, ed. John Thomas Abdy (Cambridge, 1866), p. 7 et seq; Henry Wheaton, *Elements of International Law*, ed. Richard Henry Dana (London, 1866), p. 23, §14; August Wilhelm Heffter, *Das europäische Völkerrecht der Gegenwart* (7th ed.; Berlin, 1881), §2; Johann Caspar Bluntschli, *Das moderne Völkerrecht der civilisirten Staten als Rechtsbuch dargestellt* (3d ed.; Nördlingen, 1878), p. 1.

[2] Adolph Lasson, *Das Culturideal und der Krieg* (Berlin, 1871); Lasson, *Princip und Zukunft des Völkerrechts* (Berlin, 1871), p. 48. Compare Philipp Zorn, *Das Staatsrecht der Deutschen Reichs* (Berlin, 1880-1883), II, p. 420.

branches of law, but confirmed a false view of legal science that only that system of laws deserves the title of the science of law which is applied directly in life, serves as a means of struggle for the day-to-day interests of the individual, is protected by coercive force – in a word – may be based on Roman law. Built on principles unknown to Roman jurists, often violated in practice, and in the majority of instances being of only remote interest to private individuals, international law in the eyes of a civilist was not part of jurisprudence, and therefore he did not find it possible to devote his works to it. But this view is now rejected even in Germany. Contemporary jurists and political actors are increasingly persuaded that under the existing system of social life, when the people by electing their representatives are called upon to participate in legislation and in the administration of the country, familiarity with one *Corpus juris* is far from sufficient. The Digest of Roman law does not provide an answer to many vital questions on which the comprehensive development of peoples depends. That is why new politico-legal sciences emerge, such as the science on social law (*Gesellschaftsrecht*), or the science on administration (*Verwaltungslehre*), and that is why, together with a number of others, the science of international law had achieved a high degree of development.

Roman law, however, gradually descended from the pedestal on which it had been placed in Germany by the force of recent circumstances.[3] It would be a waste of time to attempt to determine international relations of contemporary peoples on the basis of the principles of Roman law. The Romans left inimitable masters in the formulation of provisions of civil law and in the application of legal analysis which every jurist must apply to the study of law in general. In this respect Roman law gives to the science of international law that practical method, that instrument of analysis, by means of which legal norms or laws might be clarified. But one cannot seek in them a legal definition of relations existing between contemporary peoples because the Romans did not know international relations in the sense imparted to them at present. In their relations with other peoples they proceeded from the principle directly opposite to the contemporary principle: peaceful international relations in which Rome is forced to enter they deemed to be a violation of the legal order of relations in which the Romans should be with respect to other peoples; then as now international life in its peaceful manifestations was considered to be the normal order of things caused by the legitimate needs of States and their citizens.[4]

[3] Compare Lorenz von Stein, *Gegenwart und Zukunft der Rechts- und Staatswissenschaft Deutschlands* (Stuttgart, 1876), p. 48.

[4] Phillimore attached to much significance to Roman law in the field of international re-

As for the second reason, which leads to a denial of international law, as noted above it consists of a realism dominant not only in the science of history, but also in various domains of jurisprudence. Without contesting the service of the realist school to science, one cannot avoid in silence its attractiveness and shortcomings. The most remarkable and consistent proponent of this orientation, Hippolyte [Adolphe] Thaine [(1828-1893)], defined the method by which the realists might resolve the task they confronted: "Nature and history", he said, "made a choice for us"; they determined the course of our life in advance; all relations in which people may find themselves, and likewise the results of activity which ultimately come.[5] Consequently, only on the basis of a study of historical facts and circumstances may those laws of progressive development be identified under whose influence a particular society or people lives or is found. Any initiative, any arbitrariness, any chance, and any freedom of will is denied by the realist orientation. Applying this method to the field of international relations, the realist school of jurists consistently came to the conclusion that the dominance of physical force comprises the sole law of international relations; because does not historical experience prove that it determined relations between States, was the factor which almost always triumphed over law? Hence the following aphorisms with whose assistance representatives of the realist orientation resolve questions of international law: "la force prime le droit", "law without force is a dream".[6]

But is it possible to reduce international relations to the predominance of brute force as the supreme principle thereof? Is it possible to prove by positive facts that only brute force and arbitrariness should predominate and predominates in the domain of international relations? If it is essential to study the circumstances and facts among which international life is formed, then does it follow that the freedom of human will had absolutely no influence on the creation of these conditions? Of course, no. Life itself and its conditions underlie without doubt all legal relations, private and public, State and international. But those real circumstances under whose

lations. Roman law may indeed be called "written reason", but only in civil law relations. See Phillimore, note 1 above, I, p. 16.

[5] Hippolyte Adolphe Thaine, *Les origines de la France contemporaine. L'ancien régime* (Paris, 1876), preface. Compare Alfred Jules Émile Fouillée, *L'idée moderne du droit en Allemagne, en Angleterre et en France* (Paris, 1878), pp. 227, 229.

[6] Merkel, "Recht und Macht", *Schmoller's Jahrbuch für Gesetzgebung*, V (1881), p. 439. Also compare Thomas Joseph Lawrence, *Essays on Some Disputed Questions in Modern International Law* (Cambridge, 1884; 2d ed.; 1885), pp. 1-37. Also compare Ernest Nys, *Les origines du droit international* (Brussels, 1894), introduction.

influence particular legal norms and rights were generated and received a certain form are themselves a product of various causes, often coincidence and frequently a mind of genius, human will and activity. In this respect the science of international law presents many examples, well-known principles set out by some remarkable State actor, writer, or jurist, mastered by other jurists and writers, applied by the States themselves, and thus acquiring the significance of customary principles time honored by experience and the practice of entire generations. Many customary principles and rules exist in international law which were elaborated by the civilized life of peoples, respected, and applied independently of international treaties and laws solely by virtue of their inner logic and practical advantage. Such, for example, are the rights and privileges enjoyed by diplomatic agents while on foreign territory, their not being subject to the jurisdiction in civil and criminal cases of a court of that State to which they have been accredited, and so on. All these and many other phenomena of international life have nothing in common with the dominance of physical force. They are inexplicable from the standpoint of a realist orientation and can be justified only by common sense, reason, an awareness of their true advantage, and the ideas of truth and justice which should comprise the highest criteria of any law.[7]

If we leave theoretical reflections and turn to the practice of international relations in that form in which they exist at present, here we encounter a multiplicity of factors that refute the writers-jurists who suggest that there is no international law, and that in the sphere of international relations only arbitrariness and violence reign. We see that between contemporary educated peoples a correct and continuous exchange has been established of their economic, industrial, and entrepreneurial activity. Trade relations linking contemporary States have reached a scale beyond any previously existing concept. However, they have been made the subject-matter of an enormous number of international conventions and trade and navigation treaties providing conditions under which these relations should continue and contain rules on the basis of which they should occur. But economic interests are not alone in bringing contemporary peoples together and establishing legal relations between them.

Many other needs and interests exist which are pursued on the part of subjects of different States outside the limits of their fatherland but within the domain of international relations. At present, every individual who does not find the means for his existence or for the development of his abilities and forces within his own country may freely resettle in another State

[7] Cornelis van Bynkershoek, *Quaestiones juris publici* (1737), lib. I, cap. II: "*Ratio, ipsa, iuquam, ratio est juris gentium anima*".

where he, even in addition to treaties, will find full protection of personal and property rights. Not only that, every person who has settled on foreign territory may, by virtue of an act of naturalization, receive the rights of citizenship at the place of his sojourn, and such a naturalized citizen will be deemed to be a foreigner even within his own motherland.

Then contemporary peoples find it necessary to establish a certain order regulated by law also in the domain of their spiritual interests. With respect to intellectual and artistic activities, almost all western European peoples now comprise one international society within which any literary figure, scholar, artist, performing artist, or composer enjoys an identical right to defense of a court and law in the event of a violation of the literary or artistic ownership thereof.

Likewise, the interests of justice are protected by international means common to all civilized peoples. Under the contemporary development of international communication it is easy for a criminal, by fleeing, to conceal himself from legal responsibility before judges at the site of commission of the crime and go abroad. In view of this possibility to escape the deserved punishment, States are concluding cartel conventions determining the procedure for the extradition of criminals who have committed common crimes. The dominance everywhere of civil and trade laws is ensured by the recognition of the equality of rights between courts of various States whose judgments on the basis of existing treaties concerning the enforcement of foreign court decisions or according to the principle of reciprocity are considered to be valid outside their territorial jurisdiction.

Numerous congresses and conferences of representatives of various States which were held during the past and present centuries serve as evidence no less convincing not only of the actual existence but also of the legal definition of international relations. They point to the insufficiency, of which States themselves are aware, of internal legislation alone to fully ensure the legal interests of their subjects without international agreements and measures. In view of this, States enter into unions whose task is to serve the social interests of peoples. For example, the 1874 Berlin Congress established the Universal Postal Union, whose members subordinated themselves to completely identical rules relating to the use of postal communications. Telegraph conferences worked out uniform rules for the use of telegraphic relations within all States joining the telegraphic union, and so on. Even during war contemporary educated peoples deemed themselves bound by certain customs and treaty rules determining their mutual relations. The 1856 Paris Declaration defined the rights of neutral trade. The 1864 Geneva Convention established for belligerent States identical rules relating to the care of the wounded and sick by enemy personnel. On this basis of this international act any sick or wounded warrior during combat has the same right to protection and care on the part of the adversary as do own subjects of the last. The 1868 Petersburg Declaration prohibits during war the use of explosive ammunition of less than a certain weight. In 1874 at the initiative of the late Sovereign, Emperor Alexander II [(1818-1881)], the Brussels Conference was convened to determine in general all laws and customs of land warfare. Consequently, also during hostile relations contemporary States reject the principle of unlimited dominance of physical force, considering themselves bound by certain customs and agreements constraining arbitrariness. Generally speaking, the history of international relations is a continuous series of facts proving the need for a certain order in mutual relations of peoples. The idea of so-called "political equilibrium" proves that in the domain of political relations peoples considered it necessary to establish a certain order, to determine their relations by certain rules.

On the basis of the facts adduced, one cannot fail to conclude that existing international relations are determined both by customs and by formal international acts and legal principles; that is, by a number of norms, laws, which must be complied with on the part of interested States. In other words, insofar as international life is necessary, so too law is necessary regulating it, and to deny this law would be to deny those relations which exist *de facto* between peoples and which have been generated by their legal needs.

§2. Irrespective of the general orientation of the realist school denying the existence or practical significance of the science of international law, in the literature and society there are widespread special legal objections against the possible implementation and definition of legal principles and laws in the domain of international relations. These objections are based chiefly on the absence of the compulsory character of provisions of international law and, in particular, the lack of legislative power and a court common to the entire union of States.[8]

[8] The most sensible refutation of those who question the existence of positive international law must be deemed Chapter VI of the remarkable work by Karl von Kaltenborn von Stachau, *Kritik des Völkerrechts* (Leipzig, 1874), p. 158. Also the successful observations by August von Bulmerincq, *Praxis, Theorie und Codification des Völkerrechts* (Leipzig, 1874). No less noteworthy is the argumentation by Carl Bergbohm, *Staatsverträge und Gesetze as Quellen des Völkerrechts* (Dorpat, 1877), p.12, who successfully proves that the positive character of law is not determined by the actual possibility to implement it. Compare also G. Jellinek, *Die rechtliche Natur der Staatenverträge* (Vienna, 1880), p. 7; Johann Wilhelm Franz Philipp von Holtzendorff, *Handbuch des Völkerrechts* (1885-1889), p. 18.

At the head of contemporary jurists seeing the essential indicator of law in compulsion or force is the notable German jurist, [Rudolf von] Jhering [(1818-1892)], who has devoted several works to specially identifying the essence of law. In one of his works the German scholar expressly said that the "concept of law is not a logical concept, but a pure concept on force". In another place he commented: "Force is not only the means for the effectuation of law, but it becomes an organic part of the concept on law itself". Jhering proved, finally, that force represents such an essential element of law that, in the event of its absence, law itself is inconceivable, that those relations such as, for example, international relations, in which coercion has no place, will be moral and not legal relations.[9] This view has many proponents among other representatives of theoretical and practical jurisprudence.

We cannot, however, agree that such an exceptional role in determining the character of vital relations belonged to force. The fact is that the concept of law set out by Jhering is refuted by he himself in the further development of his theory. Although the noted Romanist also acknowledges that force is an essential component of law, nonetheless he proved that the strongest, in respect for its own interests, limits its own force, does not continue struggle against the adversary in perpetuity; it concludes peace, and peace, said Jhering, is the foundation of any order and law. Therefore, law is based on agreement (*auf dem Verträge*).[10]

No one will assert that this viewpoint could not be applied to international relations. And here the strongest State rather often, out of respect for own advantage, must limit its own power. In protecting its interests, it enters into agreement with other weaker peoples in order to establish order, which always is based on compliance with certain legal norms or laws. Thus, whereas civil, criminal, or State law is in general a consequence of agreements between particular parties, international order or law also are

[9] Rudolf von Jhering, *Der Kampf ums Recht* (1872); Jhering, *Der Zweck im Recht* (Leipzig, 1877), I, p. 240: "Recht ist das System der durch Zwang gesicherten socialen Zwecken"; also see I, p. 255: "das Recht ist die Politik der Gewalt". Although Jhering does not expressly deny the existence of international law, the concept of law thereof is, however, cited as authoritative evidence in support of the absence of law where there is no enforcement. Also compare Georg Friedrich Puchta, *Das Gowohnheitsrecht* (Erlangen, 1828), I, p. 142.

[10] Rather remarkable and well-founded are the objections to Jhering's theory on the essence of law advanced by Professor August Thon, *Rechtsnorm und subjektives Recht* (Weimar, 1878), p. 47. Also compare his article: Thon, "Der Rechtsbegriff", *Grünhut's Zeitschrift für das Privat- und öffentliche Recht*, VII, no. 2. Also deserving attention are Felix Dahn, *Die Vernunft im Recht: Grundlagen der Rechtsphilosophie* (Berlin, 1879); Merkel, in *Grünhut's Zeitschrift für das Privat- und öffentliche Recht*, VI, no. 2.

the result of an agreement in which States of different power and might participate.

The analogy goes further. All social relations, in the view of Jhering, have as their foundation the combination of personal purpose with the advantage or interest of another. Thus, the governmental power in a State respects the rights of its subjects with a view to ensuring own benefit or interest. But the same we see also in the domain of international relations. International life represents a number of political alliances of States, social alliances, for the extradition of criminals, for the protection of literary property, and so on, and each of them may be regarded as a combining of peoples concluded thanks to the achievement of the advantage of each by means of respect for the interests of other contracting parties. International law also is based on a compromise of the interests of States in international interaction. Any interaction of people recognizing a certain order of community life is a legal community life.

Consequently, on the basis of Jhering's theory itself, it is impossible to dispute the existence of order and law in international relations. But, in addition, the very point of departure of this theory is untrue. The scholar according to whom physical force and compulsion constitute the material appurtenance of law confuses two different things: law itself and the enforcement procedure for the effectuation thereof. The last has application usually when *jus* and *lex* are violated. Therefore, force is more an element of injustice than rights which in the normal existence thereof never generate coercive effectuation. Law ceases to exist from the moment when is ceased to be the incentive for human actions, when one is no longer aware of it. That is why the dissemination of the awareness of law is the best means to ensure its effectuation. Hence it is clear how the best application of and respect for the principles of international law is directly dependent on a knowledge thereof by those who have been called upon to be the executors and interpreters thereof.[11]

The second legal objection directed against international law is that there is no legislation in international law. If international life knows no legislative authority, say the proponents of this objection, one cannot speak of international law as the aggregate of laws determining international relations. One cannot fail to see that this objection is based on a completely incorrect understanding of the purpose and tasks of legislation. In the view of its proponents, a law issued by an established authority is the sole source of law and binding force. From this point of view, the task of the legislator

[11] Compare also Moritz August von Berthmann-Hollweg, *Civilprocess des gemeinen Rechts in geschichtlicher Entwickelung* (Berlin, 1864), I, §12.

will be to issue, or even invent, as many laws as possible and give them to its subjects, who without this will remain in a lawless state forever. On the other hand, no personal or property benefits of citizens, no law of obligations or family law will find protection and respect if, as the adherents of this view suggest, no special laws exist protecting the life, honor, and other rights of man.

One cannot agree with one or the other. Properly understood, the task of the legislator is not the invention of laws, but the good faith study and formulation of those vital relations and mutual interests of people which underlie any law. These laws arise from human nature and surrounding conditions thereof, and therefore cannot be created by legislation. They exist in and of themselves. People entered into marriage, possessed things, and concluded obligations earlier than civil laws began to determine the conditions of marriage, rights of an owner, and relations between contracting parties. Every person has the right to respect of his person, to inviolability of ownership and family, irrespective of whether law recognizes them or not. On the contrary, that law which would deny the right of a person to life, honor, and freedom would have no right to exist, would be contrary to common sense and justice.[12]

If legislative power is not the primary source of law in civil and State existence, then in the domain of international relations the absence thereof cannot serve as evidence that here no binding legal norms exist. The order of things actually established in this respect permits only one conclusion, that contemporary peoples have not yet come to that stage of development to establish a certain legislative organ above themselves whose decrees would have binding force for all peoples. Insofar as possible and desirable, the structure of a common supreme authority over States under present conditions of international relations is another question. Although [Johann Caspar] Bluntschli [(1808-1881)] called the effectuation of such an order the "beautiful dream of idealists", when all peoples will be under a common legislative authority, he did not deny the possible existence of a "world State" (Weltstaat).[13] It seems to us that under the contemporary state of international life this is an unrealizable utopia. But this circumstance does not eliminate the fact that international relations at present all the same know a certain order and, consequently, law regulating them. Those laws by which presently existing relations of peoples are determined are not the work of legislative authority but of agreements between individual States.

[12] Compare the accurate remarks of Fricker, in *Zeitschrift für die gesammten Staatswissenschaften*, I (1872), p. 92.

[13] Bluntschli, note 1 above, Einleitung, p. 4, §8-10.

The procedure operating in this respect reminds one of feudal times. Just as in the Middle Ages all so-called "coutumes" and "usages" and feudal private and State law were based almost exclusively on compromise between the suzerain on one side and the vassals on the other, between the king and the Middle Ages municipalities, so too at present the path of agreement, mutual concessions, between the contracting States is a normal means for the establishment of international laws.[14]

Finally, the last objection which jurists cite against the rule of law in relations between peoples is based on the shortcomings of a permanent and properly organized international court that would be called upon to respond to offenders of international law. The lack of such a tribunal serves, in their view, as irrefutable evidence that what is passed off as international law is devoid of any guarantee and, consequently, cannot be called law in the legal sense of this word. This objection, just as the preceding one, is flawed by an erroneous understanding of the purpose which a court has in each civilized State. It rests on the conviction that a court, when restoring a violated legal order, not only confirms the law, but also creates it; therefore, where there is no court, there cannot be law. But any court, civil or criminal, decides one task: it elicits the existing legal relations which were not fully determined, whether due to the evil will of a person or to various other circumstances; the sole purpose of a judge is to identify, by means of legal analysis, all the conditions on which the contested or violated right depends, and on this basis decide on whose side the latter is, on the side of the plaintiff or the defendant, and whether it was violated by the accused, if the case is a crime. But it is possible to imagine even such a court which in its decisions mocks any laws, divine or human. Consequently, as one existing court is not in a state to ensure legality, the absence thereof does not prove directly the absence of any law. In other words, law exists before the court and its existence does not depend on the court.[15]

In applying this point of view to international relations, we readily grasp the unfoundedness of such a view under which the shortcomings of general

[14] It is appropriate to bear in mind also instances when States solemnly declare their consent to apply principles of European international law. Such statements were made by the North American United States at the very moment of declaring their independence, and by Brazil in 1820. According to Sir William Blackstone [(1723-1780)] in England, international law is long since regarded as an integral part of English law. See W. Blackstone, *Commentaries on the Laws of England* (Oxford, 1765-1769), IV, chapter V. Compare Phillimore, note 1 above, I, p. 76.

[15] See in particular the interesting work of Wilhelm Kaufmann, *Die Rechtskraft des internationals Rechtes und das Verhältniss der Staatsgesetzgebungen und der Staatsorgane zu demselben* (Stuttgart, 1899).

judicial power is cited for all peoples as testimony that international law itself does not exist. This shortcoming proves only that the consent which underlies international law has not yet developed to the degree necessary to establish a permanent judicial authority for the resolution of all disputes which arise between States. For this a material change of contemporary international relations is necessary, and in particular more consent, more mutual concessions on the part of States than have been noted up to the present.[16] However, the development in the present century of the arbitration of international disputes shows that contemporary States often found it more advantageous for themselves to establish a court for the settlement of their disagreements than other violent means to resolve them. Of such courts, especially noteworthy are the Geneva Arbitration Tribunal founded in 1871 on the basis of an agreement between England and the North American United States in the Alabama case: it awarded England to pay an enormous sum of damages for those illegal actions which this power allowed within its own waters during the internecine war in North America. The arbitration of the dispute between England and the United States relating to the Bering Sea, completed in 1893 with confirmation of the principle of the freedom of the high seas deserves even more attention. Finally, in 1897 an international arbitration tribunal was founded under the chairmanship of the author of the present book to resolve a celebrated dispute between Great Britain and the United States of Venezuela.

However, not arbitration, but war remains the usual means of settling international disputes. But does this fact prove the absence of international law? Not at all. The history of court proceedings shows us that underlying the most ancient judicial proceeding are those very principles which dominate now in disputes between States. Given the undeveloped state of social life in ancient times, every person protected his right by his own force. The dominance of mob law proves, of course, the uncultured state of society; but it would be unjust to conclude from this that the members of this society did not know any law, did not comply with customs or laws. In the Middle Ages a court also existed, established by sovereign authority. However, subjects of the State continued to have recourse to combat as a means for the settlement of their disagreements. To a certain degree, international war at present is such a judicial duel. The similarity between them lies not only in the fact that in both instances the decision lies with force, but also in the existence of certain rules which are complied with

[16] Only we doubt that sometime an international court might be structured according to the design of Count Leonid Alekseevich Kamarovskii [(1846-1912)]. See Kamarovskii, О международном суде [On an International Court] (Moscow, 1881), p. 519. This project is too complex and not practical.

when using this force. Thus, war is not a denial of law; on the contrary, it is itself subject to certain laws which have been consecrated by custom and international agreements. Thus, international relations exist which require the need for a legal definition and an aggregate of norms and laws exist comprising international law. Agreements between States, customary principles, and finally legal order which was established by the force of vital needs serve as the sources of the rules which should dominate in the domain of international relations. The initial grounds of international law are embedded in a common source of all legal and political sciences, of which the English thinker [Sir Francis] Bacon [(1561-1626)] spoke in the following eloquent words: "In nature there is a certain source of truth and justice from which all laws of a civil society arise, just as water takes the color and taste of various strata of earth through which it flows, so too the laws of a civil society differ by localities and States in which they have been planted, although all have the same source".

Despite all the variety of political institutions and the civil and criminal laws of contemporary civilized States, the same source underlies their rights and legislation – the idea of truth and justice inherent to human nature. International law has the same source from which all other branches of law emanate. But the difference between the last and international law is that international law develops principally by means of agreements between States as members of an international community, whereas State, civil, and criminal law is the result of life, culture, and politics of each individual people. The difference of geographical position, economic state, cultural conditions in which peoples are discover their influence on the development of their internal system and law; and if despite this, one and the same legal and moral principles underlie the law of various peoples, then it should follow that international law, insofar as it is binding for these peoples, has grounds identical with their own law. In other words, it may be effectuated only on the part of peoples who are more or less at an equal stage of development of civil and State life: only these peoples have a legal consciousness materially the same.[17]

II. Definition of Concept of International Law

§3. The rich literature of international law still does not have a precise and generally-accepted definition of its own subject-matter. The existing definitions of international law are distinctive for their diversity

[17] Compare Holtzendorff, note 8 above, §7, whose observations are distinguished by great clarity and accuracy.

and for often being contradictory to one another. Ambiguity, differences, and contradictions noted in this respect may be explained by general considerations and by circumstances specially relevant to international law.[18]

A scientific definition of any subject-matter presents difficulties.[19] Indeed, for a definition of science to give a complete and clear concept of the subject-matter being studied it must, in a few words, embrace all its distinctive attributes and all the basic principles on which it depends and from the point of view of which its distinctive features can be correctly explained, those particular phenomena that are associated with and conditioned by it. This task is not easily resolved.

Another reason concerns the science of international law itself: its relative youth. International law is a young science. It has found grounds for itself, acquired a certain form, and become the subject-matter of study on the part of jurists and public figures no earlier than the seventeenth century. Under these conditions it is excusable that its concept and definition have been insufficiently strengthened and not acquired that precision characteristic of the older legal sciences – civil, criminal, and State law.

In connection with the last circumstance, an incorrect designation for it has dominated for a long time. The common name by which it is now known was established not so long ago. The name which it initially bore did not correspond to its subject-matter or to its true content.

When in the sixteenth century jurists first began to occupy themselves with international law, they attempted to find some positive legal grounds for the new science. Influenced by an orientation that distinguished that time, they adopted Roman law as the source of its provisions and rules. The last had served as the foundation of the civil laws of European States;

[18] We confine ourselves to citing some definitions given by authoritative representatives of the science of international law. Hugo Grotius, *De jure belli ac pacis* (Paris, 1625), lib. I, §XIV: "*Jus gentium est quod gentium aut multarum voluntate vim obligandi accepit*". Emer de Vattel, *Le droit des gens ou principes de la loi naturelle appliqués à la conduite et aux affaires des nations et des souverains, préliminaires* (Leiden, 1758), §6: "Le droit des gens n'est originairement autre chose que le droit de la nature appliqué aux nations". Henry Wheaton, *Eléments du droit international* (5th ed.; Leipzig, 1874), I, p. 23: "Le droit international tel qu'il est compris par les nations civilisées est l'ensemble des règles de conduite, que la raison déduit, comme étant conformes à la justice, de la nature de la société qui existe parmi les nations indépendance, en y admettant toutefois les définitions ou modifications qui peuvent être établies par l'usage et le consentement général". Compare also Phillimore, note 1 above, I, §§8-9; Heffter, note 1 above, §1; Bluntschli, note 1 above, Einleitung, §1.

[19] "*Omnis definitio in jure civili periculosa est; parum est enim ut non subverti possit*". Digest lib. 50, XVII, §202.

royal authority was enhanced on that foundation and the State system of western Europe was formed; it was comprehensively studied in the universities; in a word, Roman law dominated everywhere. Naturally, the early representatives of the science of international law turned to it so that its undoubted authority would consecrate the tenets of their science. They borrowed the name international law from it and taught that *jus gentium* is international law.

But in fact this definition represents a complete confusion of heterogeneous concepts. *Jus gentium* is the aggregate of philosophical principles and general civil laws of various countries. Its subject-matter comprises domestic, private relations between individuals in the sphere of their personal, right to a thing, law of obligations, and family law relations. But it is evident that the subject-matter of international law is not these relations, but relations between independent States.

Little by little the writers on international law were convinced, however, that the Roman *jus gentium* did not correspond to the concept of international law. The English scholar, [Richard] Zouche [(1590-1661)],[20] was the first to identify precisely that international law is not the law of nations – *jus gentium* – but the law between nations – *jus inter gentes*, and hence the contemporary names of international law gradually emerged. In the French language it is presently called droit international,[21] in English – international law,[22] in German – Völkerrecht or Internationales Recht. According to the 1835 Statute on Universities, it was known in Russia under the name all-people's law [общенародное право]; but now it is called international law [международное право].[23]

By international law we understand the aggregate of legal norms determining the conditions of the achievement by peoples of their vital aims in the sphere of their mutual relations.

International law, being the aggregate of legal norms, has law as its subject-matter, and not moral or religious laws by which peoples are guided or were guided in their mutual relations in various epochs of their life. Moral principles and religious views, without doubt, have an impact on

[20] Richard Zouche, *Juris et judicii fecialis sive juris inter gentes et quaestionum de eodem explicatio* (1651).

[21] The name *droit de gens* means more the theory of international law.

[22] Compare Jeremy Bentham, *Principles of Morals and Legislation*, chapter XIX, section 25, note; Louis Renault, *Introduction à l'étude du droit international* (Paris, 1879), p. 14.

[23] Holtzendorff, note 8 above, §2.

international life, but they do not comprise the subject-matter of the study of the science of international law.

International law, moreover, determines the conditions under which peoples may achieve certain vital goals set for themselves. In other words, the laws, customs, and international treaties comprising international law are conditions, compliance with which is necessary so that peoples might satisfy their needs by way of international exchange. Therefore, they must be respected by peoples. But then these conditions or laws themselves, evidently, depend on the goals pursued by the peoples and, consequently, must change as these goals change. Consequently, the basis of international law is the factual, real, vital relations of peoples at a given time and, from this point of view, every international law has a reasonable basis and right to exist insofar as it corresponds to the actual, reasonable, vital relations between peoples.

If this proposition is well-founded, then from the following conclusions important for a comprehension of international law may be drawn.

If particular vital relations of peoples constitute the grounds of international law, it is necessary to recognize that the science of international law has as its task to constantly follow a change of these relations. Only then will it stand at the height of its calling, when the principles proclaimed by it will not be coercion rather than a response to the legal needs of peoples, when their development will not constrain the progress of international life; in a word, when this life and international law will be in full concord with one another. Moreover, if life always remains a criterion for international rules and laws in force, if the propositions set out in the science of international law must constantly illuminate and regulate the actual state of things dominant in the domain of international relations, then this order will provide content to international law. Finally, it also follows that the system of the science of international law is determined not only by those rules and laws which have been developed and adopted by States or jurists, but also by vital relations which actually have been established between peoples.

The tasks and purposes pursued by States in their mutual relations are diverse. They may be identified only by an analysis of existing international relations. History and contemporary life point, however, to certain general, basic reasons which bring peoples together, oblige them to renounce mutual enmity and isolation, and unite in an aspiration to achieve general humanitarian, cultural, and political goals.

To those elementary forces uniting peoples belong, without doubt, identical religious beliefs and ideas which often reconciled enemy States, forced peoples to listen to the voice of human conscience and recognize the feeling of truth and justice, and therefore persuaded them to enter into agreements in order to achieve common cultural interests by their combined forces.

Common intellectual and moral aspirations unite peoples in respect for those highest benefits, the possession of which is a primary condition for the spiritual development of man and the social progress of a people. An awareness by a particular people of their common tribal origin always has served as grounds for better mutual understanding and rapprochement.

But the economic interests and trade relations of peoples have long played an especially noticeable role in international life. Thanks primarily to these relations and interests, the hostile relations and isolation of States, long supported by legislative and governmental measures and by the worldview of peoples, have been mitigated. Finally, an awareness of the commonality of political interests results in States combining aspirations for identical international goals.[24]

These are the main factors determining international relations. They all serve as an expression of one common force, the power of which is not capable of combating legislation hostile to international relations, nor inherent prejudices, nor wild concepts and barbaric habits of peoples. This force consists of an awareness by peoples of their spiritual and material needs, whose satisfaction they cannot achieve by themselves within their territories. Only as peoples come to such an awareness and their aspirations and interests exceed the means provided by their own country, do they seek their satisfaction outside their own State and must enter into relations with other peoples. One may say in general that the development of an awareness on the part of a particular people of their own needs is a measure for their participation in international turnover, and *vice versa*: the greater or lesser variety and complexity of international relations of a State represent the best evidence of the degree of its culture and civilization.

§4. According to the aforesaid definition of international law, actors in the sphere of international relations are politically organized peoples or States. They pursue in their mutual relations the most vital interests as determined in their domestic activity. In this respect international life is closely and organically linked with State life.

Indeed, the task of every State is to grant to its subjects all means for the fullest development of their spiritual and physical capabilities and forces. All representatives of the science of State law so define the reasonable goal

[24] Compare Robert von Mohl, "Die Pflege der internationalen Gemeinschaft als Aufgabe des Völkerrechts", in Mohl, *Staatsrecht, Völkerrecht und Politik* (Tübingen, 1860), I, p. 579.

of the existence of a State. From this ultimate goal, States naturally derive the duty for any State authority, unless it is in a position through its own efforts and within its own territory to create conditions under which its subjects might satisfy their material and moral interests, to seek these means and conditions outside its own territory within other States. But not a single educated people can find all the means for its existence and development solely within its own State. That is why all contemporary peoples, understanding their vital tasks, maintain relations between themselves and enter into relations in order to establish mutually those conditions under which they truly might find satisfaction of all their needs.

From this arises international activity (international administration) of States – legislative, administrative, and judicial – directed towards ensuring the said conditions for the creation of protection of foreigners by means of law and court, recognition of personal and property inviolability of representatives of foreign powers, and so on. How States resolve their various tasks in the domain of international relations we shall see below. We note for the moment that the more they are aware of their duties with respect to their own subjects and the more they treat them with respect for their rights and legal interests, the less there will be arbitrariness in the mutual relations of States, and the better the peaceful and lawful flow of international life will be ensured. Shortcomings and gaps inherent in contemporary international law are to be explained to a significant degree by the absence of legality within the States themselves and the unsatisfactory orders dominant therein.

In essence, international law may be divided: into public international law and private and criminal international law. The first has as its subject-matter the determination by legal norms of direct relations of States with one another in the domain of international turnover; the second determines the legal status of subjects in the domain of international relations generated by private law interests and the need for the criminal protection thereof.

§5. Together with States to which the sovereign direction of international relations appertains, there exist various kinds of social circles, social groups, societies, partnerships, and companies that take an active part in international life and are in constant relations between themselves, despite the territorial boundaries separating the States. Finally, private individuals play an eminent role in international relations, and history presents many examples of them giving these relations a certain direction, despite the intentions and desires of the State authorities.

The significance of all these actors in the domain of international relations may be expressed by the general proposition that the more social interests develop within a State, the greater respect the State authorities have for the reasonable needs of society, the more peoples come together, and the more international life develops more luxuriously. The degree of participation thereof in international life determines the degree of the development of social interests within a State.

The works of noted jurists – Lorenz von Stein, Robert von Mohl, Heinrich Rudolph Hermann Friedrich von Gneist (1816-1895) – identified positively that the life of States is concentrated primarily in activity, the life of social circles, classes into which every people is divided, and therefore changes to which the State existence of a people is subjected, the structure and administration of the country, always depends on the relations which social classes have vis-à-vis State authorities.[25]

When applying this proposition to international relations, we necessarily come to the conclusion that the extensive development of contemporary international relations and communication is to be explained by the unusual power which social interests have at present and those aspirations that permeate various social circles in contemporary States. For them, territorial boundaries are merely a restraint obstructing the coming together of peoples. On the other hand, if social interests primarily unite peoples in the aspiration for common cultural aims, if the development of relations between them depends on this, then one must acknowledge that such development is conceivable only between peoples who are at approximately an identical stage of cultural and social development. Where the significance of social forces and interests is nil, there cannot be developed international relations; there governments will not be under the influence of social classes, and will not devote any attention to the reasonable interests and aspirations of society and the representatives thereof. On the other hand, where society dominates the State without limitation, where the State is absorbed by society and the supreme power is a blind instrument in the hands of some separate social class in the nature of the Indian caste or contemporary clique, there international turnover may be either prohibited under threat of severe punishments or exploited for the purely egoistic estates or for mercenary purposes.

On the contrary, when the relations of society and the State are properly set, when the State authorities promote the normal development of social interests within the set limits, social aspirations lose that national harshness in the domain of international relations, that narrow antagonism typical within a State. In other words, social international relations significantly

[25] Compare especially Lorenz von Stein, *Geschichte der socialen Bewegung in Frankreich von 1789 bis auf unsere Tage* (Leipzig, 1850-1855), I, Einleitung; Heinrich von Gneist, *Der Rechtstaat* (Berlin, 1879), p. 8.

facilitate peoples in general ceasing to treat one another with contempt, with a feeling of dismissive arrogance which prevails in relations between peoples socially uncultured and underdeveloped. It is not self-righteous isolation and boasting of national distinctiveness that testify to the cultural life and civilization of a people, but, on the contrary, an awareness of one's own shortcomings and needs and an understanding of the great importance that, for their satisfaction, the international exchange of ideas, products of economic and industrial activity, and in general relations with other peoples have.

III. History of International Relations and Law

§6. The task of the essay which follows on the development of international relations and law is not an account of naked facts and phenomena of international life, nor an enumeration of all wars, diplomatic negotiations, or treaties between various peoples beginning from Antiquity to the present time, but the character of the ideas which dominated at a particular time and determined the form and content of relations between States and the law applied to them. Facts, by their nature, are transitory and changeable; they often are the result of arbitrariness or chance. On the contrary, ideas which permeate a certain historical epoch, which underlie all facts, filling it, make it possible to analyze, to find oneself within an enormous mass of special conditions and circumstances in which the life developed of both an individual people and all peoples in aggregate taking part in the European political system. In this respect, ideas play the role also of engines, the levers of law, acting in international relations in various epochs and periods of its existence, which serve as principles, in the sense of [Charles Louis de Secondat, Baron de la Brede et de] Montesquieu [(1689-1755)], with respect to the forms and orders of State life.[26]

The internal existence and political system of States have, as noted above (§§3-5) a powerful impact on the character of international relations. Only by knowing the domestic life and State institutions of a country can one understand the principles and rules which guide it in relations with other peoples. The present essay assumes these institutions and this life are known. But it indicates and constantly has in view the inextricable link which exists between them and the mutual relations of peoples in all epochs of their history.

Finally, the law of the progressive development of international relations serves as the basic law of the entire history of international law, whose

[26] Charles de Montesquieu, *De l'esprit des lois*, liv. III, chap. I and II.

prominent features will be presented below. It gives us the possibility to connect and understand, as a single whole, individual phenomena which are encountered in a particular epoch of international life, and these very epochs and periods into which we divide its history. The closest and direct expression of this law is one principle which passes through the entire historical life of peoples, namely –the principle of respect for the individual. The degree of recognition, which a person finds on his own, always determines the measure of development of international relations and law at a certain time. If this respect is considerable, if the individual is deemed as such to be a court of civil and political human rights, then international life presents a high degree of the development of order and law. And, on the contrary, we do not find in the mutual relations of States either legal order or respect for legality if the life dominant in States is a denial of inalienable rights inherent to man.

The justness of this position is confirmed by the history of international relations. As we shall see below, in Antiquity, the East, the Greek States, and Rome respect for the individual did not exist at all. Accordingly, the international relations of the ancient world were not developed at all; as a general rule, States were in hostile relations with one another and waged endless wars of destruction.

In the Middle Ages we see the dominance of the law of the fist, violence, and arbitrariness. But the peoples of the Middle Ages contributed the principle of the individual to international relations, proclaiming that principle to be a source of individual and political freedom. Thus, in this epoch we must seek the initial embryos of international law. Moreover, thanks to the spread of Christianity, a new doctrine takes hold in the Middle Ages, that not the link of a person as a subject with the State establishes certain personal and property rights thereof, but the affiliation of a person to the Catholic Church. Finally, little-by-little this doctrine extends to all Christians, without distinction of profession of faith, and in modern times, in an epoch of the unprecedented development of international relations, it has become an axiom that any foreigner in general, whatever his profession of faith, and irrespective of the conclusion of treaties on this account, must be deemed in every educated country a subject of certain personal and property rights.

§7. The history of international relations and law are usually divided into periods representing supposedly the degree of the progressive movement of international life and the legal norms determining it. On the basis of salient facts accepted as bounds separating one epoch from another, the history of international relations is divided by various writers sometimes into seven periods, sometimes four, sometimes three, and so on.[27] But this approach does not withstand scholarly critique. Of course, the history of international relations presents a multiplicity of noteworthy facts and events, but the various epochs thereof are not determined by them. The foundation of a proper division of the history of international relations must be not individual facts, as significant as they may have been, and not great events, as influential as their consequences were, and not important international acts, as significant as their content was. In the history of international relations the bounds of various epochs or periods are noted for the replacement of some leading ideas by others.

In terms of ideas that characterize various epochs of the development of international relations, the history of international law may be divided into three periods. We concisely indicate the distinctive indicia and duration of each.

The first period encompasses the ancient world, Middle Ages, and modern period up to the mid-seventeenth century or to the 1648 Peace of Westphalia. During this long time, relations between States were determined primarily by the principle of the greatest disunity of peoples and the dominance of physical force between them. Not only the peoples of the ancient East, but also the Greeks and Romans were imbued with the idea that they represent isolated and unique States which did not need international relations because within their territories they had everything for the satisfaction of their needs. Therefore, any other people, even the closest neighbors, were regarded as a natural enemy who must be conquered, enslaved, or destroyed.

The idea of physical force achieved its highest development in the Middle Ages. At that time we see the complete, unlimited, and pervasive dominance of arrogation and the law of the fist. One may say that life in the Middle Ages was nothing other than a continuous series of wars waged not only between States, but within them, between various parts of the territory and between individual subjects. "War is the law of feudalism", rightly noted [François] Laurent [(1810-1887)].[28] Under these conditions, of course, one could not speak of an international legal order or awareness by peoples of their rights and duties.

Despite the said general character of international relations in the Middle Ages, however, new principles and orientations developed gradually and

[27] Compare Henry Wheaton, *Histoire des progrès du droit des gens* (3d ed.; Leipzig, 1853), who divides into four periods; Carlos Calvo, *Le droit international théorique et pratique* (4th ed.; Paris, 1887-1896), into seven periods.

[28] François Laurent, *Histoire de droit des gens et des relations internationales* (Brussels, 1861-1870), VII, p. ix.

led to new ideas in the field of international relations. The Middle Ages did not differ from Antiquity in general principle, but new factors of social and State life could not fail to operate beyond the limits of States in their international relations. The Christian religion and the Church, which replaced ancient polytheism and spread throughout all of Europe, had such significance. Christianity and the Church favorably influenced social, State, and international relations. The peoples of the Middle Ages, to be sure, were in constant strife with one another, but were aware that they were brothers in faith, were identically subject to the authority of the Roman Catholic Church – the Pope, and that solidarity of religious beliefs and a common moral worldview united them in a single spiritual society. That is why they often entered into alliances with one another so that with combined forces they defended against common dangers, especially to protect the interests of the Church and religion. The Crusades and wars against the Arabs and Turks show that an awareness of a certain spiritual communion had developed between peoples of the Middle Ages. Being members of one Church, recognizing the spiritual authority over them of the Roman pontiff, States naturally mitigated their mutual enmity and moderated the struggle between them under the influence of the conciliatory activity of the Church. In this respect the Middle Ages comprise a transitional step to the second period.

The second period of the development of international relations and law begins from 1648 and continues to the beginning of the nineteenth century, or to the 1815 Congress of Vienna. During this period, the dominance of physical force and isolation between peoples cedes place to a new principle – the idea of political equilibrium.

The Congress of Westphalia, which brought an end to the Thirty Years War, represented an unprecedented example of virtually all western European peoples combining into one general peace assembly in order to discuss not only their mutual relations, but also the internal structure of individual countries. The fact of such an assembly obviously demonstrated that the European States had come to an awareness, finally, by the force of events of the need to bring an end to the disastrous wars and establish some kind of order in international relations.

Indeed, the treaties of Westphalia determined the principles on the basis of which a new international life should have been built. These principles consisted of the so-called system of political equilibrium of States. Underlying the new order of international relations was the principle by virtue of which the autonomy and independence of each individual people should not be subjected to the slightest danger on the part of other peoples.

At the end of the second period – namely, the time of the "Great French Revolution" of 1789 until the 1815 Peace Congress in Vienna – the system of political equilibrium, if it does not lose its strength in general as a principle of international relations, significantly pales before new ideas proclaimed by the Revolution and disseminated throughout Europe by Napoleon's armies. Having significantly changed the internal state of civilized peoples, their social existence and State institutions, the basic principles of the French Revolution are receiving in the nineteenth century the significance of a circulating coin and serve as a lever in the domain of contemporary international relations. Thus, the period from 1789 to 1815 is transitional from the second to the third and last period of international law.

The third period continues from 1815 to the present day. During this epoch, the principle of nationality is proclaimed and applied. According to this principle, people of one tribal origin speaking a single language, having identical morals and a common historical past, and professing a common religion, should comprise one State and one people.

Moreover, this period is characterized by an unusual rise of trade and economic relations between peoples and respective development of ways and means of international communication, among them: post, telegraph, railways, and others.

These and similar manifestations of a developed international life have flourished thanks to the dominance of order and legality, the increasing stability within contemporary States, and also the lengthy external peace which peoples have enjoyed after the sanguinary wars of the French Revolution and the First Empire.

The Crimean campaign of 1854-1856 violated peace and put various political questions which affected the entire European system established at the 1815 Congress of Vienna. Therefore, the 1856 Paris Peace Treaty which ended the Crimean War forms a turning point in the third period and divides that period into two sections, of which the second began from 1856 and continues down to the present. This period is full of remarkable events which changed materially both the internal orders and, especially, the international status of various States of western Europe and Russia, and should open a new epoch in the history of international relations.

What idea will serve as the guiding principle of international relations in the new coming period of their development is a question for the future, to decide which in advance is not possible. But any lawyer and statesman who reasonably understands the purpose of international relations and grasps in the correct way the tasks and goals of States, the dominant principle of the future can only be the idea of law in the broadest sense of the word.

Neither the idea of disunity nor the idea of inclination to physical force, nor the idea of political equilibrium, nor, finally, the principle of nationality can be deemed to be guiding principles of a properly structured international life. The idea of law is the guiding principle thereof.

First Period
From Antiquity to Peace of Westphalia

A. Ancient Times

§8. We begin an account of international relations in Antiquity with a general characterization of relations into which various peoples of the ancient world entered and then consider separately how these relations developed and which concepts were connected with them in the ancient East, Greece, and Rome.[1]

The view exists in the literature that international law arose when international relations began.[2] The proponents of this view assert that

[1] Doctrinal manuals on the history of international relations are rather abundant. In addition to well-known capital works on world history, there are special manuals for studying the history of international relations and law. The following serve as the basis of our historical survey:

Robert Plumer Ward, *An Enquiry into the Foundation and History of the Law of Nations in Europe from the Time of the Greeks and Romans to the Age of Hugo Grotius* (London, 1795). 2 vols.

Karl Theodor Pütter, *Beiträge zur Völkerrechtsgeschichte und Wissenschaft* (Leipzig, 1843).

Mauritius Müller-Jochmus, *Geschichte des Völkerrechts im Alterthum* (Leipzig, 1848).

Henry Wheaton, *Histoire des progrès du droit des gens en Europe depuis la paix de Westphalie jusqu'au congrès de Vienne* (Leipzig, 1853). 2 vols.

Christophe de Koch and Frédéric Schöll, *Histoire abrégée des traités de paix entre les puissances de l'Europe depuis la paix de Westphalie etc.* (Paris, 1817). 15 vols.

Guillaume de Garden, *Histoire générale des traités de paix etc.* (Paris, 1848-59). 14 vols.

François Combes, *Histoire générale de la diplomatie européenne* (Paris, 1854).

Nicomede Bianchi, *Storia documenta della diplomazia Europea in Italia del 1814-1861* (Torino, 1865-1872). 8 vols.

John Hosack, *The Rise and Growth of the Law of Nations, as Established by General Usage and by Treaties from the Earliest Times to the Treaty of Utrecht* (London, 1882).

Émile Chauveau, *Le droit des gens dans les rapports de Rome avec les peuples de l'antiquité* (Paris, 1891).

Horace Dominique de Barral de Montferrat, *Étude sur l'histoire diplomatique de l'Europe* (Paris, 1885). 2 vols.

Prince A. M. Ouroussow [Urusov], *Résumé historique des principaux traités de paix conclus entre les puissances européennes* (Evreux, 1885).

François Laurent, *Histoire du droit des gens et des relations internationales* (Brussels, 1861-1870). 18 vols. This is the most substantial work of all those cited above but, regrettably, the author too often repeats himself and rarely observes the boundaries of the subject-matter being studied.

Thomas Alfred Walker, *A History of the Law of Nations* (Cambridge, 1899). Vol. 1.

[2] See Fallati, "Keime des Völkerrechts bei wilden und halbwilden Stämmen", *Zeitschrift*

all peoples who enter into *de facto* relations with one another should be aware of the need to regulate them by certain legal norms or by a law. In support of this view they cited various facts borrowed from the history of ancient peoples and from the life of contemporary savage or semi-savage tribes which do indeed maintain trade relations between themselves and with foreigners, complying with certain formalities, often not going to war without the prior declaration thereof, performing various rites, and so on.[3]

As we will see below, these historical acts do not confirm the correctness of the view cited either with respect to primitive peoples or even to the Greeks and Romans.

But one cannot agree with the view that the barbaric and ancient peoples had knowledge of international law for theoretical, often *a priori*, considerations. It is worth analyzing those concepts and feelings which predominate among peoples whose history is only beginning and of which we have fully reliable information in order to be persuaded of the complete impossibility of assuming that these peoples had an awareness of the need for law or a certain order in the sphere of their mutual relations.

Primitive people not even knowing their own capacities nor the intentions of other peoples must be cautious about entering into any foreign relations. Such a people always treat their own existence as the primary task, not international relations; they require that their internal social and State systems correspond to their concepts and aspirations, be original, and exclude any interference of outside elements.

Historical facts affirm this psychological feature of the primitive life of all peoples, and in this respect such highly-educated and politically developed peoples as the Greeks and Romans are no exception.

The best Greek writers and thinkers – Thucydides, Aristotle, Dionysus of Halicarnassus – constantly referred in their works to the idea of the uniqueness of the Greek people. In their view, the Greeks were a special people, the chosen of the Divine, who had the right and should relate with contempt to other peoples. Demosthenes proved that not the Greeks, but the Barbarians, by their very nature were destined to be the slaves of the

für Staatswissenschaften (1850), p. 150; Compare with Johann Wilhelm Franz Philipp von Holtzendorff, *Handbuch des Völkerrechts* (1885-1889), §40.

[3] One may find many curious facts to characterize relations between savage and semi-savage peoples and tribes in works by Theodor Waitz, *Anthropologie der Naturvölker* (Leipzig, 1859-1872). 6 vols.; Maximilian Perty, *Die Anthropologie als die Wissenschaft von dem Körperlichen und geistigen wesen des menschen* (Leipzig, 1874). 2 vols.; Oscar Peschel, *Völkerkunde* (2d ed.; Leipzig, 1875), and others.

Hellenes.[4] Consequently, in the political and international legal sense only the Greeks were considered to be individuals having certain human rights.

Thus, the isolation and hostile relations of peoples, and not peace and not international relations characterized ancient life. These distinctive features were a natural consequence of the exclusivity and intolerance common to all ancient peoples. From this point of view, the Greeks were entirely consistent when they represented themselves as the golden age at a time when every people lived in complete isolation and did not need relations with others.

However, together with the disunity and hostility of peoples we encounter in the period of Antiquity facts of a different kind. Trade relations, migrations, and colonies were known to the ancient world. Primitive peoples recognized the duty of hospitality. In certain cities of Antiquity the rights of foreigners were ensured by a law. Do not these facts contradict the just cited aspirations of ancient peoples? Evidently, yes. We will point out below the true significance of this contradiction. We now note that the facts similar to those designated comprise one of those happy inconsistencies so abundant in history and to which human culture and civilization are greatly indebted for their development.

Isolation was the prevailing state of all peoples of Antiquity; but in many instances it was actually disturbed. First, war, which both in the consciousness of philosophers and *de facto* represented the normal order of international relations of ancient States, served simultaneously as a powerful means of bringing peoples together. During wartime, the victor invaded the territory of the adversary, carrying away prisoners of war, and by this act he destroyed his own and its isolation. Moreover, war was an instrument through which peoples became familiar with one another and, upon concluding peace, were bound by peaceful relations and distributed the fruits of their accomplishments to foreign lands. Almost until the noted Medes wars, the Greeks knew the Persians only by name; having triumphed, they bound them to proper trade relations. The campaigns of Alexander of Macedonia [356-323 BC] and the wars of the Romans brought the embryos of European culture to remote parts of Asia and Africa.

Migrations and colonization, rather widespread in the ancient world and caused by various reasons, had the same importance. The Phoenicians and the Carthaginians set up settlements in Africa, Gallia, and Spain to facilitate trading interests. The Greeks settled in Italy and Minor Asia usually as a consequence of political troubles – the struggle of the aristocrats and the

4 Euripides, Iphigenia in Aulis, 1401; Aristotle, Politik, I, 2. Compare Laurent, note 1 above, II, pp. 152, 287 et seq.

democrats within their municipalities. Colonization served for the Romans as a means of administrative unification of conquered territories with Rome.

Wars and colonization facilitated the development of peaceful relations, especially trade relations, between ancient States. In turn, these relations expanded the intellectual and political horizons of peoples and generated customs and institutions which were contrary to the general spirit of the ancient world. Trade and other international relations necessarily assume a move away from an attitude of intolerance towards foreigners, the recognition of certain rights for them, at least the right to life and property. However, ancient States in general viewed the foreigner as an enemy and refused him the defense and protection of the law.

Instead of this protection, the institution of hospitality developed among societies, which in some States was elevated to the level of a public institution.

What conclusion may be drawn from the facts cited? Can one speak of an international law of ancient peoples? We suggest not. The undoubted historical evidence persuades us that in the ancient world international relations indeed existed, even customs by which they were protected. But we have not a single fact which would demonstrate that the ancient peoples were aware of the need for proper mutual relations and for ensuring their rights. Law is always based on an awareness of the need for it.

§9. International relations of the ancient East have been imprinted with a character common to the entire ancient world. We encounter here the same isolation and mutual enmity of peoples, and also those *de facto* trade and other peaceful relations that we see among other peoples closer to us – the Greeks and Romans. But in one respect the peoples of the East are distinctive. The aforesaid features of international life in the ancient past are changed in their appearance in the East by the specific State structure in the countries, namely – a theocratic and caste structure unknown to Europe. We consider the guiding principles of relations between the peoples of the ancient East and with other peoples primarily from this point of view.

Of all the States comprising the ancient East, India has the most typical features which distinguish ancient theocracies. At the same time, the territory it occupies is unusually well endowed by nature. The wealth of India constantly was envied by conquerors and the goal of trade undertakings. Thanks to these circumstances, there was concentrated the entire international life of the Far East – peaceful and militant. Therefore, ancient India may be accepted as a model of eastern States in general and the international relations thereof in particular.

The social and State order of India was established in accordance with the religious requirements of Brahminism and then Buddhism. Religion introduced into this country the division into castes, of which one – the Brahmins – had the exclusive dominance over all the others. The vast majority of the conquered population was outside the castes and did not enjoy any human civil or political rights. These were pariahs (untouchables), whose social status was extremely humiliating.[5] Such a caste structure, of course, could not fail to exert a material influence on all international relations of India: it gave us for the first time evidence of that significance which social elements within a country have for international life.[6]

Under a State caste system, that caste which enjoys primacy over the rest of the population always concentrates in itself the plenitude of State power. Consequently, in each theocratic State a certain social class similar to the Brahmins in India is politically dominant, is sovereign with respect to the entire people. Naturally, this highest caste would use all means in order to preserve their rights as a whole so that other castes had no thoughts of dividing its rights among them: it must maintain with all their powers the immobility of the existing order of things. But international relations, familiarity with orders in other States, might easily undermine the significance and authority of the ruling class. Therefore, all external relations are prohibited in a caste State, are declared to be a violation of the basic laws of the country.

The provisions of the sacred Laws of Manu, on the basis of which India was governed, indeed prohibited, under threat of severe punishments, any relations with foreigners. Ancient India, just as Greece and Italy, collapsed into a multiplicity of separate States, each being fully isolated from the others. Relations might exist between them only as a crime, as a violation of the order established by laws, *de facto*, but not according to law. On the other hand, foreigners, according to a law, were in an identical position with pariahs; within India they were considered to be enemies who had no rights and contact with those who defiled Hindus.

But there were instances when the States of India entered into formal agreements. Usually such treaties were concluded by reason of a common danger which some external enemy threatened. With the cessation of the danger, the agreements themselves were destroyed.[7] Trade relations were established with India in a similar manner. The Phoenicians, Jews, and

[5] Christian Lassen, *Indische Alterthumskunde* (Bonn, 1844-1862), I, pp. 794-819.

[6] Compare James Talboys Wheeler, *A Short History of India, and of the Frontier States of Afghanistan, Nipal, and Burma* (London, 1880), p. 59.

[7] Müller-Jochmus, note 1 above, §35, p. 89.

Persians, for the most part by force of arms and cunning, encouraged the States of India to open their cities and receive barbarians to engage in trade. We have no facts which would prove a wish on the part of the Hindus, or an awareness of the need, for international exchange.[8]

In prohibiting external relations, the Laws of Manu contain, however, a series of behests and prescriptions relating to such relations. They deem hospitality to be one of the duties of Brahmins and direct them to render hospitality to a foreigner, even overlooking caste distinctions. Moreover, Brahmins maintained relations with neighboring Hindu peoples with the assistance of embassies. The mode of operation of envoys is described in detail. They are obliged, whenever possible, to learn the intentions of the sovereign to whom they have been sent; to bribe the ministers thereof, and if this is impossible, to poison them; they must take advantage of the dissatisfactions existing in the country to order to instigate an uprising against the local government, and so on. This kind of instruction does not override the general proposition that India was not aware of the need for proper international relations. They prove only that the force of circumstances obliged even India to disturb its own disunity. Thus, embassies had the main purpose of preventing war; that is, the protection of State security. As regards hospitality, this had practical significance only with respect to members of castes, but not foreigners in the strict sense. Finally, during war all possible cruelties and violence were permitted with respect to the enemy and in the conquered country.

Other peoples of the ancient East – Persians, Jews, Phoenicians – were guided in international relations by the same concepts as the Hindus.[9] They all were convinced that they are the sole representatives of deities on earth, that therefore they are higher than other peoples, and that relations with other peoples only offend the gods. The Egyptians were distinctive for especially extreme views: their laws prohibited journeys, not allowing any foreign customs in Egypt, and even not recognizing hospitality. Only in the relatively later period of their history did Egypt enter into relations with foreigners on the basis of treaties with their victors.

§10. If thanks to their theocratic structure the Eastern States could not further the development of international relations, ancient Greece, on the contrary, represented such favorable conditions that it would seem that

8 Laurent, note 1 above, I, p. 72: "Si l'Inde a eu droit de guerre, un système de relations internationales, il n'a pu se manifester que dans les rapports de ses populations indigènes".

9 Compare Laurent, note 1 above, I, p. 220 et seq; Müller-Jochmus, note 1 above, Cap. V.

Greece should be made the cradle of an awareness of the need for law determining the relations of peoples.

First, the geographical position of ancient Greece and the nature of the country were favorable for external relations. A coastline convenient for maritime transport, indented by many gulfs and bays suitable for anchoring, positioned on the Mediterranean Sea close to Egypt, Palestine, Minor Asia, and the former main points where in Antiquity the Phoenicians and other commercial peoples had concentrated, and finally, the natural wealth of Greece and the abilities distinguishing its population – these all should have facilitated an aspiration for international exchange and relations with foreigners.

Then, among the States themselves into which the Greek people were divided, there existed many favorable social conditions so that the Greek municipias and colonies were in constant and proper relations with one another. The peoples of Greece were bound by a community of tribal origin, spoke the same language, had more or less similar religious views and institutions, identical intellectual needs, and so on. In view of this, one might think that if not outside then within Greece extensive international relations developed – trade, economic, literary, and others, that the Greeks entered into a close union among themselves, and established an international order which would secure the interests of each individual Greek State.

But, in fact, we see completely the opposite.

Greece, unlike the Eastern theocracies, did not know a division of the people into castes: all citizens of Greek municipias were, according to law, equal as between themselves. But no matter how great the progress Greece achieved in this respect, it could not renounce another source of inequality between people in ancient centuries – the view that citizenship, and not the human individual, is the basis of the right of each individual. Slavery was built on the degree of a necessary State institution. Not recognizing for a person certain inalienable rights, irrespective of national origin and affiliation to a particular State, the Greeks could not have an awareness that in the sphere of the mutual relations of peoples complete equality must dominate. On the contrary, every Greek State, no matter how insignificant in size and population, was imbued with the conviction of its immeasurable superiority over other peoples and States. Just as Eastern peoples, the Greeks worshipped themselves, considered themselves to have higher powers and abilities, and treated all peoples of non-Hellenic origin with hatred, who they called by the contemptible name barbarians (βαρβαροι). As in the Eastern States, the last did not enjoy any rights in Greece, and they were looked upon as enemies. This view of foreigners, which dominated in Antiquity, made ensuring peace and any order in the field of external relations inconceivable for Greece.

Turning to the internal system of the Greek States, to their social and political life, we do not find therein any such kinship of social interests which would unite them politically, make one State from Greece, nor sufficient attention on the part of the Government to the social needs of the people, which always is a condition for the development of international relations.

The Greeks did not know unity within their republics. Throughout all their history an endless struggle proceeds between two social classes, between the poor and the wealthy.[10] The first comprised the indigenous population of the communities conquered by newcomers from other parts of Greece; the second were the victors, who took possession of the property of the vanquished and governmental authority. This circumstance aggravated the struggle: to the *de facto* inequality of the parties it added a natural enmity of the vanquished towards the victors, who held State power by all means in order to oppress their opponents.

The outcome of the struggle determined the structure of the State. Therefore, in Greece we encounter different forms of government at various times and among various peoples: some States were an aristocratic system, and others were organized as democracies; there also were States monarchically structured – for example, Sparta. But in all of them a sharp struggle was waged by social classes for political power.[11]

When determining the form of government of States, this struggle passed into the domain of international relations: the aristocratic party of one State was ready to help by all means the aristocrats of another in their struggle against the democrats, and *vice versa*. Thus, no unity existed either within Greek States or in their mutual relations. Envy inhered in the Greek people, which in the most critical moments of its life, when it was threatened by the danger of enslavement, only by unbelievable efforts were they forced to unite for defense against a common enemy. Under such "innate" separateness of the Greeks, as [Joseph Marie] de Maistre [(1753-1821)] expressed the position, it is understandable that the efforts of Athens and Sparta to unite the Greek States under their own hegemony ended in

[10] Wilhelm Oncken, *Die Staatslehre des Aristotles in historisch-politischen Umrissen* (Leipzig, 1870-1875), II, p. 229; Friedrich von Hellwald, *Culturgeschichte in ihrer natürlichen Entwickelung* (Augsburg, 1875), p. 268 et seq; Leopold von Ranke, *Weltgeschichte* (Leipzig, 1883), I, p. 157; Holtzendorff, note 2 above, §49.

[11] Compare Georg Friedrich Schömann, *Griechische Alterthümer* (3d ed.; Berlin, 1871), I, pp. 96, 195; Max Paul Ernst Schneidewin, *Die antike Humanität* (Berlin, 1897), p. 221.

failure: the successes achieved first by the Athenians and then by Sparta could have merely passing significance.[12]

But from the indisputable fact that the Greeks did not achieve unity either socially or politically, it does not follow that they were unaware of international relations. The spirit of separation and struggle, imprinted on all manifestations of Greek life, was not maintained by the Greeks in all its severity in the domain of international relations. The consistent and extreme implementation thereof faced an insuperable obstacle in the fact that, given the major difference in social aspirations that divided social classes within the Greek republics and in their international relations, many common vital and cultural interests united the Greek peoples, forced them to abandon mutual enmity, and they maintained close links with one another.

The international relations of the Greeks developed especially after the Dorian invasion. An awareness was generated at the time among the population of ancient Greece that, despite their political fractionalization, they nonetheless comprised one nation by language, religion, laws, and intellectual aspirations differing from the barbarians. The free political system which the Greek republics adopted after the Dorian invasion greatly facilitated the social and individual development of Greek citizens, duly reflected in international relations. With the expansion of the intellectual horizon of the Greeks and the growth of their material and spiritual interests, the limits and means of municipal life proved to be insufficient for the satisfaction of new needs. The developing social aspirations and needs insistently required international exchange and mutual relations of the Greek peoples; these were established, first *de facto*, but then were recognized by legislators and made the subject-matter of agreements by the States themselves.

Primacy of place among the Greek republics which took an active part in international turnover belonged to the Athenians. By degree of enlightenment and culture, the free Athenian population was superior to all other peoples of Greece. The rulers and legislators of Athens well understood the social needs of their people and treated them with full respect. Therefore, it is no surprise that this educated republic, more than the other Greek States, was aware of the complete injustice and disadvantage of their isolation and quickly came to the realization of the need for international relations and tolerance of foreign peoples. In this respect the Athenians represented the fullest juxtaposition to aristocratic Sparta and to all the Dorian republics under its influence. Moreover, as the last sought by legislative and

[12] Joseph Marie de Maistre, *Du pape*, liv. IV, chap. II. Compare Laurent, note 1 above, II, p. 18.

governmental measures to maintain the old status quo, they obstructed with all their resources the international relations of their citizens by expelling all foreigners from their country. The Athenians pursued a different policy: they saw the foundation of their power in maritime relations and trade; they opened their own territory to all foreigners and took pride in the fact that all those oppressed and persecuted in other lands found refuge and protection under Athenian laws. In both cases, the dissimilar social and State structures of the people revealed their influence on the conditions of international life.

We point out the following of the individual social reasons which facilitated a mitigation of the hatred between Greek peoples and served to bring them together.

An awareness of a common national origin is always one of those connecting elements in international life which generates in peoples a feeling of kinship and solidarity of aspirations and interests. This was born in the Greeks no earlier than the Dorian conquest; at least before that time they had no common name which would have distinguished them from all other peoples. On the contrary, now the entire population of Greece, whatever State it belonged to – Dorian or Ionian – is called Hellenes. Understandably, this conviction of the national unity of Greece should have moderated their mutual hatred and enmity. Whereas previously each insignificant Greek settlement organized in the form of an autonomous State considered itself to be a chosen people, a center to which all other peoples should gravitate, with the development of an awareness of the common origin of Greeks, this view carried over to the entire Greek people. It is higher than all other peoples, and not an individual part thereof. On this basis, the subjects of the various Greek States, although they continue to consider as foreigners those from outside their own city but within related Greek municipalities, everywhere they find a certain recognition of their rights. In any event, they are distinct from the barbarians, by whom the Greeks understood only the subjects of non-Greek States who remain in Greece deprived of any rights until the end of Greek history.[13]

The influence of religion in the ancient world, under the dominance of polytheism, was in general one of those conditions which separated peoples. In Greece, however, when the Dorians subjected to their political authority those initial tribes and imposed on them their own special religious cult, little by little common and even identical religious confessional views and rites developed in all States and acquired the significance of factors allaying the alienation and hostility which divided the Greek peoples. A strong influence was exerted in this sense by religion on all of Greek life through

[13] Laurent, note 1 above, II, pp. 45, 103, 287 et seq.

two powerful organs which enjoyed universal respect in Ancient Greece – the oracles in Delphi and the Olympic Games.[14] The religious veneration with which the Greeks treated both institutions had favorable consequences for their international relations. In celebrations in honor of Jupiter which occurred at Olympus, the divided and hostile Greeks found unity and peace. As regards the Delphic oracle, its advice often united the Greeks into a single people for common undertakings, mitigated the barbarity of international wars, and finally promoted the dissemination in Greece of hospitality and respect in general for exiles from other States.[15]

One of the distinctive features of the Greek people as a whole was civilization and culture in the broadest sense of this expression. It encompassed all parts of Greece and was, of course, that element of the social life of the Greeks which united them into a single whole. All Greek States were proud of their poets, philosophers, orators, and artists, and these people enjoyed honor not only from the people among whom they were born and lived, but throughout the entire country, wherever the news of their genius, intelligence, works, and activity reached. Such widespread admiration for the representatives of knowledge and art served as conclusive evidence of the commonality of cultural aspirations and interests of the Greek peoples, whose creation was a stable foundation for their mutual links and respect.

Finally, among the social factors which determined the international relations of the Greeks, trade played an important role.[16] Initially, commercial and industrial activity did not find in Greece all the conditions which would have favored their development. First, the Greeks saw in this kind of occupation something humiliating, unworthy of the high calling of citizen of a free republic, and therefore granted economic and trade turnover exclusively to the lower, enslaved class of the population, known by the name of Μετοικι and Περί, who did not enjoy political rights.[17] Second, in the view of the ancient Greeks, the sole legitimate route for trade relations was the land; they considered the sea to be a natural barrier erected by the gods for the purpose of preventing any contact between peoples. On this basis they for a longtime felt an irresistible aversion to maritime communication, and their trade was generated not in the maritime cities, but on land boundaries

14 Laurent, note 1 above, II, p. 79 et seq.

15 Compare Fustel de Coulanges, *La cité antique* (Paris, 1864), Introduction, chapter XI. See especially Schneidewin, note 11 above, p. 209.

16 C. de Montesquieu, *De l'esprit des lois*, liv. XX, chap. II: "Toutes les unions sont fondées sur des devoirs mutuels. Mais si l'esprit du commerce unit les nations il n'unit pas de même les particuliers".

17 Schömann, note 11 above, I, pp. 212, 329, 373; Müller-Jochmus, note 1 above, §49, 50.

with other States. Despite, however, such prejudices constraining trade relations, the trade of the Greeks, to the end of their history, flourished. The progressive growth of needs and natural self-interest proved to be stronger than all prejudices: they inclined Greek citizens to indulge themselves with all their resources in increasing their property by way of maritime trade which, in the absence in Antiquity of artificial means of communication, was the best means of intercourse with faraway lands.[18]

Robbery at sea, or piracy, was closely linked with trade turnover not only of the Greeks, but in general of all commercial peoples. This fact confirms the general situation that particular international relations always represent a mirror precisely reflecting the domestic state of societies in a certain epoch of their existence, and likewise the principles which underlie their social and political system. In ancient times power was the guiding principle of social and State relations. As a universal principle, power is closely linked also with international trade relations which existed in Antiquity, and we see that the Greeks, just as other ancient peoples, deemed trade not only to be an instrument for coming closer together with other peoples and a peaceful means of acquiring wealth, but also as a means of plundering the weak, not at all reprehensible either from the viewpoint of morality or law.

The extensive development of piracy in Ancient Greece, to which the State authorities themselves often turned, even in such a highly educated and humane republic as Athens, enables us to say that if the commercial interests and social needs of the Greek peoples in general actually served as the basis for uniting them, then the Greek States did not consider it necessary to recognize the legitimacy of these aspirations or believe themselves obliged to contribute to their development and provision through the law. The most that the State authorities in Greece did to their benefit was to treat them with tolerance, compelled by the irresistible force of the needs of the State and its citizens.

If the attitude of the Greek States towards the legitimate and reasonable aspirations of their peoples was actually determined not by the conviction of their being lawful and of advantage to the State, but by the unalterable force of particular circumstances, the real significance of those agreements and treaties sometimes concluded between individual Greek republics is understandable. Thus, on the basis of treaties, called συμβολα, the subjects of various allied and friendly Greek States enjoyed the right of free sojourn within the territories of the contracting parties, and disputes which arose between these people and natives were resolved in the procedure established

[18] Compare Oncken, note 10 above, II, p. 183; Jean-Marie Pardessus, *Collection des lois maritimes antérieures au XVIII siècle* (Paris, 1828), I, Introduction, p. vii.

by these treaties. Only a few such treaties are known. The number of treaties under which the contracting Greek republics mutually granted civil rights to their citizens and, in the view of [François] Laurent [(1810-1887)], even political rights, to enjoy on foreign territory is small. Such an alliance is called an isopolyte. Beyond any doubt, these international obligations did not contemplate the satisfaction of social interests or the need for relations of private individuals belonging to different States, but were a consequence only of a need which the State authorities were unable to resist, and not an awareness of the need in general for international order and law.[19]

In this same sense the ancient Greek States promoted the international relations of their own citizens variously. We know that in general the adverse status of foreigners in the ancient world generated the custom of hospitality, which mitigated the situation to some extent. Hospitality also existed in ancient Greece: the Greeks recognized their duty to protect the inviolability of life and property of foreigners who requested protection. But, unlike the eastern States, private hospitality acquired in Greece the character of a public institution – a custom protected by State authorities. Moreover, for the purpose of ensuring the rights of foreigners in Greek States a special category of officials was established called *proxenos*. These were individuals elected initially at the initiative of those most interested, subsequently by governments, to give protection and defense not only to a certain guest, but in general to all subjects of a foreign State on their territory.[20]

Finally, Greek colonization served as an instrument for spreading peaceful international relations of Ancient Greece.

Numerous colonies of Greeks founded in Europe, Asia, and Africa were obliged for their origin primarily to the invasion of the Dorians against the Peloponnese; then the domestic quarrels and political infighting which occurred between various parties in all the Greek republics made it unpleasant or even impossible for the losing side to remain in their motherland. Politically, such colonies were fully autonomous; but in resettling from their homeland, the colonists brought across to the foreign country the cultural concepts of their homeland, its education, gods, and usually introduced the same State institutions for which they had struggled in Greece. The population of the Greek colonies permanently retained close

[19] Compare Karl Dietrich Hüllmann, *Handelsgeschichte der Griechen* (1839), p. 193; Laurent, note 1 above, II, p. 114. See especially Rudolf von Scala, *Die Staatsverträge der Alterthums* (Leipzig, 1899).

[20] Alexandre de Miltitz, *Manuel des Consuls* (London, 1837-1841), I, p. 11; Müller-Jochmus, note 1 above, §47.

links with the metropolitan and, accordingly, not only disseminated the principles of Greek culture and civilization among the peoples, but also maintained peaceful relations between the Greek States themselves.

The said grounds and conditions which inspired the peoples of Ancient Greece not only to renounce their isolation and enmity, but to maintain mutual peaceful relations, raises the question: did not the ancient Greeks respect certain general principles of law in mutual relations; did they not know international law in the sense of an aggregate of legal norms, laws, determining the order of international relations? This question remains controversial in the science of international law.[21] But despite evidence which leads certain scholars to affirm this proposition, the majority of contemporary writers support the view that international law in the true meaning of the words was unknown to the ancient world in general or to the Greeks in particular.[22]

One must agree that this view is correct: first, the survey of international relations of the ancient Greeks set out above is persuasive that the relations of the Greek peoples existed only by way of exception from the general, normal order of things; second, those arguments on which the proponents of the contrary view rely do not withstand serious critique.

We dwell on the principal arguments adduced in support of international law existing in ancient Greece.

Some writers of past and present centuries were attracted by the so-called Amphictyonic League arranged between Greek peoples and which, these writers assumed, were political alliances of international significance.[23] But the real role of this kind of alliance was not such. The origin of the Amphictyon in Greece is to be explained solely by religious reasons. The so-called alliances of neighboring cities and Greek States were temples built from common resources in honor of a particular divinity by a general council chosen from among their citizens to supervise the construction and administer the rites therein; they were mutually obliged to protect the

[21] Wilhelm Wachsmuth, *Jus Gentium quale obtinuerit apud Graecos ante bellorum cum Persis gestorum initium* (Berol., 1822) and Müller-Jochmus, note 1 above, p. 106, and others attempt to prove the existence of international law among the Greeks. But their arguments are unconvincing and cut across the entire worldview of the peoples of Antiquity. This view was refuted by A. W. Heffter, *De antique jure gentium prolusio* (Bona, 1823).

[22] August Wilhelm Heffter, *Das europäische Völkerrecht der Gegenwart*, §6; Johann Caspar Bluntschli, *Das moderne Völkerrecht der civilisirten Staten* (Nördlingen, 1868), Einleitung, p. 12; William Oke Manning, *Commentaries on the Law of Nations*, ed. Sheldon Amos (rev. ed.; London, 1875), p. 9; Laurent, note 1 above, II, p. 117.

[23] Gabriel Bonnot de Mably, *Observations sur l'histoire de la Grèce* (1733), V, p. 10; Laurent, note 1 above, II, p. 80.

repository and privileges, often quite significant, against all other peoples. It is evident that the Amphictyonic League and its elected council were formed solely in the interests of faith, not of politics and law; the council managing the temple property pronounced its decisions not in the name of the allied States, but the divinity to whom the temple was dedicated. From the standpoint of the history of international relations, the Amphictyon only reflects the influence of religious views and interests on the mutual relations of States, for although these alliances were created specially for religious purposes, they did affect relations between the Greek States: just as other social factors, they brought peoples together and softened their isolation.[24]

Other evidence that the ancient Greeks had knowledge of international law some writers see in the fact that the ancient Greek peoples arranged their mutual relations on the principles of an order known in modern times as a system of political equilibrium of States.[25] In confirmation of this view, reference is made to various facts represented by the history of Greece. Thus, *inter alia*, they assert that during the Hegemony struggle between Thebes and Sparta, the Athenians concluded an alliance with the Thebians, being convinced that they, the weaker side, needed assistance, but when Epaminondas [(418-362 BC)] defeated his adversaries at Leuctra, the Athenians saw danger for the equilibrium of Greek States in the might of Thebes and therefore withdrew from the alliance. However, this fact, and likewise other facts borrowed from the history of ancient Greece, are hardly persuasive and actually prove that the Greek peoples were aware of the need to balance their mutual forces to maintain international order. It is evident that the alliance of Athens with Thebes had as its reason not this awareness, but was generated by the force of circumstances: they clearly showed that unless Athens helped the neighboring Thebians and the last were defeated, the political independence of Athens would be threatened by unavoidable danger on the part of their primeval enemy – Sparta. The best refutation of the opposite view is another fact from Greek history: the behavior of Sparta and Athens during the war of the Greeks against Philip II of Macedon [(382-336 BC)]. This war ended with the decisive triumph of the Macedons, thanks to the Greek peoples lacking an understanding of common political interests.

If the grounds on which the adherents of the existence of international law in Ancient Greece rely are erroneous, and if the factors actually forcing the Greek peoples to enter into relations operated on States only by their

[24] Compare Bürgel, *Die Phyäisch-Delphische Amphiktyonie* (1877); Max Duncker, *Geschichte des Alterthums* (5th ed.; Berlin, 1878), I, p. 33.

[25] Wheaton, note 1 above, I, p. 14; David Hume, "On the Balance of Power", *Hume's Essays*, VII.

natural power, without any awareness on the part of the last about the need for such relations and the order thereof, we must say that the ancient Greeks did not have international law.

§11. Ancient Rome, and especially Roman law, played a prominent role in the domain of international relations. Some scholars see in Roman law the initial source of all contemporary international law. But a closer consideration of Roman international life and an analysis of their legal concepts concerning the relations which should exist between peoples will show how correct these views are.

When comparing Ancient Rome and Ancient Greece, and Romans and Greeks, with one another, one is struck by the deep differences in the historical role and fate of the two peoples and the principles that they followed in international relations. The geographical and topographical position of both countries differs: whereas Greece is indented by innumerable gulfs and bays which generated trade and international relations, Rome is not directly adjacent to the sea. But more striking is the completely opposite cultural and political aspirations and inclinations which distinguished the Romans and the Greeks. The Greeks by their nature strove for discord in all aspects of their life; they were afraid of and avoided any combination under common authority. The separation of Greek tribes gave them the opportunity to extensively develop their intellectual, moral, and in general spiritual capabilities and strengths: it encouraged that diversity and wealth of literature, poetry, and arts which made Greeks immortal. Not so in Rome. The ancient Roman people were imbued with the idea of political unity, which they sought to achieve even in international relations. This political ideal of Rome had an impact on its historical fate. Whereas the historical task of Greek life was to enrich the spiritual treasure-house of mankind, in the Roman State there was no question of the spiritual side of individual and social life: in this respect Rome merely took advantage of the achievements of peoples who had left the stage of world history. But the Roman people fully realized another historical purpose to which they were called: it contributed the principle of unity to the ancient world, having combined all existing States under its sovereign authority.[26]

That basic principle by which ancient Romans should have been guided while pursuing their historical calling clearly appeared, so to say, from the first day of their existence. The well-known legend of how the founder

[26] Compare Wilhelm Christoph Friedrich Arnold, *Cultur und Recht der Römer* (Berlin, 1868), Einleitung; Hellwald, note 10 above, p. 324; Laurent, note 1 above, III, p. 4; Jhering, *Geist des römischen Rechts auf den verschiedenen Stufen seiner Entwickelung* (4th ed.; Leipzig, 1878-1880), I, p. 310.

of Rome was born of Mars, the god of war, and was nourished by a she-wolf, conceals a profound idea. It shows that the first representative of Rome was a representative of brute physical power, that principle before which all peoples of Antiquity should have bowed and which the Romans consistently implemented in all their relations, both private and State, and in international life. Indeed, if the spear (*hasta*) served for Romans as a symbol of the right of ownership, if on the basis of the laws of the XII Tables *nexum* led to the enslavement of an unpaid debtor to his creditor, if in family life *pater-familias* was an unlimited ruler over the household, if, finally, a foreigner had no civil rights within Rome and the single word *hostis* meant, for Romans, enemy and foreigner, then all this was merely a partial expression of a basic principle of the Roman *jus civile* –the law of force.[27] The same principle in the State life of Rome was expressed in the concept *majestas Populi Romani* – the absolute power of the Roman people. Accordingly, power in international relations was the sole measure for determining the rights and duties of Romans to other peoples.

The strict implementation of one principle and its expression in absolute legal formulas permitting no deviations comprised, of course, one of the merits of the Roman *jus civile*, but also was a major shortcoming. It made Roman law a real embodiment of the idea of physical power, imparted to it a severe formalism and merciless logic which did not allow it to be mastered by other peoples. The civil law of the Romans had to be significantly softened in order to achieve worldwide significance, so that other peoples might take advantage of the rich fruits of Roman legal life, and its change in this sense is due solely to the strength of international relations into which Rome entered and which forced Rome to abandon its original, albeit consistent, but narrow legal views.

The international relations of ancient Romans, just as of other peoples, cannot be correctly understood without an understanding of the domestic orders which dominated in their social and State life. Friendly and hostile relations between the "eternal city" and other peoples were under the noticeable influence of these orders. In this respect the political history of

[27] Cicero, *De officis*, I, 11-13; The definition of the Laws of the XII Tables is known: "*Adversus hostem aeterna auctoritas*". On the meaning of the word "hostis", see Theodor Mommsen, *Römische Forschungen* (Berlin, 1864), I, p. 349; Otto Karlowa, *Der römische Civilprozess zur Zeit der Legisactionen* (Berlin, 1872), p. 222; Dirksen, *Übersicht der Versuche zur Erklärung der XII Tafelgesetze*, p. 262; Müller-Jochmus, note 1 above, §69; V. E. Grabar, Римское право в истории международных правовых учений: элементы международного права в трудах легистов XII-XIV вв. [Roman Law in the History of International Legal Doctrines: Elements of International Law in the Works of Legists of the Twelfth to Fourteenth Centuries] (Iur'ev, 1901).

the Roman people represents two materially different epochs – the time of republic rule and the period of the Empire, which are dissimilar not only in State institutions, but also in their social character; this, in turn, affected the international relations of Rome. We consider each of these periods separately.

§12. In the epoch of the Roman republic the most powerful influence on the policy of the Senate and on all relations of Romans with other peoples was the persistent struggle between the patricians and the plebians, between the poor and the wealthy classes of the Roman population. Here we cannot determine where the plebians originated and what generated their opposition to the estate of patricians. One may agree with recent Romanists that the class of plebians consisted mostly of descendants of those peoples vanquished by the Romans and forced to become part of the Roman State.[28] This origin of the plebians placed them in a grave, lawless, and subordinate position with respect to the patricians. The way out could only be the persistent and implacable struggle to which the plebians resorted, seeking political and civil equality with the ruling class. This struggle passed through various phases. Guided by an awareness of their personal interest, the patricians little by little ceded to the legitimate demands of their adversaries and, finally, agreed to complete equalization of the rights of the plebians with their own privileges.

The consecutive concessions which the patricians made to the plebian estate were closely linked with the gradual change in the attitude of Romans toward other peoples. As antagonism in Rome softened between the struggling social classes, the Roman State became more unified in its social structure and social interests, and the political might of the Roman republic grew, as did the successes of its expansionist policy in Italy and far beyond. The merger of the patricians with the plebians led to Rome achieving full internal development, made it the master of the entire world, and the previous isolation and intolerance toward other peoples became, in the full sense of the word, cosmopolitanism in the domain of international relations. The last period of Republican Rome represents complete unity within a State of the major social aspirations and classes. The decline of the international power of Rome commences from the moment of the breakdown of Roman society.

The historical task of Rome precluded the possibility of peaceful international relations and was a denial of international law. It assumed

[28] Berthold Georg Niebuhr, *Vorträge, über alte Geschichte an der Universität zu Bonn gehalten* (Berlin, 1849), I, p. 66 et seq.; Fustel de Coulanges, note 15 above, p. 297 et seq.; Ferdinand Walter, *Geschichte des römischen Rechts bis auf Justinian* (3d ed.; 1860), I, p. 27 et seq.

endless hostile conflicts of Rome with all peoples who did not wish to bow down before its power and recognize its authority. Accordingly, the history of international relations of the Romans in the epoch of the Republic is a series of wars for the purposes of conquest, beginning with Italy and then beyond. These wars, one may say, were not interrupted by peace. The so-called peace treaties which the Senate concluded were in reality armistices which for Rome served as a transitional stage to the final enslavement of their adversaries.[29]

In the successive course of these conquests the Romans were guided by an identical policy with respect to all peoples: some were subject to the absolute severe law of the victor, with the complete destruction of their independence and rights; on the contrary, others under conquest retained certain privileges and united with Rome rather than experience the grave fate of the vanquished. The first were primarily peoples far from Rome who lived outside Italy; the second were the population of the Italian peninsula.[30]

The policy of the Roman Senate with respect to Italian peoples was in general distinctive for prudent caution and moderation. The interest of the Romans required this first and foremost: if they wanted to continue with their conquests, then of course they should be concerned about the security of their closest borders and not encircle themselves with enemies who, at the first failure of Rome, would rise up against it. Moreover, various social reasons contributed to the fact that the peoples of Italy, in comparison with the non-Italian population, enjoyed a privileged status under Roman authority: the inhabitants of Latium, Samartia, and other tribes which populated Italy shared the same origin as the Romans, a common language, and similar religious views, morals, and customs. These conditions inclined the Romans to tractability, all to the advantage of immediate neighbors and fellow tribesmen. On this basis the Italian cities subdued by the Romans received the rights of municipis (*jus municipii*) from the victors. The inhabitants of municipii cities might freely come to Rome, engage there in safe crafts and trade, and enjoy certain rights (*jus connubii* and *jus commercii*) equally with Roman citizens.[31]

The municipii rights of Italian cities, however, did not retain the significance of privileges for long. As the domestic power of Rome strengthened and Roman authority extended beyond Italy, these rights were

29 Ward, note 1 above, I, p. 192.

30 Müller-Jochmus, note 1 above, §79.

31 Joachim Marquardt, *Römische Staatsverwaltung* (Leipzig, 1873), I, p. 23. But the inhabitants of *municipii* had no political rights in Rome: neither the *jus suffragii* nor the *jus honorum*.

sought by the inhabitants of Roman provinces; on one hand, all the peoples who were first under the power of Rome on a treaty basis subsequently were subordinated to its law, to the will of the Roman Senate.

With the final conquest of the Italian cities, the international relations of the Roman Republic expanded: it set about the conquest of those lands far from Rome, called Roman provinces. Considering those principles by which the Roman people were guided with respect to States and tribes which occupied these regions, one notes the fundamental change in policy: international relations were determined solely by an awareness of its political power and superiority over all other peoples, and accordingly the vanquished come to be in a completely powerless position, subject to the unlimited arbitrariness of the conqueror. This change of Roman policy was reflected in international treaties and acts which the Roman Senate entered into with foreign States, both those not subject to Roman authority and those conquered.

§13. From the standpoint of international law, those agreements of the Romans with other peoples concluded on the principles of equality and mutuality (*foedera aequa*) are of the greatest significance. Treaties of this kind were concluded with a fully independent people whose friendship was of interest to Rome or with an adversary who Rome did not have the power to ultimately defeat and make safe. The Romans concluded treaties of alliance, peace, friendship, and hospitality with these peoples, on the basis of which the subjects of a particular party had within the territory of an ally certain rights that made peaceful sojourn and activity possible in a friendly foreign country.[32] But treaties called equal were far from always being so. The treaties of alliance concluded by the Romans usually prescribed duties and rights only to the benefit of the Romans without any respective obligations on their part. As Roman arms enjoyed success, as the power of Rome grew, the number of unequal treaties (*foedera non aequa*) increased and treaties of peace, friendship, and hospitality were rarely encountered. This phenomenon is explained by the fact that as Roman dominance expanded, the extent of Roman international relations declined; on the other hand, Rome's power gradually grew so that no competitors could resist it. Therefore, by the end of the republican period all the said treaties ceded place to the Roman law that applied to other peoples and permitted neither transactions nor agreements: one law determined the status, rights, and

[32] Marquardt, ibid., I, p. 24. Such treaties established international relations, known in ancient Greece as isopolite.

duties of peoples conquered by Roman arms. Such was the outcome of the international policy of republican Rome.[33]

§14. It is evident that the Romans of the republican period should not, in principle, have permitted peaceful international relations, the more so order and law which would have regulated them. But it would be a mistake to suppose that in reality they did not have such relations; that they recognized rights only for themselves and excluded foreigners from using the defense and protection of their laws and court; that, in a word, every foreigner within Rome was actually an enemy. No, just as all the ancient world, the Roman people were not consistent in the field of international relations. The force of circumstances and the power of needs beyond their will forced Rome not only to renounce enmity towards other peoples, but to recognize certain rights for them, to create special institutions in favor of their subjects, and, finally, in view of international relations, even to change their severe civil law.

The severe legal attitudes of Romans towards foreigners as defined in the Laws of the XII Tables over time were significantly softened under the influence of the following principal conditions.

Thanks to the diverse relations, turnover, and transactions between private individuals, Roman citizens, and subjects of other States, the need arose in Rome to find a way out of that formal legal order established by strict Roman law, according to which all such relations and transactions were outside the law. The easiest way out of this abnormal state of affairs was private hospitality, on the basis of which every foreigner in Rome might choose from among Roman citizens a patron who was the protector and defender of all rights with respect to the guest. With the development of relations with foreigners, and especially familiarity with Greek culture and civilization, the view formed in Roman society that hospitality is the highest virtue of which each educated citizen can only be proud.[34] From society and individuals this elevated concept of hospitality passed to the government and, finally, received sanction in a law.

Roman law formulated a number of provisions determining the duties of the State with respect to the subjects of those peoples who bore the title "Friends of the Roman People" (*amici populi Romani*). On the basis of

[33] Holtzendorff, note 2 above, §58.

[34] Mommsen, note 27 above, p. 321 et seq: "Hostis ist der Ausländer, der auf Rechtsschutz Ansprach macht". Laurent, note 1 above, III, p. 66 et seq. Compare Aristide Eustatziu, *De la condition des étrangers en droit romain, en droit français et en Roumanie* (Paris, 1880), chapter II.

jus hospitii, each member of such a friendly people was considered to be a guest of the Roman State: he lived at the expense of the State treasury and enjoyed special honors prescribed by a law. But this special protection was granted only to those peoples who lived in Italy or within the Roman provinces. Rome never entered into such relations with barbarians.

The institution of hospitality embedded in society and recognized by a law further secured the rights and interests of foreigners in Rome. By ensuring the personal and property inviolability of a guest, Rome did not, however, provide the means for the judicial protection of the foreigner's interests. Disputes arising between foreigners or between them and Roman citizens were not subject to the jurisdiction of the city praetor (*praetor urbanus*) because *de jure* he did not know foreigners and the *jus civile* did not give him any rules for the settlement of their litigation. The patron, as the protector of the guest, received the right to bring suit (*legisactio*) in Roman court for the benefit of the foreigner. Finally, thanks to peace agreements with other peoples, a special office was established – *praetor qui inter peregrinos jus dicit* – for litigation in which the interests of foreign subjects were engaged.[35]

If foreigners found protection in ensuring their rights within Rome which was in sharp contradiction with all the basic principles of the Roman State system and legislation, that was only because the Romans needed relations with other peoples. The developing needs of society, material and spiritual, could not find satisfaction either within the walls of the "eternal city" and its surroundings or even within Italian territories: they generated peaceful trade relations of Rome with the provinces and even with the far away East. In this respect the wars and conquests of Rome served as an instrument not only of enslaving other peoples, but of a rapprochement with them, becoming familiar with their culture and civilization, the products of their intellectual and industrial activity, which passed to Rome and became the subject-matter of the needs and way of life of citizens.

Whether the Roman people were primarily agricultural, as some writers assert, or commercial, as others suggest, is unimportant.[36] But on the basis of undoubted historical data one may say that the Romans reacted with contempt to all trade transactions and enterprises, were afraid of shipping and navigation, and shared the view dominant in Antiquity that the sea is a barrier erected between peoples by nature itself. Although not taking an

[35] Moritz Voigt, *Das jus naturale, aequum et bonum und jus gentium der Römer* (Leipzig, 1858), IV, p. 40 et seq.; Mommsen, note 27 above, II, Abth. I, p. 179; Müller-Jochmus, note 1 above, §68; Holtzendorff, note 2 above, §60.

[36] Arnold, note 26 above, p. 9 et seq.

active part in trade relations, they were fully aware of Rome's need for them: trade provided food to the Roman population and made it possible to maintain that comfort and elaborate luxury so highly appreciated by Roman aristocrats even in republican times. For these reasons the Romans were persuaded not to renounce their prejudices with respect to commercial activity, but to protect its development by ensuring the rights of merchants in Rome itself and rendering assistance to them beyond its limits. Thus, in order to cleanse the Mediterranean Sea of pirates, who often interrupted any communication of the capital with its provinces, Rome undertook wars against the pirates repeatedly and succeeded in significantly restricting the development of piracy, which flourished in Antiquity.[37]

Finally, one cannot fail to point out one of those many facts that led Rome out of its seclusion and prompted peaceful relations with other peoples – the structuring of colonies.[38] The Roman colonies differed significantly from the Greek. They owed their origin not to political troubles within the State, as with the Greeks, but to administrative considerations, types of better government distant from Rome and the regions just conquered. To this end Roman legions and citizens were sent there; they received in ownership part of the land of the conquered people and were obliged to watch over peace in their district. Thus, the composition and purpose of the Roman colonies were military: the colonies served as a "bulwark of Roman power", as [Marcus Tullius] Cicero [(106-43 BC)] expressed it. But in reality, just as the colonies of Greece, they had great cultural and educational significance: they spread among the conquered peoples Roman enlightenment, language, political and especially legal views of Romans, customs, morals, and others.

§15. The period of Imperial autocracy materially differed in domestic and international relations from the epoch of republican Rome. When imperial power replaced the republic, the Roman people had resolved their historical task. Virtually the entire *orbis terrarum* was subject to its authority, and the "eternal city" was more concerned with internecine strife within its possessions than with new conquests. However, domestic cosmopolitan views on relations between constituent peoples were not encountered during any other period of Antiquity or the Middle Ages; these peoples were granted the right of citizenship.[39]

[37] Compare Laurent, note 1 above, III, p. 247 et seq.

[38] Marquardt, note 31 above, I, §35.

[39] Laurent, III, p. 275: "L'empire romain donne la paix au monde mais cette paix était plus apparente que réelle".

In the Imperial epoch the social and State unification of various territories subject to Rome was completed, the beginnings having been laid during the Republic. The high culture and civilization of the Roman people – language, education, and political and legal views – were rapidly assimilated in the provinces, and during the Imperial period the provincials did not differ from the Romans and the Italians in cultural and social respects. The sole distinction dividing them was the political inequality which the patrician nobility stubbornly upheld. The Roman emperors, however, and primarily those who came from among the democrats, little by little erased this last distinction between the victors and the vanquished; one after another they extended the right of citizenship belonging to the Roman and Italian population to individual provincial cities and regions. Finally, the Constitution of [Marcus Aurelius] Antoninus Caracalla [(188-217)] equated in political rights the entire Roman population without exception.

Thus, Imperial Rome became a single internally compact and politically organized body, all parts of which were subject to uniform laws, court, and administration. One could no longer speak of international relations within the Roman Empire: all relations between individual parts thereof, within the boundaries of its territory, occurred not between members of different peoples, but between subjects of one State. Relations with European barbarians and Asian peoples not subordinate to Rome were episodic, incidental, and exceptional.

In concluding the survey of international relations of the ancient Romans, one question remains: did they have knowledge of an international law whose rights and duties should be respected in mutual relations between States? The resolution of this question is not solely of historical or purely scientific interest; it has great practical importance because many writers on international law still seek among Roman jurists the grounds for settling not only various legal questions between private individuals who are subjects of different States, but also misunderstandings and disputes between States themselves.[40]

We shall consider the major arguments in favor of the Roman people and jurists thereof having a concept of international law in the contemporary sense of the word.

During the Republic, and even earlier, a special branch of law was known in Rome, the so-called *jus feciale*, consisting of various formulas and rites applicable in the event war was declared by the Roman Senate or treaties

[40] Phillimore, note 1 above, I, p. 31: "The Roman law may in truth be said to be the most valuable of all aids to a correct and full knowledge of international jurisprudence of which it is, historically speaking, the actual basis". Also see Müller-Jochmus, note 1 above, p. 134: "Das Völkerrecht wurde in Rom zum Gesetz".

concluded by a special class of *fecial* priests who acted as representatives of the Romans in their international relations. On this basis certain scholars suggested that the relations of the ancient Romans with other peoples were determined by principles of law, that the interference of the *fecials* prevented unjust wars and ensured compliance with treaties.[41] In this view, the *fecials* were not only mediators in negotiations of their State with other peoples, but also decided questions of war and peace.

The sources, however, do not affirm this high opinion of the *fecials*; they do not provide a single example of the *fecials* refusing to perform instructions given by the Senate or consuls. On the contrary, they always agreed. We must conclude that either all wars of the Romans against other peoples were just and reasonable, or that the *fecials* were always persuaded of the complete legality of these wars and consented to them. But it is difficult to admit both. History shows that far from all Roman wars were based on right and justice. Therefore, one must concur with another view – that the *fecials* performed solemn rights in certain instances prescribed by the *jus feciale*, as officials, without any assessment of the reasons and motives which caused them, and that consequently the application of *jus feciale* was an empty ceremony which testified to the extreme formalism of the Roman people, but in no way to an awareness of the need for law and order in international relations.[42] Also unconvincing are the conclusions drawn from the existence among the Romans of certain concepts relating to the inviolability of the person of envoys (*legati*).[43] The Romans sent and received embassies from foreign States. But they were aware of their personal inviolability as much as all peoples were aware of it, even semi-wild tribes of inner Africa.

In the obscure news that has come down to us about ancient international arbitrators, called *recuperatores*, no evidence is seen that the Romans had knowledge of international law. *Recuperatores* were understood to be individuals chosen by the Roman people and others with whom they entered into a treaty in order to resolve disputes which might arise between

[41] Hugo Grotius, *De jure belli ac pacis* (1746), lib. II, cap. XXIII, IV: "*ita sententiarum eas sequendas quae plurimus praestantissimisque nitantur auctoribus. Sic Romani veteres non nisi consulto collegio fecialium ad id instituto, Imperatores Christiani vix nisi anditis Episcopis, bella suscipiebant, ut si quod esset quod religionem posset injicere, ejus monerentur*". Also see Ward, note 1 above, I, p. 189.

[42] On the real significance on the Roman *feciales*, see Marquardt, note 31 above, III, p. 398 et seq. Also compare André Weiss, *Le droit fetial et les fétiaux à Rome* (Paris, 1883).

[43] Caesar, *De bello Gallico*, III, 9: "*Legati, quod nomen apud omnes nations sanctum inviolatumque fuisset*". Compare Müller-Jochmus, note 1 above, §71, p. 150.

the subjects of these peoples or misunderstandings between the States generated by the performance of a treaty. However, both the rights and duties, and the appointment of such arbitrators, seems on the basis of the sources to be ambiguous. One matter is undoubted, that they were confirmed not otherwise than on the basis and occasion of the conclusion of treaties and, consequently, if one allows that instances of their appointment actually occurred, this was due to exceptional circumstances and rarely happened. As arbitrators between subjects of different States, *recuperatores* were made superfluous when the *praetor peregrinus*, who considered all litigation in which foreigners participated, began to develop his own judicial activity.[44]

Evidently the most convincing argument in favor of the fact that the Romans knew international law was the Roman *jus gentium*. Indeed, the existence of this "law of peoples" gives grounds to rather competent contemporary writers to support the view that the *jus gentium* of the ancient Romans is the contemporary international law of civilized peoples.[45] But in fact the sense and meaning of *jus gentium* is completely otherwise.

The initial legal views of the Romans and their strict *jus civile* were distinctive for a spirit of extreme exclusiveness and barbarism which did not make it possible to apply Roman laws to foreigners or to disseminate them among other peoples who were subordinate to Rome. Little by little, however, under the influence of developing international relations, these views changed, and the narrowly national Roman civil law increasingly acquired a universal character. As the Romans extended their dominion and came into contact with other peoples and their political institutions, laws, and customs, Roman jurists were persuaded that those legal principles which they considered to be exclusively their own existed among other peoples with whom the Romans had no relations, whom they held in contempt, and against whom they waged merciless war. On the basis of this experience they saw that, in addition to the civil law peculiar to a certain people, general principles of this law determined family and property relations and relations of obligations materially identical in all peoples – the *jus gentium*.[46] Such

44 Sell, *Die Recuperation der Römer* (Bonn, 1837), p. 139 et seq; Voigt, note 35 above, IV, p. 136; Karlowa, note 27 above, Cap. V: "Die Recuperationsprozesse"; Müller-Jochmus, note 1 above, p. 145; Laurent, note 1 above, III, p. 29.

45 Also see Voigt, note 35 above, II, Abth. I, p. 24, Anmerkung.

46 The classical definition of *jus gentium* in Gaius (Inst. I, 1) is well known: "*Quod vero naturalis ratio inter omnes homines constituit, id apud omnes populous peraeque custoditur vocaturque jus gentium, quasi quo jure omnes gentes utuntur. Et populus itaque Romanus partim suo proprio, partim communi omnium hominum jure utitur*". Compare fr. 17 D. 50, 7. De legationibus.

an all-people's law has as it source obviously not legislative power, but natural reason (*naturalis ratio*); that is, human nature, its legal interests and needs. It is understandable that the more Roman jurists penetrated into the awareness of the commonality of legal concepts among all peoples, the more they refrained from applying the old, formal explications of their own *jus civile*, the more the voice of justness (*aequitas*) had an advantage over strict law (*jus strictum*).

It follows that the *jus gentium* played an enormous role in the history of Roman law. Having absorbed the general humanitarian principles underlying the law of all peoples, it was disseminated not only in the ancient world, but made a source of the civil laws and legal education of contemporary educated peoples. But the *jus gentium* has as its subject-matter not international relations, but the aggregate of basic legal principles determining relations between private individuals and common to all peoples.[47] Therefore, it cannot serve as evidence of the existence of international law in the ancient world or as a source from which principles could be gleaned for determining contemporary international relations.[48]

B. Middle Ages

§16. The history of peoples of the ancient world and their international relations can be traced from the moment of the emergence of these peoples until their death. It is incomparably more difficult to determine the foundations of the international orders that dominated in the Middle Ages, when the presently existing civilized States were born and the beginnings of the modern international system arose.

In the fifth century the Western Roman Empire collapsed, and its place was taken by barbarians from the north of Europe.[49] The fate that befell the most powerful of the monarchies of Antiquity was the inevitable consequence of its internal decline. Having subjected the entire ancient world to its authority, the conquering people ceased their social and State

[47] Compare Savigny, *System des heutigen römischen Rechts*, I, §22, p. 111. Also see on the concept *jus gentium* the superb work by Voigt, note 35 above, I, p. 64 et seq, 399 et seq.

[48] To see in the abstract discourses of Cicero, *De officiis*, I, 11; *De legibus*, III, 20, an integral "theory of international law" as does Wheaton, note 1 above, I, p. 17, and Carlos Calvo, *Le droit international théorique et pratique* (1887-1896), I, p. 3, seems utterly impossible to us.

[49] There is no place here to analyze the various theories of the origin of feudalism and the reasons for the fall of the Western Roman Empire. The original view of Fustel de Coulanges, *Histoire des institutions politiques de l'ancienne France* (Paris, 1878), I, p. 317 et seq flies in the face of many positive facts.

development and could not preserve that international significance achieved in the preceding epoch.

Imperial Rome in many respects stood lower than republican Rome. That world which the Empire had planted was in reality the process of its breakup and a sign of coming death. The Roman Empire was evidence of its utter moral, economic, and political powerlessness. Already in republican times, the fatigue of military service and an aversion to it had become noticeable among Roman citizens. [Gaius] Julius Caesar [(100-44 BC)] was forced to turn to his enemies – the barbarians, in order to complement his legions (*laeti*). In the Imperial epoch the German princely armed force was the best Roman force and served as the sole support of the imperial throne.[50] Moreover, the demoralization and extinction of the Roman population reached such magnitude in the Empire that there were not enough hands to cultivate the land, and the Imperial government did not find other resources to support a declining agriculture than assistance from those barbarians; it caused colonists from among them to settle and cultivate the empty Roman lands (*coloni*). Thus, within the Roman Empire, in its very heart, were concentrated larger masses of their former enemies who, having become the *de facto* administrators of the Roman State, did not hesitate to eliminate the title of Roman emperor and share his power among their own kings.[51]

The fall of the western Roman Empire and final division of the Roman Empire had as its outcome the division of the ancient civilized world into two halves, the historical fate and international role of which differed materially. The Eastern, or Byzantine, Empire, especially after the separation of the Greek Church from the Roman, isolated itself from the western European peoples and found an arena to achieve autonomous political goals in Eastern Europe and Asia Minor. The conquest of Constantinople in the fifteenth century by the Turks widened the chasm separating the life of the peoples of southeastern Europe from the State and international orders in western Europe.

Who were those peoples who occupied in the west of Europe the place of civilized Romans and who are known in history under the general name of barbarians? A description of these peoples enables us to comprehend the social and political structure and the international relations of States of the Middle Ages.[52]

50 Laurent, note 1 above, V, pp. 40 et seq; Fustel de Coulanges, note 49 above, p. 345.

51 Fustel de Coulanges, note 49 above, p. 369: "L'empire romain ne fut donc pas renversé par ceux qui l'attaquaient, il le fut par ceux qui s'étaient faits ses soldats".

52 Compare the classical work of Augustin Thierry, *Histoire de la conquête de l'Angleterre par les Normands* (Paris, 1825).

The barbarians who destroyed the western Roman Empire and settled on its lands belonged to Germanic tribes. Just as all primitive peoples, they were distinctive for their boundless respect for physical force; they saw in force the source of any law and the foundation of private and social relations. According to the concepts of the ancient Germans, the right to existence belonged only to those who were in a state to protect it by their own forces. Respect for force was reflected in the order of justice of the barbarians: disputed property cases were decided by judicial duel. A crime was solely a violation of the interests of the victim and close relatives. The unlimited dominance of force characterizing the ancient being of the Germanic peoples was fully reflected in the feudal order. Another prominent distinctive feature of the barbarians was their aspiration for individual freedom. The Goths, Franks, Vandals, and other Germanic tribes were imbued with the idea unrecognized in the ancient world but which underlay contemporary civilization and culture – the idea of the individual and the rights thereof. Whereas the peoples of the ancient world conferred rights only on a citizen and in Antiquity a person disappeared into the State, among the barbarians, on the contrary, every free individual considered himself a person to whom certain rights belonged. Man himself was a subject of law and bore these rights wherever he went. The last were determined by the principle of the individual, not by local or territorial laws. In its consistent implementation, the principle of the individual is destroyed by the State. From the standpoint of absolute individual freedom, which comprised the idea of the barbarians, the social and State order should be regarded as a barrier, fetters, constraining human beings. For barbarians – man, his personal freedom, his rights were everything; the State was nothing.[53] This principle of individualism gave birth to centrifugal aspirations in the social and State relations of the peoples of the Middle Ages which left their imprint of all feudal life of western Europe. But if the predominance of the personal principle forced social order and State power to disappear in the Middle Ages, on the other hand, one must see enormous progress for social and State life and for international relations, in the recognition and implementation of this principle. Respect for the individual and the interests and rights thereof must necessarily underlie any order. The task of the historical life of the western European peoples – the establishment of correct mutual relations between the individual and public authority – might be resolved only thanks to the barbarians who first brought this principle to European life.

Finally, the third factor that developed the social and State existence of the peoples of the Middle Ages was the Christian religion. Unlike the

[53] Savigny, *Geschichte des römischen Rechts im Mittelalter* (1815-1831), I, cap. III.

religious faiths of the ancient world, which never served as an element ameliorating human relations or eradicating the division and enmity of peoples, Christianity, disseminated among the barbarians by peaceful preaching and by force of arms, united the western European peoples into a one church society and forced them to share identical religious views and beliefs as the initial and common source of their spiritual development, intellectual life, and moral concepts. The cultural influence of Christianity, without doubt, moderated the harsh social and State life of western Europe and moderated international relations of the Middle Ages, formed on the basis of purely Germanic principles, as noted above. With the gradual unification of the peoples of the West into one spiritual religious society and with the development of the power of the Head of the Roman Catholic Church, the creation of common cultural, social, and political tasks underlying all Christian States intensified. These tasks were resolved under the strong pressure of the Roman curia: its canon law was to serve as a model for civil and criminal laws of the peoples of the Middle Ages. It interfered in the domestic affairs of States and ultimately appropriated the right to be the supreme resolver of conflicts and disputes between various peoples.

§17. Having in view the said common elements of life in the Middle Ages, it is not difficult to determine to what social and political results they led and how the international relations were arranged of the western European States in the epoch here considered.

Among the *de facto* conditions within which the said elements operated, the attitude of the barbarians to the subdued peoples within the western Roman Empire played an important role. The barbarians could not and did not consider it necessary to change or to destroy the culture, social system, or political institutions and laws which existed in the occupied Roman possessions. The Germanic kings confined themselves to subjecting the population of these territories to their own State authority, levied taxes, and took some lands for distribution on certain conditions to their own comrades-in-arms. But this was not all. The barbarians fell under the inevitable influence of the developed culture and civic-mindedness which they found in the conquered provinces; they gradually assimilated the orders and law, were hospitable, and became the successors of the Romans in their culture and enlightenment which, in turn, have come down to the present.[54]

[54] Ibid., III, cap. XVI; Laurent, note 1 above, V, p. 87 et seq; Fustel de Coulanges, note 49 above, p. 361 et seq.

The invasion of the Germanic peoples into Italy, Gaul, and other Roman regions led to the expansion of urban settlements. The last naturally forced the peaceful population to seek refuge in fortified cities, which served as some defense against plundering by savage conquerors. Thus, the rich embryo of urban life was placed, whose development so strongly contributed to an increase of royal power and the structure of existing States.

Of those peoples who entered the scene of world history during the invasion of the barbarians, some – such as the Goths and Lombards – had fleeting political and international significance; others, on the contrary, enriched European cultural life with new principles and during the Middle Ages played a leading role in international relations. Among the last were the Franks. Having made themselves a settled and dominant population in Gaul, they little by little established an order of social and State life from which the principles of the social and political system of modern France developed. No less noteworthy was the international position of the Frankish monarchy. It was determined by the special relationship of the Franks to the Roman Catholic Church and its representative, Clovis I [(466-511)], who accepted the Christian faith, became a zealous disseminator of Christianity among the other Germanic peoples, and a fervent defender of the interests of Roman Catholicism. For his zealousness in matters of faith he received the honorary title from the Pope of "firstborn son of the Church" (*filius primogenitus ecclesiae*). This title was passed on to French kings.

The close alliance between the Frankish people and the Roman Catholic Church contributed to elevating the authority of the Roman primate and to the dissemination in the west of Europe of the ideas of ancient Rome which the Roman curia advanced.

The Empire of Charlemagne [(748-814)] was based on this alliance; he received the Roman crown from the hands of the Pope in the year 800, being solemnly proclaimed the head of all Christian peoples of western Europe. The newly arisen Empire was to be the center of all political and international life and to resurrect that unity of the civilized world destroyed by the barbarians. During the time of Charlemagne, his Empire truly had this significance. The new Emperor was well aware of his appointment as the first-born son of the Catholic Church: he waged war continuously against the Germanic and Slavic heathens who encircled his Empire and by force of arms placed Christianity and the basis of social order and law between them. In negotiations with the Byzantine emperor, Charlemagne supported the international autonomy of the western European world and his own authority as its representative. In relations with the Caliph Harun al-Rashid [(763/766-809)] he proclaimed the supremacy of the Christian world-outlook over the religious prejudices of the Muslim peoples.

The unity of the Carolingian Empire found its sole support in the genius of its first representative. After serious quarrels and internecine wars under the grandchildren of Charlemagne, the Empire of the Franks ultimately dissolved into France, Germania, and Italy (843), never to be combined for a lengthy period.

§18. After the division of the Empire of Charlemagne, an irresistible aspiration to break up and localize sovereign State authority existed in all States into which the Empire dissolved. More than 55 different provinces which enjoyed significant independence from the central government were counted in France during the tenth century, and the division of State territory intensified. The same was noted in Italy, where the process isolating individual parts of the State led to the formation of a large number of autonomous urban republics. But in no country did the political fractionalization reach the scale as in Germany: there not only provinces and cities became sovereign, but also each castle; each baron endeavored to withdraw from general State authority and pursue an independent political existence.

A feudal order developed under the influence of these centrifugal aspirations in the west of Europe. Underlying this was the principle that every individual possessing sufficient material resources in order to maintain his rights is a representative of political authority – a sovereign to whom all other individuals are subordinate who do not dispose of such resources. The personal dependence of the weak on the strong is the distinctive feature of the entire feudal system. The extent of this dependence determined the social status and rights of a person not finding protection in the authority of the government, which did not exist in feudal times. Thus, every individual should count on himself and his own power. Only in his own home, castle, family, and circle of close comrades-in-arms were his rights and interests secured. All relations became personal, direct, and vassal relations in that epoch. A vassal was bound with respect to his suzerain and knew only him. The grounds of vassal status were the possession of land and the relations of subordination arising therefrom.[55]

The military and agricultural aristocracy stood at the head of feudal society, the members of which appropriated all the prerogatives of sovereign State authority. Each feudal seigneur enjoyed within his possessions the exclusive right to issue laws and collect taxes; judicial authority and monetary regulation belonged to him; he declared war and concluded peace

[55] Compare François Guizot, *Histoire de la civilisation en Europe*, pp. 81, 92; Henry Brougham, *Political Philosophy*, I, p. 271 et seq; Laurent, note 1 above, V, p. 228.

at his discretion.[56] The rest of the population of the western European States comprised in significant number individuals nominally free but actually lacking the opportunity to exercise their rights and the predominant, in terms of population, estate of serfs who the feudal masters disposed of without limitation.

Under these circumstances, the feudal aristocracy, given the absence of firm central State authority, became the governing class during the epoch here considered, all other estates being dependent on it except for part of the estate of the clergy. It is easy to understand how the domestic orders were established in western Europe under these circumstances. Having force as the foundation, the dominion of the feudal aristocracy was a denial of any organized State life, legal order, and legality. No feudal lord turned to sovereign authority in order to receive satisfaction for offence caused to him, but waged war at own risk and entered into an agreement with his own offender. The entire history of State life during the Middle Ages is an uninterrupted series of private wars undertaken by members of the feudal aristocracy not only to resolve mutual misunderstandings and disputes, but to satisfy the passion for war, which as Laurent said, is the "poetry of the existence of peoples" during the time of feudalism.[57]

The right of private war which belonged in the Middle Ages to every natural and juridical person brought anarchy to the domestic life of western European peoples and led to the coarsening of morals, to the reign of the law of the fist (*Faustrecht, droit du poing*) – the highest expression of the principle of the individual dominant in feudal times, of individual power embedded in right and law. The extreme development of this principle had the favorable consequence for social relations of the Middle Ages that persuaded those persons who did not see the foundation of right in the law of the fist or, by reason of inadequate power, could not rely on this means of self-defense, of the need for agreements and alliances in order to pursue their interests and secure their rights by common efforts. As an awareness of the solidarity of spiritual and material rights of individual persons and the need for protection against the feudal lords spread in society through the combined forces of all those interested, the States of the Middle Ages divided themselves into a multiplicity of individual social groups: into city communities, corporations, guilds, or shops linked by identical property interests of the participants or by common goals of industry or trade.

[56] Hippolyte Taine, *Les Origines de la France contemporaine*, I, p. 9: "Dans la langue du temps, le noble est l'homme de guerre, le soldat (miles), et c'est lui qui pose la second assise de la société moderne".

[57] Laurent, note 1 above, VII, p. xi, 173 et seq.

The social and State system of the western European peoples of the feudal epoch materially influenced international relations in the Middle Ages. If feudal existence in western Europe was characterized by the fall of governmental authority and isolation of various social classes and groups into autonomous political organisms hostile to one another, then the international relations in the Middle Ages of both individuals and independent communities and States were sealed by the lack of order and legality and the predominant significance of flagrant physical force.

Just as within feudal States, constant warfare was pursued between peoples of the Middle Ages. Peaceful relations were a rare exception, and if they were maintained, it was thanks to the initiative and concern of private individuals or social classes, and not to the protection of State authority. Trade relations at this time were obstructed as much by wars waged by feudal lords as by robberies committed by knights, in order to defend against which merchants had to form armed detachments or hire mercenaries.

The failure to ensure peaceful international relations in the Middle Ages is evident, *inter alia*, from the grave situation in which foreigners found themselves in feudal Europe: their life and freedom depended on the discretion of those masters on whose land they were situated. According to customs of the Middle Ages, the feudal lord was considered to be the sole heir of all property of a deceased foreigner which remained on the territory of the feudal lord. This right, known as *droit d'aubaine*, existed in western Europe, albeit in moderated form, until the nineteenth century.[58]

To the barbarity of feudal existence the western European States were indebted for another inhuman custom which long remained in force – coastal law (*droit de naufrage*).

According to the common view which dominated in the Middle Ages, all that was cast into the coastal sea constituted the legitimate booty of local inhabitants. Therefore, mariners who suffered shipwreck were seized by local seigneurs and not only deprived of the remnants of their property, but often lost their freedom and life. This appalling abuse of force generated protests even in the Middle Ages. Despite prohibition by the popes and assemblies, and likewise instructions of the government, coastal law *de facto* existed to the eighteenth century and was eliminated only when the maritime States established a firm governmental order ensuring precise compliance with laws.[59]

[58] Compare Montesquieu, note 16 above, liv. XXI, chap. XVII; Berner, in J. C. Bluntschli, *Deutsches Staatswörterbuch*, V, p. 86 et seq.

[59] Pütter, note 1 above, p. 120 et seq; Wheaton, note 1 above, I, p. 89 et seq.

The arbitrariness and violence which distinguished private and social life in the Middle Ages was especially manifest during wars, which during this period were constantly waged by private individuals, possessors of castles, and States. Wars in the Middle Ages featured all possible cruelties and savagery, which is to be explained not only by the barbarism of the feudal lords, the passion of illiterate and militant people to shed blood and destruction, but also by the character of feudal conflicts: usually these were limited conflicts over personal matters and the rivalry of neighbors; these aggravated the struggle and imparted tinges of personal revenge. Feudal chivalry did not stop at any violence during combat and did not recognize any laws and customs which would limit the use of force; it did not even consider the precise execution of a word given to the enemy to be a duty: perfidy was one of the most abused means of waging combat, to which sovereigns themselves frequently had recourse.[60]

§19. The principles of European international law were born and developed under the general conditions of social life of the western European peoples of the Middle Ages. Even though the feudal States of western Europe disintegrated into numerous independent castles, communities, and provinces, the population of these lands and sectors were linked by identical social needs and aspirations. The social system of States of the Middle Ages were in their fundamentals more or less identical. We see in all feudal territories those same estates, communities, corporations, domestic life, aspirations, and interests both on the European continent and in England.

The feudal agricultural and military aristocracy was the ruling class in all western European States of the Middle Ages. The aristocracy was not reminiscent of either the Indian caste system or of the Roman patrician. It was organized on the basis of the personal link of the vassal and his suzerain. Consequently, affiliation to a high estate in the Middle Ages depended not so much on birth or national origin as on personal abilities and merits of the person.[61] Thanks to personal service underlying the entire feudal structure – first, there was not such an insuperable precipice between aristocrats and members of other estates as in the ancient eastern States or in Rome. History

[60] One may find many examples of such cruelties and perfidy in Ward, note 1 above, II, pp. 47, 268 et seq; Pütter, note 59 above, pp. 87, 114, et seq. Compare John Reeves, *Reeves' History of the English Law* (new ed.; London, 1869), I, p. 53 et seq; Ernest Nys, *Études de droit international et de droit politique* (Brussels, 1896), p. 75 et seq.

[61] Laurent, note 1 above, VII, p. 334 quoted the words of Pope Gregory VII [(1015-1085)] that pagan and Christian Rome triumphed because "*non tam generis aut patriae nobilitatem, quam animi et corporis virtutes perpendendas adjudicaverit*". Compare also Laurent, ibid., VII, p. 33 et seq and p. 349 et seq.

shows many examples of Germanic emperors and various kings of feudal European States granting high titles and offices to persons of low origin. In this respect the Roman church greatly influenced the lessening of the aristocratic spirit, the church hierarchy relying solely on personal abilities, excluding the principle of birth or origin.

On the other hand, the identical organization of the European aristocracy of the Middle Ages served as a link between the feudal aristocracies of various European States. A vassal of the King of France did not feel alien within the Germanic Empire or Italian possessions; personal valor equated him with the feudal lords of those lands. He remained there a member of a high estate of the Middle Ages having common interests – to protect his authority, privileges, and independence against infringements by royal authority.

The cosmopolitanism of the feudal aristocracy was most highly expressed for all western European peoples of the Middle Ages in the institution of the knighthood. Its origins are explained by the aforementioned principle of personal service.

When creating the high social status of feudal lords, the holding of office or rendering of service led to the formation in the European States of the Middle Ages of an aristocracy of intelligence, virtue, and personal abilities and powers of an individual. The knights who comprised such an aristocracy made it their duty to protect the church, defend the weak and oppressed, widows, and orphans wherever the knight was. This common goal made all knights brothers to one another, whatever their birth or national origin; knights knew no territorial boundaries and were the first to proclaim the ideas of truth and justice in the field of international relations.[62]

Another social class which existed in the Middle Ages – the trade and industrial estate – was concentrated in all western European States in fortified cities or communes defended by mercenaries or own armed citizens. Given the dominance everywhere of the law of the fist and the weakness of governmental authority, the urban communities of Germany, France, and Italy assumed the internal administration of their own affairs

[62] Compare especially the superb work of the Belgian jurist, Ernest Nys, *Les origines du droit international* (Paris, 1894); Ward, note 1 above, II, cap. XIV: on the influence of chivalry, p. 155 et seq – Laurent, note 1 above, VI, p. 206 et seq; Pütter, note 59 above, p. 93 et seq – Henry Thomas Buckle, История цивиизации в Англии [History of Civilization in England] (1863-1864), I, p. 457. Instances of knights violating their word and the commission of inhumane cruelties against an enemy do not, of course, refute the moral and cultural significance of the institution of knighthood. Compare also: Baron Mikhail Aleksandrovich von Taube, История зарождения современного международного права (Средние века) [History of the Birth of Contemporary International Law (Middle Ages)] (Spb., 1894).

and foreign relations. Just as feudal aristocrats, they had the right to declare war, conclude peace, enter into negotiations and agreements with other autonomous communities and private individuals.

Taking advantage of this right, cities entered into alliances with one another in order to combat those elements of social life of the Middle Ages which denied the need for peaceful international relations and in order to achieve common industrial and trade goals by their combined forces.

The noted Hanseatic League, to which all the major commercial centers of Western Europe belonged, was based on the community of social interests of urban inhabitants in the Middle Ages. The cities comprising this League established an autonomous government which had its own army and fleet, but also protected its commercial relations against attacks of individual feudal lords and waged war against States not coping with the opinion, interests, and wishes of the governments concerned.[63]

As regards the peasant estate, its status in the Middle Ages of western Europe was everywhere, in essence, identical: the peasants were in serf dependence on those feudal lords on whose territory they lived, and if they left these lands and resettled in another State, they did not receive freedom there, but developed serf relations with the new landholder. Only cities little by little changed their view on serfs and began to authorize rural inhabitants to settle within a commune, recognizing their full personal freedom.

In addition to the said social elements, the Roman Catholic Church and its representatives – the popes – contributed to the peaceful development of the peoples of the Middle Ages and the establishment of close cultural links between them. The Crusades were caused and supported by the spiritual authority of the Church and its primates. The popes repeatedly assumed the role of arbitrators and resolved disputes between various European monarchs, between the Germanic Emperor and imperial cities and officials, and between vassals and their suzerains. They convoked church assemblies and often issued and confirmed decrees on the Peace of God (*Treuga Dei*) for the purpose of limiting feudal quarrels and arrogation. The embryo of new better international orders is evident in those behests of assemblies and popes which abolished the use of coastal law.[64]

Finally, the unlimited dominance of arrogation within feudal possessions and constant wars and plundering by feudal lords forced private individuals

[63] See Mikhail Nikolaevich Berezhkov, О торговле Руси с Ганзою до конца XV века [On the Trade of Rus with the Hansa to the End of the Fifteenth Century] (Spb., 1879), Chapter III; Pütter, note 59 above, p. 141 et seq; Ward, note 1 above, II, p. 276 et seq.

[64] Ward, note 1 above, II, chap. XIII; Laurent, note 1 above, VII, pp. 265, 356, 381 et seq; Pütter, note 59 above, p. 120 et seq.

and societies to resort to mutual agreements to better secure their rights and legal interests. On the basis of treaties, individuals and urban communities obliged themselves not to use force in the event any misunderstandings arose between them, but would apply to arbitrators for the peaceful settlement of the dispute. Private obligations replaced absent governmental authority and to some extent secured order. Entire peoples or parts of a State sometimes, under the pressure of external circumstances, entered into such agreements. For example, cities and possessions within the Germanic Empire, in view of the danger of conquest by the Turks, for a time renounced in the fifteenth century the right of private wars and recognized a certain authority for the Germanic Emperor within his territories.[65]

But neither the social interests and aspirations in the Middle Ages, nor the spiritual authority of the Catholic Church, nor the private treaties and temporary agreements of States were able to ensure stable peace and order in the mutual relations of the European nations of the Middle Ages. The essential conditions for proper and peaceful international turnover were a sole and firm governmental authority and organized legal order within States guaranteeing security and the rule of law within State territory. The conditions did not exist in the west of Europe. To be sure, royal authority in France during the fourteenth century adopted various measures to order to terminate the dominance of the law of the fist. Philip the Fair [Philip IV (1268-1314)] in 1303 prohibited any arrogation on the part of French citizens, but this law could be binding only with the destruction of feudalism in the French kingdom.[66] The law of the fist dominated in Germany until the sixteenth century, where judicial duel was used to decide civil and criminal violations. Only in England was the rule established comparatively earlier that the king is the sovereign protector of peace and law throughout the entire country and that he who violates legal order offends the royal majesty.[67]

§20. If during the Middle Ages State authority did not exist in the contemporary meaning of this expression, it could not exist in international relations, as understood now. International relations of the Middle Ages occurred between private individuals, cities, and independent parts of feudal lands, but not States, which are the subjects of contemporary international

[65] Laurent, note 1 above, VII, p. 185.

[66] Ibid., VII, p. 181.

[67] Rudolph Gneist, *Selfgovernment: Communalverfassung und Verwaltungsgerichte Englands* (3d ed.; 1871), pp. 103, 888 et seq.; Gneist, *Der Rechtstaat* (Berlin, 1879), p. 38 et seq.

law. Hence the predominance of brute force and anarchy among western European peoples as distinctive attributes of the Middle Ages.

International relations of the Middle Ages transition into another period and are organized on the basis of order and law under the influence of declining feudalism and the birth of royal power in western Europe.

Many forces took part in the destruction of the feudal system of western European States. Without doubt, the Crusades accelerated the fall of the feudal order.

The general character of international relations of the Middle Ages presented above shows that all relations between European peoples in the Middle Ages had force as a guiding principle; that is, that principle which reigned in the form of arrogation and the law of the fist in the domestic life of feudal States. Obviously, there could be no thought of the rule of law and legal order in the international relations of that time. Nonetheless, as noted above, new elements of social and State life were generated in the Middle Ages which, gradually developing, led to order and the rule of law between contemporary educated peoples. International relations in that epoch confirm the proposition expressed by Guizot that not brute force, but ideas and moral forces concealed in the manifestations of physical power, governed human societies.[68] This truthfulness of this proposition was demonstrated by the Crusades.

The universal movement of western European peoples to the East for the purpose of liberating the grave of the Lord from the hands of infidels reduced the isolation in which these peoples lived, developed a closer-knit community formed around a religious idea, and, finally, familiarized them with the life and works of eastern countries through enduring trade relations. In this respect the Crusades encouraged the development of a peaceful international life in the European West. They also strongly influenced the domestic system of feudal States, political and social. The feudal order had disintegrated the State and social unity of the European peoples, creating a State within a State, placing a military aristocracy in the position of governmental authority, and leaving other social classes in anarchy. The Crusades, on the contrary, forced all estates of the Middle Ages to coalesce in a Christian brotherhood of people and common religious interests. In a word, they equalized the social classes of the Middle Ages and created the internal unity of States – an essential condition of order in international relations.[69]

68 Guizot, note 55 above, p. 219.

69 Ibid., p. 200: "De même que les croisades sont un événement européen, de même, dans chaque pays, elles sont un événement national". Compare also p. 215. See Laurent, note 1

The political authority of vassalage was undermined by jurist-legists of the Middle Ages who had entered the service of monarchs and sincerely struggled for law and the unity of State authority. Brought up on Roman law, they were implacable enemies of the privileges of the feudal aristocracy and helped to establish the principle that one law should dominate within State territory issued by royal power, and that the application of this law should be the duty only of royal courts, excluding the jurisdiction of feudal lords. But most of all, the final abolition of feudalism was facilitated by the alliance between monarchs and urban communes to struggle against the willfulness and violence of the feudal lords.

The urban communities played a major role in establishing State unity in the West of Europe and in the development of principles serving as the basis of contemporary international law. Whereas in the Middle Ages one might find some awareness of the need for State order and the implementation of the principle of statehood, of course not in the German Empire divided into several hundred individual possessions nor in France, where powerful vassals, dukes, and counts reduced the political significance of the king. The principles of governmental civilization, the relations of the authorities and the subjects, and ensuring order through the structured administration of justice were recognized first in communes of the Middle Ages and from these narrow territories were extended to States.[70]

In the domain of international law urban communities rendered no less service. Because they took an active and independent part in international trade turnover, by force of circumstances they developed customs which governed maritime trade and came to comprise the international law of the sea. The municipalities of various western European commercial cities of the Middle Ages had long since, under sundry names, issued collections of maritime trade customs.[71]

The alliance of royal power with urban communes was justified by the community of their political interests against feudal lords and the rich material resources which the commercial cities might deliver to monarchs.

above, VII, p. 293 et seq. Compare Heinrich von Sybel, *Geschichte des ersten Kreuzzuges* (2d ed.; Leipzig, 1881), p. 193 et seq; Hans Prutz, *Culturgeschichte der Kreuzzüge* (1883).

[70] Compare the superb work by the French historian and diplomat: René de Maulde-la-Clavière, *La diplomatie au temps de Machiavel* (Paris, 1892). 3 vols.; Francisco Pi y Margall, *Les nationalités. Essai de philosophie politique* (Paris, 1879), p. 68: "La cité est une nation en petit. Elle a sont culte, ses lois, son gouvernement, son administration, ses tribunaux, ses finances, son armée; elle a son organisme, son État".

[71] Compare Pardessus, note 18 above. See below the section "Sources of International Law".

But whereas the said alliance led everywhere in Europe to raising royal authority and the founding of a new political order, this reform operated variously in different western European States.

In France the creation of national unity developed on firm foundations thanks to the age-old war which the French people pursued, upholding their political independence against English kings. This struggle forced the French to combine their forces, seek a common center in a unified national authority, and see the ideal State structure within absolute political centralization. Therefore, the kings of France, after a steadfast struggle against the feudal aristocracy, were able to found in their own State a strong monarchical power unknown throughout the rest of Europe. Stable national unity made it possible for the French monarchy within about three or so centuries to play the primary role in international relations.[72]

State authority was organized differently in England. In no country had feudalism been so deeply rooted and left so many traces to this day as in the English kingdom. But there feudalism had a different character than on the European continent. After the conquest of England by the Normans, William the Conqueror [(c. 1028-1087)] did not introduce in pure form those feudal orders established in France. He well understood that these orders destroy State unity and make royal authority illusory. On this basis he gave English lands to his own comrades-in-arms on condition of vassal dependence on him alone as the supreme protector of peace and order throughout the country. Thus, in England the king remained the active head of the entire State; on the other hand, feudal landholders were equated in their subordination to the king and became one of his subjects. The development of an awareness by the English people of a solidarity of its interests with respect to the power of the king was an outcome of this system of feudal relations in England, and when John Lackland [(1166-1216)] indulged himself in flagrant violations of the liberties of the kingdom, all the estates acted against him and forced the signature of the *Magna Charta libertatum*.[73]

That is why, whereas in France State unity developed in the sense of the absolute power of its sovereign, the English State order was formed in the sense of a community of interests of the king and the people, in the sense of respect on the part of the government for the legal rights and aspirations of its subjects. The difference in the international policy of both States is explained by this: whereas the kings of France found it possible to

[72] Compare Jules Michelet, *Histoire de France* (Brussels ed.), IV, liv. V; Guizot, note 55 above, p. 249 et seq; Buckle, note 62 above, I, p. 466 et seq.

[73] Leopold von Ranke, *Englische Geschichte*, I, p. 45 et seq; Catharine Macauley, *History of England from the Accession of James the Second* (London, 1856), I, p. 48.

pursue their dynastic interests and personal views in international relations and to give the property and blood of their people for this, in England the same could not be said. The English Government, by reason of its political structure, was forced to set as the only goal of its international relations the advantage and needs of the English people. Given the insular position of England and the entrepreneurial nature and energy of its inhabitants, trade and industrial relations became a special vocation in the international turnover of the English nation, thanks to which it withstood a series of bloody and lengthy wars against other peoples.

In Germany feudalism took extreme forms and flourished up to the sixteenth century. German emperors, diverted by a sustained struggle against papal authority, could not prevent the fracturing of the State and little by little became nominal representatives of the German Empire, powerless and torn apart by domestic disagreements and international wars. Not having the power to maintain internal order in the country, the emperors sacrificed Germany to intrigues, international wars, and interference used by other European powers to their advantage.

Italy was a country in which the feudal order expressed itself initially in the formation of various commercial republics such as Pisa, Amalfi, Genoa, Venice, and others. With the assistance of trade turnover, these achieved noteworthy wealth and power. But within these municipalities irreconcilable struggle proceeded between the people's and aristocratic parties, depleting the prosperity of the city and sacrificing them to a conqueror. Therefore, the greater part of the Italian republics disappeared, and only Venice and Genoa retained their independence until the late eighteenth century. After that, Italy represented a multitude of independent weak States who served as an enticement and battlefield for various foreign conquerors, ultimately and for a lengthy period weakening the Italian people.

As for Spain, until the fifteenth century the greater part of its territory was under the power of the Moors, who administered the country on principles completely inconsistent with general European civilization and culture.

Irrespective of the reasons cited, the Renaissance had great influence on the domestic existence and international relations of European States. In the West of Europe familiarity spread with the scientific and artistic works of classical antiquity, on the basis of which the general intellectual life of the western peoples was formed, and the products of their intellectual activity were actively distributed. Moreover, the invention of printing, gunpowder, the compass, the introduction of standing armies[74] and various geographical

[74] Buckle, note 62 above, I, p. 151 et seq.

discoveries contributed to changing the system of the Middle Ages and the formation in Western Europe of new social, State, and international orders.

In completing this account of international relations in Antiquity and the Middle Ages, it remains only to conclude that during the first period the law of physical force indeed was the guiding principle of all international relations.

Second Period
From Peace of Westphalia to 1815 Congress of Vienna

A. International Relations from Peace of Westphalia to First French Revolution

§21. After the fall of the feudal system, Western Europe was a society of independent States in which the anarchy and law of the fist ceded place to respect for law and the dominance of unified royal power.

In the sixteenth century the peaceful life of these States was shaken by a Reformation movement which arose first in Germany but quickly embraced the entire north and west of Europe. The Reformation had tremendous international significance. It divided the European peoples into two hostile camps which engaged in an obstinate and lengthy struggle.

The Thirty Years War, religious in origin, abounded in consequences of a purely political nature. As it continued, the international aspirations of States came to the fore. States which according to their historical traditions, according to the profession of faith of their monarchs and their subjects, should be implacable enemies of the Reformation instead, in view of their worldly interests, became adversaries of the Roman Catholic Church. The Prince of the Church, Cardinal [Armand Jean du Plessis, Duke of] Richelieu [(1585-1642)], in the name of the "first-born son of the Roman Catholic Church" concluded an alliance with the King of Sweden, Gustavus Adolphus II [(1594-1632)], who took under his protection the Protestant movement in Germany. This shows what a sharp change occurred in relations between the State and the Church in the new period as compared with the Middle Ages. During and after the Thirty Years War, religion was reduced to second place, and the orientation of international politics thenceforth was determined solely by State goals.

The Thirty Years War was ended by the Peace Treaty of Westphalia concluded on 24 October 1648. Both the procedure for conclusion of this Act and the preliminary negotiations which preceded it reflected the awareness on the part of States and their representatives of the novelty of the matter undertaken and the unusual nature of its status.[75]

The peace negotiations had begun in 1634; the preliminary conditions were accepted by the parties in 1645. The governments and sovereigns who took part in the Thirty Years War were well aware of the baneful results to which it had led and the extent to which these might increase with the further continuation of the war. Force of circumstances obliged them to bring an end to shedding blood and one way or another to enter into an agreement. But peace could be concluded only with the common consent of the parties and on conditions responsive to the true state of affairs and the aspirations that had inspired the belligerents. The new order which ought to be established in international relations was ambiguous, contrary to all their concepts and historical traditions. In the preceding life of the European peoples there had not been a single precedent either in Antiquity or in the Middle Ages where the representatives of different States had discussed their affairs in common and established procedures binding on all peoples.[76] Therefore, all meetings and the exchange of ideas between plenipotentiaries of the European governments before convening the Congress of Westphalia and the Congress itself bore the character of inexperience, doubts, and childish apprehensions of the honor and dignity of the States represented being prejudiced.[77]

After lengthy negotiations, the plenipotentiaries of virtually all European powers except Russia, Poland, and England finally assembled at the Congress, whose sessions took place in two cities close to one another: Osnabrück and Münster. This division into two meetings arose from the impossibility of combining around a single table the representatives of Sweden with the papal curia. Therefore, the plenipotentiaries of Sweden, the German Empire, and various other Protestant States assembled in

[75] Garden, note 1 above, I, p. 134 et seq; Gaëtan de Raxis de Flassan, *Histoire générale et raisonnée de la diplomatic française* (1811), III, p. 220 et seq; Friedrich von Raumer, *Geschichte Europa's seit dem XV-ten Jahrhundert* (1834), III, p. 614 et seq; Horace Dominique de Barral de Montferrat, *Étude sur l'histoire diplomatique de l'Europe* (Paris, 1880-1885), I(1), p. 1; and others.

[76] Compare Karl Fischer, *Geschichte der auswärtigen Politikk und Diplomatie im Reformationszeitalter 1455-1556* (Gotha, 1874), p. 151 et seq.

[77] Montague Bernard, *Four Lectures on Subjects Connected with Diplomacy* (London, 1868), p. 21 et seq. Compare also Raumer, note 75 above, III, p. 618. For five years comic negotiations continued as to who should first arrive in Münster and in what sequence; who first ascended the stair and entered the conference hall; who was first seated to the right and left of the chairman; what titles to give the representatives of various States, and so on.

Osnabrück; the representatives of the papal curia, Venice, the German Emperor, France, and others gathered at Münster.

The most important provisions of the Westphalia peace treaty may be expressed as follows:[78]

1) The mutual relations of the two Christian churches – Protestant and Roman Catholic – must be determined by that position in which church societies were on 1 January 1624. The binding force of the 1555 Augsburg Peace Treaty was confirmed. However, a certain discretionary power of each sovereign was legitimized with respect to those church societies which existed within his territory because the basic rule of the Augsburg Peace – *cujus regio, ejus religio* – gave sovereigns the right to evict all foreigners from their country.

2) States within the German Empire, numbering 355, received full independence on one condition – not to conclude international treaties which would be contrary to the benefits of the other German States.

3) The Swiss Union and the Netherlands, which to that time had enjoyed *de facto* independence, were formally recognized as autonomous States.

4) The territorial increments of France and Sweden, as victorious parties, consisted of the accession to the first of part of Alsace and, to the second, a large part of Pomerania and the cities of Wismar, Rostock, and others. Moreover, France received rights of suzerainty over ten free Imperial cities within Alsace, including Strasbourg.

The general significance of the Westphalia peace treaty for international relations may be summarized as follows. First, its immediate significance lay in the fact, unprecedented in the past, that the combining of European States into a single international society which was so aware of the solidarity of its interests that it was considered essential not only to consult about common affairs, but to even determine the domestic order in States that are part of this society. Second, it gave formal sanction to that schism in the spiritual unity of western European peoples with the estrangement of the Protestant church from the Roman Catholic. Third, the recognition of the autonomy of the numerous German possessions ensured international and State impotence for a long time of the German Empire and opened broad expanse for the interference of all European powers in its internal affairs. Fourth, the Peace of Westphalia affirmed the international primacy of France, which strove to reduce its age-old rivals – Austria and the German Empire – and enhanced Sweden, which became an active player in the international affairs of Europe

[78] Johann Gottfried von Meiern, *Acta pacis Westphalicae publica* (Hanover, 1734-1736). 6 vols.

until internal troubles, quarrels, and egoism of political parties deprived it of any influence on the European continent.

§22. International events in the second half of the seventeenth and in the eighteenth centuries cannot be understood without having in view the State and social system established in the States of Western Europe.

The political order which arose in the continental European States on the ruins of the feudal system should have led to the enhancement and structuring of one-person royal power on those principles which underpinned the political authority and rights of feudal lords. Monarchs were made the successors of all prerogatives which the feudal seigneurs enjoyed with respect to their own lands and the population on those lands. Whereas the feudal lords considered their private property to belong to them in fee, the king, having taken away feudal sectors, considered State territory to be his property which he might dispose of at his discretion. If the population of feudal possessions treated their lord as protector who in return for protection rendered demanded unconditional subordination to his authority, then it was the same with respect to the king, whose will became the sole law for his subjects. The principle thus developed on the continent of Europe of unlimited royal rule who application in individual cases, to be sure, concealed liberal forms, but was presented as a requirement for the good of the State, the interests and needs of the people, but which in sustance was old, of the Middle Ages. In France this order was called "enlightened despotism",[79] and among German jurists and historians it was given the name "police State".

The absolutism of royal power found stable support in the social structure of European States, which in this epoch was more or less the same in all western peoples of the continent.[80] The estate of the nobility, endowed with vast privileges and not obliged to bear any duties to the country, was formed from the feudal aristocracy. Side by side stood the clergy, the highest stratum of which was undistinguishable from the nobility in social status, rights, and privileges.[81] The status of the third estate and agricultural class differed. The commercial class, the representatives of industry, knowledge, and art,

[79] Here is the response of Louis XIV to the Paris Parliament of 3 March 1766: "C'est en ma personne seule que reside l'autorité souveraine ... C'est à moi seul qu'appartient le pouvoir législatif sans dépendance et sans partage. L'ordre public tout entier émane de moi ...".Thaine, note 56 above, I, p. 16; Gneist, note 67 above, p. 155 et seq.

[80] Alexis de Tocqueville, *L'ancien regime*, p. 68: "... dans toute l'Europe alors, les mêmes droit féodaux, précisément les mêmes, se retrouvaient".

[81] Thaine, note 56 above, I, p. 21; Tocqueville, note 80 above, p. 150 et seq.

might with honor and advantage for the country take part in administration, but access to senior posts was closed to them. As for the peasants, they comprised the taxable base on which the State existed and the highest estates maintained their brilliance and idleness; in contrast to the last, the peasants had some duties and no rights.

The government was on the side of the nobility and the clergy. It brought representatives of a particular class closer to the throne, allowed some to hold senior court and State offices, embellished them with all possible honors, and closely linked their interests with its own. Relying on the contribution and unyielding obedience of these classes, royal power could pursue its own personal wishes and dynastic interests within the State.

The social order which formed in continental European States in the seventeenth and eighteenth centuries was rarely reflected in the international relations of that time. Those purposes to which absolute royal power aspired within the State also guided its international policy.

The personal and family interests of sovereigns dominated in the international relations of the seventeenth and eighteenth centuries over other tasks of States. Social needs and aspirations were not satisfied in any continental European State; moreover, they could not find respect in international relations. In the eyes of European monarchs of that epoch, subjects had no rights with respect to State authority represented by the person of the sovereign. Unlimited royal power arbitrarily disposed of the property and life of its subjects. This lack of respect for the rights of an individual in domestic administration materially influenced the general character of international relations in the period here considered. Endeavoring with all their resources to undertake their own personal egoistic purposes, sovereigns did not recognize any rights for foreign peoples and their sovereigns and did not sort out the resources necessary to achieve the tasks set for themselves. Machiavellianism was the slogan of foreign policy and the scale for determining the binding nature of international treaties.

Nonetheless, just as within States the most arbitrary regulations of the government were justified by considerations of the well-being and benefit of the people, so too in international relations all wars and seizures of foreign possessions, supposedly not unjust and unscrupulous, were concealed under the guise of justness and right, being solemnly proclaimed in royal manifestos and decrees. State officials of this epoch cited Hugo Grotius in their diplomatic acts with admiration, the father of the science of international law, and referred to the most elevated principles of morality and law in order to conceal the most scandalous violations of basic rights of peoples.[82]

France played the main role in the international relations of European States after the Peace of Westphalia. The predominant influence of France in European affairs was especially strong at the end of the seventeenth and early eighteenth centuries when Louis XIV ascended to the throne. The personal royal policy that dominated on the continent of Europe throughout the period here considered found in that sovereign the most typical representative.

Territorial acquisitions, expansion of the boundaries of his own State at the expense of neighboring powers – this was the task which Louis XIV set for himself. It was addressed by diplomatic negotiations and by seizures and wars which filled the entire reign of this remarkable sovereign.[83]

Circumstances were auspicious for the King of France. The State structure of France enabled him to expend without control all the resources of his people; he disposed of enormous material resources left to him by predecessors; he bult the best army and navy. The other European States, on the contrary, either were nothing militarily, such as the States of Holland, or represented, as did the German Empire, social collapse and political impotence.[84] With generous subsidies, Louis XIV forced the German sovereigns to obey him unquestioningly and in the same way supported an alliance with the government of Kings Charles II and James II of England and with the Kingdom of Sweden.

Under these conditions, Louis XIV began his first war against Spain, which refused to cede the Belgian provinces voluntarily; these were demanded by the King of France on the ground that they comprised the legitimate inheritance of his wife as the only daughter from the first marriage of Philipp IV [(1605-1665)] of Spain (*par le droit de dévolution*). The war for the Belgian provinces was ended by the Peace of Aachen (1668), thanks to the alliance and mediation of Holland, England, and Sweden. On the basis of this Peace, Louis XIV acquired twelve Flemish cities and their environs.[85]

[82] Bernard, note 77 above, p. 78.

[83] Macauley had some perceptive words to say about Louis XIV: "In his dealings with foreign powers he had some generosity, but no justice …, he broke through the most sacred ties of public faith without scruple or shame whenever they interfered with his interest of that, what he called his glory". Macauley, note 73 above, I, p. 199.

[84] Compare Ranke, *Abhandlungen und Versuche* (Leipzig, 1872), p. 4 et seq.

[85] Ranke, *Französische Geschichte* (Leipzig, 1869), III, p. 231 et seq.

Annoyed by the interference of the Dutch Republic, at whose initiative the aforesaid triple alliance was formed, in 1672 Louis XIV declared war on Holland, having the English and Swedish kings as his allies. On the side of Holland were: the German Emperor, Denmark, Spain, and Brandenburg. Under the 1678 Peace Treaty of Nijmegen, Louis XIV received the Franche-Comte, having displayed surprising skill in disuniting his adversaries and in subjecting each individually to his conditions.[86]

The successful peace at Nijmegen encouraged the King of France to further conquests. In 1680 he founded special judicial commissions – *chambres de réunions*, for the purpose of investigating which lands were in fief dependency on districts belonging to France under the treaties of Westphalia, Aachen, and others. The princes of the German Empire and representatives of the Alsace and Flemish cities appealed to these courts for evidence of their legitimate rights to independent existence, the slightest doubt serving as a pretext for combining their possessions with French territory. By this means Louis XIV seized a significant number of cities and villages in Germany and in the Spanish Netherlands.[87]

In vain the King of Spain and the Dutch States submitted representations and protests to the court of Versailles against such appalling violations of the rights of independent States: Louis XIV ignored them. Convinced of this own strength and the weakness of other States, he continued to dispose of foreign possessions arbitrarily. Without declaring war, he besieged and occupied the city of Luxembourg; Strasbourg suffered the same fate.

After the 1688 English Revolution, the attitude of the continental European States towards France gradually changed. Of all the sovereigns of that time, only the Stadtholder of the Dutch Republic, William, Prince of Orange [(1650-1702)], saw the common danger for all States of the insatiable ambition of the King of France and had the courage to oppose, as much as possible, his claims to unlimited dominion in Europe. He considered the best means of stopping the conquests of Louis XIV to be the practical implementation of the political equilibrium of States through the conclusion of a general alliance between the European States to protect their autonomy and independence against the infringements of an ambitious monarch. But these alliances gave little to the Dutch Stadtholder until he was invited, in 1688, to take the vacant English throne.

As the King of England, William of Orange disposed of sufficient influence, power, and resources to form an all-European coalition which,

[86] Jean Dumont, *Corps universel diplomatique du droit des gens* (Amsterdam, 1726-1731), VII(1), p. 350; Macauley, note 73 above, III, p. 122.

[87] Arsène Legrelle, *Louis XIV et Strasbourg* (4th ed.; Paris, 1884).

thanks to his efforts, was organized in 1689 during the war of Louis XIV against the German Empire. In addition to the last and England, the alliance included Holland, Brandenburg, Sweden, Denmark, Spain, and Savoy. But the coalition did not succeed in defeating Louis XIV. The last succeeded again in dividing the allies and prescribed his peace conditions to each. The Ryswyck Peace Congress in 1697 confirmed the possession of Strasbourg for France and enriched her with significant territorial additions at the expense of Spain.[88]

The peace in Ryswyck was a triumph for French policy thanks to the lack of unanimity in the actions of the allies. The full burden of the war fell on England and the Dutch States; the German Emperor and the imperial princes exhibited an extreme lack of action and indifference not only to general European interests, but to their own advantage. This failure of the Empire and the sovereigns within it to understand its own interests so upset William of Orange that he decided not thereafter to link the interests of the English people with their interests. After the Ryswyck peace, he changed his policy, and in 1698 at The Hague he concluded a treaty with Louis XIV to divide the Spanish possessions in view of the imminent death of the childless Charles II [(1661-1700)] of Spain.[89] But the agreement could not be implemented. Angered by the project to divide his kingdom, Charles II, after the death in 1699 of the Bavarian prince heir to the throne who had been initially appointed as his successor, drew up a will in favor of the grandson of Louis XIV, Philip, [Duke of] Anjou [(1683-1746)]. When Charles II did die in 1700, Philip of Anjou, with the consent of the King of France, was declared the legitimate sovereign of all the Spanish lands, both European and beyond the ocean.[90]

Having accepted the will, Louis XIV violated a separate treaty concluded with the King of England and aroused the apprehension of all European States regarding the equilibrium, for Philip of Anjou and his descendants might combine the Spanish and French crowns into one person. Therefore, a coalition once more formed against France in which there participated: the German Empire, England, Holland, Prussia, Portugal, and Savoy. Only Spain took the side of the King of France.

[88] Dumont, note 86 above, VII(1), p. 381 et seq; Macauley, note 73 above, IV, p. 788, gives an accurate account of the procedure for conducting diplomatic negotiations at the Ryswyck Congress.

[89] Ranke, note 73 above, VII, p. 152 et seq; Dumont, note 86 above, VII(1), p. 442 et seq.

[90] François-Auguste-Marie-Alexis Mignet, *Négociations relatives à la succession d'Espagne sous Louis XIV* (Paris, 1835-1842), I, Introduction, p. lx et seq. Compare Wheaton, note 1 above, I, p. 115 et seq.

The War of the Spanish Succession (1701-1713) brought France to virtual exhaustion. A series of decisive failures of the French forces forced Louis XIV to sue for peace, ultimately concluded at Utrecht in 1713. The defeated king nonetheless achieved his main goal: Philip of Anjou was recognized as the King of Spain. But thanks to the maintenance of European equilibrium, the Utrecht Peace Treaty determined that France and Spain could never be united under one crown.[91] Moreover, Spain ceded the Belgian provinces to Austria and, in addition (by the 1814 Treaty of Baden), Lombardy and Naples. England acquired Gibraltar, with the Spanish Government retaining an option of first purchase if England for any reason wished to withdraw from the possession of this fortress. France ceded part of its North American colonies to England and obliged itself to raze the fortifications at Dünkirchen [Dunkirk].[92]

After the conclusion of the Utrecht Peace Treaty, material changes occurred in the international system of European States. Louis XIV died in 1715, and France for some time ceased to be a threat to European peace. Sweden, elevated by the genius of Gustavus Adolphus to the level of a first-class European power, was exhausted by the continuous wars of Charles X and Charles XII; in the early eighteenth century, thanks to dissensions of the oligarchic parties over the possession of State power, Sweden withdrew from a leading role in foreign policy. A new powerful State – Russia – for the first time entered into vital relations with Western Europe and, having been victorious in the Great Northern War against its primordial enemy, the Swedes, finally confirmed its own position in the family of cultured European peoples.

§23. Before the eighteenth century the relations of Russia with western States were a rare phenomenon and of a special character. These relations will be understood if one has in view the conditions under which the Russian State was formed. The geographical position of medieval Russia to a significant degree obstructed the development of its relations with western

[91] This provision of the Utrecht Treaty was newly confirmed by diplomatic correspondence between England and France from 1842 to 1847 on the occasion of the marriage of the French Prince, [Antoine] Duke of Montpensier [(1824-1890)] to the sister [Infanta Luisa Fernanda] of the Queen of Spain, Isabella [II (1830-1904)]. William Beach Lawrence, *Commentaire sur les Éléments du droit international: et sur l'Histoire des progrès du droit des gens Henry Wheaton* (Leipzig, 1868-1880), II, p. 209 et seq; Phillimore, note 1 above, III, p. 207.

[92] Dumont, note 86 above, VIII(1), p. 339; Alexandre de Clerq, *Recueil des traités de la France* (Paris, 1880), I, p. 1; compare Garden, note 1 above, II, p. 305 et seq.

peoples.[93] From the thirteenth century to these disadvantageous conditions should be added the invasion of the Tatars, who for two or so centuries disengaged Russia from Western Europe. When the Russian lands little by little assembled around Moscow and formed a State under the sovereign authority of a Tsar, Russia could not quickly act in the role of a subject of international relations. The closed social and State system of Moscow and the insufficient cultural development of its population made these relations impossible and superfluous. Sinification corresponded to the morals and views of Russian society, becoming at the same time a slogan given to it by the government.[94]

On their part, the western European States shunned Muscovites and treated them with hostility. One cannot fail to see the principal reason for this estrangement and enmity in the differences of basic elements of spiritual life of one and the other. The separation of the Greek and Roman churches led to peoples professing Orthodoxy, thanks to the influence of the catholic pontiffs, ceasing to be considered as Christians in the west of Europe and fully-fledged members of European international society. That is why Kievan and then Muscovite Russia maintained relations not with the Latin West, but almost exclusively with Byzantium, with whom it was united by the community of religious faith and, subsequently, when one or the other was subjected to conquest by Asian barbarians, also political interests.

The said unfavorable circumstances were the reason that neither the Russian State nor the Russian people were for a long time aware of the need for international relations. Therefore, until the eighteenth century, when the sovereign authority of the Muscovite State finally became aware of certain goals and interests connecting it with western States, Russia played for the most part a passive role in the field of international relations. Such relations arose at the initiative of foreigners and usually were hoping to achieve commercial advantage or exploitation of the Russian people and the natural wealth of the country. There was and could not be rapprochement between Russian and foreign individuals in the absence of common cultural or political interests.[95]

93 See the accurate comments of Anatole Leroy-Beaulieu, *L'empire des Tsars et les Russes* (Paris, 1881), I, chapters I and III.

94 [Grigorii] Kotoshikhin [(c. 1630-1667)] wrote: "As for the travel of the Muscovites, except those who are sent by edict of the Tsar or for trade with those passing by, to travel is not permitted for any matters". G. Kotoshikhin, О России в царствовании Алексея Михайловича [On Russia in the Reign of Aleksei Mikhailovich] (1840), p. 24.

95 See Aleksandr Gustavovich Brikner, Русские дипломаты-туристы в Италии в XVII

The initial relations of Russia with England were of such a character.[96]

They began in 1553 when the merchant [Richard] Chancellor [(d. 1556)] arrived in Kholmogor and sent a request to the Tsar in Moscow to permit trade in his State. Having received a charter for free trade, Chancellor returned to England, where the Muscovy Company was created for commerce with the unknown Moscow lands. Frequent trips to Moscow by English merchants and even envoys followed; for its part, the Moscow Government sent its representatives to England. By the beginning of the seventeenth century reference was made to the English consul in Moscow. The principal subject-matter of these international relations remained the commercial interests of the English, who advocated not only a trade monopoly within Russia, but also the right of transit through Russia to Persia and India.[97] No earlier than the seventeenth century the relations between England and Moscow changed their character. Convinced of the power and wealth of the English State, the Muscovite tsars began to turn for assistance to England against its malevolent enemies – Sweden and Poland. England did not refuse its services, constantly having in view new commercial advantages. Thus, the Stolbovo Peace (1617) between the Russians and the Swedes was concluded with the mediation of an English plenipotentiary, John Merrick [(c. 1559-1638/39)], who afterwards demanded significant privileges for trade of the English in Muscovy. During the reign of Aleksei Mikhailovich [(1629-1676)], friendly relations with the English cooled for some time as a consequence of news which reached the Tsar about the execution of King Charles I. Aleksei Mikhailovich issued an Edict under which English merchants were banished, together with the consul "for such an evil deed", from Moscow; thereafter they were permitted to arrive only in Archangel and to trade only upon the payment of duties. Friendship was renewed upon the restoration of the Stuarts to the throne; from then on the

столетия [Russian Diplomats-Tourists in the Seventeenth Century] (M., 1878), p. 6 et seq.

[96] F. F. Martens, Собрание трактатов и конвенций, заключенных Россиею с иностранными державами [Collection of Treaties and Conventions Concluded by Russia with Foreign Powers] (Spb., 1874-1909). 15 vols. (hereinafter: F. F. Martens, Собрание трактатов и конвенций [Collection of Treaties and Conventions]), X, Introduction; Iurii Vasil'evich Tolstoi, Первые сорок лет сношений между Россией и Англией 1553-1593 гг. [First Forty Years of Relations between Russia and England 1553-1593] (Spb., 1875), Introduction.

[97] However, sometimes questions of a different nature were raised. In 1569 [Petr G.] Sovin was sent to London as an envoy and ordered to put, *inter alia*, the following question to Queen Elizabeth [(1533-1603)]: "What if, sovereign, some misfortune occurs from enemies, would he be permitted to come to England? Likewise, if the same were to happen to the Queen, she might freely come to Russia".

Moscow Government was more circumspect about the annoying English importunities concerning new trading privileges so prejudicial to Russian traders and to the treasury.

The relations of Russia with Austria, just as with England, did not begin at the initiative of the Muscovite tsars. The Holy Roman Emperor, Friedrich III [(1415-1493)] sent an embassy to Moscow in 1489 requesting the hand for his nephew, Albrecht, Margrave of Baden [(1456-1488)] of one of the daughters of the Grand Prince Aleksandr Vasil'evich, as well as a prohibition against the Pskovites making raids in Livonia. In that same year the Prince of Moscow sent to Austria the Greek Trachaniot with colleagues for negotiations on free intercourse between both States and mutual embassies.

Thus were born permanent diplomatic relations of Russia with Austria, which strengthened over time. The friendliness of relations between the two States was supported, first and foremost, by their geographical position; during the period here considered they were separated by possessions of other States hostile to them, and therefore had no occasions to enter into border conflicts, rather natural between neighboring powers. One important reason for the rapprochement between them was that both States had identical enemies and friends. Indeed, the entire history of Austria proceeds in seizures and acquisitions of neighboring lands with the assistance of marriages, gifts, and conquests which did not always make peoples happy that they acceded by these means. Thus, Belgium and Hungary had many reasons to be dissatisfied with their fate under Austrian authority. Constant troubles and plots arose in these lands opened broad scope for interference in Austrian affairs by neighboring States, Poland and Turkey. The last seized to its advantage a large part of Hungary, and by virtue of the 1545 Treaty of Adrianople, Emperor Ferdinand I [(1503-1564)] was forced to pay annual tribute to the Sultan. Russia had similar unfriendly relations with respect to Poland and Turkey. The grand princes and tsars of Moscow had reason to be apprehensive about the designs of the Polish people for the independence of Russian territory. Poland repeatedly interfered in the internal affairs of Russia and succeeded in seizing many western and southern regions. Naturally, the Moscow princes were sworn enemies of Poland and sought an alliance against Poland with Austrian sovereigns. The Moscow Government was no less hostile towards the Turks, under whose authority were, on one hand, Russian peoples of the same faith in the Balkan Peninsula and, on the other – restless Crimean Tatars who ravaged Russia with their raids. In the struggle against the Ottoman Empire, Russia was again the natural ally of Austria.[98] It is not, therefore, surprising that agreements of alliance

98 See for details relating to the historical development of the relations of Russia with

were constantly concluded between the two powers during the sixteenth and seventeenth centuries directed against their common enemies, Poland and Turkey, and that relations between them remained amicable.[99]

Exceptionally, trade relations existed between Great Novgorod, Pskov, and Smolensk, on one side, and German commercial cities within the Hanseatic League, on the other. They arose in the twelfth century at the initiative of entrepreneurial German traders who carried to the said Russian cities their "households" and lived in a military situation, constantly apprehensive of attacks by the "northern barbarians". But it must be said that the Germans valued Russian markets. They enjoyed extensive trade rights and privileges in Russia which gave them the full opportunity to exploit the Russian people. All aspirations of the German merchants were directed towards an expansion of their freedoms at the expense of the interests of Russian trade and preservation for themselves of a monopoly of trade turnover with Russians. They were not interested either in the social system or the political goals of Great Novgorod or remote Moscow and did not inspire in Russians any desire to become familiar with life beyond the sea. Their mutual relations were confined solely to trade and had no political significance. They ceased in 1478, when with the destruction of the freedoms of Novgorod the German presence, by order of the Grand Prince, was closed and abolished.[100]

On the contrary, relations between the Russian State and the Duchy of Prussia and the Brandenburg Margravinate established in the sixteenth century had political interests as their foundation.

The Duchy of Prussia and the Brandenburg Margravinate achieved their position in the East, using the words of [Leopold von] Ranke [(1795-1886)], by three main instruments: the sword the plough, and the cross. By force of arms, they enslaved the obstinate population of Prussia, by the cross they spread Christianity among this population, under the cover of which culture and civilization developed; finally, by the plough they laid the beginnings of a civil society. Having confirmed their independent political existence on these foundations, both German countries combined under one scepter in the sixteenth century, and at the same time the Elector of

Austria the Introduction to volume one of F. F. Martens, Собрание трактатов и конвенций [Collection of Treaties and Conventions].

99 Fiedler, *Die Allianz zwischen Kaiser Maximilian I und Vasilji Ivanovich, im Jahre 1514* (Vienna, 1863) (Sitzungsbericht der Wiener Academie der Wissenschaften).

100 See Berezhkov, note 63 above, especially Chapter VI et seq; Nikolai Ivanovich Kostomarov, Очерк торговли московского государства в XVI и XVII ст. [Survey of Trade of the Muscovite State in the XVI and XVII Centuries] (Spb., 1862).

Brandenburg was persuaded that an alliance with Moscow represented the most appropriate means of upholding independence against his enemies – Poland and Sweden.

The Kingdom of Poland held Prussia in suzerainty; its possessions were divided by Prussia and Brandenburg. After the merger of the last under the authority of the Elector, the principal goal of the policy of the Berlin Government was liberation from fiefdom relations with Poland and enrichment from the possessions of that State. Pursuing similar goals, the Brandenburg Electors naturally found sympathy and alliance from the Muscovite State. A new basis for rapprochement between them in the seventeenth century was identical hostile relations with neighbor Sweden, who had taken possession of Pomerania and the Baltic territories, which later moved away from it to Prussia and Russia.

Thus, the close rapprochement between Moscow and the Brandenburg Electorate was generated by common vital interests and political aspirations of both States. During the sixteenth and seventeenth centuries the relations of alliance between them were strengthened by diplomatic relations and treaties.[101]

Relations commenced in the sixteenth century between Russia and The Netherlands. During the reign of Grand Prince Vasilii Ivanovich [(1479-1533)], Dutch merchants, thanks to gifts, received an instrument providing for freedom of arrival and trade in the Muscovite State. Just as the English, the Dutch came for negotiations with the tsars and sent an embassy to Moscow for the sole purpose acquiring possible extensive trade rights and privileges.

The relations of Russia with France, by reason of the remoteness of these States from one another, were not extensively developed during the Muscovy period. But these relations were noteworthy because for the first and sole time they were generated at the initiative of the Moscow Government.[102] Upon the advice of the Carnolian ambassador, Baron [Sigismund von] Herberstein [(1486-1566)], Grand Prince Vasilii Ivanovich in 1518 sent an instrument to the King of France requesting assistance against Poland. The King replied with an expression of readiness to render any assistance to the sovereign of Muscovy, but in fact undertook nothing. Also unsuccessful was

101 See Martens, Собрание трактатов [Collection of Treaties], V (Spb., 1880), Introduction.

102 "Résumé historique des relations politiques de la Cour de France avec celle de Russie des le XVII siècle jusqu'au traité de Paris en 1814" (from the Moscow Main Archive of the Ministry of Foreign Affairs). Rambeau, *Recueil des instructions. Russie* (1890), I; F. F. Martens, Собрание трактатов и конвенций [Collection of Treaties and Conventions], XIII, Introduction.

an embassy sent to France by Tsar Mikhail Fedorovich [(1596-1645)] in 1615 with complaints against Polish and Swedish seizures and attacks. The first French embassy arrived at Moscow in 1629: its purpose was to ensure trade rights of the French in Russia, but found it superfluous to enter into an agreement of alliance between France and the Tsar of Muscovy against the Poles. The Moscow Government again sent an embassy to Versailles in 1667 on this subject-matter, once more unsuccessful, but this time thanks to the rudeness of the Moscow ambassador, [Petr Ivanovich] Potemkin [(1617-1700)], who made all possible difficulties for the French court.

The relations of Russia and England, which arose incidentally during the reign of Ivan the Terrible, developed constantly in the sense of peaceful trade. The English succeeded in obtaining exclusive trade and navigation rights, which they enjoyed unobstructed until the end of the nineteenth century. Political interests moved to the forefront in the relations of Russia with England in the reign of Empress Catherine II [(1729-1796)].[103]

The relations of Russia with Sweden were more important and complex. The beginning of these relations goes back to the thirteenth century. The Battle of the Neva opened a series of sanguinary conflicts between the two neighboring peoples who fought for the possession of Northern Rus and the coasts of the Baltic Sea. One may say that from the thirteenth to the eighteenth centuries war was normal in the mutual relations between Russia and Sweden. Therefore, all treaties concluded between them during this period were peace treaties or, more accurately, armistices suspending war for a brief period. Alliances between the two States were a rare exception.

Age-old relations of hostility between Sweden and Russia were resolved by the Great Northern War (1700-1721). On the basis of the Peace Treaty of Nystad (1721), Russia acquired Estland, Lifland, Ingria, the island of Ezel [Saaremaa], part of Karelia, and Finland with the city of Vyborg; other conquered Finnish regions were returned to Sweden. The Russian Government, however, obliged itself not to interfere in internal Swedish affairs and confirmed those privileges and rights which the nobility and urban population of the Baltic territories had enjoyed under Swedish authority.

The Nystad Peace ensured permanent and proper relations with Western Europe. Russia became an essential member of European international society and throughout the eighteenth century not a single more or less serious international question was resolved without Russian participation.

[103] F. F. Martens, Собрание трактатов и конвенций [Collection of Treaties and Conventions], X, Introduction. Compare also: Vasilii Nikiforovich Aleksandrenko, Русские дипломатические агенты в Лондоне в XVIII веке [Russian Diplomatic Agents in London in the XVIII Century] (Warsaw, 1897). 2 vols.

§24. Another power which advanced to the forefront in the eighteenth century and acquired major significance in the field of international relations was Prussia. We pointed above to the conditions which contributed to the elevation of Prussia and Brandenburg in the sixteenth and seventeenth centuries. The aspiration of the Electors of Brandenburg to expand and enhance the political significance their State among the other European powers involved Prussia in a struggle against Austria for predominance in the German Empire. Elector Ferdinand I was crowned in 1701 as the King of Prussia and held this title notwithstanding initial protests of the German Emperor. Taking advantage of propitious circumstances following the death of the German Emperor Charles VI (1740), Friedrich II of Prussia increased his possessions at the expense of the Austrian crown.

On the basis of the Pragmatic Sanction issued by Charles VI, all lands within the Austrian monarchy were to pass to the undivided possession of his eldest daughter, Maria Theresa. This act violated the procedure for succession to the throne in Austria, and it could have been reasonably anticipated that the European powers would not permit the death of the last Hapsburg to be used to make claims to the Austrian succession. To avoid the division of his lands, Charles VI imparted to the Pragmatic Sanction the character of an international act. With great sacrifices, monetary and cessions of land, he achieved the recognition and guarantee of the rights of his daughter by all the major European States.[104]

But the powers who signed the acts of guarantee of the Pragmatic Sanction did not find it convenient to honor their promises. As soon as Charles VI passed away, Bavaria, Saxony, Prussia, Sardinia, and Spain immediately declared their rights to various parts of the Austrian possessions. In alliance with France, the claimants to Austrian possessions formed a coalition against Maria Theresa and, on the basis of a treaty concluded in 1741 at Nymphenburg, agreed to the partition of her State.[105]

The King of Prussia, Friedrich II, pursued his claims most energetically. Not denying the binding force of the Pragmatic Sanction which he had confirmed, he considered his rights to Lower Silesia to be beyond doubt and considered it just to occupy this Austrian region with his own forces. Thus commenced the First Silesian War (1740-1742), unsuccessful for Austria, who pursuant to a peace treaty at Breslau (1742) agreed to the accession of Silesia and the County of Glatz. These acquisitions by the King

[104] Compare Ranke, *Zwölf Bücher preussischer Geschichte* (Leipzig, 1874), V, Book 10; Laurent, note 1 above, XI, p. 232 et seq.

[105] G. F. Martens, *Recueil des traités*, Suppl., I, p. 721.

of Prussia were confirmed by the peace at Dresden (1745),[106] which ended the Second Silesian War between Austria and Prussia (1744-1745), thanks to the intervention of Russia in order to defend the possessions of its ally, the King of Poland.[107]

At the same time, Maria Theresa waged war against France, Bavaria, and Spain, who also coveted territorial acquisitions. This, the War of Austrian Succession (1741-1748), ended more happily for Austria than the Silesian wars with the 1748 Peace Congress at Aachen, held with the participation of Austria, England, Holland, and Sardinia, on one side, and France and Spain, on the other. On the basis of the Aachen Peace Treaty, all conquests made during the War for Austrian Succession were returned, but Austria ceded to Don Philipp [(1720-1765)], the son of Philipp V [(1683-1746)], King of Spain and Elizabeth Farnese [(1692-1766)] its Italian possessions – Parma, Piacenza, and Guastalla, and to the King of Sardinia – part of Lombardy; the King of Prussia was guaranteed the possession of Silesia and Glatz.[108]

The Aachen peace did not establish in the west of Europe that order of things which would have satisfied the wishes and interests of the governments. Austria could not forget the loss of Silesia; France, having lost its entire fleet in the war against England, could not hold any of the territories that it had conquered. Therefore, after the peace in Aachen, the European States again prepared for war and continued to negotiate with one another about the conclusion of new treaties of alliance.

The Russian Government had ample reasons to be distrustful and apprehensive of the King of Prussia. The growing power of Prussia and ambitious plans of conquest of Friedrich II worried Empress Elizaveta Petrovna [(1709-1762)] and inspired her to seek an alliance with enemies of the King of Prussia. When the last violated the Breslau peace treaty, one of the guarantors of which was Russia, the head of Russian policy during the reign of Elizaveta Petrovna, Chancellor [Aleksei Petrovich] Bestuzhev-Riumin [(1693-1766)], finally persuaded the Empress that the vital interests of the Russian State required that limits be placed on the seizures of the King of Prussia, who sought to shake European political equilibrium.[109]

[106] Friedrich August Wilhelm Wenck, *Codex juris gentium* (Leipzig, 1781-1795), I, p. 739; ibid., II, p. 194.

[107] Ranke, *Zur Geschichte von Österreich und Preussen, zwischen den Friedensschlüssen zu Aachen und Hubertusburg* (Leipzig, 1875), p. 65 et seq.

[108] Clerq, note 92 above, I, p. 65; Wenck, note 106 above, II, p. 333 et seq.

[109] "This King", wrote the Chancellor to Count [Mikhail Illarionovich] Vorontsov [(1714-1767)] on 1 August 1744, "being the closest and strongest neighbor of this Empire [Russia] is therefore naturally the most dangerous, even though he is not of such a fickle, acquisitive,

In addition to these political considerations, personal enmity between the Empress and the King of Prussia, insulted by her feminine self-esteem, significantly contributed to the rupture between Russia and Prussia.

Elizaveta Petrovna entered into a defensive alliance in 1746 with Maria Theresa against Prussia and when, by the efforts of Count [Wenzel Anton, Prince of] Kaunitz [-Rietberg (1711-1794)] the Austrian Government, having changed its age-old policy, concluded the Versailles treaty of alliance with France in 1756, Russia adhered to this alliance in the same year.[110]

However, in 1747 the Queen of Hungary and Bohemia [Maria Theresa] concluded a secret agreement with the Elector of Saxony, August III [(1696-1763)] concerning the partition of the Kingdom of Prussia. Having received news about the coalition against him, Friedrich II unexpectedly moved into Saxony in August 1756 and occupied Dresden. The papers of the Dresden Archive seized by Prussian forces confirmed the suspicions of the King of Prussia.[111]

At the outset, thus, of the Seven Years War (1756-1763), Austria, Germany, Saxony, France, and Russia took part on one side, and on the other Prussia in alliance with England. The War brought Friedrich heavy losses. By the end of 1761, the complete exhaustion of Prussia and a series of defeats inflicted on Prussian forces made his situation hopeless. The death of Elizaveta Petrovna and the accession to the Russian throne of Peter III [(1728-1762)] in 1761 saved Friedrich II. The new Russian emperor, who admired the Prussian military system and Friedrich II personally, immediately ordered the cessation of military actions on the part of Russia and concluded a peace treaty with Prussia on conditions specified by Friedrich himself.[112]

Russia, as a result, withdrew from welcome military successes in an extremely expensive War without any reward. The ascension to the throne of Catherine II obstructed the execution of the treaty of alliance between Peter

restless, and outrageous character and disposition as was [Friedrich II]". F. F. Martens, Собрание трактатов [Collection of Treaties], V, p. 337 et seq. On the other hand, Friedrich II wrote in 1748 to Count Finkelstein in St. Petersburg: "Croyez moi, tout bien compté, nous n'avons pas besoin de l'empire muscovite et nous pouvons très bien vivre sans ce dernier". *Politische Correspondenz Friedrich's d. Gr.*, V, No. 2974.

110 F. F. Martens, Собрание трактатов и конвенций [Collection of Treaties and Conventions], I, Nos. 17 and 20.

111 Frédéric II, *Histoire de la guerre de Sept ans. Pièces justificatives*; Ranke, note 107 above, p. 224 et seq.

112 F. F. Martens, Собрание трактатов и конвенций [Collection of Treaties and Conventions], I, No. 29; V, No. 215.

III and Friedrich II, under which Russian forces would join with Prussian for joint actions against Austria and its allies.[113] Catherine II confined herself to confirmation of the peace concluded with Prussia but did not wish to maintain an offensive alliance either with Maria Theresa or with Friedrich II. On the contrary, she exerted every effort to reconcile the adversaries, and her insistence was successful. In 1763 Austria and Prussia signed the Hubertsburg Peace Treaty, which finally confirmed Silesia and the County Glatz for Friedrich. In that same year a peace treaty was concluded at Paris between England, France, and Spain under which virtually all French colonies in America passed to England.[114]

The unparalleled struggle which Friedrich II waged with honor during the Seven Years War not only solidified for Prussia the authority of a first-class European power, but gave Prussia within the German Empire a significance equating her with Austria. Constant antagonism between Austria and Prussia in the affairs of Germany, which was forced to seek allied assistance from neighboring Russia, was noticeable from this time forward.

§25. These three powers were brought together more closely by the Partition of Poland undertaken first in 1773, second in 1793, and bringing an end to the existence of this republic in 1795.

Various views exist in the historical literature as to which of the three powers took the initiative to partition Poland. But all writers are agreed that the principal reason which led to this event was the "deformed" State structure of the *Rzeczpospolita* which made Poland an anarchical country and enabled foreign governments to constantly interfere in its internal affairs.[115]

In any event, the idea of partitioning Poland undertaken in the eighteenth century was nothing new. Back in 1573 the German Emperor proposed to the Tsar of Muscovy, Ivan the Terrible, that Poland be partitioned. During the second half of the eighteenth century, the obvious political fall of the Polish republic generated several projects for its partition. The Porte proposed to divide Poland with Austria in 1769. A year before Prince Kaunitz elaborated an original plan for joining parts of Poland to Prussia in exchange for removing Silesia from Austria.

113 Ibid., V, p. 389 et seq.

114 G. F. Martens, *Recueil des traités*, I, p. 136, 197. [William Pitt, Earl of] Chatham [(1708-1778)] accurately noted: "France lost America to Germany".

115 F. F. Martens, Собрание трактатов и конвенций [Collection of Treaties and Conventions], II, No. 30, Historical Introduction.

The following favorable political circumstances contributed to implementation of the plan to partition Poland in 1772. In 1768 Turkey declared war against Russia, which was rather successful for Russia. Upon the conquest of Moldavia and Wallachia in 1770, Catherine II offered peace to Turkey on condition of recognizing the independence of the Danube principalities and the Crimean Tatars. In view of Austria's interest in this matter, Catherine II sought the mediation of the Cabinet in Vienna. But the last declined, having determined that the peace proposals of the Russian court were not in Austrian interests. In reality, the Viennese Cabinet could not forget that Catherine II had not renewed the 1746 treaty of alliance with them and had drawn closer to the King of Prussia, having concluded an alliance with him in 1764 under which Friedrich II was obliged to assist with money and forces in the event of the attack by another power on Russia.[116] With a view to counteracting the peace conditions offered to Turkey by Catherine II, Austria offered an alliance to The Porte. Thus, war between Austria and Russia seemed inevitable. The King of Prussia was to take part in this War as an ally of Russia. However, Friedrich wanted nothing more than to keep the peace, so essential for his State after a series of destructive wars during the first half of his reign. Seeking a way of preventing a rupture between Austria and Russia, he settled on a combination that should have satisfied his own interests and the interests of adversaries.

Back in 1769 Friedrich had sent to Count [Nikita Ivanovich] Panin [(1718-1783)] a project for the partition of Poland known as the Linarski Plan, which was ignored by the St. Petersburg court. These plans found a more favorable reception in Petersburg after Austria, during a complete peace with Poland, occupied two Polish provinces and seized the salt mines of Bochnia and Wieliczka. Friedrich II reckoned that if Austria would be offered recognition of these seizures and join them to several Polish frontier regions, it would undoubtedly refrain from a militant policy both with respect to Russia and Prussia, and the peace between Russia and the Porte would be secured on advantageous conditions. In view of this, the King of Prussia sent his brother, Prince [Friedrich] Heinrich [Ludwig (1726-1802)] to St. Petersburg in 1771; in personal negotiations with the Empress he demonstrated the great advantage of the proposed Plan.

The final resolution of this question depended on the view which would prevail at the Vienna court. Personally, the Empress-Queen Maria Theresa opposed the partition of Poland. But the leader of Austrian policy, Prince Kaunitz, and the young German Emperor, Jozef II [(1741-1790)] found this

116 Полное собрание законов Российской империи [Complete Collection of Laws of the Russian Empire] (1st series), No. 12119.

participation to be favorable for Austria. They were greatly worried that the Vienna Cabinet would remain outside the agreement already existing on this matter between Russia and Prussia. Therefore, when at the end of 1771 the Austrian court was acquainted in detail with the project for partition, its consent was not long in coming. At the outset of 1772 complete unanimity had been established between the two governments, which led to the First Partition of Polish possessions.[117]

Thanks to the agreement relating to Poland, the Vienna court no longer opposed the peace conditions proposed by Catherine II between Russia and the Porte. On these conditions, the belligerent powers concluded the 1774 Peace Treaty of Kuchuk-Kainardzhii which secured for Russia a leading role on the Balkan Peninsula, retained until the 1856 Peace of Paris.[118]

The fortunate war against Turkey and the successful Partition of Poland elevated the status of Russia to the point that Petersburg became the center in which threads were connected of diplomatic negotiations concerning all European affairs. The great German powers fighting among themselves for supremacy in the German Empire especially had to court Catherine II. The influential role of the Russian Empress in this struggle was noted in 1778 on the occasion of the dispute between Austria and Prussia over the Bavarian Succession: Austria succeeded in concluding with the heir of the late Bavarian Elector, the Pfalz Elector Karl-Theodor [(1724-1799)], a convention under which the last ceded to Austria a significant portion of Bavaria. Immediately afterward, Austrian forces occupied and administered the ceded territories as though it were their own country. Friedrich was resolved not to permit such strengthening of Austria. When negotiations with Austria led to nothing, he advanced forces, and in 1778 a Prussian army of one hundred thousand was sent to Königgrätz, fortified by the Austrians. However, a real war between Prussia and Austria was prevented by the intervention of Russia, to whom both sides turned for mediation. In view of its alliance with France, Austria also invited Russia to take part in the mediation.

Catherine II settled the dispute. At her suggestion, in 1779 a Congress assembled at Teschen and drafted several international treaties.[119] On the basis of the main treaty, Austria concluded peace with Prussia and renounced

[117] F. F. Martens, Собрание трактатов и конвенций [Collection of Treaties and Conventions], II, Nos. 30, 31, 32, 33, 34, 44, 45, 48, 49, 50, 51, 52.

[118] Полное собрание законов Российской империи [Complete Collection of Laws of the Russian Empire] (1st series), No. 14146; G. F. Martens, *Recueil des traités*, II, p. 286.

[119] F. F. Martens, Собрание трактатов и конвенций [Collection of Treaties and Conventions], II, No. 35.

its claims to Bavarian territory. The other conventions annexed to the main act determined the territorial composition of various German States who had joined the dispute of the Bavarian Succession. At the request of the contracting parties, all these acts were guaranteed by the mediating powers. Russia, however, became surety for the Peace Treaty of Westphalia and the order of things created by it in the west of Europe because the Peace of Teschen renewed the force of that major treaty, and likewise the treaties of Breslau, Dresden, and Hubertsburg.

In North America a war of the colonies against England broke out in 1774, with the formation in 1776 of the independent North American states. This event was reflected in the international relations of the European States. Under the influence of strong public sympathy for the colonies struggling for their independence, the King of France, Louis XVI, concluded an alliance with the American republic and declared war against England, who having ended the War under the 1783 Peace Treaty of Versailles, was forced to recognize the independence of the colonies which had fallen away.[120] On the basis of the constitutions of the new power across the Atlantic, European international law was deemed to be an integral part of the State laws thereof.

B. On International Relations from the 1789 French Revolution to the 1815 Congress of Vienna

§26. The unsatisfactory international position which France occupied at the end of the eighteenth century was one reason for the dissatisfaction and hostile mood of the French people against its own government that found its outlet in the 1789 Revolution.[121]

The French people could not forget that thanks to the inability of their rulers it had lost the pre-eminent significance in Europe which it had under Louis XIV. During the eighteenth century, France was deprived of its two main allies – Sweden and Poland. The French Government accepted that the Ottoman Empire, which for centuries had served as the mainstay of French influence in the East, had been defeated by and surrendered to Russia. The alliance with the Austrian Habsburgs and the pathetic role which France played during the Seven Years War convinced the French of the utter bankruptcy of their government, in its lack of skill and inability to maintain the glorious traditions of French policy. To be sure, the struggle for the freedom of the North American colonies was successful for France, but did

[120] G. F. Martens, *Recueil des traités*, III, p. 553.

[121] Compare the capital work by the talented French writer: Albert Sorel, *L'Europe et la revolution française* (Paris, 1885-1892). 5 vols.

not enhance the credit of the French Government in the eyes of the people: on the contrary, it demonstrated the power of French society and incited in the people a hope of conquering their own political freedom destroyed by an absolutist regime.

The revolutionary movement which enveloped France acquired international significance from the very outset. When the National Assembly was convened in France and Louis XVI was forced to renounce the prerogatives of unlimited royal power and to sign a constitution, doubt was increasingly raised in other States whether it was possible to be indifferent to the new order of things. The French emigrants who flooded European courts tirelessly proved that the revolutionary fire of France threatened all monarchies of Europe. The statements and actions of the revolutionaries themselves affirmed this significance of the French Revolution. The decrees of the revolutionary republic were an appeal to the European peoples to rise up against their sovereigns in alliance with and with the assistance of the French people. The leaders of the Convent openly proclaimed that treaties concluded by tyrants could not bind the sovereignty of the people. The French republic clearly sought to make a revolution throughout all of Europe.[122]

The first coalition of European States against France was formed in 1793 under these circumstances. The powers which took part were afraid of the spread of revolutionary ideas and wished to take advantage of the anarchy dominant in France in order to expand their possessions at France's expense. But the coalition did not succeed either in stopping revolutionary propaganda or in enriching themselves. The allied powers demonstrated complete moral and political bankruptcy in the struggle against the French republic. The mercenary calculations and egoistic aspirations divided the allies, and their forces did not fight with enthusiasm for interests alien to them, whereas the French were enthusiastic in defending the new ideas and their independence. A series of defeats suffered by the allies forced the coalition to be dissolved.[123]

[122] [Jacques Pierre] Brissot [(1754-1793)] declared in the National Assembly on 22 December 1792: "La souveraineté des peoples n'est point liée par les traités des tyrans". Jean Marie Hêrault des Séchelles [(1759-1794)] exclaimed: "Partout où il y a un trône, nous avons un ennemi". See Thaine, *La conquête jacobine*, p. 124. The Decrees of the Committee of 10 November and 15 December 1792 are well known: "Guerre aux châteaux, paix aux chaumières". Laurent, note 1 above, XV, pp. 177, 246; Phillimore, note 1 above, I, p. 469.

[123] Barral de Montferrat, note 75 above, I(2), chapter III; Jean François Guillaume, comte de Bourgoing, *Histoire diplomatique de l'Europe pendant la révolution française* (Paris, 1886), IV.

Russia did not take an active part in the first common alliance of European States against the revolution. The uprising in Poland and uncompleted affairs with Turkey prevented Catherine II from satisfying the insistent request of the Austrian court to send a Russian corps to the Rhine. But the Empress did not sympathize with the revolutionary movement in France and was well aware of the danger it threatened to the European order and common interests of monarchies. In view of the successes of French forces and the failures of the allies, she decided finally to send her forces to the theater of war; but death prevented her from fulfilling this intention.[124]

Dissension between the allied States at war with republican France was on display in 1795 when, secretly from Austria, Prussia entered into negotiations with the French Government and concluded the Basel Peace Treaty.[125] By virtue of this Treaty, Prussia renounced further participation in the coalition against France and assumed the duty not to obstruct the left bank of the Rhine being the boundary between France and the German Empire.

Austria remained alone against the victorious French colonel, Napoleon Bonaparte, and after severe losses had to agree peace conditions dictated by the victor. According to the peace concluded at Campo Formio in 1797, Austria ceded Belgium and Lombardy to France, receiving in exchange for these regions Venice with Istria and Dalmatia conquered by Napoleon. In addition, Austria was obliged to withdraw its forces from various German fortresses, including Mainz, on the Rhine, as a result of which the left bank of this River could be occupied by the French.[126]

In order to discuss the peace conditions between the German Empire and France, a Congress was convened in 1797 at Rashtatt, where officials of the Empire recognized the cession of the left bank of the Rhine to France.[127]

The peace concluded between Austria and France was not a long one. The plans of conquest which the French successfully pursued in Italy, Egypt, and Syria and the republican orders which they introduced in the conquered lands were the reason for a new war coalition against France in which Austria, England, Turkey, and Russia participated (1798-1799).[128]

124 F. F. Martens, Собрание трактатов и конвенций [Collection of Treaties and Conventions], II, pp. 281-282.

125 Clerq, note 92 above, I, p. 232.

126 Ibid., I, p. 335; Léopold Neumann, *Recueil des traités conclus par l'Autriche avec les puissances étrangères, depuis 1763 jus'quà nos jours* (Leipzig, 1855-1912), I, p. 576.

127 Clerq, note 92 above, I, p. 345.

128 See the superb work by Heffter, *Der Rastatter Congress und die zweite Coalition*

§27. Having ascended to the throne, Paul I expressed the wish to maintain peace with all States, including revolutionary France. But soon he had to withdraw from the position of neutrality with respect to the French republic, whose government not only did not respect its undoubted rights, but inflicted one insult after another. Russian forces under the leadership of [Alexander Vasil'evich] Suvorov [(1729/30-1800)] were sent to Italy, where they achieved a number of brilliant victories over the French. These victories, however, did not bring the slightest advantage to Russia or its allies. Having achieved, thanks to Suvorov, significant success in Italy, the Austrian Government hastened to take advantage in order to secure their reward from lands conquered by the Russians. When Emperor Paul I declared that he could not allow territorial increment to Austria other than by the common consent of the allies, the Vienna Cabinet set itself the task of interfering in the orders of Suvorov and created all possible difficulties so as to paralyze the military plans of the Field Marshall. In view of the systematic opposition of the Austrian court, by order of Paul I the Russian forces separated from the Austrians and moved into Switzerland. There the small army of [Alexander Mikhailovich] Rimskii-Korsakov [(1753-1840)] was abandoned by the Austrian generals at a critical moment and suffered defeat near Zurich. Suvorov succeeded in saving the remnants of his army only thanks to his genius and exceptional endurance and the valor of Russian forces.[129]

Angered by the perfidy and ambiguous behavior of Austria, in October 1799 Paul I renounced the alliance and broke diplomatic relations with Austria. Friendly relations between Vienna and Petersburg were renewed only with the ascension of Emperor Alexander I to the throne. In a notable instruction of 10 September 1801 given to the Russian ambassador in Vienna, Alexander I set out in detail the basic principles of the political system which he intended to follow in relations with foreign States: "I will never accept the slightest participation in internal troubles in other States, whatever the form of government chosen by peoples at their own wish; they may be in complete amity with my Empire if in relations with me they are guided by the same spirit of justice".[130]

(Bonn, 1878-1879). 2 vols.

[129] Dmitrii Alekseevich Miliutin, История войны России с Францией в царствование императора Павла I в 1799 году [History of the War of Russia against France in the Reign of Emperor Paul I in 1799] (Spb., 1852-1853). 5 vols.

[130] F. F. Martens, Собрание трактатов и конвенций [Collection of Treaties and Conventions], II, p. 374 et seq. Compare, especially for the history of the relations of Russia with France in this epoch F. F. Martens, Собрание трактатов и конвенций [Collection of

As a result of the Russian Emperor's categorical refusal to participate in the coalition against France, Austria again had to make peace with the enemy on conditions dictated to it. A new peace was concluded at Luneville in 1801. Austria confirmed the conditions of the Campo Formio Treaty and recognized the Ardèche and Rhine rivers at the boundaries of France.[131]

A mediation occurred the next year between France and England. Under the 1802 Amiens Peace Treaty, England returned all French colonies conquered by it, but did not return the Island of Ceylon to the Dutch or the Island of Trinidad to the Spaniards.[132]

In 1804 Napoleon took the title of Emperor of France. France then changed its international policy. The French Empire no longer propagandized revolutionary ideas, no longer waged a struggle against monarchical orders and the remnants of feudalism, but clearly endeavored to destroy to its advantage the autonomy of all other European nations. Emperor Alexander I was convinced by bitter experience that his idea expressed in 1801 about the inviolate right of every people to freely dispose of their own internal affairs could not be undertaken with respect to France so long as Napoleon exercised full power. The hypocritical and impertinent attitude of the French Emperor towards all submissions of the Russian Government, the arbitrary violation of treaties, and finally the unceasing seizures on his part of the possessions of others – all these circumstances inspired Alexander I to enter into an alliance with England, who against from 1803 fought against France, tried to persuade others powers to follow its example, and formed a coalition for a common struggle against French infringements.[133]

The third coalition thus formed in 1805 against France was made up of England, Russia, Austria, and Sweden; it did not lead, just as the preceding coalition, to the goals set by the allies, despite the fact that Prussia joined. After the unfortunate Battle of Austerlitz (1805), Austria concluded the Pressburg Peace in 1805 with Napoleon, ceding to France the Tyrol, Venice, and Dalmatia – in all about 1,000 square miles with three million inhabitants.[134]

Treaties and Conventions], XIII (Spb., 1902).

131 August Fournier, *Gentz und Cobenzl* (Vienna, 1880), p. 40 et seq; Neumann, note 126 above, II, p. 1; Clerq, note 92 above, I, p. 424.

132 G. F. Martens, *Recueil des traités*, VII, p. 404; Clerq, note 92 above, I, p. 484.

133 F. F. Martens, Собрание трактатов и конвенций [Collection of Treaties and Conventions], II, Nos. 54 and 56.

134 Neumann, note 126 above, II, p. 185; G. F. Martens, *Recueil des traités*, VIII, p. 388.

Having destroyed the resistance of Austria, Napoleon undertook a number of measures to finally make western continental Europe subject to his will and break the resistance of England. In 1806 he founded the Rhine Union of sixteen German States and declared himself to be the Protector of these States under his unconditional sway. Under these conditions, the existence of the German Empire was made impossible, and it was *de facto* abolished.

Against his most malevolent enemy – England, Napoleon introduced in 1806 a measure known in history as the "continental system". By two decrees, Berlin and Milan, he declared a blockade of the British Isles, communication with which was prohibited under pain of punishment; English subjects on the continent were declared to be prisoners of war; English property was subject to confiscation; trade in English goods was forbidden. Napoleon by agreements and threats forced European States to join the continental system. But England did not submit. On its part, England established the "starvation system", having declared a blockade of all ports and coasts of France and allied powers and ordered the confiscation of any ship and cargo destined for one of these ports.[135]

Russia, in alliance with England, continued the war against Napoleon. At the same time, the Emperor of France learned about a secret agreement between these powers and the King of Prussia in 1805. Therefore, in 1806 he began military actions against Prussia and, after a series of decisive defeats of Prussian forces, occupied Berlin. The Russian Army was unable to stop the victorious advance of the French and suffered defeat at Friedland. Then Friedrich Wilhelm III [(1770-1840)] and Alexander I entered into peace negotiations with Napoleon, the treaty being signed at Tilsit in 1807 during a personal meeting of the three monarchs. Prussia was deprived of 2,700 square miles of territory with five million inhabitants. The ceded lands were joined partly to France and partly to new States created by Napoleon – the Kingdom of Westphalia and the Duchy of Warsaw. Russia acquired the Białystok region, but had to adhere to the Continental System.[136]

At Tilsit Alexander I not only made peace with Napoleon, but also concluded an alliance with him. The last was confirmed at a Congress in Erfurt (1808), where both emperors agreed to divide Europe between

135 Gabriel Massé, *Le droit commercial dans les rapports avec le droit des gens et le droit civil* (3d ed.; Paris, 1861), §244. See also F. F. Martens, О праве собственности во время войны [On the Right of Ownership During War] (Spb., 1869), p. 49.

136 F. F. Martens, Собрание трактатов и конвенций [Collection of Treaties and Conventions], XIII, p. 276 et seq. Heinrich von Treitschke, *Deutsche Geschichte*, I, p. 264 wrote: "indeed, only out of respect for the Tsar did Napoleon confine himself to performing only half of his firm decision to destroy Prussia".

themselves, Russia receiving complete freedom of action with respect to Sweden and the Ottoman Empire and the French emperor becoming the ruler of western European States.[137]

Indeed, after the Tilsit peace, Napoleon saw no obstacle to his ambitions. He treated European States as his vassals. In the event of the slightest resistance to his will, French forces occupied their lands. Under these conditions, Austria again took up arms, not finding any other way to preserve their independence against the infringements of the French emperor. Thus a new war commenced between Austria and France (1809). Alexander I performed the obligations assumed at Tilsit and, for his part, declared war against Austria. Russian forces occupied Galicia. In a battle at Wagram the Austrians were beaten and under the Schönbrun (or Vienna) treaty (1809) gave 2,058 square miles of their possessions with 3.5 million inhabitants to France; part of Galicia went to Russia.[138]

Only one State now remained on the European mainland which might resist Napoleon and restrain his ambitious notions. For unlimited dominion in Europe, Napoleon had to put an end to Russia. After the Schönbrun Peace, Napoleon began to disrespect his obligations with regard to the Russian sovereign, so that a rupture between them was inevitable. But the calculations by the French emperor of an easy victory over his ally were not justified. The War of 1812 led to the complete rout of the French Army and Napoleon's flight from Russia.

Alexander I decided not to conclude a peace with France so long as it was not introduced within his former historical boundaries. The immediate task of Russian policy after the expulsion of the French from Russia was to unite the European States into a single alliance to struggle for freedom, order, and quiet in Europe.[139] On the basis of the Kalisch Treaty (1813), Prussia joined the existing coalition of England, Sweden, and Russia against Napoleon. Austria allied itself with Russia after the failed Prague Congress.[140]

[137] Paul Hassel, *Geschichte der preussischen Politik 1807 bis 1815* (Leipzig, 1881), I, p. 273 et seq. Compare Albert Vandal, *Napoléon et Alexandre I. La paix de Tilsit* (Paris, 1891-1893). 2 vols.

[138] Clerq, note 92 above, II, p. 143. Compare F. F. Martens, Собрание трактатов и конвенций [Collection of Treaties and Conventions], III, p. 33 et seq.

[139] In the Russian Government at the time there were two opposed views relating to the policy of Russia after the expulsion of the French. See F. F. Martens, Собрание трактатов и конвенций [Collection of Treaties and Conventions], III, p. 93 et seq.

[140] Ranke (ed.), *Denkwürdigkeiten des Staatskanzlers Fürsten von Hardenberg*, IV, p. 357 et seq; Wilhelm Oncken, *Österreich und Preussen im Befreiungskriege* (Berlin, 1876), I, p. 269; II, p. 163; Bailleu, in Sybel, *Historische Zeitschrift*, no. 1 (1877), p. 139 et seq; F.

The Battle of Leipzig forced other German states to withdraw from the alliance with Napoleon and join the coalition. In early 1814 an enormous allied army passed over the Rhine and invaded France. At Chaumont the major allied powers (Russia, Austria, Prussia, and England) concluded a new treaty affirming the need for the allies to continue the war against the French emperor so long as he failed to accept the peace conditions proposed and not to enter into separate negotiations with him nor sign a peace other than with common consent.[141]

The war of all Europe against Napoleon ended with the entry of allied forces into Paris, the removal of the French emperor from the throne signed at Fontainebleau, and the ascension to the throne of Louis XVIII [(1755-1824)], a representative of the old Bourbon dynasty. Then the first Paris Treaty of Peace was concluded between the allied powers and France,[142] on the basis of which its territorial boundaries were restored in that form which they existed on 1 January 1792; Prussia's former possessions were returned to it; Austria received Venice and Milan for Belgium, which was to be united with The Netherlands in a single State; Germany was to be organized in the form of a confederation.

A Congress was convened at Vienna for the final determination of the peace conditions, distribution of conquered lands, and arrangement of the political system of Europe. Its work was approaching an end when news was received of Napoleon's escape from the Island of Elba, landing in France, and ceremonial entry into Paris. By a Declaration of 13 March 1815, eight European powers solemnly deemed the Napoleon Bonaparte who had returned to France to be outside the protection of "civil and social relations, and likewise the enemy and the destroyer of peace". Napoleon, said this remarkable document, "betrayed himself to public opinion".[143]

F. Martens, Собрание трактатов и конвенций [Collection of Treaties and Conventions], III, p. 111 et seq.

141 Neumann, note 126 above, II, p. 440.

142 Clerq, note 92 above, II, p. 414; Документы для истории дипломатических сношений России с западными державами европейскими от заключения всеобщего мира в 1814 до конгресса в Вероне в 1822 года [Documents for the History of Diplomatic Relations of Russia with Western Powers from Conclusion of Universal Peace in 1814 to the Congress of Verona in 1822] (Spb., 1823-1825), I, p. 1 et seq; Полное собрание законов Российской империи [Complete Collection of Laws of the Russian Empire] (1st series), No. 25587.

143 Léonard Chodźko [Comte de Angeberg pseud.] and [Jean Baptiste Honoré Raymond Capefigue], *Congrès de Vienne et les traités de 1815* (Paris, 1864), p. 912.

For one hundred days Napoleon was once more a common danger to all of Europe, and the great allied powers united for war against the violator of European peace. The Battle of Waterloo finally decided the fate of Napoleon; he was forced again to renounce the throne and exiled to the Island of St. Helena. The second Paris Peace concluded in the aftermath reduced French territory to the boundaries which it possessed in 1790; France had to pay a Contribution of 700 million francs, and was subjected to occupation for five years by 150,000 allied forces in order to make the return of Napoleon to the French throne impossible and to ensure the preservation of the new order of things in France created by the allies.[144]

§28. It is evident from the foregoing survey of political relations of the European States that from the Peace Congress of Westphalia to the beginning of the nineteenth century wars and divisions of the possessions of others comprised the exclusive subject of attention by sovereigns and their ministers. Power and arbitrariness, however, were not the sole factors of international relations in this period. Together with countless examples proving disrespect for the independence of foreign States and the failure to perform obligations most solemnly assumed, we have evidence that during the seventeenth and eighteenth centuries the European civilized peoples recognized the legal force of international law not only during peacetime, but during wartime.

We point to certain major positive legal principles which were developed in international relations of this epoch and became an integral part of international law.

First, an important result of the foreign policy activity of the European States after the Peace of Westphalia and those private and general agreements into which they entered with one another during this period was the precise identification of the basic rights belonging to States and the sovereign authorities as subjects of international law. Moreover, the need for permanent diplomatic relations and negotiations between States embedded in consciousness and practice the necessity to respect the personal and property inviolability of envoys, their extraterritoriality, and other privileges which constitute the law of embassies.[145]

[144] Clerq, note 92 above, II, p. 661; Documents, note 142 above, II, p. 25; Полное собрание законов Российской империи [Complete Collection of Laws of the Russian Empire] (1st series), No. 25984.

[145] The universal outrage aroused in Europe by the insidious murder of French envoys at the 1799 Rastadt Congress consolidated the awareness of the inviolability of diplomatic agents. See Heffter, note 128 above, II, p. 312 et seq.

The international law of the sea achieved a high level of development in this period. On 28 February 1780, Catherine II issued the notable Declaration of Armed Neutrality in which the following binding principles during warfare at sea were proclaimed: 1) war does not terminate peaceful international intercourse between ports of belligerent and neutral States; 2) enemy property on a neutral ship is inviolate unless it constitutes military contraband; 3) by military contraband is understood the articles enumerated in Articles 10 and 11 of the 1766 Treaty of Commerce between Russia and England; 4) for the validity of a blockade of a port it is essential that access thereto be actually terminated by an enemy squadron in proximity; 5) the said principles should serve as the grounds for a legal proceeding. This Declaration received the significance of a generally-binding international law because it was accepted by and obliged the majority of European powers, except England, to defend by force against any violator. At the initiative of Emperor Paul I in 1800 the Second Armed Neutrality was concluded with merely a change in the definition of blockade and the addition of new rules concerning the inspection of a ship.[146]

In addition, during the second period the view on mutual relations of belligerents during war on land changed significantly for the better: prisoners of war were not converted into slaves; they were recognized as legitimate enemies with regard to whom an adversary has certain rights, but also duties; on the basis of individual treaties concluded between States in the event of war, medical personnel and military hospitals enjoyed a certain inviolability from belligerents, and so on.[147]

Finally, the general principle which underlay all diplomatic negotiations, congresses, and wars originating in the seventeenth and eighteenth centuries – the idea of political equilibrium –shows that States were sensitive to the insistent need for an international order which would ensure their national independence and their legitimate interests and rights.

After the Peace of Westphalia, sovereigns and their representatives no longer found it possible, as before, to undertake international acts without explaining the reasons for them, having at least the appearance of justice and right. The equilibrium of States was principally such a reason. In the name of this principle, States entered into alliances and formed coalitions; for the sake of this they declared war and divided the territories of others. The entire task of international policy of the seventeenth and eighteenth

[146] Martens, note 135 above, p. 251 et seq.

[147] G. F. Martens, *Recueil des traités*, II, p. 74; F. F. Martens, Собрание трактатов и конвенций [Collection of Treaties and Conventions], II, Nos. 37 and 38. See in particular ibid., IX, p. 259 et seq. Also Martens, note 135 above, p. 241 et seq.

centuries consisted of maintaining equilibrium. But at the same time the idea of political equilibrium served as a justification for all possible violence and seizures, violations of law and the basis for illegal claims on the part of monarchs and their advisors.[148]

It is evident that the equilibrium of States, as understood in the second period, if it referred to the awareness by European educated peoples of their close interests and mutual dependence on one another, then it could not serve as grounds for determining their mutual rights and duties and the establishment of an international legal order. The system of political equilibrium was based on a political idea serving as a distinctive instrument for all possible seizures and unjust attacks.

The European political system created by the Westphalian Peace Congress was destroyed by the conquests of the French Revolution and the Empire of Napoleon I. The European States having triumphed by uniting against them, they laid the beginnings of the new international order existing today. The role and significance which revolutionary and Imperial France had in this respect is fully explained by the radical restructuring of its social and State system thanks to the 1789 Revolution. The new social and political orders established in France after 1789 replaced the old monarchical regime and were the cause of transformations in the internal existence of the European peoples, duly reflected in international relations.

Considered from this standpoint, the wars and conquests of Napoleon had enduring international significance. Napoleon won in Europe less by force of arms and more by the propaganda of new free ideas proclaimed by the Declaration of Rights of Citizen and Man. The French forces spread these ideas in those States which they occupied and everywhere met the sympathies of peoples for the free political orders which they established in the conquered lands. Napoleon brilliantly understood the significance of propaganda: in instructions and manifestos he constantly declared that war is being waged against feudal orders detested by all peoples and he wished to base his own authority not on the enslavement of peoples, but on their sympathy.

148 "Political equilibrium" is first mentioned in the 1713 Treaty of Utrecht. But over time the concept of equilibrium constantly changed and was defined variously. See, for example, the definitions of Prince Charles Maurice de Talleyrand- [Périgord (1754-1838)], in *Correspondance inédite du prince de Talleyrand* (Paris, 1881), preface, p. xvi. Compare Friedrich von Gentz, *Fragmente aus der neuesten Geschichte des politischen Gleichgewichts in Europa* (Leipzig, 1803), p. 71 et seq. In addition, Bernard, note 77 above, p. 97; August von Bulmerincq, *Das Völkerrecht oder das internationale Recht: Systemisch dargestelt* (2d ed.; Freiburg i B., 1889), p. 40 et seq; Phillimore, note 1 above, I, p. 483.

That is why initially the French did not encounter that hatred and resistance on the part of western European peoples on which their sovereigns had counted. But the character of the struggle between the last and Napoleon changed in 1813. From that time in Germany, Italy, and Spain the people's enthusiasm reached unprecedented scales; all their peoples collected around the monarchs for a war for freedom and independence of their States. This change is explained, on one hand, by the fact that peoples were convinced of the true intentions and goals of Napoleon, who aspired more to enhance his personal imperial power than to secure the well-being and interests of his subjects, and on the other, by those promises which were given to peoples by their sovereigns with regard to the political orders, free administration, and legislation to ensue upon the liberation from the French yoke. The struggle of peoples for freedom and rights of which they were aware led to the fall of Napoleon.

Third Period
From Congress of Vienna to Present Time

A. International Relations from 1815 Congress of Vienna to 1856 Paris Peace

§29. On the basis of the first 1814 Treaty of Paris, the contracting powers agreed to convene a Congress at Vienna for the final determination of territorial acquisitions made during the recent War and the grounds on which the European political system destroyed by the conquests of the French Revolution and Empire of Napoleon should rest. The sessions of this major Congress were opened on 1(13) November 1814 with the personal participation of three monarchs – Russian, Austrian, and Prussian – and the representation of virtually all European States.

Three kinds of views were identified at the Congress, the plenipotentiaries of the powers considering it possible to resolve complex and difficult questions subject to discussion.

The first view, a representative of which was the Austrian Chancellor, [Klemens Wenzel Nepomuk Lothar, Prince of] Metternich- [Winneburg zu Beilstein (1773-1859)], denied the need for any general principle and firm plan for structuring the fates and mutual relations of European peoples: all should be decided by the circumstances, diplomatic intrigues, and compromises. According to this view, international relations and diplomatic negotiations must be determined only by the principle of chance.[149]

The point of departure for the second approach was the principle of legitimacy (*principe de légitime*). It sought to build a European system on historical law, on those principles which dominated in Europe before the French Revolution. Prince [Charles-Maurice de] Talleyrand [(1754-1838)] was the principal proponent of this approach, the plenipotentiary of France who successfully combined the new principle with the principle of political equilibrium and demonstrated that both principles should serve as the basis of a stable international order of Europe. The majority of State officials taking part in the Congress of Vienna shared the views of the French diplomat thanks to the brilliant and witty argumentation of Talleyrand in support of his opinions and because a large portion of the members of the Congress feared revolutionary movements and wished nothing more than the restoration of the old legitimate order of things.[150]

Above these views on the task and significance of the Congress of Vienna were the views of the noted Prussian Minister, [Heinrich Friedrich Karl vom und zum] Stein [(1757-1831)], which Emperor Alexander I shared as well. The last expressed them well in general instructions of 13(25) May 1815 supplied to all foreign Imperial missions. European policy, according to these instructions, had to set itself the task "to study and conform to the moral situation of various peoples in order to determine in accordance with the common point of view the territorial composition, internal orders, and likewise the mutual relations of States, the combination of which should comprise from that time the great European family". Respect for the rights and interests of peoples – that is the principle which, in the view of Alexander I, should guide the Congress of Vienna. The allied governments, following this principle, should have granted to the peoples the "advantages of the governmental system"; then satisfied people's interests "would impart to the decisions of the Congress that stability and force of permanency which cannot be secured for them by any other guarantee".[151]

But these lofty ideas were far from consistently implemented. The religious-mystical approach so clearly expressed in the Act of the Holy

[149] Compare *Mémoires du prince de Metternich* (Paris, 1880), I, p. 30 et seq; Treitschke, note 136 above, I, p. 604 et seq.

[150] *Correspondance*, note 148 above, pp. 223, 447, 463; *Mémoires de Talleyrand*, II, p. 272 et seq; Friedrich Brockhaus, *Das Legitimitätsprincip* (Leipzig, 1868).

[151] F. F. Martens, Собрание трактатов и конвенций [Collection of Treaties and Conventions], III, pp. 210-211.

Alliance of 14(26) September 1815 was led by the actions and instructions of Alexander I at the Congress of Vienna.

The subject-matter of this Act, as was solemnly declared by the sovereigns who signed it, was to "open in the face of the universe their unshakeable determination both in the administration of the States entrusted to them, and in political relations with all other governments, to be guided by no other rules than by the commandments of holy faith, love, truth, and peace".[152] It is understandable that this decision could not be reconciled with the need to conform to the legitimate interests of peoples and to introduce a constitutional form of government in the European States. For the sake of maintaining peace and friendship with his allies, Alexander I often departed from those principles which he considered to be just and favored principles and measures proposed at the Congress by Talleyrand and Metternich that he did not like.[153]

However, the principle of legitimacy so celebrated at the Congress of Vienna also could not be applied strictly. Together with the diplomatic intrigues of Metternich, it led to the fact that States who participated in the Congress found it difficult to come to an agreement on the most important issues under discussion. The firm decision of Alexander I to join the entire Duchy of Warsaw to Russia and the demand of Prussia with regard to the Kingdom of Saxony encountered such a hostile rebuff on the part of the other powers that in early 1815 a rupture between the allies was inescapable. Austria, England, and France also concluded (3 January 1815) an offensive and defensive alliance against Russia and Prussia to which Holland and Bavaria adhered, and only the return of Napoleon from the Island of Elba forced the great allied powers to combine again and end their sessions at the Congress peacefully.[154]

The Act of the Congress of Vienna was signed on 28 May (9 June) 1815. Its main provisions concerning territorial changes of the European States consisted of the following.[155] Russia received the Duchy of Warsaw, except for Poznan Province, which went to Prussia. Part of Galicia joined to

[152] G. F. Martens, *Nouveau Recueil*, II, p. 656; F. F. Martens, Собрание трактатов и конвенций [Collection of Treaties and Conventions], IV(1), No. 99. Compare Mémoires, note 149 above, I, p. 210.

[153] Edmondo Mayor, *Il trattato della Santa Aleanza e la signora di Krüdner* (Torino, 1883).

[154] Clerq, note 92 above, II, p. 447. Compare *Correspondance*, note 148 above, p. 211; *Mémoires*, note 149 above, II, p. 474 et seq.

[155] F. F. Martens, Собрание трактатов и конвенций [Collection of Treaties and Conventions], III, Nos. 79-96; Angeberg, note 143 above.

Russian possessions by virtue of the 1809 Treaty of Vienna was returned to Austria; the southern part of the Duchy of Warsaw with the City of Krakow constituted an autonomous and perpetually neutral Krakow Republic under the special protection of Russia, Austria, and Prussia. It existed until 1846, when by decision of the three said powers, it was joined to Austrian possessions.

Austria was restored to its former possessions that belonged to it prior to the Campo Formio, Luneville, and other treaties, and in addition acquired the remaining part of Venice and extensive regions comprising Lombardy.

Prussia obtained almost half of the Kingdom of Saxony; lands taken from Prussia under the Tilsit peace were rejoined to it; moreover, its possessions were increased by many cities and units lying on both banks of the Rhine and other German lands.

All sovereign German sovereigns and free cities, and also the Austrian emperor, Prussian, Danish, and Dutch kings founded a perpetual alliance under the name of the German Union managed by a Diet under the chairmanship of an Austrian plenipotentiary. The former Belgian provinces were combined with Holland into one State under the name Kingdom of the Netherlands. It was to serve as a bulwark against the expansionist plans of France.

Switzerland received back the regions removed from it and Swiss territory was recognized as neutral in perpetuity.

The former Republic of Genoa was joined with the Kingdom of Sardinia. The northeastern provinces which belonged to the King of Sardinia were declared to be neutral, just as Switzerland.

Negotiations proceeded at the Congress of Vienna on the development of peaceful and proper relations between peoples. These questions included: freedom of navigation on rivers; trade in negroes; and the rank of diplomatic agents.

As regards the first question, taking into account the important commercial significance of those navigable rivers which flow through the possessions of several States or serve as their boundaries, the Congress of Vienna developed a number of articles on the basis of which navigation through all such rivers was declared to be completely free to the commerce of all nations; moreover, fiscal rights and police duties which riparian States have with respect to these rivers were precisely determined. These provisions subsequently were applied to all major European rivers that have the significance of commercial arteries for international exchange.

With regard to trade in dark-skinned persons, the powers promulgated a Declaration at the Congress of Vienna which abolished forever this inhuman sector of trade. This Declaration was developed in special international conventions which determined general measures on the part of governments that should have promoted the real cessation of trade in negroes.

Finally, the Congress of Vienna developed a special statute relating to diplomatic agents. With a view to preventing in the future the onerous disputes between representatives of various powers in foreign States, first, the classes of diplomatic agents were determined and, second, their mutual relations when taking seats, signing, and concluding treaties.[156]

§30. The general character of international relations of the European States after 1815 reflects the mood of European peoples from the time of their liberation from the French yoke. Hopes for extensive State reforms inspired by the solemn proclamations of governments during the war for independence rapidly were replaced by general disenchantment.[157] The Congress of Vienna and subsequent reactionary measures adopted in common by European sovereigns finally convinced the western peoples that the promises given to them would not be honored. The natural result of the unsatisfied legitimate expectations of western European societies was everywhere the fermentation of minds, the aspiration of peoples to free themselves from feudal restraints that hindered the development of social life, and to take part in State administration.

For the standpoint of public interests, the international relations of this period represent the aggregate of phenomena causally dependent on the goals and tasks pursued by social classes within the States.

Thus, religion did not exert at this time a direct impact on international relations in the sense that a difference of faith did not cause international wars or serve as an obstacle to permanent peaceful international relations. On the contrary, an awareness of the community of religious interests is reflected during this period in the aspiration of European peoples to protect the freedom of conscience everywhere, the right of each people to profess their religious convictions and beliefs without obstruction, especially Christianity. The demand for full tolerance of faith within a State forced educated peoples to treat with sympathy and go to the assistance of a people whose religious views and faith is being subjected to oppression or forcible limitations. The history of the Greek uprising and attitude of Christian

[156] The international significance of the last provisions of the Congress of Vienna are well explained in Treitschke, note 136 above, I, p. 595 et seq.

[157] The promises of the Prussian Proclamation of 17 March 1813 are well known. See Hardenberg's *Denkwürdigkeiten*, IV, p. 390; Oncken, note 140 above, I, p. 284 et seq.

Europe to Turkey was evidence of the influence of religious convictions and spiritual aspirations.[158]

In the domain of intellectual and spiritual interests the European peoples were aware during the period here considered of common tasks linking them. As the constraints on the freedom of scientific research, press, and speech gradually fall within European States, as intellectual life, literature, artistic, and performing arts of peoples acquire greater dimensions, as the exchange of products of intellectual and spiritual labor expands, the need grows to determine the conditions of this kind of exchange. Literary conventions protecting literary and artistic property of authors were concluded.

Then economic activity, developing strongly during this period, creates one society of all the European peoples imbued with the aspiration to transform those material resources essential for man to struggle against surrounding external nature and to develop spiritual capacities and forces. Not finding on its own territory all the resources to satisfy their legitimate needs, individual peoples interact with one another as necessary, enter into international commercial intercourse, conclude trade treaties, arrange common unions – postal, telegraph, and others. The great truth is increasingly identified, that contemporary man, in acquiring and increasing his personal resources, uses the labor of all peoples, all mankind. In a word, the contemporary economic activity of peoples increasingly acquires a cosmopolitan and legal character.[159]

Finally, an awareness of tribal and national origin not only serves in the period under consideration as a factor uniting various States, but is regarded as the highest principle of the entire international order. By the power of their inner being, all the stated public interests strive for a certain organization, a specific external order and definition by law; all public elements have one goal – to influence or dominate the State. Moreover, a State is a member of the international community, and therefore it is understandable how, especially in the present century, public aspirations should impact international relations.

§31. After the Congress of Vienna, the reactionary policy of European governments has as its result kinds of international acts which were completely contrary to the public needs and aspirations of peoples. Having formed a so-called pentarchy (five powers), the great powers adopted a rule

[158] The history of the Greek uprising and relations of Christian Europe with Turkey are evidence of such influence of religious convictions and spiritual aspirations.

[159] Compare Lorenz von Stein, *Geschichte der socialen Bewegung in Frankreich von 1789 bis auf unsere Tage* (Leipzig, 1850-1855), I, pp. 287, 303 et seq.

to intervene in the internal affairs of independent States in those instances when the order established therein represented, in their view, a danger to peace in Europe.[160] Given the general hostile mood at the time of western European societies against reaction and the aspirations of peoples for political freedom, there was no shortage of occasions for such intervention.

In 1818 a Congress assembled again at Aachen, composed of representatives of the great powers; monarchs were present from Russia, Austria, and Prussia. This Congress reduced the period for the occupation of French territory by allied forces and the Contribution imposed on France was lowered. Rules developed at the Congress of Vienna relating to diplomatic agents and the definition of the rank of resident ministers were added at Aachen. Finally, a declaration issued by plenipotentiaries of the great powers with regard to negotiations at the Aachen Congress confirmed the close alliance of the participating monarchs and announced that the last deemed it to be their immutable duty to be guided in relations among themselves and with other powers by the principles of international law. Moreover, the five allied sovereigns decided to gather in the future at congresses or conferences to discuss in common both own interests and questions with regard to which other States had applied with a request for intervention.[161]

But the Aachen Congress did not resolve those issues of interest to European societies. On the contrary, both the meetings of this Congress and subsequent measures of the Vienna Cabinet which inspired European policy at the time showed that the great powers were firmly resolved not to permit in continental monarchical States either liberal reforms emanating from governments and the more so internal coups d'état in favor of social freedom and human rights. To this end a conference was held in 1819 of representatives of German states in Carlsbad and Vienna at the initiative of Austria to prevent the spread of revolutionary ideas in Germany; a number of provisions were drafted in opposition to social movements in the German Union.[162]

160 Prince Metternich expressed the motto of his own reactionary policy as follows: "L'Europe fait aujourd'hui pitié à homme d'esprit et horreur à l'homme vertueux". *Mémoires*, note 149 above, III, pp. 426, 445.

161 G. F. Martens, *Nouveau Recueil*, IV, p. 554; Documents, note 142 above, Iii, pp.351, 373 et seq; F. F. Martens, Собрание трактатов и конвенций [Collection of Treaties and Conventions], VII, Nos. 288-296. Compare Alfred Stern, *Geschichte Europas seit den Verträgen von 1815 bis zum Frankfurter Frieden von 1871* (Berlin, 1894-1897). 2 vols.

162 *Mémoires*, note 149 above, III, No. 334, p. 283 et seq; G. F. Martens (Murhard), *Recueil des traités*, IV, p. 8. Compare Stern, note 161 above, I, p. 540 et seq.

Revolutions in Spain, Portugal, Naples, and Sardinia were regarded by the great allied powers as all-European affairs which required intervention and restoration by force of the legal order of things. In 1820 the plenipotentiaries of Austria, Prussia, and Russia assembled in a Congress at Troppau and the following year at Laibach to discuss common measures against revolutionary uprisings flaring up in various European States, especially means of suppressing the revolution in the Kingdom of Naples. The Congress of Laibach decided that Austrian forces would occupy Naples and destroy the Constitution which the King of Naples had to give to his people.[163] The Spanish Revolution was discussed at the Congress of Verona (1822), and executed with respect to the revolutionary Cortes of France. This time the English Government formally refused to approve measures adopted by the Congress and constantly defended the principle of non-interference in the internal affairs of other States.[164]

An uprising of Greeks flared up in 1821 against the Turkish yoke. Initially, both Metternich and Alexander I reacted hostilely to the Greek Revolution and favored the side of the Sultan, which disturbed the Greeks. But the influence of public opinion, especially of England, rapidly forced the European governments to abandon their passive position and stand up for an oppressed Christian people. From the formation in England of the tenure in office of [George] Canning [(1770-1827)] and the ascension to the Russian throne of Emperor Nicholas I, both the Russian and English governments decided to compel Turkey to make concessions to the Greek people. At Petersburg in 1826 Russia and England signed a Protocol which obliged them to intervene in the war against the Turks and grant to Greece those rights which the Danube principalities enjoyed if their demands were not satisfied by the Sultan. The Petersburg Protocol was changed in London into an international convention in 1827 which France also signed.[165] The allied powers sent their fleets to the Archipelago in order to obstruct the

[163] Nicomede Bianchi, *Storia della diplomazia Europea in Italia dall'anno 1814 all'anno 1861* (Torino, 1865-1872), II, p. 33 et seq; Georg Gottfried Gervinus, *Geschichte des neunzehnten Jahrhunderts seit den Wiener Verträgen* (Leipzig, 1855-1866), IV, p. 148 et seq; F. F. Martens, Собрание трактатов и конвенций [Collection of Treaties and Conventions], IV(1), Nos. 122-123; Treitschke, *Deutsche Geschichte im XIX-ten Jahrhundert*, III, p. 131 et seq; Stern, note 161 above, I, p. 103, et seq.

[164] F. F. Martens, Собрание трактатов и конвенций [Collection of Treaties and Conventions], XI, p. 242, et seq; Bianchi, note 163 above, II, p. 107 et seq; Lawrence, note 91 above, II, p. 287.

[165] G. F. Martens, *Nouveau Recueil*, VII, p. 40. Compare F. F. Martens, Собрание трактатов и конвенций [Collection of Treaties and Conventions], IV(1), Nos. 130 and 131; XI, p. 344 et seq.

carriage of ammunition and military supplies to Greek coasts. The Battle of Navarin, which culminated in the burning of the Turkish and Egyptian fleet, led to the Russo-Turkish War of 1828-1829. According to the Peace of Adrianople with Russia, the Sultan had to recognize the independence of Greece, which in 1830 on the basis of the London Protocol, was declared to be a Kingdom and the Bavarian Prince Otto [Friedrich Ludwig (1815-1867)] occupied the Greek throne.[166]

The Greek uprising opened a series of internal coups d'état in European States which destroyed the old regime supported by the great powers and changed the political system of Europe created by the Congress of Vienna. The 1830 French Revolution did not generate the intervention of Austria and Russia because King Louis Philippe hastened to declare that the 1815 Treaty of Vienna was binding. The example of the French attracted neighboring Belgium. Simultaneously with the July Revolution, the Belgians rose up against the detested Dutch Government. With the assistance of France and England, they separated from Holland and, by virtue of the 1831 London treaty, Belgium was declared to be an autonomous and perpetually neutral Kingdom whose throne was occupied by Prince Leopold of Saxe-Coburg [and Gotha (1824-1884)]. The King of Holland recognized the fact of the division of his possessions only in 1839.[167]

The new revolution in France which flared up in February 1848 was a signal of general troubles in Western Europe. A people's movement in Germany generated an attempt to transform the German Union, which was the task of a Frankfurt national assembly. In Prussia, Austria, and Hungary the revolutionary movement overthrew the principles proclaimed at congresses in Laibach and Verona. The Duchies of Schleswig-Holstein rose up in Denmark for the purpose of seceding from the Kingdom of Denmark. This uprising led to war between Denmark and the German Union, which was ended thanks to the intervention of Russia, by the 1850 Treaty of Berlin, on the basis of which both duchies remained under the authority of the King of Denmark. In the Vatican the Italians banished Pope Pius IX from Rome and founded a republic. But that republic was destroyed by French forces, who, having reinstated the authority of the Pope, occupied Rome for several years.[168]

166 G. F. Martens, *Nouveau Recueil*, VIII, p. 143; Clerq, note 92 above, III, p. 557. Compare Lawrence, note 91 above, II, p. 403 et seq; Gervinus, note 163 above, V.

167 Clerq, note 92 above, IV, pp. 146, 478; Neumann, note 126 above, IV, pp. 319, 416.

168 Compare Constantin Bulle, *Geschichte der neuesten Zeit, 1815-1871* (Leipzig, 1876), II; Bianchi, note 163 above, V, p. 11 et seq.

B. International Relations from 1856 Paris Peace to Present Time

§32. The Eastern War of 1853-1856 between Russia, on one side, and Turkey, France, England, and Sardinia, on the other formally began on the occasion of a dispute concerning the Holy sites, but in reality was caused by the exclusive position created for Russia on the Balkan Peninsula by the Treaty of Kuchuk-Kainardzhi. After the belligerent powers took Sevastopol, with the mediation of the Austrian court they entered into peace negotiations, the preliminary conditions of which, concluded in Vienna, served as the foundation for the 1856 Paris Peace Congress.[169]

The 1856 Paris Treaty of Peace took away from Russia the exclusive right to protect Christians under the authority of Turkey and made it a common right of all Christian powers who signed the said Treaty. Russia had to agree to the neutralization of the Black Sea, renouncing the maintaining there of a naval fleet and building fortifications, and to destroy the fortresses which existed on the coasts of this Sea. The Bessarabian region went from Russia to the Danubian principalities. The last formed two independent principalities – Moldavia and Wallachia, under the authority of two princes selected by the population of the principalities and confirmed by the Porte. The Principality of Serbia was placed in the same position. Finally, the Treaty of Paris declared the Dardanelles Strait to be closed in perpetuity to the passage of warships. The London Convention of 13 March 1871 materially changed the provisions of the 1856 Treaty of Paris insofar as they concerned the limitation of the sovereign rights of Russia to the Russian coasts of the Black Sea and neutralization of that Sea.

After the signature of the Treaty of Paris, at the suggestion of France and England, the powers who participated in the Congress issued on 4(16) April 1856 a Declaration concerning the international law of the sea. On the basis of this important act: (1) privateering was abolished forever; (2) a neutral flag covers enemy cargo, excluding military contraband; (3) neutral cargo under an enemy flag, except military contraband, is not subject to seizure; (4) a blockade is deemed to be effective only when it is maintained by sufficient force terminating access to the enemy coast. These rules were proposed for signature also to States which did not take part in the Paris

[169] See the historical survey of diplomatic negotiations which preceded the beginning of the Crimean War in F. F. Martens, Собрание трактатов и конвенций [Collection of Treaties and Conventions], XII (Spb, 1898), No. 456. Compare VIII, No. 333; Neumann, note 126 above, VI, p. 274; Clerq, note 92 above, VII, p. 59; and [Aleksandr Genrikhovich Jomini], *Étude diplomatique sur la guerre de Crimée* (Paris, 1874). 2 vols.

Congress, and at present have been recognized by the vast majority of civilized peoples on the entire planet.

Those international issues created by the 1815 Treaty of Vienna were resolved little by little after the Paris Peace. We indicate concisely the major events which changed the political system of Europe structured on the principles of that Treaty.

The first question which arose soon after the conclusion of the Paris Peace concerned the structure of the Italian Peninsula. At the Congress in Paris, the plenipotentiary of the King of Sardinia, Count [Camillo Benso of] Cavour [(1810-1861)], submitted a memorandum in which he demonstrated that the sovereignty of Austria in the north of Italy served as a pretext for the Vienna Cabinet to constantly interfere in Italian affairs, which was not consistent with the legitimate rights of the Italian nation. Sardinia had already entered into an agreement with France on the Italian question. In 1859 the King of Sardinia, in alliance with the French Emperor, declared war against Austria, which ended in the same year with a preliminary peace between Austria and France concluded at Villafranca without any participation of Sardinia.[170] The contracting powers agreed that the boundary of Austrian possessions in Italy was the Mincio River; Lombardy was ceded to the French Emperor, who was to transfer it to the King of Sardinia; all Italian States comprised one federation under the honorary chairmanship of the Pope. The Peace of Villafranca was confirmed by the Treaty of Zurich (1859), which the King of Sardinia did sign.[171]

But the Treaty concluded at Zurich was not implemented. The people rose up in all Italian States against the existing governments and demanded unification under the King of Sardinia. [Giuseppe] Garibaldi [(1807-1882)] conquered the entire Kingdom of Naples to the benefit of Sardinia. In 1860 Italy actually was united. But formally the new order could not exist on the Italian Peninsula without the consent of the French emperor. The Convention of Turin (1860) was concluded between Sardinia and France under which the Emperor of the French recognized the force of what had transpired on condition of the cession to France of Savoy and Nice.[172]

170 G. F. Martens (Samwer), *Recueil des traités*, III(2), p. 376. Compare Bianchi, note 163 above, VIII, p. 21 et seq.

171 G. F. Martens (Samwer), *Recueil des traités*, III(2), p. 531; Neumann, note 126 above (N.S.), II, p. 281.

172 Edward Hertslet, *The Map of Europe by Treaty* (London, 1875), II, No. 313, p. 1429; No. 307, p. 1415.

The unification of Italy was completed in 1870 by the occupation of the Papal district and the City of Rome by Italian royal forces. Only the Vatican and Lateran were left in the possession of the Pope.

Gradually, a resolution was prepared of another all-European problem – the structure of Germany. A war broke out in 1864 between Denmark, on one side, and Austria and Prussia, on the other. All three powers belonged to the German Union, and the War between them was a punishment ordered by the German Diet against Denmark because of the duchies of Schleswig-Holstein. The last had become part of the Danish Kingdom on the basis of treaties which guaranteed the special structure of the duchies. But in 1863 the King of Denmark, Christian IX [(1818-1906)] issued a constitution for his State which extended to Schleswig. The German Diet saw in this measure a violation of the rights of a German State which belonged to the Union and decreed to subject the King of Denmark to punishment. Prussia and Austria assumed the execution of this punishment. Under the 1864 Treaty of Vienna, Denmark renounced the duchies of Schleswig, Holstein, and Lauenburg, which passed to the joint possession of the victor powers. But the condominium of Austria and Prussia did not last for long. A number of disputes arose between the two powers which led to war.[173]

The 1866 Austro-Prussian War finally resolved the question of which of the two great powers should have hegemony in Germany. The Battle of Königgrätz resolved this issue in favor of Prussia. The belligerent powers concluded at Nikolsburg in 1866 a preliminary peace and, in Prague, a final peace.[174] The Prague Peace Treaty eliminated Austria from further participation in the German Union; Austria renounced any rights to Holstein and Schleswig, but relative to the last Article V of the Peace Treaty provided that the population of the northern part thereof would be asked through a vote whether it wished to be joined to Prussia. The Prussian Government did not find it necessary to perform this provision. This could have served as a convenient pretext for Austria to begin a war against Prussia. In 1878 the Vienna Cabinet, however, renounced all claims under this Article.

In the 1866 War between Austria and Prussia, Italy took part against the first and Bavaria, Württemberg, Baden, Hanover, Kurhessen, Nassau, and Saxony, against the second. According to the Prague Peace Treaty, Austria should have transferred Venice to Napoleon III, and the last should cede this region to the King of Italy. The defeated German states, except Saxony, were joined to Prussia.

[173] Neumann, note 126 above (N.S.), III, No. 277, p. 516.

[174] Ibid., IV, Nos. 356 and 358.

After the Austro-German War, the German Union dissolved and in its place a North German Union was formed with the King of Prussia at the head. The south German States – Bavaria, Württemberg, Baden, and part of Hessen – at the insistence of Napoleon III remained independent States. They all, however, concluded secret treaties with the North German Union on the basis of which they were obliged to unite, in the event of war, their armies with the forces of the North German Union.

The unification of northern Germany met with great dissatisfaction in France. The public opinion in France was critical of Napoleon III, who had not succeeded in preventing the strengthening of this neighboring State. In order to rectify his mistake, the French emperor decided in 1867 to take advantage of the Luxembourg Question and entered into diplomatic negotiations to purchase Luxembourg, which belonged to Holland, but was occupied by a Prussian garrison. When this transaction was not consummated, the French emperor demanded the removal of Prussian forces from Luxembourg. Prussia delayed, and war between the two powers seemed inevitable. It was prevented by the mediation of the great powers, which at a Conference in London during 1867 decided that Luxembourg would remain in the possession of Holland but would be neutral in perpetuity. The Prussian garrison would be withdrawn, and the Luxembourg fortifications would be razed.

The rupture between France and Prussia ended in 1870 on the occasion of the candidacy for the Spanish throne of Hohenzollern Prince Leopold [Stephen Karl Anton Gustav Eduard Tassilo (1835-1905)]. The French Government, seeing in this candidacy the aspiration of Prussia to demean France, requested the King of Prussia to order Prince Leopold not to accept the proposal addressed to him from Spain. The voluntary abdication of the Prince, however, which followed at once, did not pacify Napoleon III. He decided to demand from the King of Prussia a promise that never in the future would the Prince accept the Spanish candidacy. The King, of course, refused to satisfy this request. This was the cause of the War declared by Prussia on 19 July 1870. The next year, after a series of unheard of defeats, France was forced to sign the Versailles preliminary and Frankfurt final peace treaty, assuming extremely onerous obligations. France gave the Alsace to Germany and part of Lotharingia, assumed the duty to pay five million francs as a military Contribution, and until the payment of this sum, to be occupied by German forces.[175]

[175] *Staatsarchiv*, nos. 4441, 4443, 4615 (1871), et seq. Compare Jules Joseph Valfrey, *Histoire de la diplomatie du gouvernement de la défense nationale* (Paris, 1871-1872), III, p. 103 et seq.

The most important outcome of this War for the North German Union was the accession in 1870 of the south German States and the formation in 1871 of the German Empire under the authority of the King of Prussia, who accepted the title of German Emperor.

After 1871, Europe enjoyed peace for several years. During this time, the principal attention of European governments turned to the development of trade between States on the basis of international agreements. At the initiative of Emperor Alexander II [(1818-1881)], in 1874 the Brussels Conference for the Codification of the Customs and Regulations Binding during War on Land was convened. All the European powers took part in the Conference. But the draft laws of war developed by the Conference remained without ratification thanks especially to Eastern confusions which arose in 1875.

The Herzogovina uprising, which commenced in 1875, little by little reached a scale requiring intervention of the European powers. From autumn 1875 the Porte constantly received representations from European governments encouraging it to change the order of things which existed in Bosnia and Herzogovina and to satisfy the legitimate demands of the Christian population of these provinces, but this insistence remained unsatisfied. At the end of 1875, Count [Gyula] Andrássy [de Csikszentkirály et Krasznahorka (1823-1890)] composed a draft of those transformations which the Porte had to introduce in the presence of Europe in its regions under revolt. Turkey agreed to make the proposed reforms. For their part, the insurgents presented their own conditions which, however, were not taken into account by the great powers. The blood-letting continued. In 1876 three neighboring powers communicated to the other States a developed "Berlin Memorandum" which determined those compulsory measures which, with the common consent of the powers, must be applied to the Porte if it refused to introduce the proposed reforms. England declined to accede to this Act. Moreover, the uprising embraced Rumelia; Serbia and Montenegro declared war against Turkey. In October, at the insistence of Russia, the Porte concluded an armistice, which made possible the convening of an international conference in Constantinople to determine the conditions of a final peace with Serbia and Montenegro and the preparation of reforms which the Porte was to introduce in Herzogovina, Bosnia, and Bulgaria. At the outset of 1877, the Turkish Government rejected all the proposals of the conference, and it dispersed.[176] The one means which remained to

[176] For a survey of diplomatic negotiations which preceded the War, see F. F. Martens, Восточная война и Брюссельская конференция 1874-1878 гг. [The Eastern War and Brussels Conference, 1874-1878] (Spb., 1879), chapter IV.

break down the resistance of the Porte was war, which Russia began in April 1877. The war was unsuccessful for Turkey.

In February 1878 the preliminary peace treaty was signed by plenipotentiaries of Russia and Turkey at San Stefano under which the Porte agreed to: (1) finally recognize the independence of the principalities of Montenegro, Serbia, and Romania; (2) Bulgaria was to form an autonomous principality in suzerain dependence on the Porte, whose boundary extended to Salonica; (3) transformations were to be introduced immediately in Bosnia and Herzogovina as specified by the Constantinople international conference; (4) the amount of military Contribution to Russia was determined in the sum of 1410 million rubles, but the Russian Government preferred instead of a large portion of the amount (1100 million rubles) to acquire from Turkey: on the Balkan Peninsula – Tulchin Sanjak with the right to exchange it for that part of Bessarabia which it had ceded under the 1856 treaty of Paris, and Romania; in Asia – Ardahan, Kars, Batum, Bayazid, and territory up to Saganlug.

The provisions of the treaty of San Stefano destroying the *de facto* existence of Turkey on the Balkan Peninsula caused extreme dissatisfaction in Western Europe. England and Austria-Hungary accused Russia of failing to perform obligations accepted by it before and during the War. In early 1878 a war between England and Russia seemed inevitable. A rupture did not occur thanks to the mediation of Germany, which proposed the convening of a congress to discuss the conditions of the final peace between Russia and Turkey. This proposal emanated from the notion that the San Stefano treaty might be abrogated only by the common consent of the great powers, just as had happened in 1871 when the articles of the Paris Peace were abrogated which had limited the rights of Russia with regard to the Black Sea.

The Berlin Congress, which assembled on 13 June 1878, ended its work on 13 July, when a treaty was signed that should have served as the new order of things on the Balkan Peninsula. The principal provisions of the Berlin treaty were as follows: Montenegro was recognized as an independent principality and its possessions were enlarged, but use of the port of Antivari joined to it and adjacent sea areas were significantly limited. Romania and Serbia were recognized as independent from the Porte and received territorial increments. The Principality of Bulgaria did not keep those boundaries which were assigned to it under the treaty of San Stefano. Southward of the Balkan mountain range a special province was formed under the name of Eastern Rumelia, which remained under the direct political and military authority of the Sultan, but with extensive local autonomy. Russia acquired from Romania part of the Bessarabian region; from Turkey, to Russia came Ardahan, Kars, and Batum, declared "porto franco, being primarily commercial" (Article 59). All other lands ceded to Russia under the San Stefano treaty were returned to the Ottoman Empire. The provinces of Bosnia and Herzogovina were handed over for administration to Austria-Hungary. Finally, to Persia were ceded the city and region of Qatur.

In addition to territorial changes, the Berlin treaty determined those measures which should be taken by the Porte to improve the status of Christians under its authority, over the application of which the powers would observe. The treaty proclaimed the freedom of navigation on the Danube, from the Iron Gates to the mouth, a guarantee of which would be the razing of fortresses in this space and a prohibition against warships sailing downstream from the Iron Gates. All provisions of the 1856 Paris Treaty not repealed by the Act and the 1871 London treaty were confirmed.[177]

Of recent events which occurred in America, the War between the northern and southern states (1861) had great international significance. It arose thanks to social and political antagonism long separating the north and the south of the American republic. The final rupture between them was the abolition of slavery, which the northern states demanded, not being interested economically in the existence of slavery and which the agricultural southern states decided to resist with arms in hand. The last formed an autonomous confederation, but after defeats suffered on the southern army by General [Hiram Ulysses S.] Grant [(1822-1885)], rejoined the Union in 1865 and accepted the authority of the Washington government.

France used the American internecine war to build an Empire in Mexico, the throne of which, at the invitation of Napoleon III, was taken by the Archduke [Ferdinand] Maximilian [Joseph Maria von Hapsburg-Lothringen (1832-1867)]. The Mexican People's Party rose up against the sovereign imposed and, having gained the upper hand, subjected him to a trial, according to the judgment of which the unfortunate Archduke was shot (1866).

§33. International relations in the third period increasingly take on a legal character. The principles of contemporary positive international law are developing and being confirmed. Contemporary educated governments and peoples increasingly are convinced of the inadequacies of their own forces by themselves to fully satisfy developing State needs and the need for extensive mutual intercourse and relations. In the domain of political relations the interests of the powers were discussed at congresses and

[177] Albert Friedrich Berner, *Die Orientfrage. Beantwortet durch die Verträge von 1856 und 1878* (Berlin, 1878).

conferences, whose decisions received the force of law. The public interests of States find their satisfaction in special and general treaties on various questions concerning the social relations of peoples. A result of international agreements was the establishment of positive legal principles, rules, and laws determining the mutual relations of States. The rules on international representation, maritime trade, free navigation on rivers, and others are such.

The guiding principle of international relations in the period here considered is the principle of nationality. It was proclaimed in the nineteenth century as a panacea against all international misunderstandings and confusions, as the most reasonable basis for the settlement of disputes and conflicts arising between States, and for the structuring of an order of mutual relations which was in a position to ensure the peaceful development of each people.[178]

The principle of nationality was first formulated by the French writer, Madame [Anne Louise] Germaine de Staël- [Holstein, née Necker (1766-1817)]. In one of her works[179] she expressed the idea that every State should consist of the people imbued with an awareness of its national unity, having one language, and identical morals and customs. In recent times this notion has been subjected to comprehensive development and was officially proclaimed by various State officials (Napoleon III) as the guiding principle of international policy. In Laurent's view, the "State usually is an accidental combining of individuals more assembled than combined by their own wish under one sovereign authority dominant over them". Mankind, he said, seeks to replace States that are the product of force or arbitrary transactions with States based on the natural element of nationality. The same idea serves as

178 Compare Bulle, note 168 above, II, p. 290 et seq. The literature on this question is rather abundant. We confine ourselves to pointing to a few titles. Pasquale Stanislao Mancini, *Della nazionalitâ come fondamento del diritto delle genti* (Torino, 1851); Robert von Mohl, "Die Nationalitätsfrage", in Mohl, *Staatsrecht, Völkerrecht und Politik* (Tübingen, 1862), II, p. 333 et seq; Rüdiger, "Über Nationalität", *Zeitschrift für Völkerpsychologie und Sprachwissenschaft*, III; Guido Padelletti, "L'Alsace et la Lorraine et le droit des gens", *Revue de droit international* (1871), p. 464 et seq; Richard, *Études sur les nationalités, leur formation et leurs rapports* (Geneva, 1870); Bulmerincq, note 148 above, p. 53 et seq; Julius Neumann, *Volk und Nation* (Leipzig, 1888); Michel Bréal, "Le langage et les nationalités", *Revue de Deux Mondes.*, 1 December 1891. In Russian literature, see Aleksandr Dmitrievich Gradovskii, Национальный вопрос в истории и литературе [Nationality Question in History and Literature] (Spb., 1873).

179 [G. de Stael, *De l'Allemagne* (1810). The first printing of 10,000 copies was ordered destroyed by Napoleon Bonaparte; the reprinting in 1813 achieved considerable renown – WEB].

the point of departure for all contemporary Italian literature on international law.[180]

What did those writers understand by nationality who saw in it the basis of the contemporary international system? The most successful definition of nationality belongs to the Italian scholar, [Pasquale Stanislao] Mancini [(1817-1888)]. By nation he understood a natural society of individuals who, as a consequence of common territory, origin, morals and language, are united by the unity of life and imbued with a social consciousness.[181] This social awareness forced contemporary peoples to endeavor to form individual national political organisms which, in the view of proponents of the idea of nationality, combined all the necessary conditions for the establishment of a stable international order. The recent history of European States, say the nationalists, confirms the aspiration of peoples for freedom and independence. They point out that the uprising of the Greeks arose thanks to an awareness by the Greek people of their common tribal origin, language, religion, and morals. On the same basis Belgium seceded from Holland; Italy combined into a single kingdom; finally, the German people eliminated their political division created by the Treaty of Vienna and organized themselves into a single Empire.[182]

It is evident that the proponents of the nationality idea juxtaposed the national State to the State formed historically and encompassing various nationalities. This juxtaposition is understandable if one bears in mind the means by which State possessions are increased or reduced during a period of unlimited royal autocracy. The idea of nationality is a protest against the arbitrary disposition of the fate of a particular people, against the sale of State territory together with its population, or giving it away as dowry and similar transactions customary in times past. It is also justified by the

[180] Laurent, note 1 above, XVIII, p. 523 et seq. Also see François Laurent, *Droit civil international* (Brussels, 1880-1881), I, p. 62 et seq; Augusto Pierantoni, *Storia degli del diritto internazionale in Italia* (Modena, 1869); Pierantoni, *Geschichte der italienischen völkerrechts-literatur von August Pierantoni*, transl. Leone Ranconi (Vienna, 1872); Luigi Palma, *Del principio di nazionalità nellà moderna società Europea* (1886); József Eötvòs, *Der Einfluss der herrschenden Ideen des XIX. Jahrhunderts auf den Staat* (Leipzig, 1854), I, p. 31 et seq.

[181] "Una societa naturale di nomini da unità di territorio, di origine, di costumi e di lingua conformati a communanza di vita e di coscienza sociale". Mancini, *Diritto internazionale* (Naples, 1873), p. 37.

[182] Richard Böckh, *Der Deutschen Volkszahl und Sprachgebiet in den europäischen Staaten* (Berlin, 1870), pp. 1-47; Adolph Wagner, *Elsass: eine deutsche Provinz* (Berlin, 1870). Compare also Ernest Renan, *Qu'est ce qu-une nation?* (Paris, 1882); Jomini, note 169 above; Bernhard Becker, *Der Missbrauch der Nationalitätslehre* (Vienna, 1867).

demand which may be justly made to the contemporary State that it treat the nationality element with full respect, those natural nationalities which exist within its limits. The less that these nationalities find satisfaction of their legitimate requirements in a particular State, the stronger will be their aspiration for liberation from under its authority and the formation of an autonomous State or unification with a State more akin to it in nationality composition and understanding of its reasonable goal. But a single-tribal State will have such an attractive force insofar as it gives guarantees with its domestic social system and culture of the free development of the human personality and full respect for the ideals of which civilized peoples are aware.

Without denying the impact on international relations of nationality links and agreeing with the duties of every government to respect the rights and interests of all their subjects whatever their national origin and whatever national language they speak, we all the same cannot adhere to the view that the national composition of a State serves to secure order and law in the domain of international relations. Not to mention that the implementation of the principle of nationality should lead to a radical change of the political map of Europe and consequently inescapably cause international wars, we have no guarantee that the "national States" formed will be imbued not only with an awareness of domestic unity but with respect for the legal order in their mutual relations, that they will recognize mutual rights and duties. To see a panacea in the principle of nationality for the settlement of all international difficulties seems to us to be an unfounded and dangerous conviction in its exceptional supremacy over all guiding ideas of our time.[183] The principle of nationality, lacking a historical foundation, creates nothing stable, but is in a position to destroy much. If it were applied to Italy, it does not follow that it can be applied everywhere with benefit for peoples and with respect for alienable requirements of truth and justice.

The international power of a community of tribal origin always is proportional to the power of solidarity of common cultural aspirations. No sacrifices made in favor of fellow-tribesmen, no legends, no fair accusations of ingratitude are able to bind one-tribal peoples firmly together if at the same time they are not united by the same cultural interests, the same State

[183] Absolutely correct is the assessment of the views of the Italian school of nationalists made by Padelletti: "La théorie de nos publicists sur ce point, sans compter qu'elle est bien loin d'être unanime et uniforme, est Presque partout vague, inexacte incertaine dans ses développements et jamais pratique dans ses conclusions extrêmes". *Revue de droit international*, III, p. 477. Also compare Vladimir Sergeevich Solov'ev, Национальный вопрос в России [The National Question in Russia] (1891).

ideals, the same understanding of political freedom, and in general the same respect for the high benefits of human civilization.

IV. Development of Science of International Law

§34. The science of international law and its development are closely linked with international life, with those real relations between States which exist in various epochs. This link is explained, on one hand, by the inevitable influence of surrounding circumstances on the concepts and view of writers who have devoted their works to international law and, on the other hand, the impact of the theoretical views of these writers on the views and activity of governments.

The majority of writers, when describing international relations in a certain epoch, cite the teachings of jurists who lived at the time. We did not adhere to this system, wishing to make it possible to trace the organic development of the theory of international law. But we do not lose sight of the dependence of this last on the practice of international relations. In the survey above the history of international relations should be seen as the groundwork for the historical development of the science of international law.

The various epochs of the theoretical elaboration of international law may be divided into three periods that differ materially from one another.

The first period encompasses the time when the embryonic science of international law established its initial foundations. The creator and early representatives thereof did not find another scale for determining relations between States except abstract nature, the essence of the State. Mutual rights and duties of States were logical conclusions from this nature; international law was natural law.

In the second period jurists were persuaded that attempts to establish any rules binding on States by means of philosophical abstraction were hopeless. Having renounced natural law, they turned to the real relations of States and deduced norms and laws actually complied with in international practice. The science of international law acquired a purely positive character that excluded a critical attitude towards facts and phenomena of international life.

The new orientation which emerged in the third period rejected the extremes of both the preceding schools. Not considering it possible to base its doctrines on abstract principles contrary to reality, it also did not impart exclusive significance to history, legend, and existing practice which the positivists ascribed to them. On the contrary, the followers of this orientation proceed from the facts and positive data, but recognize the freedom of autonomous assessment thereof, the scientific classification and critique from the standpoint of general principles. Thus, they combine the principles of natural law with principles of positive law. The best contemporary representatives of the science of international law belong to this school.

The said three chief orientations in the scientific development of international law correspond fully to those periods into which we divided the history of international relations.

During the first period, as we have seen, the relations of peoples were determined by physical force, which indicated the limits of their mutual rights. In deducing the rights of a State from its nature, representatives of natural law logically came to the same principle of force as the foundation of mutual relations of States. They taught that the most powerful State has the most rights. But just as the unlimited dominion of brute force was softened during the first period of international relations by the authority of the church, so too natural law insisted on limiting the absolute rights of a State in the name of religion, conscience, and honor.

The same correlation between science and life is noticeable during the second period of the development of international relations. In this epoch the political system of Europe is based on the equilibrium of States, according to which *de facto* relations, once established between States, should not be subjected to the slightest change disturbing the *status quo*. Adherents of the positivist orientation have in view only *de facto* mutual relations of States and do not permit any critique which would question the principles to be applied in practice and illuminated by history.

Finally, during the third period, together with the principle of legitimacy celebrated at the Congress of Vienna, the idea of nationality takes hold. Thus, two principles operate simultaneously, of which one requires recognition of established facts and historically-formed States, and the other – respect for natural nationalities in the name of the high principles of freedom and independence. For their part, the representatives of the science of international law in modern times attempt to identify positive legal principles which should guide States in their mutual relations, taking into account not only history, actual circumstances, and real life conditions, but also the requirements of scientific truth and developing legal consciousness of the educated world.

A. Period of Domination of Natural Law

§35. In the following concise survey of the history of the science of international law we sketch and critically assess the general features of the doctrine and system of the main representatives of each of the three orientations.[184]

The remarkable Dutch jurist and State official, Hugo Grotius (1583-1645), is considered to be the father of the science of international law. However, this noted writer had predecessors who were aware of the need to determine international relations by legal means. Among the jurists preceding Grotius who attempted to create a theory of international law was the Spanish writer, Francisco Suarez [(1548-1617)]. In his *De legibus ac Deo legislatore* he distinguished the *jus gentium* from natural law (*jus naturale*). In his view, Christian States should determine their mutual relations by treaties and customs, the aggregate of which comprises a law distinct from *jus naturale*. These thoughts he did not develop in detail nor did they receive clear and precise expression.

Superior to him was Alberico Gentili [(1552-1608)], an Italian who died in England. He wrote *De jure belli* (1583), in which he set out the requirement that States determine their mutual relations not by actually existing rules and not by considerations of politics, but by certain legal norms which should be recognized by all European peoples.[185]

International law became an autonomous legal science only from the appearance of Grotius, *De jure belli ac pacis* (1625).[186] Grotius was

[184] The following works may serve as aids on the scientific literature of international law:

Diedrich Heinrich Ludwig Freiherr von Ompteda, *Litteratur des gesammten sowohl natürlich als positiven Völkerrechts* (Regensburg, 1785). 2 vols.

Carl Albert von Kamptz, *Neue Literatur des Völkerrechts seit dem Jahre 1784* (Berlin, 1817).

Robert von Mohl, "Die neuere Literatur des Völkerrechts", in *Geschichte und Literatur der Staatswissenschaften* (Erlangen, 1855), I, p. 337 et seq.

Karl von Kaltenborn von Stachau, *Kritik des Völkerrechts* (Leipzig, 1847).

August von Bulmerincq, *Die Systematik des Völkerrechts, von Hugo Grotius bis auf die Gegenwart* (Dorpat, 1858).

Bulmerincq, *Praxis, Theorie und Codification des Völkerrechts* (Leipzig, 1874).

Vsevolod Pievich Danevskii, Очерк новейшей литературы по международному праву [Survey of Recent Literature on International Law] (Spb., 1876). The best survey of the history of the literature to the present was compiled by a Professor of Brussels University, [Alphonse Pierre Octave] Rivier in Franz von Holtzendorff (ed.), *Handbuch des Völkerrechts* (Berlin, 1885-1889), I, pp. 395-523. Also see Ernest Nys, *Le droit de la guerre et les précurseurs de Grotius* (Brussels and Leipzig, 1882); Nys, note 62 above.

[185] The best edition of Gentili was prepared by Thomas Erskine Holland, a Professor of Oxford University. [Martens refers to Alberico Gentili, *De iure belli libri tres*, ed. T. E. Holland (Oxford, The Clarendon Press, 1877) – WEB].

[186] Biographical data on the remarkable Grotius can be found in the most recent French translation by Paul Louis Ernest Pradier-Fodéré (Paris, 1867), I, p. xiii, in three volumes. The best edition of Grotius with much commentary was by William Whewell, Cambridge,

impelled to write his work by the terrors and misfortunes generated by the Thirty Years War. It inspired Grotius to put the question: should not Christian peoples during warfare between themselves be subject to certain laws restraining the animal passions of humans? To resolve this question, Grotius turned to the history and literature of various peoples of the ancient world and the Middle Ages. The enormous number of facts and opinions of authoritative thinkers and jurists which he collected persuaded him that if Christian peoples had the right to wage war, they were obliged to limit their arbitrariness and violence by respect for inalienable rights which arise from human nature.

Grotius devoted his work primarily to questions of war. But with a view to identifying these questions more precisely, he undertook a close examination of the principles on which law is based in general and, in particular, international law.

Grotius insisted that every State must be aware of its legal duties with respect to other States. Just as the law of an individual State has the purpose to protect the well-being of its subjects, he said, so a law exists whose subject-matter is the prosperity of States in general and determines their mutual relations. This is international law. It not only justifies itself by advantage to States, but arises from the undoubted precepts of justice.

But the theoretical substantiation of international law in Grotius is casuistic. He divided all law into natural (*jus naturale*) and positive (*jus voluntarium*); the last is subdivided into human law (*jus humanum*) and divine law (*jus divinum*). Human law comprises the civil law (*jus civile*) and international law (*jus gentium*). The binding force of the last rests on the agreement of the wills of all or several peoples.[187] In favor of the existence of legal norms binding on States in their mutual relations Grotius cited the following consideration: if, he said, many persons living in various places and at various times share similar opinions on a certain subject-matter, their unanimity should be ascribed to a universal reason: it may arise either from conformity to the laws of nature, or from universal agreement of humans. The first serves as a source of natural law; the second, of international law.[188]

Thus, according to Grotius, prescriptions of international law should be derived from customs and international treaties in which the consent of peoples is expressed. But in his day treaties between States which might be

1853, in three volumes.

[187] Grotius, *De jure belli ac pacis*, lib. I, cap. I, §XIV: "*Jus gentium est quod gentium omnium aut multarum voluntate vim obligandi accepit*". Grotius, *Prolegomena* 17: "*inter civitas autem omnes aut plerasque ex consensu jura quaedam nasci potuerunt*".

[188] Grotius, *Prolegomena* 40.

considered to be generally binding did not exist; he deliberately overlooked the international life and politics contemporary to him, a critical attitude towards which might have engaged persecution. Therefore, Grotius confined himself to an expression of the wish that international law, having treaties and customs as sources, was positive law in the true sense. In reality, the principles of international law which he set out were confirmed by evidence borrowed from the history and literature of times past. His book abounds in references to Jewish, Greek, and Latin authors. But understandably positive international law of the seventeenth century could not be based either on the sayings of thinkers, orators, and poets, however ingenious and profound or found in the practice of the ancient world and Middle Ages. Adhering to his methods, Grotius condemned himself to philosophical, abstract reflections in which, to be sure, the noble and humane feelings of the author are salient, but which were not able to identify positive elements of international law.

As regards the system which Grotius followed in his work, one can hardly say it was a system of international law. The diverse questions on which he touched were considered solely with respect to the law of war; war generated his work, and the order and essence of his argumentation was affected by war.[189]

But despite all the shortcomings, Grotius' work exerted a truly amazing impact on the life contemporary to him.[190] Gustavus Adolphus [King of Sweden] always carried it with him on his campaigns, together with the Gospels, which served him as a manual. Upon the publication of this work, chairs were founded in various German universities to study it. Finally, Grotius' work was the progenitor of two orientations – philosophical and positivist – in which the science of international law subsequently developed.

Initially, the abstract orientation dominated. It proceeded from the fiction developed by Grotius that a certain natural law inheres in human nature, the source of which is in the reasonable essence of things which therefore is binding in and of itself, irrespective of any utilitarian considerations or behests of the authorities. In this orientation, called natural law, one must see the spiritual aspiration of the best people of the seventeenth and eighteenth centuries contrasted with the materialist interests which dominated in the politics of that time, the requirements of moral nature and justice. The more that arbitrariness and violence reigned in international relations, the more insistently jurists proclaimed the duty of States to respect a law arising from

189 Bulmerincq, *Systematik*, note 184 above, p. 24

190 Sir Henry Sumner Maine, *Ancient Law* (London, 1861), p. 111: "the great marvel of the treatise *De jure belli ac pacis* was its rapid, complete, and universal success". Laurent, note 1 above, X, p. 477 et seq.

their reasonable nature and binding apart from any positive legislation and treaties.

The first noteworthy follower of Grotius in the abstract understanding of international la was Samuel Pufendorf [(1632-1694)].[191] He took this orientation to an extreme. Denying the possibility of the existence of positive international law because States do not recognize any authority higher than themselves, Pufendorf identified international law with natural law (*praecepta utriusque eadem sunt*). A violation of the last, especially during war, cannot be considered to be a violation of any legal duties. Therefore, relations between States in reality are not regulated by law, but by force.

In this respect, Pufendorf was similar to the views of other representatives of natural law. [Thomas] Hobbes ([1588-1679])[192] taught that relations between States are no different from the initial or natural state of man, when *homo homini lupus est*. According to [Baruch (Benedict de)] Spinoza [(1632-1677)],[193] everyone has as much right as they have power; consequently, in international relations the strong States have more rights than weak States.

Pufendorf's pupil, [Christian] Thomasius [(1655-1728)], developed this idea.[194] Agreeing with Pufendorf, Thomasius deemed international law to be part of natural law applied to States or to peoples. According to his doctrine, international treaties and customs cannot be tantamount to a law because the last assumes sovereign power, which does not exist over peoples. Consequently, in setting out international law, he denied its existence.

Beginning from the eighteenth century, natural law, while remaining the dominant orientation in science, little by little perceives in itself principles of positive law. International practice is given certain attention in a work by [Christian von] Wolff [(1679-1754)], an eminent proponent of natural law theory.[195] Wolff applied his mathematical method to his exposition of international law, through which he investigated all ethical and legal issues. It was not possible to identify by this means the basic principles of

[191] S. Pufendorf, *De jure naturae et gentium* (1672). Compare Laurent, note 1 above, XI, p. 503 et seq.

[192] Thomas Hobbes, *Elementa philosophica de cive* (1642).

[193] B. Spinoza, *Tractatus theologico-politicus* (1670); Spinoza, *Tractatus politicus* (1672), cap. II, §3.

[194] C. Thomasius, *Institutiones jurisprudentiae* (7th ed.; 1730); Thomasius, *Fundamenta juris naturae et gentium* (1705).

[195] Christian von Wolff, *Jus gentium methodo scientifica pertractatum, in quo jus gentium naturale ab eo, quod voluntarii, pactitii, consuegudinarii est, accurate distinguitur* (1749).

international law; but thanks to this method, Wolff did not omit real facts and historical experience.

Wolff divided international law into four types: (1) natural law (*jus gentium naturale*); (2) positive law (*jus gentium voluntarium*); (3) treaty law (*jus gentium pactitium*); (4) customary law (*jus gentium consuetudinarium*). Natural law he considered possible to apply to States, but not to mix it with that natural law which determines relations between individuals: the subjects of one or the other differ, and therefore are not identical in rights and duties. He deviates even more from the dominant views of the natural law school in the doctrine on positive international law. He based its binding force on a presumed agreement of peoples (*consensus gentium praesumtus*). Wolff makes tangible, so to say, this agreement as a fiction of a world State (*civitas gentium maxima*). If the purpose of life of each individual, said Wolff, is to improve his moral self, if States are formed for this purpose, then for the sake of achieving full perfection of the State it is necessary to enter into international relations; they must comprise one worldwide republic in which sovereign power (*imperium*) belongs to all together over each individual State. From the purpose of this republic arises both its justification proper and the binding nature of positive international law.[196] Unlike this last, international treaty law presumes the clear consent of peoples (*consensus expressus*) and is based on treaties between States which are binding only on the parties which concluded them. Finally, customary international law has as its source the tacit consent of peoples (*consensus tacitus*).

Thus, the theory of international law developed by Wolff did not confine itself to abstract principles of natural law, but included positive elements, customs, and treaties. The system shows that Wolff attempted to come to an organic, purely scientific, exposition of international law. Nonetheless, Wolff's doctrine is replete with blunders and fundamental errors. First and foremost, the scholastic division of law which he established was completely useless for the theoretical substantiation of international law because it gave no possibility to distinguish between positive international law based on the presumed agreement of peoples and customary international law, the basis of which is tacit; that is, the presumed agreement of peoples. The principal shortcoming of Wolff's theory lies in the fiction of the universal State which should ensure compliance with positive international law. This fiction is not consistent with the essence of international relations because

[196] "*Ex fine civitatis maximae*", wrote Wolff in his preface, "*quem perinde ac societatem inter omnes instituit ipsa natura, ut in jus istud consentire debeant gentes, non vero libertati earum relictum sit, utrum consentire malint, an nolint*".

the subordination of individual States to a common sovereign authority would destroy their independence: autonomous States become part of a federation within which international law does not operate, but a union State law. Finally, to the shortcomings of Wolff's work should be relegated the arduous Latin language in which it was written and the prolixity and murderous mathematical method which Wolff undeviatingly followed.

The Swiss, [Emer de] Vattel [(1714-1767)], thought to rectify the shortcomings of Wolff's work.[197] Deeming in general the principles and conclusions of his predecessor to be true, Vattel set as his task to make them, in language and by method of exposition, generally comprehensible. This goal he fully achieved. Written in a fine French language and free of scholastic judgments, Vattel's work enjoyed enormous success and to this day is an authority in the eyes of diplomats.

Vattel himself considered his work to be merely a reworking of Wolff. However, it would be unjust to ignore his originality. Although on the majority of questions he developed the ideas of his mentor, he did not accept unconditionally all the propositions which Wolff set out. Moreover, Vattel discarded the Wolff fiction of the universal State as not consistent with the basic condition of international order and law – the autonomy of individual States. He created his own theory justifying the binding nature of positive international law. Every social union of individuals, according to his doctrine, is based on agreement, a contract between the members of the union, and with their consent may be changed or even eliminated. The same applied to a society of peoples: it arises from an agreement of States, who retain their freedom and independence.[198] This agreement serves as the source of positive international law (*droit des gens volontaire*). But Vattel, just as Wolff, recognized the existence of natural international law which was binding in and of itself, irrespective of the will of peoples: it is a necessary and immutable law, because it is a natural law based on human nature and only applicable to relations between States. Consequently, Vattel did not distinguish between natural law and international law; on the other hand, it is unclear how he distinguished natural international law from positive, for the last, in Vattel's opinion, also arises from nature and, consequently, is a necessary and immutable law.[199]

The lack of firm principles and the constant contradictions are a material shortcoming of Vattel's work. Moreover, he devoted a significant part of his

[197] Emer de Vattel, *Le droit des gens, ou principes de la loi naturelle appliqués à la conduite et aux affaires des nations et des souverains* (1758).

[198] Ibid., livre I, chap. II, §16.

[199] Ibid., Préliminaires, §6 et seq. Compare Laurent, note 1 above, XI, p. 507 et seq.

book to discourses not relevant to international law.[200] But when individual questions are considered, one encounters sensible remarks of genius, the proper interpretation of facts known to him from history and contemporary practice, and in general love-of-fellowmen views on the mutual relations of States during war. The great merit of Vattel is that he disseminated in official spheres and in the public a familiarity with the principles of international law; from a scientific point of view, he had no merits which would justify ascribing to him on matters of international law an authority equal to Grotius and other leading lights of this science.

B. Period of Predominance of Positivist Orientation

§36. The extreme position of the natural-philosophical school caused a reaction on the part of those jurists who deemed customs, treaties, and the practice of international relations to be the sole source of international law. The writers of this orientation not only absolutely denied natural law, but for them every kind of theoretical generalizations and principles suggested to States in a manual were an insult to governmental authority acting autonomously in the field of foreign policy.

The positive orientation, which reached its apogee in the eighteenth century, had noteworthy representatives in the second half of the seventeenth century. In 1650 the English jurist, Richard Zouche, published the first textbook on international law, which deserves attention in many respects.[201]

By international law Zouche understood the law determining the relations of peoples and monarchs between themselves; the *jus gentium*, he said, is nothing other than natural law; that is, the aggregate of general legal norms which are based on the nature of things and therefore are encountered among all peoples. He distinguished between general and special international law. The first arises from the general consent of peoples; the second has as its basis treaties linking specific States. The existence of one or the other Zouche attempted by confirm by historical facts and positive data from the international life contemporary to him, which compared favorably with Grotius. He is superior to the last also in the sense that he considers in detail various issues of international law and sets them out systematically, in an

[200] Thus, the first part of the book is titled: "De la nation, considérée en elle-meme" and occupies almost a third of Vattel's entire work, which has as its subject matter: the duties of a nation towards herself; the constitution of a State; the duties and rights of a sovereign; the principal objects of a good government; religion, agriculture, commerce, money, piety, justice, and so on.

[201] Richard Zouche, *Juris et judicii fecialis sive juris inter gentes et quaestionum de eodem explicatio* (1650). He was the first to use the term *jus inter gentes* instead of *jus gentium*.

order borrowed from Roman private law. But in endeavoring to substantiate his conclusions primarily with empirical data, Zouche could not confine himself to the contemporary practice of international relations because the facts from that domain were considered a State secret. It remained to turn to the history of the ancient world, especially to Roman law, and Zouche seriously demonstrated that the *jus feciale* of the Romans was a source of contemporary international law.

Another jurist of the eighteenth century, [Samuel] Rachel[(1628-1691)], belonged to the positive school; he polemicized with Pufendorf, defending the autonomy of international law.[202]

Rachel recognized three kinds of law: private law, which determines relations of private individuals with one another; State law, which determines relations between citizens and the government; and finally, international law, which establishes norms for relations between States. Given that there is no higher power over autonomous peoples, international customs and treaties which States conclude serve as the source of international law. Consequently, international law is an arbitrary law in the sense that it is based on the clear or tacit consent of peoples; therefore, it cannot and should not be mixed with natural law, as Pufendorf and his followers do. Just as Zouche, Rachel divided international law into general and special (*jus gentium commune et jus gentium proprium*); the first is recognized by all or, at least, the majority of educated peoples and arises from international customs; the second is binding on two or several States which have concluded treaties. Finally, the ultimate purpose of international law Rachel saw in its general advantage for all States, and in this respect he may be considered to be a predecessor of [Jeremy] Bentham and other, especially English, writers who proclaim interest or material benefit of peoples to be the principal foundation of international law.

The considerable merit of Rachel is that he struggled against those who denied positive international law and demonstrated that it may be based on practice and historical data. His views found followers, including [Gottfried Wilhelm] Leibniz [(1646-1717)], [Johann Wolfgang] Textor [(1638-1701)], and other philosophers and jurists. But Rachel, just as Zouche, was not free from the influence of Roman law, and although he distinguished international law or *jus gentium* in the sense of the Romans, he did not fully understand the difference between the two so as to avoid confusing both.

The initial efforts to prove the autonomy of international law and to establish it on firm positive data were made more difficult by the

202 Samuel Rachel, *De jure naturae et gentium: dissertationes duae* (1676). Only the second discourse has international law as its subject-matter.

inadequacy of those materials that should have served it as sources. So long as international treaties and diplomatic negotiations were not published for general information, positive international law had no real foundation, and the scientific treatment thereof could not be undertaken satisfactorily. Facts from the domain of foreign relations were made more or less generally accessible no earlier than the Congress of Westphalia. From that time forward, governments considered it useful to appeal, through the press, to public opinion of their own and foreign peoples, and to prove the justice of their claims and political measures they published in the French language documents, memoranda, reports, justifications, and accusations of their adversaries. Thanks at the same time to the development of periodicals, newspapers, and journals discussing political issues, the principles which States should follow in international relations were increasingly identified. At the end of the seventeenth century, it became customary to publish memoirs in which State officials and diplomats described their activities in detail and the course and purpose of international negotiations in which they took part or concerning which they had information. But the principal source for knowledge of the guiding principles of policy and the contemporary status of international relations was, of course, treaties and conventions which were published officially and issued in the form of collections by various writers.[203] Thus, precious material was accumulated from which one might glean positive legal principles comprising international law.

Now the representatives of the positive orientation had firm support for building the science of international law on principles of practice and treaties. Indeed, in the eighteenth century a number of writers emerged who devoted their efforts to identifying these principles. But the development of the materials of positive international law was extremely unscientific. It

[203] The first attempt to collect international treaties was made in France in the sixteenth century by Tillet; in the seventeenth and following centuries the number of such collections was very large. We name here the major treaty collections published at this time:

Jean du Tillet, *Recueil des guerres et traictez d'entre des roys de France et de l'Angleterre* (1577).

Gottfried Wilhelm Leibniz, *Codes juris gentium diplomaticus* (1693); continued as *Mantissa codicis juris gentium* (1700).

Jacques Bernard, *Recueil des traités de paix* (Amsterdam, 1700). 4 vols.

Jean Dumont, *Corps universel diplomatique du droit des gens* (Amsterdam and The Hague, 1726-1731). 8 vols. Supplements by Jean Barbeyrac and Jean Rousset de Missy (1739).

Friedrich August Wilhelm Wenck, *Codex juris gentium recentissimi* (Leipzig, 1781-1795). 3 vols.

The most recent treaty collections will be indicated when setting out the sources of law (§43).

consisted almost exclusively of collecting and stating facts without a critical assessment or drawing any conclusions worthy of the being considered to be principles of international law.

[Gabriel Bonnot de] Mably [(1709-1785)] wrote in this spirit.[204] In his work on European international law he cited a mass of diverse documents relating to international relations; but the facts from this domain and the provisions of treaties comprising the entire content of his work were not placed in a system nor illuminated by scientific generalizations and critique.

The most typical representative of the purely positive orientation was a German scholar, Johann Jacob Moser [(1701-1785)].[205]

In his numerous works Moser was constantly true to the method he adopted – not engaging in any "philosophizing" and not entering into a critical consideration of events and governmental acts. The "judgments of private individuals about State and international affairs", wrote Moser, "one must recognize to be useless and often improper". Accordingly, he confined himself in his works devoted to international law in good faith of all facts known to him and treaties concluded between States, drawing the most uncomplicated conclusions; he made not the slightest attempt to generalize or to expand upon these conclusions or to connect them with some theoretical reflections. His system represented a mixture of the principles of international law with principles of State law. Moser's sole merit lay in the accumulation of an amazing quantity of material for the study of international law, which he gleaned from not only official acts, but also the periodical press of his time.

In the person of Moser the positive orientation achieved its extreme limits and should have convinced positivists that the method adopted by them was unsustainable. The task of further development of the science of international law obviously consisted of an organic combination of the positive and the philosophical orientations. The noted Dutch jurist, Cornelius von Bynkershoek attempted to resolve this task.[206] He did not leave an integral system of international law, but when considering various special

[204] G. B. de Mably, *Droit public de l'Europe* (Paris, 1747). 2 vols.

[205] J. J. Moser, *Grundsätze des jetxt üblichen europäischen Völkerechts in Friedenzeiten* (1750); Moser, *Grundsätze des jetxt üblichen europäischen Völkerechts in Kriegzeiten* (1752); Moser, *Versuch des neuesten europäischen Völkerrechts in Friedens- und Kriegszeiten, 1777-1780*. 10 vols. Moser published as "Annexes" to these works a collection of his articles, coming to eight volumes. Biographical data on this productive writer is to be found in Mohl, note 184 above, II, p. 401 et seq.

[206] C. van Bynkershoek, *Quaestiones juris publici* (1737); Bynkershoek, *De foro legatorum tam in causa civili quam criminali* (1721).

issues he pointed to that scientific method which writers on international law should follow.

In the very division of the sources of international law Bynkershoek was an undoubted prophet of the new, purely scientific, orientation in this branch of jurisprudence. He considered to be the main grounds of international law: first, customs (*usus*) and morals (*mores majorum*); second, the agreement of peoples (*consensus populorum*) expressed in morals and in customs, and in international treaties. All these positive grounds of international law are confirmed with rather successful generalizations of historical facts and contemporary data. But Bynkershoek did not confine himself to the methods of the positive school; he also identified the significance of philosophical analysis, an instrument of which is reason (*ratio*) based on the very nature of things. Reason should be a natural aid when investigating questions of international law: "*Ratio, ipsa, inquam, ratio juris gentium est anima*".[207] Bynkershoek marked the path to which contemporary representatives of the science of international law adhere.

C. Period of Combination of Philosophical Principles with Elements of Positive International Law

§37. If the abstract or natural-philosophical orientation deprived the science of international law of real power and credit in the eyes of State officials, then as we have seen, the school of positivists fell into the opposite extreme: it turned science into a servant of practice, a defender of all its shortcomings and abuses. The authority of science could be elevated only by the conciliatory combination of both methods, by the correct correlation of the date of experience and philosophical speculation. Such was the orientation of the third period, contemporary to us, of the development of the science of international law.

The forefather of the new, truly scientific, method of investigating questions of international law was the well-known Georg Friedrich von Martens [(1756-1821)], Professor of Göttingen University, subsequently a representative of the Hanover Government attached to the Union Diet at Frankfurt-on-Main.[208] Martens considered the abstract discourses on

[207] Bynkershoek, ibid. (1737), lib. I, cap. II.

[208] G. F. von Martens, *Primae lineae juris gentium Europaearum practici* (Göttingen, 1785); G. F. Martens, *Précis du droit des gens moderne de l'Europe, fondé sur les traités et l'usage* (Göttingen, 1789) – there were many editions, of deserving attention are those edited by Silvestre Pinheiro-Ferreira (Paris, 1831) and Charles Vergé (Paris, 1864). On the legal scholarship of this writer, see Mohl, note 184 above, II, p. 460 et seq.

issues of international law to be useless, but also opposed the mechanical collecting of the facts of international life without drawing general guiding principles from them. It seemed to him that the science of international law would only rise to the height of its calling when by means of abstraction and critique it would identify, on the basis of international customs, treaties, and historical examples, those legal norms by which contemporary States can and should determine their mutual relations.

Martens recognized the existence of positive international law, basing himself, in accordance with his method, on analyses of numerous treaties, international customs, and general legal consciousness of civilized peoples, demonstrating the undoubted *de facto* agreement of peoples and governments with regard to the general conditions of a lawful international life. The genius and erudition with which Martens drew general conclusions from the mass of historical facts of all countries and all times should be no surprise – that international law is not a domain where arbitrariness dominates but, on the contrary, that States recognize certain rights and duties, in compliance with which only the correct course is possible.

Martens imparted to his research and conclusions a completely scientific form in one harmonious system which surpassed the systems of many luminaries of the science of international law. He began an exposition of positive international law with the doctrine concerning its subjects, which were the European civilized States, then passed on the means of acquiring international rights and determined the rights of States relating to territory and relations relating to obligations arising from treaties; war he considered as a means of settling international conflicts. Finally, the large collection of treaties published by Martens and the thorough development of certain special issues of international law gave him one of the most honored places in the ranks of authoritative writers on international law.

However, neither Martens' works nor his orientation were free of mistakes and partisanship. First, he had a complete misconception about the essence of philosophical international law, saying that it is only the application of natural law determining the relations between individuals and to relations of States with one another. Next, in all of Martens' works there is a lack of independent critique and, on the contrary, an excessive addiction to facts. He did little to comprehend and generalize the positive historical data he collected and gave that data significantly more space than speculation.

During the first half of the nineteenth century, the orientation to which Martens adhered was dominant in the science of international law. The works of English and American jurists especially suffered from the lack of a critical attitude towards the sources of positive international law. These writers concentrated on demonstrating that a particular rule or institution defended by them had existed since time immemorial and, moreover, rested on the agreed opinions of authorities. Whether it corresponded to the requirements of contemporary international life and developmental laws thereof – the question does not even occur to them. Moreover, the writers of the Anglo-American School are not distinguished for the objectivity of their studies of the principles of international law: political and patriotic reflections often cloud their views and place them in opposition to the humane and progressive aspirations of the jurists of continental Europe.

The North American diplomat and jurist, [Henry] Wheaton, occupies an eminent place in the ranks of the notable representatives of this School.[209]

By positive international law he understands the aggregate of legal rules derived from the nature of international society and necessary for determining the mutual relations of States, with those limitations and changes introduced by custom or universal agreement. It is evident that Wheaton did not confine his research to the narrow sphere of treaties and practice of the intercourse of States but took under advisement the "nature of international society", which cannot be revealed without identifying the essence of international relations. Just as Martens, however, Wheaton did not distinguish precisely between philosophical and positive international law. Similarly to his predecessor, Wheaton gave greater weight to facts over ideas, not differing in depth of thought or logical nature of conclusions. But Wheaton's method was original in that he usually first set out some philosophical principles, general propositions, and then accompanied them with selected facts and customs of international life confirming them. It is obvious that it is impossible by this means to reveal the essence of positive international law because the abstract principles advanced by Wheaton, in essence *petitiones principii*, assume to be proved that which needs to be proved.

The work of the contemporary writer, [Sir Robert Joseph] Phillimore, is incomparably superior: *Commentaries upon International Law*.[210] They encompass the entire domain of international law, giving evidence of a basic familiarity with continental literature and continental international relations, which is not always possible to find in the works of other English

[209] Henry Wheaton, *Elements of International Law* (London, 1836). 2 vols.; French editions of 1848 and 1852; Richard Henry Dana edition of 1866; Boyd edition of 1878 in London. Also see Lawrence, note 91 above, in four volumes. Wheaton's work was translated into the Chinese language.

[210] Phillimore, note 1 above; the second edition appeared in 1871-1874; the third edition began to be issued in 1879 but by reason of the author's death was not completed.

jurists; finally, Phillimore drew attention to those questions of international law which were not studied by his predecessors; for example, the relations of the Roman curia with Catholic States.

His entire work is divided into two main sections: the first three volumes treat legal relations between States, the violation of which is a legitimate occasion for demanding satisfaction by a particular means or for beginning military actions. Here are considered the rights of States as subjects of international relations, objects of international law, law of war and neutrality (public international law). Volume IV sets out international private and criminal law, the violation of which, Phillimore suggests, does not provide legitimate grounds for declaring war.[211] Of the individual issues, the English jurist dwells in detail on the doctrine concerning sources of international law and, *inter alia*, deems to be binding those provisions drawn from the very nature of international relations. But he gives especially important significance to Roman law, calling it "written reason" and the best aid for acquiring precise and full knowledge of international law. One cannot fail to see in such an understanding of Roman law, to which international relations was unknown, the fundamental error of Phillimore unfavorably reflected throughout his entire work. Also unfounded was his division of international law into the said two sections because the entire domain of private-law international relations is under the same guarantee of governments as direct relations between States. These shortcomings do not diminish, however, the superior scientific significance of Phillimore's work; he to this day remains one of the most honored authorities of the science of international law.[212]

§38. The science of international law found talented and diligent German scholars and is significantly obliged to them for their research. In contrast to Anglo-American jurists, the German literature of the first half of the nineteenth century sought to impart a philosophical character to the

[211] "The obligations *juris privati inter gentes* are not – as the obligations *juris publici inter gentes* are – the result of legal necessity, but of social convenience, and they are called by the name of Comity – *comitas gentium*". Phillimore, note 1 above, I, §16, p. 12.

[212] Of the works by Anglo-American jurists, there are deserving of special attention: Sir Travers Twiss, *The Law of Nations Considered as Independent Political Communities* (Oxford, 1861). 2 vols.; the last edition was 1884. James Kent, *Kent's Commentary on International Law*, ed. John Thomas Abdy (Cambridge, 1866); Henry Wager Halleck, *International Law; or, Rules Regulating the Intercourse of States in Peace and War*, ed. Sherston Baker (London, 1878). 2 vols.; Edward Shepherd Creasy, *First Platform of International Law* (London, 1876); William Edward Hall, *A Treatise on International Law* (4th ed.; Oxford, 1895); Thomas Alfred Walker, *The Science of International Law* (London, 1893).

study of positive international law. The philosophy of international law arose in Germany as part of the philosophy of law in general. [Immanuel] Kant, [Johann Gottlieb] Fichte, and [George Wilhelm Friedrich] Hegel made international law a section of their philosophical systems, developing its concepts from higher philosophical principles. Other German scholars occupied themselves with the philosophical treatment thereof; that is, subjected actual international relations to comprehensive research and on this basis attempted to create one organic integral system of positive international law.

Noteworthy among the followers of the first method were: [Johannes Baptista] Fallati [(1809-1855)], Gelschner, and Lorenz von Stein.[213] The best representatives of the second orientation were: Heinrich Bernhard Oppenheim [(1819-1880)], Heffter, and Bluntschli. We confine ourselves to briefly indicating the merits and shortcomings of the works of these three last writers on international law.

Oppenheim wished to set out a system of international law, but his work[214] does not address all questions of international law; the system he adopted is distinctive, however, for its simplicity and deserves attention. But the success of the work is greatly harmed by the author's political discourses about contemporary international practice, completely inappropriate in a scholarly treatise.

Heffter's textbook enjoys an excellent and well-deserved reputation.[215] The German scholar treated legally and with full knowledge of the matter vast material of positive international law, having demonstrated a basic familiarity with the extensive literature on the subject-matter. But one cannot agree with Heffter's system.

Heffer divided his work into three main parts: (1) international law during peace; (2) international law during war; and (3) forms of international intercourse, in which the rights and duties of diplomatic representatives and measures of protecting the social interests of States are set out. It is evident that this last part relates entirely to the peaceful state of international life and should not be set out specially. Moreover, when compiling the law of peace and law of war as separate parts of international law, Heffter gives occasion to suppose that war is an autonomous order of legal relations between States

[213] On the views of these writers, see Kaltenborn von Stachau, note 184 above, p. 160.

[214] Heinrich Bernhard Oppenheim, *System des Völkerrechts* (1845; 2d ed.; 1866).

[215] August Wilhelm Heffter, *Das europäische Völkerrecht der Gegenwart auf den bisherigen Grundlagen* (1844; 7th ed.; 1881); Heffter, *Le droit international public de l'Europe*, transl. Jules Bergson (Paris, 1866); Heffter, Европейское международное право, transl. Baron K. F. Taube, with Preface by F. F. Martens (Spb., 1880).

and not a means of protecting international rights, which in reality is what it is.

As for Bluntschli, in his work on the contemporary international law of civilized States set out in the form of a Code,[216] he wished to give practitioners in the sphere of international relations a convenient manual, having formulated, in the form of concise provisions, the basic principles of international law and indicating under each the reasons explaining these provisions. Bluntschli achieved his purpose: his codification manual became widely-known and contributed to the dissemination of familiarity with international law. The work of this likeable scholar (died in 1881) is imbued to a high degree with an enlightened and humane view of international relations, but suffers from the shortcoming that one often finds – the provisions do not formulate principles of international law in force, but the *pia desiderata* of the author.[217]

The literature of international law in Italy has recently become extensive. The point of departure for the doctrines thereof is primarily the principle of nationality which, as we saw above, is proclaimed by the best Italian jurists – Mancini, [Augusto] Pierantoni [(1840-1911)], Luigi Palma

[216] Johann Caspar Bluntschli, *Das modern Völkerrecht der civilisirten Staaten als Rechtsbuch dargestellt* (Nördlingen, 1868; 3d ed.; 1878); Bluntschli, *Le droit international codifié*, transl. Charles Lardy (Paris, 1895); Bluntschli, Современное международное право цивилизованных государств, изложенное в виде кодекса И. Блюнтчли, transl. V. A. Ul'ianitskii and A. Lodyzhenskii; ed. Count L. A. Kamarovskii (Moscow, 1876); Bluntschli, *Gong fa hui tong:* [10 juan], transl. William Alexander Parsons Martin (Beijing, [1880]). 5 vols.; Bluntschli, *Kongpŏp hoet'ong: Kwon 1-10*, transl. William Martin (Korea, [1896]). 3 vols.

[217] The following recent works of German literature deserve attention: Neumann, *Grundriss des heutigen europäischen Völkerrechts* (Vienna, 1877; 3d ed.; 1885); Bulmerincq, "Völkerrecht", in Heinrich von Marquardsen, *Handbuch des öffentlichen Rechts der Gegenwart in Monographien* (Tübingen, 1883), I(2); Peter Resch, *Das europäische Völkerrecht der Gegenwart* (Graz, 1885); Franz von Holtzendorff, "Das europäische Völkerrecht", in Holtzendorff, *Encyclopädie der Rechtswissenschaft* (Leipzig, 1870), I; Hermann Johann Friedrich Schulze, *Grundriss zu Vorlesungen über Völkerrecht* (Heidelburg, 1880); Adolf Hartmann, *Institutionen des praktischen Völkerrechts in Friedenszeiten* (Hanover, 1874; 2d ed.; 1878); Dr. Quaritsch, *Compendium des europäischen Völkerrechts* (2d ed.; Berlin, 1875); Franz von Liszt, *Das Völkerrecht* (2d ed.; Berlin, 1902); Liszt, Международное правов систематическом изложении, transl. Vladimir Emmanuilovich Grabar (Iur'ev, 1902); Karl Gareis, *Institutionen des Völkerrechts* (2d ed.; Giessen, 1901). Of special scholarly value is the *Handbuch des Völkerrechts* edited by Baron Holtzendorff in four volumes between 1885 and 1889 in collaboration with other jurists. Finally, within the school of German jurists must be numbered Professor James Lorimer, of Edinburgh University, who published his *The Institutes of the Law of Nations* (London, 1883-1884) in two volumes, translated in a single volume as *Principes de droit international*, transl. Ernest Nys (Brussels, 1885).

[(1837-1899)], and others[218] as the supreme principle of the new European international law. However, the idea of nationality, false in the sense which the said writers impart to it, found opponents among Italian scholars in the person of [Conte Terenzio] Mamiani [del Rovero (1799-1885)] and especially [Guido] Padelletti [(1843-1878)],[219] who contrasted it to the principle of autonomy and independence of States as subjects of international law. Whatever the case, the Italian literature on international law endeavored to reach the height of contemporary trends in scholarship and tactfully treated all questions arising in international life.

In French literature, rich in monographs on various questions of international law, there were no attempts until recently to systematically set out this science. The gap was thought to have been filled in 1877 by two French scholars: [Théophile] Funck-Brentano [(1830-1906)] and [Albert] Sorel [(1842-1906)], who published a concise textbook on international law.[220]

But their experiment could not be called successful: they rather provided a series of publicist essays on international law during peace and war than a scientific account of the principles of positive international law.[221]

Finally, a work by the South American jurist and diplomat, [Carlo] Calvo,[222] has recently received extensive distribution. This work is distinguished by a wealth of cited facts from the domain of international relations of the European and American States, but insufficiently generalizes

[218] See on Italian contemporary literature: Pierantoni, note 180 above; Pierantoni, *Trattato di diritto internazionale* (Rome, 1881), vol. 1 of 4. Compare Pasquale Fiore, *Trattato di diritto pubblico internazionale* (Milan, 1865); Fiore, *Nouveau droit international public suivant les besoins de la civilisation moderne*, transl. Paul Pradier-Fodéré (Paris, 1868-1869). 2 vols.; Giuseppe Carnazza Amari, *Trattato sul diritto internazionale pubblico di pace* (Milan, 1875).

[219] Terenzio Mamiani del Rovero, *D'un nuovo diritto pubblico europea* (1859); Guido Padelletti, *Revue de droit international*, III.

[220] Th. Funck-Brentano and A. Sorel, *Précis du droit des gens* (Paris, 1877), reviewed by F. F. Martens, Сборник государственных знаний [Collection of State Knowledge], V. Paul Pradier-Fodéré, *Traité de droit international public* (Paris, 1889-1897). 7 vols. This work is enormous, but distinctive for lightness of content and incoherence of the system. Also see Robert Piédelièvre, *Précis de droit international public* (Paris, 1894).

[221] Superior in scholarly merit to the work by Funck-Bretano and Sorel is the small study by the talented French scholar, Louis Renault, *Introduction à l'étude du droit international* (Paris, 1879). Compare Henry Bonfils, *Manuel de droit international public* (1894; 3d ed.; 1901, edited by Paul Fauchille).

[222] Carlo Calvo, *Derecho internacional teorico y pratico* (1868); Calvo, *Le droit international théorique et pratique* (2d ed.; 1870; 2 vols.; 3d ed.; 1881; 4 vols.).

these facts and treats them critically from the standpoint of general guiding principles of law: too large a place is given to political practice to the detriment of an autonomous theoretical treatment of the subject-matter. The work of the noted Swiss jurist, Alphonse Rivier [(1835-1898)] on the principles of international law, for depth of thought, enormous erudition, and remarkable clarity, merits special attention.[223]

Russian literature is rather sparse for autonomous works encompassing the entire system of international law. The basic principles of this science have been set out in the following:

(1) D. I. Kachenovskii (Professor of Kharkov University) – Курс международного права [Course of International Law] (1863-1866. 2 vols.); an uncompleted work which dwelt on the history of international relations in the Middle Ages).

(2) A. N. Stoianov (Professor of Kharkov University) – Очерки истории и догматики международного права [Survey of the History and Dogmatic of International Law] (1875); published according to the Notes of Kachenovskii.

(3) M. N. Kapustin (former Professor of Moscow University and Administrator of St. Petersburg Educational District) – Обозрение предметов международного права [Survey of the Subject-Matter of International Law] (1856) and Международное право: конспект лекций [International Law: Conspectus of Lectures] (1873); the first is significantly obsolete, but the second is remarkable as an attempted autonomous systematization of the entire science of international law, but too concise to serve as a manual for familiarization with the subject-matter of the science.

(4) [Anton] Bialecki (Professor of Warsaw University) – О значении международного права и его материалов [On the Significance of International Law and the Materials Thereof] (1872); useful for familiarization with various views of representatives of foreign literature relating to international treaties, customs, governmental regulations, and other sources of international law.

(5) [Petr Evgen'evich] Kazanskii – Учебник международного права публичного и гражданского (вместо литографированного издания лекций) [Textbook of Public and Civil International Law (in place of a lithographed edition of lectures)] (Odessa, 1902); the author reveals great erudition, but his system of exposition and scientific conclusions generate serious doubts.

223 Alphonse Rivier, *Principes du droit des gens* (Paris, 1896). 2 vols.

V. Task and Purpose of Science of Contemporary International Law

§39. The history of international relations demonstrates the existence of common social and cultural interests between civilized peoples and the need for legal norms regulating these interests; the historical development of the science of international law leads to the conviction that the system of rules developed only exerts a creative impact on practice when it is based on the study of actual relations which peoples have during a particular epoch under the protection of the general law which they have created. Proceeding from this information, one may say that the task of the science of contemporary international law consists of identifying the legal consciousness of contemporary educated peoples expressed in the aspiration to ensure their legitimate spiritual and material interests through an exchange of services, mutual assistance, and agreement.

In reality, the reasonable needs of peoples were not always the subject-matter of international politics; they did not always constitute the content of those negotiations, legal transactions, or treaties concluded between States. But the lack of understanding on the part of State authorities of the essential social and State needs of their people or insufficient respect for them always leads to the result that international obligations quickly discover their own obvious unfoundedness and are subject either to change or to violation. Only those treaties withstand the onslaught of circumstances and serve the development of international relations which have been concluded by States in awareness of and for the sake of satisfaction of the rights and for the benefit of their peoples.

In the same way, the scientific processing of international law should be directed not towards the creation of artificial systems having no foundation in the present or inconsistent with the solidarity of interests and aspirations of contemporary educated States, but should pursue one goal – to establish, on the basis of these relations, principles of international order that are consistent with the common cultural tasks and emanating from the full mutuality of rights and duties of civilized peoples. Obviously, such an order cannot have as its supreme principle the sovereign independence of every individual State because this principle inevitably leads to the dominion and justification of exclusive interests contrary to law in the domain of international relations. Underlying the scientific system of contemporary international law must be the idea of an international community, according to which every autonomous State is an organic part of an single whole connected with other States by common interests and rights.

Considering the contemporary international order from this point of view, the science of international law will have as its subject-matter only positive legal norms developed by the legal consciousness of contemporary educated peoples duly reflected in international customs, treaties, and practice of the mutual intercourse of States. The personal views of a particular scholar, no matter how sublime, humane, and worthy of respect, should not be confused with international law in force. But in separating our desiderata from the principles and laws assimilated by practice, we do not exclude a critical attitude towards the existing order. Only it is impossible to acknowledge that the correct scale for such criticism is not the principle of political equilibrium nor the idea of nationality, for they are not principles which provide the legal foundation for the mutual relations of States. The idea of law is the sole possible guiding principle when considering the positive principles of international law from the standpoint of *de lege feranda*. There is no place within a scientific system for political considerations.

The legal principle was adopted by the States as the guiding principle of their mutual relations. The great allied powers assembled in the Congress at Aachen issued a Declaration of [3 (15) November 1818] which, *inter alia*, provided that the "monarchies entered into the alliance recognize as their chief immutable duty in all relations between themselves and with other powers to comply with undeviatingly the provisions of international law".[224] One may only regret that the States, having proclaimed this principle, did not always find it necessary or possible to actually be guided by it.

VI. Basic Features of System

§40. Each scientific system should satisfy two main requirements: first, it should encompass the entire domain of questions subject to study; and second, introduce in the last a certain order imbued with one general idea. Thus, inasmuch as the subject-matter of the science of international law is the aggregate of vital relations existing between contemporary educated States, the system of international law obviously should be the system of these relations and not those laws and principles that in the course of time have been developed in international life.

[224] Detailed critiques of Stoianov and Kapustin were published by the present author in the Журнал гражданского и уголовного права [Journal of Civil and Criminal Law] (1876) and in the Сборник государственных знаний [Collection of State Knowledge], II. Also see Danevskii, Пособие к изучению истории и системы международного права [Manual for the Study of History and System of International Law] (Kharkov, 1892). 2 vols.

The majority of representatives of the science of international law ignore this essential condition for the proper systematization of international law. They substantiate its system either on the basis of Roman law or on incidental and personal considerations having nothing in common with the objective grounds of the science.[225] A systematic dominates in works devoted to a general survey of international relations and law that is borrowed from Roman civil law. When applying it to international law, jurists, of course, wished to fully communicate their legal character and impart great certainty to the tenets of their science, but in fact they completely distorted the meaning and autonomous significance of inter-State relations and the law applicable to them.

The system to which we intend to adhere is as follows.

We shall consider all questions of international relations and the science of international law from the standpoint of the idea of an international community. It underlies the contemporary international order and should be the highest principle in the science of international law which justifies and links all provisions it contains. Having established this principle on positive data, we set out analytically the inalienable rights that belong to States as members of the international community – as subjects of international law in their mutual relations – with respect to their territories, and finally – as contracting parties entering into international obligations. All these questions, being basic for international law, comprise the General Part of our system.

In the Special Part we consider those real vital relations which unite contemporary educated peoples and provide content to the international administration of States. To the subject-matter of international administration we relegated: first, the interests of entire peoples, both various social classes and individuals in the domain of spiritual life, religious, intellectual, and aesthetic; second, international administration in the sphere of physical life, State, social, and individual economic activity; third, the regulation judicially of civil and criminal legal relations having as their purpose the protection of legitimate rights belonging to a State and subjects within another's possessions (international private and criminal law). Finally, the last section of the Special Part will set out the law of war and the law of neutrality determining the legitimate means which States have to protect their interests and rights as belligerent and neutral powers.

225 Памятники дипломатических сношений [Monuments of Diplomatic Relations], II, p. 370; F. F. Martens, Собрание трактатов и конвенций [Collection of Treaties and Conventions], VII, No. 291.

VII. Space of Operation of International Law

§41. Contemporary international law is the product of the cultural life and legal consciousness of the peoples of European civilization. As the history of international relations shows, common social tasks pursued by peoples in mutual intercourse and identical moral and legal views assimilated by them – these are essential conditions of an international legal order – initially developed in Europe and still are far from existing in all States of the globe. Accordingly, the spatial operation of international law is confined to those peoples who recognize the basic principles of European culture and are worthy of the name educated peoples.[226]

The unique social and State conditions in which peoples of the Muslim faith live, and also pagan and wild tribes, do not make it possible to apply international law in intercourse with these uneducated or semi-educated peoples. International relations rest on the idea of community, which is inconceivable without solidarity of interests and common aspirations uniting peoples. Moreover, the Muslim lands are administered solely on the basis of the Koran, which treats peoples of other faiths with hostility and intolerance. As for the barbarian tribes, they not only do not feel the need for international intercourse, but usually do not even have a firm social organization and definite territorial boundaries. One cannot, therefore, say that maintaining intercourse *de facto* between educated and uneducated peoples is not subject at all to the determination of law. We suggest that they should be subject to the prescriptions of natural law; that is, the aggregate of certain principles arising from the moral and reason of man. Natural law requires that a word of honor is performed so that the life, honor, and property of another is respected, so that evil instincts cede place to noble motives: it is evident that such a law applicable to intercourse of uneducated peoples does not assume either solidarity of interests or an awareness of the need for mutual intercourse, and consequently does not identify with the provisions of international law. But it is undoubted that civilized States should set an example to peoples of a lower culture in the good faith performance of obligations assumed.[227]

226 See, for example, the strange system of Johann Ludwig Klüber, *Droit des gens modern de l'Europe* (Paris, 1861).

227 That is why down to the present they speak of European international law, although this classification is inaccurate in that contemporary international law extends to the civilized States of America which, following the example of the Northern United States, declared it to be binding on itself.

Against the exclusion of Turkey and certain other Asian States from the international community existing between the European educated peoples it is objected that the last not only enter into *de facto* intercourse with these States, but conclude treaties of peace, alliance, and trade with them and, moreover, Turkey was solemnly recognized at the 1856 Paris Congress as a fully-fledged member of the family of European peoples (Article VII, Treaty of Paris). These objections only demonstrate that those who wish to extend international law to uncivilized States are not aware of the positive grounds of the contemporary international order based on mutuality and confuse natural law with positive international law. The reference to Article VII of the Treaty of Paris cannot be considered to be persuasive because the great powers, having proclaimed the equality of the Sublime Porte with other European governments, at the same time declined its request to abolish consular jurisdiction and Capitulations operating in Turkey and not consistent with the domestic sovereignty which is recognized for every civilized State that is a member of international society. The jurisdiction of consuls also exists in Persia and China, for these States too, just as the Ottoman Empire, do not provide all the guarantees essential to ensure the interests and rights of foreigners present among them. So long as material changes do not occur in laws and in the political and social order prevailing in the East, the said States will not enjoy in international intercourse the rights belonging to educated peoples.[228]

While insisting on the position that only States approximately identically developed culturally and socially may be subjects of contemporary international law, we do not want by this to say that international law is based solely on Christian principles and is binding only in relations between peoples of the Christian faith. No, it may be recognized and complied with irrespective of religious faiths predominant in a country, but it is necessary that the people involved or the classes leading them share the views on the reasonable goals of human existence and the purpose of the State developed by the age-old culture of civilized European peoples.

We therefore cannot concur with the opinion expressed by Bluntschli that the operation of international law is not confined only to European civilized peoples, that its domain is the entire world, that it coincides with the law of all mankind. Such a noble and elevated cosmopolitanism deprives international law of any political foundation and practical significance; he

[228] With regard to the cardinal issue of the spatial operation of positive international law there is a complete confusion of concepts in the contemporary literature: one author cites another or refers to the "authority" of another without any critique. Compare Phillimore, note 1 above, §28, p. 23; Theodore Dwight Woolsey, *Introduction to the Study of International Law*, §5; Heffter, note 21 above, §7; G. F. Martens, note 1 above, §8, et seq.

converts international law into a series of ideal legal norms unrealizable under contemporary conditions. As John Stuart Mill rightly noted,[229] to apply European international law to uneducated peoples means to understand law stupidly, the basis of which is mutuality; that is, the practical condition which forces civilized States to treat with respect their joint rights and interests and which have no place in intercourse with uneducated peoples.

VIII. Relations of International Law to Other Legal and Political Sciences

§42. The position that the science of international law holds among other legal and political sciences is determined by its subject-matter, task, and purpose. International law serves as an expression and sanction of a community existing between all aspects of the individual life of educated peoples. Accordingly, the science of international law, with its complete autonomy, is organically linked with other sections of jurisprudence having as their subject-matter private, social, and State legal life.[230]

I. Without any doubt, international law differs in content from civil and criminal law. But given the contemporary development of international relations, both civil and criminal law find their highest protection in international law. Indeed, the codes and statutes determining private law relations are insufficient to guarantee respect for the rights of individuals and their judicial protection outside a particular country. For this, the mutual recognition by States is necessary of the binding force of foreign laws within their territorial limits. Thus, private international law is an essential supplement to the civil law of every civilized State. Contemporary governments are fully aware that the domestic legal order depends to a significant extent on the respect which criminal laws find on the part of other States. For the sake of ensuring internal order and safety, they enter into agreements on the mutual extradition of criminals and assist one another in identifying persons guilty and determining the fact of crimes. The principles flowing from this are the subject-matter of international criminal law.

II. In the historical survey of international relations we attempted to indicate the link between the social life of peoples and the character of

[229] This position is demonstrated in greater detail in F. F. Martens, О консулах и консульской юрисдикции на Востоке [On Consuls and Consular Jurisdiction in the East] (Spb., 1873), p. 513 et seq. Also see F. F. Martens, Россия и Англия в Средней Азии [Russia and England in Central Asia] (Spb., 1880), pp. 10-23, also published in the French, German, and English languages.

[230] John Stuart Mill, *Dissertations and Discussions: Political, Philosophical, and Historical* (London, 1859), I, p. 161; III, p. 166.

their international activity. If the international community and the internal kinship of peoples is based on the community of their social elements, it is understandable that the relationship between international law and social law is close. Those domestic laws which determine the social system and the mutual rights and duties of social classes and the State obviously should influence the law ensuring the social interests of every people in the field of international relations.

III. The same should be said of State law. Domestic State orders are always reflected in the order existing in international relations. Contemporary positive international law cannot be understood without knowing the State law in force of educated peoples. On the other hand, if the reasonable goal of every State is to establish that order within a country which would ensure the comprehensive development of personal qualities and abilities of each subject, this goal may be achieved only by means of international intercourse, the exchange of services, and the mutual assistance of States as subjects of international law.

IV. The doctrine of the external relations of States or politics is commonly placed beside that of international law. The subject-matter of the study of international law and foreign policy is not the same: the first sets out those laws and legal principles by which international relations are administered; the second teaches the art of the satisfaction, by the most advisable means, of international interests created by geographical position, cultural system, or political life of the State. When seeking the appropriate means for achieving reasonable goals of the State in the field of international relations, politics should first and foremost be guided by those legal norms which international law provides because the failure to comply with them would be contrary to the reasonable interests being pursued. In other words, international policy should be lawful if it truly wishes to satisfy not egoistic and ambitious interests, but legitimate needs of the people, thanks to whom international law exists.[231]

V. Finally, international law should not be confused with diplomacy and the law of diplomacy. Diplomacy does not differ materially from foreign policy, and its name indicates the persons who dedicate themselves to foreign policy should base their activity on the study of positive data of international treaties (*diploma*) regulating the mutual relations of States.[232]

[231] Compare Heffter, note 21 above, §4; Renault, note 220 above, p. 27; Kachenovskii, Курс международного права [Course of International Law] (Kharkov, 1963-1866), I, §6; Holtzendorff, note 217 above, pp. 47-68.

[232] Compare Klüber, note 226 above, §7; Pradier-Fodéré, *Cours de droit diplomatique à l'usage des agents politiques du Ministère des affairs étrangêres des États européens*

If diplomacy and diplomatic law have become synonyms of arbitrariness and cunning, then this is thanks to the distortion of simple and reasonable concepts on the purpose of international relations and the tasks of diplomacy justified by the reason and history of international law.

IX. Sources of International Law

§43. Independent States forming an international union do not subject themselves to a sovereign authority which would determine their mutual relations by its own laws; they also are not subject to responsibility before an international tribunal for a violation of international law. The basis of legal norms determining international relations is solely an awareness by civilized States of the need for international legal order and their voluntary agreement arising therefrom to recognize its binding character.[233] This awareness and agreement receive their external expression (or formulation) in international customs and treaties, diplomatic negotiations, legislation, governmental regulations, and, finally, judicial decisions. Insofar as the said acts and customary principles are a true reflection of the legal consciousness of States, they may be considered to be sources of contemporary positive international law.

I. Those rules and procedures which are established in international relations on the basis of the constant and uniform application to instances identical in essence are called international customs. As norms of international relations, customary principles have enormous practical and legal significance.[234]

From the practical side, the importance of international customs is evident from the fact that many basic institutes and provisions of international law have no protection other than the tacit agreement of States to their recognition and compliance. International treaty and ambassadorial

et américains (Paris, 1881), I, p. 1: "la diplomatie est l'art des négociations". Pradier-Fodéré's definition of diplomatic law, however, is mistaken, as a "branche du droit public externe". The law of diplomacy is not a part of international law. See the perceptive remarks of Bernard, note 77 above, p. 111 et seq.

233 [Herrenius] Modestinus: "Omne jus aut consensus fecit aut necessitas constituit aut firmavit consuetudo". Compare Heffter, note 1 above, §3, 8; Phillimore, note 1 above, I, p. 14 et seq; Creasy, note 212 above, p. 65 et seq.; Bluntschli, note 216 above, §13 et seq.; Holtzendorff, note 217 above (1870), I, p. 934 et seq.; Holtzendorff, note 217 above, pp. 77-156.

234 Bynkershoek, *Quaestiones juris publici*, III, 10: "*Jus gentium oritur e pactis tacitis et praesumtis, quae ratio et usus inducunt*". *De reb. belli* praef.: "*Ut mores gentium mutantur, sic mutatur jus gentium*". Phillimore, note 1 above, I, p. 38 et seq.

law arose and were confirmed by custom. Next the rights which monarchs and, in general, representatives of the sovereign authority enjoy during sojourns on foreign territory, and likewise the etiquette of mutual relations, developed by themselves and retained force without any formal sanction. The international law of the sea, beginning with the rules on the shipment of goods, marine insurance, relations between skippers and seamen, and ending with the rights of central trade – all arose in the Middle Ages, initially in the form of customs, which were then recorded in special collections, and finally became part of the legislation of various States. The majority of legal norms constituting the law of war until recently were not formulated either by international treaties or by State legislation, remaining in the form of customs. Finally, in the domain of private international law one may point to the extremely important principle: *locus regit actum*, which also is based on the force of custom.[235]

From the standpoint of law, international customs have great significance. Whereas customs existing in a State prove that persons guided by them are linked with one another by a community of moral and legal world outlook and vital interests, the same may be said about international customs: their recognition and respect on the part of States is evidence of that mutuality of interests of educated nations and the identical legal consciousness uniting them on which contemporary international law is based.

The process of the formation of international customary norms explains to us the very essence of international law and the highest source of its binding force. Unlike customs operating in private and social being of peoples and generated by the dark instinct of the masses and immutable force of circumstances, international customary rules are established more by calculation, on the basis of speculation, consciously. Often those principles which little by little are confirmed in international practice as customary rules initially are proclaimed as a reasonable principle of international relations by some leading jurist or noteworthy political figure. Thus, the origin of international customs is confirmed by the position set out by us above, that an awareness of the need for legal order in the field of international relations is the true source of international law.[236]

[235] The major collections of international customary principles are the following: Rolls d'Oléron (twelfth century); Consolato del Mare (fourteenth century); Guidon de la mer (sixteenth century). Compare Pardessus, note 18 above, I; Ferdinand Perels, *Das internationale öffentliche Seerecht der Gegenwart* (Berlin, 1882), §3.

[236] In this sense the observation of Woolsey is completely correct: "Self-protection and intercourse are the two sources of international law". Woolsey, note 228 above, Introduction, §6 footnote.

II. By international treaties in the meaning of sources of international law we understand any kind of obligation mutually assumed by States – whether expressed in treaties and conventions or in notes and declarations. Such agreements of States represent primarily a source whose study is essential for a complete understanding of existing international legal relations.[237]

International treaties in this sense may be divided into two major kinds: some formulate legal norms binding on States respected in practice as principles of international law; others, on the contrary, are transactions between two or several States concerning their private interests.

Recognition of principles of international law has been attested to on the part of States in a number of remarkable acts having the force of laws for international society. Among these are: the Declaration of Catherine II on the Armed Neutrality and confirmation of its principles in the 1856 Paris Declaration; the 1864 Geneva Convention for the amelioration of the condition of the wounded in the field during war; the postal and telegraph unions, and others. All similar acts were generated not by struggle and agreement of opposing interests of the parties, but by States aware of the need to precisely determine those legal rules which, being binding, are ambiguously expressed in customs or special international agreements.

There belong to treaties of the second kind which represent compromises between various interests of the contracting parties: treaties on peace, commercial treaties, cartel, literary, and consular conventions, and so on. Concluded by individual governments for the sake of satisfying the interests of the contracting parties, such treaties evidently may not serve as sources of international law which extend their operation to all educated States. However, when comparing cartel conventions with one another or navigation treaties and other treaties concluded between various States, we note that they usually are similar not only in their grounds, but often in their details. Thus, the legal order established in the sphere of mutual relations between certain contracting parties in reality is a general order joining all States and consisting of relations of obligation between them. Considered from this standpoint, the special agreements of States undoubtedly should be deemed to be a source of positive international law.[238]

[237] Carl Bergbohm, *Staatsverträge und Gesetze als Quellen des Völkerrechts* (Dorpat, 1877), §77 et seq; Jellinek, *Die rechtliche Natur der Staatsverträge* (Vienna, 1880); Renault, note 221 above, p. 32 et seq.

[238] From this point of view, collections of treaties are of special significance. We indicate the major collections: G. F. Martens, *Recueil des traités* from 1761 to the present, with supplements by Saalfeld, Murhard, Samwer, and Hopf; from 1887, Felix Stoerk. *Das Staatsarchiv* by Aegidi and Klauhold; *Archives diplomatiques* from 1861; Individual States have their own special treaty collections, such as: Austria-Hungary – Neumann, note 126

Here it is necessary to eliminate one misunderstanding. The binding force of international treaties not protected by means of enforcement is based on the voluntary limitation their will by those States which enter into the agreement. It is evident that such self-limitation cannot be assumed with respect to States which have not signed the particular treaty.[239]

III. Diplomatic negotiations and acts which prepare the resolution of questions arising between States or determine the mutual position of States at a particular time and under certain circumstances serve as an important aid for explaining legal orders in the field of international relations.

IV. National laws and governmental measures, insofar as they have as their subject-matter relations transcending the limits of State territory, also may and should be deemed a source familiarizing with principles of international law. In the contemporary legislation of educated peoples many provisions generated by international relations are essentially identical, such as, for example, laws on foreigners arriving in the country, consuls, maritime laws, and so on. Rather often international relations provided the initial impetus for certain legislative works in a State or to a change of legislation inconsistent with treaties whose content, in turn, depends on orientations and views dominant in the administration of a country. In a word, the interaction between the domestic life of a State and its international relations is an indisputable fact.[240]

above, 1763-1856, and New Series from 1856; France – Clerq, *Recueil des traités* since 1763; England — Hertslet, Complete Collection; United American States – John H. Haswell, *Treaties and Conventions concluded between the United States of America and Other Powers since July 4, 1776* (Washington, 1889); Russia – Martens, Собрание трактатов [Collection of Treaties] (Spb., 1874-1909). 15 vols. Also see Michman Vashkevich, Сборник действующих трактатов и конвенции, имеющих отношение к военному мореплаванию [Collection of Treaties and Conventions in Force Relating to Naval Navigation] (Spb., 1885); Сборник действующих трактатов, конвенций и соглашений, заключенных Россией с другими государствами и касающих различных вопросов частного международного права [Collection of Treaties, Conventions, and Agreements in Force Concluded by Russia with Other States and Concerning Various Questions of Private International Law] (Spb., 1889-1896). 4 vols.; Japan – *Treaties and Conventions Concluded between the Empire of Japan and Foreign Nations 1854-1874* (Tokyo, 1874). In general, see Ferdinand von Martitz, "Les Recueils des traités internationaux", *Revue de droit international* (1886), p. 168 et seq.

239 Therefore the view of Bluntschli that a decision of a "European congress" is binding on all States, even those who formally did not adhere to it, is completely wrong.

240 Compare Bergbohm, note 238 above, p. 102; Phillimore, note 1 above, I, p. 34 et seq; A. Bialecki, О значении международного права и его материалов [On the Significance of International Law and the Materials Thereof] (Warsaw, 1872), p. 219.

V. The significance of judicial practice for international law will be understood if one has in view that civil and criminal courts of civilized States have been called upon to decide not only issues relating to private international law and criminal law, but often cases which concern public international law, for example, the lack of jurisdiction over diplomatic agents, the liability of monarchs under suits against them by private individuals, and so on.

Certain special courts in a State have an expressly international character. Prize courts are founded by a belligerent State to consider cases concerning captured property of subjects of enemy and neutral States (on prizes) and which are guided not by local laws but by international law. Collections of decisions of such courts provide rich material on all questions of international law, both war and peace. But one should not see in them, as English and American jurists do, an immutable truth not allowing even doubts. Mixed international courts have the same significance, founded in Egypt in 1874 from indigenous subjects and individuals recommended by European governments to consider commercial cases, as well as civil and criminal trials in which the parties are foreigners or persons of different nationalities.

VI. Finally, the history and science of international law are a means for eliciting the true meaning of existing treaties and international customs; they make it possible to imagine in pure form the legal consciousness of peoples expressed in treaties and customary norms, and therefore undoubtedly belong to the sources of international law.[241]

X. Codification of Principles of International Law

§44. Positive international law based on the aforementioned sources suffers from one material shortcoming – the absence of certainty and authenticity of its provisions. Moreover, the publication of such generally-binding international acts as the 1856 Paris Declaration or the 1864 Geneva Convention shows that this shortcoming can be eliminated by the codification of international law. Convinced of the possibility of drawing up a code to determine the mutual relations of States, various attempts were made to resolve this task.

The need to combine the entire aggregate of the principles comprising international law into one organic whole, in the form of a law, has long been on the agenda. [Jeremy] Bentham [(1748-1832)] had thought of

[241] Phillimore, note 1 above, p. 43: "History is a record of the injustice, evil passions and folly as well as of the justice, virtues, and wisdom of Nations".

this, but undertook merely a sketch of an international code which, in his view, should exist.[242] The question which he raised found support among many jurists. Our compatriot, Dmitrii Ivanovich Kachenovskii, Professor at Kharkov University, submitted a remarkable memorandum to the London Law Society in 1862 in which he demonstrated the need for the codification of international law undertaken by the common efforts of jurists of developed countries. The Italian scholar, Augusto Parodo, first set out private international law in the form of the articles of a law.[243] A more successful experiment at producing a digest of international treaties in a single law belongs to [Alphons von] Domin-Petruschevecz [(1835-1871)].[244] Of the most recent works of this kind, that by Bluntschli deserves special attention,[245] having inspired the New York professor, [Francis] Lieber [(1798-1872)][246] to prepare "field instructions" and a draft international code by Dudley Field, a legislator from the state of New York.[247]

Recently, however, these attempts encountered strong objections on the part of authoritative scholars who categorically dispute the feasibility and even the desirability of such codification. Opponents of the reform included: Holtzendorff, Bulmerincq, Bergbohm, and certain other jurists[248] who borrowed the main arguments against codification from the classical work by Savigny.[249]

Applying the propositions advanced by Savigny to international law, they say that: (1) the codification of international law, having severed its organic link with the life and legal consciousness of peoples, has ceased to develop; (2) if one succeeded more or less in successfully codifying civil and

242 John Bowring (ed.), *The Works of Jeremy Bentham* (London, 1843), VIII, p. 538 et seq.

243 Augusto Parodo, *Saggo di codificazione del diritto internazionale* (Torino, 1851).

244 Alphons von Domin-Petruschevecz, *Précis d'un code du droit international* (Leipzig, 1861).

245 Bluntschli, note 216 above (3d ed.; 1878).

246 Francis Lieber, *Draft Outlines for the Government of Armies of the United States in the Field* (1863); see the Annex to Bluntschli.

247 David Dudley Field, *Draft Outlines for an International Code* (New York, 1872; 2d ed., 1876). Compare Leone Levi, *International Law: With Materials for a Code of International Law* (London, 1888).

248 Holtzendorff, note 217 above (1870), I, p. 768; Bulmerincq, note 148 above, p. 180 et seq; Bergbohm, note 238 above, p. 70 et seq.

249 F. C. von Savigny, *Vom Beruf underer Zeit für Gesetzgebund und Rechtswissenschaft* (1814).

criminal law, this was only because the compilers of these codes had in hand ready material in civil and criminal laws which the codifiers of international law do not have; (3) an essential preliminary condition for establishing the international law in force that should be included in a code must be the comprehensive scholarly processing of treaties directed towards the explanation of homogeneous definitions to which the wills of the majority of educated States have agreed; only upon the completion of this preparatory work could one embark upon the codification of international law. However, so far the study of the extensive material consisting of treaties is nil; finally (4) they refer to the best scholarly works on international law set out in the form of a code, with their gaps, contradictions, lack of objectivity, and other shortcomings to demonstrate the untimeliness of this kind of work.

We do not fully concur with these objections; in our view, the codification of international law is not only desirable, it is essential. What is the principal task of any codification? Obviously, it is to precisely determine what is a positive right, a law, and what is not binding. Codification is, first and foremost, a cleansing exercise liberating the law in force from ambiguities, contradictions, and obsolete norms; among all peoples it has served as the best means for familiarizing with law, with those rights and duties which belong to each; finally, it always encouraged respect in government and in society for law, precisely determined and known to all. These reflections justifying codification have greater significance in the field of international law than in civil and criminal law.

In fact, the opponents of codification of international law pretend that it is not enough to recognize the generally binding force of international customs and laws in order to truly be guided by them in all cases; on the contrary a thorough and close familiarity with international norms is required which, however, is least common in those areas that are called upon to administer international relations. If this proposition is correct, then the need for the codification of international law flows logically from it; by stating international laws in force, it provides to practitioners that source from which they easily glean all the reliable information needed and applicable to a concrete matter. Bluntschli's work may serve as an example, which set out all international law in the form of a code; thanks to its form, the work was widely distributed and, of course, contributed to familiarization with the principles of international law more than all the multi-volume works of his predecessors; even the Government of China published it in a translation into their language, to be used as a convenient manual in intercourse with civilized States. The military practice of educated peoples is even more persuasive as to the benefit of the codification of international law. In the wars which occurred recently the belligerent parties in principle recognized the laws and customs of war as binding on themselves; but disputes constantly arose about the true sense and meaning of such because a code of the law of war did not exist adopted by all governments; many cruelties and pathetic violations of military customs would have been avoided if the armies and population of the belligerent States had precise knowledge about the laws of war.[250]

But we agree that the codification of international law is a complex and difficult task which hardly can be performed successfully by the efforts of one individual. At least the attempts undertaken are convincing that even leading jurists experienced in legislative work, such as Bluntschli and Dudley Field, are not in a position to cope with this task. It is essential in order to resolve it to combine the legal scientific forces, and given that international law is developed by the cultural life of various peoples, it is desirable that scholars of all educated nations be involved in this common labor. From this point of view, it seemed desirable to found private societies in various European States for the purpose of studying questions of international law. If a permanent link is maintained between such societies, and if they jointly and amicably will act on the public opinion of civilized peoples in the sense of enlightenment and guidance, then ignorance and dark forces having nothing in common with the real interests of peoples will probably dominate less in international relations. This kind of association now exists. At Ghent in 1873 the Institute of International Law was founded by scholars from various countries with a view to promoting through the collective efforts of its members the progress and gradual codification of international law.[251]

[250] See the development of these arguments in Martens, note 176 above, p. 47 et seq. Compare Holtzendorff, note 217 above, §36.

[251] Here is an excerpt from the Statutes of the Institute of International Law:

Art. 1. "L'Institut de droit international est une association exclusivement scientifique et sans caractère officiel. Il a pour but de favoriser le progrès du droit international: 1) en travaillant à formuler les principes généraux de la science, de manière à répondre à la conscience juridique du monde civilisé; 2) en donnant son concours à toute tentative sérieuse de codification graduelle et progressive du droit international; 3) en poursuivant la consécration officielle des principes qui auront été reconnus comme étant en harmonie avec les besoins des sociétés modernes" …

Art. 3. "L'Institut se compose de membres, d'associés et de membres honoraires".

Art. 4. "L'Institut choisit ses membres parmi les hommes de diverses nations qui ont rendu des services au droit international, dans le domaine de la théorie ou de la pratique". See *Annuaire de l'Institut de droit international (1879-1880)*.

Founded in 1873, the Association pour la réforme et la codification du droit international pursues partly the same purposes as the Institute: its members may be all those interested in questions of international law. No intellectual qualification is required.

There is no doubt that the codification of the principles of positive international law comprises a task to the resolution of which the Institute of International Law may bring great benefit. In expressing its impartial opinion on a particular controversial international issue, it may indeed serve as the articulator of a "legal conscience" of the civilized world, and its moral authority will be contested by no one. All the major and most noteworthy works of the Institute relate solely to the domain of codification.

At various annual meetings the Institute completed the following codification works, *inter alia*: a statute for the arbitration of international disputes; a draft convention relative to the basic principles of private international law; a draft convention relative to the rules for enforcing decisions of foreign courts; a draft international prize statute, and many others.

No doubt the most remarkable and contemporary were the resolutions of the Oxford meeting of the Institute (1880) relating to the rules for the extradition of criminals and the manual composed at this meeting on the laws of war on land. Finally, it should be added that at its meeting in The Hague during 1875 the Institute energetically favored the codification of the laws of war undertaken by Russia at the Brussels Conference, and one must conclude that this competent society of the most well-known contemporary representatives of the science of international law found that the codification of the principles of international law not only was possible, but even devotes to this task virtually all of its attention and labors.

The Institute repeatedly took the position that neither diplomatic negotiations nor works of jurists could serve as the enlightened conscience of civilized peoples because individual legal scholars too often are attracted by their personal sympathies and feelings of a narrow, albeit legitimate, patriotism, whereas diplomats and practical State officials of necessity consider all of international relations from the standpoint of the exclusive advantage and political views of a concrete State.

The Institute of International Law, regarding its main task as the codification of international laws, set itself the goal of communicating to the discretion of all European governments the drafts of organic international acts in order to generate in States an awareness of the need to embark upon the path of proper codification.

We hope that this lofty goal will be achieve in the near future.

Finally, in 1880 the Russian "Society of International Law" was founded in St. Petersburg, also setting for itself the goal "to patronize all efforts for the codification of the principles of international law".

The international conferences convened at The Hague by the Dutch Government for the codification of the principles of private international law obliges us to hope that the peoples will take slow but true steps towards the said lofty goal.[252]

[252] See the General Part, §48, note 8 below.

General Part

CHAPTER 1
LAW OF INTERNATIONAL INTERACTION

I. Concept and Definition of Law of International Interaction

§45. The majority of representatives of international law are of the view that the rights and duties belonging to States in the domain of external relations have as their sole basis sovereignty, mutual autonomy, and independence of States. We reject this view because logically it leads to insoluble legal conflicts between legislation and the interests of individual peoples.

The idea of State sovereignty points only to the fact that a State is a unique legal person; it does not make it possible to identify in what relations States are with one another, what duties and rights unite them. From the standpoint of autocracy of a State, enmity and hostility are understandable, which usually existing peoples share, being closed off from one another. But not one contemporary civilized State can imagine itself in a similar primitive position. The "permanent relations" in which educated peoples find themselves forces the last to mutually limit the unconditional application of its own autocracy thanks to the achievement by common forces of those benefits which go beyond the means or jurisdiction of the territorial State authority. In other words, the need for a peaceful and structured international life of States arises from the need for their international relations and turnover, and not the sovereignty of States.

The international community is a free union of States for the achievement by common actions of the full development of their forces and satisfaction of their reasonable needs. The aggregate of legal norms determining the realization of the idea of the international community comprises the law of the international community; this is international law.[1]

The international community is necessary given the purpose of the State. According to its reasonable purpose, the State must facilitate with all of its

[1] Robert von Mohl, "Pflege der internationalen Gemeinschaft als Aufgabe des Völkerrechts", in Mohl, *Staatsrecht, Völkerrecht und Politik* (Tübingen, 1862), I, p. 579 et seq; Karl von Kaltenborn von Stachau, *Kritik des Völkerrechts* (Leipzig, 1847); Van Kriecken, "Über die Begriffe Gesellschaft, Gesellschaftsrecht und Gesellschaftswissenschaft", *Grünhut's Zeitschrift* (1883), pp. 34-74; Georg Jellinek, *Die Lehre von den Staatenverbindungen* (Vienna, 1882), p. 91 et seq. Compare Witold Zaleski, *Zur Geschichte und Lehre der internationalen Gemeinschaft* (Dorpat, 1866); Mikhail Nikolaevich Kapustin, Международное право: Конспект лекций [International Law: Synopsis of Lectures] (Iaroslavl, 1873), §§5-9; Welzhofer, *Der europäische Völkerverein. Seine Entwickelung und Zukunft* (Berlin, 1897).

might the comprehensive development of its subjects. No State has all the means to perform this calling by confining itself to the sphere of its internal life. In order for itself and its citizens to fully flourish, States must enter into relations with one another, seek the resources they lack within foreign possessions, and for their part assist each people in the achievement of their legitimate goals. States depend upon one another in the realization of their vital tasks. The extent of their mutual dependence is determined by the degree of their cultural development and civic mindedness. The more complex and diverse the needs of the people, the more it needs international relations; the better the State is aware of its goal, the more actively will international turnover be maintained. Only within the international community can a State realize the animating idea thereof and its vital purpose.

When entering into international relations, every State naturally represents autonomous interests, legal concepts, moral views, and the culture in general of its people. It enters the society of States with the entire aggregate of those special inherent attributes which express its internal, personal national life. The international community does not destroy the individuality of peoples. On the contrary, they come to an awareness of their distinctive features, their national originality. Just as an individual natural person, only in society with other persons does an understanding penetrate of the personal abilities and forces peculiar thereto, so a concrete people receives the means of self-cognition in the international community. By means of constant relations with other peoples, it comes to understand its own individual character, its own forces, its own shortcomings, its own legitimate needs and means of satisfying them, in a word, fully develops its own person.[2]

Therefore, when considering States as subjects of international law not separately, in and of themselves, abstracted, but in interaction with one another as members of an "international union" or "international association", we do not ascribe to this community the character of a *Weltstaat* or *civitas maxima* of Wolff. The international community is a free society of peoples joined by the solidarity of certain interests and aspirations. It not only does not abrogate, but gives the highest sanction to the independence of individual States. Without the existence of the international community, such States as Belgium, Switzerland, Holland, or Denmark would be inconceivable. Insignificant politically, they would not preserve national independence from the infringements of the Great Powers. Whereas at present they

[2] Compare Heinrich von Treitschke, *Die Gesellschaftswissenschaft: ein kritischer Versuch* (Leipzig, 1859), p. 63; Dmitrii Ivanovich Kachenovskii, Курс международного права [Course of International Law] (Kharkov-Moscow, 1863-1866), I, p. 13 et seq.

are recognized as fully-fledged members of international society, and Switzerland and Belgium even were declared to be perpetually neutral, this is without any doubt because contemporary educated peoples are aware of themselves as members of a single international community which they all identically need for the full development of their self-identity.

In its essence this community does not differ from any other human society: it is based on a State combining itself for its own purpose with the benefit and interest of other States. From this point of view, all members of the international union are autonomous and have equal rights. The ideal procedure for their mutual relations is established when each people is imbued with the conviction that the international community exists for the State and the State for the international community.

II. Development of Idea of International Interaction

§46. The development of the idea of the international community is the history of international relations in general and each civilized people in particular. It shows that peoples have been in relations with one another long since, but the international community has developed only recently.

Societies of States did not exist either in Antiquity or during the Middle Ages because the peoples of that time were not aware of the need for mutual assistance and the organized exchange of products of intellectual labor and industrial activity and were not conscious of the common law regulating international relations. This consciousness was born and developed in conditions of contemporary international life. It found support particularly in the extensive development of the material interests of peoples and international trade turnover generated by them, which have achieved an enormous scale in modern times.

However important in and of themselves were the economic interests and relations joining contemporary peoples, they are merely one factor under whose impact the international community was established. The last is a result of the entire culture and civilization of educated States. It was developed by an awareness, increasingly embedded in peoples, of the community of the most diverse aspirations and requirements of human life, both personal and social and State among various peoples dissatisfied within the boundaries and resources of individual States. Therefore, underlying the international community were not only economic activity and trade relations, but the aggregate of all social interests which join civilized States to one another.

A fact well-known to us serves as evidence of this, that the international community encompasses only peoples of European civilization, who, as

[François] Guizot [(1787-1874)] correctly observed, are distinctive by the diversity of their ideals, aspirations, and features and the entire external world surrounding the European peoples.[3] All these various aspirations, spiritual and material, distinguish the European educated States from the Eastern and Muslim peoples; taken together, they comprise that cement which binds these States, and only them, into one international union.

It follows that the necessary condition for the progress of the international community is the mastery and development by States of all the basic elements of European civilization and culture. The extent of participation of each people in the international community always corresponds to the degree of its enlightenment and civic-mindedness. If the social and State life of a people has achieved a high degree of prosperity, unless it encounters obstacles in the yoke of political arbitrariness or in the all-embracing influence of religious views, or in the obscuratanism of society, such a people will always be imbued with an awareness of the need not only of the exchange of the works of nature and their own labor with other peoples, but also the mutual assistance of peoples in all spheres of human life and activity. Only on this condition can those diverse international relations of both individuals and of social classes, and of entire peoples, be established which occur at present among the union of States of Christian or European education. For uncivilized peoples, the idea of an international community is incomprehensible.

The initial relations of Russia with the European peoples may serve as an illustration of this situation. As we have seen, the Russian State was in relations with foreigners from the early thirteenth century. Moscow concluded treaties, sent and received embassies, permitted the English and Dutch to trade in Russia, and so on. But it would be mistaken on this basis to consider the Muscovite State a member of the international community and to assert that the Russian people and its Government understood at that time the need for international turnover and relations with western powers. The external relations of Russia of that epoch were *de facto*; Moscow's cultural conditions and social and political system made impossible permanent and proper relations with European peoples on the principles of equality and mutuality. Such relations began no earlier than the reign of Peter the Great and only under Catherine II were on a firm footing. What do we see?

The more the desire was strengthened in the Russian Government and people to be an actual member of the international community, the more they sought to take advantage of historical experience and the fruits of the labors of European States. The Russian Government renounced claims

[3] François Guizot, *Histoire de la civilisation en Europe*, p. 3.

declared by Moscow to be recognized as higher and better than all other States. The Russian people were no longer afraid, as in the past, that Russians sent abroad, "having learned the faith and customs of the States there, would begin to lose their faith". On the contrary, it became aware of its shortcomings, its rudeness, imbued with a self-awareness, and aspired to reach the level of civic life and culture at which other, more enlightened peoples, stood.

III. Basic Principles of Law of International Interaction

§47. International society is the foundation of the entire international legal order. The basic principles of law regulating international relations arise from the tasks and goals of the international community.

The international community has as its task to serve the satisfaction of reasonable vital needs of its members, both entire States and social classes and individuals. Its goal is to structure an international legal order which would secure the peaceful and comprehensive development of peoples on condition of full respect for their national interests.

Is such an order possible? Will not the interests of one people directly conflict with the legitimate needs of other peoples? The existence of the contemporary international community proves that such an order is possible: it acquired the vital experience of peoples and is based on a conscious need to respect other's interests in order to ensure respect for its own.

On the basis of the tasks and purposes of the international union of States, the basic principles of the law of the international community may be expressed in the following propositions:

1) The international community is a legal order between peoples which should ensure autonomy and the full development of each State in connection with the rights and interests of others. There is no sovereign authority therein which would dispose of the fates of the peoples belonging to it and specify to them vital goals and means to achieve them.

2) Every State is above all obliged to have in view own advantage and protect by all forces the inviolability of their autocracy because it acts within a community thanks to the better satisfaction of its interests and full development of national distinctiveness. An international community would be contrary to the aims of its existence unless it secured the advantages and well-being of its members and the full independence thereof.

3) Therefore, a State is not obliged to expend the resources which it needs itself for the general benefit of the international union. This is completely understandable in view of the fact that the subjects give their forces and their property for the express needs of their country, and not for other peoples.

But this principle does not vitiate the international community based on the idea of mutual aid and assistance because only on condition of satisfaction of own needs can the needs of others be satisfied.

4) The international community embraces not only States, but extends to social classes and individuals.

5) All international activity (or administration) of States during peace and war is conceivable and the goals of achieving it only when an international community exists.

6) Mutual agreement between States represents the best means for identifying the rights, duties, and tasks of members of the international community.[4]

IV. Basic Tasks of International Interaction

§48. The international community, as already noted, must serve the satisfaction of reasonable vital requirements of its members. Various interests whose satisfaction assumes the mutual assistance and aid of States may be reduced to three main groups corresponding to the three kinds of subjects that are actors in international relations. The subject-matter of international activity of States, as members of an international union, may be: first, tasks relating to the organs of State power of each people; second, those goals which various social groups existing in States pursue in the international domain; and finally, third, economic and spiritual interests of individuals, subjects of States.

We consider separately each of these three categories of tasks lying on States as members of the international community.

A. In the Domain of Mutual State Relations

The international community manifests its operation in all functions of sovereign power realized within individual States.

a) *In the sphere of legislation.* The influence of the international community on the internal legislation of States is enormous, although not always recognized. The domestic law of every State, legislative and customary, is usually regarded as the best evidence of the uniqueness of a people's life. But is the positive law of each people the result solely of its legal consciousness? How is it possible to speak about the mutual impact of

[4] Compare Frederic Seebohm, *De la réforme du droit des gens* (Paris, 1873), p. 35 et seq; Mohl, note 1 above, p. 593 et seq.

foreign peoples on one another in such a primarily personal and autonomous activity of each State as legislation?

Moreover, positive facts prove that contemporary States may satisfactorily resolve the tasks of internal legislation not otherwise than being aware of themselves as members of an international union. They must necessarily take into account the diverse international turnover in which they themselves and their subjects participate; they must regulate by legislation those interests which peoples pursue in mutual relations. That is why the influence of the international community is salient in the legislation of those States which most keenly relate to the legal needs of their subjects, which understand international relations as an instrument of the cultural development of the people.

A noteworthy example of this influence is the recent legislation of the Kingdom of Italy. The 1865 Civil Code issued in Italy is a notable attempt to set out in individual provisions of a law the principles of private international law which arise from the principle of the international community and were based previously on the theories of jurists and judicial practice. These principles were adopted by the Italian legislators for the sake of ensuring international intercourse as principles entirely consistent with the interests and views of the Italian people.

To what extent international relations can change historically and uniquely formed legal norms is shown by contemporary English legislation. For many centuries the view dominated in England that an English subject could never withdraw from subjecthood (once a subject, always a subject). Thus, many thousands of Englishmen who emigrated abroad and were naturalized there continued to be considered as lawful subjects in England and in the event of an international war were subject to the risk of being convicted as traitors. On the other hand, however long they were in England, foreigners always remained foreign subjects in the eyes of English legislation. This view, inconsistent with an international community, cardinally changed in 1870 with the issuance of an Act of Parliament under which any Englishman may renounce the subjecthood of England and foreigners, after a five-year sojourn on English territory, might acquire all civil and political rights of Englishmen.[5] Moreover, the 1870 Act relative to the conditions for the conclusion of cartel conventions by English executive authorities, until then rather constrained, also serves as

5 John Cutler, *The Law of Naturalization: as amended by the Naturalization Acts 1870* (London, 1871).

evidence of the favorable impact exerted by international relations on the obsolete legal views of the English Government and people.[6]

The development of Swiss legislation from 1848 to the present cannot be understood when considered solely from the standpoint of the domestic life of Switzerland. The revision of the Swiss Constitution in 1874, which led to the strengthening of the Confederation over the autonomy of the cantons, was significantly indebted for his success to international relations. They required that Switzerland, as a fully-fledged member of the international community, actually have the possibility of performing its duties in relations with other States, and for this it was essential that the Council of the Confederation concentrate international intercourse of the Confederation in its hands with the limitation of the rights on individual cantons in this respect.[7]

Other States offer no fewer examples of legislative acts generated by the requirements of international life. We note the Russian law of 10 February 1864 on the acceptance of foreigners as Russian subjects issued in view of the need to give a certain legal status to foreigners who are in Russia and engage in peaceful, industrial, or trade activity. The provisions of the Russian Statute on Civil Procedure relating to the execution of decisions of foreign courts (Article 1273 and others) are an echo of the legislative provisions and views of judicial practice existing on this question in other educated States.

The recent codes in general were developed in contemporary States on the basis of the comparative study of legislation of various civilized peoples because the last are permeated with more or less identical legal views, the eliciting of which constitutes the principal task of legislative activity.

But the impact of the international community on the legislation of States is not exhausted by the examples cited. Common international interests, especially trade, constituting the subject-matter of permanent relations and transactions between subjects of various States generated attempts to introduce common international legislation on those questions which most often arise in the sphere of international, particularly commercial, turnover. Insistence on similar legislation was felt especially strongly in the former German union comprised of many independent States, each of which had its own special laws. With a view to easing relations between their mutual subjects, in 1848 an all-German Bill of Exchange Statute was issued, and then an all-German Trade Statute (1861). The question was recently raised concerning the issuance of all-European laws concerning financial and trade

[6] Louis Renault, *Étude sur l'extradition en Angleterre* (Paris, 1879).

[7] See *Annuaire de législation étrangère*, VI, p. 537 et seq; VII p. 568 et seq.

transactions concluded by subjects of different States. Hence the proposal of the German Government in 1878 to all European States concerning the issuance of a general statute on the bill of exchange. The Dutch Government back in 1874 proposed to issue a general law relating to the execution of foreign civil and commercial courts. Both proposals were adopted rather sympathetically by a majority of powers.

In 1893 the Dutch Government proposed anew to the European powers a general council to develop the basic principles of private international law. This proposal was sympathetically adopted by thirteen European powers, and the first conference held in The Hague in 1893 and the second in 1894. An act was signed at these two conferences called a "Protocole final" which contained basic principles relating to the operation of laws on marriage, divorce, inheritance, trusteeship, and guardianship, preliminary securing of a suit, and others. Although the entire Hague act has not yet received the binding force of an international treaty, its enormous practical and scientific significance will be discovered, without doubt, in the nearest future and will be strengthened each year, even bypassing the sanctioning thereof by a formal international agreement. In November 1896 an international convention was signed at The Hague in which part of the provisions of the Hague Conference concerning the execution of letters rogatory, preliminary securing of suits, and so on were included. Russia also acceded to this act in December 1897, which at present is binding on fourteen States who participated in the Hague conferences on questions of private international law.[8]

Finally, in 1900 the Third Hague Conference on private international law assembled, which drew up draft international conventions relative to the conditions for the conclusion of marriages, divorce, trusteeship over youth, and inheritance. In June 1902 ten European States signed all these conventions, except for the draft convention on the law of inheritance. Russia did not sign any of these conventions. In the summer of 1903 the Fourth Conference was to assemble at The Hague in order to determine, *inter alia*, laws relating to competition, but assembled only in 1904.

b) *In the sphere of administration*. Internal administration is, without doubt, the domain of activity of the sovereign power of every State which should be completely free from interference on the part of other States. But obliged to be guided in the resolution of administrative tasks exclusively for the benefit of own subjects, no government has sufficient resources for the

[8] The decisions of the Hague conferences were circulated by the Dutch Government as: *Actes de la Conférence de La Haye chargée de réglementer diverses matières de Droit international privé* (La Haye, 1893, 1894, and 1900).

full satisfaction of their legal needs. The resources lacking it acquires with the assistance of other States, members of the international community. The union of States has as its task to assist its members in the satisfaction of all common administrative interests and the concrete administrative needs of a particular country.

Every State must have those governmental institutions and organs needed for the purposes of its administration. But by mutual agreement of States, in addition international administrative institutions exist with competence and resources separate from local territorial authority. These completely autonomous institutions have been generated by interested States convinced that they are not in a position to resolve various tasks with their own governmental organs and power which have international significance and, moreover, are put by the reasonable interests of their own subjects. In view of this, they refrained from exercising their administrative rights which previously were regarded as an inalienable State monopoly of every independent State, or they were forced under the pressure of other governments to recognize the existence of some international institution.

Among the international organs of administration is the Rhine Navigation Commission, founded in 1831 and transformed in 1868. It had not only purely administrative tasks, but also judicial rights.[9] In 1856 the Danube European Commission was founded, and the Commission for navigation on the Danube of riparian States. The first has its own flag, which covers the inviolability of personnel of the commission and the buildings and property belonging thereto; it enjoys various police rights, may inspect all vessels sailing the Danube, impose penalties, recover a determined duty, and so on.[10] A telegraph and postal bureau ("international secretariats") were founded in Berne to maintain uniformity in conditions for the operation of the postal and telegraphic State monopoly of all States who joined the international postal and telegraphic unions. Also relegated to the category of international administrative institutions is the Geneva "committee for assistance to wounded warriors", and the Paris Metric Commission, Constantinople sanitary inspectorate, and other institutions operating on the basis of the special international agreements.[11]

[9] Karl von Martens and Ferdinand de Cornot, Baron de Cussy, *Recueil manuel et pratique des traités, conventions et autre actes diplomatique* (Leipzig, 1846-1857), IV, p. 271.

[10] F. F. Martens, Собрание трактатов и конвенций, заключенных Россиею с иностранными державами [Collection of Treaties and Conventions Concluded by Russia with Foreign Powers] (Spb., 1874-1909). 15 vols. (hereinafter: F. F. Martens, Собрание трактатов и конвенций [Collection of Treaties and Conventions]), IV(2), No. 160, p. 751.

[11] Ibid., IV(2), No. 174, p. 1050; Gustave Moynier, *Étude sur la convention de Genève*

Necessary in particular was international assistance to States in the performance of various administrative tasks within the jurisdiction of State organs. It is not possible to enumerate these tasks. Questions arise in each branch of administration – spiritual, physical, economic life of peoples – which require for their resolution the participation, assistance, and aid of members of an international association.

A State would not achieve its purpose relative to the spiritual development of its subjects if its territory were closed to the education, scientific ideas, or works of artistic activity of foreign peoples, or if it prohibited visits to educational institutions of other States or to participate in scientific international congresses. The regulation of resettlements, counteracting epidemics and cattle plagues, measures against starvation, and other physical calamities acquire an international character. The stronger the industrial life of a people develops, the more urgent is the securing thereof by international treaties and institutions.[12]

Finally, civilized peoples need international relations to preserve their autonomous political existence. A government which does not observe and take advantage of inventions and improvements in military technology and art in other States will deprive its country of necessary means of defense. Sinification leads not only to ruinous stagnation in all spheres of life, but also to the danger of losing national independence.

c) *In the domain of judicial power*. Mutual assistance of States in civil and criminal justice is becoming more necessary with each passing day. From the standpoint of State sovereignty, it is inexplicable and should not take place; it is understandable and legitimate only as an expression of the idea of an international community. In fact, whereas the establishment and administration of justice is the direct task of the autocrat of a State, the strengthening of international relations increasingly requires concessions and services in judicial matters to the benefit of other States. No contemporary State is in a position by itself to protect respect for law and procedure within the country; this is a task of the international community. No local court can be guided only by territorial laws and confine itself to resolving those disputes which arise between native subjects. The conflict of national

pour l'amélioration du sort des militaires blessés dans les armées en campagne (1864 et 1868): droit des gens (Paris, 1870); Maurice Block, *Dictionnaire général de la politique* (Paris, 1873-1874), see the entry for: Régime sanitaire, II, p. 808. Compare in particular: P. E. Kazanskii, Всеобщие административные союзы государств [General Administrative Unions of States] (Odessa, 1897). 3 vols.

[12] For the development of these ideas, see the Special Part, Chapter III.

legislation regarding criminal and civil cases is insoluble other than on the basis of principles of international law.

In the domain of civil justice, contemporary States consider themselves bound to recognize those legal relations established on the basis of and within the limits of the operation of foreign legislation. If there are disputes concerning these relations, the territorial judicial authority is guided by the principles of domestic and of foreign law. The principle of the mutual recognition and interaction is especially discovered in agreements between States relating to the enforcement of foreign court decisions.

The protection of the legal order by punitive powers requires in many instances the joint action of States. In order to discover the criminal or to obtain evidence of his guilt often it is necessary to request foreign courts to take witness testimony or state certain facts. A guilty person who has committed a crime in one State may conceal himself on the territory of another; then negotiations are initiated concerning extradition, the conditions of which comprise the subject-matter of cartel conventions concluded by States.

Finally, the Permanent Court of International Arbitration founded in 1899 at The Hague expresses the need for civilized States to introduce the rule of law over arbitrariness and justice over violence in international relations. The more often the Hague international court will settle international conflicts by an arbitral proceeding, the more stable the international legal order will become.

B. In the Domain of Social Interests

§49. If international law were actually based on the absolute autonomy of individual States, the question of their mutual duties in relation to various domestic societies might not arise. These societies would not have international significance; their activity would affect only that State in which they had been organized. But we already have had occasion to point to the active role which social interests play in the development of international relations. It is understandable that social groups as powerful factors of international interaction must find assistance and respect for their interests on the part of all educated States. The law of the international community determines which social groups may participate in international relations as juridical persons and of what that assistance may consist which they have the right to count on from a foreign State authority.

Civilized States, as members of the international community, in principle should recognize as legally existing all those societies which are recognized as such in their own State.

On this basis, no societies, partnerships, or companies formed against the will of their government, nor authorized by a law, or in general not enjoying the rights of juridical persons in their own country should not be considered to be legal unions on another's territory. Members of such societies should remain, in the eyes of a foreign government, individual private persons; otherwise, this clearly violates the sovereign rights of a foreign State.

Social groups and classes legally existing in a State have the right to promote their interests in other States.

One cannot enumerate those societies which enjoy international protection. The most important of such unions are, without doubt, churches existing in all States. The assistance rendered to their goals by a foreign authority often has assumed enormous proportions, as the expedition of the French forces (1848) shows, for example, to benefit the Pope. Scientific-literary societies *de facto* or on the basis of international agreements have the right to take measures for the defense abroad of the interests of their members. Other societies, various trading companies, estates, shops, and communities, may take advantage of protection in foreign States and, as recognized juridical persons, may possess property, defend their rights in a judicial proceeding, and so on.

C. In the Domain of Relations of Individual Subjects

§50. The international community gives to every individual the right to seek satisfaction of his vital and legal needs everywhere within the domain of international turnover. On this basis, States, as members of an international association, are obliged not to refuse the protection of the law and local authorities to any person within their territory, whatever State he may be a subject of. We saw above how this principle of respect for the human individual in and of itself serves as a scale for the recognition of the development of the citizenship of States and their mutual legal relations.

At present, educated States make provision for the protection by law and court of all foreigners. For the better protection of the freedom of relations and rights of their own subjects, they conclude treaties: commercial, consular, settlement, navigation, and so on. Uncivilized States, such as China, Siam, or Morocco, even by force of arms are compelled to respect the legal interests of individuals. In the event of the failure to recognized human rights, educated governments undertake common international measures. We will not mention the total expulsion of foreigners from a State.

Moreover, contemporary States render, on the basis of treaties or *de facto*, material assistance to those foreigners who need it because of various misfortunes. A treaty was concluded between Russia and England (9

October 1880) on the protection and issuance of inheritances remaining after seamen who died on a ship or on the territory of either State. On the basis of agreements between Austria and Switzerland, Switzerland and France, and other powers, mutual subjects of the Contracting Parties who have experienced misfortune receive assistance from the local State treasury.[13] But in addition to the treaties, contemporary peoples consider themselves bound by a duty of mutual assistance, and in the event of war, flood, fires, starvation, and other calamities hasten to ease the situation of those victims, donating their labor and resources to a general humanitarian cause.

V. Organization of International Interaction

§51. The need for the organization of international interaction arises from the essence of the unie, the association of peoples. If States are aware of their being linked by a community of certain interests, as members of an international community, if, when participating in international congresses and conferences the powers manifest their will, adopt decisions, and act, then one must conclude that they feel the need to change the *de facto* community, uniting them into a formal legal order.

An international community would make no sense if the mutual relations of States represented an *état sauvage* ([Jean-Jacques] Rousseau [(1712-1778)]). But although in possession of all the attributes of a legal order, the society of States does not know or need a permanent organized international authority. It remains, in essence, and must be a free association of independent States based on complete respect for the individuality of each people and determined by the principles of international law. The principle of the independence of States underlies the community. International congresses and conferences serve as its organs; it has no legislative, executive, or judicial authorities, as a State has.

Therefore, the attempts to organize an international community in the sense of a State, or in the form of a worldwide monarchy, or worldwide republic should be treated with care. It is unlikely that some international community would organize itself according to projects and plans drawn up at various times by analogy with the forms of a State.

Underlying this type of project are proposals whose realization is inconceivable and entirely undesirable. They all assume either a complete reworking of the political map of Europe or the subordination of autonomous

[13] See *Journal du droit international privé*, VII, pp. 27, 620; Léopold Neumann, *Recueil des traités et conventions conclus l'Autriche avec les puissances étrangères, depuis 1763 jusqu'à nos jours*, nouvelle suite (Leipzig, 1855-1912), IV, p. 4 et seq; VIII, p. 254 et seq.

States to a common sovereign authority. They may be divided into two categories: one is based solely on ideal reflections, completely ignoring the existing legal order of things; the others, on the contrary, proceed from real data and partly take into account the basic conditions of international interaction. We will indicate the more noteworthy attempts of both kinds.

A. To projects of international organization of the first kind are relegated numerous plans drawn up for the purpose of ensuring perpetual peace.

The King of France, Henry IV [(1553-1610)], insofar as known from the notes of his Minister, the [Maximilien de Béthune, 1st] Duke of Sully [(1560-1641)], thought in order to prevent international wars one should organize from the European States one great "Christian republic". It would be composed of fifteen States with significantly changed boundaries. France and England would enlarge their possessions at the expense of Holland. Spain would be enclosed on its peninsula, but would acquire Portugal. Bohemia and Hungary would be separated from Austria as independent kingdoms. Autonomous confederations would be formed in the north of Italy from various territories. The Muscovite State and Turkey would be excluded entirely from the unie. A general council would manage all the affairs of the republic, composed of 60 plenipotentiaries from States. It was to be concerned with not only the peaceful settlement of disputes arising between Christian peoples, but not allow tyrannical rule within States and defend tolerance towards Catholics and Protestants. With the Muslims there should be perpetual war by the republics until their complete expulsion from Europe. In addition to a General Council, six local councils were designed from representatives of a certain number of neighboring States for the discussion of their special affairs.[14]

In 1713 the [Charles-Irénée Castel] Abbé de Saint-Pierre [(1658-1743)] submitted to the Congress of Utrecht his project for perpetual peace. Just as the Plan of Henry IV, it was structured on the possibility and advantage of the formation from European States, not excluding Russia, of a single league or unie similar to the old German Empire. A common Diet was to serve as the legislative and judicial organ of the unie and have enforcement authority with respect to all its members. The last never could oppose their interests to the common interest or secede from the unie. Their mutual rights were to be determined by a common constitution, changes of which might be made only by unanimous decision of members of the Diet. Individual

[14] François Laurent, *Histoire du droit des gens et des relations internationales* (Brussels, 1861-1870), X, p. 248 et seq; 287 et seq; Leopold van Ranke, *Französische Geschichte*, II, p. 143 et seq; Theodor Kükelhaus, *Der Ursprung des Planes vom ewigen Frieden in den Memoiren des Herzogs vom Sully* (Berlin, 1893); compare Ernest Nys, *Les origines du droit international* (Paris, 1894), p. 389 et seq.

disputes between States were to be settled on the merits thereof; but on questions concerning the discovered inheritance of lands, the Diet should be guided by the principle of the equilibrium of States. The league would serve as a guarantee against conquests and internal revolutions, which are to be suppressed by the interference of the allied powers.

The example of Germany, said Saint-Pierre, proved as well as possible that the plan set out was not a utopia. Its advantage was undoubted; it ensured to each State its possessions and rights and, at the same time, eliminated all pretexts for armed conflicts of States. But obviously this organization proposed by Saint-Pierre would transform an international unie into a State unie; it deprived peoples of their highest good – their independence, their right to dispose of their own fates within and outside the State.[15]

Saint-Pierre's ideas were developed by Jean-Jacques Rousseau and many other writers and thinkers of the eighteenth and nineteenth centuries.[16] Among others, [Jeremy] Bentham [(1748-1832)] saw a means of rescuing the European powers from continuous wars in a permanent congress of deputies who should decide by a judicial proceeding all international disputes and expel from the European unie any State not obeying the judgment of the Congress. In order to enforce a decision of the Congress, each State should assign to a common international force a certain contingent of its forces. In order to prevent wars, Bentham deemed it necessary to: 1) reduce the number of permanent forces; and 2) liberate the colonies from the metropolitan.[17]

At the very end of the eighteenth century and beginning of the [nineteenth] century the idea of a federation of European States was defended by [Immanuel] Kant [(1724-1804)] and [Johannes Baptista] Fallati [(1809-1855)].[18] Distinctive means to ensure "perpetual peace" were proposed by our compatriots – [Vasilii Fedorovich] Malinovskii [(1765-1814)],[19] who

[15] Here is the title of Saint-Pierre's proposal: *Projet de traité conclu pour rendre la paix perpétuelle entre les souverains chrétiens, pour maintenir toujours le commerce entre les nations et pour affirmer beaucoup davantage les maisons régnantes sur les trônes* (Utrecht, 1713). 3 vols. Compare Gustave de Molinari, *L'abbé de St. Pierre, membre exclu de l'Académie française, sa vie et ses œuvres* (Brussels, 1857).

[16] Henry Wheaton, *Histoire des progrès du droit des gens en Europe depuis la paix de Westphalie jusqu'au congrès de Vienne* (Leipzig, 1853), I, p. 329 et seq.

[17] John Bowring (ed.), *The Works of Jeremy Bentham* (London, 1843), II, p. 546 et seq.

[18] Immanuel Kant, *Immanuel Kant's Sämmtliche Werke*, ed. Karl Rosenkrantz and Friedrich Wilhelm Schubert (Leipzig, 1838-1842), XII, pp. 229-291; J. B. Fallati, "Die Genesis der Völkergesellschaft", *Zeitschrift für die ges. Staatswissenschaft* (1844).

[19] V. F. Malinovskii, Рассуждение о мире и войне [Discourse on Peace and War] (Spb., 1803).

proved that all evil lies in envoys, who must be eliminated, and Prince Platon Zubov [(1767-1822)], who wrote at the end of the eighteenth century a fantastic project on the partition of Europe.[20] On this basis of this project, all Europe would be partitioned between fifteen States. Austria would be completely abolished; all Germany, Austria, Denmark, and Sweden would accede to Russia. The capitals of the first degree in the Russian Empire would be: Petersburg, Berlin, Vienna, Constantinople, Astrakhan, and Moscow. Cities of the second degree would be: Hamburg, Copenhagen, Stockholm, and so on. It is difficult to imagine anything so fantastic.

B. To projects of the second kind based on real data and better reflecting the requirements of reality one may relegate:

a) *Attempts to construct a worldwide monarchy*. The most eminent representatives of the Roman Catholic Church clearly aspired to this goal in the Middle Ages (Pope Gregory VII [(1015-1085)], Innocent III [(1160/61-1216)], and others) and certain sovereigns, for example Charles V [(1500-1558)], Louis XIV [(1638-1715)], and Napoleon I.[21]

b) *Projects of organizations of an international society on the principles of representation*. Unlike the aforesaid plans, the authors of these projects do not require either arbitrary changes and then forcible protection of established boundaries of States, nor the absorption of independent peoples into confederations or a State unie. Insofar as possible, they turn attention to the *de facto* and vital conditions, not allowing States to be bound by such an organization but allowing a freer combination of States with subordination to an all-European congress and international court. The projects of [Johann Baptist] Sartorius, [Félix Marie Louis Pierre Esquinou de] Parieu [(1815-1893)], [James] Lorimer [(1818-1890)], Bluntschli, and one reigning monarch were such.

The Swiss scholar, Sartorius, proved that peace and the development of civilized peoples may be achieved only by means of establishing a worldwide representative republic.[22]

Parieu pointed to the possibility of founding an international commission composed of representatives of governments and people's assemblies of individual States.[23]

20 P. Lebedev, Графы Никита и Петр Панины [Counts Nikita and Petr Panin] (Spb., 1863), p. 301 et seq.

21 Laurent, note 14 above, X, p. 16.

22 Johann Baptiste Sartorius, *Organon des vollkommenen Friedens* (Zurich, 1837). Compare Leonid Alekseevich Kamarovskii, О международном суде [On an International Court] (Moscow, 1881), p. 309.

23 Johann Caspar Bluntschli, *Das moderne Völkerrecht der civilisirten Staten* (Nördlin-

Lorimer, a professor of Edinburgh University, suggested two projects. On the basis of the first (1871), plenipotentiaries of States (two from each) would assemble annually in Belgium or Switzerland and form a congress to decide international questions. The votes of the deputies are not equal, but commensurate with the real significance and importance of the States represented. The number of votes belonging to each State is determined by the size of its population, net revenue, and imports and exports. The congress itself decides whether a particular question is international or purely of a territorial character. It may enforce its decisions by force of arms. The congress appoints members to an international court and refers there those matters which should be decided in a judicial proceeding. Appeals against the judgments of the court lie to the congress. According to the second project (1877), the international congress sits in Constantinople and consists of a chamber of deputies and a Senate; the international court is situated there; they dispose of an international enforcement army composed of contingents from various States.[24]

Bluntschli also based his project on the representation of States. In his view, States might be subject to a council in which sovereigns personally sit or their plenipotentiaries and a senate consisting of deputies of people's assemblies; judicial matters should be decided by an international court.[25]

Finally, one of the monarchs reigning in a great Empire proposed the following organization: for a "European Empire civilization or synarchy" three councils must be established in Europe: council of national churches; council of national States; and council of national communities. The first should represent religious and intellectual life – wisdom and science; the second, political and legal life – truth and justice; the third, the economic life of peoples – civilization and labor. The members of these councils would be elected.[26]

gen, 1868), §108.

[24] *Revue de droit international*, III(1871), p. 1 et seq; IX (1877), p. 161 et seq. For a detailed and recent account of the Lorimer plan, see James Lorimer, *The Institutes of the Law of Nations: A Treatise of the Jural Relations of Separate Political Communities* (Edinburgh, 1883-1884), II, p. 183, especially p. 279 et seq.

[25] Bluntschli, "Die Organisation des europäischen Staatenvereins", in *Gegenwart*, nos. 6, 8, and 9 (1878).

[26] See [Joseph Alexandre, Marquis Saint-Yves de l'Alveydre (1842-1909)], *Mission actuelle des souverains par l'un d'eux* (Paris, 1882), p. 181 et seq. The author of this curious work is called the Emperor of Brazil.

One may object to all these projects that they impart to the international community the form of a State organization and therefore will hardly ever receive practical realization.

c) *Structure of international relations on the basis of political equilibrium.* Without presenting certain plans of international organization, some writers view international relations as a political system which is supported by the preservation of an equilibrium between States (Heffter, Montague Bernard). States are members of this system and are obliged together, materially and morally, to counteract seizures by the strongest and any dangerous change of existing political relations. The shakiness of this principle has been demonstrated above.[27]

d) *Pentarchy (five-powers).* Since the Congress of Vienna, five Great Powers have stood at the head of the international unie (Russia, Austria, Prussia, England, and France), who considered themselves to have the right not only to decide international questions, but also to interfere in the internal affairs of other States. Underlying their unie and hegemony was the moral idea that the Christian peoples are obliged to maintain peace between themselves and defend the legal order within States. But it is worth recalling the history of the congresses at Troppau, Laibach, and Verona in order to be convinced that the Pentarchy was a violence against their legal rights and interests of the peoples. It proves only that not all the powers have *de facto* identical significance and status in international society. In suppressing the autonomy of other peoples, it violated the idea of absolute equality of States, as members of the international community, and therefore could not be deemed to be a just and desirable form of organization thereof.

In view of the fact that State institutions of contemporary peoples are not identical, that they are far from perfection, and that carrying them over to an international unie in any event is not consistent with the internal autonomy of States, the majority of writers refuse to arrange the international community on the State principle. Guided by these considerations, many writers confine the organization thereof to the structuring of an international court (Fiore, Kamarovskii).[28] It must be said that such attempts are less consistent than projects of perpetual peace because if an international tribunal should exist which is competent to decide all international conflicts in general and for the absolute enforcement of its judgments, there are no grounds to build

[27] August Wilhelm Heffter, *Das europäische Völkerrecht der Gegenwart*, §5; Montague Bernard, *Four Lectures on Subjects Connected with Diplomacy* (London, 1868), pp. 63, 87 et seq.

[28] Pasquale Fiore, *Sul problema internazionale della società giuridica degli stati* (Torino, 1878); Kamarovskii, note 22 above, p. 461 et seq.

an international congress as a permanent legislative institution. Moreover, such an international court would exert little influence on international relations unless it disposed of material force ensuring the enforcement of its decisions. The creation of an international enforcement army would hardly be possible.

On the basis of these reflections, one may only wish for the development of those foundations created in 1899 by the Hague Peace Conference of a Permanent Court of Arbitration for the consideration by an arbitration court of conflicts which arise between States. It would be very desirable that powers in dispute turn more often to such a court. But the Hague arbitration tribunal is a court to which powers have recourse voluntarily and enforcement of its awards is not ensured by a special enforcement army, but by an advance solemn obligation in good faith and unconditionally to subordinate oneself to its awards and execute them. There is no doubt that achieving the establishment of a permanent binding court over States is unlikely to be possible.

VI. Organs of International Interaction: Congresses and Conferences

(a) Concept of Congress and Conference

§52. While retaining the freedom of association of independent States, the international community has certain general institutions which represent the embryos of its organization. Such significance appertains to international congresses and conferences, the authority and power of which, pursuant to the voluntary agreement of States, extends to the entire international unie.

International congresses and conferences are organs of the international community, but not of the individual States which have sent their representatives there.

The justness of this position is confirmed by numerous historical examples and positive data. The congresses of Westphalia (1648), Vienna (1815), Paris (1856), and Berlin (1878) might have been held and led to certain results only because the States taking part in them were aware of their solidarity, as members of the international community. The general order of things established by them was developed by the mutual consent and concessions of States in view of and thanks to the satisfaction of international interests. Toleration, freedom of navigation, repeal of trade in negroes, mitigation of the calamities of war, and other principles of contemporary international law proclaimed by various conferences and congresses were the products of the historical life of all civilized peoples and are an expression of their common legal consciousness. In a word, neither the assembly of congresses nor the procedure of their meetings, nor their decisions will be understood unless one has an international community in view whose interests they represent.

International congresses and conferences are in essence international meetings of representatives of independent States to discuss their common affairs and interests.

(b) Difference between Congresses and Conferences

The majority of writers do not distinguish between congresses and conferences.[29] But they must be distinguished. On the basis of historical precedents, their distinction is manifest in: 1) the identity of the representatives of States participating in particular international meetings; 2) the subject matter of their discussions; and 3) the purposes subject to achievement.

As regards representation, either the sovereigns themselves are present at international congresses, as has been true repeatedly (congresses: Vienna, Aachen, Troppau, Laibach, and others) or their first ministers, and in general those representatives of States who have the powers to conclude treaties and agreements comprising the subject-matter of discussion at the congress. On the contrary, delegates of governments appointed *ad hoc* with a casting or consultative vote take part in conferences, rarely ministers and never sovereigns. The subject-matter of discussion at congresses is questions concerning important vital interests of States and the entire international unie; conferences discuss existing obligations and their construction or prepare the decision of some important and difficult matter; for example, the 1874 Brussels conference was convoked to identify the laws of war. Finally, the purposes of a congress and conference differ. The first has the task of deciding controversial questions, preventing war and misunderstandings between States, and in general ensuring the preservation of the international legal order; the second – not proclaim new principles, but only develop existing principles; not decide controversial questions of international relations and law, but prepare their resolution.

[29] Compare Bluntschli, note 23 above, §108 et seq; Heffter, note 27 above, §240, p. 464; Carlos Calvo, *Le droit international théorique et pratique* (1887-1896), I, p. 452; Paul Pradier-Fodéré, *Cours de droit diplomatique à l'usage des agents politiques du Ministère des affairs étrangêres des États européens et américains* (Paris, 1881), II, p. 421; Witold Zaleski, *Die völkerrechtliche Bedeutung der Kongresse* (Dorpat, 1874), p. 4; Mikhail Nikolaevich Kapustin, Международное право: конспект лекций [International Law: Conspectus of Lectures] (1873), §8.

It should be added that at present governments are far from being aware of the grounds on which congresses and conferences may be distinguished. Therefore, in practice some of the international assemblies which had fully the character and importance of congresses were called conferences.

(c) Clerical Work of Congresses and Conferences

Regarding the ceremonial side of both, they developed the following principal provisions.

1. *Procedure of convocation.* The creation of international congresses and conferences, as history and contemporary practice show, may emanate from various parties.

First, the proposal concerning the convocation of an international assembly may come from any third mediating power.

This procedure has been repeatedly applied in practice. In 1779 Catherine II invited Austria and Prussia, in dispute over the Bavarian succession, to appoint plenipotentiaries to settle the dispute at a Congress in Teschen. An 1813 Prague Congress, not held, was convoked at the initiative of the Vienna Cabinet with a view to negotiations on a final peace between Napoleon I, on one side, and Russia and Prussia, on the other. The Austrian Government played such a role with respect to Russia and its adversaries – France, England, and Turkey during the Crimean War. With the mediation of Napoleon III in 1866, a preliminary Nikolsburg peace treaty was concluded between Prussia and Austria.

Second, the occasion for a convocation may be the interested States directly involved in the dispute.

All peace congresses which brought an end to war without the interference of third powers were arranged at the initiative of the belligerents themselves.

Third, in the absence of occasions for conciliatory mediation, the question of convoking a congress or conference may be initiated by each power for the consideration and resolution of common international affairs.

Thus, in 1863 the Emperor of France suggested to all European courts to assemble at an all-European congress to discuss the state of affairs in Europe and to eliminate occasions for possible embarrassment in the future. This grandiose plan concealed the wish of Napoleon III to force other States and France to interfere in Polish affairs and was rejected by the powers.

2. *Participating States.* Only interested independent States enjoying full sovereignty may participate in congresses and conferences. Semi-independent States, for example, Egypt, Bulgarian Principality, and so on, are represented at international assemblies by those powers having sovereignty over them. In addition to those directly interested, mediator-

powers and all others take part in congresses and conferences if the subject-matter of discussion has general significance for peoples. In any event, the power whose affairs are involved must participate.

This basic rule of justice is not always observed. Not to mention congresses which occurred at the beginning of the eighteenth century, even recently international assemblies are encountered at which plenipotentiaries of States directly interested were not admitted. An example is the Paris Conference (1869) which discussed mutual misunderstandings between the Ottoman Empire and the Kingdom of Greece on the occasion of an uprising in the Regno di Candia. Representatives of the Great Powers and Turkey participated, but the Greek plenipotentiary was invited only to give answers to questions put by the conference.[30] Similarly, the preliminary meetings of the Constantinople Conference (1876-1877), convoked at the initiative of England, to discuss the final conditions of a peace between Serbia, Montenegro, and Turkey and reforms of local government in Bosnia, Herzogovina, and Bulgaria, occurred without the participation of a representative of the Turkish Government. The Porte had grounds to consider such a course of action by the European powers as violating its honor and dignity. Finally, the protest of Romania against the decisions of the 1883 London Conference convoked to discuss navigation on the Danube, to which it was not invited, seems wholly valid because, as a Danubian power, Romania had a legal right to take part in the discussion of the procedures for navigation on the Danube.

3. *Representation.* The persons attending congresses and conferences differs, as we have seen. Either the sovereigns themselves or their plenipotentiary ministers participate in congresses, whereas at conferences governments appoint their delegates or even commissars, who bring the decisions of the conference to the information of their government. The number of representatives sent from each State to particular assemblies is at the discretion of the governments.

4. *Subject-matter of meetings.* In this respect, congresses and conferences also differ from one another. To enumerate all questions which might and should be subject to consideration of international assemblies is not possible. History shows that not only the relations of States, but also internal State orders, have been discussed at congresses and conferences. Such interference can never be justified. In principle, both organs of the

[30] Prince [Aleksandr Mikhailovich] Gorchakov [(1798-1883)] had every reason to be upset by this violation of a "basic principle of justice". He wrote on 12(24) December 1868 to Paris: "Si la Turquie est admise, la Grèce devait l'être aussi. La conférence étant un arbitrage, il serait contre toute équité de n'admettre qu'une des parties en litige". See *Annuaire de l'Empire de Russie* (1870), p. 177 et seq.

international community, congresses and conferences should confine themselves solely to matters affecting the unie of States.

5. *Procedure of meetings*. In comparison with earlier times, the clerical work of contemporary congresses and conferences is distinctive for the lack of empty formalities and ceremonies which made international assemblies in the seventeenth and eighteenth centuries so difficult. The external aspect of diplomatic congresses has been significantly simplified.

They are opened by the election of a chairman, who usually is the first plenipotentiary of that State on whose territory the assembly is taking place. This is a mark of respect to the local authorities whose hospitality the representatives of the other States are enjoying.

The customary rule of the election as chairman of a person representing the local authorities was violated in recent times only in three instances: at the Brussels Conference (1874), when the plenipotentiary of Belgium declined the chairmanship, proposing to render this honor to the representative of Russia, at whose initiative the conference was convoked; at the Constantinople Conference (1876-1877), the preliminary meetings of which occurred under the chairmanship of the Russian plenipotentiary as "*doyen du corps diplomatique*";[31] and at the Hague Peace Conference (1899), which occurred under the chairmanship of the Russian plenipotentiary out of respect for the initiative of Russia.

Upon the election of the chairman, an exchange and verification of credentials take place. The assemblies are conducted orally and directly. Sometimes special commissions are established from members of the assembly to study individual questions and prepare the decision, or for the final formulation of decisions already adopted. A protocol is drawn up concerning each session. If the assembly was convoked at the suggestion of mediator-powers, the role of mediator belongs to its plenipotentiary; all meetings occur with the direct participation thereof; documents and correspondence concerning the case are communicated to him and, in the event of disagreement, he attempts to bring the parties to a conciliation agreement.

6. *Adoption of decisions*. Draft decisions of congresses and conferences are subject to voting. Each State participating in an assembly has one vote. Decisions are adopted by a majority vote. However, the opinion adopted by a majority of the assembly does not have unconditional binding force for the minority. Imposing it by force would contradict the principle of the independence of States. In view of this, the efforts of the congress should

[31] See "Actes de la conference de Bruxelles", Protocol No. 1, *Annuaire diplomatique de l'Empire de Russie* (1877), p. 237 et seq.

be so directed to persuade the minority to withdraw its opposition and agree with the majority. In the absence of unanimity, the purpose of the conference will not be achieved, and it must be considered to be unconstituted.

7. *Enforcement of decisions*. There is no executive authority in an international unie which might enforce the decisions of congresses and conferences. The execution of their decisions depends entirely on the States who participated in and adopted their decisions. Sometimes this is formally assigned to one of the participants in an international assembly or undertaken by the aggregate forces. The question of the resources and methods for ensuring the execution of decisions of congresses and conferences remains open.

Chapter 2
Subjects of International Law and International Relations

I. General Remarks

§53. Independent nations or States of European civilization are direct subjects of international law and actors in the domain of international interaction.

In the domain of international relations the State is regarded as one indivisible whole, as a legal personal which has relative to other States certain rights and duties. The State, as a whole, acts as an actor which, pursuing in interaction with other States tasks set for itself, gives direction and protection to international relations. International law is the result of the aggregate efforts and interaction of formed States. In relations between States those forms are elaborated in which international relations are formed, and those procedures are established and principles are created, by which relations are determined of both entire nations and individual subjects thereof.

Neither monarchs, nor private individuals, nor societies participating in international relations should be considered to be subjects of international law.[1] Monarchs and diplomatic agents (envoys) act in the international world in the role of and with the rights of representatives or plenipotentiaries of a State: they do not have autonomous international rights. As regards private associations and individuals, they conduct their own international turnover under the control, patronage, and even responsibility of the State authority in whose subjectship they are.

II. The State as International Person

§54. Each State participating in international interaction possess the same legal capacity and dispositive legal capacity as an individual natural person in the sphere of private relations. In this sense a State is a person; that is, an essence which not only has certain inherent rights, but may acquire others, protect them, and enter into various kinds of legal obligations.

But as a subject of international law, a State is not some kind of special person differing from that studied in the science of State law. International

[1] Henry Wheaton, *Elements of International Law*, ed. Richard Henry Dana (8th ed.; London, 1866), §19 – a different view.

law takes the State as it is, as developed by history and determined by State law. The definition given by Cicero remains one of the best definitions of the State for its precision and clarity.[2]

International law may be satisfied by this simple definition of the State. It does not consider the internal structure of States. To be sure, the existing political orders always exert a certain influence on international relations: they promote the development of international turnover or serve as a restraint on them. But it is not for the science of international law to determine these orders, to identity their merits and relative perfections. All States, whatever form of government they have, are identically subjects of international law.[3]

The same for political power, the actual power belonging to a people, is not determined in aggregate by international law. As subjects of international law, all States are equal between themselves. Certain rights and corresponding duties worked out by history and the existing international order belong to all of them. But, of course, the strongest, most enlightened or economically prosperous State in fact always will have more resources to take advantage of its rights than a weak and culturally undeveloped State.

The rights of international personality belonging to a State assume the aforementioned basic indicia of a subject of international law. In order to participate in international interaction it is absolutely essential that a particular people be situated on a certain territory and subject itself to an organized political power. Therefore, nomadic tribes or various kinds of social groups may not be considered to be subjects of international law as they were not influential in an international respect (see Introduction above).[4]

The Italian scholar, Mancini, proved that subjects of international law are nations, and not States, as they are determined by State law. But a nation being, in the words of Mancini, a "natural union of people connected by virtue of the unity of their territory, origin, customs, and language, communion of life, and social consciousness", this is not a State.

[2] "*Respublica est coetus multitudinis juris consensu et utilitatis communione sociatus*". De republica, lib. I, p. 25.

[3] Robert Joseph Phillimore, *Commentaries upon International Law* (London, 1854-1861), I, p. 81: "It is a sound general principle, and one to be laid down at the threshold of the science of which we are treating, that International Law has no concern with the form, character, or power of the constitution or government of a State, with the religion of its inhabitants, the extent of its domain, etc.".

[4] Notwithstanding the authoritative reflections of Sir Travers Twiss in the *Revue de droit international*, XV, pp. 437-442, 547-563; XVI, p. 237 et seq, it nevertheless seems to me that the "Association africaine internationale" cannot be considered to be a subject of international law and could not found a State and act with the rights of an independent power.

If a nationality, understood as an ethnographic whole, amalgamates into one political union; that is, exists on one territory and under one sovereign power, then it may be a subject of international law. In other words, in order to be a subject of international law, a nation must be made by a people, as a State.[5]

Finally, personality may be ascribed to a State in the sense that it dies away, leaves the field of world history, and departs from international interaction. State law cannot make provision for this fact; international law must. History knows multiple examples of the death of States. The ensuing of this event raises the question of the inheritance of a deceased State as to its rights and duties resolved in international law.

III. Division of States

§55. All existing civilized States are members of the international community and subjects of international law; but the degree of their international independence is not the same; some States possess full international sovereignty and are not part of any other than general international dependence on one another; others, on the contrary, without ceasing to be subjects of international law, are in relations which more or less limit their sovereignty. Finally, there are States internally autonomous but undoubtedly not autonomous in international relations: these are semi-dependent States which are not subjects of international law. Thus, an international autocracy of States represents modifications and hues on the basis of which existing States may be divided into *genera* and *species*.

International law distinguishes simple States, complex, and combined.

A. A simple State is not bound by special international ties with any other State; it is a single political organism having the full right of international representation.

B. A peculiarity of complex States is that they are a combination of several States connected by certain common institutions or by one sovereign power. The activity of this last may be limited by some international relations or extend to internal administration. On this basis complex States are divided into the following types:

a) A union of States (*confoederatio civitatum, confederation d'États, Staatenbund*) is that form of combination in which subordination to

[5] Pasquale Stanislao Mancini, *Diritto internazionale* (Naples, 1873), p. 42. See §33 above. Compare August von Bulmerincq, *Das Völkerrecht oder das internationale Recht: Systemisch dargestelt* (2d ed.; Freiburg i B., 1889), §16.

common institutions does not exclude internal and external autonomy of the combined States.

b) A combination of several States under one sovereign power (*unio civitatum*) is a different *genus*.

α) *Personal combination* (*unio personalis*). States combined in this form are linked with one another by another person of the sovereign or reigning dynasty governing them.

β) *A real combination* (*unio realis*). Here the link between States is expressed not by the person of the sovereign or dynasty, but in a certain community of life of the States themselves united forever.

γ) *Union State* (*État fédéral, Bundesstaat*). These States may enter into a permanent combination under one authority insofar as the State formed by them is itself a subject of international law. Members of such a union State subordinate themselves to the sovereign union authority which usually is established by their mutual agreement and manifests its operation especially in the domain of international relations which it administers.

δ) *Semi-independent States* (*États mi-souverains*). They legally comprise part of another State. More or less autonomous in the domain of internal administration, they in international relations depend completely on the power of another State. The similarity between them and members of a union State is that none have international personalities but, unlike them, the dependence of members of a union State does not have an international, but a State, character. Such semi-independence of States is found in various ways. As we shall see below, semi-independent States are creations solely of international relations, but not the aspirations and forces of peoples.

The diverse political forms cited, materially influencing the international dispositive legal capacity of States, should be taken into consideration and clarified by positive international law.

A. Simple States

§56. From the standpoint of international relations and law, simple States (Russia, England, France, Belgium, and others) may be considered to be types of autonomous and fully-fledged members of the international community. They do not depend either in internal or in their external relations on any foreign authority and operate in all instances as unified and indivisible political organisms.

Such States may consist of various parts without losing through this their organic unity in international relations. For example, colonies often have their own parliaments and forces but, not enjoying autonomous international representation, are considered to be an integral part of their metropolitans. Therefore, all colonial States (as England, Portugal, and others) are simple individual international persons.[6] A State may also include various accessioned (or incorporated) regions without losing the character of a simple State. An example of this is Great Britain, combined with Scotland and Ireland into one kingdom on the basis of Acts of 1707 and 1800.[7]

Russia and Poland. The view has been expressed in western European literature that Poland cannot constitute an inseparable part of Russia in common with the status of other regions and governates. The full accession of Poland to the Empire supposedly would not be justified either by the "acts of the Congress of Vienna or on some other legal grounds"; that, on the contrary, this accession violates the Vienna treaties which created for the Poles a privileged status within the Empire. "The dominion of Russia is maintained", wrote Calvo, "by force of arms", and Poland retains its legitimate right to be liberated.[8]

This view is refuted by the facts and, first and foremost, by the actual meaning of the Act of Vienna. By virtue of Article I of this Act, the Duchy of Warsaw was declared to be in an "inextricable link" with Russia "in perpetuity". "His Imperial Majesty", this Article continues, proposes to give, at his discretion, a domestic system to this State (that is, to the Duchy) which has the status of a special administration. It is evident from a comparison of these provisions and even more from the Congress of Vienna that the privileged and national administration of Poland was conditioned by its accession to Russia, on which Emperor Alexander I insisted by right of conquest and none of the allies objected to in principle. On the contrary, they strongly objected to Alexander's wish to give Poland a constitutional system.[9] In any event, the last was given on the aforesaid condition, which in

6 August Wilhelm Heffter, *Das europäische Völkerrecht der Gegenwart auf den bisherigen Grundlagen* (7th ed.; Berlin, 1882), §20 erroneously considers England to be a united State.

7 Johann Caspar Bluntschli, *Das moderne Völkerrecht der civilisirten Staten* (Nördlingen, 1868), §79 errs by including "colonial States" (*Colonialstaaten*) in the category of semi-independent States. Australia and Canada are indissoluble parts of the Kingdom of Great Britain.

8 Carlos Calvo, *Le droit international théorique et pratique* (1887-1896), I, §48. Wheaton, note 1 above, §43; William Beach Lawrence, *Commentaire sur les Éléments du droit international: et sur l'Histoire des progrès du droit des gens Henry Wheaton* (Leipzig, 1868-1880), I, §303 et seq; Phillimore, note 3 above, I, p. 14 et seq. Compare also Georg Jellinek, *Die Lehre von den Staatenverbindungen* (Vienna, 1882), p. 71.

9 For details, see F. F. Martens, Собрание трактатов и конвенций, заключенных Россиею с иностранными державами [Collection of Treaties and Conventions Conclud-

1813 was violated by the Poles, who rose up against the Russian authorities. Therefore, in the Manifesto issued in 1832 after the uprising was suppressed, Emperor Nicholas I had grounds to declare the Poles to be guilty of failure to perform the conditions previously agreed and himself, as the victor, to be free to take measures with respect to Poland as required by the interests of Russia. The 1862 Polish uprising led, again on "legitimate grounds", to the system which Poland has at present. In a word, Russia possesses the former Duchy of Warsaw and other Polish regions and considers them to be an integral part of itself by right no less than Prussia has with respect to the Province of Poznan or the German Empire has to Alsace and Lotharingia.[10]

B. Complex States.

a) Union of States

§57. A union of States is an international combination in the full sense of the word: it is based on commonality of interests and respect for the internal and international autonomy of the members of the union. The last retain the right of international representation together with representation of the entire union; they all may conclude treaties and send embassies, with one limitation, that international transactions concluded by them or instructions

ed by Russia with Foreign Powers] (Spb., 1874-1909). 15 vols. (hereinafter: F. F. Martens, Собрание трактатов и конвенций [Collection of Treaties and Conventions]), III, p. 213; IV(1), p. 427 et seq.

[10] In 1863, on the occasion of the last Polish uprising, western European cabinets (including in Vienna) also attempted to prove that Russia violated the 1816 Vienna treaties by disposing of the Kingdom of Poland at its discretion. Prince Metternich rather surprisingly refuted these arguments in a letter of February 1840 (see F. F. Martens, Собрание договоров [Collection of Treaties], IV(1), pp. 527-528). "The Emperor Alexander", said Prince Metternich, "restored the Kingdom of Poland in 1815 and, having arranged it, gave it institutions. The structure of this Kingdom and its institutions were placed by this same monarch under the moral guarantee of the Act of the Congress of Vienna. In 1831 the Kingdom of Poland rose up and, having proclaimed its renunciation of the Tsar, at the same time destroyed the constitution given by Alexander. This undertaking had no success. A struggle commenced on the field of battle, and the Emperor Nicholas was the victor. As the victor, His Imperial Majesty determined the fate of the country. Which of the two, Tsar or Poland, violated the Act of the Congress of Vienna? Obviously, this was Poland! What is the legal position, in view of these events, of those who signed this Act? To now defend the structure given in 1815 by the Emperor Alexander … would be the equivalent of asserting that the violation by one of the Contracting Parties does not unbind the hands of the other". Compare the Memorandum attached to the Despatch of Prince Gorchakov to Baron Brunnov in London of 26 August 1863, *Annuaire diplomatique de l'Empire de Russie* (1864), p. 219 et seq.

given to diplomatic agents are not contrary to the interests of the entire union and its individual members; as regards their internal autonomy, in principle they are not subject to any limitations. A union arises according to a mutual agreement of the States comprising it with a view to satisfaction of common international interests.

The sole peculiarity of a union of States is not the mixture therein of State and international elements.[11] A union should not represent this mixture; on the contrary, in a normal structure it protects the external security of its members and promotes the development of the autonomous internal administration. A model structure of a union State is a prototype of that organization of an international community of which one may dream and whose implementation one may hope for during the further development of international relations. Regrettably, the enormous cultural-international significance of a union of States has still not been elicited in the literature.[12]

There have been organized in the form of a union of States: Netherlands General States (1580, 1609-1795); Swiss Confederation to 1798 and again from 1803 to 1848; North American United States from 1776 to 1787; finally, the German Union (1815-1866).

Closest to a pure type of union of States was the German Union founded in 1815.

The structural basis was the already noted 1814 Peace Treaty of Paris, which provided (Article 6): "The states of Germany shall be independent, and united by a federative bond". Accordingly, the Congress of Vienna prepared an Act of union structure for Germany, added to in 1820 and subsequent years.[13]

[11] Bluntschli, note 7 above, §70, for an opposite view.

[12] Compare the few perceptive comments in Lorenz von Stein, *Die Verwaltungslehre* (Stuttgart, 1865-1868), II, p. 97, and Heinrich von Treitschke, *Historische und politische Aufsätze* (3d ed.; Leipzig, 1876), p. 446 et seq. Also compare John Caldwell Calhoun, *A Disquisition on Government: and, A Discourse on the Constitution and Government of the United States*, ed. Richard Kenner Crallé (Columbia, 1851), p. 111 et seq; Phillimore, note 3 above, I, p. 133 et seq; Siegfried Brie, *Der Bundesstaat* (Leipzig, 1874); Léopold Neumann, *Grundriss des heutigen europäischen Völkerrechts* (2d ed.; Vienna, 1877), p. 19; Paul Laband, *Das Staatsrecht des Deutschen Reiches* (Tübingen, 1876), I, p. 70 et seq; Heffter, note 6 above, §19, 20; Brie, *Theorie der Staatenverbindungen* (Stuttgart, 1886); Hugo Preuss, *Gemeinde, Staat, Reich als Gebietskörperschaften* (Berlin, 1889).

[13] Aleksandr Dmitrievich Gradovskii, Германская конституция [The German Constitution] (Spb., 1875-1876), I, p.13 et seq; Henry Wheaton, *Histoire des progrès du droit des gens en Europe depuis la paix de Westphalie jusqu'au congrès de Vienne* (Leipzig, 1853), II, p. 132 et seq. On how diverse opinions may be even on the character of the 1815 German union, which undoubtedly was a union of States, see the curious information in the dispatches of Baron von Bismarck from Frankfurt-on-Main published in Heinrich Ritter

Germany was organized in the form of a confederation or union of 38 (later, 33) independent states "for external and internal security". The States mutually guaranteed their possessions which were part of the Union. Only lands with Germanic population were among such possessions. Therefore, Italy, Hungary, and the Slavic lands from Austrian regions were not included, nor were Poznan or eastern and western Prussia included from Prussian lands. On the other hand, the Danish King (as Duke of Holstein and Lauenburg) and the Dutch King (the possessions of Luxembourg and Limburg) were members of the Union.

The Diet served as the organ of the Union, composed of representatives from the individual German states with sessions held at Frankfurt-on-Main. It may rightly be called a "permanent congress of German states". The Diet had two forms of sessions: a permanent council (*Engerer Rath*) and a plenary assembly (*Plenum*): Austria presided over both. The Diet had special duties: (1) to care for the international interests of the entire Union; (2) the Diet had an active and passive right of embassy; (3) the right to declare war and conclude treaties in the name of the Union; (4) mediation in all claims of foreign powers against a member of the Union. But the autonomy of individual States which were members of the Union was not eliminated: they retained their sovereign international rights and internal sovereignty.

Such was the system of the German Union, which for always remains a remarkable example of international organization with full respect for the autonomy of individual states.

The Austro-Prussian War of 1866, having removed Austria from being part of Germany, led to the destruction of the Union. In 1867 the North German Union was founded of 22 states situated north of the River Main. Prussia received predominant influence there and strengthened the bonds of Union ties. Thereafter, all efforts of Prussian policy were directed to converting the German Union into a Union State under the primacy and leadership of Germany.

The contemporary system of Germany is developing along this path. The Constitution of the North German Union served in many respects as a model for the organization of the German Empire, formed in 1871 from 22 monarchical and 3 republican German states and the Imperial region of Alsace-Lotharingia.

The structure of the new Empire continues to be disputed by jurists. The majority of writers consider it to be a Union State; others suggest that it is

von Poschinger, *Preussen im Bundesstag 1857-1859* (Leipzig, 1881-1883), III, pp. 192, 196 et seq.

a Union of States which have retained to a significant extent their domestic and international autonomy. The last view is, in our opinion, more correct.[14]

On the basis of the 1871 Constitution, Imperial affairs were in the charge of: 1) the Emperor of Germany (King of Prussia); 2) Union Council; and 3) Reichstag. The representation of the Empire as an international person belonged to the Emperor: he had the right of active and passive embassy and the right to declare war and conclude treaties with foreign powers. But these rights did not abolish fully the international representation of the members of the Empire. All were recognized to have the right to appoint their own plenipotentiaries at foreign courts, although understandably they could not enter into any international obligations or negotiations contrary to the interests of the Empire or its members. The Union Council, which expressed the sovereignty of individual German governments and consisted of their representatives, had its own special "foreign affairs committee" whose membership included plenipotentiaries from Bavaria, Württemberg, and Saxony and two members from other States chosen by the Union Council. According to a law, this committee convened in all cases when it was necessary to adopt important international measures and was to supervise the foreign policy of the Imperial Chancellor. The extent to which it actually performed this task is a question of fact. But its existence, with the right of diplomatic intercourse belonging to German states, demonstrates that the German Empire is a Union of States, and not a Union State. The creator of modern Germany, Prince [Otto von] Bismarck, expressed this very thought, having recognized the "federative foundation" (*föderative Grundlage*) of the German Empire created by union treaties between German States, the sanctity of compliance with which he imputed to the duty of the German emperors.[15]

[14] Compare Heinrich Tinsch, *Das Recht der deutschen Einzelstaaten bezüglich des Abschlusses völkerrechtlicher Verträge mit besonderer Berücksichtigung ihrer Stellung im Reichs* (Erlangen, 1882); Laband, note 12 above, I, p. 72; Robert von Mohl, *Des deutsche Reichsstaatsrecht* (Tübingen, 1873), p. 29 et seq; Hermann Johann Friedrich Schulze, *Lehrbuch des deutschen Staatsrechts* (Leipzig, 1886); Georg Meyer, *Staatsrechtliche Erörterungen über die deutsche Reichsverfassung* (Leipzig, 1872), p. 12 et seq; Ludwig von Rönne, *Das Verfassungs-Recht des Deutschen Reichs* (Leipzig, 1872), p. 29 et seq; Gradovskii, note 13 above, II, p. 16 et seq.

[15] Otto von Bismarck, *Gedanken und Erinnerungen* (Stuttgart, 1898), I, p. 356-357, et seq.

b) Combined States

§58. α) Personal combination. This form of combination is based solely on the community of the dynasty ruling in States or on the fact that they are under the authority of a single sovereign. Such a combination may be more or less continuous and does not destroy the international personality of each of the combined States: they may have various international representation, conclude treaties separately and autonomously, even go to war with one another. But actually the personal combination always significantly influences the international policy of the combined States. This terminates with the dynasty itself, or with the ensuing of that moment when the procedure for accession to the throne in both States makes their further combination impossible. Separation also may be the result of war between them.[16]

History knows many examples of the personal combination of States. Thus, of the German emperors elected in 1520 the Spanish King Charles V combined Spain and Germany under his power so long as he did not abdicate the thrones (1556). The English kingdom consisted of the personal combination of the Elector of Hanover from 1714 to 1838, when Queen Victoria ruled in England and on the basis of the law on succession to the throne operating in Hanover could not occupy the throne of Hanover. The King of Prussia was the head of the Principality of Neuchatel until the accession of the last in 1857 to Switzerland.[17] Finally, Holland and Luxembourg were until 1890 in a personal combination under the authority of the House of Orange-Nassau (Act of Congress of Vienna, Article 67; London Protocol of 11 May 1867).[18] From 1885 the "State of the Congo" was founded at the Berlin African Conference, consisting of a personal combination with the King of Belgium.

β) Real combination. States combined in this form may enjoy complete autonomy in the sphere of internal administration, but be a single person

16 Grotius, *De jure belli ac pacis*, I, 2. 7; Georg Friedrich von Martens, *Précis du droit des gens moderne de l'Europe, fondé sur les traités et l'usage* (Göttingen, 1789), I, §16 et seq; Phillimore, note 3 above, I, p. 96; Heffter, note 6 above, §20; Edward Shepherd Creasy, *First Platform of International Law* (London, 1876), p. 136 ; Lawrence, note 8 above, I, p. 268; Bluntschli, note 7 above, §74.

17 See the Treaty of 1857 relating to Neuchatel in G. F. Martens, *Recueil des traités*, VII (1875), p. 103: "Traité conclu entre l'Autriche, la France, la Gr. Bretagne, la Prusse, la Russie et la Suisse pour faire cesser les droits de souveraineté de la Prusse sur la principauté de Neuchâtel et le comté la Valangin, signé à Paris le 26 mai 1857".

18 L. de Hardog, "Das Staatsrecht des Königreichs der Niederlande, in Heinrich von Marquardsen", *Handbuch des öffentlichen Rechts der Gegenwart* (Freiburg, 1883-19?), IV(1).

in the domain of international relations. In principle, a real combination is the result of an agreement between two equal political organisms: self-government of some province or domain does not establish and does not serve as evidence of a real combination thereof with the State of which in reality it is an organic part. Externally, a real combination is usually reflected in the existence of certain organic institutions common for both States, but never depends on a dynasty. It is terminated either by a new treaty between the combined States or by force of arms.[19]

1. Of modern States, AUSTRIA AND HUNGARY are a real combination. Their combination is proved as follows: the will of Emperor Ferdinand I 1543, Statute of Emperor Leopold I 1703, in particular the Pragmatic Sanction of Charles VI 1734, and the Pragmatic Law of Franz II issued in 1804. All these acts established the indivisibility in perpetuity of the two States. The uprising of 1848 and the final defeat of the Hungarian nationalist party gave occasion to the Government in Vienna to once more affirm this indivisibility. The proponents of a contrary view, defending the personal combination of Austria and Hungary, refer, *inter alia*, to the 1867 reform which introduced the presently operating system of Austro-Hungarian dualism and supposedly established the international autonomy of Hungary.[20] But such a conclusion is not confirmed by the acts on which dualism is based. On the contrary, underlying these acts without any doubt is the notion that Austria and Hungary constitute in indivisible State in perpetuity under the influence of the Austrian Emperor and Hungarian King representing the international interests of both Austria and Hungary together.

2. NORWAY AND SWEDEN also are in a real, and not a personal, combination, which is evidenced by the following positive facts.[21] Beginning from 1536 to

[19] Bluntschli, note 7 above, §75; Johann Ludwig Klüber, *Droit des gens moderne de l'Europe* (2d ed.; Paris, 1874), §27.

[20] Jellinek, note 8 above, pp. 79, 221, 226 et seq; Theodor ritter Dantscher von Kollesberg, *Der monarchische Bundesstaat Österreich-Ungarn und der Berliner Vertrag nebst der Bosnischen Vorlage* (Vienna, 1860); Th. Funck-Brentano and Albert Sorel, *Précis du droit des gens* (Paris, 1877), p. 39; Travers Twiss, *The Law of Nations Considered as Independent Political Communities: On the Right and Duties of Nations in Time of Peace* (2d ed.; Oxford, 1884), I, §38; Lawrence, note 8 above, I, p. 272 et seq; Jules Joseph Valfrey, *L'Empire constitutionnel d'Autriche et ses lois fondementales* (Paris 1868); Hermann Ignaz Bidermann, *Die rechtliche Natur der österreichisch-ungarischen Monarchie* (Vienna, 1877).

[21] For another view, Phillimore, note 3 above, I, §74; Funck-Brentano and Sorel, note 20 above, p. 39. Compare Jellinek, note 8 above, p. 223 et seq; Twiss, note 20 above, I, §40. Lawrence, note 8 above, I, 268.

1814, Norway was combined with Denmark under the authority of the King of Denmark representing both in international relations. In 1814 thanks to assistance rendered by allies in the struggle against Napoleon by the Swedish heir, Prince [Jean-Baptiste] Bernadotte [(1763-1844)], Norway acceded to Sweden. The Norwegians did not wish to obey this decision, and only after an armed conflict, concluded a Treaty in the City of Moss determining the mutual relations of these two States. On the basis of the Moss Convention, Norway preserved internal autonomy, but recognized the King of Sweden as the Head and representative in international relations. Moreover, the Convention provided that when the present dynasty ruling in Sweden and Norway come to an end, in this event the Swedish and Norwegian peoples should each select a candidate for the Swedish-Norwegian throne and, if the choice does not fall on one person, then their plenipotentiaries shall assemble in a determined city and choose one Sovereign. It is evident that the link between the two States does not depend on the dynasty but should exist permanently and, consequently, is a real tie. Whereas in the past Norway sought to have its own Minister of Foreign Affairs and its own diplomatic and consular representation abroad, it is evident that Norway seeks full separation from Sweden. Foreign States which have received diplomatic agents and consuls appointed by the Government in Christiana would have thereby recognized the full international independence of Norway – republic or kingdom, if the Norwegian people choose their own special king. The King of Sweden ceases to rule Norway from the moment of the existence of this country as an international person with its own right of embassy and consulate.

According to some writers,[22] Russia and the Grand Duchy of Finland are in a "real" combination. Underlying a real combination usually is a mutual agreement of the combined States. However, Finland came to Russia on the basis of the Fredrikshamn Peace Treaty (1809) concluded between Russia and Sweden.[23] Article 4 of this Treaty provides: "All these (Finnish) provinces, with inhabitants, cities, ports, fortresses, villages, and islands,

[22] As, for example, Heffter, *Das europäische Völkerrecht der Gegenwart auf den bisherigen Grundlagen*, ed. Friedrich Heinrich Geffcken (7th ed.; Berlin, 1882), §49. A completely correct view is found in Jellinek, note 8 above, pp. 70-71. Compare Nils Eden, *Die schwedisch-norvegische Union und der Kieler Frieden* (Leipzig, 1895); Herman Ludvig Rydin, *Unionen och Konungens sanktionsrätti Norska grundlagsfrågor* (Uppsala, 1885); Alphonse Rivier, *Principes du droit des gens* (Paris, 1896), I, p. 98.

[23] Karl von Martens and Ferdinand de Cornot, Baron de Cussy, *Recueil manuel et pratique des traités, conventions et autre actes diplomatique* (Leipzig, 1846-1857), II, 938; Полное собрание законов Российской империи [Complete Collection of Laws of the Russian Empire] (1st series), No. 23882; Lawrence, note 8 above, I, p. 342.

and likewise with all fields, will belong in full ownership and sovereignty to the Russian Empire and remain acceded thereto". It is evident that the Grand Duchy of Finland is an integral part of Russia, a province thereof. It has its own constitution and various autonomous institutions recognized in 1809 and subjected to material limitations from 1899 down to the present.[24]

§59. (γ) *Union State*. From the standpoint of international law, a union State should satisfy two basic conditions: 1) possess supreme union power and be a single international person; 2) being a single subject of international law, it should deprive of this character the States subordinate to the common union authority.[25]

When applying this definition to the present German Empire, we must say that it is not a union State because it does not remove international representation from its individual members. But it is on the path to a union State. The history of the origin of union States in general shows that they are formed from a union of States under the pressure of international needs. They are the result not only of a community of economic, social, and national interests or geographical position as of the international status of a certain group of peoples generating the merger of their forces in order to protect external security. In the name of this purpose, they renounce their international rights and subordinate themselves to a common sovereign power.

1. **Swiss Confederation**. Switzerland was recognized formally as an autonomous State in 1648 and represented a union of thirteen autonomous cantons. During the wars against the French Revolution, the status of Switzerland was complicated. Six new cantons became part of Switzerland in 1798. All the Swiss cantons were independent States and subjects of international law: they had the right autonomously to conduct diplomatic relations and conclude treaties, especially "military Capitulations" on the basis of which they supplied various courts with crack troops from among their subjects. The status of the cantons changed on the basis of constitutions of 1798 and 1803. The Helvetic Republic was formed from all the cantons

[24] Compare Leo Mechelin, *Précis de droit public du Grand-Duché de Finlande* (Helsingfors, 1886); also his article in Marquardsen, note 18 above, IV; Kesar Ordin, Покорение Финляндии [Subjugation of Finland] (Spb., 1889). 2 vols. For a critique of this work, see Professor Johan Richard Danielson, Соединение Финляндии с Российскою Империею [Joinder of Finland with the Russian Empire] (Spb., 1890); Hisinger, *On the Validity of the Fundamental Laws of Finland* (Stockholm, 1892).

[25] See especially Jellinek, note 8 above, pp. 253-314. Compare also Brie, "Zur Lehre von den Staatenverbindungen", in *Grüdhut's Zeitschrift für das Privat- und öffentliche Recht*, XI, p. 85 et seq.

under the authority of a Union Diet which assembled regularly in Freiburg, Bern, Solothurn, Basel, Luzerne, and Zurich. The chairman of the Diet and head of the Union in international intercourse was the Landammann of the canton of that city where the Diet met.

This system was changed at the Congress of Vienna. The new constitution (1815) added three cantons to the existing 19, and they all received the guarantee of inviolability and of neutrality in perpetuity. The goal of the Union was to protect the freedom and independence of the entire Union and each canton. The Tagsatzung, composed of delegates from the cantons, conducted the affairs of the Union and held sessions in turn at Bern, Zurich, and Luzerne. The canton of that city in which the Tagsatzung assembled was the "governing canton". The Tagsatzung managed international intercourse, but the cantons retained the right to conclude conventions, such as the military Capitulation, on the police, and on economic interests.

The 1815 structure proved to be unworkable. It excessively separated the Swiss cantons in domestic and especially international relations, and in Switzerland there was greater awareness of the need, in view of international interests, to merge into a single whole under strong Union authority. Thus commenced the struggle between the centralists and autonomists, which has continued throughout the entire history of Switzerland.

A new constitution was issued in 1848, on the basis of which Switzerland was declared to be a Union State composed of 25 cantons. International relations, the declaration of war, the conclusion of peace and treaties were concentrated in the hands of the Union authorities, the cantons being deprived of the right to conclude a military Capitulation, but maintained their right to enter into agreements on international matters concerning the vicinity, police, or economic interests so long as these were not contrary to the interests of the entire Swiss State. All relations of the cantons with foreign powers happen through the Union Council and its President, who serve as organs of the Union executive power. Legislative power belongs to a federal assembly consisting of a "national council" and a "council of cantons".

The 1848 Constitution was reviewed in 1874 and changed to expand the rights of the Union authorities with respect to the cantons on the naturalization of foreigners in Switzerland.[26]

2. **North American United States**. The history of the structure of this State convincingly demonstrates the power of that influence which

[26] Bluntschli, *Geschichte des schweizerischen Bundesrechts* (2d ed.; Stuttgart, 1875); Antoine Cherbuliez, *De la démocratie en Suisse* (Paris, 1843); Orelli, "Das Staatrecht der Schweiz", in Marquardsen, note 18 above, IV(2); see *Staatsarchiv*, no. 5177 (1874).

international interests have on the transformation of a Union of States into a Union State.

Under a Constitution of 1778, the North American states constituted a Union of States. Each state was an independent State and international person. It is understandable that the actions of the representatives of the states in the field of international relations often were contrary to those purposes which the highest Union authority – the President of the states – pursued in this sphere. The central government had no means to protect the international interests of the Union and encourage their development: he had neither an army nor financial resources at his disposal.

This impossible – from the standpoint of international relations – structure of the states was quickly felt and generated agitation in favor of establishing a more stable order securing the integrity and inviolability of each republic. Thanks to the efforts of [Alexander] Hamilton [(1757-1804)], [James] Madison [(1751-1836)], and other remarkable political figures, in 1787 a new constitution was adopted which organized the states into a Union State.[27] On the basis thereof the internal autonomy of the states remained, but in international relations the republic is a single indivisible whole and a subject of international law.[28]

The central organs of the states are: the Washington Congress, consisting of the Senate and the House of Representatives, and the President, who is the head of executive power of the Union. The Senate has a special "Committee on Foreign Relations". All the diplomatic relations of the Union are managed by the President with the decisive exclusion of individual states from autonomous international representation. The "Committee on Foreign Relations" supervises the foreign policy of the President. Thus, the North American United States represent a type of Union State as a special type of international person.[29]

3. **United States of Venezuela**. In 1810 these former Spanish colonies declared themselves to be independent and, after twenty years of war, their

[27] Compare Joseph Story, *Commentaries on the Constitution of the United States* (Boston, 1833), §243-271. Alexis de Tocqueville, *De la démocratie en Amérique* (Paris, 1836); Calhoun, note 12 above, pp. 132, 201 et seq.

[28] The Constitution of the North American United States begins with the following words: "We the people of the United States".

[29] Compare Johann Jacob Rüttimann, *Das nordamerikanische Bundesstaatsrecht verglichen mit den pollitischen einrichtungen der Schweiz* (Zurich, 1872), II, §351-382; Hermann von Holst, *Verfassung und Demokratie der Vereinigten Staaten von Amerika* (Düsseldorf, 1873). 3 vols.; Eugen Schlief, *Der Verfassung der Nord-Amerikanischen Union* (Leipzig, 1880); Holst, "Das Staatsrecht der Vereinigten Staaten von Amerika", in Marquardsen, note 18 above, IV(3).

independence was recognized by Spain. At present, the United States of Venezuela consist of twenty states, four territories, two colonies, and a Union region in which Caracas, the capital of the Union, is located. The President is elected for six years and administers the international relations of the states.

4. **United States of Brazil** (*Estados Unidos de Brazil*). In 1889 the Emperor of Brazil, Dom Pedro II [(1825-1891)] was deprived of the throne, and Brazil was declared to be a republic, which still exists. This republic consists of twenty states and is administered by a president (elected for four years), a Senate (three senators from each state and from the capital), and a chamber of deputies (one per 70,000).

5. **Argentine Republic**. It became independent in 1816 and consists of fourteen states, autonomous in internal administration, and represented in international relations as a single whole by a central union authority. Its system is similar to the Constitution of the North American States.[30]

§60. δ) SEMI-INDEPENDENT STATES. They are in essence the creation solely of international relations and order: their existence is explained by the insistent need to find a *modus vivendi* among particular States which averted an inevitable conflict between them; this compromise between opposing interests at a particular moment did not find a final settlement. In this sense, semi-independence is a transitional step from complete State dependence to full international sovereignty, or *vice versa*, as merely a transitional and temporary form has its own *raison d'être*. Considered from the standpoint of the science on the State, this is *non sens* because the concept of the State excludes any non-autonomy.

A material indicator of the semi-independent State is the subordination of its external relations to foreign State power; in its domestic administration it is for the most part completely autonomous. Usually, such a State pays tribute to its suzerain, the amount of which is determined either by mutual agreement or by the Treaty creating the semi-independent State.

The payment of tribute is not an absolute indicator of lack of autonomy. There have been instances when one State paid tribute to another but retained complete international sovereignty. Thus, at the outset of the present century the Washington Government paid a certain amount annually to the Bey of Algiers in the form of ransom to prevent the capture and sale into slavery of American seamen by the Algiers pirates, not finding it convenient to go to war against them; but through this the North American United States were not, of course, in vassal dependence on the Bey of Algiers.

[30] Phillimore, note 3 above, I, p. 163; Calvo, note 8 above, I, p. 189.

The semi-independence of a State is found in various forms: (1) it may arise from the protection of a State over others established usually for the purpose of ensuring the external security of the protected people who are obliged for this to subject themselves to control on the part of the protecting Government in the domain of diplomatic relations;[31] (2) this may be reflected in vassal relations of a State similar to those in which vassals were found to their own suzerain in the Middle Ages. In either instance the autonomy of international relations of the State is similarly limited.[32]

Caused by concrete and passing political circumstances, semi-independence terminates together with these circumstances. A dual fate may confront the State: either by way of normal development it becomes completely independent, becomes a subject of international law, or under unfavorable circumstances finally subjects itself to that State under whose protection or suzerainty it is found.[33] The first form of development, as facts and history show, prevails in the East, in those States which have been created by European diplomacy from the Provinces of the Ottoman Empire; in the West usually the protection of European powers leads to the complete deprivation of independence of the protected States, as happened, for example, with the Krakow Republic.

Of existing States, the following are in a state of semi-independence:

1. Egypt. The contemporary position of this State deserves special attention in view of the Suez Canal, which has worldwide significance as an artery of international commerce of European States with the East.

The legal status of Egypt is determined by the 1840 London Convention concluded between Austria, Russia, Prussia, and England and accepted by Turkey.[34] France did not participate in the agreement and tried to prevent it. The London Convention confirmed the order of things established in

[31] Compare on the international protectorate, *inter alia*, the following: Ed. Engelhardt, *Les protectorats anciens et modernes* (Paris, 1896); François Gairal, *Le protectorat international* (Paris, 1896); Edgard Rouard de Card, *Les traités de protectorat conclus par la France en Afrique* (Paris, 1897); Paul Pic, "Influence de l'établissement d'un protectorat sur les traités antérieurement conclus avec des puissances tierces par l'État protégé", *Revue générale de droit international public* (1896), p. 613 et seq.

[32] John Austin, *The Province of Jurisprudence Determined*, pp. 201-208; Miloš Boghitchévitch, *Halbsouveränität. Administrative und politische Autonomie seit dem Pariser Vertrage 1856* (Berlin, 1903).

[33] "Suzerainty" is the limited sovereignty of the dominant State over the semi-independent government.

[34] G. F. Martens (Murhard), *Recueil des traités*, 1, p. 158 ; Léopold Neumann, *Recueil des traités et conventions conclus par l'Autriche avec les puissances étrangères, depuis 1763 jusqu'à nos jours* (Leipzig, 1855-1912), IV, p. 453.

relations between Egypt and the Porte from the time of the appointment of the Egyptian Governor, Mehemet-Ali (1806).

The noted Pasha destroyed the Mameluks who had dominated in Egypt, introduced order in the country, ensured the development of its industry and trade, and created an armed force which made it possible to consider himself a full lord over the domain he administered. In 1832 Mehemet-Ali rose up against the Sultan, conquered Syria, defeated the Turkish forces in Asia Minor, and prepared to move against Constantinople. Apprehensive about the integrity of the Ottoman Empire, the European powers decided to interfere in the Turkish-Egyptian quarrel.[35] Thanks to the sending to Minor Asia of a Russian auxiliary corps, Mehemet-Ali made peace with the Sultan, who granted him autonomous administration not only of Egypt, but also Palestine and Syria. This peace was quickly violated by the Porte, and in 1838 again began war against the recalcitrant governor. The defeats sustained by the Turkish Army generated the protection of the western powers, who forced Mehemet-Ali to cease military actions and subordinate himself to the decisions of the Conference assembled in London in 1840.[36]

The main decisions of the London Conference consisted of the following: (1) in domestic administration the Egyptian Viceroy or Khedive enjoys autonomy, but governs "in the name of the Sultan"; (2) the Egyptian army and fleet are considered to be part of the Ottoman Armed Forces; (3) banknotes issued by the Egyptian treasury have on one side the image of the Sultan and, on the other – the Khedive; (4) Egypt pays the Porte a certain tribute; (5) all international relations of Egypt should proceed through the Constantinople Government, and treaties concluded by the last are binding on the Egyptian Viceroy.

There was no more war between Egypt and the Porte after 1840, but the rights of the Khedive gradually expanded. On the basis of the firman of the Sultan of 1866, the Egyptian throne was declared to be hereditary in a direct descending line of the reigning house (Mehemet-Ali). A firman of 1873 gave to the Khedive the right to conclude international conventions on trade issues.[37] With the opening of the Suez Canal, the international

35 See F. F. Martens, Собрание трактатов и конвенций [Collection of Treaties and Conventions], IV(1), p. 435 et seq; p. 468 et seq. Compare: Anton Prokesch von Osten, *Mehmed-Ali. Vize-König von Aegypten* (Vienna, 1877).

36 See F. F. Martens, Собрание трактатов и конвенций [Collection of Treaties and Conventions], IV(1), pp. 475 et seq.

37 See the English "Blue-Book": Firmans granted by the Sultans to the Viceroys of Egypt, 1843-1873 (Egypt No. 4, 1879). At present the Egyptian tribute to the Sultan is 750,000 pounds sterling.

significance of Egypt came more to the forefront. In Egypt, mixed courts were arranged in which Europeans participate for the consideration of cases between subjects of European States and natives. As a consequence of the financial distress of this country which became so serious that the Khedive was not in a position to pay interest on the loans he had contracted, a permanent financial commission having supervision over the management of the revenues and expenses of Egypt was created by representatives of the States most interested in this question – England and France.[38] The influence of European governments in the internal affairs of this State was reflected visibly in 1879 when at the instigation of France and England and with the consent of other European governments, the former Khedive, Ismail-Pasha [(1830-1895)], had to be removed from the throne in favor of his son, Tevfik-Pasha.

In view of the international significance of Egypt, and especially in view of the 1840 London Treaty, which remains in force, the legal status of the Egyptian Government determined by this Treaty should be inviolate both for Turkey and for any other power; it is the creation of a European agreement and only by means of such agreement can be changed or abrogated.[39]

2. PRINCIPALITY OF BULGARIA. The international status of Bulgaria is determined by the 1878 Treaty of Berlin.[40]

On the basis of the Preliminary Peace of San Stefano (Articles 6-12), Bulgaria should form a "self-governing principality paying tribute with a Christian government and land force" (Article 6). The Statute for the administration of Bulgaria was to be worked out by an assembly of noteworthy people under the supervision of a Russian commissar and in the presence of an Ottoman commissar. The prince is elected by the population and confirmed by the Porte with the consent of the powers. He might not be elected from the members of a reigning dynasty of the Great European Powers (Article 7). The Turkish forces should be withdrawn from Bulgaria and all previous fortresses therein destroyed (Article 8). The boundaries of Bulgaria encompass a vast territory, beginning from the Danube to Salonika, so that Constantinople was cut off by Bulgarian possessions from

[38] Compare the financial report of the Englishman, [Sir Stephen] Cave [(1820-1880)], *Staatsarchiv*, XXX, No. 5759).

[39] From this point of view the collective Anglo-French Note of 7 January 1882 does not agree with the existing international obligations. See Edmond Plauchut, *L'Egypte et l'occupation anglaise* (Paris, 1889); Wilhelm Kaufmann, *Das internationale Recht der egyptischen Staatsschuld* (Berlin, 1891).

[40] Compare the article of Bluntschli, in *Revue de droit international* (1881), p. 570 et seq.

Makedonia and Thessalonika which remained under the authority of the Porte.

The Treaty of Berlin elaborated these provisions of the San Stefano Peace which concerned the international legal status of the Principality of Bulgaria, namely: (1) the Principality received autonomy in internal administration, but was placed under the primacy of the Sultan, to whom tribute had to be paid (Article 1); (2) the Bulgarian prince elected by the population is confirmed by the Sublime Porte with the consent of the Powers (Article 3); (3) treaties on trade and navigation and all agreements in force between the Porte and foreign powers retain force for Bulgaria; just as the rights of consular jurisdiction and established Capitulations and customs remained in force (Article 8); (4) the Principality, as part of the Ottoman Empire, is obliged to bear a determined share of the State debt of the Empire (Article 9); (5) natives of the Principality of Bulgaria traveling to or residing in other parts of the Ottoman Empire do not enjoy exemptions and privileges of foreign subjects, but are subject to Ottoman authorities and laws (Article 12).

These provisions show that Bulgaria is not an autonomous subject of law in international relations: it depends on the Porte and is placed under the control and protection of the Great Powers which signed the Treaty of Berlin. The Congress of Berlin determined which principles should underlie the State law of Bulgaria: an organic Statute of the Principality drafted by a Bulgarian assembly should ensure all citizens equality before the law, despite the difference in religious professions of faith and teachings; all Bulgarian natives and foreigners enjoy freedom of external celebration of any religious services (Article 5). Therefore, religious persecution which a Bulgarian government might permit in its country may cause interference on the part of the Great Powers.

The boundaries of the Principality of Bulgaria established by the Treaty of San Stefano were subjected to significant change. From the single Principality of Bulgaria assumed by this act, the Treaty of Berlin formed two regions: Bulgaria and Eastern Rumelia. The Balkans serve as the boundary between them, with the inclusion in Bulgaria of the Sanjak of Sofia (Article 2).

Upon the conclusion of the Treaty of Berlin, the assembly of noteworthy people of Bulgaria convened in Tarnovo and founded a representative government from the principalities and elected Prince Alexander of Battenberg [(1857-1893)] as the Bulgarian Prince.[41]

[41] For the text of the Bulgarian Constitution, see *Staatsarchiv*, XXXVI (1879), no. 7081. At present the Bulgarian territory encompasses a space of 63,865 square kilometers, with

In July 1881 the Bulgarian Prince performed a coup d'êtat, abolishing the National Assembly and founding a State Council in its place. Serious misunderstandings arose with the Porte with regard to payment of tribute by the Principality and especially from the question concerning its diplomatic agency in Constantinople. Following the example of the former semi-independent Serbian and Rumelian princes, the Bulgarian prince had a special agent attached to the Porte for the defense of its interests and relations in general with the government of the Sultan. For several months the Bulgarian plenipotentiary filled his office and was recognized by the Porte; but in most recent times a "Bureau for Privileged Regions" was founded in Constantinople – the Levant, Samos Islands, Candia, Eastern Rumelia, and the Principality of Bulgaria – and to it the agent of Bulgaria was proposed to have recourse in all matters. Thus, the principality was placed on the same level as Turkish provinces, but not equal to them in rights and status. The Bulgarian Prince rightly protested against such actions of the Turkish Government and finally diplomatic relations were terminated entirely.

In September 1882 the Porte withdrew its unjust demand and agreed to recognize for the Bulgarian agent the right to communicate directly on matters of the Principality with the Porte.

The Bulgarian Principality was united in 1886 with Eastern Rumelia in the person of the Prince appointed also as Governor-General of the said province. The present Bulgarian Prince, Ferdinand [Maximilian Karl Leopold of Saxe-Coburg (1861-1948)] was recognized from spring 1896 in his rank by the Sultan and all the great powers. Bulgaria received the right to conclude international trade and navigation agreements with foreign powers. Bulgaria concluded such trade conventions with Austria, France, and England and, in 1897, with Russia.

3. Eastern Rumelia. To the south of the Balkans, the Congress of Berlin created a special province called "Eastern Rumelia", which not a semi-independent State proper, but a region under the political and military administration of the Sultan. The autonomy of this province, however, and protection which it enjoys on the part of the Great European Powers, placed it in reality virtually in the same international status as the former Danube Principality and Serbia.

The Treaty of Berlin left Eastern Rumelia under the "direct political and military power" of the Sultan under conditions of an "administrative autonomy" (Article 13). It had a Governor-General of the Christian faith who is appointed for 5 years by the Sultan with the "consent" of the Powers (Article 17). The internal order of the province is protected by a native guard

a population of 2,650,000 inhabitants.

with the assistance of the police, whose officers are appointed by the Sultan. The Sultan has the right to be concerned with the defense of the sea and land boundaries of the region, erection of fortresses, and maintenance therein of forces; but the use of irregular forces (*bashi-bazouk*) is prohibited. When passing through the region, regular forces may not make stops (Article 15). The Governor-General was granted the right to call up Ottoman forces in the event of an external danger or internal disorders. The Sultan gives explanations about the reasons for this measure to representatives of the European Powers in Constantinople (Article 16).

The Statute of Eastern Rumelia was worked out by a European commission jointly with the Porte; it was promulgated by a firman of the Sultan and communicated by the Sultan to the European powers.[42] On the basis of this Statute, Rumelia has a representative "Regional Assembly" which, together with the Governor-General, autonomously carries out the entire administrative and judicial administration of the region. But the Governor-General cannot enter directly into relations with foreign powers. All treaties, conventions, and international agreements, whatever their properties, concluded by the Porte are binding on Eastern Rumelia (Article 21).

The aggregate provisions of the Treaty of Berlin concerning Rumelia are completely persuasive that this province has an international character. The sovereignty of the Porte with respect to it is so limited in the domain of internal administration and placed under such constraining conditions for their effectuation that Eastern Rumelia may be considered *de facto* a semi-independent region left by decision of the international congress within the Ottoman Empire. Its international character and merger with Bulgaria, as Bluntschli says, is a matter for the near future. The prediction of the late Professor of Heidelberg University was realized earlier than expected: in September 1885 the population of Eastern Rumelia proclaimed its unification with the Bulgarian people, which in March 1886 received recognition on the part of the great European powers at the Constantinople Conference, on the basis of which the Prince of Bulgaria was appointed Governor-General of Eastern Rumelia for five years. This term received tacit continuance subsequently, and the Prince of Bulgaria now administers Eastern Rumelia.[43]

42 For this Statute, see *Staatsarchiv*, XXXV (1879), no. 7064.

43 *Revue de droit international*, XII (1881), p. 580. Eastern Rumelia occupies a space of 32,221 square kilometers and has 1,100,000 inhabitants.

§61. 4. BARBARIAN POSSESSIONS: TUNISIA, TRIPOLI, AND ALGIERS. Of these three possessions, only the first may be considered a semi-independent State.

TRIPOLI, beginning from 1835, was transformed into a Turkish province without any special rights and privileges. Its Governor-General is appointed and replaced by the Porte.

Previously a nest of pirates, ALGIERS, after being conquered by the French in 1830, acceded to France and is governed on the basis of special law as a French region.[44]

As regards TUNISIA, recent events have generated a dispute between France and the Porte relative to its international status. In the view of the French Government, Tunisia has long since been a completely independent State and in no way connected with the Ottoman Empire. On the contrary, the Porte considers the Bey of Tunis to be its vassal. Without going into the arguments advanced in defense of one view or the other, we point out certain facts proving that until recently the Bey of Tunis himself considered he was subject to the Sultan and was considered as such on the part of other States.

After the conquest of northern Africa by the Turks in the sixteenth century, the Tunisian Bey succeeded in preserving his great autonomy. However, they did not deny the sovereignty of the Sultan and even paid him tribute, which he called a "voluntary offering". The dependence of Tunisia on the Porte was recognized by the Great European Powers. In the event of violence caused to their subjects on the part of Tunisian bandits, they had recourse with appeals and demands for satisfaction most often to the Turkish Government rather than to the Tunisian Bey. Thus, on the basis of the 1791 Treaty of Sistova, Austria obliged the Porte to terminate the piracy of the Tunisian corsairs and remunerate those Austrian subjects who suffered from their depredations.[45] The Russian Government, as is evident from the 1792 Treaty of Jassy (Article 7) and 1826 Akkerman Convention (Article 6), also precisely considered the Sultan to be responsible for the robbery by the Tunisians. Finally, the Porte constantly calls the Bey the Governor-General of Tunis and gives him an investiture. The inheritance of this title in the descending line of the Bey was confirmed by a firman of the Sultan in 1871. The fact of the dependence of Tunisia on the Ottoman Empire was manifest at various times more or less consciously, despite whoever occupied the

[44] Compare the curious work by Sir Robert Lambert Playfair, *The Scourge of Christendom. Annals of British Relations with Algiers Prior to the French Conquest* (London, 1884).

[45] Neumann, note 34 above, I, p. 454.

Tunisian throne and who reigned in Stambul. Under a weak Government of the Sultan, energetic Beys might, of course, ignore their dependence on the Porte and concluded autonomous treaties with European powers. But in view of the data cited above, the vassal *de jure* relations of Tunisia vis-à-vis the Porte can hardly be in doubt.[46]

After the expedition of French forces in April 1881 against the Khroumirs, the status of Tunisia changed. France concluded a Treaty with the Bey (11 May 1881) which delivered the Tunisian possessions under its protection.[47] On the basis of this Treaty, the Bey recognized the protectorate of France; French forces occupy for a time points selected by them in Tunisia (Article 2), and the French Minister-Resident is made an intermediary in relations of the Bey with foreign powers (Article 5).

These provisions show that Tunisia at present is a semi-independent State in relations with France, but not Turkey. Just as all semi-independent States which are part of the Ottoman Empire were created by means of a general agreement among the European powers, relations of France with Tunisia might also be determined only by this means. In view of the undoubted rights of Turkey in Tunisia, such a position is irrefutable. In 1882 the European powers agreed to the proposal of France to consider the Capitulations in Turkey to be repealed and French jurisdiction to be legally operative. Only England entered a reservation: it wished to recognize the repeal of the Capitulations only after the French courts prove themselves in fact to be fully constituted. But as of 31 December 1883 the English Government agreed to recognize their subjects in Tunisia as within the jurisdiction of French courts.

5. Samos Islands. These are a privileged Turkish province, but not a semi-independent State. The special position thereof within the Ottoman Empire was created by a Law of 1832. They have a Governor from among the Christians and enjoy certain other preferences which, however, are not protected by any international agreement and therefore may be repealed by the Porte.

6. Syria. In 1860 the Christian population of this region was subjected to the savagery of Muslims, which inspired a Paris Conference assembled on this occasion to decide about sending a corps of French forces for establishment in the Levant (Syria) of order and protection of the lives of

[46] Compare *Staatsarchiv*, XXXIX (1881), nos. 7447, 7469, 7478, 7470, and others. The contrary view of the French Government is defended, *inter alia*, also by Ed. Engelhardt in the *Revue de droit international*, XII (1881), pp. 331 et seq. Compare Phillimore, note 1 above, I, p. 121 et seq; Lawrence, note 8 above, I, 257.

[47] *Staatsarchiv*, XXXIX, no. 7479.

Christians. After that, a European commission in 1864 drafted a Statute for this province which determined that the Governor-General thereof would be chosen by the Porte with the consent of the European powers and have rights and duties precisely designated in this Statute with respect to the local Christian population. The Porte did not have the right to freely repeal this Statute.[48]

7. San Marino. This microscopic republic (16 square kilometers with 9,535 inhabitants) is situated within the Papal region and under the patronage of the Pope; from 1862 it is a protectorate of the Italian Kingdom; exists from the fifth century as a semi-independent State.

8. Andorra Republic. (5,231 inhabitants). Lies on the slopes of the Pyrenees. Until 1868 was deemed a protectorate of France and the Bishop of Urgell (in Spain); to the first it paid tribute of 960 francs, to the second, 841 francs. In 1868 Andorra passed under the protection only of France, but from 1881 the French Government again shared its rights with the Bishop of Urgell. Both patrons appoint their commissars (*viguiers*) in Andorra obliged to watch over the order and peace of the republic.

9. Principality of Monaco. Located on the French Riviera; until 1861 was under the protection of Sardinia, and now France. In 1861 the Prince ceded to the last for 4 million Roquebrune and Menton. French customs authorities operate in Monaco.

10. Khiva Khanate. For many centuries Khiva served as a den of robbers who plundered Russian caravans and sold captured merchants into slavery. The position of the Khanate militarily is advantageous, encircled on all sides by inaccessible deserts, forced repeatedly to suffer expeditions against Khiva inadequately supplied by the Russian Government. Finally, in 1873 it was taken by General [Konstantin Petrovich von] Kaufman [(1818-1882)] and, according to the peace concluded in that same year (24 August), the Khanate was delivered into vassal relations with Russia. The Khan of Khiva declared himself (Article 1) to be the "loyal servant of the Emperor of All the Russias". He renounced the right to maintain direct relations with neighboring princes and khans. He would never "conclude either commercial treaties or other treaties with these princes and khans and he would never take part in hostile actions against them other than with the knowledge and authorization of the high Russian leadership in

[48] See *Annuaire diplomatique de l'Empire de Russie* (1862), pp. 99-104; (1868), pp. 141-190. Compare Calvo, note 8 above, I, pp. 177, 187. Lawrence, note 8 above, I, p. 122. On the basis of Article 23 of the Treaty of Berlin, the Porte obliged itself "to introduce the organic Statute of 1868 on the Islands of Crete in good faith" with changes which would be deemed to be just. "Similar statutes' should be introduced with certain exceptions in other Turkish regions.

Central Asia". At present, the Khan enjoys administrative autonomy in his possessions: to appoint his own officials, collect tribute, and so on, but his diplomatic relations have been placed under the control of the Governor-General of Turkestan.[49]

In a royal Rescript in the name of the Khan of Khiva of 21 December 1902 the sovereign Emperor expressed "special satisfaction" with regard to the Khan's decision to remain at the head of the administration of the Khanate, in spite of his unhealthy condition. "As a mark of my favor", continued the Rescript, "I give to you the title 'Grace', and to your son, Sendu-Asfendiar-Tur, the title 'Highness'". By this Act the Khanate of Khiva was finally recognized to be under the sovereign protection and control of Russia.

11. Bukharan Khanate. On the basis of an 1873 treaty, Bukhara entered into close trade relations with Russia, which after the opening of the Trans-Caspian Railway became so close that at present the entire trade turnover of the Khanate is dependent on Russian credit and Russian credit institutions. The political dependence of the Bukharan Khanate on Russia cannot be doubted. The Emir of Bukhara is a General in the cavalry of the Russian Army and with respect to his Muslim subjects his sovereign authority is exercised freely.

12. Indigenous princes in English India. Various treaties concluded by the English authorities with these princes show that the administrative autonomy which they enjoy was given to them on condition that they do not enter into any kind of international transactions, even in alliance with one another, except the English Government.[50]

13. Indian tribes on the territory of the North American United States. As aborigenes, they in reality are the owners of the American continent. The Washington Government and Supreme Court in principle recognize this is their right, but declare that they must be under the exclusive protection of the United States. On the basis of judicial decisions and treaties, the Indian tribes have the right to freely manage their internal affairs, but may not enter into any relations with foreign powers.[51]

[49] See *Staatsarchiv*, XXVI, no. 3738.

[50] The trial of the Gaekwad of Baroda, tried and disgraced by judgement of an English court in 1875, elicited in relief the subordinate status of the Indian princes. See 7 Blue Books on this trial: Report of the Commission appointed to inquire into the Administration of the Baroda State. 1873-1875. Compare also Creasy, note 16 above, p. 94.

[51] The view of Calvo, note 8 above, I, §69, is curious, suggesting that the Indian tribes possess land in the United States "by right of occupation" (*droit d'occupation*). The opposite position is more just, because the Americans occupied the territory belonging to the initial population of America.

§62. Many of those States which are in a semi-independent position have lost this character: they either were incorporated in, or formed, autonomous States. The history of such States plainly proves that semi-independence is a transitional step towards complete dependence or to full independence. It gives, moreover, many indications with whose assistance one may definitely elicit the status of presently existing States linked by protection. In view of this consideration, we consider it not superfluous to say several words about States formerly semi-independent.

1. Romania. The old States of Moldavia and Wallachia comprising Romania were conquered by Turkey in the fifteenth century. By a number of Capitulations concluded with the victors (1460, 1511, 1634) the Romanian hospodars ensured for themselves complete autonomy in internal rule. They sought that Turkey would promise not only not to interfere in their internal affairs, but also not settle in Romania. The dependence of the principalities on the Porte was reflected solely in the fact that the hospodars freely chosen by them were confirmed by the Sultan and paid him a determined tribute in the Capitulations.[52]

Such were the initial relations of Romania with the Porte on the basis of treaties concluded between them. But these treaties were little respected on the part of the Turkish authorities. In flouting their obligations, the Porte constantly interfered in the governing of the principalities and introduced procedures not consistent with the Christian beliefs of Romanians. Turkish arbitrariness and violence found a response in Russia, which at the time of the Peace of Kuchuk-Kainardzhi (1774) assumed protection and defense of the Christians of the Balkan Peninsula. By the 1812 Treaty of Bucharest (under which Russia acquired Bessarabia) and the Akkerman Convention (1826), Moldavia and Wallachia, complete internal autonomy was guaranteed. This was affirmed by the 1829 Treaty of Adrianople. Finally, in 1830 Count [Pavel Dmitrievich] Kiselev [(1788-1872)] was sent as a commissar of the Russian Government to Romania, where he furthered the structure and the industry and the trade prosperity of the principalities.[53]

The protection of Russia over the Danubian principalities was recognized without dispute until the Crimean War. This was changed by the 1856 Treaty of Paris in the sense that the rights exercised solely by Russia became the rights of all the powers which signed the treaty. The

[52] Compare the articles of Arntz, Engelhardt, and Bluntschli in *Revue de droit international*, IX, p. 18 et seq; XI, p. 532 et seq; XII, p. 410 et seq. Compare F. F. Martens, *Mémoire sur le conflit entre la Grèce et la Roumanie. L'affaire Zappa* (Athens, 1893).

[53] See Andrei Parfenovich Zablotskii-Desiatovskii, Граф П. Д. Киселев и его время [Count P. D. Kiselev and His Time] (Spb., 1882), I, p. 314 et seq.

last determined that both principalities remain under the sovereign authority of the Sultan with retention of independence in internal administration, but without the right to enter into direct diplomatic relations with other States. The Porte obliged itself immediately upon the conclusion of the treaty to create consultative assemblies (*divans*) in both principalities for the discussion of those transformations which should be introduced into the structure of the principalities. Finally, this structure was elaborated by the Paris Conference (1858). The Great Powers provided that both principalities would be called by a common name, "United Principalities of Moldavia and Wallachia", but each would have separate State institutions and its own hospodar elected by the population from native Romanians and confirmed by the Sultan. The amount of tribute to be paid by the Porte was specially determined for each principality. This unnatural division was not realized in practice, however. In 1859 both principalities elected one person as their own hospodar, Colonel Cuza, who entered into the administration of Romania under the name Alexandru Ioan [Cuza] I [(1820-1873)]. The Great Powers agreed to the unification of the principalities, which officially were named the "Romanian Principality".

In 1866 the party, being dissatisfied with Cuza, forced him to abdicate from the throne and to leave Romania. In his place was elected in the same year Prince Karl-Ludwig Hohenzollern, who after certain vacillations was recognized by the Great Powers and then by the Porte.

The new Romanian Government steadfastly sought to reduce whenever possible those duties which its semi-independence imposed on the principality. Thus, it appropriated the right to enter into direct diplomatic relations with foreign powers. Finally, in May 1877, when Russian forces crossed the boundary of the Danubian principalities (on the basis of the April convention with the Romanian Government), Romania proclaimed its independence and declared war against the Porte.

On the basis of the Treaty of San Stefano (Article 5), the Porte recognized the absolute independence of Romania. The Treaty of Berlin (Article 43) also recognized it, but under the following conditions: first, the principality cedes back to Russia part of the Bessarabian region separated from it under the 1856 Treaty of Paris (Article 45); second, the principality ensures to subjects of all Powers trading and otherwise sojourning in Romania complete equality without distinction of profession of faith and recognizes freedom of conscience and worship for all persons within the limits of its possessions (Article 44). Thanks to this condition, Romanian legislation, rather unfavorable especially for Jews, after strong agitation was finally changed to satisfy the requirements set by the Treaty of Berlin.

In spring 1881 the chamber of people's representatives and Senate of Romania proclaimed their prince to be the King of Romania. This title is recognized at the present time by all the European Powers.

2. SERBIA. It was conquered by the Turks in 1454 and, just as Romania, concluded several treaties with the Porte which secured for the Serbs a certain share of internal autonomy. But the administrative autonomy of Serbia was never as extensive as in Romania. Only thanks to the protection of Russia did Serbia come to be in a position of a State semi-independent from Turkey.[54]

The 1812 Treaty of Bucharest and the 1826 Akkerman Convention laid a firm basis for Serbian self-government, confirmed in their provisions concerning Serbia by a firman of the Sultan in 1830. Serbia received the right to autonomously take possession of its internal affairs with the duty to pay tribute to the Sultan and not enter into relations with foreign powers. Serbian fortifications were occupied by Turkish garrisons. The status of Serbia as a semi-independent principality is confirmed by the 1856 Treaty of Paris. In 1867 Serbia strove so that the powers forced the Porte to withdraw their forces from Serbian fortifications. In the recent Russo-Turkish War Serbia took an active part as an ally of Russia and in 1877 declared itself independent.

According to the San Stefano peace (Article 3), Serbia is deemed to be independent, which was confirmed in the Treaty of Berlin (Article 34), having laid down, however, as a condition of its independence ensuring freedom of conscience and profession of faith in the Serbian principalities (Article 34) and not changing commercial relations with foreign States before the conclusion of the new treaties, and so on (Article 37). At present, Serbia is a fully independent State under the authority of Prince Milan [I (1854-1901)] from the Obrenovič dynasty, who accepted in February 1882 the title of King.

3. IONIAN ISLANDS. Upon liberation from the authority of the Turks, they were a protectorate of England (from 1815 to 1864).[55] The English Lord High Commissioner on site conducted the internal affairs of the islands; internal relations remained in the exclusive jurisdiction of the London cabinet.

The relations of the islands with England are characterized by a curious incident which occurred during the Crimean War. An English cruiser

[54] See Benoit Brunswik (intro.), *Recueil de documents relatifs à la Serbie* (Constantinople, 1876).

[55] Phillimore, note 3 above, I, p. 100 et seq; Lawrence, note 8 above, I, p. 231 et seq; Jellinek, note 8 above, p. 129.

captured a Greek ship with contraband sailing under the flag of the Ionian Islands. When discussing the legality of this capture, the English Prize Court decided that, although the Ionian Islands are a protectorate of England, they might remain neutral in the event of war with other powers.

In 1863 the English Government voluntarily renounced any power over the Ionian Islands in favor of the Greek Kingdom, an integral part of which they continue to remain to the present time.

4. Krakow Republic. This was created by the 1815 Vienna Treaty, which declared the city of Krakow with the appurtenant region to be "in perpetuity a free, independent, and completely neutral" city under the protection of Russia, Austria, and Prussia (Article 6). The formation of this Republic is explained by the disagreements which arose at the Congress of Vienna between Austria and Russia with regard to the division of the Duchy of Warsaw. The Great Powers granted political independence to Krakow on condition that it not serve as a refuge for political agitators and Polish emigrants dissatisfied with the orders in neighboring States. This condition was not fulfilled, and therefore the three protectorate powers, in view of constant disorder which Krakow caused to them, decided in 1846 to unify it with the Austrian possessions.[56]

Addition: on Montenegro. The international status of the Principality of Montenegro until 1878 remained extremely uncertain.

Both certain publicists and powers (England at the 1878 Congress of Berlin) enumerated Montenegro among the semi-independent States with respect to Turkey. In reality, it was never subject to the Porte, did not pay tribute thereto, and its prince was not confirmed by the Sultan. When a representative of the Ottoman Empire at the 1856 Paris Congress, Ali-Pasha, declared *inter alia* that Montenegro is dependent on the Porte, a State paying tribute to the Sultan, and representatives of the other powers did not object to this statement, the Prince [Nikola I Petrovič-Njehoš] of Montenegro [(1841-1921)] immediately protested this statement, proving that the principality was always independent. The actual position which Montenegro always took with respect to Turkey serves as the best refutation of the claims of the Porte.[57]

In the San Stefano peace treaty the Porte "finally" recognized the independence of the Principality of Montenegro (Article 2) and agreed to a

[56] See F. F. Martens, Собрание трактатов и конвенций [Collection of Treaties and Conventions], III, pp. 319, 358, et seq; especially IV(1), pp. 471, 472, et seq; p. 525 et seq.

[57] Compare Jean Vaçlik, *La souveraineté du Monténégro et le droit des gens moderne de l'Europe* (Leipzig, 1858). In this pamphlet the complete independence of Montenegro is proved since the most ancient times.

significant expansion of its territory at the expense of its regions (Article 1). Especially important for the Principality was the acquisition of the port of Antivari which opened for Montenegro direct access to the sea.

The provisions of the Treaty of Berlin materially changed the status of Montenegro. According to Article 26 of the Treaty, "the independence of Montenegro is recognized by the Sublime Porte and by all those of the High Contracting Parties who had not hitherto admitted it". Religious freedom is ensured in the Principality for all persons. Antivari acceded to Montenegro on the following conditions: Dulcinjo is restored to Turkey, the commune of Spica is incorporated in Austria; Montenegro may not have warships or a navy; the port of Antivari and in general all the waters of Montenegro remain closed to warships of all nations. The fortifications between the lakes and the coast on Montenegrin territory must be razed and may not be rebuilt. Police, maritime, and sanitary supervision in Antivari and along the entire Montenegrin coast is provided to Austro-Hungary. The Principality must introduce its own maritime laws operating in Dalmatia; the Austro-Hungarian consuls shall render protection to Montenegrin trade.

These provisions were not fully performed by Turkey, which declared that it could not transfer Gusinje and Plav, the populations of which together with the Albanians rose up against accession to the Principality. Therefore, on 28 November 1880, with the consent of the Powers, a new convention was concluded between the Porte and Montenegro, on the basis of which the last received, together with Gusinje and Plav, part of the regions of Zemskaia and Vermosskaia with the port of Dulcinjo.

The Treaty of Berlin evidently places Montenegro in a worse position than it occupied previously: from a factually independent State as it was before the war with Turkey, the Treaty returned it to a State under the law of the protecting Austro-Hungary, which has, of course, the force and resources to make its protection felt. One must concur with the view of Bluntschli,[58] Montenegro with 285,000 inhabitants cannot under the conditions created for it by the Treaty of Berlin fail to fall under the influence of the neighboring Great Power and it is difficult for it to preserve its political independence.

IV. Conditions of Existence of States as International Persons

§63. The foundations of a State are well-known, what fundamental requirements it must satisfy in order to be considered a subject of

[58] *Revue de droit international*, XI (1880), p. 284. Also see the diplomatic correspondence on the occasion of the transfer of Dulcinjo in *Staatsarchiv*, XXXVIII, nos. 7203-7286.

international law: it must be a society of people living on a determined territory under one sovereign power. The absence of any of these conditions is sufficient for the particular organization not to be considered a State and subject of international law. Therefore, any political party, albeit a belligerent (Hungarians in 1849, Poles in 1862) or a church society, may not be deemed to be subjects of international law.

Concrete States comprising an international association are the products of a certain historical process; they are subject to its operation at each given moment of their existence. In this sense, each State arises, develops, grows, declines, and dies away. A State is "immortal" only in the sense that its being does not emanate from the existence of the present subjects: generations of citizens are replaced by others, but the State continues to exist.

It is not the business of international law to investigate the process of the development of States. But in members of the international community recognizing respective concrete States, the community must have in view that influence which inevitably is exerted on their international status, the material alterations or changes of their mutual rights and duties to which they are subjected in their development. Such facts as the formation of new States, or important changes in the territorial or personal composition of existing States, or, finally, the death of a State, generate certain relations between members of an international union which must be regulated by international law.

A. Recognition of New States

§64. A State, being a product of the development of a people's self-awareness, may arise under the most diverse conditions. It may be created by the will and efforts of any State figure or conqueror; may be theocratic; may develop from family relations in the form of a patriarchal State or have its foundation in ownership relations as a feudal State; may be formed by means of colonization, revolt, and so on. All these forms of origin of a State have no international significance and are not subject to analysis by the science of international law. They comprise the subject-matter of the history of State law or of universal history. The very fact of the origin of a State is another matter. Each newly-formed State wishing to participate in international interaction with the rights and duties of international personality must be recognized as such on the part of other States; its origin becomes a question of international law. Proper international relations are conceivable only between States recognizing one another. The need for such recognition arises from the very concept of an international community.

From the standpoint of international law, the recognition of a State may arise in three main instances: 1) as a consequence of the separation of part of a nation forming an autonomous political organism; 2) as a consequence of the creation of one State from several regions; and 3) as a consequence of the adoption of a new title by the Head of State.[59]

For example, thirteen states of North America who separated from England and declared themselves to be independent (4 July 1776) were recognized as such by France in 1778; the South American colonies of Spain and Portugal, after continuous warfare with their metropolitans, formed individual States, recognized to be such in 1825 by England; Belgium proclaimed its independence from Holland and was recognized by the Great Powers in 1830.

There may serve as examples of States formed from several regions belonging previously to other States or constituting separate States: Westphalia and other States created by Napoleon I, and also the Mexican Empire, which Napoleon III built for the Austrian Archduke Maximilian.

Negotiations were conducted on the recognition of new titles: Friedrich I, who adopted the title of King of Prussia; and Peter I [(1672-1725)] on the title of Emperor of All the Russias.

Recognition assumes the internal independence of a newly arisen State, but does not create it. A State arises and exists autonomously. Recognition thereof merely states its birth. Therefore, one cannot see in an act of recognition "moral interference" in the internal affairs of another State, as Phillimore asserts. On the contrary, in principle recognition is always nothing more than formal certification of a certain fact which has occurred.

As is well-known, Switzerland was solemnly recognized to be independent at the 1648 Congress of Westphalia, having been autonomous in reality by the fourteenth century, and so too the 1783 Treaty of Versailles, in recognizing the independence of the United States of America, merely affirmed the state of affairs which had existed in that country from 1776; Belgium, having satisfied all the conditions of an autonomous State, was recognized to be such by the 1830 London Conference. Hungary, to the contrary, did not receive recognition of its independence in 1849 by reason of the absence therein of elements of a stable autonomous political organization.

Recognition is official (formal) or *de facto* (informal). Official recognition is expressed in official acts, such as: decrees of congresses, declarations

[59] Compare Phillimore, note 3 above, II, p. 16 et seq; William Edward Hall, *International Law* (Oxford, 1880), p. 77 et seq; Calvo, note 8 above, I, §79 et seq; Bluntschli, note 7 above, §28 et seq. See especially Rivier, note 22 above, I, p. 57 et seq; p. 392 et seq.

issued by one or several governments, appointments of consuls or diplomatic agents, in general at the beginning of proper international relations. *De facto* recognition is displayed at the outset of proper international relations with a new State without any prior ceremonial declaring of this decision.

Each State is free to declare the international independence of a State being formed and is not obliged to anticipate recognition thereof on the part of other more interested States. But, of course, it is better if recognition were to be given earlier than others by that government which is most directly interested.

History knows many examples of States from whose territory a certain part of the population have separated and formed an autonomous State rather reluctantly agreeing to its recognition.

For example, Portugal separately completely from Spain in 1640, but this fact was recognized by the Spanish Government only in 1668; despite this, other powers respected the *de facto* independence of the Lisbon Government and maintained correct relations with it. The independence of the States of the Netherlands was recognized by Spain only at the 1648 Congress of Westphalia. The London Conference (1827) recognized the independence of Greece from Turkey at a time when the Turkish Government continued to view the Greeks who had revolted as subjects of the Sultan. Belgium separated from Holland in 1830, but the last recognized this fact only in 1839. England recognized the independence of Italy in 1860, when Francesco II [(1836-1894)] of the Two Sicilies was still in Gaeta and did not contemplate abdication.[60]

Finally, recognition may, in addition, be conditional or unconditional. An example of conditional recognition is the provision of the 1878 Treaty of Berlin concerning the independence of Romania, Serbia, and Montenegro.

The legal consequences of recognition are of a dual nature, depending on whether it followed on the part of all States or only some. In the first instance the recognized State becomes a fully-fledged member of the international community; in the second – proper international relations are maintained by the new State only with the powers which recognized it. The act of recognition has, in any event, enormous moral significance and influence, especially if it followed a still uncompleted struggle of a State with the part of the territory which separated from it. In many instances this was regarded as a *casus belli* with that power which issued it; for example, England so viewed the recognition by France of the son of James II Stuart

[60] See the remarkable 1860 dispatch of Lord [John] Russell [(1792-1878)] in Phillimore, note 3 above, II, p. 29.

[(1633-1701)] as the King of England and later French recognition of the independence of the North American states.[61]

B. Influence of Internal State Coups d'État

§65. The domestic State orders undoubtedly determine the *de facto* position which a particular State occupied among other nations; but in and of itself transformations or coups d'état in a State do not change its legal status, rights, or duties with respect to other States.[62]

If all States, whatever their form of government, are part of the international community, then of course every State is free to change its domestic order, structure, and administration at its own discretion and need. All State transformations, however material and in whatever spirit they were undertaken, are issues of domestic policy and not international law. It is only necessary that a particular people existed as an independent political organism having all the attributes of a State. Such a people under new internal orders retains its quality of international personality and will be a subject of international law. Changes within a State do not cause it lose its former international rights or acquire new ones.

This general principle was expressed by the five Great Powers in the London Protocol of 19 February 1831, which gave formal sanction to the independence of the Kingdom of Belgium. There it was said: "according to the general basic principle, treaties do not lose their binding character irrespective of the changes to which the internal organization of peoples have been subjected".[63]

[61] Recognition of a new title usually was given only on condition of a non-reduction of the title and honorary rights of other sovereigns. Compare, for example, the "Declaration of 8 July 1742 of the Russian Court that recognition by the Court of Vienna of the title of Emperor for Russian sovereigns did not change either the existing ceremonial or the rights of Austria". See F. F. Martens, Собрание трактатов и конвенций [Collection of Treaties and Conventions], I, No. 15; t. V, No. 20.

[62] Compare Grotius, note 16 above, lib. II, c. IX, 8; Emer de Vattel, *Le droit des gens* (1758), liv. II, chap. XI; James Kent, *Kent's Commentary on International Law*, ed. John Thomas Abdy (2d ed.; Cambridge, 1878), p. 95 et seq; William Oke Manning, *Commentaries on the Law of Nations*, ed. Sheldon Amos (London, 1875), p. 98 et seq; G. F. Martens, note 16 above, I, §128; Phillimore, note 3 above, I, pp. 169, 186 et seq; Heffter, note 6 above, §28, 50; Bluntschli, note 7 above, §40 et seq; Calvo, note 8 above, I, §81 et seq.

[63] "D'après ce principe d'un ordre supérieur, les traités ne perdent pas leur puissance quelsque soient les changements qui interviennent dans l'organisation intérieure des peuples". See G. F. Martens, *Nouveau Recueil*, XI, p. 209 et seq; Compare Rivier, note 22 above, I, p. 283 et seq.

The extreme necessity and reasonableness of this rule are understood. If the force of international obligations depended upon a particular dynasty reigning or a particular form of government, then a change of government or overthrow of a dynasty would serve as a clear means of freeing a people from the duty to perform treaties concluded by them.[64]

Numerous examples may be cited from history which illustrate the proposition set out above. During the first and second English revolutions (1649 and 1688), neither the English people, nor Lord Protector Cromwell, nor William of Orange denied that the treaties concluded by Charles I and in general by the Stuart dynasty were binding. In turn, the Stuarts restored in the person of Charles II (1660) recognized the binding force of treaties concluded by Cromwell. The 1789 French Revolution fundamentally changed the "ancien regime" of France; nonetheless, the National Assembly of 1790 did not consider itself to be freed of obligations placed on France by international treaties of Louis XIV and his predecessors because France continued to exist as a single State. To be sure, this principle found strong opponents in the 1791 National Assembly and in individuals of the Convent (see Introduction, §26), who proclaimed that treaties concluded by "tyrants" were not binding on France. But the European powers justly saw in a violation of these treaties a violation of their rights and joined together for armed combat against a common enemy. The same occurred when [Alphonse Marie Louis de Prat de] Lamartine [(1790-1869)], the former Minister of Foreign Affairs of the Second French Republic (1848) announced the Declaration in which in eloquent phrases he rejected the binding nature of the 1815 Vienna treaties for France; the Great Powers energetically protested such a Declaration, proving that the said treaties might be abrogated only by mutual agreement of the States.

An exception is those international obligations whose force by their very essence or by agreement between the parties depends upon the existence on a certain throne of a particular dynasty or monarch: with the dynasty losing the throne or with the death of the sovereign, this kind of obligation terminates.

In 1535 a Capitulation was concluded between the Sultan of Turkey and Francis I, King of France, whose duration, by will of the contracting parties, was limited to the "life of the monarchs" who signed it. Louis XIV concluded a treaty with James II Stuart on the basis of which he was obliged to assist him with forces and money in the struggle against the English people until James II was back on the English throne: the treaty

[64] Phillimore, note 3 above, I, §36, rightly observed: "This good faith is the great moral ligament which binds together the different nations of the globe".

was binding only for the two said sovereigns as their personal affair. The treaties concluded by Napoleon III with the Mexican Emperor, Maximilian, had the same personal character.

On the basis of the foregoing, the influence which an interregnum exerts on the international status of a particular State will be understandable. A dynasty newly ruling cannot fail to recognize the international obligations duly concluded during the interregnum if only the last was viable. In international relations a usurper who *de facto* held power is considered to be the legal representative of his people. Therefore, the international acts adopted by him as Acts performed in the name of the State are binding on the legitimate government which is restored to power.

On this basis Charles II, King of England [(1630-1685)], recognized the treaties concluded by Oliver Cromwell [(1599-1658)]. The Bourbons restored to the French throne in 1814 had to recognize as binding on them many of those international treaties which Napoleon I had concluded as Consul and Emperor. [William I], the Elector of Hesse [(1743-1821)], who intended not to perform the treaties concluded by the King of Westphalia, the usurper with regard to him, at the insistence of the Great Powers who returned his former possessions (in 1814), had to recognize the legality of those treaties. On the contrary, those international acts are not binding on a legitimate government which were undertaken by the head of a party or part of the population which rose up against it, without having achieved autonomy and not existing as an independent whole. The uprisings of [Andrew Thaddeus Bonaventure] Kościuszko [(1746-1817)] in Poland (1794), Daniele Manin [(1804-1857)] in Venice, and [Lajos] Kossuth [(1802-1894)] in Hungary (1849) were of this nature.

C. Significance of Territorial Changes of State

§66. The political organization and State structure of a people constitute a necessary condition of the existence of a State as an international person. An equally real basis is its territory, that space of land on which the people lives and which is subject solely to its sovereign power. If changes in a State order may have meaning in the field of international relations, then the more so the changes influence the mutual relations of States whose territory is affected. The system of internal administration, in principle, is the affair of each individual State, autonomously determined by it and concerning it alone. On the contrary, territorial changes always change borders separating particular States and neighborly relations: therefore, they always are reflected in the mutual legal relations between States.

Changes in State territory may be one of three types: 1) a particular State may be completely deprived of its territory and its existence terminated; 2) it may lose part of its possessions; 3) it may enlarge its territory by the accession of new possessions. In each of these instances special legal relations arise for States as members of the international community.

§67. 1. *State territory is lost.* A State without territory is inconceivable: deprived of its territory, a State ceases to exist, leaves the international community. The usual and primary instance of this kind happens when one State with its entire population accedes to another and thereby ceases to exist as an independent international person.

History is abundant with examples of such accessions, peacefully and by conquest. The autocratic Muscovite State was formed by the subordination of appanage principalities to Moscow, the accession of Great Novgorod and Pskov, the conquest of the Kazan, Astrakhan, and other realms. Scotland and Ireland became part of a single English kingdom. Napoleon I conquered many States and created autonomous republics, kingdoms, and dukedoms from them. The King of Prussia by a Proclamation of 1866 declared the accession to Prussia of Hanover, Kurhessen, Nassau, and Frankfurt-on-Main.

Other instances of the "death" of a State cited by Heffter and Phillimore are extremely rare and hardly possible at the present time: 1) when all citizens comprising a State die out or are eradicated; 2) when citizens of a particular State cease to constitute a political union as a result of oppressions, evictions, or banishment from their native land, as was so with the Jews and other peoples of the ancient world.[65] It is difficult to imagine that something similar could happen in our times.

The legal consequences of the absorption of one State by another remind us of the relations arising between private individuals by way of inheritance: a State acceding to another's State territory taking the place of a "dead" State fully enters into its legal personality and its rights and obligations.[66]

The following basic principles relating to succession to international rights and duties have been developed historically and recognized by theory and practice: 1) a State to which one or several States have acceded remains a

[65] Heffter, note 6 above, §24; Phillimore, note 3 above, I, p. 168; Bluntschli, note 7 above, §60; Schlief, "Das Völkerrecht und die legalen Aenderungen der Ländervertheilung", *Archiv für öffentlichen Recht*, XIII, p. 189 et seq; S. Kiatibian, *Conséquences juridiques des transformations territoriales des États sur les traités* (Paris, 1892). Compare in particular, Rivier, note 22 above, I, pp. 63, 138, 172-217.

[66] Compare Max Huber, *Die Staatensuccession* (Leipzig, 1898).

single subject of international law with one vote when deciding international questions; 2) in principle all international rights and obligations which the "dead" State had pass to the "heir". It cannot be said that succession occurs "insofar as the existence and continuation of such obligations is possible", because this limitation is too elastic.[67] Only those rights and obligations of the acceding State whose existence without the independence of the last is inconceivable do not pass to the State to which accession was made.[68]

The inheritance which the State receives from the accession to it of another's territory consists of active and passive rights. The *beneficium cum inventario* is not applicable in international law; that is, a State-heir may not stipulate as a condition that it assumes obligations of the acceding State insofar as they are beneficial. To it pass all obligations and rights of the acceding people. They consist of three types of rights and property: 1) all international obligations and treaties; 2) *domaine public*, such as: governmental institutions, offices, barracks, prisons, railways, ports, cities, and so on; 3) treasury ownership in the narrow sense; that is, capital and property of the treasury.

There pass to the State to which accession has been made, first, all international obligations and treaties. Therefore, it is obliged to assume the debts of the acceding State, to pay interest on them, and to repay them in that procedure and amount which has been determined by the laws of that State. All commercial treaties and other international treaties concluded by the acceding State are binding on the State to which accession was made.

Second, the State to which accession has been made is the heir of the *public domaine* of the acceding people. To it pass the possessions and dispositions of this *domaine* and the right to regulate it by its laws and regulations; in a word, in the domain of public law relations a State may act at its discretion in its own interests and advantage. This right extends to all that serves the satisfaction of State needs; for example, stocks of weapons, military ammunition in the acceding State, and so on.

Third, the treasury ownership of the State which ceased to exist goes as a whole to the full disposition of the State-heir: money, forests, lands, and

67 Bluntschli, note 7 above, §50. Compare also Calvo, note 8 above, I, §102.

68 Prior to the accession of Courland to Russia, it was in vassal relations with Poland. When in 1794 there were negotiations between Russia and Prussia concerning the Third Partition of Poland, the Prussian Minister, Count [Christian August Heinrich Kurt] Haugwitz [(1752-1832)], said to [Magnus Maximilian Count von] Alopeus [(1748-1822)], the representative of Russia at the Court of Berlin: "Ce duché étant un fief de la Pologne ne peut exister comme tel, dès que la Puissance suzeraine cessera d'être". From an unpublished Letter of Alopeus to Vice Chancellor [Ivan Andreevich] Count Osterman [(1725-1811)] of 22 August (2 September) 1794.

immoveable and moveable property in general of the old treasury becomes its ownership.

Recent history presents several interesting instances of the application of the principles just set out. The Kingdom of Sardinia, having joined to itself in 1860 other Italian States, assumed their obligations (all State debts) and received the right to their *public domaine* and treasury ownership. Having terminated (1870) the independent existence of the Papal domain, the Italian Government assumed the duty to pay interest on State loans and to perform international obligations which had been concluded by the Popes as secular sovereigns. Exactly the same with Prussia, which by a Law of 22 September 1866 destroyed the international independence of Hanover, Kurhessen, Nassau, and Frankfurt-on-Main and declared itself to be responsible for their debts and all international obligations. After a three-year heroic struggle, the Transvaal and Orange republics in South Africa lost their international independence and acceded to England. The aforementioned principles should apply fully to these South African republics without a violation of the legal rights of subjects of neutral States having lawful interests in the conquered Dutch republics.[69]

§68. 2. *State territory is reduced in size*. A reduction of the territory of a particular State may be more or less significant; in any event, a State is not deprived through this of its political independence and remains a subject of international law. Therefore, no matter how vast the provinces that have fallen away from the State, all former international obligations nonetheless remain.

Prussia, for example, after the Tilsit Peace (1807), was deprived of almost a third of its possessions, but did not cease to exist as an independent kingdom and therefore should have performed international obligations concluded by it under other conditions. The Kingdom of Saxony lost half of its territory on the basis of the Act of Vienna (1814), but was not released from international obligations while remaining an independent State. Austria was deprived after 1859 of Lombardy – its richest region; in 1866 it lost Venice, but its international obligations remained in full force. The same may be said about France after 1815 and 1871, and about Turkey after 1829 or 1878.

State territory is reduced either as a consequence of an unfortunate war or internecine warfare. In the first instance, usually part of the territory of

[69] On the fate of neutral railway companies in the Transvaal, see Mallarmé, "Étude sur la condition juridique des chemins de fer privés sud-africains depuis l'annexion du Transvaal", *Revue générale de droit international public* (1903), p. 282 et seq.

the vanquished State is joined to the possessions of the victor; in the second – the separated provinces or colonies form a new State or are combined with existing States. Most important and difficult to resolve is the question of the transfer of international obligations of the main State to the provinces which separated from it after internecine warfare.

Under the general rule, internecine warfare should remain a dispute solely between the directly interested parties. A legitimate government has the right to take all measures to restore its authority and to resist the aspiration of the mutinous region to achieve independent existence. Any interference by neutral powers will be an unwelcome intrusion into the internal affairs of the particular State.[70] An internecine war, however, may acquire international significance. Occurring in an adjacent neighboring State, it makes necessary the adoption on the part of the last of measures ensuring the inviolability of its territory. Commercial interests of neutral powers may be disturbed by the internecine warfare. Understandably, in these instances third States will not remain uninvolved spectators. The question is under what conditions do they have the right to declare that the rebellious region is an independent State.

The existence of an autonomous State is a question of fact; it may be stated only on the basis of circumstances in which the particular people actually find themselves. When applying this requirement to the region in revolt, neutral governments, before proclaiming it to be independent, must be convinced, must confirm whether what they intend to confirm are indeed facts. Only by this means may one verify the true status of the belligerent parties and in good faith recognize their mutual autonomy.

The Message of President [Hiram Ulysses S.] Grant [(1822-1885)] in 1875 relating to the Island of Cuba resolved the issue in this sense. In reply to the demand of certain members of the Washington Government to declare the Cubans who had revolted to be independent of Spain, Grant declared that so long as open combat continued between the metropolitan and the colony, he did not consider that he had the right to interfere in an internecine war. The significance of an internecine war was demonstrated with special clarity in correspondence between the envoy of the Northern states, [Charles Francis] Adams [(1807-1886)], and Lord [John] Russell on the occasion of the recognition in 1863 of the independence of the South by the London Cabinet. Finally (in 1849), the Washington Government withdrew its recognition of the independence of Hungary after an agent sent

[70] Compare the dispatch of Prince [Aleksandr Mikhailovich] Gorchakov [(1798-1883)] to Baron [Eduard de] Stoeckl [(1804-1892)] in Washington of 28 June 1861 and 9 January 1862 on the occasion of the internecine war in the United States, in the *Annuaire diplomatique de l'Empire de Russie* (1862), p. 104 et seq.

by it (one Mann) reported that the Hungarian revolutionary government was not viable.[71]

One can therefore not agree with the view that neutral governments may according to law immediately recognize a region in revolt as an independent State and take its part in an internecine war.[72] In this event the interference would be recognition of a fact that had not been finally determined, and the governments would assume an inappropriate role of judge of the justness of an internecine war. But, on the other hand, one cannot refuse to outside powers the right to support *de facto* relations, especially trade, with the province or colony in revolt and take measures for the protection of its subjects within the limits of legitimate interests.

For this purpose, England, France, and Russia sent their own consular agents to Greece, which was struggling for freedom against the Turkish Government.

From the files of the State Archive we cite the following relevant instance of interest. In 1811 an American, [Courtland] Parker, arrived in St. Petersburg with a view to establishing proper commercial relations between Russia and the South American colonies which had separated from Spain: Caracas, Venezuela, and Santa Fe. The State Chancellor refused formal recognition of the independence of these colonies but all the same made a submission to the State Council in the sense that "the opening of trade relations with the said provinces, not representing any inconveniences for us (Russia), should be authorized provided that this decision is based precisely on the general rules of the firmly-based system established for neutral powers"(sic!). But the State Council did not agree with the view of the State Chancellor. By a majority of 21 to 4, the Council decreed "that so long as the governments of the three provinces requesting to enter into trade relations are not firmly established and solemnly recognized by us, the solicitations of the American Parker should not be satisfied". Emperor Alexander I affirmed the opinion of the majority on 27 October 1822.

This decision of the State Council must be deemed to be well-founded. No interests of Russian subjects existed in the aforementioned three colonies which were requesting the patronage of Russia. In the absence of this condition, the entry of neutral powers into trade relations with the

71 Wheaton, note 1 above, p. 34 et seq, notes 15 and 16; Hall, note 59 above, p. 75; Calvo, note 8 above, I, §83.

72 Vattel, note 62 above, liv. II, chap. VI, §56; Henry Wager Halleck, *International Law; or, Rules Regulating the Intercourse of States in Peace and War* (New York, 1861), p. 73 et seq; Wheaton, note 1 above, I, §23; Lawrence, note 8 above, I, p. 213 et seq; Bluntschli, note 7 above, §47 et seq.

uprising provinces would justly be regarded by the legitimate belligerent government as interference and a political demonstration.

The completed separation of part of the territory from the main skeleton of a State leads to the following legal consequences. Those international obligations which lie specially on the separated region remain and are no longer on the State to which that region belonged. These obligations may be local or personal. To the first are relegated, for example, private-law obligations relating to the possession of railways which are situated in the separated part of the State. They usually are regulated by mutual agreement of the interested States.

Thus, the 1871 Frankfurt Treaty determined the rights and duties of the German Union with respect to the railways of Alsace and Lorraine: it should either assume all private-debt obligations lying on these railways or purchase them for a determined amount.

State debts pass in a certain part to the separated region.

For example, Belgium bound itself (Article 13, 1839 Belgian-Dutch Treaty) to pay 5 million annual rent on account to the State debt of Holland formed between 1815 and 1830. On the basis of the 1859 Zurich Treaty, Sardinia assumed payment of part of the Austrian-Lombardy debt. Bulgaria (Article 9, Treaty of Berlin) was obliged to assume part of the State debt of Turkey, which had to be determined by the Porte by agreement with the powers.

As regards personal obligations falling on the State that annexes a region or on a new State formed from the provinces which separated, they do not have special significance. However, those belonging to the population of the ceded locality relating to the profession of a particular faith or the rights of foreigners present in this locality must retain their force under the new government insofar as they are not contrary to the interests of the entire population because the government always has the right to establish that order within its territory which is beneficial to the entire people.

§69. 3. *State territory increases.* The question of an increase of State territory is closely connected with the question of its reduction. Usually a State expands its territory at the expense of the possessions of others, so that if one territory is increased, another is decreased; therefore, the legal consequences of a reduction or increase of territories correlate fully. It remains to add several words to what was said about these consequences in §68.

In joining part of the territory of another to one's own, a State acquires with respect to it all rights of sovereignty, as in the event of the accession of an entire State; the relevant principles have been indicated above (§67).

Those rights and obligations which specially appertain to the acceded possessions, such as, for example, the debts and debt demands thereof, pass in particular to the acquiring State. On the other hand, the joining part receives all rights and assumes all duties of the new whole.[73]

The accession of the possessions of others may be unconditional or conditional. Misunderstandings might arise relating to the conditions of accession, best prevented by a mutual agreement of the interested States which usually underlie territorial acquisitions.

Thus, in the Treaty of Berlin (1878) the conditions were determined in detail on which part of the Ottoman territory of Serbia, Montenegro, and Romania were acquired. Principalities were obliged to respect the religious freedom of all persons within their own possessions (Articles 27, 35, 44); Serbia and Montenegro assumed part of the Ottoman debt (Articles 33 and 42). We indicated above on what conditions Montenegro joined the port of Antivari and surrounding region to itself. In exactly the same way, Sweden in the Treaty of Nystad (1721) stipulated certain privileges and rights to the benefit of the population of the Ostsee Territory ceded to Russia. The Grand Duchy of Finland passed to Russia under the 1809 Friedrichsham Treaty also on certain conditions.

In practice the question is repeatedly raised about the time during which conditions of such type are binding on a State and the consequences of a violation thereof. The view exists that a State is bound by them forever, and if they are violated, the right to further possession of the acquired territory is lost. It is difficult to agree with this view. First, the population of the territory joined on conditions may by its behavior give legitimate occasion for the failure to comply with privileges stipulated to its benefit; second – and most important – the perpetual binding nature of these conditions is contrary to the natural law of the development of social and State life to which all peoples are subject.

V. International Attributes of State

§70. By international attributes of a State we understand qualities inherent to States, without which they are inconceivable in the domain of international relations and on which their mutual rights are based. Such grounds and necessary attributes are: 1) sovereignty, 2) dispositive legal capacity, and 3) equality of rights. All three appertain to every State participating in international interaction and are assumed by this interaction.

[73] Bluntschli, note 7 above, §59; Lawrence, note 8 above, I, p. 214; Hall, note 59 above, p. 85.

a) *Sovereignty*. The independence of a State is expressed in sovereignty or supremacy in the sphere of internal administration and in international relations.

In the domain of international relations sovereignty has no "size", as in State administration. A difference is immediately discovered as the State enters into relations with other peoples and wishes to conclude obligations and enjoy international rights: then by the course of events it is forced to make concessions, respect the legal interests and rights of other peoples, and should refrain from any absolute exercise of its sovereignty. The absolute principle of sovereignty in the sense of State right is determined in international interaction by the mutual relations which exist between and are limited by peoples.

The sovereignty of a State is a necessary presumption of their international personality: legal relations may be established only between States autonomous in internal administration and independent (in the degree indicated above) in its external activity. Semi-independent States are an anomaly. A people which has lost its sovereignty is subordinated to the operation not of international law, but State law, and, on the contrary, the community which acquired sovereignty becomes a subject of international law.[74]

b) *Dispositive legal capacity*. A State, as an international person, must express its own will and act. Without dispositive legal capacity, a State can neither direct its own relations with its own people nor enter into agreements with other States, nor implement the tasks of international administration. The legal capacity of States coincides with the dispositive legal capacity thereof. Once a State has been formed and recognized as a member of the international community, it cannot lack dispositive legal capacity. Periods of maturity limiting dispositive legal capacity are not applicable to States.

Semi-independent States, which remind one of natural persons under trusteeship or guardianship by reason of their limited dispositive legal capacity, are exceptions. The status, for example, of the Egyptian Government is such, controlled in financial affairs by a specially appointed English advisor on finances, or the Tunisian Bey, whose diplomatic relations on the basis of a Treaty with France of 12 May 1881 must pass through a French resident minister accredited to and attached to the Bey. Logic and justice require that such non-autonomous States be responsible for their actions to foreign governments insofar as their dispositive legal capacity is free. The European powers under whose guardianship they are situated

[74] Jellinek, note 8 above, p. 16 et seq.

must be responsible to a certain extent for the actions of the Government of the Egyptian Khedive or Tunisian Bey.

This view is partly affirmed by practice. When in 1871 a well-known builder of railroads, [Bethel Henry] Strousberg [(1823-1884)], having concluded a contract with the Romanian Government to rebuild the railroads did not receive it as a consequence of the failure of the Romanian chamber to confirm it, appealed to Prince [Otto von] Bismarck [(1815-1898)],who made a submission on this matter not only to the Bucharest Cabinet, but also to the Porte, demonstrating that it was liable for the actions of its vassal State. From this standpoint, the [Russian] Government viewed the Porte as responsible for piracy by subjects of the Barbary possessions, and the 1826 Akkerman Convention formally obliged the Turkish Government to pay remuneration to those Russian who suffered from these pirates.

c) *Equality of rights*. Just as individuals, citizens, are equal before the law, so independent States are equal before international law: they all have certain basic rights which may be enjoyed and which should be mutually respected. The equal rights of States arise from the concept of an international community; in this sense it is a "theoretical" principle. But it would be unjust to say the principle had no practical importance and to deny its positive grounds.

The principle of equality of rights of States was superbly formulated by the North American [Charles] Sumner [(1811-1874)] at a session of the Washington [United States] Senate on 27 March 1871. Here are his words: "nothing can be done to a small or weak nation that would not be done to a large or powerful nation, or that we would not allow to be done to ourselves".[75] The community uniting contemporary educated peoples requires that they recognize mutual equal rights.

If equality is not always respected in practice, the power of this principle is not shaken. The practical view of Funck-Brentano and Sorel, who say that "in addition to instances when the equality of States actually finds application, it is an empty word",[76] is refuted by the fact of an international community being inconceivable without its members being equal. Likewise unfounded is Lorimer's view, who sees in the principle of absolute equality of the rights and duties of States a principle that is false in theory and unrealizable or inconceivable in practice; he structured both his projects of

[75] Bluntschli, note 7 above, §81; Calvo, note 8 above, I, p. 386. [Martens misstates the date as 23 March 1871, whereas the passage was declared on 27 March 1871 and appears in Sumner's San Domingo Resolution of said date. See *The Works of Charles Sumner* (Boston, 1875-1883), XIV, p. 169 – WEB].

[76] Funck-Brentano and Sorel, note 20 above, p. 401.

an international organization on the principle of the "*de facto* inequality" of States.[77]

But the legal principle of the equality of rights of members of the international community does not exclude their *de facto* inequality – inequality in power, size of population, wealth, and others. Private individuals also must be equal before the law; civil equality is a great "theoretical" principle achieved by European civilization; but not all private individuals have the identical possibility to take advantage of their legal rights, to apply them. "Great" powerful States possess substantial means to realize their rights, more than small and powerless States. But it does not follow that the former may by right prescribe laws to powerless peoples.

The claims of some States to be called "great powers", from the standpoint of international law, is not based on anything, although this name is recognized for them in view of their special political power and international significance. But in any event the attempts of these States to dispose of the fate of others, to interfere in their internal affairs, and to manage their international interests can be justified by nothing.[78] Such interference does not arise from the principle of equality of rights because it does not require that all States have identical orders and exercise their international rights "identically". A State is free in the sphere of internal administration and may grant more rights to its subjects on its territory than to foreigners and may give greater privileges to subjects of some States than comparatively to others. Finally, the principle of equality between States does not repeal the ranks and titles of States and their representatives established by international practice and especially by the provisions of the Congress of Vienna and other congresses of the nineteenth century, which, moreover, do not promise the holders thereof any authority in international relations.

§71. According to the principle of sovereignty, every State has the right to accept that title which it wishes; but in order to acquire international significance, it needs recognition on the part of other States. It is essential

[77] James Lorimer, *Revue de droit International* (1877), p. 165. This view is expressed less sharply by the distinguished Professor of Edinburgh University in *The Institutes of the Law of Nations: A Treatise of the Jural Relations of Separate Political Communities* (Edinburgh, 1883-1884), I, p. 105 et seq.

[78] On the basis of a Protocol signed at Troppau on 19 November 1820, the plenipotentiaries of the three northern great powers declared that the "allied powers" (that is, Austria, Russia, and Prussia) exclude from the European alliance any State which as a consequence of a "revolt" was subjected to changes. See F. F. Martens, Собрание трактатов и конвенций [Collection of Treaties and Conventions], IV(1), No. 122.

for such recognition that the dignity and rank combined with the title which a State adopts correspond to the place and status that it actually occupies in the international community; a State that is politically insignificant cannot claim a title and rank belonging to large States.[79]

The powers which took part in the 1818 Congress of Aachen refused a royal title to the Elector of Hesse, finding that the request of the Elector concerning this title "is not justified by sufficient grounds". On the contrary, the royal title of the Electors of Brandenburg, adopted in 1701 by Friedrich I [(1657-1713)], was recognized by all the powers because the international significance which Prussia then enjoyed fully corresponded to this title. The same may be said about the Russian title of emperor adopted by Peter the Great in 1721 upon the conclusion of the Nystad Peace and recognized at various times by the European cabinets.[80] In recent times the Proclamation of the English Government (1876) on the adoption by the Queen of Great Britain of the title "Empress of India" was communicated to all powers and accepted by them without question. The powers agreed to the recognition of the Romanian Principality and Serbia as kingdoms (1881-1882). In 1897 the Korean King adopted the title of Emperor, which has not yet been recognized by the European States.

The ambiguity of the rank of sovereigns has generated constant altercations between representatives of various powers over precedence or *droit de préséance*. The history of the sixteenth, seventeenth, and even eighteenth centuries is replete with examples of disputes, often comic, but which sometimes seriously disturbed the peace of Europe as to who should preside at an international meeting, in what sequence one should preside, or sign a treaty, or be admitted to an audience with the sovereign, and so on.[81] These endless disputes drew the attention of the Pope, who at the request of those in dispute and by virtue of the highest authority ascribed to themselves by Roman pontiffs, determined the ranks and titles of sovereigns.

The regulation issued by Pope Julius II [(1443-1513)] in 1504 is completely erroneous; according to it, first place should belong to the

[79] Compare the interesting work by Frederick Henry Marshall, *International Vanities* (London, 1873), in which numerous curious facts are cited testifying to the amusing vanity of States in their mutual relations.

[80] Holland and Prussia recognized before others in 1722. See F. F. Martens, Собрание трактатов и конвенций [Collection of Treaties and Conventions], V, No. 204. The Court of Vienna (Austria) in 1744; France in 1762; and Poland only in 1764.

[81] Marshall, note 79 above, p. 17 et seq, 95 et seq. Compare Catharine Macaulay, *History of England*, IV, p. 788; Ernest Nys, *Les origines du droit international* (Brussels, 1894), p. 332.

Roman Emperor, and then followed: the king of Rome, the king of France, Castile, Aragon, Portugal, England, and so on. No mention was made of the Muscovite tsar. On the basis of recent studies, neither Pope Julius II nor other Roman popes issued similar regulations binding on States.[82]

At present, the rank and ceremonial rights of sovereigns are determined by the aforementioned customary and treaty rules:

1) Until the present various monarchs have held religious titles granted to their predecessors by Roman pontiffs for special services to the Church. Thus, the king of France was called the "*roi très chrétien*", or "*filius primogenitus ecclesiae*"; the king of England – "*defensor fidei*"; the Emperor of Austria as the king of Hungary – "*Majesté Apostolique*"; the king of Spain – "*roi catholique*"; the king of Portugal – "*roi très fidèle*"; and the former Polish kings were titled "*rois orthodoxes*".

2) The Catholic States recognize precedence for representatives of the Pope – a custom not binding on Russia and Protestant States.

3) First place among autonomous States is occupied by those to which *honneurs royaux* belong. These are: empires, kingdoms, grand duchies, and great republics – French, Swiss, and North American (previously Venice and the Dutch States). To privileges combined with *honneurs royaux* are relegated: the title "*Majeste*", special arms, various ceremonial rights and the right to send diplomatic agents of the first class – *ambassadeurs*. Complete equality of rank and ceremonial rights is recognized between emperors, kings, and republics. Switzerland does not appoint ambassadors by own choice, but does not lack this right. It should be noted that kinship and family relations between sovereigns, just as political alliances, do not change the sequence of places and ranks of States.[83]

The title of emperor has no formal advantages over the title of king. Attempts to establish a difference between them in theory and to thereby justify a preference which in practice is usually accorded to the title of emperor to date have not been successful.

Bluntschli saw this difference in the "universal" meaning of empire and its domination over "several peoples". But both history and positive facts are contrary to this view. England has long since ruled over many peoples and, of course, has worldwide significance; however, it bears the title of kingdom.[84] Prussian kings did not change their title to emperor despite the

[82] Nys, *Études de droit international et de droit politique* (Brussels, 1896), p. 211 et seq.

[83] Statute of the Congress of Vienna, 7(19) March 1814, relating to diplomatic agents, Article VI. See F. F. Martens, Собрание трактатов и конвенций [Collection of Treaties and Conventions], III, p. 529 et seq. Compare: Rivier, note 22 above, I, p. 286; II, p. 22 et seq.

[84] The term "British Empire" reflects the principle of the international unity of all English

fact that it enjoyed great international significance from the time of Friedrich (II) the Great. Finally, the German Emperor is at present the head of a unified German people which have comprised an empire since 1871. Bluntschli's remark that "imperial rank" does not affect the "title of emperor" does not eliminate the misunderstanding.[85]

4) Semi-independent States must be below independent States and, in any event, cede priority to that State on which it is dependent.[86]

5) Certain rules have been developed which indicate the rank of States with regard to mutual relations and correspondence between sovereigns, and also maritime salutes.[87]

6) Special agreements between particular States concerning rank are recognized by other powers, as for example – an agreement on precedence between sovereigns who are part of the old German Empire.

7) A change of the form of government does not change the rank of a State. England enjoyed royal honors under Cromwell and under the Stuarts; the most recent French Republic remains a "great power".[88]

VI. Basic International Rights of States

§72. The basic rights of States are inextricably connected with the international attributes of the last and, consequently, with the entire status of States as international persons. They belong to each independent State, whatever its political power, size of its territory, or obligatory relations to other peoples. Without these rights, States are not in a position to achieve a reasonable purpose of international life; without them, they are not members of the international community. The acquired rights of States are created by treaties and depend on circumstances and time; basic rights are inherent to States, inalienable, and always must be present.

A State may not renounce its international rights without denying itself its own independence. Therefore, treaties violating or abrogating basic rights

possessions.

85 Bluntschli, note 7 above, §85-86.

86 Compare Bluntschli, ibid., §93. It is unclear how, in the view of Bluntschli, the North American state of Virginia may be considered a semi-independent State and why semi-independent States with respect to non-suzerain powers may be in an equal status with them "according to their significance in the family of nations"?

87 See Phillimore, note 3 above, II, §34; Calvo, note 8 above, I, §318 et seq; G. F. Martens, note 16 above, §158-163.

88 Wheaton, note 8 above, II, chap. III, §152 et seq; David Dudley Field, *Outlines of an International Code* (2d ed.; New York, 1876), §16-17; Heffter, note 6 above, §27-28.

of States are illegal and not binding. Such treaties are possible only under two conditions: 1) if a State is powerless to restore its violated right, or 2) is in a state of complete collapse. A State possessing instincts of life sooner or later will cast such limitations aside and restore its international personality to the full extent. Because basic rights are inextricably connected with the existence of States, any infringement thereof is a *casus belli*.

These basic rights are: 1) the right to self-preservation; 2) the right of territoriality; 3) the right of independence; 4) the right to respect and honor; 5) the right to international communication; and 6) the right of coercion.[89]

§73. 1. *Right of self-preservation*. This right arises directly from the fact of the existence of a State. Just as man, a State has the right and is obliged to protect its life by all means at its disposal. The right to self-preservation consists not only of the right to resist an attacker, but also the right to prevent an unavoidable threatening danger. The duty of a State is to take advantage of this right: a people not wishing to defend its own life has no right to autonomy.[90]

From the right of self-preservation arises the need for a State to have resources to protect its own life. To these belong: 1) the aggregate of armed land and sea forces; 2) fortresses and fortifications of all kinds; 3) international defensive and offensive alliances. In general all means of defense not connected with an infringement against the independence of other non-hostile peoples are legal. The purpose of measures taken under the pretext of self-preservation should not be adverse to the autonomy of another peaceful State or violate the basic conditions of its life.

The behavior of England with respect to Denmark in 1807, when Copenhagen was subjected to bombardment only because the Danish Government refused to perform a completely illegal demand of the English – to immediately place its fleet at their disposal which, as they thought, might be delivered to Napoleon I and be used against England – was an

[89] Heffter, note 6 above, §29 et seq; Twiss, note 20 above, I, p. 143 et seq; Wheaton, note 8 above, II, chap. I, §60 et seq; Hall, note 59 above, p. 226 et seq; Creasy, note 16 above, p. 147 et seq; Calvo, note 8 above, I, p. 224 et seq; Léopold Neumann, *Grundriss des heutigen europäischen Völkerrechts* (2d ed.; Vienna, 1877), §8; Adolf Hartmann, *Institutionen des praktischen Völkerrechts in Friedenszeiten* (Hanover, 1874), §7-17.

[90] Compare Lorenz von Stein, *Die Lehre vom Heerwesen: Als Theil der Staatswissenschaft* (Stuttgart, 1872), p. 4 et seq; Friedrich Adolf Trendelenburg, *Naturrecht auf dem Grunde der Ethik* (Leipzig, 1868), §152, 177, 195; Rudolf von Jhering, *Der Zweck im Recht*, I, p. 416 et seq.

example of the pathetic abuse of force concealed under the guise of self-defense.[91]

The conditions for the application of the right of defense by States have much in common with the principles applied with respect to the self-defense of private individuals. The self-defense of a State should not be unlimited: it begins from the moment of an actual attack or from the moment of clear threatening danger. From this standpoint, one cannot consider to be illegal the attack by Friedrich II on Saxony in 1756 because before undertaking this, the King of Prussia had in his hands evidence of the hostile schemes of the Elector of Saxony.[92]

To adhere to a different view on this question means to open the door to all possible violence and seizures. In the eighteenth century clear wars of conquest were justified by the need to counteract a violation of the political equilibrium. Another matter was the undoubted aspiration of a particular people for a worldwide monarchy: in this event the States had to take common defensive measures for self-preservation.[93]

Measures of self-preservation may be adopted within or outside the territory of a State which is threatened by an attack or danger.

The following instances may serve as examples. In 1838 the local authorities in English Canada during an uprising received reliable information that the warship *Caroline* was being outfitted on American territory with the participation of subjects of the United States to deliver military supplies and armed personnel to the Canadians who had rebelled. The Government of Canada ordered the dispatch of a military unit across the Lake, which seized the warship, disarmed it, and then launched it over Niagara Falls. The Washington Government instituted a dispute in this matter, accusing the Canadian authorities of a violation of the territorial integrity of the United States, but refrained from a demand for satisfaction, after which the English Government proved that these actions were caused by necessary defense.[94]

Another instance occurred in 1873, when an uprising took place on the Island of Cuba. The Spanish detained the *Virginius* on the high seas sailing under an American merchant flag and ordered people removed from the

[91] The contemporary English jurist, [William Edward] Hall, note 59 above, p. 230, found it possible to justify the behavior of England, sharply condemned by many English writers. Compare Archibald Alison, *History of Europe*, VI, p. 474.

[92] Leopold von Ranke, *Zur Geschichte von Österreich und Preussen*, p. 224 et seq.

[93] Bluntschli, note 7 above, §99.

[94] Phillimore, note 3 above, I, p. 255; Hall, note 59 above, p. 227.

vessel to be hanged on the grounds that the captured ship had been hired by the rebellious Cubans to carry arms and ammunition to them. The American Government protested the stopping of its vessel and punishment of its crew, relying on the fact that the high seas were free to all, but terminated the dispute when it was proved that the measure taken was self-defense and it was determined that the vessel itself had no right to fly the American flag.[95]

Protection of the rights and interests of either the State directly or of some social class, or of individuals is the subject-matter of defensive measures. The operation or duration of the application of these measures is determined by the significance and duration of the attack or the danger itself.

Finally, it is evident that any limitation of the right of self-preservation is a positive infringement on the existence of a people and should be regarded as a temporary absurdity.

Many examples are encountered of such limitations. In the eighteenth century, France obliged itself by the treaties of Utrecht (1713), Aachen (1748), and Paris (1763) not to fortify Dunkirk; according to the 1815 Paris Treaty, it obliged itself not to restore the fortifications of Huningue; Russia, on the basis of the 1856 Paris Peace Treaty, should have razed the fortifications on the coasts of the Black Sea, not erected new ones, and not maintained a naval fleet on the Black Sea. At the insistence of the Russian Government, these limitations were revoked in 1871. In the 1878 Treaty of Berlin there were several such restrictive Articles: Bulgaria obliged itself to raze old fortresses within its limits and not construct new ones (Article 11); the right to have naval vessels and to build fortifications on the Bojana River and along the coast was taken away from Montenegro (Article 29); in order to ensure freedom of navigation along the Danube it was provided to raze all fortresses and fortifications along the River from the Iron Gates to the mouth and a prohibition to erect new ones; no naval vessels might sail in this space except *stationnaires*, which had the right to ascend only to Galati (Article 52).

§74. 2. *The right of territoriality* (*jus territoriale*). It has a direct link with the right of self-preservation and consists of the exclusive dominance of a State over all the space of its territory. Therefore: 1) no State has the right to extend its authority over another's territory or undertake there any governmental actions. Foreign territory gives asylum to all persons persecuted in their own State. Forces and naval vessels of belligerent

[95] Theodore Dwight Woolsey, *Introduction to the Study of International Law* (5th ed.; London, 1878), Appendix No. 3; Hall, note 59 above, p. 232 et seq; With regard to the *Virginius* affair, see *Staatsarchiv*, XVII-XVIII, nos. 5284-5427.

powers stop at the boundaries of foreign territory. 2) Any action of a State diminishing or limiting the territorial authority of another State gives to the last a legal occasion to take repressive measures.

Every State has the right to demand that foreign powers not incite its subjects to an uprising, to secession from the State, or to eviction. The Manifesto of Catherine II (1763) which invited subjects of Prussia and other German States to resettle in Russia was regarded by the German governments as a violation of their legal rights.[96] Austria also considered an invitation sent by the Russian Government to Austrian Slavs concerning their resettlement in the south of Russia in the "New Serbia" colony to be disrespect for their territoriality and their interests.[97]

3) All persons and property, especially immoveable, on the territory is subject to the territorial laws and jurisdiction.

4) No State should violate the natural conditions and relations in which another State has been placed by nature. That which nature gave to all may not be appropriated by an individual State to its ownership. If, for example, a river flows through the possessions of several States, no one of them has the right to change its direction to the prejudice of the others.

The occupation or accession of part of another's territory is, without doubt, a material change of the operation of the right of territoriality of a particular State which justifies rebuff and a demand of satisfaction. Chapter III contains a more detailed consideration of the right of a State to territory.

§75. *Right of independence*. This basic international right of a State is an expression of State sovereignty and is exercised: 1) in full freedom of the internal system and administration of the State (change of form of government, issuance of laws, appointment of officials, system of local government, and so on); 2) in the right autonomously to administer international relations (direction of foreign policy, appointment of diplomatic and consular agents, conclusion of treaties, development of armed forces, and others).

[96] In a Report (unpublished) of Prince [Iurii Vladimirovich] Dolgorukov [(1740-1830)] from Berlin of 14(25) October 1763 it was said that the move of Prussian subjects to Russia was being delayed by all means on the part of the Prussian Government, which had ordered its border authorities not to allow the resettlers to pass. Measures were even taken so that the Manifesto was not made known. Полное собрание законов Российской империи [Complete Collection of Laws of the Russian Empire] (1st series), Nos. 11880, 11881, and 11896.

[97] The Austrian envoy in St. Petersburg, Baron [Johann Franz von] Pretlack [(1708-1767)], even accused the Russian envoy attached to the Court in Vienna of inciting Serbs to resettle and demanded that he be forbidden to do so. See F. F. Martens, Собрание трактатов [Collection of Treaties], I, p. 184.

When proclaiming the full internal and external independence of a State, one must remember that the right to own independence always corresponds to the duty to respect another's independence. One is inextricably linked with the other. France under Napoleon I generated the events of 1814 and 1815 relating to disrespect for the independence of other peoples.

§76. *On interference*. The unrequested entry into the affairs and mutual relations thereof by interested parties in a dispute is called interference. If States in dispute themselves request a third power to settle their dispute, we will have not interference, but mediation. It is evident that unrequested intrusion in another's affairs, in essence the action itself, is not the right of any State; therefore, it is impermissible to speak about a "right of interference"; interference admissible in a few instances is justified by completely exceptional circumstances, but not by a right in the legal sense.

It may be: 1) interference in the internal affairs of another people, or 2) in external relations existing between concrete powers.

The reasons for interference are various. In particular, often said to be a justification for interference is the need for self-preservation, the need to perform a treaty concluded, and an appeal for interference on the part of parties in dispute. So long as both parties agree to interference, there will be, as we said, mediation. Either diplomatic notes or force of arms serve as means of interference.

We consider both types of interference separately.[98]

I. *Interference in internal affairs*. On both the concept and limits of this kind of interference in the literature on intervention there are extremely diverse and vague views which open up a wide field for arbitrariness in their interpretation and application. Nonetheless, the majority of contemporary writers speak of interference as an exception from the normal order of international relations, and they all deny the "right" of interference, which at the outset of the present century belonged to the category of uncontested truths. In such a change of views one cannot fail to see a great triumph to the advantage of law. The task of contemporary science on this question lies

[98] The literature on this question, controversial in its time, is very rich. Compare Phillimore, note 3 above, I, p. 463 et seq; Hall, note 59 above, §88; Heffter, note 6 above, §44; Bluntschli, note 7 above, §474; Lawrence, note 8 above, II, p. 489 et seq; Amari, "Nouvel exposé du principe de non-intervention", *Revue de droit international* (1873); John Stuart Mill, *Dissertations and Discussions: Political, Philosophical, and Historical* (London, 1867), III, p. 153; Hermann Strauch, *Zur Interventions-Lehre* (Heidelberg, 1879). A detailed analysis of this question is found in Rivier, note 22 above, I, p. 389 et seq. For Russian literature, see Count L. A. Kamarovskii, Начало невмешательства [Principle of Non-Interference] (M., 1874).

in the elimination of those exceptions from the principle of non-interference which authoritative publicists still allow and which often undermine the force of the principle itself.

When considering the question of interference in internal affairs it is not so important to distinguish occasions for interference as it is to distinguish between the subjects and objects thereof. Interference is perceived to be different depending on whether it is applied in relations between civilized States or in relations of these last with uncivilized peoples.

a) In relations between civilized peoples interference is in principle not permitted: it is always illegal because it contracts the independence of States. Moreover, it does not achieve its purpose, humiliating the government to the benefit of which it was undertaken, and irritating and insulting the people against which it is directed. The history of the early nineteenth century is the best evidence of the justice of this position.[99] That is why now interference is not defended even by political actors.

From this point of view, all exceptions from the principle of non-interference are dangerous. However, we do not deny that special instances are possible when interference in internal affairs of an educated State may happen. These are instances when interference is caused by the interests of the international community. We allow, by way of exception, collective interference and insist on common actions undertaken against a particular State by mutual agreement not only of two or three powers, but of all the leading powers.

One may relegate the following to instances of such interference: 1) when interference is based on a treaty, for example, when certain States assumed a guarantee to secure the system of a particular country. Thus, the guarantee of *liberum veto* in the sejms of the Polish Republic accepted by Russia, Austria, and Prussia justified the interference of these powers in the internal affairs of Poland. In and of itself, of course, this guarantee for preservation in another State of the existing orders is a completely abnormal phenomenon. But if it is based on a treaty, it cannot be denied. 2) If an internal State coup d'état violates positive legal rights of other powers: the threat of such a violation was, for example, the declaration of [Alphonse de] Larmartine [(1790-1869)] in 1848 concerning the 1815 Vienna treaties not being binding on republican France. As is known, this caused an energetic protest of the interested governments. 3) If the interference is caused by the interference of another State (counter-interference).

[99] Compare the Protocol of the Congress in Troppau of 7(19) November 1820. F. F. Martens, Собрание трактатов и конвенций [Collection of Treaties and Conventions], IV(1), No. 122, p. 282; *Mémoires de prince de Metternich*, III, pp. 417, 441 et seq.

b) In relations of civilized people with non-civilized peoples, interference finds full application in the aforementioned three instances; but, in addition, with respect to Turkey, China, Korea, and other Asian States the interference of an educated power is legal in principle when the Christian population of those territories is subjected to barbaric persecution and massacre. In this instance the community of religious interests and considerations of love-of-fellow-men justify interference; that is, the principle of natural law which in general determined the relations of educated and uneducated peoples. In relations between civilized powers this reason, contrary to the views of Bluntschli and Phillimore, should not have application because an educated people gives to its subjects the legal provision of religious freedom.[100]

II. *Interference in external relations*. The principal occasions for such interference usually are: violation of treaties and, especially, the need to preserve political equilibrium. Here, in principle, we acknowledge the duty of non-interference in all instances when relations between concrete powers do not directly violate the interests of the international community: otherwise, interference destroys that autonomy which must necessarily appertain to every State in the domain of international relations. Therefore, interference in external relations is legal if it is undertaken for the purpose of putting to an end the clear aspiration of a particular State to establish a worldwide monarchy. A violation of treaties serves as a legal occasion for interference, once the last have the force of generally-binding international laws. It is difficult to point to other similar instances. But one must have in view that interference in external relations differs materially from interference in internal affairs. The last almost always is an infringement on the independence and national autonomy of a people, whereas the first in and of itself does not have such a character because the existing civilized States are in their mutual relations closely linked and depend on one another. Only it is in no way possible to recognize for one State or an alliance of States, in the nature of a Pentarchy, the exclusive right to interfere in the mutual relations of other powers or supervise all international relations which occur within a certain part of the continent or part of the globe.

§77. The North American United States claims to direct the foreign relations of all American States. There is an aphorism: "America belongs to the Americans". The United States long ago took the position "America belongs to the North Americans – Yankees". They prohibit Chile, after almost a two-year successful war against Peru and Bolivia, to join to itself some part of Peruvian territory. In November 1881 they declared to the

[100] Bluntschli, note 7 above, §478; Phillimore, note 3 above, I, §409 et seq.

Government of Chile that "contrary to the laws that should prevail in relations between educated peoples, there is set as a *conditio sine qua non* of peace the accession of possessions to Chile which indisputably belonged to Peru".

Relying on its fictitious right of dominance in America, the Washington Government protested the slightest attempt of the interference of Europe in the affairs of American States. It is well-known that the Mexican expedition of Napoleon III in 1866 ended in catastrophe, *inter alia*, thanks to the Government of the United States insisting on the removal of French forces from Mexico. But the Washington Government went even further and recently does not recognize for European States even the right to enter into agreements between themselves on those arteries of world trade and international relations which are in America and are of special importance for powers having possessions or colonies in America. The former Washington Secretary of State, [James Gillespie] Blaine [(1830-1893)] in his Circular (October 1881) and dispatch to the American envoy in London (19 November 1881) struggled to prove that the Isthmus of Panama, in particular the canal to be cut through it, must be under the exclusive control of the United States, even contrary to the treaty concluded on this subject-matter between England and the United States in 1850 (the so-called Clayton-Bulwer treaty).[101]

Finally, in a session of 7 January 1889, the Washington [United States] Senate decreed to invite the President to declare to all European governments that any participation by them in building the canal through an Isthmus of Central America would be deemed on the part of the United States as harmful to the interests and prosperity of that State. Most recently, in 1895, the Washington Government, referring to the Monroe Doctrine, interfered in a dispute between England and Venezuela relating to their mutual frontier possessions in Guinea. President [Stephen Grover] Cleveland [(1837-1908)] considered it possible to establish a demarcation commission from citizens of the United States to demarcate the English and Venezuelan possessions without a request from England. Ultimately, it happened that in February 1897 an agreement between Venezuela and England, with the participation of the United States, transferred this confused dispute for the resolution of an arbitration tribunal.

We shall return to this question in the Special Part of our system. Here we touch only upon the principled aspect of those views which the Washington Government pursued in its relations towards the European States in America.

[101] Phillimore, note 3 above, I, pp. 244-251.

European international law, which the North American States formally recognized as binding upon itself, absolutely did not permit any one people to exclusively dominate within a certain continent. In particular, the Washington Government could not exclude from America those European powers which possess territories there or have colonies and which therefore must be considered to be part of the American States. Even less admissible were claims of the States from the standpoint of the international community. The last did not create for one American State any special privileged position with respect to other States. Finally, these claims found no explanation even in the Monroe Doctrine.

The so-called doctrine on non-interference formulated by the President of the United States, [James] Monroe [(1758-1831)], in his message to the Congress of the United States of 2 December 1823, underlay all subsequent protests of the Washington Government against the interference of European powers in the affairs of America.

Of what does this noteworthy doctrine consist? The Message by Monroe may be expressed in the following three main propositions: 1) the European powers have no right to interfere in the internal affairs of the American States as the Pentarchy interfered, for example, in the affairs of Naples or Spain; 2) the Message did not determine precisely what the counteraction of the United States to such interference would consist of, but merely stated that the last would be considered a threat and danger to the States; finally, 3) colonization in America was declared to be inadmissible on the grounds that the entire American continent was already under the authority of civilized governments.

It is sufficient only to read these three propositions in order to see the complete impossibility of avoiding the conclusion that the United States had the right of supervision over the external relations of all American States. It must be noted, moreover, that the "Monroe Doctrine" was merely the opinion of the head of the executive branch in the United States in 1823 and, although it never received the force of law, all the same in recent times directs the policy of this State. However, it cannot have the binding force of an international law for European civilized States.[102]

§78. 4. *Right to respect and honor*. A State as an international person should enjoy the same right to honor and moral dignity as a moral human being. Any infringement on this honor gives the right to demand satisfaction.

[102] Wheaton, note 1 above, p. 98 et seq; Lawrence, note 8 above, II, p. 310 et seq. See in particular Maurice Delarnë Caron de Beaumarchis, *La doctrine de Monroë* (Paris, 1898). Compare F. F. Martens, «Американские впечатления» [American Impressions], Вестник Европы [Herald of Europe] (November 1902).

A State which is not in a position to protect its own honor loses the right to respect and, moreover, to its own independence, which always coincide.[103]

There arise from the right to respect and honor of a State:

1) The necessity to respect the symbols of the national honor of a State, such as: flag, arms, title. An insult of these marks is an insult of the State.

To the desecration of State honor are relegated: the use of another's title or arms: it always is caused by hostile relations between States. Thus, the king of France looked upon the English with enmity during the Hundred Years War and for a lengthy period after titled himself the "kings of France". Mary Stuart [Queen of Scots (1542-1587)] borrowed the Arms of the Queen of England and paid for this with her head. Insult of the flag was always considered to be one of the grave crimes against the honor of the State.

When in 1784 an Austrian vessel wishing, contrary to treaties, to enter the Schelde was shelled by a Dutch battery, [Emperor] Joseph II [(1741-1790)] considered himself to be insulted and demanded satisfaction from the Dutch States. The desecration of the Russian flag in Ancon by the Austrians in 1799 led to a complete rupture between Russia and Austria. The Chinese Government had to give satisfaction to England, whose flag was subjected to shelling by Chinese on the River Peiho (1860).[104]

2) States demand respect also for persons who represent them in international relations. An insult of monarchs or diplomatic agents may cause a war.

Any action in general directed against the honor of another State or expression of contempt is a violation of the basic right of a State to respect and honor.

On the other hand, the honor ascribed to each State does not allow the commission of dishonorable actions with respect to other States. States in no event should protect the contraband trade of their subjects, forge credit notes or coins, incite subjects of another State against the legal government, and so on.

§79. 5. *Right of international communications*. This right arises from the very essence of international interaction and underlies international law; in the absence of international relations, it is evident there would be no legal norms which apply to them.

103 Phillimore, note 3 above, II, p. 41 et seq; Heffter, note 6 above, §32.

104 See F. F. Martens, Собрание трактатов и конвенций [Collection of Treaties and Conventions], II, p. 372. D. A. Miliutin, История войны России с Францией в царстовование императора Павла I в 1799 году [History of the War between Russia and France in the Reign of Emperor Paul I in 1799] (Spb., 1852-53), II, p. 447 et seq.

The right of international communications has significantly lost its previous practical importance, at least with respect to civilized States. One cannot suggest that some contemporary educated State wished to isolate itself from other peoples and sought to cease any relations with them. On the contrary, they all find it necessary to take advantage of their right: they allow foreigners to enter their territory, support trade and other international turnover of their subjects, conclude treaties for this purpose, and so on.

One cannot, however, agree with all the conclusions that contemporary scholars draw from the right of international communications. Heffter, for example, asserted[105] that no power may refuse to permit the subjects of a friendly State to its territory, once their identity has been verified. It seems to us that the duty for a State to accept foreigners under all circumstances does not arise from the right of international communications. The international community leaves to each government the freedom to determine those conditions (passports, necessity of legitimation, and so on) in compliance with which international communications may occur within its territory. These conditions may be convenient or inconvenient for foreigners, but they are legal as an expression of territorial power and not contrary to the right of international communications. Therefore, in principle, a State has the right to expel any foreigner who does not subject himself to the conditions laid down for the sojourn thereof by local laws.

Heffter cites other examples of the illegal limitation of international communication, *inter alia*, an attempt of a people to starve another people by terminating intercourse with them: it is unlikely such instances are possible at present.

More important in practice is the question of the right of international communications of educated States with uncivilized or semi-wild peoples. It is asked whether educated powers have the right by force to oblige an uncivilized State to renounce its isolation and open its territories and harbors to communications with foreigners? To this question one must answer negatively: there exists no mutuality between educated and barbaric peoples, there is no international community, and consequently cannot be mutual rights and duties relating to international communications. Natural law, binding in their relations, excludes any violence not caused by the illegal behavior of the barbarians.[106]

6. *Right of coercion.* The right to protect by all legal means its rights and interests with respect both to other States and the subjects thereof inheres in every State as an international person. The right of coercion is immanent to

[105] Heffter, note 6 above, p. 76.

[106] Calvo, note 8 above, I, p. 450 et seq.

all actions and measures of States in their mutual relations. It is latent during peacetime, when the legal interests and rights of a State are respected. It enters into operation from the moment a serious international conflict arises and exceptionally dominates during time of war.

VII. Sovereigns as Subjects of Rights in International Relations

§80. Many authoritative writers in the science of international law expressed the view that sovereigns and presidents of republics are international persons and, just as States, should be considered to be subjects of international law.[107] This view is unfounded, for international relations are exclusively relations established under the protection and responsibility of States, and therefore the law which determines them has autonomous peoples as its sole subjects. But the sovereignty of States is expressed in the person of monarchs: the sovereign is the first representative of his people in foreign relations and in this capacity enjoys a certain international status which must be acknowledged.

The rights belonging to monarchs in foreign relations are rather significant. Many of them, as we shall see below, are at odds with the territorial authority of the State within which a foreign monarch is situated. Moreover, various honors and ceremonial rights appertain to monarchs.

On the basis of custom, sovereigns reigning in different States are deemed to be members of a single "family". According to this fiction, they maintain kinship relations in form. They inform one another about ascension to the throne, appoint special plenipotentiaries to be present at coronations and other ceremonies in honor of a sovereign, and notify one another about all joyous and grievous events in their family life. They call one another "brothers" in correspondence.[108] Finally, as members of a single "family", monarchs recognize mutually those titles of honor and titles which have been conferred on them by the laws of their States.

Presidents of republics have a different international status in comparison with sovereigns. To be sure, all States, whatever form of government they have, are equal in international relations, and from this point of view the presidents of republics, as representatives of their States, should enjoy the

[107] Phillimore, note 3 above, II, p. 127; Heffter, note 6 above, §48; Bluntschli, note 7 above, §125 et seq; G. F. Martens, note 16 above, §164 et seq.

[108] Compare the exceedingly interesting correspondence between Catherine II and Joseph II published as Alfred Ritter von Arneth [ed.], *Joseph II und Katharina von Russland. Ihr Briefwechsel* (Vienna, 1869).

same international rights as monarchs. Certain jurists resolve the question in this sense. Such a theoretically justified equality, however, is not fully implemented in practice, and it must be said on a completely lawful legal ground. The fact is that presidents on the basis of the structure of republican States are in essence only the representatives of executive authority, and not the sovereign power, which is concentrated in the people. As persons elected to a presidential post, they in international relations above all have the character of private individuals and only on the basis of and within the limits of a legal power are persons representing their people. That is why they are not numbered among members of the "family" of sovereigns and do not enjoy all honorary rights belonging to sovereigns.

As regards other international rights recognized for monarchs, they extend to presidents of republics insofar as these persons have been empowered to be representatives of their States in international relations. The right of representation and exterritoriality are relegated to such rights.

§81. a) *The right of representation* (*jus repraesentationis omnimodae*). The right of representation of sovereigns is based on the assumption that the supreme power of the State is concentrated in the person of the sovereign. Understandably, in every concrete instance when this right is applied, there must be *de facto* and *de jure* grounds justifying the said assumption. If a particular sovereign does not possess sovereign rights or is deprived of the throne, he may not claim to special privileges which are combined with the international status of a reigning sovereign: such a sovereign will not be the representative of his people, and his will is not the will of the State.

At present, monarchs reigning in constitutional States may not speak of themselves as Louis XIV did: "*L'état c'est moi*". On the basis of constitutions of various western European States a king is merely the "head of executive power". In this capacity he acts also in international relations. All sovereigns reigning in representative monarchies have been limited in their international acts by the formality of a counter-signature of responsible ministers, the consent of chambers to international treaties concluded, the independence of courts, and so on. The actions of sovereigns violating the conditions and forms prescribed by law will obviously be an excess of power and may not be binding on the State.

Thus, every monarch has as much a right of international representation as the laws of his country recognize for him; the internal legislation of each State determines the grounds and limits of this right.[109]

[109] Johann Ludwig Klüber, *Droit des gens moderne de l'Europe* (1874), §49; Heffter, note 6 above, §53-54; Wheaton, note 1 above, §95; Phillimore, note 3 above, II, §101; Hall, note

Likewise, does internal legislation determine who should at a particular time be considered to be the sovereign in the country and its representative? It is not the business of foreign governments to resolve this question. Whatever feelings they have for the reigning monarch or particular form of government, they must recognize and respect the legal representative of the people in the person of the head of the other State. Refusal of such recognition is an insult of the State.

In the event of an internecine war and usurpation the difficulty may arise of whom to recognize as the representative of the State – the head of the rebelling party, or usurper, or the previous legitimate government? According to the principle of non-interference, foreign States are obliged to refrain from any participation in the internecine strife of another people and not to render assistance to any of the belligerent parties. They must await the outcome: the final triumph of a certain party gives to it the disposition of sovereign authority in the State, and then the question resolves itself as to who will be the representative thereof in international relations. Both in this event and when seizing the throne, no foreign power is deemed to be the judge as to who is right, the legal or illegal accession of the sovereign to the throne – this is a matter for the people where the revolution occurred. For international relations only the existence of the State and its *de facto* representation are important. Therefore, who actually possesses power over the people is the sole representative thereof in international relations. Such possession of power assumes that the particular government enjoys recognition by its own people.

How does one determine whether such recognition exists? It may be *de facto*, namely when a people unquestionably is subject to the power of a particular person either formally, when the people (as, for example, in France in 1852) expresses consent by universal suffrage (*suffrage universel*). And in fact, in another instance when the power of a person is undoubtedly real power, and is recognized as such in the domain of international relations.

The history of European States is replete is examples which confirm the theoretical principles mentioned. During the seventeenth century in Russia, the tsars, such as Mikhail Fedorovich in 1613, informed European States of the ascension to the throne and requested they be recognized as sovereigns. Such notifications during the eighteenth century on the part of reigning Russian sovereigns became the general rule. Elizaveta Petrovna, having ascended to the Imperial throne (1741), immediately declared this to European cabinets and insisted not only on recognition of this fact, but also of the title Empress of All the Russias and all related rights of honor. During

59 above, p. 137 et seq.

the reign of Henry VII [(1457-1509)] in England, an Act of Parliament was issued (1494) which provided that the King of England must be considered to be actually King no matter how he took the throne, whether by way of succession or by election, and the principle was always applied as a rule by the English people.[110] The Protector [Oliver] Cromwell, Charles II Stuart, and William III of Orange were identically the representatives of England with full legal capacity and full dispositive legal capacity. In France Napoleon I replied to the sovereigns who did not wish to recognize him as the sovereign head of the French people that he needed recognition as much as the sun needs recognition. Ludwig-Philip and Napoleon III, who actually possessed sovereign power and were recognized by the French people, combined in their hands the right of international representation of France, which was respected by other States. But when the "government of national defence", which after 4 September 1870 actually was at the head of the French, entered into negotiations with Prince Bismarck on the peace conditions, the German Chancellor in a dispatch of 14 January 1871 demanded that this government receive formal recognition on the part of representatives of the French people who had gathered in the National Assembly.[111] The National Assembly also had to confirm the preliminary Frankfurt peace treaty.

These facts show that under certain circumstances one must be convinced and have a guarantee that a government acting in the name of the people is actually a people's government and may bind its State by international treaties. Finally, Victor Emmanuel [II (1820-1878)] in Italy was recognized as King of the Italians as soon as order was established in that country.[112]

If legislation and the order existing in a country both determine who should be recognized to be its representative, it follows that a sovereign who is deprived of or who has renounced the throne cannot have the right of representation. Treaties concluded by such a sovereign have no binding force for the people.

Therefore, the treaties concluded by Louis XIV with James II – who had been removed from the English throne – could not bind the government

[110] Phillimore, note 3 above, II, p. 16 et seq.

[111] See *Staatsarchiv*, XX (1871), no. 4283. By a Circular Note of 26 August 1874 Prince Bismarck proposed to the European powers that the Government of Marshall [Francisco] Serrano [Dominguez Cuenca y Pérez de Vargas, 1st Duke of la Torre (1810-1885)] in Spain be recognized. Many powers accepted this proposal, but Russia disagreed, having doubts as to the stability of this Government. This doubt was soon justified.

[112] Russia recognized the Italian Kingdom and Victor Emmanuel as King of a unified Italy much later than others. This was in 1862. See the Circular Note of Prince Gorchakov of 6 August 1862, *Annuaire diplomatique de l'Empire de Russie* (1863), p. 127.

of William III, who took the throne left by James. It also is evident that [Charles Philippe] Count of Artois [(1757-1836)], bustling about Europe to arrange a coalition against the French Republic in order to restore the Bourbons, could not assume obligations in the name of France, whose republican government had not empowered him for this mission. Exactly the same for Napoleon III, who did not have the right to carry on negotiations in the name of France after the Sedan debacle, when he was removed to Germany as a prisoner of war and dethroned by a revolutionary party on 4 September 1870. Peace negotiations were conducted with him: they were not successful, but if a peace treaty had been signed by the prisoner-ex emperor or by the Empress Eugénie [de Montijo (1826-1920)], it would not have been binding on France, which after 4 September was governed by and fought against the German army through the Léon Gambetta [(1838-1882)] government alone.

Finally, on the same basis, the King of the Netherlands could not after 1831, when Belgium formally separated from Holland, bind the Belgians by its treaties.

Every sovereign actually possessing power and recognized by his people enjoys by virtue of the right of representation all honors and other rights and privileges which are recognized in general for the supreme head of a people. The failure to recognize these rights, for example, titles, belonging thereto according to the laws of his State or failure to name him in correspondence by the usual name "brother" is an insult of the people which he governs.

Napoleon III could not forgive Emperor Nicholas I for not calling him, in his letter, "brother" (*Sire et bon frére*), but "good friend" (*Sire et bon ami*),and this offense was in reality one of the reasons which caused the Crimean War that led to the 1856 Treaty of Paris.[113]

§82. b) *Right of extraterritoriality* (*droit d'exterritorialité*). On the basis of international custom and judicial practice, the right of extraterritoriality is recognized for sovereigns, by virtue of which they are not subject, while on another's territory, to the operation of local laws and authorities. The fiction was created in explanation of this law that sovereigns while in another State continue to remain on their own territory. This fiction must be understood as a figurative expression of an exceptional status which sovereigns enjoy abroad: it should by no means by taken as the basis of the right of extraterritoriality because the interests of international relations are solely such.

[113] [Baron Aleksandr Genrikhovich Jomini], *Étude diplomatique sur la guerre de Crimée (1852 à 1856)* (Paris, 1874), I, p. 97.

The right of extraterritoriality belongs to a sovereign under the following conditions: 1) if he is recognized as a sovereign on the part of the territorial authorities; 2) unless he is prohibited from entering foreign territory; 3) unless the territorial authority is at war; 4) if the sovereign wishes to take advantage of this right: he may renounce it, traveling or staying abroad incognito, as a private individual.

Peter the Great behaved in this way, making his first journey in western Europe under the name of the nobleman, Peter Mikhailov.

But a sovereign who wished to remain incognito does not lose the right to declare his title at any time and, having rejected incognito, enjoys all the privileges conferred on a sovereign. Thus, the King of Holland, who resided in Vevey (Switzerland) as a private individual, was sentenced in one instance to pay a fine but not subjected to levy after he officially declared his title.

5) No sovereign enjoys the right of extraterritoriality in that State where he is in service.

There arise from the right of extraterritoriality: 1) the sovereign is not subject to the jurisdiction of local police authorities; 2) exemption from the payment of duties and taxes; and 3) is not within the criminal and civil jurisdiction of local courts.[114]

The basis of these privileges is the rule: *par in parem non habet potestatem*; but, as we now shall see, they are far from having an absolute character.

1) The extent of the sovereign not being subject to police regulations of the territorial authority depends on the requirements of public security. Therefore, all regulations of the local police are binding on him if the failure to execute them would threaten this security.

2) As for taxes and duties, the sovereign is exempted only from those which have a more or less personal character and may conflict with the external dignity of the Head of State. All other duties and charges, for example, postal and telegraph, on immoveable property, for the conclusion of contracts of purchase-sale, and others are paid by sovereigns equally with private individuals.

3) As for monarchs not being within criminal jurisdiction, there are no disagreements among the representatives of science or judicial practice:

[114] Compare G. F. Martens, note 16 above, II, p. 11 et seq; C. van Bynkershoek, *Traité du juge compétent des ambassadeurs tant pour le civil, que pour le criminel*, transl. Jean Barbeyrac (The Hague, 1723), chap. III, p. 17 et seq; Phillimore, note 3 above, II, p. 129 et seq; Bluntschli, note 7 above, §137; Rivier, note 22 above, I, p. 417 et seq.

this is recognized by all.[115] But at present this does not have great practical significance. In fact, it is difficult to imagine that a sovereign would commit a criminal offense on a foreign territory. Rather he might be guilty of a political crime. In this event diplomatic negotiations are initiated between the interested States, and if the matter is not settled by this means, a war may commence; but a crime will not be the subject-matter of a criminal examination. The trial and punishment of Conrad [III, King of the Holy Roman Empire (1093/94-1152)] and Mary Queen of Scots were cases of political revenge.

Nonetheless, many jurists cited as legitimate grounds for commencing a criminal prosecution against a foreign monarch the criminal behavior thereof in another State. If a sovereign conducts himself as a "robber", said Bynkershoek, one must behave towards him as an enemy.[116]

4) More controversial is the limits of civil jurisdiction over monarchs. The old writers defended the principle that the sovereign, by virtue of his right of extraterritoriality, cannot be a defendant or plaintiff in foreign courts: but certain judicial decisions established a gap in this principle, especially in recent times. On the basis of these decisions, a dual character is distinguished in the person of the sovereign: the sovereign and a private individual. As sovereign, a foreign sovereign is exempt from civil jurisdiction; as a private individual – he is not exempt; for example, when the suit arises from possession of immoveable property, the conclusion of trade transactions, and so on.[117]

Usually, civil courts have not recognized their competence to consider suits which were brought against a foreign sovereign as the supreme Head of State.

In 1851 a suit was brought against the Queen of Portugal in the Lord Mayor's Court "as the reigning sovereign and sovereign head of the Portuguese people". The Lord Mayor's Court declared itself to be not competent to adjudge that the plaintiff should pay court costs. That same

[115] Bynkershoek, note 114 above, p. 24 et seq; Phillimore, note 3 above, II, p. 131 et seq; Wheaton, note 1 above, §95; Heffter, note 6 above, §42; Bluntschli, note 7 above, §141; Hall, note 59 above, §49.

[116] Bynkershoek, note 114 above, chap. XVIII: "Si un prince agissant en vrai brigand, ne respecte ni la vie, ni les biens, ni l'honneur de tous ceux qu'il lui prend fantaisie d'insulter, s'il porte partout l'horreur et l'effroi … il est permis certainement de se saisir de sa personne et peut-être, même de le faire mourir".

[117] François Laurent, *Droit civil international* (Brussels, 1880-1881), III, p. 44 et seq; Phillimore, note 3 above, II, p. 134 et seq; Hall, note 59 above, p. 139; Lawrence, note 8 above, III, p. 420 et seq; Bluntschli, note 7 above, §139-140; Ludwig von Bar, in *Journal du droit international privé* (1885), p. 645 et seq.

court on the same grounds refuse to consider a suit brought against the Spanish Queen to pay on a cheque of the Spanish State treasury. But a suit of the Duke of Braunschweig against the King of Hanover in 1844 was accepted by the court because it was brought against the King of Hanover in his capacity as the Duke of Cumberland and, consequently, a subject of Queen Victoria.[118]

French judicial practice also adheres to the aforementioned distinctions. In 1847 a Seine court rejected a suit of one Solon, who demanded from the Egyptian Viceroy, Mehemet-Ali, the sum of 100,000 francs of losses incurred by Solon for failure of the defendant to perform a contract concluded by him; the reason for the rejection was the lack of competence of French courts to decide suits filed against a foreign government.[119] Exactly the same in 1872 when a Paris appellate court deemed itself to lack competence to award the sum of 51,479 Francs to a diamond merchant, Lemaitre, to be recovered from the Emperor of Austria, Franz Joseph, for an Order commissioned by the Emperor Maximilian of Mexico on the grounds that such a commission was a governmental act, into the consideration of which the French court did not have the right to enter.[120] In 1870 on the same grounds a Parisian court rejected a suit of Massé, a French subject, who demanded the sum of 500,000 francs from the Emperor of All the Russias for losses incurred by the plaintiff from the closure of a trading establishment in Petersburg enforced by the local police.[121]

Deserving of attention from Belgian judicial practice is the arrest imposed by judgment of a court (1876) on a Turkish cannon in Antwerp harbor at the request of an instigator who had a suit against the Turkish Government and wished to secure it. The Turkish Embassy in Brussels protested this measure and turned to a Munich professor, [Franz Joachim Wilhelm Philipp von] Holtzendorff [(1829-1889)], requesting an opinion. The last demonstrated that the Belgian courts could not judge the Turkish Government, and therefore the prohibition placed on the cannon was illegal, and it was removed.[122] An English appellate court in 1892 considered itself to lack competence in a suit filed by Mighell, an Englishman, against the Sultan Iogorsky on the grounds that a foreign monarch is always not within

118 Phillimore, note 3 above, II, p. 136.

119 Ibid., II, pp. 138, 608 et seq.

120 *Revue de droit international*, IV, p. 656; V, p. 245 et seq.

121 Calvo, note 8 above, I, p. 568.

122 *Holtzendorff's Jahrbuch des deutschen Reiches* (1877), I, p. 179 et seq.

the jurisdiction of an English court, not excluding instances when he is traveling as a private individual.

On the other hand, one may cite many instances when a foreign court deemed itself competent to consider suits brought against a foreign monarch or government. These are instances when the public character of the defendant did not come to the forefront, when the sovereign or government acted in the interest of or in the capacity of private individuals.

Thus, in 1870 a Paris court considered itself to have competence to award to the spouses Casalini a certain amount which they recovered from the Queen of Spain and her husband. In 1872 the Seine court accepted a suit filed against the Queen of Spain by the jewelers Mellerio for the payment of diamonds delivered to the defendant. In this case it was proved that the Queen ordered the jewels personally for herself and her daughter, with no relation to the Spanish crown, and that at the time the Queen no longer occupied the Spanish throne. On this basis, the court ordered the defendant to pay, and the judgment was affirmed by a Paris court. Likewise, the Seine court, by a decision of 3 March 1875, rejected a suit by the Turkish Government filed on the basis of Article 2078 of the Code Civil against creditors of Turkey for the sale of a pledge given by it.[123]

According to established practice, a court recognizes itself to be competent when the sovereign himself brings suit against a private individual. The House of Lords spoke in this sense in 1833 on the occasion of a suit filed by the King of Spain.[124]

The decisions cited show that if courts give priority to the public character of a sovereign or government against which suits are brought, they are not inclined to recognize their absolute lack of civil jurisdiction. It is difficult to state in each individual instance whether the sovereign acted as a private individual or as the representative of sovereign power, but to ascertain this difference, as practice shows, is nonetheless possible.

In any event, one cannot agree with the view that the principle of no civil jurisdiction over monarchs is accepted "unanimously" by authorities on international law.[125] An extensive interpretation of this principle is, in particular, contrary to the constitutional laws of States because on the basis thereof a sovereign is not in all his actions and not under all conditions the sovereign representative of the people.

123 *Revue de droit international*, V (1873), p. 246; Laurent, note 117 above, III, p. 74; Lawrence, note 8 above, p. 428; *Annuaire de l'Institut de droit international* (1877), p. 229.

124 Phillimore, note 3 above, II, p. 142; Calvo, note 8 above, I, p. 541.

125 *Holtzendorff's Jahrbuch*, note 122 above, p. 181.

The majority of contemporary jurists allow certain limitations on the principle of sovereigns not being subject to civil jurisdiction. First, no one denies that a sovereign who possessed an immoveable in a foreign State is subject, on the principle of *lex rei sitae*, to a local court in all cases concerning this ownership. But if this immoveable was acquired, with the authorization of the territorial authority, by a foreign government for some State need and is operated in view of this need, the jurisdiction of the local court will be an exception, and not the general rule. Second, if a sovereign serves in a foreign State or engages there in trade or crafts, he is subject on the general grounds to the jurisdiction of the local court. Finally, third, jurisdiction of local courts is allowed, as said above, when suits are brought by foreign governments themselves.[126]

For example, in 1868 the Seine court accepted a suit filed by the Washington Government against the French supplier, Arman, and decided it not in favor of the plaintiff: the court deemed the "United States and President Johnson" to have unfoundedly filed the suit and awarded court costs against them.[127]

The fact that local courts consider themselves to be competent in the event suits are brought by foreign sovereigns or governments themselves, requires the question to be put: if jurisdiction is recognized in this instance, why is it not recognized when a private individual brings suit against foreign monarchs? There are simply no convincing legal arguments against such recognition in many instances. Why, for example, did a Brussels court refuse to consider a suit brought against the Austrian Emperor as trustee of the Princes von Thurn and Taxis? The sovereign, just as any private individual, should be subject to civil jurisdiction for the actions of persons under his trusteeship. If the king is merely the "head of executive power", his actions undertaken outside this role, of course, may be within the jurisdiction of civil courts. Not removed from civil jurisdiction, of course, are all possible legal transactions which the sovereign concludes as the representative of the treasury.[128]

[126] Compare the Rules prepared by the Institute of International Law relating to jurisdiction over suits against foreign States and sovereigns in *Tableau générale de l'Institut de droit international*, p. 116 et seq.

[127] Lawrence, note 8 above, II, p. 427; also compare John Westlake, *Private International Law* (London, 1880), §182.

[128] See in particular Laurent, note 117 above, III, pp. 60, 96, et seq; Jean Jacques Gaspard Foelix, *Traité du droit international privé: ou, du conflit des lois de différentes nations en matière de droit privé*, ed. Charles Demangeat (4th ed.; Paris, 1866), I, p. 419 et seq; Heffter, note 6 above, §118.

The Ruling Senate, by decision of 7 April 1893, re: Agarkov, who brought suit against the Italian Government in the person of its Ministry of War for 10,000 rubles for illegally taking possession of his lands in the Tauride Governate and the arrangement thereon of a cemetery for the remains of Sardinian soldiers who died during the Crimean War, deemed the Italian Government to be within the jurisdiction of Russian courts in this case on the grounds that all suits relating to land ownership are subject to the territorial court.

Thus, from a legal point of view, the right of civil jurisdiction over monarchs should be construed in a limited sense. But practical grounds exist which justify its extensive application: 1) decisions of courts decreed against sovereigns are difficult to enforce; and 2) may even generate unfavorable consequences for the territorial authority. These practical considerations do not, of course, eliminate the need for properly raising the legal question.

If reigning sovereigns are not within the jurisdiction of civil courts only as sovereigns, then sovereigns deprived of the throne obviously do not have any right to this privilege: it may be recognized for sovereigns only as a courtesy (*courtoisie*) or favor of the territorial authority to particular persons, but not by right.

VIII. International Status of Members of Family and Suite of Sovereign

§83. Members of reigning houses and persons belonging to the suite of a sovereign do not enjoy, while on foreign territory, either the right of extraterritoriality or, in particular, exclusion from court jurisdiction, although certain writers also assert that they should enjoy these to the same extent as the sovereign. They defend these rights in particular for the spouse of the reigning sovereign and the heir to the throne.[129] But none of these persons can be considered either to be the supreme Head of State or even the representative of executive power, and there are no decisive grounds to recognize the requested rights. Whereas in practice such recognition occurs, this serves only as a mark of special friendship to the foreign State or to the Head thereof, and is not a duty arising from principles of international law. The same is so of recognition of various kinds of honorary titles and rights belonging to family members of sovereigns; this is a matter of mutual friendly relations between States and a courtesy which is not subject to determination by the science of international law.

[129] Heffter, note 6 above, §55; Bluntschi, note 7 above, §145 et seq.

Moreover, persons who comprise the suite of a sovereign may not claim extraterritoriality. But in theory and practice doubt arose as to what relation these persons should have to their sovereign while on foreign territory? Does the right of extraterritoriality impart to the sovereign any rights over persons accompanying him?

Phillimore says that for sovereigns traveling in a foreign country "a certain amount of jurisdiction" over members of their suite should be recognized.[130] Having regard to the fact that persons constituting the suite of a sovereign do not enjoy the right of extraterritoriality and that the extraterritoriality of the sovereigns themselves cannot be understood in the sense that they exercise on foreign territory all rights which they have in their own country, one cannot concur that sovereigns may have the right to try members of the suite.

History, to be sure, knows examples of traveling monarchs conferring this right on themselves. Queen Christina [(1626-1689)] of Sweden, while in France during 1657, ordered that her Chamberlain, [Marchese Giovanni Rinaldo] Monaldeschi [1626-1657] be executed.[131] This incident gave occasion for jurists to express their reflections as to whether Christina had the right while in France to judge and punish a person belonging to her suite. Some writers justified the behavior of the Queen by her extraterritoriality, overlooking that Christina back in 1654 had abdicated and therefore in 1657 was no longer a reigning queen having the right to extraterritoriality. Even if one agrees with Phillimore that extraterritoriality gives a right of jurisdiction to a reigning sovereign – which, as we have seen, is not true – then in this case common sense and legal logic indicate that a sovereign may not have on foreign territory more rights than on his own. From this point of view, no punishment of a criminal character arbitrarily imposed by a sovereign on members of his suite would be tolerated by territorial authority because in all States it must be a consequence only of the judgment of a legal trial. But this is not enough. If even a foreign monarch might, according to the laws of his own State, arbitrarily punish his subjects, he is not permitted to exercise this right in another civilized State because none of them permits foreign jurisdiction within their limits. That is why neither the Persian Shah nor the Turkish Sultan, while traveling in Europe, could display here their absolute rights over members of their suite.[132]

[130] Phillimore, note 3 above, II, p. 131.

[131] Charles de Martens, *Nouvelles causes célèbres du droit des gens* (Brussels, 1843), II, Appendix No. IV.

[132] Laurent, note 117 above, §117; G. F. Martens, note 16 above, II, §172; Klüber, note 109 above, §49; Vattel, note 62 above, liv. IV, chap. IX, p. 124. For a different view, see

IX. Social Classes as Subjects of Rights in Domain of International Communication

§84. When setting out the doctrine on international communication (Chapter I), we pointed out the importance that various social groups in States have for international relations, and likewise the tasks that lie in relation to them on the States connected by international communication. The last require that States mutually respect those rights which belong to social classes on the basis of the laws of the place of their origin. Thus, social groups, partnerships, and companies deemed to be legally existing in their own States operate in the domain of international relations as subjects of certain rights which they exercise everywhere that only European international law is recognized. These rights may be protected by treaties, but international communication and international law give the highest sanction to them.

The rights undoubtedly belonging to societies in international relations do not, however, make these societies subjects of international law. Every society is a subject only of those rights which have been recognized by State law. The last determines the legality of the existence of the particular social group: international law – its law and dispositive legal capacity in international relations. International law may not recognize that a particular society exists unless this was recognized by State law, or accept it as an autonomous political organism unless it is such according to principles of State law.

Thus, a society combining identical religious professions of faith is not a State and therefore may not claim international independence identical with a State or recognition of itself as a subject of international law. From this standpoint, the claims of the Roman curia to sovereignty in the domain of international relations declared in the name of the supremacy of the Pope over the Roman Catholic Church are completely unfounded because the last has in various States a legal status of merely a society recognized by local law. On this basis the Concordats; that is, contracts which the Roman curia concludes with governments are not, in essence, international treaties, but agreements between a State as a subject of international law and the representative of a society for which the State recognizes certain rights.

A society unified by bonds of identical national or tribal origin also may not be a subject of international law. As a natural society, a nation must be under the protection of a State law and State authority: to recognize it as

Bluntschli, note 7 above, §147.

having autonomous international rights would be to infringe on the rights of the State. The same should be said about all other social unions.

The following basic rights belong in international relations to each legal society: 1) the right to recognition on the part of all civilized States of the legality of its existence; 2) the right to day-to-day pursuit of its legal purposes under conditions and within limits laid down by the territorial authority; and 3) the right to defense of its legal rights before courts of a foreign State. The rights of a territorial government with respect to foreign societies are determined by the laws of each State; they are similar to a great extent with rights in respect of foreigners (see below), but should be interpreted even more broadly.

X. Private Individuals as Subjects of Rights in Domain of International Communication

§85. Similar to societies, private individuals are not subjects of international law but have certain rights in the domain of international relations which derive from: 1) the human person in and of itself; 2) from the status of these persons as the subjects of a State.

A. Human Rights in International Relations

All contemporary civilized States are agreed that man is a person, that is, a subject of certain inalienable rights which should be respected in their mutual relations. Therefore, every person, irrespective of subject affiliation or nationality, finds protection of his person and property throughout the entire spatial operation of international law. The ultimate purpose of the State and the purpose of international relations is the protection of the person.

Respect for the individual is, without doubt, that attribute which distinguishes with special clarity contemporary States from ancient ones. Whereas in Antiquity slavery was an institution *juris gentium* – enjoying the protection of the law and court of all peoples, international law proclaims as an inalienable truth that no person may be in the ownership of another, that slavery should not exist. The rule "*L'air fait libre*" received the force of law in all contemporary educated States.

In the domain of international relations Russia adhered to this principle, and its enormous services to the cause of the cessation of human trafficking are undoubted. But Russian judicial instances of serfdom Russia could not explain how the entry of a foreign slave on to Russian territory populated by several tens of millions of serfs made him free. The following interesting case extracted from the Archive of the Ministry of Foreign Affairs may serve as the best illustration. In 1820 a negro, Domingo Ivanov, submitted a request to the St. Petersburg Governor-General, Count [Mikhail Andreevich] Miloradovich [(1771-1825)], in which he explained that he and two brothers were forcibly removed from Brazil by the Portuguese Consul General, Lopez, to St. Petersburg, who released him to serve, but then kept him with himself, subject him to all kinds of tortures, as a slave. Referring to an Edict of 17 August 1815, "by which all immigrants from abroad, from different nations, shall be free from slavery",[133] the negro Ivanov requested that he be recognized as free from slavery and protected against Lopez. The Portuguese envoy, as the superior of the Consul General, submitted the negro's passport and evidence that he had been purchased by Lopez in Brazil, together with other slaves. The lower [надворный] court deemed the evidence submitted by Lopez to be sufficient to confirm his right of ownership to the negro. The chamber of the civil court decided otherwise on the grounds that evidence concerning the right of ownership required by the Edict of 20 October 1783 was not submitted. Finally, the Ruling Senate confirmed the decision of the civil court, "finding that the Portuguese Consul, Lopez, took possession of the negro Domingo Ivanov after the purchase thereof supposedly in Rio Neiro; but did not submit evidence of such purchase except a translation from the passport, which mentioned three slaves sent to their destination, and that Domingo Ivanov was one of them is not explained". Thus, the negro Ivanov received freedom only because of the lack of evidence of the right of ownership by the Portuguese General Consul.

For civilized States slavery is so detestable an institution that an international campaign is being waged against it. In this respect the facts proving that contemporary peoples share solidarity in their aspiration to destroy slavery everywhere are instructive. Common international measures which have been taken by States to achieve this goal undoubtedly confirm that unconditional respect for the individual is precisely that principle by which European peoples are guided in their external relations.

The history of measures directed towards the abolition of slavery everywhere shows that three kinds of efforts were made by States to ensure human rights in international relations. First and foremost, States took common measures to prevent such trade by Europeans, which was practiced in particular in barbarian possessions and in Central Asia. Trafficking in dark-skinned people required the most persistent and systematic struggle, which had great significance for the European States themselves thanks to

133 This Edict of 17 August 1815 is not in the Полное собрание законов Российской Империи [Complete Collected Laws of the Russian Empire].

the colonial policies which dominated in the eighteenth century. Finally, in recent times trafficking in Chinese (coolies) is developing, which for the sake of the interests of civilization must, in turn, generate decisive measures to bring this to an end.

a) *Struggle against trafficking by Europeans*. We have had occasion to mention treaties which were concluded by various States with the barbarian beys and with Turkey in order to stop or, at least, paralyze, insofar as possible, the most terrible consequence of privateering in the Mediterranean Sea – the sale into slavery of mariners captured by pirates. The United States of America paid tribute to the Bey of Algiers annually to liberate seamen from the terrors threatening them. Only in the last century, thanks to England and France, was piracy and trafficking by whites, which flourished along the northern coasts of Africa, finally terminated.

To the English Government belongs the honor of energetic initiative in this matter. In 1816 it ordered [Edward Pellew,1st Viscount] Exmouth [(1757-1833)], Commander-in-Chief, Mediterranean, to deliver to the Bey of Algiers an ultimatum regarding the release immediately of all white slaves in Algiers. When this demand was not respected, Exmouth, in performance of his instructions, bombarded the coastal cities of Algiers, after which the Bey agreed to: 1) abolish slavery forever in Algiers; and 2) release to the English all Europeans and former slaves in that country. The conquest of Algiers by the French in 1830 brought an end forever to the enslavement of whites in northern Africa.[134]

Russia played the same role in the Black Sea and recently in Central Asia. The Caucasus and Asia Minor have for a long time been dens of traders who purchased slaves and then sent them to Constantinople. Insofar as possible, the Russian Government obstructed this commerce. In 1817 and 1818 serious misunderstandings arose between Russia and the Porte regarding the stopping of Turkish vessels in the Sevastopol harbor carrying slaves destined for sale in Constantinople. The Russian authorities detained the ships and cargo and declared the slaves to be free. Regarding the insistent demands of the Porte concerning remuneration to the owners of the living commodity, the Emperor Alexander I categorically declared that any slave who entered his territory received freedom.[135] But Russia had few

[134] Phillimore, note 3 above, I, p. 345. According to a Convention concluded on 2 March 1882 between England and Persia, English vessels received the right to stop vessels under the Persian flag if they were suspected of engaging in the slave trade. Captured slaves were freed, and Persian mariners trading in slaves were transferred to a Persian court.

[135] From the Archive of the Ministry of Foreign Affairs.

resources to combat this evil so long as the Caucasus had not come into Russian possession.

The Russian Government in Central Asia still is waging an unceasing campaign against the custom in that country of kidnapping people for sale into slavery. In order to deter raids made on Russian possessions by neighboring barbaric tribes populating Central Asia, Russia was forced to make periodic military expeditions to the steppe and conquer the foreigners. There are Articles in peace treaties concluded by Russia with conquered Central Asian khanates, Khiva, and Bukhara (1873) that obliged the vanquished khanates to liberate slaves and abolish slavery thereafter.[136] The recent campaign by General [Mikhail Dmitrievich] Skobelev [(1843-1882)] against the Turkmens had as its result, in addition to liberating several thousand slaves, an obligation assumed by that people not to capture Russian subjects anymore and sell them into slavery.

b) *Abolition of trade in negroes.* We do not dwell here on the most curious history of trade in dark-skinned people and the development of the extent thereof, which finally generated criminal and police measures in various States with a view to limiting and terminating it. We indicate only the most salient moments of this history.[137]

Trade in negroes began in 1443, when the Portuguese for the first time exchanged captured Moors for stronger negroes better able to work in the colonies. The English Government soon was convinced of the great advantage of this labor force. For several centuries the English used every effort to concentrate trade in negroes in their own hands. Finally, on the basis of the Treaty of Utrecht (1713) they received a monopoly on the delivery of negroes to the Spanish colonies in America. But at the end of the last century [eighteenth], this role, humiliating for England, generated the most virulent protest in English public opinion. Thanks to agitation by such noteworthy people as [Thomas] Clarkson [(1760-1846)], [William] Wilberforce [(1759-1833)], William Pitt [the Younger (1759-1806)], [George] Fox [(1624-1691)], and others, the English Government had to agree not only to the abolition of trade in negroes in their own colonies, but to exert every effort so that other powers would decide to put an end to it.

136 Article 17, Treaty with Bukhara: "To please the Sovereign Emperor of All the Russias and for the great glory of His Imperial Majesty, the most honorable Emir, Seid-Muzefar decreed: henceforth within the limits of Bukhara the shameful trade in people contrary to the laws of humanity shall cease forever". Article 17 of the peace treaty with Khiva is similar.

137 Compare Leone Levi, *The History of British Commerce: and of the Economic Progress of the British Nation, 1763-1870* (London, 1872), pp. 36, 195; Nys, note 82 above, p. 245 et seq.

Acting in accord with the wish of the English people, the London Cabinet, supported by virtue of a separate Article in the first 1814 treaty of Paris by France, insisted at the Congress of Vienna on the eight powers obliging themselves to take measures for the complete and final abolition of the evil which for so long emptied Africa, humiliated Europe, and sorrowed mankind.[138] More than that, the English plenipotentiary, Lord [Robert Stewart, Viscount] Castlereagh [(1769-1822)] proposed to eliminate slavery: 1) an obligation of the powers not to allow the carriage to themselves of colonial goods from those localities in which slavery had not been abolished by the expiry of a certain period; 2) the establishment of supervision over the African coasts and recognition of the right of inspection of ships suspected of carrying negroes; 3) establishing in Paris a "permanent committee" of representatives of the great powers for control over the execution of the measures adopted against slavery.

The meeting on this question of the plenipotentiary powers at the Congress of Vienna ended with the signature of a Declaration of 27 January (7 February) 1815. The powers solemnly declared the urgent need to rapidly cease the trade in negroes, but did not indicate the time when this should be done nor the means by which it would be accomplished.

The negotiations continuing afterwards between the powers led to the development of two completely opposite systems for struggle against this embedded evil. One, which the North American States and France defended, proceeded from the principle of the full sovereignty of every State and opposed the control of foreign governments, especially the inspection of ships suspected of carrying negroes. The other, English, system, on the contrary, viewed the termination of slavery as a matter for all the peoples; it sought that governments, for the sake of a lofty task set for themselves, abandon petty fears for their independence and, in particular, the inviolability of their merchant fleet. Convinced of the practicality of their system, the English Government made every effort to incline other powers to the conclusion of treaties which would authorize the mutual inspection of ships.

The efforts of England were crowned with success. England has concluded more than forty treaties on the basis of this system: for example, in 1822 with Spain and the Netherlands; in 1824 with Sweden; in 1826 with Portugal; in 1831 and 1833 with France; in 1841 with Austria, Prussia, and Russia. The Treaty of 1841 determined in detail those measures which should be applied for the real termination of slavery; it was renewed in

[138] F. F. Martens, Собрание трактатов и конвенций [Collection of Treaties and Conventions], III, pp. 495 et seq.

1879, when the German Empire acceded. England concluded a treaty with the United States in 1862 on this basis of this same treaty.[139]

The participation of Russia in the 1841 treaty may seem incomprehensible in view of the fact that it is difficult to imagine the possibility of Russian subjects engaging in the trade in negroes. Emperor Alexander I openly expressed himself in this sense at the Congress of Vienna: he agreed to support the humane efforts of England, but refused to assume special obligations to prosecute Russian slave traders. Emperor Nicholas I shared the same view. But in 1838 the English Minister at the Court of St. Petersburg, [John Ralph] Milbanke [(1800-1868)], informed the Ministry of Foreign Affairs that two Russian vessels had been detained in Havana with a cargo of negroes. One vessel was named "*Golubka*" or "*Golubchik*". According to an investigation rapidly done in Odessa, it turned out that the "*Golubka*" or "*Golubchik*" was a Spanish vessel purchased by an Odessa merchant, who denied that he had any notion of illegal trade on the part of the skipper. Nearly a year elapsed, and by a Note of 22 May (3 June) 1839 the English envoy reported to the Russian Government that near Barcelona an English warship stopped a brig under the Russian flag named "*Golubchik*" obviously engaged in the slave trade. The envoy rightly suggested that the "Golubchik" and the "Golubka" were the same vessel. The vessel captured by an English cruiser was convoyed to Portsmouth and placed at the disposition of Count [Nikolai Dmitrievich] Kiselev [(1802-1869)], the Russian envoy to the Court of St. James. Count Kiselev protested energetically to Lord [Henry John Temple, 3d Viscount] Palmerston [(1784-1865)] against the arrest of a Russian vessel on the high seas and the escort thereof to an English port. But Lord Palmerston took advantage of this incident to express the hope to Count Kiselev that this case might persuade His Imperial Majesty of the need to assist other powers in measures to bring an end to the slave trade.[140] This hope was fully vindicated in 1841, although the investigation of the case determined that the sale of the Spanish vessel to the Odessa merchant, who was Spanish by origin, was completely fictitious and the entire crew and

139 Wheaton, note 1 above, p. 203 note.

140 The Note of Count Kiselev to Count [Karl Robert von Reichsgraf von] Nesselrode [(1780-1862)] of 29 August (10 September) 1839. Palmerston wrote to Count Kiselev on 15 August 1839: "This case may be thought by the Emperor to afford valid reasons to induce His Imperial Majesty to concur with the other Powers of Europe in a Treaty, which will prevent the Russian flag from begin hereafter used for purposes of Slave trade". This entire matter is extracted from the Archive of the Ministry of Foreign Affairs. See F. F. Martens, Собрание трактатов и конвенций [Collection of Treaties and Conventions], XII, p. 168 et seq.

skipper of the ship were Spaniards. It only remained unclear how it received the right to fly the Russian merchant flag.

The principal conditions of the 1841 treaty and other similarly named acts were as follows: 1) cruisers sailing near African coasts were permitted to stop and inspect suspicious vessels; 2) vessels detained while carrying negroes should be sent to the port of that State whose flag they flew (or to another port, depending on the condition), and there the court should determine the punishment that followed to the slave trader; 3) the captured guilty vessel is confiscated and a certain remuneration to the cruiser is assigned from the value thereof; 4) trade in slaves is equated to maritime piracy (Articles 1411 and 1630, Statute on Punishments).

The services of England in the cessation of trade in negroes were great. In 1808 England declared this trade to be illegal within its possessions. At the suggestion of Lord [Henry Peter] Brougham [1st Baron Brougham and Vaux (1778-1868)] in 1824, the Parliament of England issued a law which deemed trading in slaves to be piracy. By 1838 England had freed 780,993 negroes in its colonies and paid plantation owners twenty million pounds sterling for them.

Slavery was abolished in the North American United States in 1865; in Brazil, in 1871; finally, on the Island of Cuba in 1877.

But despite the enormous sacrifices made by almost all States, slavery continued to exist; from the western coast of Africa, this trade moved eastward. Now cruisers often capture vessels of slave traders which carry their cargo to Egypt, Arabia, and other countries and do so more or less openly. That is why Germany, Austria, Russia, and England found it necessary in 1879 to renew the 1841 treaty, and the London Anti-Slave Trade Society agitated in favor of the execution by all powers of the Declaration of the Congress of Vienna and those conventions which it concluded to counteract the slave trade.[141] The most recent and most remarkable international act in the campaign against the slave trade is the "General Act" of the 1874 Brussels anti-slavery conference. An entire system of measures is contained therein for the final eradication of trade in negroes. These measures concerned not only maritime, but equally land, transport. The campaign against slave traders moved on to within the African continent, and the right to inspect suspicious vessels on the high seas is merely an auxiliary means of the campaign of civilized States against an evil from which Africa still suffers.

141 The history of diplomatic negotiations on the prohibition of trade in negroes and the contemporary state of this question is best set out in Ferdinand von Martitz, "Das internationale System zur Unterdrückung desafrikanischen Sklavenhandels in seinem heutigen Bestande", *Archiv für öffentliches Recht von Laband and Stoerck*, I, p. 1 et seq.

c) *Trade in coolies*. This has received considerable impetus in recent times. Chinese are called "coolies", recruited by various traders in Chinese ports and sent to America and to Pacific Ocean islands, where they must work, performing contracts signed by them, in the full sense of the word as negroes.

Recent history shows many disturbing facts relating to the recruitment and exploitation of "Chinese slaves"; but they so far have not generated sufficiently strong and common measures directed towards the termination of this new type of slavery. To be sure, in 1866 the Chinese Government itself issued a law which was to regulate the hiring of "coolies" in order to prevent frauds when they concluded contracts; but England and France saw in this completely legitimate and just measure a violation of their own trade interests secured by the contracts and opposed the application thereof.[142]

§86. At present, all educated States recognize for man, as such, irrespective of the status of subject or nationality, certain basic rights which are inextricably connected with the individual, namely:

1) *The right to existence and development of the natural person* – consequently, the right to the acquisition of the means necessary for the maintenance of life, physical labor, trade turnover, engaging in crafts or otherwise legally; in this respect, each person enjoys complete freedom within the limits decreed by a law.

2) *The right to the development of one's spiritual and intellectual abilities and forces*; consequently, the right to use all resources which a country has for the education of a person and the satisfaction of his egoistic aspirations, such as: schools, libraries, museums, and others.

The assistance which a State renders to every person in the domain of the economic activity and spiritual life thereof comprises the special task of international administration (see Special Part, Section I, Chapter II).

3) *To every person belongs the right of communication and free movement within the limits of the international union of States*. The attachment to the land consecrated by customs of the Middle Ages and laws for the *glebae adscripti* is contrary to the general order of things and to the legal and moral concepts dominant in contemporary educated States. According to the order binding States to one another, the right to resettlement (emigration) should be deemed to be an inalienable human right; the abolition of this right goes against international law.

[142] Compare Karl Gareis, *Das heutige Völkerrecht und der Menschenhandel* (Berlin, 1879), p. 30 et seq. Also see Ferdinand Lentner, *Der schwarze Kodex. (Code noir). Der afrikanische Sklavenhandel und die Brüsseler General-Akte v. 2 Juli 1890* (Innsbruck, 1891).

Other inalienable human rights arise from the aforesaid rights recognized for every person in the domain of international relations: the right to inviolability of the person, life, honor, and health, the right to possess ownership, to enter into obligations, the right to conclude a family union, and so on. The limits and conditions of the use thereof are considered in international criminal and private law. Suffice it to note here that if States truly considered these rights to be inherent in the human person and sanctioned by the international community, then many instances of the conflict of legislation and mutual flouting of States, explicable only by excessive exaggeration of the significance which governments attach to territorial law or simply by their discretion, would be eliminated.[143]

B. On Rights of States with Respect to Subjects and Foreigners

§87. In the domain of international relations, a man is not only a person with inherent basic rights, but also the subject of a State which has with respect to him certain rights and duties, and a foreigner with respect to whom the territorial authority has certain rights and duties. Thus, certain basic rights belong to the State: 1) relative to its own subjects abroad, and 2) relative to foreigners present on its territory.

a) *With respect to subjects*. The State autonomously determines those rights and duties which it has with respect to its own subjects, but the legal relations between it and these persons are demarcated by the limits of State territory. If it transcends these limits – which under the contemporary development of international relations happens rather frequently – this must be determined from the standpoint of the international community and the law regulating it. Such are the relations of the State to those subjects who are abroad or in general support international turnover. From the standpoint of international law, these relations are in the following form:

1) During sojourn abroad, subjects remain subordinate to the sovereign authority of their State. They must on foreign territory execute domestic laws and all instructions of their government insofar as, of course, this is actually possible in view of the laws issued by local authorities and binding on foreigners on its territory. If therefore a subject commits an ordinary crime or crime against the State outside his fatherland, he may be brought to responsibility in his own country even if he already has been tried and punished for the crime in a foreign State.

143 Heffter, note 6 above, §58a.

2) It follows from the very essence of relations of a subject that subjects may not in any event resort to the protection of a foreign government against domestic authority. Such recourses to a foreign State constitute treason against the State and should be rejected.

3) State authorities have the right at any time to summon their subjects from abroad (*jus avocandi*) when this is found to be necessary. The occasion for a summons may be the performance by a subject of military duty or some other legal duty making the presence thereof in the native country necessary; the declaration of war against that State in which he resides; and so on. But because a foreign government in general should not interfere in relations existing between a particular State and the subjects thereof, however important the reasons for the summons, they are not obliged to assist in its performance.[144]

Thus, during the Franco-German War a few Prussian subjects in Russia, despite the summons of their Government, did not return to the fatherland in order to take part in the war, and although they obviously did not perform their legal duty, they were not and could not be forcibly sent back to Prussia. Such a duty of their emigration might lie on the Russian Government only on the basis of a special agreement on this subject-matter with Prussia; but such an agreement in and of itself would not be justified either by international law or by those normal relations which ought to exist between a government and its subjects.

Governments may require of foreigners who have expressed a wish to receive naturalization the preliminary submission of a certificate concerning their performance in their motherland of all legal duties, especially military duty. But such a requirement may be explained only by the wish to prevent any international misunderstandings.

4) A State has a duty to protect its subjects and their legal interests against the infringements of foreign governments. For this purpose, all States have diplomatic and consular agents abroad whose chief duty is to be the defenders of the rights and interests of their compatriots. When and within what limits such protection should be rendered are not usually determined by State laws. In this respect every government should be guided primarily by an awareness of its dignity and the general duty to represent its subjects in international relations.

It is impossible to enumerate all instances when the protection by a State of its subjects occurs: each legitimate interest of a subject violated

[144] Very curious data may be found relative to the *jus avocandi* during the past century in *Politische Correspondenz Friedrich des Grosses* (Berlin, 1879-), VI, no. 512; VII, nos. 4042, 4073, 4129, et seq.

by local authorities may justify this protection. In practice, the following instances most often generate it.

Every subject abroad must be defended by local courts with respect to illegal infringements against his person, ownership, and other undisputed rights. As we have said, they all arise from the essence of international relations and for those nothing needs to be provided in international treaties or provisions of domestic legislation. Refusal to recognize them is denial of justice. Therefore, if local courts do not wish to protect them, without doubt the fatherland authorities are obliged to protect their victim subject and to demand that the foreign government treat them with the same respect as subjects of other States.

Often commercial enterprises of its subjects, especially the unfounded refusal of some government to pay interest and to repay debt on foreign loans concluded by it, have appealed for the protection of their State. In the last instance the possessors of securities issued by a foreign State often insisted their governments not only interfere by diplomatic means in their support, but even on measures of enforcement. Such statements were made, for example, by English and French subjects with respect to the insolvency of Turkey, Egypt, and Portugal, who did not wish to pay debts incurred by King Dom Miguel [I, of Portugal (1802-1866)] in 1832.[145] How a government should treat such petitions was masterfully resolved by Lord Palmerston in his dispatch of January 1848. He said that if Englishmen give their capital to a foreign State in hope, of course, of profit from the transaction, they must take into account the risk to which they are inevitably subjected in the event of the debtor's insolvency. Not having taken this circumstance into account, they must reconcile themselves to the misfortune understood by any speculator who is mistaken in his assumptions.[146]

The logical conclusion from these considerations is that the English Government does not consider itself bound to protect those of its subjects who entrusted their capital to another State and suffered from its bankruptcy. The French Government holds the same view. Both England and France, if they have taken it upon themselves recently to protect their subjects who are creditors of Turkey, then only by friendly petitions in their support to the Porte or the Sultan. The interference of England and France in the affair

[145] Compare Henri Becker, *Emprunt D. Miguel (emprunt portugais de 1832)* (Paris, 1874-1875).

[146] "It is therefore simply a question of discretion", the dispatch says, "with the British Government whether this matter should or should not be taken up by diplomatic negotiation, and the decision of that question of discretion turns entirely upon British and domestic considerations". See Phillimore, note 3 above, II, p. 10; Hall, note 59 above, p. 236, et seq.

of Egypt was generated less by concern for the Anglo-French creditors of [Khedive] Ismail-Pasha [(1830-1895)] than by considerations of high policy. Other commercial enterprises arranged by subjects in other States lead to the same consequences; for example, the building of railroads, plants, and others: they generate active protection of their government only if the interests of subjects are violated contrary to the laws of that country where the enterprise was built.

b) *With respect to foreigners*. The legal status of foreigners in a State is determined by domestic legislation and by international treaties. We will consider these act in their place; here we attempt to identify the general basic rights which the territorial authorities have with respect to foreigners according to principles of international law.

1) Every State, by virtue of its sovereignty, undoubtedly has the right to determine the conditions under which it agrees to allow foreigners on its territory. In this respect the autonomy of the local authorities is limited only by the following requirements of the international community: not to declare foreigners to lack rights on their territory and to be outside the protection of the law, and also not to subject them to expulsion from the country, as was done in Sparta. The adoption of such measures by a State would be equivalent to a refusal to participate in international relations and declare oneself to be outside the international community.[147]

2) With regard to the territorial authority, foreigners in a State are temporary subjects (*subditi temporarii*). They are subject to both the jurisdiction of this State and to all orders binding in general on native subjects and specially for foreigners. These orders may be disadvantageous and inconvenient; may diverge fundamentally from the orders operating in other States; may even be unfounded from the standpoint of policy and the State economy; but unless they are contrary to international treaties, foreigners are obliged to obey them; it is their business to foresee their legal status in the country in which they wish to be.

From this point of view, a protest will not be deemed to be appropriate declared by the English Government regarding the exile from Petersburg in 1881 of an English subject, the Jew Levinson, who violated the law on Jews in force in Russia. The London Cabinet initially called the measure adopted

[147] How widely the Russian Government of the eighteenth century viewed this question is known. Compare the Edict of Catherine II of 22 July 1763 with the Manifesto "on permitting all foreigners to settle where they wish and of the rights given to them". Полное собрание законов Российской империи [Complete Collection of Laws of the Russian Empire] (1st series), No. 11880. Compare nos. 11881 and 11896. The Belgian law on foreigners of 6 February 1885 deserves attention and even borrowing. See *Archives diplomatiques*, no. 1 (1886), p. 69.

by the Russian Government with respect to Levinson as not consistent with treaties concluded between Russia and England, nor with principles of international law, nor with the conditions of international relations which should exist between educated States. To this one may object that every State is free to take with respect to foreigners all measures which it finds advisable so long as they do not violate treaties and do not exclude absolutely international relations with them.[148]

There are, by way of exception, not subject to territorial laws and authorities: monarchs, diplomatic agents, military ships and auxiliary forces which, as organs or representatives of their States, enjoy the right of extraterritoriality. In this question lies the essential difference between civilized and uncivilized States: in the last foreigners to a significant degree are not subject either to the territorial authority or to the local court (see Special Part, Chapter I, §24-26).[149]

3) As temporary subjects, foreigners are obliged not to violate the local legal order. In the event of a violation by them of the criminal or police laws of the country, they are subject to all the consequences established for a violation in a law and may not claim in this respect privileges in comparison with indigenous subjects. Thus, they are tried for crimes by local criminal courts, even extraordinary courts if such exist in the State. They may be on general legal grounds subjected to arrest and confined in ordinary places of confinement. One may not speak of special prisons for foreigners or the duty of a local authority to notify the appropriate government about the arrest of particular subjects.[150]

Political émigrés do not enjoy any privileges in the slightest in comparison with other foreigners: there are no grounds for them to demand special protection of the territorial authority. The Swiss Government,

[148] Indeed, as is evident from the dispatch of [George Leveson Gower, Earl] Granville [(1815-1891)] to the English ambassador in St. Petersburg of 28(16) December 1881, the English Government itself was convinced, upon a new attentive study of this matter, that English Jews did not have more rights in Russia than Russian Jews themselves enjoyed in the Empire, and that Articles 1 and 11 of the 1858 commercial treaty in force might grant to British subjects only rights which Russian laws recognize for Russian subjects.

[149] What extraordinary privileges in this respect are imposed by European and American powers on uncivilized States may be seen in the 1880 Madrid Convention with respect to Morocco. See *Archives diplomatiques*, no. 7 (1885), pp. 62 et seq.

[150] The best definition of the mutual rights and duties of a State and foreigners can be found in the Rules of the Institute of International Law adopted by the Geneva Congress of its members in 1892 as: Règles internationales sur l'admission et l'expulsion des étrangers. See the *Tableau générale de l'Institut de droit international* (Geneva, 1891), p. 136 et seq. Compare also Alfred Chantre, *Du séjour et de l'expulsion des étrangers* (Geneva, 1891).

for example, looks at political émigrés thus, especially in recent times, repeatedly reminding émigrés who have taken refuge in Switzerland that they may enjoy the hospitality of the country only on condition of full respect for laws and governmental measures binding without exception on all persons residing on Swiss territory. Political émigrés in England are in exactly the same position.

But not all duties to be performed by local subjects may be extended to foreigners Arriving temporarily on foreign territory, foreigners remain subjects of their own State according to law. Therefore, they must be free from all those local duties which are not in accordance with their legal relations to their own State or which assume being a local subject, for example, military duty, electoral office, and others.

4) All foreigners have the right to free exit from a State provided they fulfilled their obligations with respect to private individuals and the local authorities.[151]

[151] On foreigners in Russia, see Dmitrii Vladimirovich Tsvetaev, «Иностранцы в России в XVI-XVII вв.» [Foreigners in Russia in the XVI and XVII Centuries], Русский вестник [Russian Herald], no. 12 (1887), pp. 1-46; Tsvetaev, Из истории иностранных исповедании в России в XVI и XVII вв. [From the History of Foreign Confessions in Russia in the XVI and XVII Centuries (Moscow, 1886) – reviewed by Aleksandr Nikolaevich Pypin in Вестник Европы [Herald of Europe] (January 1888).

CHAPTER 3
STATE TERRITORY AND INTERNATIONAL ROUTES

I. On State Territory in General

§88. Territory is an expanse of land and water subject to the exclusive sovereign power of a State. State power with respect to territory is territorial authority: it is discovered in the sovereign dominion over a certain territory and over everything situated on it (*Quidquid est in territorio est etiam de territorio*).[1]

There is no need to prove that both territory and exclusive power over it of a certain people are absolutely essential for the existence of a State: without them, and without citizens populating the territory, a State is inconceivable and cannot be a subject of international law.

It follows from the concept of State territory that it included not only the land, but also water expanses – seas, lakes, rivers – which are subject to the authority of the State. The composition of territories differs in another respect: the possessions of some States form a compact mass, some an indissoluble whole; others, on the contrary, represent uncoordinated parts, more or less remote from a common State center; for example, colonies. This does not change the principle: all territorial possessions of a State, wherever situated, are regarded in international law as a single undivided whole under one sovereign authority. Here is not the place to point to the strategic or, in general, political significance which the geographical position of its territory has for a State, the integral nature or fractionalization of its possessions, or their geometrical form: these are all questions of military science and politics, but not of international law.

Sovereign and exclusive dominion over all its possessions belongs to the territorial authority. In this sense territory is an object of international

[1] Georg Friedrich Martens, *Précis du droit des gens moderne de l'Europe* (1801), I, §72; August Wilhelm Heffter, *Das europäische Völkerrecht der Gegenwart*, §65; Johann Caspar Bluntschli, *Das moderne Völkerrecht der civilisirten Staten* (Nördlingen, 1868), §276; Robert Joseph Phillimore, *Commentaries upon International Law* (London, 1854-1861), II, p. 264ff; Travers Twiss, *The Law of Nations Considered as Independent Political Communities: On the Rights and Duties of Nations in Time of Peace* (2d ed.; 1884), I, p. 105; David Dudley Field, *Outlines of an International Code* (2d ed.; 1876), §27; William Edward Hall, *International Law* (Oxford, 1880), p. 134; Carlos Calvo, *Le droit international théorique et pratique* (1887-1896), I, p. 312; August von Bulmerincq, *Das Völkerrecht oder das internationale Recht: Systemisch dargestelt* (2d ed.; Freiburg i B., 1889), §43; L. A. Shalland, Юридическая природа территориальнго верховенства [Legal Nature of Territorial Sovereignty] (Spb., 1903), vol. 1.

ownership of the State: every State alone disposes of and uses its own territory, not allowing the interference of other States. With respect to private property situated on the territory, to the State belongs the sovereign right of protection and disposition; that is, the aggregate of public rights, but not ownership on the principles of private law; not *dominium*, but *imperium*. Unlike this ownership, the right of territorial authority to property of its subjects and foreigners in the State or possessing an immoveable there is called *dominium eminens*. From it there arise: 1) the right of the State to levy taxes on private ownership; 2) the right to alienate it in forms of public use (right of expropriation); 3) when extremely necessary, for example, during military actions, the right to completely destroy it without remuneration to the owner.

Finally, with respect to those lands which are part of the territory but belong to no one, which have not been colonized, or have been abandoned by their possessors, the territorial authority has the right to take possession (occupation); it not only disposes of such lands by right of State authority, but also possesses them, as a private owner. Therefore, the appropriation of unoccupied lands without the authorization of the State should not occur; such lands are "masterless things" (*res nullius*) which, according to the doctrine of Roman jurists, belong in ownership "to the first who takes possession thereof". As part of State territory, they belong first and foremost to the territorial authority, on which depends the determination of on what conditions it agrees to give them into the possession of private individuals.

This view has enormous practical significance for those States, such as the North American United States, which occupies vast territory to such an extent that full occupation of all the space is possible only over many years. Adhering to this principle that lands comprising the North American territory are subject to the sovereign authority of the states, the Washington Government entirely consistently extends its authority to those which are in the possession of the Indians: it either acquires these lands by purchase or occupies them without remuneration to the possessors.[2]

II. Boundaries of Territory

§89. The importance of the precise determination of the boundaries of a State does not require special explanations. The boundary of a territory designates the limits of the dominion of territorial authority and operation of a law of the particular country: it indicates where the authority of one State

[2] Compare Schlief, "Die staatsrechtliche Stellung der Territorien innerhalb der Nordamerikanischen Union", *Archiv für öffentliches Recht*, IV (1889), p. 314.

ends and the authority of another begins. Consequently, from the standpoint of internal administration one must want a demarcation between States which does not give rise to any doubts. It is even more essential for peace and structured international relations because border conflicts generated by ambiguous boundaries not only create misunderstandings between States; they also serve as a restraint preventing the development of international frontier turnover.

The State boundaries usually are divided in the science of international law into two kinds: 1) physical or natural boundaries, and 2) conditional or treaty (artificial) boundaries.

1) Seas, rivers, mountains, steppes, and shoals are relegated to the category of natural boundaries.

In times past it was supposed that nature itself established natural boundaries, that they always and unconditionally separate States and need not be within their territories. Moreover, they were used to best sketch territorial possessions – those which give to a people all resources for the satisfaction of their needs and the development of their forces. Therefore, the view was formed that every people who had reached the natural limits of their territory would have no grounds or right to further expansion; and, on the contrary, should endeavor with all its forces to acquire new lands if the possession thereof did not coincide with a feature assigned to it by nature. On the basis of this view, a certain theory was developed of the "natural boundaries" of States which found talented proponents, especially in France. How well-founded was this theory is best shown by the fact that even its proponents could not agree how nature itself had established boundaries as final, even for their own homeland: the opinions concerning the French "natural boundaries", not to mention others, strongly diverged from one another.[3]

The following principles applicable to the natural boundaries of States dominate in positive international law.

With regard to maritime boundaries, it is accepted, as a general rule, that coastal States extend their authority over the sea to a distance of cannon shot from shore. This principle is expressed in the aphorism uttered by Bynkershoek: "*terrae dominium finitur, ubi finitur armorum vis*" or "*quousque man e terra imperari potest*".[4] They suggest that in this expanse

[3] Compare Maurice Block, "Dictionnaire de la politique v. 'Frontières naturelles'", in Escher, *Handbuch der practischen Politik* (Leipzig, 1863), I, p. 94.

[4] C. von Bynkershoek, *Quaestiones juris publici*, cap. VIII. De dominio maris, cap. 2; Phillimore, note 1 above, I, p. 235 ; Theodore Dwight Woolsey, *Introduction to the Study of International Law*, p. 50. In particular, the remarks in Ferdinand Perels, *Das internationale*

of sea a State is in a position to maintain its authority. But because the breadth of this space given the constant improvements in artillery cannot be permanent, States either must issue laws or enter into agreements on the basis of which the maritime boundary extends a certain number of miles from the coast. If coastal States overlap in a maritime boundary, a median line should be drawn to separate them.[5]

In Antiquity and the Middle Ages the sea in particular was considered to be an obstacle created by nature to separate people. But given the contemporary development of maritime relations, one may say that the sea "erects a wall between enemies and raises a bridge that joins friends".

Rivers are considered to be a second natural boundary. If States are separated by a river, the line passing along the middle of the river is accepted as the frontier feature between them. On navigable rivers this line passes along the thalweg (or channel).[6] Understandably, with a change of the river course the position of the river frontier feature does not change. The old course remains in the event of the complete change of the direction of the river.

Rivers have never not served as natural barriers separating peoples. On the contrary, the settlement of peoples along the basins of the major rivers shows that they have from time immemorial been a means for bringing people closer together. Their character is the more salient in recent times when navigable rivers flowing through the territories of different States are in the full sense of the word arteries of international communication. On this basis one may say about frontier rivers that: 1) they by their very nature are intended to join and not separate States; 2) the freedom of navigation along them ensured by treaties arises from the difficulty of the territorial department of riparian States to demarcate them; 3) an agreement between the riparian States is undoubtedly essential for such delimitation. This all demonstrates that a river in reality may serve only as an artificial treaty boundary, but not as a natural boundary. The strategic significance of rivers is beyond question.

If States are separated from one another by mountains, the boundary is considered to be the line forming the mountain peaks or the line of the watershed. Just as the seas, mountains are not a natural wall which disengages

öffentliche Seerecht der Gegenwart (Berlin, 1882), p. 24.

[5] Compare the English Law of 1878, "Territorial Waters Jurisdiction Act"; Ludwig Gessner, *Le droit des neutres sur mer* (2d ed.; Berlin, 1876), p. 22. See below §§99 and 100.

[6] Compare Article IV, 1809 Fredrikshamn Treaty concluded between Russia and Sweden: "Dans le cours des rivières de Tornéa et de Muonio, les iles situées à l'est du Thalweg appartiendront à la Russie, et celles à l'ouest du Thalweg à la Suède".

States: thanks to the digging through of tunnels and railways, even the highest mountains are no longer an insuperable obstacle to international communication.

Finally, steppes and shoals, without doubt, constrain communications between States and in these senses may still be considered to be natural boundaries, but to avoid disputes over this feature which separates States an agreement is absolutely necessary.

It remains to conclude that the so-called "natural" boundaries do not themselves comprise a frontier separating States, but have this significance only on the basis of treaties deciding in which direction a boundary should pass. In other words, natural boundaries have a treaty, artificial character. Only conditional boundaries are recognized, and of them it would be more just to say, rather than speak of natural boundaries, that they have been established by nature itself, by the force of circumstance, than by the natural order of international relations to which all contemporary educated States are subject.

2) Artificial or treaty boundaries are determined in acts of demarcation which States conclude and consist of a conditional mathematical line whose points and direction are designated by names of isolated terrain features, numbers of points placed on a map, watershed lines, and so on. Columns, ditches, floating buoys, and others serve as external boundary marks. The precise determination thereof and especially the maintenance of marks by which it may be recognized are rather important because disputes and conflicts constantly occur between the population and the frontier authorities.[7]

Note. In recent times the publicists have pointed to special, so-called "social", boundaries separating States. They showed that when drawing boundaries between States it is necessary to draw attention to economic and social conditions in which the inhabitants of the separated region are found. One cannot separate from a State part of any locality representing as a whole, with all of its population, a single economic unit. The natural consequence of such separation is the destruction of the well-being of the territory not justified by a wise policy of States; moreover, forcibly separated parts will always seek to be reunited and may give occasion for conflicts undesirable and dangerous for international peace. In favor of the theory of "social

[7] See the demarcation acts relating to Poland in F. F. Martens, Собрание трактатов и конвенций, заключенных Россиею с иностранными державами [Collection of Treaties and Conventions Concluded by Russia with Foreign Powers] (Spb., 1874-1909). 15 vols. (hereinafter: F. F. Martens, Собрание трактатов и конвенций [Collection of Treaties and Conventions]), II, Nos. 50 and 52.

boundaries" may be cited many reasonable arguments fully deserving the serious attention of governments.[8]

III. On Means of Acquisition of Territorial Possessions

§90. A State, as an international person, has the right to acquire and alienate territorial possessions and any kind of ownership belonging to it. Within what limits a State exercises this right is a question resolved by the domestic legislation of each country.

The means of acquiring international ownership may be divided into two kinds: original (*acquisitio originaria*) and derivative (*acquisitio derivativa*). The principles developed in Roman law are applicable fully to both.[9]

1) *Original means of acquisition.* All means by which one State increases its international ownership without depriving another of its possessions are so-called. To these are relegated: increment, limitation, and taking possession.

a) *Increment* (*accessio*). This means of acquisition does not have great significance for a State. In those extremely rare instances when State territory grows by increment, the principles accepted in civil law may, speaking generally, serve as grounds. To such instances belong: raising of the seabed, formation of an island on a river, and alluvium (*alluvio*). All such kinds of natural increments are in the ownership of the coastal State.

Therefore, when islands were formed in the mouths of the Mississippi River and England declared the islands to be its own, first seen by an English ship, the Washington Government rightly objected to these claims because the islands were situated in the mouth of a river belonging to the United States. An increment to territory may be a consequence of human labor; for example, such work has long since been carried out in Holland for the purpose of drying out lands covered by lakes or by sea waters.[10]

b) *Limitation* (*usucapio*). Unlike private law, international relations permit the operation of limitation within restricted limits. The significance thereof in this domain may be expressed in the following propositions:

[8] Compare Inama Sternegg, *Tübinger Zeitschrift für die gesamte Staatswissenschaft*, XXV, nos.3 and 4.

[9] Eugène Ortolan, *Des moyens d'acquérir le domaine international* (Paris, 1849); Karl Friedrich Heimburger, *Der Erwerb des Gebietshoheit. Eine staats- und völkerrechtliche Studie* (Karlsruhe, 1888).

[10] Phillimore, note 1 above, I, p. 282; Twiss, note 1 above, I, p. 171; G. F. Martens, note 1 above, §45; Bluntschli, note 1 above, §288; Alphonse Rivier, *Principes du droit des gens*, I, p. 179.

1) International law does not recognize a period of limitation because a State possesses a particular territory so long as it may and deliberately maintains its sovereign authority over it.

2) In the domain of international relations there are no instances of a violation of the running of limitation. State authority may be *de facto* deprived of its possession, but may always strive to return it one way or another.

3) In international relations only a time immemorial limitation has valid significance (*antiquitas, vetustas, cujus contraria memoria non existit*). The entire political map rests on it, the entire existence of civilized and uncivilized States. The force of time and the sanction of history force all claims and accusations to be silenced which in their day may have given occasion for violence and injustice committed by States in order to expand their territories. In this sense, the words "*beati possidentes*" are no longer applicable. An accomplished fact covered by the limitation of time immemorial is legitimate under international law.[11]

c) *Taking possession* (*occupatio*). Taking possession is understood as the occupation by a State of lands belonging to no one; that is, territory not under the authority of other States. The history of the application of this means is rather instructive, for it created the political power and financial, industrial, and commercial significance of many contemporary peoples.[12]

In the fifteenth and sixteenth centuries, when the most significant discoveries were made of new lands, States took possession of these lands, disagreed among themselves in resolving the question of what, in fact, space the power of government should encompass to whose benefit the discovery was made. For the most part, the discoveries were made from the seacoast and did not proceed into the depths of the country: however, States in whose name coastal points were occupied declared themselves to be the masters not only of the coastal belts, but of all the lands completely unknown to them within the newly-discovered continent or island. On this basis, the Portuguese claimed all of Africa, the Spaniards all of South America, and the English, North America; the last as a consequence of the Venetian [John] Cabot [(c. 1450-c. 1500)] traveling in 1496 with his ships along the American coast from 56° to 38° N. lat.

It is natural that under such an extensive interpretation of taking possession, governments often were in conflict over a particular territory

[11] This question is discussed in detail by Grotius, *De jure belli ac pacis*, lib. II, cap. IV; Emer Vattel, *Le droit des gens*, liv. I, chapter XIV; liv. II, chapter XI; Phillimore, note 1 above, I, chapter XIII; Hall, note 1 above, p. 100; Heffter, note 1 above, §12, 13.

[12] Heinrich Ahrens, *Cours du droit naturel ou De philosophie du droit* (1868), II, p. 125.

which each considered to be its by right of first discovery. They sometimes turned to the Popes for the settlement of their disputes, who did not hesitate to give entire countries to the use of various peoples. By a Bull of 1454 Pope Nicholas V gave all of Guinea in Africa to Portugal, with the right to subdue inhabiting barbarian tribes and prohibited other European peoples from undertaking conquests there. On the basis of a Bull of Pope Alexander VI, issued in 1493, the Spaniards received in ownership all lands discovered by them or which might be discovered by them to a distance of 100 miles westward and south of the Azores Islands and Cape Verde. By a treaty concluded in 1494 between Spain and Portugal a boundary line was drawn from the North to the South Pole at a distance of 370 miles west of Cape Verde in order to delimit the Spanish and Portuguese possessions and claims. As for the risky orders of the popes concerning newly discovered lands, they were constantly disputed by various parties well into the sixteenth century.[13]

Until recently, the question of taking possession was purely of historical interest. But since 1878, thanks to the growth of colonial aspirations in France, Germany, and England and particularly the activity of the "International African Society" founded by the King of Belgium, Leopold II [(1835-1909)], rather significant lands were occupied by Europeans in Africa, especially on the coasts of the Congo and islands in the Pacific Ocean. The conflicts which emerged from this led to an awareness of the need to determine mutual territorial claims and the conditions of the validity of occupation. To this end the Berlin African Conference was convoked in October 1884, ending in February 1885 with the signature of a noteworthy international act.[14]

On the basis of the decisions of the Berlin Conference and contemporary international law the following conditions must be present to validly take possession as a means of acquiring international ownership.[15]

[13] Phillimore, note 1 above, I, §231. Compare especially Ernest Nys, *Études de droit international et droit politiques* (Brussels, 1896-1901), I, p. 203.

[14] The history of recent colonization aspirations of the European powers in the Berlin Conference are set out in Fedor Fedorovich Martens, «Африканская конференция в Берлине. Колониальная политика современных государств» [African Conference in Berlin. Colonial Policy of Contemporary States", Вестник Европы [Herald of Europe], no. 11 (November 1885), pp. 186-224; no. 12 (December 1885), pp. 512-522. It also was translated into the French language and published at Brussels in 1886 with additions. Also see *Archives diplomatiques*, nos. 5-9 (1885).

[15] Charles Salomon, *L'occupation des territoires sans maître* (Paris, 1889). Compare also Adam, "Völkerrechtliche Okkupation und deutsches Kolonialstaatsrecht", *Archiv für öffentliches Recht*, no. 2 (1891); Eval'd K. Simson, О завладении по международному праву [On Taking Possession under Principles of International Law] (Spb., 1894).

1) In the subjective respect, it is necessary that taking possession be in the name of and with the consent of a State authority. If it is performed by officials or State organs, there may be no doubt which people should be considered to be the owner of the land occupied. Taking possession undertaken by private individuals requires confirmation on the part of the government to whose benefit it ensued.

2) Taking possession is valid if the State unambiguously intended to subject the land to its authority and to use that space which it discovered, occupied, and joined to its territory. Outwardly such an intention (*animus possidendi*) is expressed by raising the State flag or arms and other symbolic acts on the newly-discovered land: by the establishment thereon of a governmental order, sending forces, erecting fortifications, and so on.

3) The object of taking possession may only be lands belonging to no one and regions inhabited by barbarian tribes. One must be aware that with respect to the last, civilized States, to their shame, rarely acted with truth and justice worthy of educated and Christian peoples. As history of the colonization of South and North America testifies, European governments in the majority of instances were convinced that it was only necessary for some adventurer to arrive in a country inhabited by savages for it to come into the "ownership" of the State in whose name this person wishes to act. The Washington Government is an exception, which, as already has been said, usually remunerated those Indians whose lands pass to the territory of the states and who thereby are deprived of their undoubted property.[16]

4) The limits of taking possession are determined by the *de facto* possibility for a government to maintain its authority to the space occupied. There the authority of the State does not manifest itself; there is no taking of possession because occupation is obligatory insofar as it is valid. What indicia prove the operation of State authority is a question to be decided for each individual instance according to local customs and by those means which at the time are in the hands of the occupier.[17]

Therefore one cannot set out as a general principle, as Bluntschli does, that an occupier has the right to consider as its possessions not only points occupied by it, but all lands which, together with these points, "by their nature" comprise a single organic whole. Thus, for example, a State which

[16] Henry Wheaton, *Elements of International Law*, ed. Richard Henry Dana (8th ed.; London, 1866), p. 69, n. 24; Bluntschli, note 1 above, §280; and especially Rivier, note 10 above, I, pp. 140, 188-197.

[17] Vattel, note 11 above, liv. I, ch. XVII, §208.

took possession only of the mouth of a river possesses, in Bluntschli's view, the entire course thereof.[18]

The facts may, however, be contrary to this assertion, and in that instance what stands out as an unconditional rule will not find any application: only actual taking possession creates certain rights for the occupier and imposes respective duties on other States.

5) A power occupying some region with a view to taking possession is obliged by diplomatic channels to bring this to the information of other States. The boundaries of the region taken possession of should be designated approximately in this act of notification (*acte de notification*).

These rules are confirmed by various examples from the history of international relations. There may serve as such: 1) the dispute between Spain and the United States relating to Louisiana;[19] 2) the dispute between England and the United States over Oregon territory; it ended in 1846 with the conclusion of a convention;[20] 3) the occupation in 1879 by French forces of Matakong Island off the western coast of Africa (England and France);[21] 4) the dispute between Russia, on one side, and England and the United States, on the other, with regard to the Edict issued by Emperor Alexander I of 4(16) September 1821.[22] On the basis of this Edict, all space, ports, and bays along the entire northwestern coast of America, beginning from the Bering Strait up to 51° N. lat., as well as the Aleutian and Kurile islands, beginning from the Bering Strait to the southern cape of Urupa Island, that is, to 45°50′ N. lat. (§1), was declared to be Russian territory. Foreign vessels were prohibited from approaching Russian coasts within a distance of less than 100 English miles.

This Edict encountered energetic protest on the part of the Washington and English governments, which proved that the regulation of the Russian Government violates "all generally-recognized principles of international law and customs". The Russian Government justified the Edict by the need to protect the interests of the Russian-American Company and based it on the "right of first discovery, first occupation, and uninterrupted possession" of the said islands and water expanse. But Emperor Alexander I, wishing to prevent a conflict with the United States, ordered Russian cruisers not to

[18] Bluntschli, note 1 above, §282.

[19] Phillimore, note 1 above, I, p. 278 et seq.

[20] Calvo, note 1 above, I, §217.

[21] *Journal de St. Petersbourg*, 1 April 1879.

[22] Полное собрание законов Российской империи [Complete Collection of Laws of the Russian Empire] (1st series), No. 28747.

go too far out to sea in order to pursue contraband trade and the delivery of weapons. Moreover, he agreed to enter into negotiations on this matter.

In 1824 Russia withdrew its excessive claims and concluded conventions with the United States and with England in 1825 which essentially paralyzed the operation of the 1821 Edict.[23]

§91. 2. *Derivative means of acquisition.* To the category of means of acquiring international ownership called derivative belong all by which one State acquires from another part of its territory freely or forcibly ceded by it. Free cessions of territories were extensively practiced in times past, when monarchs looked upon State possessions as their own. Presenting territories as a gift, the exchange thereof for other possessions, sale, or designation as dowry were a common phenomenon in the Middle Ages and early Renaissance. "Happy" Austrian marriages even became a saying. In contemporary States, both constitutional and absolute, State territory is no longer deemed to be in the "ownership" of the sovereign: it is the indivisible ownership of the whole people and may be alienated not otherwise than on the basis of a law. The agreement of parliament is needed for the cession of possessions by States with a representative form of government.

A general indicator of derivative means of acquisition is a treaty or mutual agreement between States acquiring and alienating a certain territory. There are relegated to the category of derivative means: purchase, voluntary cession, and acquisition by right of conquest.

a) *Purchase-sale*. At present, this is a means of acquisition very exceptional and rarely practiced in international relations. In any event, it is admissible only on one condition: that the purchase not extend to the population. In the event of the sale of territory, the inhabitants populating it receive the right to leave during a determined period.

Examples of the purchase of territory which have happened recently include: the acquisition by the United States of Russian-American possessions sold by Russia for $7,200,000 and the purchase by it in 1868 of the Danish islands of St. Thomas and St. John (for $1,500,000). The last purchase was not confirmed by the Washington Senate.[24] A new convention

[23] Of the papers in the Archive of the Ministry of Foreign Affairs relating to this interesting matter, the dispatch of Count Nesselrode to the Russian envoy in Washington, Mr. [Petr Ivanovich] Poletika [(1778-1849)], and the Instruction to Baron [Diderick Jacob van] Tuyll [van Serooskerken (1772-1826)], appointed to resolve this dispute in Washington, of 27 June 1823, deserve attention. See F. F. Martens, Собрание трактатов и конвенций [Collection of Treaties and Conventions], XI, p. 304 et seq.

[24] The Washington Government, contrary to the laws of the United States and the principles of international law, did not find it necessary to submit the convention concluded for

was concluded in 1901 between the United States and Denmark relating to the sale of these islands. But in October 1902 the Danish Landstang by a vote of 32 to 32 rejected this convention and the islands remained with Denmark.

b) *Voluntary cession and exchange*. They also are rarely encountered. In 1863 the Kingdom of Greece acquired the Ionian Islands from England in this way. One may also regard the transfer to France in 1860 under the Turin Convention of the counties of Nice and Savoy as a voluntary cession, at least in part. On the basis of an 1890 convention Helgoland Island was ceded by England to Germany in exchange for an increment to English possessions in Africa from Germany.[25]

c) *Conquest* (*debellatio*). This most ancient means of acquisition remains down the most frequently applied. There are necessary for a valid transfer of possession forced by conquest: 1) the consent of the contracting parties expressed in a peace treaty; 2) the *de facto* taking possession of the ceded region which is proved by its occupation and subordination of administration to the acquiring State; and finally 3) the *de facto* obedience of the population living in the locality to be transferred.

Recently this third condition has been interpreted to mean that the formal consent of the population of the territory to be alienated (plebiscite) is necessary for the legality of a cession or accession based on conquest or required by some other circumstances and considerations. An impartial evaluation of the arguments advanced both in defense and in refutation of this view convinces, however, of the complete legal unfoundedness thereof.[26]

The need for a plebiscite in the event of the cession of or accession of lands is advanced, first and foremost, as an indisputable requirement of European civilization and progress of international relations. The time has irrevocably passed, say proponents of the plebiscite, when sovereigns arbitrarily dispose of the weal of the peoples and their subjects, when their

ratification on the part of the Senate. See James Parton, *The Danish Islands: Are We Bound in Honor to Pay for Them?* (Boston, 1869); Sidney Andrews, *The St. Thomas Treaty: A Series of Letters to the Boston Daily Advertiser* (New York, 1869).

25 See *Archives diplomatiques*, no. 9 (1892).

26 Compare Felix Stoerk, *Option und Plebiscit bei eroberungen und gebietscessionen* (Leipzig, 1879), p. 39 et seq; Francis Lieber, "De la valeur des plebiscites dans le droit international", *Revue de droit international*, III, p. 139 et seq; Padelletti, ibid., III, p. 364 et seq; Robert von Mohl, *Staatsrecht, Völkerrecht und Politik* (Tübingen, 1862), I, p. 293; Rolin-Jaequemyns, *Revue de droit international*, III, pp. 172, 536; Calvo, note 1 above, I, §220; Théophile Funck-Brentano and Albert Sorel, *Précis du droit des gens* (Paris, 1877), p. 335, et seq; Guido Fusinato, *Annessione* (Torino, 1891).

personal will was the sole law for States. Given the present level of education, it is inconceivable that the population of any territory was regarded as a flock or as serfs who may be ceded to another State together with their lands contrary to their will and consent. If a people freely establishes the form of their government, if through their own elections it takes part in the legislation and administration of their country, then is it just to do violence to its freedom by an act of cession, subjecting it to a government not created by it and to laws in the issuance of which it did not participate? It is possible to avoid this injustice only by one means: granting to the population of the region to be alienated to say whether it wishes to be joined to a foreign State? If the majority of votes answer negatively, such accession should not take place.

The facts of recent practice evidently prove that governments themselves are so convinced of the justice of the said reflections that they find it necessary when transferring possessions to actually have recourse to a plebiscite. On the basis of the 1860 Convention of Turin, the population of Nice and Savoy by a national vote expressed their consent to transfer under the authority of the Emperor of France. The population of the Ionian Islands, ceded in 1863 to the Kingdom of Greece, was asked whether they wished to be subject to this State. Finally, the 1866 Prague Peace Treaty (Article 5) contained a condition that Prussia would not join the northern part of Schleswig to it against the will of the population expressed by a plebiscite.

However, close familiarity with the circumstances under which this kind of treaty was concluded makes it obvious that if States have agreed to a plebiscite, then either it was in those instances when there was no doubt about the outcome thereof or when circumstances forced them to do so.

In fact, with regard to the Ionian Islands under the authority of England it was already known before 1863 that they wished to unite with Greece; in Nice and Savoy, whose sympathies were on the side of Italy, necessary measures were taken beforehand so that the outcome of the voting would not turn out to be against accession. In these two instances the national vote was an empty form, or comedy, which brought no honor to its participants, nor to European civilization. As for the notorious Article 5 of the Prague Treaty, imposed on Prussia by mediation of Napoleon III, it was not, as is well-known, executed, and in 1878 by agreement with Austria was abolished altogether. There were no provisions on plebiscites in the 1871 Frankfurt Treaty or in the 1878 Berlin Treaty relating to any of those regions which were joined to Germany, Russia, and other States.

Thus, the facts do not prove that States were aware of the need to justify a plebiscite on their territorial acquisitions or that this itself was a reliable guarantee ensuring the freedom of the people. The theoretical reflections cited in defense thereof do not withstand criticism. From the standpoint of law, any treaty, including on the cession of territory, once it has been concluded by a competent authority is binding on all States: this is a basic principle of public international law, and there are no exceptions. The population on that part of the territory which is acceding, on the basis of a treaty, to another State must subordinate itself to its fate, not having any right to oppose its own will to the decision of the State authority. If it is agreed that a plebiscite is a necessary condition for the cession of territory when it is a consequence of an unsuccessful war, does this not mean recognition that part of the population has the right to its own "no" to compromise the fate of the entire State? Finally, from the practical point of view a mass of unresolved misunderstandings arise with respect to the application of plebiscite. In what forms should a plebiscite happen? How should the voting be structured? What if the population of the ceded region says "no"?

One matter is beyond doubt: if a belligerent knows that the outcome of a war depends upon the free vote of the population, it will force the population to say "yes"; it will carry on military actions not only against forces, but also the peaceful population, and compel it by force to agree to the accession.

It seems to us that these reflections should be convincing as to the unfoundedness of the view on the necessity of a plebiscite in international relations. Not having any legal grounds, it remains in the mouths of publicists a phrase, and in the hands of political actors, a trumpery usually concealing egoistic purposes.

Another means exists in international law which might fully satisfy the legitimate feelings of the population of the acceding region; namely, the population which must go to the other State is given the freedom within a determined period to make a choice (option) between the former and the new government. During the seventeenth and eighteenth centuries, examples are encountered of granting the right to such a choice. In recent times it has become a custom.[27]

Thus, on the basis of the Frankfurt peace (Article 2), the inhabitants of Alsace and Lorraine, which acceded to Germany, were permitted before 1 October 1871 to resettle in France and remain subjects thereof. The Treaty of Constantinople (1879) granted to inhabitants of Turkish regions which passed to Russia on the basis of the Treaty of Berlin a three-year period from the day of ratification of the Treaty (3 February 1879) during which

[27] Compare the sensible work by George Cogordan, *Droit des gens: La nationalité au point de vue des rapports internationaux* (Paris, 1879), p. 293 et seq.

they might freely leave, "selling their immoveable property" (Article 7). The last limitation usually is not encountered in other peace treaties of the recent period and may rightly be called an "obsolete condition" (*une clause surannée*).[28]

IV. On Means of Alienation and Loss of Territory

§92. In principle, territorial possessions are in the inalienable ownership of the State. But in practice no people is secure against circumstances when it, voluntarily or coerced, must renounce part of its possessions or even lose all of its territory. On this basis one may speak about the means by which States alienate or lose their international ownership.

In general all derivative means of the acquisition of possessions by one State are means of loss for another. Most often a State loses its ownership against its will. To instances of such loss are relegated: conquest and secession of part of the population.

For example, in 1857 Neuchatel separated from Prussia and became part of the Swiss *unie*; in 1860 various Italian States acceded to Sardinia; Texas in 1845 became part of the North American States, notwithstanding the protest of Mexico.

Less frequently encountered are examples of the voluntary renunciation on the part of States of possessions belonging to them. We already have referred to them when addressing derivative means of acquisition. This should also include the voluntary abandonment by a State to the mercy of fate any of its regions or islands (*derelictio*). Abandonments of possession are considered to be lost by the State and subject to taking possession as things *res nullius*.

§93. *Addition: status of Cyprus, Bosnia and Herzogovina, Kiao-chu and Port Arthur*. The Island of Cyprus and the provinces Bosnia and Herzogovina were nominally part of the Ottoman Empire, but on the basis of special treaties were occupied – the first by England, and the second, by Austria-Hungary. Thus, the legal status of these lands is completely special and without precedent in the history of international relations.

a) *Cyprus*. On 4 June 1878 a defensive and offensive alliance was concluded between England and the Ottoman Empire. The treaty of this alliance provides that in the event of the accession to Russia of Batumi, Ardagan, and Kars, England will combine its forces with the Turks in order to defend Turkish possessions. "En échange" the Sultan promised England

[28] Ibid., p. 301.

to introduce necessary reforms to the advantage of his Christian subjects and, in addition, for this purpose to supply to England the possibility to have available the means necessary to perform its obligation, and agreed to designate (désigner) the Island of Cyprus "pour être occupée et administrée par elle (l'Angleterre)".

It is evident from this provision that the Island of Cyprus was granted to England in administration, especially as a pledge that Turkey would perform its promise – to introduce reforms in its Christian provinces and, of course, as a means ensuring to England the possibility to render assistance to Turkey in the event of a new war with Russia.

According to the literal sense of the treaty, sovereign authority over Cyprus belonged to the Sultan; England exercises it *de facto*. The Island is under the administration of England, which is placed in the position of its full steward: it appoints its own officials, collects and spends duties and taxes from the local population, and so on. When comparing the *de facto* possession of the Island by the English Government and the legal authority over it by the Sultan, one must say that such a status of Cyprus from the standpoint of State and international law is extraordinary. A well-known member of the English House of Commons, [Henry] Labouchere [Baron Taunton (1798-1869)], called this a "disgraceful" means of seizure of this Island by England, for which it pays Turkey 90,000 pounds sterling annually in the form of lease payment.

In any event, from the treaty which created such an extraordinary position for Cyprus it follows that: 1) the Island was given to England only for administration: the Sultan should be considered the legitimate sovereign thereof; 2) it is occupied by England conditionally – until the introduction by the Sultan of the promised reforms: as this happens, the Island must pass again to the administration of the Turkish authorities; 3) *de jure* it remains an inextricable part of the Ottoman Empire, but the English Government has the role of an administrator – *negotiorum gestor*; 4) therefore all treaties concluded in Turkey and in force within the limits thereof are binding on the Island of Cyprus and, consequently, on England as the administrator of the Island. On this basis it should recognize within the limits of Cyprus the jurisdiction of foreign consuls created by the Capitulations of the European powers with Turkey. However, interested States agreed to the limitation thereof on the Island so long as England administers it. Finally, 5) the inhabitants of the Island of Cyprus are not English, but Turkish, subjects.[29]

[29] Nikolaos Saripolos, "La législation anglaise dans l'ile de Chypre", *Revue de droit international*, XII (1880), p. 389ff. Pietro Esperson, "L'Angleterre et les capitulations dans l'ile de Chypre", *Revue de droit international*, X (1878), p. 587 et seq. Very correct is the view of G. Jellinek, *Die Lehre von den Staatenverbindungen* (Vienna, 1882), p. 177.

Therefore, when in other provinces of Turkey outside the Island, they absolutely are subject to all Turkish laws and in particular may not claim the jurisdiction of English consuls which subjects of the English crown enjoy.

b. *Bosnia and Herzogovina.* With regard to these regions, the 1878 Treaty of Berlin provided (Article 25) that it "will be occupied and administered by Austria-Hungary". The Austro-Hungarian Government did not wish to assume the administration of the Novobazar Sanjak, and therefore the Ottoman administration remained in operation as before. But in order to ensure the existence of the new political system, and also the freedom and security of the railways, Austria-Hungary granted to itself the right to maintain a garrison, and also to have military and commercial roads throughout this part of the former Bosnian wilight.

"For this purpose the Governments of Austria-Hungary and Turkey allow themselves to stipulate the details". In execution of this last point a Convention was concluded between Austria-Hungary and Turkey on 21 April 1879 determining precisely those conditions on which the Austro-Hungarian "occupation" should occur.

Counting on the stable pacification of Bosnia and Herzogovina but not on accession to Austria-Hungary, the "occupation" to which the Congress of Berlin gave consent placed these provinces in a strange situation that could not be summed up – as Bluntschli expressed the matter – by any known legal category.[30]

On the basis of both the said acts, especially the last (1879), Bosnia and Herzogovina were placed under the following conditions:

1) There is no doubt that the Sultan is the sovereign possessor of both provinces, which remained part of the Ottoman Empire. To be sure, in this instance the power of the Turkish Padishah is in the form of "*nudum jus*"; nonetheless, as law it is not to be denied without distorting the literal meaning of the treaties concluded.

2) The Berlin Congress gave an assignment to Austria-Hungary, also recognized by the Porte, to "occupy and administer" Bosnia and Herzogovina for an indefinite period of time. According to the spirit of the

Note. From January 1879 a high English court existed on the Island in Nicosia under the chairmanship of the High Commissioner of commissioner-judges and deputy commissioners. The deputy commissioners were sent to the provinces. Moreover, assessors participate in the high court. This court eliminated the consular courts – but with the clear or tacit consent of the interested European powers. For Muslims the previous Muslim courts remained. But the High Commissioner might transfer any case from a Muslim court to the Christian high court.

30 J. Bluntschli, "Le Congrès de Berlin", *Revue de droit international*, XIII (1881), p. 585.

Berlin Congress and the 1879 Convention, such assignment is impossible to consider, however, to be free from any conditions: Austria-Hungary solemnly assumed the duty, in view of its frontier interests, and in particular thanks to ensuring a European peace, to establish an order and quiet in occupied regions, to maintain which was, as experience showed, beyond the strength of the Turkish administration. It followed that the Austro-Hungarian Government should demonstrate its ability to perform this task; otherwise, there would be no reasonable legal grounds to continue its occupation. One must hope that Austria-Hungary performs its duty.

3) The population of Bosnia and Herzogovina consists of Turkish subjects. Therefore, the Law of 3 November 1881 adopted by the Austro-Hungarian Government on the introduction of military duty in these regions and appeals to the Bosnians and Herzogovinians as subjects of Austria-Hungary is, without doubt, an act violating their conscience and express duties with respect to their legal sovereign, the Sultan.

4) The inhabitants of Bosnia and Herzogovina are subject to the Austro-Hungarian authorities so long as they are within those provinces: having departed from there, they return go the legal status of Turkish subjects obliged to obey the regulations and laws of the Ottoman Empire.

The general conclusion from these provisions is clear: Bosnia and Herzogovina are in an impossible position legally and not especially able to pacify this territory; to call it "occupation" is, at the very least, strange.[31]

c. *Kiao-chu*. At the end of 1897 the German Empire, on the pretext of satisfaction for the murder of German missionaries by Chinese rabble, seized the Kiao-chu Bay on the Shandung Peninsula. On the basis of a treaty concluded between Germany and China, the last ceded this Bay to the first with surroundings on lease and full administration for 99 years.

[31] For another view, Neumann, "L'empire austro-hongrois, La Bosnie et l'Herzégovine", *Revue de droit international*, XI (1879), p. 39 et seq. On the falsity of the aforesaid view concerning the status of Bosnia and Herzogovina I was not convinced also by the Viennese professor, [Heinrich] Lammasch [(1853-1920)] in his interesting article devoted to me: H. Lammasch, "Friedrich von Martens und der Berliner Vertrag", *Grünhut's Zeitschrift für Privat und öffentliches Recht*, XI, p. 405 et seq. Compare the accurate remarks of [Alphonse] Rivier [(1835-1898)] in the *Revue de droit international*, XI (1879), p. 144 et seq. Also Jellinek, note 29 above, pp. 115-117, and *Revue de droit international*, XVI (1884), p. 95. E. de Laveleye, *La Bosnie et l'Herzégovine* (Paris, 1886). Compare also Emil Lingg, "Die staatsrechtliche Stellung Bosniens und der Herzegowina", *Archiv für öffentliches Recht* (1890), p. 480 et seq. The author recognized both provinces as Austrian possessions (sic!!). A completely opposite opinion: Hans Schneller, *Die staatsrechtliche Stellung von Bosnien und der Herzegowina* (Leipzig, 1892); [Živojin] Peritch [Perić (1865-1953)], "Condition juridique des Bosniaques et des Herzégoviniens en pays étrangers", *Revue de droit international*, XXXIII (1901), p. 50 et seq.

d. On the basis of an Agreement (1898) between Russia and China, the last ceded to Russia in full administration and lease the ports of Arthur and Talyanvan together with water expanses adjacent to these ports and part of Liaodong Peninsula. Talyanvan is now called "Dalnyi".

V. Limitations of Right of Territoriality

§94. Every independent State, in principle, has an unlimited right of ownership with respect to its territory. It follows that State authorities are free to dispose of its international ownership, and not only to use it, but also to limit it by various kinds of obligations.

The right of territoriality may be limited by the establishment of rent, fief, and mortgage, which were practiced especially often in times past.[32]

Rents for life payable from treasury revenues were often established in the old German Empire to the benefit of mediatized and non-mediatized German princes. Thus, by decision of the Imperial Diet in 1803 the Rhine navigation duty was granted to the German archbishop primate.[33] The limitations of territorial authority by fiefdom relations comprised the general rule in the Middle Ages. Fiefs no longer exist. In former times mortgages were widely used; that is, pledges of State territory securing the obligations of a State. The Genoa Republic, for example, pledged the Island of Corsica to France in 1768, which remained a French possession after Genoa ceased to exist as a State. So too the City of Wismar was pledged in 1803 by Sweden to the Duke of Mecklenberg for the sum of 1,258,000 thalers with the right of purchase after one hundred years; that is, in 1903, if Sweden paid interest and interest on the interest for the amount of the loan. By 1903 this amount exceeded 250 million rubles. Sweden refused the purchase and renounced all rights to Wismar to the benefit of Mecklenberg. One no longer encounters such pledges.[34]

Those limitations of territorial authority which have the character of a duty or servitudes are more frequent and important.

In the domain of international relations, territorial sovereignty is already limited by the very fact of the existence of a community of States. Nature

[32] Heffter, note 1 above, §71; Calvo, note 1 above, I, §222 et seq.

[33] Léopold Neumann, *Grundriss des heutigen europäischen Völkerrechts* (2d ed.; Vienna, 1877), §19.

[34] F. F. Martens, Собрание трактатов и конвенций [Collection of Treaties and Conventions], V, §187 and 195. The 1803 treaty relating to the City of Wismar, concluded at Malmö, was printed in the Supplement to G. F. Martens, *Recueil des traités*, III, p. 488 et seq.

itself, the natural relations of being neighbors, do not make possible the complete, unlimited disposition of one's territory. Therefore, one speaks of natural international duties (*servitutes juris gentium naturales*) to which all States are subject as a consequence of the inevitable conditions of their physical existence side by side.

Thus, a river flowing through the possessions of two States may not be diverted by one of them from its natural course to the prejudice of the other.

Unlike these duties, international treaty duties (*servitutes jus gentium voluntariae*) are established by mutual consent of States and arise from the fact of international interaction. We dwell only on the last in view of the fact that natural duties in the majority of cases also are regulated by treaties: if they exist in and of themselves, the principles of civil law are applicable to them. Only international treaty duties have an autonomous legal character.

Limitations placed on a State by this kind of duty consist of either 1) they lack the possibility to exercise their territorial authority in full (*in non faciendo*); or 2) in permitting the actions of a foreign authority on their territory (*in patiendo*). The first kind of limitation consists of negative international duties (*servitutes jus gentium negative*); the second are the subject-matter of positive international servitudes (*servitutes jus gentium affirmative*).[35]

Only States may be subjects of negative and positive international duties.

The view of Heffter that international duties are established also to the benefit of "private individuals – foreigners" is mistaken, because private individuals, just as social classes, do not enjoy authority or public rights in international relations which serve as the subject-matter of international duties. In confirmation of his view, Heffter cites as an example postal regulation secured by an Act of the German Union for the Princely House of Thurn und Taxis. In reality, however, the Princes of Thurn und Taxis (Bavarian subjects) merely had an assignment to head the postal services in the Union and were nothing more than agents in this matter of various German governments which found it convenient to concentrate the postal administration in single hands: the sovereignty of German States was not diminished by such an assignment and therefore it cannot be considered to be an international duty.[36]

Only the right of sovereignty exercised by a State with respect to its territory may be the subject-matter of international duties. Private rights and

[35] Phillimore, note 1 above, I, chap. XV; Bluntschli, note 1 above, §323 et seq.; Heffter, note 1 above, §43; Edward Shepherd Creasy, *First Platform of International Law* (London, 1876), p. 255 et seq.

[36] Heffter, note 1 above, p. 104.

property of subjects may not be the subject-matter of these duties. Having as its object solely international ownership, international servitudes are of a real character. Personal servitudes, which Phillimore allows, make no sense in international relations because a State itself, as a juridical person, cannot be the object of a servitude right.[37]

By their origin, international treaty duties are of a dual kind: the grounds thereof may be either the formal consent of a State, forced or voluntary, that is, a treaty, or a period of time immemorial, that is, the tacit recognition of a particular servitude by a State. They also terminate variously: by mutual agreement of the interested powers; as a consequence of unilateral refusal to use a servitude – formal or tacit; finally, destruction of the subject-matter of the duty. With the transfer of territorial possessions to a new State, the duties thereon do not terminate, but fall on the new possessor unless it was the subject thereof.

Just as *jura in re aliena*, according to the general rule international duties which extend to all such rights without exception must be interpreted in a limited sense. A servitude may not destroy the independence of a State. In general one may say that only those servitudes have reasonable grounds are those that have been generated by a community of economic or political interests of States. Such measures as a system of railway stations on foreign territory, or the prohibition of passage of the warships of all nations through the Dardanelles and Bosphorus are justified by the international community. For a better explanation of the essence and extent of international servitudes we cite below various examples, grouped by types of those rights to whose limitation – negative or positive – they have been directed.

§95. a) *Negative international duties.* The content of negative international servitudes is the obligation of a State not to use particular territorial rights belonging thereto. The following may serve as examples of such limitations accepted by a State under a treaty.

1) Limitation of right of State to increase its army, build fortresses, and maintain warships above a determined number.

Obligations of this kind were repeatedly placed on States. On the basis of the 1713 Treaty of Utrecht (Article 10), France obliged itself not to erect fortifications at Dunkirk again, which had been razed. Russia and Turkey, according to the 1856 Treaty of Paris (Articles 11, 13, and 14) were obliged to destroy fortifications and not build new ones on the coasts of the Black Sea, and likewise not to maintain a naval fleet on that Sea. There was a

[37] Phillimore, note 1 above, I, p. 331.

series of Articles in the 1878 Treaty of Berlin limiting the rights of States in this respect. Article 52 provides:

> In order to increase the guarantees which assure the freedom of navigation on the Danube which is recognized as of European interest, the High Contracting Parties determine that all the fortresses and fortifications existing on the course of the River from the Iron Gates to its mouths shall be razed, and no new ones erected.

Pursuant to Article 11, the Principality of Bulgaria must raze all the old fortresses and not construct fresh ones. With regard to Montenegro it was provided that it should not erect any fortifications on the Boyana River, except for those which are necessary for the defense of the stronghold of Scutari. Antivari was closed to warships. Montenegro was to have neither ships of war nor flag of war. The fortifications between the lakes and the shore on Montenegrin territory were to be razed and no new ones built (Article 29).

One of the Articles of the Berlin Treaty, namely Article 59, concerning Russia gives rise to doubts. It reads: "His Majesty the Emperor of Russia declares that it is his intention to constitute Batum a 'porto-franco', essentially commercial". In view of this provision, does Russia have the right to erect maritime fortifications in order to defend Batum? Taking into account the Protocols of the Berlin Congress explaining the circumstances under which the declaration of Batum to be a free port ensued, one may say only: this port should not be transformed into a naval harbor and deprived of the significance of a free port. But it does not follow that Batum cannot be protected by a Russian armed force just as any other region within Russia is protected. It is necessary, moreover, not to lose from sight that Article 59 of the Berlin Treaty merely reiterates the declaration of the Russian sovereign made at the Congress – a declaration in which no reservations were made relative to the territorial rights of Russia over the port. These rights always are assumed for the State, and since in the present case formal renunciation of them on the part of a competent authority did not follow, then obviously they were reserved by the Russian Government and continued in full force.

Indeed, it is known that by the Highest edict of 23 June 1886 in the name of the Minister of Finances, the Sovereign Emperor declared that in view of the inconveniences caused by the existence of a free port of Batum, the free port is abolished. This regulation generated serious objections only on the part of England. But at present Article 59 of the Berlin Treaty has been repealed.[38]

[38] Compare G. Rolin-Jacquemyns, "Chronique du droit international (1885-1886)", *Revue de droit international*, no. 1 (1887).

2) Obligation of State to limit its inalienable right of jurisdiction with respect to foreigners.

Examples of such obligations are treaties of European States with Eastern States. By virtue of Capitulations concluded with Turkey, China, Persia, and other Asian countries, the subjects of European powers in those lands are subject not to the local court, but to their own consuls, who are guided by the laws of their homeland. The treaties of Russia with China – Tianjin, 1858 (Article 7) and Peking, 1860 (Article 8) – are interpreted in the sense that they impose a similar duty on Russia with respect to subjects of the Celestial Empire: Chinese who have committed a crime on Russian territory should be accompanied to the Chinese border and extradited for trial by the Chinese authorities. But circumstances and conditions in view of which the said treaties were concluded force the existence of such a duty to be denied, now positively repealed by the Edict of 8 June 1882.

3) Limitation of State authority with respect to any church or profession of faith within territory.

Of interest in this respect is the status which the Pope and the Vatican have on Italian territory. On the basis of a Law on guarantee adopted in Italy on 13 May 1871, the Pope has the "honor of a sovereign" (Article 3); the palace of the Pope and all premises which persons occupy who serve in the papal palace enjoy the right of extraterritoriality. Article 7 of the Law, *inter alia*, determined that "no Italian official may enter the Vatican". All these material limitations of the territorial rights of the Italian government are generated, of course, by the completely special international significance which undoubtedly belongs to the Pontiff of the Roman Catholic Church and the wish, in view of this significance, to deflect from the Kingdom of Italy any complaints in embarrassment of the Pope.[39]

4) Limitation of State to free alienation of its territorial possessions.

On the basis of an 1895 convention, Belgium obliged itself, in the event of the sale of the State of Congo, to recognize for France the right of first purchase. In addition, Belgium assumed the obligation not to cede or give the possessions of the State of Congo to anyone.

§96. b. *Positive international duties*. By positive international servitudes are understood the obligations of a State to permit (or tolerate) various actions within its limits performed by a foreign State authority, usually a

[39] Bluntschli, *Die rechtliche Unverantwortlichkeit und Verantwortlichkeit des römischen Papstes* (Nördlingen, 1876), p. 9 et seq. Also see Holtzendorff, "Völkerrechtliche Erörterungen zum italienischen Garantiegesetz", *Jahrbuch für Gesetzgebung*, IV (1876), p. 303 et seq.

neighbor. Most often States agree the following rights to their advantage which they might exercise on foreign territory:

1) Right to undertake within another State certain governmental actions to be performed by own officials.

To these are relegated the right of a State to pursue deserters to foreign territory. Usually powers enjoy this right mutually, determining the major conditions in treaties on the extradition of criminals. For example, in the punitive convention concluded between Russia and Austria in 1808 it was provided (Article 8) that detachments sent to pursue deserters should stop at the border, and if the deserter concealed himself beyond it, may send to search for him "no more than one or two persons" with passports to the nearest place where these people may apply to the superior with a request to send a team to search for and detain the fugitive.[40]

Sometimes States concluded treaties about the crossing, in certain instances, of their forces into foreign territory. Such a treaty was concluded in 1833 between Russia and Austria in view of the campaign being waged at the time by both neighboring powers against revolutionaries in their Polish regions. It was determined in the treaty (Article 5) that if one of the Contracting Parties needed for the success of its operations against the Poles in rebellion to have its forces cross into the territory of the other power, then such crossing would, upon its request, be permitted.[41]

Among the governmental actions to be performed on foreign territory were the arrangement in a foreign State, by agreement with it and by regulation of the interested power, of necessary customs stations, wharfs, bridges, warehouses, and the like. The right to similar structures was stipulated, for example, for Russia on the left bank of the Amu-Darya, within the possessions of Khiva and Bukhara (see 1873 treaties with the Khan of Khiva (Articles 6 and 7), and with the Emir of Bukhara (Article 4)).

The State may extend its authority to foreign territorial waters. The Turkish harbors of Klek and Sutorin in southern Dalmatia were in such a position with respect to Austria-Hungary. They previously belonged to the Ragusa Republic, which ceded them to Turkey. At the outset of the present [nineteenth] century both harbors were occupied by the French and then passed to the authority of the Austrians. Having returned them again to the Porte, Austria retained for itself, however, authority over the entire bay and adjacent Turkish shore and maintained a station there which did not allow

[40] F. F. Martens, Собрание трактатов и конвенций [Collection of Treaties and Conventions], III, p. 15.

[41] F. F. Martens, Собрание трактатов и конвенций [Collection of Treaties and Conventions], IV(1), p. 457.

even warships belonging to the Turks access to the Turkish coast. During the recent uprising in Albania, the Turkish Government only after lengthy diplomatic negotiations with the Vienna Cabinet received authorization to deliver its forces to the site of the uprising through the Klek Bay.[42] At present, Klek and Sutorin are considered to be Austrian possessions. On the basis of the Berlin Treaty (Article 29), Austria-Hungary has police, maritime, and sanitary supervision along the entire coast of Montenegro.

2) Right of State to use communication routes in another State.

In this case reference is made not to friendly services or courtesy rendered by one State to another, but about an international obligation, a servitude of travel, on a foreign territory. For example, under the 1807 Treaty of Tilsit (Article 16), Prussia was obliged not to obstruct military communications passing through its territory between the Kingdom of Saxony and the Duchy of Warsaw. Under the 1819 Act of Frankfurt (Recès de Francfort), Austrian, Prussian, and Bavarian forces received the right of passage (*droit de passage*) through Baden, Hesse, and Oldenburg possessions (Articles 6, 23, 32).[43]

3) Right of State to occupy foreign territory in event of certain circumstances ensuing or permanent occupation by forces of a foreign territory or city.

For example, the Swiss Confederation on the basis of the 1815 Treaty of Vienna (Article 92) may temporarily occupy the Provinces of Chablais and Faucigny with its forces. Both these provinces were declared, just as Switzerland, to be neutral in perpetuity, and to assure their inviolability the Congress of Vienna determined that in the event of war between the powers neighboring Switzerland, the forces of the King of Sardinia, to whom the provinces belonged, should withdraw from them and, if this proved to be necessary, might be replaced by Swiss forces. Because in 1860 Chablais and Faucigny became part of France, the servitude placed on Sardinia with respect to them should now be executed by the French Republic.

An example of an international duty consisting of the permanent occupation of a fortress by foreign forces is the occupation of Luxembourg by a Prussian garrison which continued until 1867 on the grounds that this city, which belonged to the King of the Netherlands, was declared by the Act of the 1815 Congress of Vienna (Article 67) to be in the military respect

[42] Ferdinand Ritter von Attlmayer, *Die Elemente des internationalen Seerechts und Sammlung von Verträgen* (Vienna, 1872), I, p. 113 et seq.

[43] Karl von Martens and Ferdinand de Cornot, Baron de Cussy, *Recueil manuel et pratique des traités, conventions et autre actes diplomatique* (Leipzig, 1846-1857), III, p. 432 et seq.

a fortress belonging to the German Union.[44] At the Conference in London the great powers in 1867 decided to raze the fortifications of Luxembourg and proclaimed its perpetual neutrality.[45]

VI. On the High Seas

§97. At present it is recognized as an undisputed axiom of positive international law that the high seas are completely free and that no State power can dominate it, even though actually it had the possibility there to prescribe laws to other States. It follows from this proposition that all vessels on the high seas are subject solely to the authority of that State whose flag they fly; from this arise many other important legal rules of both public and of private international law and international criminal law which incontestably have enormous significance for international maritime relations and turnover.

On what is this principle based? It is justified variously. Some writers say that the sea, as an element, cannot be subject to anyone's exclusive power and by virtue of its natural attributes or nature is the common weal of all peoples. Others, in particular, point to the impossibility of a settled way of life on the high seas and a precise determination of the boundaries separating the States thereon.

But these explanations are not persuasive. Given the contemporary development of naval forces and defense technologies, there is no doubt that vast parts of the sea and even oceans can be *de facto* occupied by a State. There is no doubt that an attribute of such occupation, once it is undertaken, might be determined no less precisely than land boundaries. The sole legal ground for the freedom of the high seas should be deemed the need to develop international turnover. The principle of freedom of the sea arises from the community and solidarity of the interests of all peoples. Nature did not establish this, but an awareness by all peoples that the sea is a natural link which joins all of them, that their well-being depends on the freedom thereof, the development of their forces, their status as members of the international community. That is why an infringement on this freedom is an infringement on the inalienable rights of peoples, is a crime against all States, and the common rebuff of such violation is completely legitimate.[46]

[44] F. F. Martens, Собрание трактатов и конвенций [Collection of Treaties and Conventions], III, p. 288. 284. and 298.

[45] Ibid., XII, pp. 370-376.

[46] Compare Ludwig Gessner, *Le droit des neutres sur mer* (Berlin, 1865), p. 15 et seq.; Perels, note 4 above, §4; Laurent-Basile Hautefeuille, *Des droits et des devoirs des nations*

The principle: "the sea is free", generally-recognized at present, diverges from those views of the high seas which dominated earlier in the laws and practice of maritime States. Despite the fact that Roman law denied the possibility of the right of ownership with respect to the high seas,[47] all the same in the Middle Ages and the Renaissance up to the seventeenth century there was no shortage of claims to exclusive ownership of the open seas and oceans. Having declared a particular sea to be under its authority, States pursued and captured foreign ships sailing within its limits, required maritime salutes as a mark of subordination, levied duties, and subordinated to their jurisdiction. Such claims were made by the: Venetian Republic to the Adriatic Sea; Genoa, to the Ligurian Sea; Portugal, to the Indian Ocean and part of the Atlantic southward of Morocco; Spain, to the Gulf of Mexico and the Pacific Ocean; England, to the seas encircling the United Kingdom and to the North Sea; Denmark and Sweden, to the Baltic Sea; finally, Turkey to the Black Sea. It was difficult to resolve on the basis of any common indisputable principle those bickerings of States which arose from these claims, and it was not surprising that the Pope was deemed to be the sole judge who awarded seas and part of the oceans to whomsoever and as he found it necessary.

A change gradually occurred in views of the high seas from the seventeenth century. The claims of individual peoples to a monopoly of maritime trade and shipping were abandoned little by little, having encountered criticism from various writers and, finally, a rebuff from the States themselves. One of the early proponents of freedom of the sea was Hugo Grotius in his work *Mare liberum* (1609). Opposing views were defended by an Englishman, John Selden, who refuted Grotius in a discourse entitled *Mare clausum* (1635).

Contemporary jurists and legislation unanimously recognized that the high seas are free, and no people may consider the sea to be in its ownership. At present, not only the oceans, but also the parts thereof connecting with the high seas are deemed to be free and generally accessible, even though they are enclosed by the possessions of one State. Certain limitations of this principle permitted in practice are justified only by the security requirements of the coastal country.

neutres en temps de guerre maritime (2d ed.; Paris, 1858), I, p. 34 et seq.; Théodore Ortolan, *Règles internationales et diplomatie de la mer* (4th ed.; Paris, 1864), I, p. 105 et seq.; Bluntschli, note 1 above, §304 et seq.; Heffter, note 1 above, §74 et seq.; Phillimore, note 1 above, §196; Hall, note 1 above, p. 115 et seq.; Ernest Nys, *Les origines du droit international* (Paris, 1894), p. 379 et seq.

[47] See l. 2 §1 Dig. De div. rer.: "*Et quidem naturali jure omnium communia sunt illa: aer. aqua profluens et mare, et per hoc litora maris*".

Therefore, from the contemporary point of view the territorial authority of a State cannot be expanded over the adjacent seas up to limits which would destroy the character of high seas peculiar to them. From this point of view, the claims of Sweden to ownership in the Baltic Sea never had grounds, for being joined with an ocean, the Baltic Sea always remained free for all States.[48] No more well-founded were the claims of the Porte to the Marmora Sea and the Black Sea, even when they were encircled by the possessions of the Turks. The same must be said about the demands of the Venetians with respect to the Adriatic Sea, England to the Narrow-Seas, and others. Unlike these seas, the Sea of Azov, although joined to the Black and Mediterranean seas, is rather a closed sea than a free sea: first, its link with the ocean is rather remote; second, it not only is encircled on all sides by possessions of Russia, but entry thereto is under Russian cannons; finally, third, by size it should be considered a gulf rather than a sea.

The Kara Sea, on the contrary, can never be deemed to be Russian. Certain Russian publicists, defending an opposite view, refer in substantiation of their opinion to the geographical position of this sea, to those climatic conditions in which it is situated, and finally to historical data. We shall consider these arguments individually. As regards geographical position, one glance at a map shows that the Kara Sea is directly connected with the Northern Ocean and completely open to the access of ships. If then it is said that the Kara Sea for nine months is ice-covered and supposedly comprises a continuation of Russia territory, one may object that ice is nowhere equated to dry land and, moreover, the freedom of the Kara Sea may interest other States, chiefly from the standpoint of navigation thereon, and this is possible only during those three months when this sea is ice-free. The argument, finally, is not convincing that Tsar Mikhail Fedorovich [(1596-1645)] issued an Edict in 1620 which concerned fishing in the Kara Sea, and this Edict encountered no objections on the part of western powers. It is evident that they forget at the time neither Russian nor European States were interested in the Kara Sea, and therefore hardly had any knowledge of the existence of the Muscovite Edict. Indeed, the question of the affiliation of the Kara Sea to Russia, one must assume, has to now engaged European States little because the regulations concerning this Sea published by the Russian Government in 1833 and 1869 generated no protest on their part. On this basis – and only on this basis – may it be asserted that the Kara Sea *de facto* belongs to Russia, but from the legal point of view it is an open and free sea.

[48] Phillimore, note 1 above, I, §179; Henry Wheaton, *Histoire des progrès du droit des gens en Europe*, I, p. 205 et seq.; Perels, note 4 above, p. 36.

Those seas which not only are encircled by the territorial possessions of one State but have no connection with the oceans are in a completely different position in comparison with open seas. These are closed seas; they are under the power of that State within whose limits they lie.

On this basis the Dead Sea in Asia belongs to the Ottoman Empire, whose possessions encircle it entirely. The Caspian Sea is also closed, and although it washes the coasts belonging to Russia and Persia, it must be considered to be Russian because in the Turkmenchai Treaty with Russia (1828) the Persian Shah, out of special respect for the Emperor of Russia, agreed (Article 8) to grant to him in perpetuity the exclusive right to keep warships on the Caspian Sea, and "no other power may have warships thereon". Accordingly, the Caspian Sea is subject solely to Russian laws and authorities.

§98. Rather important legal and practical consequences arise from the principle of freedom of the high seas. The high seas are free for the navigation and communication of all peoples. Likewise, no people may be prohibited on the high seas from fishing and other peaceful trades. If all peoples have an identical right to use the high seas, it follows that no State should subject others to its laws relating to the conditions and limits of this use nor subject foreign mariners to trial or detain and inspect foreign ships sailing on the high seas. All vessels on the high seas are subject to the jurisdiction only of their States. Ships, and especially warships and fleets, are regarded on the high seas as isolated parts of State territory; however, it would be mistaken to infer not only the right of a vessel to a place in the water, but also in the surrounding sea space at cannon shot distance. Such a conclusion is not justified.[49] States are liable for the actions of their subjects committed on the high seas. In view of this, every State is obliged to take all measures to that maritime relations, fishing, and other trades performed at sea are conducted by its subjects properly and without offence to other peoples. And because, on the other hand, all States are equally interested in the development of maritime turnover, general agreements relative to measures for the maintenance of order on the high seas, facilitating navigation and eliminating various kinds of obstacles constraining such are both desirable and essential by reason of the very essence of maritime international communication. Therefore, maritime laws and navigation treaties of various educated peoples are distinctive for their similarity. Legislative and treaty provisions relating to them will be addressed in the Special Part.

[49] Bluntschli, note 1 above, §318; Phillimore, note 1 above, I, p. 241; Perels, note 4 above, p. 47 et seq.

VII. On the Coastal or Territorial Sea

§99. By coastal or territorial sea is understood in general that part of the sea which washes the possessions of the coastal State. It is deemed to be in the ownership of this State, is considered to be a continuation of coastal territory, and is subject to its authority. The need for such recognition has been acknowledged from time immemorial and may be justified by many reasonable considerations.

First and foremost, security of the State requires that it take on the high seas at a certain distance from shore all measures that might prevent surprise attacks from without and serve as a defense during war. In disposing of authority over the territorial sea, the State also receives the possibility to administer police and sanitary supervision over ships.

Further, dominion in coastal waters gives to a State the means to successfully combat smuggling and satisfy its fiscal interests. For inhabitants of the seacoast the exclusive power of the coastal State ensures the possibility to exist by fishing. Finally, the order and safety of trade turnover itself carried on by foreigners on sea routes fully justifies allowing the authority of a State along a coastal sea belt: in former times, States with the assistance of this power might protect the coastal sea and maritime communication in general against pirates who with impunity committed robbery while remaining on the high seas.[50]

By virtue of dominion over the coastal or territorial sea, a State subjects to its own laws, court, and regulations everything found or performed within this sea. All customs and police measures established by it are binding on foreigners who arrive within this boundary. Crimes committed in ports of the State are prosecuted and punished according to its laws. All transactions which they enter into between themselves or with indigenous subjects while in these waters of the State are conducted according to the principle of the local court. In a word, for these persons and for their legal relations the law of the coastal State is as binding as the territorial law is binding for all foreigners who are on foreign territory.

In view of the extensive rights which a State enjoys with respect to the territorial sea, it is exceedingly important to determine to what distance it extends. Where does the power of the coastal State end and the high seas begin? It is clear that an increase of the extent of the coastal sea narrows the high seas to the same extent and reduces the freedom of navigation. Moreover, inasmuch as the freedom of the high seas is in the common interest of all States, individual States are interested in as large a coastal

[50] Hautefeuille, note 46 above, I, p. 232 et seq.

sea as possible. The broader its boundaries, the better are treasury revenues ensured, and the more profitable marine trades are for subjects, foreigners usually not being admitted to such in coastal waters. That is why down to the present some States declare as coastal sea expanses which in reality cross over into the high seas and thereby violate its freedom.

An example of excessive claims in this respect is the aforementioned Edict of Emperor Alexander I of 4 (16) September 1821. The Edict provided that the entire sea space from the Bering Strait up to 54° N. lat. to a distance of 100 Italian miles from the Asian and American mainlands is deemed to be a Russian sea, and foreign vessels, on pain of confiscation, were prohibited from engaging in fishing in this space. Having encountered decisive protest on the part of the North American United States and England, Alexander I had to agree to a change of his Edict. Indeed, the Russian Government also in the past century expressed an understanding of the boundaries of the coastal sea which was not justified either by international customs or by the theory of international law. Thus, on 26 January 1776 the College of the Admiralty was given an Edict to arrange a cruise of two warships and two frigates in the Northern Sea "from the White Sea to Cape Nord and the vicinity thereof, making from the squadron such a chain that no vessel might sneak in". This measure was generated by the attacks of American privateers on Russian vessels. On the contrary, "The Highest Confirmed Rules for Particular Corsairs" of 31 December 1787 (П.С.З. № 16599) recognize the power of a neutral State to a distance of cannon shot from shore.[51]

When determining the boundary of the coastal sea, the theory of international law proceeds from the position that the power of a coastal State ends where it *de facto* cannot be supported: "*Terrae dominium finitur ubi finitur armorumm vis*".[52] On this basis Bynkershoek and, following him, other jurists say that the boundary of coastal waters is determined by a cannon shot from the coast. But, as we already have had occasion to note, this scale, under constant improvements in weaponry, is a changeable and indefinite figure. Therefore, practically the question is best decided by international agreements. At present, many treaties concluded by States and likewise many writers on international law accept as the outer feature of

[51] A curious discourse on this question was drawn up by Baron [Filip Ivanovich] Brunnov [(1797-1875)] in January 1837 under the title "De la jurisdiction qu'une puissance, qui possède le rivage, est en droit d'exercer sur la mer circonvoisine". (Archive of the Ministry of Foreign Affairs).

[52] Bynkershoek, De dominio maris, cap. II.

the coastal sea a line extending to three English miles from maximum ebb tide.[53]

This definition was accepted recently by the laws of various western European States. Thus, the English "Territorial Waters Jurisdiction Act" of 1878 limits the space of coastal jurisdiction of the Kingdom to three English miles. The circumstances which generated the said Act show how important it is to know in practice where precisely the coastal sea of a State ends.

A collision which occurred not far from the English coast between a German vessel, the *Franconia*, and an English ship, the *Strathclyde*, was the occasion for the adoption of the English law. Having been holed, the English ship sank. A criminal case was instituted against the master of the German ship as a consequence of the death of one passenger on the English ship during the collision. The English tribunals could not agree as to the question of jurisdiction. The court of second instance deemed itself to lack competence in view of the absence of English laws determining the expanse of the coastal sea. Judicial practice contained numerous completely contradictory interpretations relative to the spatial operation of English territorial authority on the high seas. Under these circumstances, the Government assumed the legislative initiative on this matter and sought the adoption of the 1878 Law by Parliament.[54]

However, the final conclusion made from the provisions of certain treaties and opinions of writers was completely mistaken in the sense that the three-mile coastal or territorial sea was a generally-binding law. There is no such binding international law and cannot be. On the contrary, the Bynkershoek rule is the sole true scale for determining the power of a coastal State over parts of the high seas washing its coast. Given the contemporary development of artillery, it should be said that the power of the coastal State extending to a cannon shot from shore reaches to ten miles from the coast. The Institute of International Law approaches this reality, having declared in 1894 at its Paris session, that the territorial sea extends to six miles. This proposition was incomparably more reasonable than the fictitiously-binding law on the three-mile distance.[55] Finally, one must note that on the basis of recent international agreements of 1892, 1893, and 1894 Russia, England,

53 Bluntschli, note 1 above, §302; Heffter, note 1 above, §75; Gessner, note 46 above, p. 22 et seq.; Perels, note 4 above, p. 26; Phillimore, note 1 above, I, §98. Compare Article 283 in the Russian Customs Statute and the 1895 Statute on Prizes.

54 Perels, note 4 above, p. 86 et seq.

55 See F. F. Martens, "Le tribunal d'arbitrage de Paris et la mer territoriale", *Revue générale de droit international public*, no. 1 (1894). Debates of the Institute of International Law and rules adopted by it are in the *Annuaire de l'Institut de droit international* for 1894.

and the United American States, with a view to preventing the eradication of species of seals in the northern Pacific Ocean, agreed to recognize to ten miles from shore a right of special protection by the coastal Russian and American authorities, and to establish to a distance of sixty miles from shore a special general regime for observation over and prosecution for the illegal killing of seals.

§100. Sometimes gulfs, roadsteads, bays, and sea waters in general encircled by the possessions of a single State are called the territorial sea.[56] That such parts of the sea should be considered to be under the authority of the coastal State hardly requires evidence, for even the part of the sea adjacent to the coasts of a State, the coastal sea, is subject to the laws of the coastal country. But it is essential that the gulfs, bays, and roadsteads be actually enclosed by the possessions of one power. Therefore, even if entry to a gulf is under the authority of a particular State, but another power has dominion over the remaining shore, the State having dominion over the entry has no right of ownership to the entire gulf.

The question of whether Austria-Hungary had the right to dispose of Klek Bay must be considered from this standpoint, to which we have referred above. This Bay was adjacent to Turkish coasts, and Austria-Hungary had dominion only over the entrance to the Bay; but the Austro-Hungarian Government had no right to consider it part of its territorial waters and, consequently, restrain access of the Turks through it to their own coast. It was as much in the ownership of Austria-Hungary as of the Porte.

According to the definition advanced, there may be enumerated among the territorial seas: Gulf of Finland and Gulf of Riga, Zuiderzee, the sea between England and the Isle of Wight (The Solent). During Sweden's sway over Finland, the Gulf of Bothnia was the territorial sea of that power.[57] In 1872 the English Government issued a regulation on the basis of which the Bay of Conception in Newfoundland, jutting forty miles into the Island and having a breadth of fifteen miles, was declared the territorial sea of England. But the so-called King's (or Queen's) Chambers; that is, parts of the sea lying between the English coast and a mental line drawn between the two

[56] *Note*. Rather often publicists mix the "coastal" and "territorial" sea, designating both either by the same name of territorial sea or, not connected by any general term, as gulfs, bays, roadsteads, and so on. See, for example, Perels, note 4 above, pp. 21, 87.

[57] Heffter, note 1 above, §76a, asserted that the Gulf of Bothnia belongs at present by right of common ownership to Russia and Sweden. One can hardly agree with this view. The Gulf of Bothnia is part of the free sea.

closest capes of this coast, and also the Gulf of Mexico and Hudson Bay, cannot be deemed to be territorial seas.[58]

It should be noted that the power of the coastal State both over the coastal and over the territorial seas should not be understood in the sense of a complete exclusion of these waters from the natural arteries of international turnover. Not all vessels in these waters are subject to the laws and jurisdiction of coastal States. If any merchant ship merely passes through the line of the coastal or territorial seas, it does not become subject to the jurisdiction of the territorial authorities. For such jurisdiction it is necessary that the vessel continued its sojourn there, anchored, or commenced to unload goods.[59]

In this sense the Russian Government resolved two relevant instances which occurred in the Black Sea. In 1836 at a distance of ten miles from the coast of the Caucasus the local authorities detained an English ship, *The Lord Ch. Spencer*, which was accused of smuggling. By instruction of the Government, it was released immediately on the grounds that Russian territorial authority did not extend to ten miles. However, the Russian Government declared to the English Government that, without wishing to obstruct legitimate and peaceful relations within Russian waters or the high seas, it, however, would not allow the carriage by sea of weapons to the population of the Caucasus or their being incited to resist Russian authority. Accordingly, in 1837 the English steamer *Vixen*, detained near Sukhumi-Kale and guilty of carrying military contraband to Caucasian mountain people, was confiscated despite the protests of England and even the threat of war.[60]

As can be seen from the foregoing, the authority of a coastal State over coastal and territorial seas should be regarded not as a right of ownership, private possession, but as a right of dominion justified by State and international interests.[61]

[58] Compare Hall, note 1 above, p. 128; Woolsey, note 4 above, §56; Phillimore, note 1 above, I, pp. 220, 239; Bluntschli, note 1 above, §310.

[59] Ortolan, note 46 above, I, liv. II, chap. 7, 8; Hall (p. 126) recognizes the full right of ownership, not only the right of dominion, for territorial coastal authority: "Accordingly, on the assumption that any part of the sea is susceptible of appropriation, no serious question can arise as to the existence of property in marginal waters".

[60] From the files of the Archive of the Ministry of Foreign Affairs. Humble Reports for 1836 and 1837. Compare F. F. Martens, Собрание трактатов и конвенций [Collection of Treaties and Conventions], XII, p. 62ff.

[61] Perels, note 4 above, p. 42 et seq.

VII. On Straits

§101. There is no need to explain the significance of straits for international turnover. In view of the unobstructed communication through straits, States have since time immemorial and on many occasions entered into international agreements, especially with respect to straits connecting the high seas. The following main principles have been established in the contemporary theory and practice which determine the authority of coastal States over straits.

If a strait is within two cannon shots of the same State, it is considered to be under the authority of the last and regarded as a territorial possession thereof; if a strait is shared by two States and has a breadth of no more than six English miles, the line drawn through the middle of the strait serves as the boundary between both States.[62]

Thus, the Dardanelles and the Bosphorus, enclosed by the possessions of the Ottoman Empire, must be deemed to be Turkish straits. The Strait of Kerchensk belongs to Russia.

But to us it seems more correct from the standpoint of freedom of navigation to distinguish straits connecting two free seas from those which connect a closed sea with a free sea. A strait which connects high seas should be free to all commercial ships of all States irrespective of whether the possessions of one State enclosed it or not. Passage may be prohibited only to warships if the security of the State possessing the strait so requires. On the contrary, a strait leading to a closed sea is subject to the unlimited authority of the coastal State. The distinction made by us is the natural consequence of a general principle – freedom of the high seas.

Taking this distinction into account, it is understandable why the powers have agreed to insist on the abolition of duties recovered by Denmark from all ships which pass through the Sound Straits. In this case the duty hampered the freedom of navigation between high seas – the Baltic and German seas – and was contrary to this freedom. At the initiative of the Washington Government, the powers under the 1857 Copenhagen Treaty bought up the Sound duty for a determined amount, at the expense of which the Danish Government was obliged to maintain lighthouses and other installations essential for the safety of the passage of vessels through the Sound.

The Bosphorus and Dardanelles also connect high seas, and therefore, despite the fact that they belong to Turkey, should remain free for trade

[62] Bluntschli, note 1 above, §303; Phillimore, note 1 above, I, p. 224 et seq.; Heffter, note 1 above, §76.

relations. This freedom was formally secured first by the 1841 London Treaty and then confirmed by treaties: Paris of 1856, London of 1871, and Berlin of 1878, which gave to the Porte the right not to allow warships through the straits.[63]

VIII. On Rivers

§102. A distinction is made in the science of international law, entirely properly, between rivers flowing within the territorial possessions of one State and those which flow through the territorial possessions of different States. With regard to the first, all are agreed that they for their entire extent, from sources to mouths, are subject exclusively to the authority of that State on whose territory they are situated. As regards the second, then *stricto jure* each of the States through whose possessions the same river flows are free to dispose of and use the part thereof belonging to it at its discretion. Many States, however, have abused their right to such an extent that trade and navigation along international rivers has been made virtually impossible. In order to eliminate the consequences harmful to commerce which emanate both from abuses of territorial authority over such rivers and from the diversity of rules applicable on the same river within different States, attempts were undertaken to subject all rivers flowing through different territories to a single regime and more or less permanent rules.[64]

On the basis of the 1815 Act of Vienna, the powers in whose possessions the same navigable river flows or serves as a boundary obliged themselves, by common consent, to establish navigation rules for this river (Article 108), the statutes which thus must be drafted would have certain general rules sketched in the Treaty of Vienna. These principles ensuring full freedom of navigation on international rivers were applied to the Rhine, Elbe, and Schelde. The 1856 Treaty of Paris extended them to the Danube and, in addition, in order to develop navigation on that river, founded the European Danube Commission, endowed with respect to navigation on the lower Danube with rights which in many respects cut across the sovereignty of the territorial riparian States and did not arise from the Congress of Vienna. Indeed, the European Danube Commission, as an institution whose existence was not justified by the use of navigation, long since should have

63 Perels, note 4 above, p. 35 et seq; Wheaton, note 16 above, §190, et seq. Also compare *Staatsarchiv*, XVI, No. 3558; XX, No. 4239.

64 Wheaton, note 48 above, II, p. 184 et seq; Ed. Engelhardt, *Du régime conventionnel des fleuves internationaux* (Paris, 1879); Bluntschli, note 1 above, §312-316; Heffter, note 1 above, §77; Phillimore, note 1 above, I, §162 et seq; Hall, note 1 above, p. 106, et seq.

been closed and ceded place to a "riparian commission". Respect for the freedom of river navigation does not require the taking of measures that clearly and uselessly violate the legitimate rights and interests of riparian States. Moreover, the 1878 Treaty of Berlin not only confirmed the provisions of the Paris Treaty relating to the Danube, but elaborated them in a sense expressly violating the 1815 Act of Vienna. By the London Convention of 10 March 1883, the existence of the European Danube Commission was extended for 21 years.[65]

[65] We shall return in the Special Part to this vitally important question of navigation on international rivers.

Chapter 4
International Treaties

I. On International Treaties

§103. An international treaty is an agreement of the will of two or several States. It establishes certain obligatory relations between the States which concluded it and always has served as one of the best means for the identification and determination of legal relations, even principles of law which should dominate in international relations. Finally, it is not subject to any doubt that treaties should be complied with by the Contracting Parties: "*Pacta sunt servanda*".

Such are the general basic principles which are set out in textbooks on international treaties by all jurists.[1] But disagreement is immediately discovered if one asks: on what is the binding force of treaties based? Some writers confer on treaties primarily a morally binding character, asserting that the honor and dignity of States which have signed a treaty requires performance in good faith. Others carry over this duty from the prescriptions of religion, or say that the laws of nature direct peoples to determine mutual relations by treaties which therefore must be observed. Recently a theory has been developed in detail basing the force of treaties on the "self-limitation of will" of the States which concluded them.[2] Finally, in the opinion of Bluntschli, the binding force of international treaties arises from the "legal consciousness of the human species".[3]

All of these explanations have little evidence. So, first of all, the position advanced by Bluntschli is so flexible that it can rightly be attributed to both international obligations and to all other types of legal relations

[1] Compare Montague Bernard, *Four Lectures on Subjects Connected with Diplomacy* (London, 1868), p. 163 et seq; Robert Joseph Phillimore, *Commentaries upon International Law* (3d ed.; London, 1879), II, p. 64 et seq; Henry Wager Halleck, *International Law, or, Rules Regulating the Intercourse of States in Peace and War* (New York, 11861), chapter VIII; William Edward Hall, *International Law* (Oxford, 1880), p. 271 et seq; Georg Friedrich Martens, *Précis du droit des gens moderne de l'Europe* (1801), I, §53; Johann Caspar Bluntschli, *Das moderne Völkerrecht der civilisirten Staten als Rechtsbuch dargestellt* (3d ed.; Nördlingen, 1878), §402 et seq; August Wilhelm Heffter, *Das europäische Völkerrecht der Gegenwart* (7th ed.; Berlin, 1881), §81; Ernst Meier, *Über den Abschluss von Staatsverträgen* (Leipzig, 1877); Georg Jellinek, *Die rechtliche Natur der Staatenverträge* (Vienna, 1880); Ferdinando Laghi, *Teoria dei trattati internazionali* (Parma, 1882); Otfried Nippold, *Der völkerrechtliche Vertrag* (Bern, 1894).

[2] Jellinek, note 1 above, p. 31 et seq.

[3] Bluntschli, note 1 above, §410.

not only between States, but also between individuals and societies. No less surprising is the view that the binding force of treaties arises from the "self-limitation of will" of States. If when signing a treaty a State finds it necessary to limit its will, then, if violating it, may refer to the fact that such limitation is excessive. Finally, neither morality, nor religion, or the laws of nature obviously constitute the legal grounds justifying compliance with treaties.

The binding nature and, consequently the legal significance of international treaties is based solely on the recognition of the legal capacity of one State by another. States must recognize one another as subjects of law; they must recognize mutual rights: otherwise, any relations between them are impossible. In other words, the binding nature of international treaties arises from the concept of an international community. *Ubi societas, ibi jus est*. When entering into international relations, States are subject to the operation of immutable vital needs and relations which determine the conditions under which States are in a position to achieve their reasonable goals. These conditions take the form of legal norms, and because international treaties are a formulation of vital relations existing between States, these norms also must comprise the content of treaties concluded by States and are as binding as the treaties themselves are binding.

It follows that the purposes and relations from which international life is formed must be reflected in international obligations or treaties. In view of this, the study of treaties is not only desirable, but essential in order to become familiar with the external relations of States. Moreover, the treaties concluded for ensuring the interests of States serve as an indicator of to what degree of development the civic and cultural life of peoples which concluded them is and how properly their State order is structured. If there are no guarantees in the structure of the State for full respect of the interests of the people, then the treaties in whose name they are concluded will be perhaps a reflection of the genius or perhaps the arbitrariness of those persons who had the possibility to dispose of their fate but not the needs and aspirations of the people.

It also is evident that if the vital relations and goals determine the content of international treaties, the performance thereof is the better ensured the more those rules and norms that are established by the vital relations of States themselves are respected in the concluded circumstances. Interest and own advantage force States to conclude international treaties, and interest and advantage ensure recognition of their being binding. A court does not exist in the European international union which would enforce compliance with treaties. As regards the moral force of obligations, its significance in international relations should not be exaggerated.

In general the binding force of treaties, just as any moral or legal law, depends not so much on their actual protection as on the force of being binding which we ascribe to them and recognize for them. On this basis one may put the rule that the degree of being binding and implementation of international treaties is determined by the extent of their conformity to the real reasonable needs of States and their mutual relations.

This proposition explains why international treaties are violated so often. In justification of the proverbial fragility of treaties, usually reference is made to a circumstance that the interests and advantage of States underlying treaties often are opposed to one another and lead to conflicts. It seems to me that such "conflicts of interests", if they are not a phrase – are the result not so much the actual order of things as a consequence of mutual distrust and suspicions dividing States and especially personal passions and preconceptions with which people are imbued who direct international relations and conclude international transactions. The true reason for the frequent violation of treaties is not a "conflict of interests", but the fact that treaties often are concluded without knowledge and sufficient respect for mutual reasonable relations and advantage of the contracting parties.

The 1856 Treaty of Paris serves as evidence in those provisions which concerned Russia and ran counter to its basic rights as an independent power. Russia could and should have rejected these provisions, and she acted as predicted in advance and was well-known to the Contracting Powers at the Paris Congress.

Insofar as life itself leaves an imprint on international treaties and gives them their content, this can be seen in all the treaties which were concluded by Russia with the European and Asian peoples. For example, the treaties between Russia and Prussia, beginning from 1517 when the first treaty of alliance between them was concluded, down to the present are closely linked with the geographical position of both States and with the goals of national policy which they both pursued.[4] The same with the treaties between Russia and China, which reflect the actual conditions in which relations between them happened: both powers being neighbors, common trade interests, and so on.[5]

[4] Compare the Introduction to F. F. Martens, Собрание трактатов и конвенций, заключенных Россиею с иностранными державами [Collection of Treaties and Conventions Concluded by Russia with Foreign Powers] (Spb., 1874-1909). 15 vols. (hereinafter: F. F. Martens, Собрание трактатов и конвенций [Collection of Treaties and Conventions]), V.

[5] Compare F. F. Martens, *Le conflit entre la Russie et la Chine, ses origines, son développement et sa portée universelle* (Brussels, 1880), p. 8. Russian translation by Telesnitskii (1881).

In the absence of legislative power regulating international relations, State treaties have special significance as a source of international law (see Introduction, §43, II).

II. Conditions of Conclusion and Legal Force of Treaties

§104. In order to be valid, international treaties must satisfy certain basic conditions which relate to: 1) the persons concluding the obligation (subjective conditions), and 2) the subject-matter of treaties (objective conditions). In both respects, the following main principles have been developed and recognized in positive international law.

A. Subjective Conditions

The first material subjective condition for the validity of international treaties is that they were concluded between fully independent States. Semi-independent States do not possess the legal capacity to conclude treaties, and if in reality they bind themselves or are bound by them, it is due to their abnormal, from the viewpoint of international law, position.[6] Agreements between independent States and the Roman curia (concordats) are not international treaties because the representative of the Roman Catholic Church – the Roman curia – cannot be considered to be a subject of international law. On the contrary, treaties between uneducated States and States of European culture and civilization are called treaties, but the principles not of European international law, but of natural law, should be applicable to them.

The second subjective condition making an international treaty binding is expressed in the requirement that it was concluded by individuals empowered to bind in the name of a particular State and with observance of the procedures existing therein for this event.

In an absolute monarchy the sovereign has the unlimited right to bind his people by treaties. The exercise of this right in representative States is often left to certain formalities provided in a law, and the Head of State, without the consent of the people's representatives, cannot always be considered to have the dispositive legal capacity to sign international obligations.

[6] Compare *Staatsarchiv*, XXIX, No. 5482, an identical instruction given by Russia, Germany, and Austria-Hungary to their ambassadors at the Porte with regard to the rights of the Danube principality to autonomously conclude trade treaties.

Therefore, the government must know the domestic procedures of that State with which it wishes to enter into a treaty.[7]

International treaties are concluded in the name of sovereign State power which alone has the right to bind its people and represent it in international relations. In some instances it is difficult to decide who should be considered to be the possessor of sovereign power in a State; for example, in the case of usurpation, internecine war, the existence of two candidates for an open throne, and so on. In general, only the government has the right to enter into international treaties, which *de facto* is the representative of the State and to which the people are actually subject. The question of the origin of particular State authority does not relate to the field of international law.

Usually monarchs empower particular individuals to conclude treaties who act in the name of the State. Every treaty concluded correctly by a duly empowered person is binding on the State upon confirmation thereof in the established procedure and, *vice versa*, does not have binding force if concluded by an individual not empowered or who exceeds his powers. In the last instance the treaty will be a simple promise (*sponsio*), for the performance of which the State is not liable.

For example, the Commander in Chief of forces and heads of squadrons during war do not enjoy the right to conclude preliminary peace conditions without the formal empowerment on the part of the sovereign State authority. Therefore, if they entered into this kind of obligation, these would have no legal force. But the right to conclude armistices and various other kinds of military conventions (for example, cartels on extradition or exchange of prisoners of war) usually are within the powers of these individuals: signed by them, they are directly binding. The question of the right of the Commander-in-Chief of an army to agree to peace conditions offered to him is considered in detail by jurists especially with regard to the history of the Caudine Gorges.[8]

§105. The third subjective condition is the need for confirmation or ratification of international treaties. By ratification is understood the formal acceptance by the sovereign State authority of a treaty concluded by duly empowered persons. The authorities of international law are agreed that ratification is essential for the binding force and operation of a treaty. Before the signature of a treaty, the plenipotentiaries exchange their powers and sign it on the basis of instructions given to them. Nonetheless, it

[7] Meier, note 1 above, p. 103ff. Also compare Unger, "Über die Gültigkeit von Staatsverträgen", *Grünhut's Zeitschrift*, VI, p. 349 et seq.

[8] See especially Emer Vattel, *Le droit des gens* (1758), liv. II, §209 et seq.

will not bind the contracting parties unless ratified by a competent State authority. The right of such confirmation belongs solely to the sovereign State authority of each of the contracting parties, whoever exercises this power, whether by the monarch alone, or by the sovereign together with other institutions. Under what conditions and in what procedure should ratification follow is determined by the domestic structure of each State. But if it is given, the treaty is considered to have begun operation usually not from the moment of confirmation, but from signature by the empowered persons: "*Ratihabitio retrorahitur ad initium negotii*". Accordingly, the date and year of conclusion is designated in the treaty and entered in a separate Article, which provides that the treaty will be ratified and the exchange of ratifications will follow within some period.[9]

§106. The said rules are set out by all writers as undoubted and consecrated by custom. Disagreement begins with the question of under what conditions a refusal of ratification should be deemed to be well-founded, legitimate, and just? Can one assert that a State is free always and under all circumstances not to give its sanction to a treaty?

Some writers, for example Grotius and Pufendorf, suggest that such a refusal is illegitimate unless the plenipotentiaries have exceeded their powers. Others, such as Bynkershoek, Vattel, and Georg Friedrich Martens, say that a State is bound by a treaty concluded by its representatives unless they violated secret instructions given to them. Refusal to ratify under the last condition, although it would be in the view of these writers, a "violation of honor and good relations", cannot be called unfounded. Finally, recent jurists – Heffter, Bluntschli, Hall, Phillimore – find refusal to ratify in general to be "dangerous" in view of the "enormous importance of international acts", and therefore think that arbitrary refusal, if not from the legal then from the moral standpoint, is unjust and should not be permitted.

In order to properly resolve the question put, it is necessary, it seems to us, to proceed from the concept on the prerogatives of sovereign State power. As a principle, the general proposition must be defended that until

[9] H. Grotius, *De jure belli ac pacis*, lib. II, cap. XI, §12; C. Bynkershoek, *Quaestiones juris publ.*, cap. VII; Vattel, note 8 above, liv. II, §156; Martens, note 1 above, liv. II, §48; Johann Ludwig Klüber, *Droit des gens moderne de l'Europe* (2d ed. ; 1874), liv. II, §42; Phillimore, note 1 above, II, p. 75; Hall, note 1 above, p. 276; Bluntschli, note 1 above, §419-421; Heffter, note 1 above, §87; Christian Friedrich Wurm, "Die Ratification von Staatsverträgen", *Deutsche Vierteljahrsschrift* (1845), p. 163 et seq; G. Carnazza Amari, *Trattato sul diritto internazionale pubblico di pace* (1875), p. 758; Carlos Calvo, *Le droit international théorique et pratique* (4th ed.; Paris, 1887-1896), I, p. 654 et seq; Jellinek, note 1 above, p. 53; Unger, note 7 above, VI, p. 355 et seq.

ratification an international treaty is not a treaty proper, an act having some sort of binding force. For a treaty to be binding, ratification is as necessary as the sanction is essential of sovereign power for the legal suitability of any draft law, and as the sovereign authority may refuse confirmation of any legal provision developed and adopted by the chambers or State council, so it always has under all circumstances the right not to confirm a treaty which its plenipotentiaries signed.

But the view is mistaken that the sovereign authority can never transfer this right to any other person. In exceptional instances, exercise of the right of ratification may be assigned to certain officials or to special representatives. For example, during a war the commander in chief is sometimes given the power not only for the autonomous conclusion of cartels, but also a preliminary peace, and even the right to implement proposed peace conditions without awaiting confirmation of the sovereign. The right of sanction of treaties sometimes is entrusted to the governors of border and remote provinces; for example, in Russia the Governor-General of Turkestan enjoyed this right with respect to treaties concluded by him with Central Asian rulers, and in England, the Viceroy of East India. In 1801 a treaty concluded between Russia and France was ratified on behalf of Emperor Alexander I, by Count [Arkadii Ivanovich] Morkov [(1747-1827)].[10]

In the possibility of this kind of powers lies the difference between the sanction of draft laws and the ratification of treaties. At present, all international treaties usually are confirmed personally by sovereigns, not excluding those which are concluded by governors of remote regions, the more so that telegraph communications fully allow the actions of plenipotentiaries to be supervised in this respect.

In rare instances ratification was not essential for the implementation of treaties. For example, at the 1840 London Conference certain measures to resolve a Turkish-Egyptian conflict were implemented by a special secret Article signed by the plenipotentiaries of the powers which provided that the measures worked out would be implemented immediately without awaiting their ratification. Such hasty action by the allies was generated by completely exceptional circumstances in which Turkey found itself at the time, thanks to victories over Muhammad Ali [Pasha al-Mas'ud ibn Agha (1769-1849)].[11] It is understandable that there is no need for ratification

10 Georg Friedrich Martens, *Recueil des traités*, Suppl., II, p. 551; Alexandre Jehan Henry de Clercq, *Recueil des traités de la France* (1880), I, p. 467. See F. F. Martens, Собрание трактатов и конвенций [Collection of Treaties and Conventions]), XIII, p. 263 et seq.

11 See François Guizot, *Mémoires pour servir à l'histoire de mon temps* (Paris, 1860),

also when sovereigns themselves directly conclude a treaty with one another, the consent of a legislative institution not being required according to the form of government in their States. The rather important defensive and offensive alliance between Catherine II and Josef II was concluded in this form, they having exchanged letters of 12 April and 18 May 1781 in which the conditions of the treaty were set out in detail.[12] The Villafranca peace between France and Austria was concluded in 1859 also by personal explanations of Napoleon III with Franz-Joseph.

§107. Refusal of ratification not only is permitted, but absolutely essential in the following main instances: when plenipotentiaries who have signed a treaty exceeded their powers; when a competent State institution – a parliament, congress, or State council – does not give consent to the adoption of the treaty; when a material change has occurred in the circumstances under which the treaty was signed (if, for example, the sovereign in whose name and empowerment the negotiations were conducted, was deprived of the throne or if the subject-matter of the treaty was destroyed, and so on); finally, when it turns out that the signature of the treaty was the result of coercion over the will of the plenipotentiaries or was a consequence of their deceit or error.

The consent of the chambers has importance in particular: the failure to approve the treaty always is regarded as a legal reason for refusal of ratification. But it essential that the chamber or other competent institution be given the possibility to express their opinion; that is, were actually asked about the treaty. Sometimes this is lost from view.

The President of the United States, [Grover] Cleveland [(1837-1908)] in 1885 refused to submit for the ratification of Congress the Act of the Berlin African Conference signed by two plenipotentiaries of the United States on the grounds that this Act placed on the republic the duty to guarantee the inviolability of the State of the Congo. The United States should, according to the words of a Presidential message, confine its activity only to America. Curiously, at that time the sole and first diplomatic agent attached to the Government of the State of the Congo was a Mister Tisdale, appointed by the Washington Government.

The aforementioned convention of 1867 concluded between Denmark and the United States on the sale to the last of the islands of St. Thomas and St. John which belonged to Denmark was not ratified. In both States the

IV, p. 324ff.

12 See F. F. Martens, Собрание трактатов и конвенций [Collection of Treaties and Conventions], II, No. 36.

convention, as had been provided, had to receive confirmation within six months of its signature. The Danish Government actually ratified the treaty within the designated period, confirming it in the established legislative procedure and even setting about performance, having issued a proclamation on transfer of the islands to the United States. However, the chairman of the Senate Foreign Relations Committee in Washington, the well-known [Charles] Sumner, refused to submit it for discussion of the Senate. The Washington Government had to agree a new period for ratification.[13]

On the other hand, if the sovereign authorities confirm the treaty without asking the competent institution, the contracting party has the right to demand performance because it is not its business to enter into a consideration of whether the co-contracting government, in confirming the treaty, violates its own laws.

Therefore, the Washington Government, having concluded a treaty in 1831 with France for the payment of 25 million francs for losses caused to the [United] States during the Napoleonic wars and to issue a bill of exchange for part of the amount, after the French Government commenced performance of the treaty and its ratification, considered itself to have the right to insist on payment under the bill of exchange despite the fact that the French chambers had not ratified this treaty.[14]

But if a treaty is not ratified by one of the contracting parties, the other does not have the right to behave as if ratification had actually ensued.

On this basis the United States would have behaved illegally if it has agreed with the proposal of its Government to consider a treaty binding on Spain which was concluded in 1819 between it and the United States, ignoring the fact that this treaty, not confirmed by the Cortez, had not been ratified by the Spanish Government.

As we noted, without ratification a treaty is not binding. If before ratification thereof one of the parties set about performance and ratification did not follow, it may return to the former state of affairs. Refusal of ratification restores the *status quo ante* insofar as, of course, this is actually possible. Therefore, it would be more reasonable not to perform anything stipulated in the treaty earlier than final ratification thereof.

If the right to refuse ratification of an international treaty undoubtedly belongs to the sovereign authorities of a contracting State, then on the other hand it is no less undoubted that such refusal must relate to the entire treaty

[13] See §91 above. James Parton, *The Danish Islands: Are We Bound in Honor to Pay for Them?* (Boston, 1869), p. 43; Eugene Schuyler, *American Diplomacy and the Furtherance of Commerce* (1886), p. 23. Compare also Meier, note 1 above, pp. 163-211.

[14] Calvo, note 1 above, I, §708.

and not to particular parts thereof. Such partial ratification in the form of a statement on recognition of the binding nature of only certain Articles of a signed treaty has not been permitted until recently and would clearly be nonsense.

However, the French Government, under the pressure of idle speeches by members of the Chamber of Deputies, refused in 1891 to ratify the entire General Act of the 1890 Brussels antislavery conference. Of 100 Articles, it excluded 24 and only 76 Articles were ratified by the French Government. It is highly desirable that this unfortunate and unparalleled fact not be imitated in the future. From the standpoint of common sense and practice only the complete refusal of ratification of an international act signed by plenipotentiaries is permissible.

§108. The rule has been established with regard to the operation of ratification that it has retroactive force, namely – makes the treaty binding from the moment of signature by the plenipotentiaries. *Ratihabitio retrorahitur ad initium negotii.*

This is a generally-recognized rule proclaimed as an axiom by all writers on international law and completely without foundation. If an international treaty before ratification is nothing more than a draft obligation or simple promise lacking legal force, then obviously it is impossible to treat it as valid from the moment of signature, which does not make the treaty binding. The operation of a treaty may and should commence only from the moment of ratification.

In conclusion, we cite several instances when States have refused ratification. From Russian history we may point to the following relevant examples: 1) The Treaty of 2 March 1711 between Russia and Prussia was not ratified by the King of Prussia, as [Count Gavriil Ivanovich] Golovkin [(1660-1734)] reported: "Because this treaty is not advantageous to the Prussian court, and it is dangerous to rebel against the Swedes, so as not to annoy them this treaty must remain invalid".[15] 2) Convention of alliance with Prussia, 13(24) September 1712, again not ratified by Friedrich I, who this time referred to his plenipotentiary exceeding his powers. The real reason, as in the first case, was the fear of the King of Prussia to enter into open struggle against the Swedes.[16] 3) The Treaty of 13 December 1732 between Prussia, Austria, and Russia on facilitating the election to the Polish throne of the Portuguese Prince [Infante] Manuel [Count of Ourém (1697-1766)]

[15] See F. F. Martens, Собрание трактатов и конвенций [Collection of Treaties and Conventions], V, p. 88, Annex §1, p. 379.

[16] See Ibid., V, p. 90, Annex §2, p. 386.

and a Prussian prince to the Courland Duchies, and also the accession to Prussia of certain German territories, was not ratified by Charles VI [(1685-1740)] on the grounds that the imperial envoy had no powers to conclude such a treaty. As a consequence, the Treaty did not acquire legal and binding force for any of the contracting parties.[17] 4) The treaty of alliance between Russia (Peter III) and Prussia (Friedrich II) of 8(19) June 1762 remained unratified as a result of a coup d'état which occurred in Russia on 28 June (ascension to the throne of Catherine II).[18] 5) The treaty of 20 July 1806 concluded between Russia and France was not ratified by Emperor Alexander I because the Sovereign found that his plenipotentiary, [Petr Iakovlevich] Ubri [(1774-1847)], exceeded the powers given to him.[19] 6) The Treaty of Livadia between Russia and China concluded at St. Petersburg on 20 September 1879 with the mediation of the Chinese ambassador, Chonghou [(1826-1893)], and ratified by the Russian Emperor, but did not enter into force as a result of the Peking Government not ratifying it, accusing its ambassador of exceeding his authority.[20]

In addition, the three instances below of the failure to ratify concluded treaties which occurred recently are noteworthy: 1) A treaty was concluded in 1841 between England, France, Russia, Austria, and Prussia relating to general measures for the termination of the slave trade. Having failed to achieve the consent of the French chambers, which considered the right to inspect merchant ships stipulated by the English to be incompatible with the honor and dignity of the French merchant flag, the Government of the King of the French, Louis-Philippe I [(1773-1850)], refused ratification thereof. This refusal, not in itself containing anything illegal, was respected by the other powers, but the former First Minister of France, [François Pierre Guillaume] Guizot [(1787-1874)], sent him reflections with whose substantiation one must positively disagree. Guizot demonstrated that every government is free to give or not its sanction to a treaty signed by the

[17] See Ibid., I, p. 64, Annex §1, p. 311 et seq.

[18] Ibid., V, Annex §3. Compare Sergei M. Solov'ev, История России с древнейших времен [History of Russian from Ancient Times], XXV, p. 88 et seq.

[19] See F. F. Martens, Собрание трактатов и конвенций [Collection of Treaties and Conventions], XIII, Annex. G. de Garden, *Histoire générale des traités de paix et autres transactions principales entre toutes les puissances de l'Europe depuis la paix de Westphalie* (Paris, 1848-1887), IX, p. 308 et seq.

[20] Martens, note 5 above, p. 67 et seq.

plenipotentiaries thereof entirely at its own discretion and without justifying the refusal by any plausible arguments.[21]

It is hardly possible to defend this view because if the right of ratification constituted the undoubted prerogative of sovereign State power, the exercise of this right assumes sufficient reasonable grounds justifying its use in the eyes of the other contracting parties; refusal to ratify arbitrarily or through caprice is not just and is unworthy of a State.

2) The 1869 London treaty between England and the United States relating to the Alabama question, concluded by fully empowered persons, was not confirmed by the Washington Congress and therefore remained without ratification.

3) In 1876 a convention was concluded between England and China at Chifu, on the basis of which trade in opium was limited, but for this the English received certain new privileges and rights. The Chinese Government imprudently partly performed this convention before ratification, and because the London Cabinet ultimately did not ratify, English subjects succeeded in partly using the advantages which the convention granted and to repeal which the Chinese Government was unable to do.[22]

§109. The fourth subjective condition comprises the free will of the contracting parties. Agreement is essential for the force of treaties, the unity of will of the contracting parties relative to those obligations which they mutually or unilaterally assume. Mistake and deceit, destroying this unity, make an international agreement invalid. In this respect State treaties do not differ from private-law contracts. But they are materially different in another respect: in legal transactions between private individuals coercion always vitiates the binding force of the contract; on the contrary, international treaties concluded by forcible means are binding in principle, such as, for example, all peace treaties.

This proposition is based on a general presumption of the freedom of action of States in their mutual relations. A State which is defeated in war against another power and under the pressure of its misfortune signed a peace treaty in reality does not have complete freedom, but formally it remains free, having the choice between continuation of the war and the conclusion of peace. In declaring war, it should foresee the inevitable consequences of

[21] Guizot, note 11 above, VI, chapter XXXVI, p. 161.

[22] William Frederick Mayers, *Treaties between the Empire of China and Foreign Powers* (Shanghai, 1877), p. 44; Fry, "China, England and Opium", *Contemporary Review* (January 1878), p. 313; Theodore Christlieb, *Le commerce Indo-Britannique de l'opium et ses effets* (Paris, 1879).

defeat and know that in the event of no success it must agree to those peace conditions which the victor lays down. In this sense the peace treaties are treaties lawfully compelled and must be complied with.[23]

But a treaty will not be valid if natural persons empowered to conclude it or a sovereign are subjected to coercion or fright and under the influence of this circumstance sign the treaty. In this case the will of those persons who act in the name of the State is under the pressure of coercion which excludes the possibility of a free decision, and therefore the treaty cannot be binding.

The obligations signed by the King of Spain, Ferdinand VII [(1784-1833)] in 1807 at Bayonne on abdication and others which the threats of Napoleon I forced were compelled and therefore invalid. On the contrary, the peace treaty which the King of France, Francis I [(1494-1547)], concluded while imprisoned in Madrid in 1526, and also the act of abdication signed by Napoleon I at Fontainebleau (1814), were a consequence of the force of circumstances, but not physical force or threat directed personally against these sovereigns and consequently may not be considered to lack binding force.

Precisely the same, if Napoleon III, in 1870, during the confinement at Wilhelmshöhe and continuing to remain the Emperor of the French, signed a peace treaty with Germany, that treaty would have been valid insofar as he was not compelled by violence against the person of the imprisoned Emperor.[24]

Finally, the fifth subjective condition is the mutuality of the expression of will. It is essential for the validity of a treaty that the proposal made by one party be accepted by the other. Only on this basis may one speak of the unity of will of the contracting parties which is assumed by treaties. But there is no need that the proposal directly precede its acceptance. One may point to cases, rare to be sure, when consent was given in advance of the proposal.

Thus, the Declaration of Sweden of 7 November 1772 on the preservation of peace encompassed the adoption of a counter-declaration by Denmark, which followed two days later (9 November 1772).[25]

[23] Heffter, note 1 above, §85-98; Bluntschli, note 1 above, §408.

[24] Henry Wheaton, *Elements of International Law*, ed. Richard Henry Dana (8th ed.; London, 1866), §267; G. F. Martens, note 1 above, liv. II, chapter II, §58; Léopold von Neumann, *Grundriss des heutigen europäischen Völkerrechts* (2d ed.; 1877), §28.

[25] G. F. Martens, *Recueil des traités*, III, p. 248; Suppl., II, p. 170.

B. Objective Conditions

§110. The subject-matter (*causa*) of international obligations may be all that appertains to the domain of international relations and turnover. But in and of itself, of course, every State may oblige itself only relative to those things and rights which *de facto* or *de jure* are at its disposition and power. Thus, the subject-matter of an international treaty is determined by the dispositive legal capacity of the States which concluded it. International treaties are subject to the following requirements with respect, in particular, to their object.

First, it is essential that the physical and moral possibility existed for the performance of the international treaty. Obligations not physically performable and immoral do not have legal force. One can reasonably wish only what is actually possible; the ought is only the possible morally.

If many treaties in reality clearly violate these conditions, especially obliging immoral actions, this does not prove that they were possible and permissible from a legal point of view.

Bluntschli enumerates those instances when treaties should be deemed to be invalid on the basis of their subject-matter. Treaties establishing slavery or protecting it; declaring foreigners *ex lex*; abolishing freedom of the high seas; prescribing religious oppression; finally, treaties establishing worldwide dominion – do not have force.[26] Of course, such treaties may not be considered to be binding. But many of them are inconceivable and, moreover, hardly exhaust all instances of the legal unsuitability of treaties with respect to their content.

As a general rule encompassing all such kinds of treaties, one may lay down the proposition that any treaty limiting or destroying the basic rights of a State is not binding on it morally enough so as not to make an attempt to abrogate it. On the contrary, the burdensomeness of a treaty, its unsuitability or *laesio enormis*, should not serve as grounds for a refusal to perform it.

Second, in essence a treaty is binding only for the parties which concluded it. No State entering into a treaty may, without powers, bind a third power. It is not important what the subject-matter or content is, collective treaties are binding only on their contracting parties.

Accordingly, the 1785 treaty between Prussia and the United States, which had great significance in view of the fact that the contracting parties obliged themselves to respect the private property of their subjects mutually during war on land and at sea and renounced the right to issue letters of marque, was binding only on those two powers. The Paris Declaration of 16

[26] Bluntschli, note 1 above, §411, 412.

April 1856 finally abolished privateering, but was not formally accepted by the North American United States, Mexico, and Spain and was not binding on those States.

Third, a right already ceded under a treaty to a certain State may not be ceded anew to another State.

France in 1740, justly from a formal standpoint, refused to recognize the right of Maria-Theresa to the throne of Charles VI because it already was obligated in favor of Bavaria not to give consent to the procedure of succession to the throne established by the Pragmatic Sanction. In 1774 the Porte obliged itself to recognize primacy of place for the Russian ambassador after the Austrian internuncio, but because this place had been secured for the representative of France in Constantinople in 1604, then with respect to Russia the Porte obviously could not perform its obligation.

III. On Participation of Third Powers in Treaties

§111. According to the general rule, a treaty is binding only on the contracting parties. The participation of third powers therein arises as a result of the entry or accession to the main parties of an outside State to which the obligations concluded by them extend to the third power. This accession is voluntary or coerced, formal or informal (semi-official), and revealed in the form of: 1) good offices; 2) mediation; 3) adhesion; 4) accession; and 5) interference.[27]

1) *Good offices* (*bons offices*). These are rendered at the good wish of a third power or at the request of the contracting parties and consist of arranging an agreement between the last, inclining them to a peaceful end to the dispute, or in an entreaty by one contracting party to the benefit of the other. A government rendering "good offices" does not participate in the treaty and is not a party to the obligation. There are many examples of the conclusion of international transactions through the "good offices" of an outside State, and it would be superfluous to cite them.

2) *Mediation.* Compared with good offices, this type of participation in a treaty by a third power is more definite. The mediating power participates in negotiations formally, usually by invitation of both parties or one of them, in rare cases autonomously, and endeavors to arrange an agreement on the basis of its proposals. Its role ceases only after the conclusion of a treaty or as a result of the complete failure of the negotiations. It does not ensure the performance of an obligation assumed during its mediation, but may become a party on the basis of a special act of accession to the treaty.

[27] Compare Calvo, note 9 above, I, §685; Heffter, note 1 above, §88.

As an example of mediation, one may cite the participation of Catherine II in settling the dispute between Austria and Prussia regarding the Bavarian succession. Thanks to the mediation of the Russian Empress the Teschen treaties (1779) were concluded, to which she herself acceded, having assumed formally a guarantee of their performance.[28] Napoleon III acted in this same role in 1866, without the invitation of the parties, and insisted on the signature by Austria and Prussia of the Nikolsburg preliminary peace treaty.

Finally, Germany was the mediator with regard to the convocation of a Congress in Berlin and the conclusion of the 1878 Treaty of Berlin. Comparing the action of the last with the role of Napoleon in the Austro-Prussian War, one must note that mediation may be exercised in various forms and have a various character. Prince Bismarck himself defined his own role as a mediator in 1878, saying that he only performed the duties of an "honest broker" for the parties in dispute. Mediation imposed on counter-parties loses the actual meaning of mediation and passes into interference.

3) *Adhésion*. This is a formal statement by a power concerning the recognition of a certain treaty being binding on it which already has been concluded by States. This statement is usually by invitation of the contracting parties and extends only to certain principles set out in the treaty or to part of the obligations assumed by a third State unconditionally or with reservations. Adhesion in general is less than the solemn acceptance of a treaty, such as accession, and often leads to the last.

For example, many powers initially "adhered" to the Declaration of Empress Catherine II of 28 February 1780 on the principles of the international law of the sea, declaring that they recognized these principles as agreeing both with their interests and with the legal consciousness of civilized peoples; then, at the suggestion of Catherine, these same powers concluded formal acts (treaties and conventions) with Russia and obliged themselves mutually to protect the principles proclaimed in the Declaration with all their sea and land forces (First Armed Neutrality). This was "adhesion" to the Act issued by Catherine.

The 1856 Paris Declaration signed by eight powers at the Paris Congress was then communicated to all States, who virtually all "adhered" to it, but did not accede because there were no special treaties between them determining the conditions (similar to the Treaties of Armed Neutrality) under which this Declaration must be complied with. It does not, of course, follow from this that the Paris Declaration was less binding than the Declaration of

[28] F. F. Martens, Собрание трактатов и конвенций [Collection of Treaties and Conventions], II, No. 35.

Catherine II because the form of recognition changes nothing of the essence of the legal obligation.

4) *Accession.* By this Act is understood the formal and solemn entry of a third power into a treaty, acceptance of it as a whole on completely equal rights with the main contracting parties. It is essential for the validity of such an Act that it be accepted by the initial contracting powers.

The recognition by various States of the 1815 Vienna treaties, Act of the Holy Alliance, and others as binding on them followed in this form.

5) *Interference (intervention).* We already have said (§76) that interference, unlike mediation, should be considered as any kind of undesirable intrusion by parties into negotiations occurring with respect to the conclusion of a treaty or with an agreement already made. It always has a coercive character and, in principle, should not happen. It is lawful only in one case: when a concluded treaty or negotiations violate the legal rights of another power.

Precisely from this point of view that the interference of England and Austria-Hungary in the relations of obligation between Russia and Turkey established by the preliminary San-Stefano peace treaty of 1878 should be discussed. As the grounds of its protest against the provisions of this treaty, it alleged a violation by Russia of the 1856 Treaty of Paris, which placed the fate of the Ottoman Empire under the collective protection of the powers which participated in the Paris Congress.

IV. On the External Form of International Treaties

§112. The external form for international treaties does not have remotely the same importance which it has in the private law of obligations. We do not speak of a particular form for treaties being binding because in the domain of international relations there is no sovereign authority which might prescribe compliance with any forms. And indeed, international obligations are concluded in the most diverse forms.[29]

In general, one may say that the external form of international treaties is determined by the importance of their content and the means of concluding them. But whether they are called treaties or conventions, protocols, or diplomatic notes, they are identically binding for the States which signed them.

[29] G. F. Martens, note 1 above, §58; Adolf Hartmann, *Institutionen des praktischen Völkerrechts in Friedenszeiten mit Rücksicht auf die Verfassung, die Verträge und die Gesetzgebung des Deutschen Reichs* (1874), p. 135; Theodore Schmalz, *Europäisches Völkerrecht in acht Büchern* (Berlin, 1817), p. 52; Bluntschli, note 1 above, §417; Neumann, note 24 above, §29.

Therefore, the view expressed by some public officials is unfounded that a declaration is not an international act equivalent to a treaty and is not binding. They assert that a declaration proclaims certain general principles whose reasonableness States which adhere to or issue them state by their signatures without, however, binding themselves to always comply with them.

But the facts are contrary to this view.

The binding character of the Paris Declaration Respecting Maritime Law is not contested by any State. In general, the 1868 Petersburg Declaration on the non-use during war of explosive bullets with a weight of less than 400 grams is also recognized and respected as is any treaty concluded by States. The binding nature of the Declaration of 1(13) January 1885 relating to the extradition of criminals between Russia and Prussia also is beyond question.

As practice shows, international treaties may be concluded even by the exchange of letters between sovereigns. The important obligations relating to the political interests of Empress Catherine II and the Emperor of Germany, Jozef II, were concluded in this form.[30]

As noted above, the various names of international treaties have no influence on either the character of the obligations assumed by States or on their force. Usually those international treaties which are concluded in especially solemn forms and instances such as, for example, the end of a war (peace treaty) are called treaties.

They begin: "In the name of the Holy Trinity" if concluded between Christian powers or – in treaties with the Porte – "In the name of Almighty God". Then follows an account of the circumstances and occasions which generated the conclusion of the treaty and the name of the plenipotentiary powers which participated in the negotiations. The offices, titles, and orders belonging to these persons are enumerated. The treaty itself is set out in the form of individual Articles and signed by the plenipotentiaries. Ratification is undertaken upon the conclusion of the treaty by the personal signatures of the heads of State.

As for conventions, in form they are less solemn and commence directly with an account of the reasons for which the Articles are set out and the signature of the plenipotentiaries follow. Ratification is necessary and given in the same form as for treaties.

[30] See F. F. Martens, Собрание трактатов и конвенций [Collection of Treaties and Conventions], II, §36.

All international treaties are written at present in the French language. Only England remains true to its language and gives all instructions to its plenipotentiaries and communicates notes in English.

There was controversy in works on international law as to whether a State is obliged by oral treaties? Because no generally established forms for international treaties exist, the obligations of States assumed orally are entirely possible and should be performed just as written obligations. There are no legal grounds to contest their permissibility and binding character in the domain of free international relations.[31]

In practice, sometimes such treaties are concluded. An alliance was formed in 1697 between Russia and Prussia orally. Peter the Great and the Elector of Brandenburg, Friedrich III [(1657-1713)], at a personal meeting in Pilau gave a solemn promise "so that in a convenient and necessary case, to help each other with all our forces against all enemies, and especially against the Swedes". Then, having shaken hands, the sovereigns exchanged kisses and sealed their treaty by an oath.[32]

Although oral international treaties are possible also at present, nonetheless the constitutional procedures in contemporary States are not favorable for their conclusion.

V. Types of International Treaties

§113. Attempts have repeatedly been made in the science of international law to divide (or classify) international treaties into certain types. But the experiments made so far of this kind have not been very successful.

Hugo Grotius tried to establish a division of treaties which would satisfy the special essence of international relations of obligation. Such a division was, in his view, the separation of treaties into: 1) treaties by which obligations are determined arising from natural law; and 2) treaties supplementing those obligations with new ones unknown to natural law.[33] But precisely which duties have natural law as their source is impossible to determine because of the ambiguity of the concept of natural law itself.

More recently, Heffter divided treaties into the following three types: 1) constitutive treaties (*Constitutiv-Vertrage*), on the basis of which States acquire certain rights, such as treaties on boundaries, partition, loan, and

31 G. F. Martens, note 1 above, §49; Heffter, note 1 above, p. 190; Klüber, note 9 above, §141.

32 See F. F. Martens, Собрание трактатов и конвенций [Collection of Treaties and Conventions], V, §183, p. 52.

33 Grotius, note 9 above, lib. II, cap. XV, §5.

so on; 2) regulatory treaties (*Regulatorische Vertrage*), by which political and social relations of States are regulated, for example, treaties on the conditions of mutual relations between States; finally, 3) partnership or alliance treaties (*Gesellschafts-Vertrage*), binding States to common actions for the sake of achieving a certain goal.[34]

But this division is extremely contradictory. All treaties, both constitutive and others, identically create certain rights and impose duties, and also they all, and not only regulatory treaties as Heffter supposes, regulate the "conditions of the mutual relations of States".

In Bluntschli's view, treaties may be divided into: 1) obligations concluded directly between two or several States; and 2) contracts and transactions which are concluded between subordinate officials and places.[35] This division is even more unsuccessful because States themselves, obviously, cannot conclude contracts; these are concluded in its name by various empowered persons; but all treaties, by whomsoever they were concluded, usually are confirmed by the sovereign State authority.

Many writers divide international treaties simply into treaties and conventions. They see the distinction between treaties and conventions in that the first require constant uninterrupted actions on the part of a State; on the contrary, the second are performed by one certain act.

Vattel, [Georg Friedrich] Martens, Wheaton, and, of Russian scholars, Professor [Vladimir Iakovlevich] Stoianov [(1826-1888)], adhere to this classification.[36] Stoianov said that of all the divisions of treaties, this is the simplest and most advisable; he adds that, unlike treaties, "someone's real right to things is established" by conventions.

One may note with regard to this division that it in general is based on the incidental fact of the greater or lesser solemnity of the form and means of concluding treaties, and not on the different character of their content. Moreover, this division, as Stoianov in particular understands it, is completely unfounded from the legal point of view. One cannot agree that all conventions are implemented "once", nor that they establish "someone's right to a thing". For example, cartels on the extradition of criminals are called conventions, but establish no right to a thing. Conventions concluded in the interests of justice, protection of literary and artistic property, naturalization, and many others create nothing of the kind.

34 Heffter, note 1 above, §89.

35 Bluntschlli, note 1 above, §442.

36 Vattel, note 8 above, liv. II, §153, 192; G. F. Martens, note 1 above, §58; Wheaton, note 24 above, §268; A. N. Stoianov, Очерки истории и догматики международного права [Essays on the History and Dogmatics of International Law] (1875), p. 447.

Finally, there is a view that international treaties may be divided into real and personal. By the first is understood treaties binding States as juridical persons; by the second – treaties which bind only the monarchs who signed them. This distinction no longer has practical significance because the vast majority of treaties are concluded by States as subjects of international law; the number of personal treaties concerning the interests of sovereigns alone is virtually nil.

By content, irrespective of their external form, international treaties may, in our view, be divided only into political and social. All international obligations, whatever their form and however they may be called, fall under these two categories, which have a precisely determined character and differ completely from one another.[37]

To the category of political treaties belong all treaties concerning the interests and rights of States, for example, treaties on the territorial possessions of States, international duties, rights and duties with respect to the high seas, all peace treaties, and others. Social treaties have in view the satisfaction of social interests and cultural needs of the people as a whole and of individual social classes and individuals. To these should be relegated conventions on literary property, extradition of criminals, naturalization, rights and duties of various spiritual societies, and especially international commercial treaties and treaties on navigation and shipping

In view of the foregoing on the influence of social interests on international relations, it is understandable that the increased number of social international treaties is the best evidence of the development of international relations and turnover. The view of the well-known English jurist and public figure, Montague Bernard, that the number of treaties in general is declining and that the fewer there are, the better for international law, is more paradoxical than well-founded.[38] The reduction of the number of treaties in general does not show the development of peaceful international relations, but rather the reduction only of treaties with political content. Indeed, the number of political international treaties, comparatively speaking, is declining. This can be seen in particular in the treaties of alliance, which were concluded in the seventeenth and eighteenth

[37] G. Jellinek, *Die Lehre von den Staatenverbindungen* (Vienna, 1882), p. 106, proceeds from the same basic provisions and came independently to the same conclusions. He divided international treaties into administrative (*Verwaltungs-vertrage*) and political (*politische*) treaties. The first coincide with "social" treaties under our classification. Jellinek, whose work appeared several months after the appearance of the first Russian edition of the present volume and before the appearance of the German edition thereof, could not have known the system adopted by us.

[38] Bernard, note 1 above, p. 194.

centuries in profusion. Some monarchs of those times were in alliance with nearly all States. Defensive and offensive alliances were concluded for a period of time and without such period, against certain States or against all powers. Treaties of alliance frequently were violated, and therefore rarely served the cause of peace and the development of international relations. The first and second Armed Neutralities were concluded for the express purpose of protecting peaceful commercial relations against infringements by naval belligerents, especially England. At present, formal alliances are rare and exceptional. Contemporary States are aware that alliances will be established by themselves through mutual interests that bind them, and not by any political combinations devoid of a real foundation.

VI. Performance of International Treaties

§114. Just as private obligations, international treaties must be performed in good faith. Without this condition, they would have no decisive influence and sense. Performance *bona fide* assumes consent to not only the letter, but also the spirit, of the treaty. The distinction allowed by some writers in the performance of the main and the secondary treaty provisions is unfounded.[39] Because all Articles of a treaty are identically signed and confirmed by the sovereign authority, a violation of one, albeit not important, is equivalent to a violation of the entire treaty. In view of the primary importance of international treaties, it is never sufficient to categorically insist on the provision: "*Pacta sunt servanda*". Suspension of performance or the failure to perform may be permitted, but only with the consent of all the contracting parties.

This principle was expressed and sealed by the signature of the major European powers at the 1871 London Conference in an Annex to the Protocol of the sessions of 5(17) January. It was said: "The plenipotentiaries of Northern Germany, Austria-Hungary, Great Britain, Italy, and Turkey, gathered today in Conference, recognize as a material principle of international law that no power may free itself from obligations of a treaty or change the provisions thereof other than with the consent of the contracting parties reached by means of amicable agreement".

Such are the basic principles relative to which theory and practice are agreed. As regards the means and forms of the performance of international obligations, they are determined by domestic legislation and the administration of each country. In any event, a State which has signed a

[39] G. F. Martens, note 1 above, §59. See the critical remarks of Silvestre Pinheiro-Ferreira. Also compare Hall, note 1 above, p. 295.

treaty and given its ratification is obliged to promulgate it and in general to take all measures to achieve and ensure its performance.[40]

In constitutional States those treaties which require for their validity the consent of chambers are not subject to publication before that consent follows. In Russia all treaties are published for general information by the Ruling Senate just as laws or the Highest approved opinions of the State Council.

The failure to publish treaties may be equivalent to the failure to perform them. Therefore, each party to an obligation has the right to demand of the other that a treaty concluded between them was brought to the information of those obliged to perform them. Secret articles and treaties are not published, but, of course, they should be communicated to all places and persons whom they may concern.

VII. International Means of Securing Treaties

§115. The lack of an international court and the impossibility of applying enforcement measures to States for the performance of assumed obligations have since time immemorial inspired a search for the best means to secure treaties concluded. As history and international practice show, for this purpose they have resorted to various means, of which some are applied to this day, and others have been withdrawn from use and are merely of historical interest. We consider the principal means of this kind and show how valid they are from a legal point of view.[41]

1. *Oath.* This was the usual means of securing international treaties in the Middle Ages and Renaissance.

Thus, the oral treaty of 1697 between Peter the Great and the Elector of Brandenburg, Friedrich III, was sealed by the joint solemn oath of these

[40] Meier, note 1 above, p. 329. With regard to the moment of entry of a treaty into operation, compare, for example, Article 8 of the 1879 Russo-German convention "on direct relations between judicial institutions of the Warsaw Judicial District and the German border judicial instances in civil and criminal cases": "Elle sera exécutoire à dater du trentième jour après sa promulgation dans les formes prescrites par les lois en vigueur dans les territoires d'État des Hautes Parties contractantes".

[41] Phillimore, note 1 above, II, p. 77; Heffter, note 1 above, §96; Vattel, note 8 above, liv. II, chap. XV, §225; Calvo, note 9 above, I, §701.

sovereigns.[42] An oath was last applied to a treaty between Switzerland and France, concluded at Solothurn in 1777.[43]

The practical uselessness of this means is obvious. As purely a religious rite, an oath may bind only persons who take it, but in no event a State, as a juridical person, which is the sole subject of international law. Even in the Middle Ages the oath was greatly discredited by the indulgences given by the Popes for money.[44]

2. *Hostages* (*otages*). Just as the oath, the use of hostages to secure treaties was common in the Middle Ages.

The last known instance of the use of this means relates to 1748, when two English peers were required to be sent to Paris as hostages for the performance of the Treaty of Aachen, concluded that same year between France and England.[45]

This means is no longer used because it does not achieve the goal. In fact, a State to which hostages are given has only one right with respect to them – to keep them until the performance of the treaty. It may not torment or execute them. And what is gained by depriving hostages of their life with respect to the obligation concluded?

Now hostages are taken sometimes during war when special conditions are performed, of which we will speak when considering the law of war.

3. *Pawn and pledge* (occupation). The pawn of things (moveables) with a view to securing performance of a treaty was rarely encountered even in times past. Perhaps the sole example of such a transaction was the pawning by Poland of its crown diamonds to Prussia.[46] A pledge has a certain practical significance now. It consists of the occupation by forces of one State on part of the territory of another so long as the last does not perform its obligation.

Pledge was often used in times past, and down to the present is deemed to be a valid means. In 1713 Peter I gave defeated Stettin [Szczecin] with all of Swedish Pomerania to the King of Prussia on condition that he openly stand on the side of Russia in the war against Sweden and would protect

[42] F. F. Martens, Собрание трактатов и конвенций [Collection of Treaties and Conventions], V, p. 52.

[43] Klüber, note 9 above, §155.

[44] Grotius, note 9 above, II, 13.

[45] Friedrich August Wilhelm Wenck, *Codex juris gentium recentissimi* (1781-1795), II, p. 352.

[46] Karl Gottlob Günther, *Europäisches Völkerrecht in Friedenzeiten nach Vernunft, Verträgen und Herkommen* (Altenburg, 1793), II, p. 153; Phillimore, note 1 above, II, p. 79; G. F. Martens, note 1 above, §63.

these possessions from the Swedes.[47] Prussia in 1808 was forced to pledge to Napoleon I the fortress of Stettin, Kostrzyn, and Głogów until the payment of a Contribution of 140 million francs. On the basis of the 1815 Treaty of Paris, the allied forces were to occupy the eastern departments of France until it paid a Contribution of 700 million francs. The 1871 peace treaty of Versailles also provided for the occupation of part of French territory by German forces, serving as security for the payment by France to Germany of a Contribution of five billion.[48]

Cases happen, in addition, when the government gives to private individuals – its creditors – a particular source of State revenues in the form of a pledge which secures the proper repayment of the loan and interest. The English and French creditors of Turkey and Egypt, for example, use such pledges.

The legal relations between pledgor States and the pledgeholder do not fit fully under the civil law concept of pledge. The differences lie both in the subject-matter and in the operation of this kind of obligation. The subject-matter of an international pledge is the territory of the State, and not private ownership. As in private-law relations, an overdue pledge usually is subject to sale, and in international pledge, in the event of failure to perform the obligation, the pledged (or occupied) territory is combined with the possessions of the occupier. We already have addressed above (Chapter I, §87) the status of private individuals who are creditors of a State: the granting to them of a pledge on the part of a government does not change this status.

The right of pledge terminates with the performance of the obligation which it secures, or earlier by mutual agreement.

4) *Suretyship* (*guarantee*). Of all the international means of securing treaties, this most satisfies its purposes. It is based on the real awareness by States of the solidarity of their interests, in view of which they assume an obligation to secure, separately or jointly, the performance of a particular treaty, to defend the rights of a particular people, or to protect a certain state of affairs (*status quo*). In essence an act of guarantee is an additional treaty and its fate is linked with the main treaty.[49]

47 F. F. Martens, Собрание трактатов и конвенций [Collection of Treaties and Conventions], V, No. 187.

48 Bluntschli, note 1 above, §428.

49 Phillimore, note 1 above, II, Chapter VII; Hall, note 1 above, p. 287; Bluntschli, note 1 above, §431; Heffter, note 1 above, §97; Wheaton, note 24 above, §277; Neumann, note 24 above, §35a; Calvo, note 9 above, I, §702; Milan Milovanowitch, *Les traités de garantie au XIX siècle* (Paris, 1888).

By its content an international suretyship is one of the following three main types:

1) Suretyship to protect a certain status quo. For example, the European powers down to the present guarantee the perpetual neutrality of Switzerland, Belgium, Luxembourg, Ionian Islands, and the State of the Congo.[50]

2) Suretyship for the performance of a certain action, for example, the payment of a debt. Thus, the 1833 Greek loan was guaranteed by France, England, and Russia; the Turkish loan of 1855 – by England and France.[51]

3) Suretyship to protect a certain domestic system of a people. For example, the Convention of 1775 between Russia, Austria, and Prussia guaranteed the inviolability of the old Polish Constitution. The powers whose delegates took part in drafting it guaranteed performance of the organic Statute of Eastern Rumelia.

One must note that this third type of suretyship is not normal because every State must remain independent in its internal affairs. A suretyship to protect a particular State order within a people usually was a pretext for interference in its affairs.

With respect to form, a simple and complex guarantee are distinguished.

A simple suretyship is when a third State alone gives surety for the performance of a particular treaty. For example, Maria Theresa guaranteed a treaty of alliance between France and Denmark on 4 May 1758.[52] In this case the surety-State autonomously determined when the moment ensued for insisting on performance of the guarantee treaty.

The complex form of a suretyship is, first, in the form of a mutual guarantee by States of the inviolability of their possessions or rights.

An example is the 1833 Münchengrätz Convention on the basis of which Russia and Austria, jointly guaranteed to one another the peaceful and quiet possession of the Polish provinces (Article 1). In 1807 Russia and France, under the Treaty of Tilsit, mutually gave surety for the integrity of the possessions belonging to them.[53]

Second, a collective guarantee is a general suretyship by several States to preserve a certain *status quo* or the inviolability of possessions and rights of a particular people.

[50] Jellinek, note 1 above, p. 135; August von Bulmerincq, *Das Völkerrecht oder das internationale Recht: Systemisch dargestelt* (2d ed.; Freiburg i B., 1889), p. 200.

[51] Karl von Martens and Ferdinand de Cornot, Baron de Cussy, *Recueil manuel et pratique des traités, conventions et autres actes diplomatiques* (1846-1857), V, p. 341.

[52] F. F. Martens, Собрание трактатов и конвенций [Collection of Treaties and Conventions]I, No. 25, p. 265.

[53] Ibid., IV(2), No. 136; XIII, No. 493.

By a treaty of 1832, England, France, and Russia together guaranteed the preservation of the independence of Greece. The 1815 treaties of Vienna and the London treaties of 1831, 1839, and 1867 provided for the perpetual neutrality of Switzerland, Belgium, and the Duchy of Luxembourg. In 1856 Austria, France, and England concluded a treaty on guaranteeing the inviolability of the Ottoman Empire.

A suretyship is generated either by the interests only of the powers directly participating therein or the interests of the entire international community. In the first instance, the act of guarantee is usually a supplementary treaty to the main document; in the second – an autonomous act. The circumstances and conditions of a guarantee arising may be identified only by studying the history of concluding it in each individual instance.

The operation of a suretyship is various. If a guarantee is generated only by the interests of the surety States, they are obliged to perform their debt either singly or together at the demand of the State whose rights they guaranteed. If there is no agreement between the sureties on common actions, then each surety may perform its debt separately. There is no unanimity either in theory or in practice with regard to the operation of a collective guarantee.

In 1867, on the occasion of the adoption by the Government of England of a suretyship for the perpetual inviolability of Luxembourg, [Edward Smith-Stanley, 14th Earl of] Derby [(1799-1869)], in the House of Lords, resolved the question of the consequences of this Act for England. In his view, England had assumed the duty, in the event of an infringement against Luxembourg, to act in common with other guarantors, but one is by no means obliged to sacrifice oneself in favor of performance of the suretyship. This interpretation is, however, contrary to the facts.[54]

During the Franco-Prussian War, when the neutrality of the Kingdom of Belgium was endangered, the English Government proposed to all powers who had guaranteed the integrity of Belgium to confirm this formal act anew. The interested cabinets declined this proposal, finding that the material obligations were sufficiently clear and did not require a new definition. England, however, was not satisfied and concluded special treaties with France and Prussia which provided that in the event of an attack on Belgium by one of these powers, the English forces would join with another for joint action against the aggressor.

Indeed, under a collective guarantee assumed by the powers in view of national interests, they all are obliged to perform the suretyship together, but in the event of disagreement, each individually retains the right

[54] Hall, note 1 above, p. 289.

of interference and even is obliged by itself to assist the exercise of the guarantee under own pain and risk.

What are the measures assumed by a surety in order to perform its obligations is purely a question of fact. In no case can it be demanded of a surety that he sacrifice his own life in order to protect another's independence. *Ultra posse nemo tenetur*. Nor can it be required to perform any immoral or physically impossible action.

A suretyship terminates by agreement between the guarantors: as a consequence of the renunciation of the suretyship by that State to whose benefit it was concluded; the expiry of the period of operation of the treaty; and finally, the destruction of the object of the guarantee.

VIII. On Interpretation of International Treaties

§116. The early writers dwelt in detail on those rules by which ambiguous or doubtful treaties should be interpreted. These rules they borrowed from Roman law.[55]

While completely agreeing that the principles of civil law are applicable to the interpretation of treaties, nonetheless, the danger of extending them too much to international treaties must be avoided, for the subjects, objects, and operation of treaties differ from private-law obligations. We confine ourselves to setting out the major rules absolutely applicable to the interpretation of treaties.

All international treaties must be interpreted *bona fide*: always it is necessary to assume that the States who signed it had in view its good faith interpretation and performance. The contracting States, if they have agreed between themselves, are the best interpreters of treaties.

The interpretation of treaties consists in an explication of: 1) the words, and 2) the elements, thoughts, and content of the treaty.

An interpretation of the words consists of an explication of: a) the literal meaning of the words, b) their grammatical construction, and c) the logical connection between the words and sentences.

The content of treaties is construed by a determination of: a) the historical origin of the treaty; b) the agreement of its provisions with the ruling principles of international law, and c) the intentions, purposes, and spirit of the treaty.

[55] Grotius, note 9 above, lib. II, cap. XVI; Vattel, note 8 above, liv. II, chapter XVII; G. F. Martens, note 1 above, §52; Phillimore, note 1 above, II, chapter VIII; Heffter, note 1 above, §95; Calvo, note 9 above, §713; Hall, note 1 above, p. 281.

It goes without saying that when interpreting words one must understand them in the ordinary sense, and not in some strange and impossible meaning. Contradictions between individual articles are eliminated by the application of logic and explication of the intention of the contracting parties. It also is understandable that any special provision of a treaty repeals or limits the operation of a general provision; that a doubtful provision should be interpreted in a sense less burdensome for the obliged party, and so on.

There are many examples of the application of these rules in practice. We cite one taken from the files of the Archive of the Ministry of Foreign Affairs.

In 1845Austria requested Emperor Nicholas I to be an arbitrator in its dispute with Sardinia, which arose from a convention concluded between them in 1751. The Sardinian Government authorized the transit carriage of 4,000 centners of salt from Genoa to the Tessin [Ticino] Canton. Austria protested, referring to the Act of 1751, which prohibited trade in salt between Sardinia and the Swiss cantons. When the Sardinian Government began to prove that transit trade was not prohibited by the treaty of 1751, which, moreover, was no longer binding, Austria increased the duties on Piedmont wines. Emperor Nicholas did not assume the duties of arbitrator, but expressed the view that under the spirit of the disputed convention, right was on the side of Sardinia, and literally – on the side of Austria.[56]

IX. Termination of Operation and Binding Nature of International Treaties

§117. The binding force of a treaty is destroyed if when concluding it any of the subjective or objective conditions of its legal fitness are violated, to which we referred to above. For example, clear fraud, mistake, or coercion over the person of a plenipotentiary make the treaty void. In this respect the principles of the civil law of obligations are applied to international treaties. But treaties are not subject to any prescriptions of civil law with regard to the obligatory forms of concluding treaties.

The operation of an international treaty terminates according to law as a consequence of: 1) the performance of an act established by a treaty unless the last obliges a constant action; 2) the ensuing of a resolutive provision; 3) the ensuing of the period for which the treaty was concluded; 4) the joint or, if so authorized by the treaty, unilateral renunciation of the treaty; 5) the perishing of the object; 6) the death of an obliged subject. It is assumed in

[56] Despatch of Count Nesselrode to Count [Paul von] Medem [(1800-1854)] in Vienna of 13 July 1845 and Humble Report of Count Nesselrode of 2 July 1846.

the last instance that the treaty was concluded by a sovereign and concerned the personal interests thereof. Above we noted that treaties personally concluded by monarchs are virtually never encountered at present; finally, 7) the treaty no longer being binding by reason of a material change of circumstances in view of or thanks to which it was concluded.[57]

Of the instances enumerated, some explanation is required: first, the conclusion of treaties for a period; second, the change of conditions under which States assume obligations.

Treaties concluded for a period usually are distinctive for the certainty of the mutual rights and duties of the parties and the voluntary nature of the agreement. Upon the expiry of the period, such treaties often are renewed, the possibility of their renewal often specially stipulated in a separate article providing that both contracting parties have the right to prolong the operation of the treaty and that party which does not so wish is obliged to inform the other by at least a year before expiry of the period; otherwise, the treaty is considered to be tacitly prolonged for a year.

There is this kind of condition, for example, in the conventions on literary property concluded by Russia with France and Belgium for ten years. Upon the expiry of nine years the Russian Government, it seems, wished to renounce these conventions, but only in 1895 declared to France and Belgium that it renounced compliance with the convention concluded with the first power in 1861 and the convention concluded in 1862 with Belgium.

All trade treaties, navigation treaties, treaties on the extradition of criminals, and others belong to the category of fixed-term treaties. Peace treaties, on the contrary, are concluded "in perpetuity". This condition, together with a characteristic attribute of peace treaties – their coerced conclusion – leads to such treaties usually being violated soon after their signature. In view of this, one must agree in principle with the suggestion of John Stuart Mill who, on the occasion of the refusal of Russia in 1870 to perform certain articles of the Treaty of Paris, demonstrated how ridiculous it was to bind a State with "eternal" obligations. He expressed the view that it was reasonable to oblige a people only by a treaty concluded for a definite period not exceeding the life of one generation.[58]

[57] Bluntschli, note 1 above, §450; Heffter, note 1 above, §99; Jellinek, note 1 above, p. 30; Vattel, note 8 above, liv. II, §296; G. F. Martens, note 1 above, §60, 61; Hall, note 1 above, p. 292.

[58] John Stuart Mill, "Treaty Obligations", *Fortnightly Review* (1 December 1870); also see the accurate remarks of G. Rolin-Jaequemyns, *Archives de droit international*, I, p. viii.

Indeed, it makes no sense to limit, the more so to completely abrogate, by a peace treaty any fundamental right for an "eternity". But to set a more or less precise period for such treaties to be binding is, all the same, difficult. Better beforehand to foresee the possibility of the revision thereof and to set a time, depending on the conditions.

With regard to a change of circumstances under which the conclusion of a treaty proceeded, it should be noted that the last is always signed with the tacit assumption that it will have force so long as the conditions under which it was signed remain unchanged. This so-called *clausula rebus sic stantibus*, to be sure, often concealed an arbitrary violation of treaties and was understood in the sense that any change of circumstances entails a legitimate basis for termination of the operation of a treaty. But abuses do not, of course, prove that the rule itself had no significance. It follows from the essence of international treaties that a State may reasonably oblige itself only in view of a State goal, and any obligation concluded by it exists so long as it is consistent with this purpose. Therefore, the operation of a treaty terminates under such a change of the mutual provision of the parties which makes the said purpose unachievable and the further recognition of the treaty places the State in danger.

An illustration of the correct application of the clause *rebus sic stantibus* is the following. In 1855 Austria concluded a concordat with the Roman curia, on the basis of which the last received extensive rights within the Austrian Empire, especially with reference to public education. In 1870 Pope Pius IX [(1792-1878)] proclaimed the dogma of the infallibility of the Roman pontiff. In and of itself, of course, this fact fundamentally changed the mutual relations of the representative of the Roman Catholic Church and the States, and in view of this change the Austrian Government had the right to renounce the concordat concluded under completely different circumstances.[59]

X. Addition: International Obligations from Permitted and Impermissable Actions

§118. Heffter first carried over the doctrine of civil law on obligations *quasi ex contractu* and *ex delicto* to the sphere of international law.[60] His service in this respect is undeniable. Indeed, there are not only formal agreements in international relations, but also various kinds of actions having nothing in common with treaties that led to the same consequences as

59 See *Staatsarchiv*, Nos. 4938, 4939, and 4940.

60 Heffter, note 1 above, §160; Neumann, note 24 above, §36b.

treaties. Heffter's theory on this question suffers only from the shortcoming that civil law is mixed with international law.

I. Obligations *quasi ex contractu*. They are rarely encountered in international relations. Among the examples of such obligations, Heffter cites, *inter alia*, a case of *negotiorum gesto* with an international character giving a right to remuneration, namely – when some foreign sovereign or republican government assumes a regency in a country by reason of the youth or lack of legal capacity of its sovereign. It is unlikely that something similar could occur at present. The duty of remuneration of a State for an occupation by forces and administration of foreign territory caused by wartime circumstances might serve as an example of an international obligation *quasi ex contractu*.

Thus, for example, Russian forces and officials at the end of the last Eastern war remained for more than a year in Bulgaria and Eastern Rumelia with a view to protecting these provinces and maintaining order. This fact created for Russia the right to remuneration recognized by the Treaty of Berlin; but it would have existed also without such recognition.

II. Obligations *ex delictu*. A crime gives the right to the victim to remuneration for the material damage and moral offense caused thereto. Although in the domain of international relations one cannot speak of crimes committed by a people, violations are possible of a right establishing, as also in private relations, an obligation of the party at fault to remunerate material, to return a thing, or to give moral satisfaction to a victim State.

A violation of another's right in international relations may be committed by: 1) States or sovereigns themselves; 2) officials, and 3) private individuals.

Of these instances, the first two are the simple. There is no doubt that if the rights of a State are violated by another State, the Head thereof, or officials, the victim people has a right to demand compensation of losses and satisfaction from the party at fault.

When the Russian envoy in London, [Andrei Artamonovich] Matveev [(1666-1728)], was stopped on the street in 1708, pulled out of a carriage, and imprisoned for the failure to pay a debt of fifty pounds sterling, Peter the Great immediately demanded satisfaction. The English Government did not object to this demand and not only released Matveev at once, but issued a law on the English authorities not having jurisdiction over diplomatic agents, a list of which was sent to Peter with a ceremonial embassy.

More controversial is the responsibility of a State for a crime committed by its subjects. On the basis of generally-recognized principles of law, a private individual is, in principle, liable for all crimes or violations of a right of which he is guilty. He is subject to trial in a foreign State if he is situated there and the crime was committed within its limits; if he leaves his homeland or is guilty of a crime against a foreign State committed on homeland territory, he is punished according to its laws. One may speak of the responsibility of a State for the actions of its subject only if it, at the request of the interested party, does not take any measures to prosecute and punish the guilty person. In this instance solidarity is established between the State authority and the private individual who is the offender. Then the question acquires an international character and is resolved by diplomatic means.

Finally, in the field of international relations impermissible actions exist which identically violate the interests of all peoples, and therefore should be prosecuted everywhere. To these are relegated: piracy, the slave trade, destruction of marine cables, and damage in general to international communications.

INDEX

Aachen, Congress of (1818), 105, 139, 177, 229
Aachen, Peace of (1748), 72, 83, 234
Abdy, John Thomas, 1, 133, 217
Adam, -, 277
Adams, Charles Francis, 222
Adrianople, Treaty of (1545), 78
Adrianople, Treaty of (1829), 107, 208
Agarkov, -, 253
Ahrens, Heinrich, 276
Ährenthal, Aloix Lexa von, lv
Akkerman Convention (1826), 204, 208, 210, 227
Alabama arbitration, 11, 318
Albrecht, Margrave of Baden, 78
Aleksandr Vasil'evich, Grand Prince, 78
Aleksandrenko, Vasilii Nikiforovich, 81
Aleksei Mikhailovich, Tsar, 76, 77
Alexander I, Emperor, ix, x, 91-94, 100, 101, 106, 186, 187, 223, 258, 279, 300, 313, 317
Alexander II, Emperor, xlix, liv, 6, 112
Alexander III, Emperor, lvi
Alexander VI, Pope, 277
Alexander the Great, of Macedonia, 27
Alexandre, Joseph, 174
Ali-Pasha, 211
Alison, Archibald, 233
Alopeus, Magnus Maximilian Count von, 220
Amari, Giuseppe Carnazza, 136, 236, 312
Amiens Peace Treaty, 92
Amos, Sheldon, 38, 216
Amphictyonic League, 38, 39
Andrássy, Count Gyula, 112
Andreevskii, Ivan Efimovich, xxxiv
Andrews, Sidney, 281
Angeberg, comte de: see Chodzko
Anglo-Ottoman Treaty of Alliance (1878), 284, 285
Anglo-Russian Treaty of Commerce (1766), 97
Anglo-Russian Treaty on Inheritance (1880), 169, 170
Anglo-Venezuelan arbitration (1897), 239
Anti-slavery treaties, 260, 261
Antoine, Duke of Montpensier, 75
Aristotle, 26, 27
Armed Neutrality, Declaration of (1780), 97, 147, 322, 328
Armed Neutrality, Second (1800), 97, 328
Arneth, Alfred Ritter von, 243
Arnold, Wilhelm Christoph Friedrich, 40, 46
Arntz, -, 208
Attlmayer, Ferdinand Ritter von, 294
August III, Elector of Saxony, 84
Austerlitz, Battle of, 92
Austrian Succession, War of, 83
Austro-Russian Convention on deserters (1808), 293
Austro-Russian Convention on frontiers (1833), 293
Austro-Turkish Convention on occupation (1879), 286, 287

Bacon, Sir Francis, 12
Baden, Peace of (1814), 75

Baikov, Aleksandr L'vovich, lvii
Bailleu, -, 94
Baker, Sherston, 133
Bantysh-Kamenskii, Nikolai Nikolaevich, xlix
Bar, Ludwig von, 249
Barbeyrac, Jean, 128, 248
Barral de Montferrat, Horace Dominique de, 25, 68, 89
Basel Peace Treaty (1795), 90
Bavarian Succession, 88, 178, 322
Beaumarchais, Maurice Delarnë Caron de, 240
Becker, Bernhard, 116
Becker, Henri, 266
Belgian-Dutch Treaty (1839), 224
Bentham, Jeremy, xiii, xiv, 14, 127, 149, 150, 172
Berezhkkov, Mikhail Nikolaevich, 61, 79
Bergbohm, Carl, xxiv, xxvi, 6, 147, 148, 150
Bergson, Jules, 134
Bering Sea arbitration, 11
Berlin African Congress (1885), 191, 277, 278, 314
Berlin Congress (1874), 5
Berlin Congress (1878), 113, 176, 287
Berlin Memorandum (1876), 112
Berlin, Treaty of (1850), 107
Berlin, Treaty of (1878), 200-203, 206, 209-212, 215, 225, 234, 282-284, 286, 291, 292, 294, 305,, 306, 322
Bernadotte, Prince Jean-Baptiste, 193
Bernard, Montague, xxii, 68, 72, 98, 145, 175, 307, 327
Berner, Alfred Friedrich, 58, 114
Berthmann-Hollweg, Moritz August von, 8
Bestuzhev-Riumin, Aleksei Petrovich, 83
Bialecki, Antoni, xii, 148
Bianchi, Nicomede, 25, 106, 109
Bidermann, Hermann Ignaz, 192
Bismarck, Otto von, 188, 190, 227, 246, 322
Blackstone, Sir William, 10
Blaine, James Gillespie, 239
Block, Maurice, 167, 272
Bluntschli, Johann Caspar, xi-xiv, xxii, xxxiii, liv, 1, 9, 13, 38, 58, 135, 142, 145, 148, 150, 151, 173, 174, 177, 186, 188, 191, 192, 195, 200, 203, 208, 212, 214, 216, 219, 220, 223, 225, 227, 230, 231, 233, 236, 238, 243, 248, 249, 253-255, 270, 275, 278, 279, 286, 289, 292, 296, 298, 301, 303, 305, 307, 312, 319, 320, 323, 326, 331, 336
Böckh, Richard, 116
Boguslavskii, Mark Moiseevich, xlvi
Bonfils, Henry, 136
Bowring, John, 150, 172
Boyd, Alexander Charles, 132
Bréal, Michel, 115
Breslau, Treaty of (1742), 82, 88
Brie, Siegfried, 188, 194
Brikner, Aleksandr Gustavovich, 76, 77
Brissot, Jacques Pierre, 89
Brockhaus, Friedrich, 100
Brougham, Henry, 56, 262
Brun, M. I., xlvii
Brunnov, Baron, 187, 300
Brunswik, Benoit, 210

Brussels Antislavery Conference (1890), 316
Brussels Conference (1874), 6, 112, 153, 177, 180, 262
Bucharest, Treaty of 1812), 208, 210
Buckle, Henry Thomas, 60, 65, 66
Bukharan-Russian peace treaty (1873), 259
Bukhe, E. A., liv
Bulle, Constantin, 107, 115
Bulmerincq, August von, 6, 98, 115, 120, 122, 135, 150, 184, 270, 332
Bürgel, -, 39
Butler, W. E., xxiv-lvii
Bynkershoek, Cornelis van, xi, xxi, 4, 129, 130, 145, 248, 249, 272, 300, 301, 312

Cabot, John, 276
Caesar, Gaius Julius, 49, 52
Calhoun, John Caldwell, 188, 196
Calvo, Carlos, xii, 21, 51, 136, 177, 186, 197, 206, 207, 214, 216, 220, 223, 227, 231, 232, 242, 250, 270, 279, 288, 312, 315, 321, 329, 331, 334
Campbell-Bannerman, Henry, lv
Campo Formio, Peace of (1797), 90, 92
Canning, George, 106
Capefigue, Jean Baptiste Honoré Raymond, 95
Capitulation, 195, 208, 217, 285, 292
Caracalla, Marcus Aurelius Antoninus, 48
Card, Edgard Rouard de, 198
Carnegie, Andrew, lv
Caroline, 233
Casalini, -, 251
Caspian Sea, 298
Castlereagh, Lord Robert Stewart, Viscount, 260
Catherine II, Empress, ix, xxxii, lx, 81, 84-87, 90, 97, 147, 160, 178, 235, 243, 267, 314, 317, 322-324
Cave, Sir Stephen, 200
Cavour, Camillo Benso of, 109
Chancellor, Richard, 77
Chantre, Alfred, 268
Charlemagne, vii, 55, 56
Charles I, King of England, 77, 217
Charles II, King of England, 217, 218, 246
Charles II, King of Spain, viii, 72, 74
Charles V, 173, 191
Charles VI, Emperor, 82, 192, 317, 321
Charles X, King of Sweden, 75
Charles XII, King of Sweden, 75
Charles Philippe, Count of Artois, 247
Chaumont, Treaty of (1814), 95
Chauveau, Émile, 25
Cherbuliez, Antoine, 195
Chodzko, Léonard, 95, 101
Chonghou, Ambassador, 317
Christian IX, King of Denmark, 110
Christina, Queen of Sweden, 254
Christlieb, Theodore, 318
Cicero, Marcus Tullius, 41, 47, 51, 183
Clarkson, Thomas, 259
Clayton-Bulwer Treaty (1850), 239
Clerq, Alexandre de, 75, 83, 90, 92, 94-96, 101, 107, 108, 148, 313
Cleveland, Stephen Grover, 239, 314

Clovis I, 55
Cogordan, George, 283, 284
Combes, François, 25
Concordats, 255, 337
Congo, State of, 191, 292, 314, 332
Congress of Vienna (1815), 22, 23, 95, 99-105, 107, 119, 175, 176, 186, 187, 191, 195, 230, 260, 262, 294, 295
Conrad III, King, 249
Constantinople conference (1876/77), 180
Constantinople Treaty (1879), 283
Copenhagen, Treaty of (1857), 304
Cornot, Ferdinand de, Baron de Cussy, 166, 193, 294, 332
Coulanges, Fustel de, 35, 42, 51, 52, 54
Crallé, Richard Kenner, 188
Creasy, Edward Shepherd, 133, 145, 191, 207, 232, 289
Crimean war, 23, 108, 178, 208, 210, 211, 247, 253
Cromwell, Oliver, 217, 218, 231, 246
Cutler, John, 163
Cuza, Alexandru Ioan, 209

Dahn, Felix, 7
Dana, Richard Henry, 132, 182, 278
Danevskii, Vsevolod Pievich, xxxv, 120, 139
Danielson, Johan Richard, 194
Dantsher von Kollesberg, Theodor ritter, 192
Danube Commission (1856), 166, 305, 306
Danube navigation, 179, 234, 305, 306
Dardanelles, Straits of, 108, 290, 297, 304, 305
Dead Sea, 298
Demangeat, Charles, 252
Demosthenes, 26
Dionysus of Harlicarnassus, 26
Dirksen, -, 41
Dogger Bank incident, li, lii
Dolgorukov, Iurii Vladimirovich, 235
Dom Miguel I, of Portugal, 266
Dom Pedro III, 197
Domin-Petruschevecz, Alphons von, xiii, 150
Don Philipp, 83
Dresden, Treaty of (1745), 83, 88
Dumont, Jean, 73-75, 128
Duncker, Max, 39

Eden, Nils, 193
Edward VII, King, lv
Eliashevich, F., l
Elizabeth I, Queen of England, 77
Elizaveta Petrovna, Empress, viii, 83, 84, 245
Emir of Bukhara, 293
Engelhardt, Ed., 198, 205, 208, 305
Eötvòs, József, 116
Epaminondas, 39
Esperson, Pietro, 285
Eugénie de Montijo, Empress, 247
Euripedes, 27
Eustatziu, Aristide, 45
Eyffinger, A., lv

Fallati, Johannes Baptista, xii, xiv, 25, 26, 134, 172
Fallières, Armand, lv
Farnese, Elizabeth, 83
Fauchille, Paul, 136
Ferdinand I, Emperor, 78, 82, 192
Ferdinand VII, King of Spain, 319
Ferdinand, Prince of Bulgaria, 202

Fichte, Johann Gottlieb, xii, 134
Fiedler, -, 79
Field, David Dudley, xiii, 150, 231, 270
Fiore, Pasquale, 136, 175
First Silesian War, 82
Fischer, Karl, 68
Flasson, Gaëtan de Raxis de, 68
Foelix, Jean Jacques Gaspard, 252
Fouillée, Alfred Jules Émile, 3
Fournier, August, 92
Fox, George, 259
Francesco II, of Two Sicilies, 215
Francis I, King of France, 217, 319
Franco-Danish Treaty (1758), 332
Franco-Tunisian Treaty (1881), 205, 226
Franconia, 301
Frankfurt, Act of (1819), 294
Frankfurt, Treaty of (1871), 224, 282, 283
Franz II, Emperor, 192, 314
Franz-Joseph I, Emperor, lv
Fredrikshamn Peace Treaty (1809), 193, 194, 225, 273
Friedrich I, of Prussia, 214, 229, 316
Friedrich II, of Prussia, 82-84, 86, 231, 233, 317
Friedrich III, Emperor, 78
Friedrich III, Elector of Brandenburg, 325, 329, 330
Fry, -, 318
Fujinami, Nobuyoshi, xxiv
Funck-Brentano, Théophile, xii, 136, 192, 227, 281
Fusinato, Guido, 281

Gaekwad of Baroda, 207
Gairal, François, 198
Gaius, 50
Gambetta, Leon, 247
Garden, Guillaume de, 25, 68, 75
Gareis, Karl, 135, 263
Garibaldi, Giuseppe, x, 109
Geffcken, Friedrich Heinrich, 193
Gelschner, -, xii, 134
Geneva Convention (1864), 5, 147, 149
Gentili, Alberico, xi, 120
Gentz, Friedrich von, 98
Gervinus, Georg Gottfried, 106, 107
Gessner, Ludwig, 273, 295, 301
Giers, Nikolai Karlovich, xlix
Giolitti, Giovanni, lv
Gneist, Heinrich Rudolph Hermann Friedrich von, 18, 62, 70
Golovkin, Gavriil Ivanovich, 316
Golubchik, 261
Gorchakov, Aleksandr Mikhailovich, xxxii, xlix, 179, 187, 222, 246
Gorovtsev, Aleksandr Mikhailovich, xlix
Grabar, Vladimir Emmanuilovich, xxxvii, xli, l, 41, 135
Gradovskii, Aleksandr Dmitrievich, xxxiv, 115, 188, 190
Grant, Hiram Ulysses S., xvi, 114, 222
Granville, George Leveson Gower, Earl, 268
Gregory VI, Pope, 59
Gregory VII, Pope, 173
Grey, Edward, lv
Gribovskii, Viacheslav Mikhailovich, xlviii
Grotius, Hugo, xi, xxii, 13, 49, 120-123, 191, 216, 276, 296, 312, 325, 330, 334

Guillaume, Jean François, comte de Bourgoing, 89
Guizot, François, 56, 63, 65, 160, 313, 317, 318
Günther, Karl Gottlob, 330
Gustavus Adolphus II, King, 67, 75, 122

Hague conferences on private international law, 165, 166
Hague peace conference (1899), 176, 180
Hall, William Edward, 133, 214, 223, 225, 232-234, 236, 244, 245, 249, 266, 270, 276, 296, 303, 305, 307, 312, 328, 331, 333, 334, 336
Halleck, Henry Wager, 133, 223, 307
Hamilton, Alexander, 196
Hanseatic League, 61, 79
Hardenberg, -, 103
Hardog, L. de, 191
Hartmann, Adolf, 135, 232, 323
Harun al-Rashid, Caliph, 55
Hassel, Paul, 94
Haswell, John H., 148
Haugwitz, Christian August Heinrich Kurt, 220
Hautefeuille, Laurent-Basile, 295, 296, 299
Heffter, August Wilhelm, xii, xvi, xviii, xxii, xxiii, 1, 13, 38, 90, 91, 96, 134, 135, 142, 144, 175, 177, 186, 188, 191, 193, 216, 219, 231, 232, 236, 241-244, 249, 253, 264, 270, 276, 288, 289, 296, 301, 302, 304, 307, 312, 319, 321, 325, 326, 329, 331, 334, 336-338
Hegel, Georg Wilhelm Friedrich, xii, 134
Heimburger, Karl Friedrich, 275
Hellwald, Friedrich von, 32, 40
Henry IV, King, xiv, 171
Henry VII, King, 246
Hêrault des Séchelles, Jean Marie, 89
Herberstein, Sigismund von, 80
Hertslet, Edward, 109, 148
Hisinger, -, 194
Hobbes, Thomas, xi, 123
Holland, Thomas Erskine, liii, 120
Holst, Hermann von, 196
Holtzendorff, Johann Wilhelm Franz Philipp von, xviii, 6, 12, 14, 26, 32, 45, 46, 120, 135, 144, 145, 150, 152, 250, 251, 292
Holy Alliance, Act of (1815), 100, 101
Hosack, John, 25
Huber, Max, 219
Hubertsburg Peace treaty, 85, 88
Hüllmann, Karl Dietrich, 37
Hume, David, 39

Iablochkov, Tikhon Mikhailovich, xliv, xlvi, xlvii
Il'in, A., xxv
Infanta Luisa Fernanda, 75
Infante Manuel, Count of Ourém, 316
Innocent III, Pope, 173
Institute of International Law, 152, 153, 268, 301
International African Society, 277
Iogorsky, Sultan, 250
Isabella II, Queen, 75
Ismail Pasha, 200, 267
Ivan the Terrible, Tsar, 85

Ivanenko, Vitalii S., xxviii-lvii
Ivanov, Domingo, 257
Ivanovskii, Ignatii Ioakinfovich, xxviii, xxxii, xxxiii
Izvolskii, Aleksandr Petrovich, xlix

James II, King, 72, 215-217, 246, 247
Jassy, Treaty of (1792), 204
Jellinek, Georg, 6, 147, 157, 186, 192-194, 210, 226, 285, 287, 307, 312, 327, 332, 336
Jhering, Rudolf von, 7, 8, 40, 232
Johnson, Andrew, 252
Jomini, Aleksandr Genrikhovich, 108, 116, 247
Jozef II, Emperor, 86, 314, 324
Julius II, Pope, xvii, 229, 230

Kachenovskii, Dmitrii Ivanovich, xii, xiii, 137, 144, 150, 158
Kalisch treaty (1813), 94
Kaltenborn von Stachau, Karl von, 6, 120, 134, 157
Kamarovskii, Leonid Alekseevich, xli, xlii, 11, 135, 173, 176, 236
Kamptz, Carl Albert von, 120
Kant, Immanuel, xii, xiv, 134, 172
Kapustin, Mikhail Nikolaevich, xii, 137, 139, 157, 177
Kara Sea, 297
Karl-Ludwig Hohenzollern, Prince, 209
Karl-Theodor, Elector, 87
Karlowa, Otto, 41, 50
Kaufman, Konstantin Petrovich von, 206
Kaufmann, Wilhelm, 10, 200
Kaunitz-Rietberg, Wenzel Anton, Prince of, 84-86
Kazanskii, P. E., 137, 167
Kent, James, 1, 133, 216
Kerchensk, Strait of, 304
Kerenskii, A. F., xxxvii
Khan of Khiva, 206, 207, 259, 293
Kiatibian, S., 219
Kiselev, Nikolai Dmitrievich, 261
Kiselev, Pavel Dmitrievich, 208
Klüber, Johann Ludwig, 141, 144, 192, 244, 254, 312, 325, 330
Koch, Christophe de, 25
Korf, Sergei Aleksandrovich, lvii
Kościuszko, Andrew Thaddeus Bonaventure, 218
Kossuth, Lajos, 218
Kostomarov, Nikolai Ivanovich, 79
Kotoshikhin, Grigorii, 76
Kross, Jaan, xvii, xxix, xxx, xxxii, xxxiii
Kuchuk-Karnardzhii, Treaty of (1774), 87, 108,208
Kükelhaus, Theodor, 171

Laband, Paul, 188, 190
Labouchere, Henry, Baron Taunton, 285
Lackland, King John, 65
Laghi, Ferdinando, 307
Laibach, Congress of (1821), 106, 107, 175, 177
Lamartine, Alphonse Marie Louis de Prat de, 217, 237
Lammasch, Heinrich, 287
Lamzdorf, Vladimir Nikolaevich, xlix
Lardy, Charles, 135
Lassen, Christian, 29
Lasson, Adolf, 1
Laurent, François, 21, 25, 27, 30, 33-35, 37, 38, 40, 45, 47, 50, 52, 54, 56, 57, 59-64, 82, 89, 115, 116, 122, 123, 125, 171,

173, 191, 192, 249, 251, 252, 254
Laveleye, E. de, 287
Lawrence, Thomas Joseph, 3
Lawrence, William Beach, 75, 106, 107, 132, 186, 205, 206, 210, 223, 225, 236, 240, 249, 251, 252
Lebedev, P., 173
Legitimacy, principle of, 100, 101
Legrelle, Arsène, 73
Leibniz, Gottfried Wilhelm, 127, 128
Lemaitre, -, 250
Lenin, Vladimir Il'ich, xxxvii
Lentner, Ferdinand, 263
Leo, Alfred, xxiv
Leopold I, Emperor, 192
Leopold II, King, l, 277
Leopold, Hohenzollern Prince, 111
Leopold, Prince of Saxe-Coburg, 10
Leroy-Beaulieu, Anatole, 76
Lesment, L., xxix, xxx
Levi, Leone, 150, 259
Levin, David Borisovich, xl
Levinson, -, xix, 267
Lieber, Francis, xiii, 150, 281
Linarski Plan, 86
Lingg, Emil, 287
Liszt, Franz von, 135
Lobanov-Rostovskii, Aleksei Borisovich, xlix
Lodyzhenskii, A., 135
London Conference (1827), 215
London Conference (1830), 214
London Conference (1840), 199, 200, 313
London Conference (1867), 295
London Conference (1871), 328
London Conference (1883), 179
London, Convention of (1871), 108
London, Convention of (1883), 306
London Protocol (1831), 216
London Protocol (1867), 191
London, Treaty of (1831), 107, 333
London, Treaty of (1839), 333
London, Treaty of (1841), 305
London, Treaty of (1867), 333
Lopez, Consul General, 257
Lord Ch. Spencer, The, 303
Lorimer, James, xiv, 135, 173, 174, 227, 228
Louis XIV, viii, 70, 72-75, 88, 173, 217, 244
Louis XVI, 88, 89
Louis XVIII, 95
Louis-Philippe I, 317
Ludwig-Philip, 246
Ludwig, Prince Friedrich Heinrich, 86
Lunts, Lazar Adol'fovich, xlv-xlvii

Mably, Gabriel Bonnot de, xi, 38, 129
Macauley, Catharine, 65, 72-74, 229
Madison, James, 196
Madrid convention (1880), 268
Maine, Sir Henry, 122
Maistre, Joseph Marie de, 32, 33
Malinin, S. A., lii
Malinovski, Vasilii Fedorovich, xiv, 172, 173
Mallarmé, -, 221
Malyshev, Kronid Ivanovich, xlvii
Mamiani del Rovero, Conte Terenzio, xii, 136
Mancini, Pasquale Stanislao, xii, 115, 116, 135, 183, 184
Mandelstam, Andrei Nikolaevich, xlix, lvii
Manin, Daniele, 218

Manning, William Oke, 38, 216
Manu, laws of, 29, 30
Margall, Francisco Pi y, 64
Maria Theresa, Empress, viii, 82-86, 321, 332
Marine cables, destruction of, 339
Marquardsen, Heinrich von, 135, 194-196
Marquardt, Joachim, 43, 44, 47
Marshall, Frederick Henry, 229
Martens, August, xxx
Martens, Charles de, xxvii, xxxii, 166, 193, 254, 294, 332
Martens, Edith, xxx
Martens, Fedor Fedorovich, xxiv-xxvii, 77, 79-81, 84, 85, 87, 90-95, 97, 100, 101, 105, 106, 108, 112, 134, 136, 140, 143, 148, 152, 166, 186, 187, 199, 208, 211, 216, 228-230, 235, 237, 240, 241, 260, 261, 274, 277, 280, 288, 293, 295, 301, 303, 309, 313, 314, 316, 317, 324, 325, 330-332
Martens, Friedrich Wilhelm, xxix, xxx
Martens, Georg Friedrich, xi, xxvii, xxxii, 82, 85, 87, 88, 92, 97, 101, 105-107, 109, 130-132, 142, 147, 191, 198, 216, 231, 243, 248, 254, 270, 275, 288, 312, 313, 319, 323, 325, 326, 328, 330, 334, 336
Martens, Heinrich, xxx
Martens, Johannes, xxx
Martens, Julius, xxx
Martens, Karl: see Martens, Charles de
Martens, Nikolai, xxx
Martens, Teresa Wilhelmina, xxix, xxx
Martin, William Alexander Parsons, 135
Martitz, Ferdinand von, 148, 262
Mary, Queen of Scots, 241, 249
Massé, -, 250
Massé, Gabriel, 93
Matveev, Andrei Artamonovich, 338
Maulde-la-Clavière, René de, 64
Maximilian, Archduke, 114, 218, 250
Mayers, William Frederick, 318
Mayor, Edmondo, 101
Mechelin, Leo, 194
Medem, Paul von, 335
Medvedev, D. A., xxxvii
Mehemet-Ali, 199, 250
Meier, Ernst, 307, 311, 315, 329
Meiern, Johann Gottfried von, 69
Mellerio, Jewelers, 251
Merkel, -, 3, 7
Merrick, John, 77
Metternich-Winneburg zu Beilstein, Klemens Wenzel Nepomuk Lothar, Prince of, 99, 101, 105, 106, 187, 237
Meyer, George, 190
Miakinin, A., xxv
Michelet, Jules, 65
Mighell, -, 250
Mignet, François-Auguste-Marie-Alexis, 74
Mikhail Fedorovich, Tsar, 81, 245
Milan I, Prince, 210
Miliutin, Dmitrii Alekseevich, 91, 241
Mill, John Stuart, xii, xxiii, 143, 236, 336
Miloradovich, Mikhail Andreevich, 257
Milovanowitch, Milan, 331

Miltitz, Alexandre de, 37
Modestinus, Herrenius, 145
Mohl, Robert von, 16, 18, 115, 120, 130, 157, 162, 190, 281
Mommsen, Theodor, 41, 45, 46
Mondaleschi, Marchese Giovanni Rinaldo,254
Monroe, James, 240
Montesquieu, Charles de, 19, 35, 58
Morkov, Arkadii Ivanovich, 313
Moser, Johann Jacob, xi, 129
Moss Convention, 193
Moynier, Gustave, 166, 167
Muhammad Ali, 313
Müller, Gerhard Friedrich, xlix
Müller-Jochmus, Mauritius, 25, 29, 30, 35, 37, 38, 41, 43, 46, 48, 50
Münchengrätz Convention (1833), 332
Murav'ev, Mikhail Nikolaevich, xlix
Murzanov, N. A., xxviii

Nakamura, Shingo, xxiv
Napoleon I, Emperor, ix, 23, 90, 92-95, 98, 99, 101, 115, 173, 178, 214, 218, 219, 232, 236, 246, 319
Napoleon III, Emperor, 110, 111, 114, 115, 178, 214, 218, 239, 246, 247, 282, 314, 319, 322
Nationality, principle of, 115-117, 136
Nesselrode, Karl Robert von Reichsgraf von, 261, 280, 335
Neumann, Julius, 115
Neumann, Léopold, 90, 92, 95, 107-110, 135, 147, 148, 170, 188, 198, 204, 232, 287, 288, 319, 323, 331, 337
Nicholas I, Emperor, 106, 187, 247, 335
Nicholas II, Emperor, xxxvii, l, lviii
Nicholas V, Pope, 277
Niebuhr, Berthold Georg, 42
Nijmegen, Peace of, 73
Nikbin, Moshen, xxiv
Nikola I, of Montenegro, 211
Nikolsburg, Treaty of (1866), 110, 178, 322
Nikol'skii, Dmitrii Petrovich, lvii
Nippold, Otfried, 307
Nobel peace prize, liv, lv
Nolde, Boris E., xlvii, xlix, lvii
North German Union, 189, 190
Nymphenburg, Treaty of (1741), 82
Nys, Ernest, 3, 59, 60, 120, 135, 171, 229, 230, 259, 277, 296
Nystad, Treaty of (1721), 81, 225, 229

Oldenberg, Petr Georgevich, liv
Ompteda, Diedrich Heinrich Ludwig Freiherr von, 120
Oncken, Wilhelm, 32, 36, 94, 103
Oppenheim, Heinrich Bernhard, xii, 134
Ordin, Kesar, 194
Orelli, -, 195
Ortolan, Eugène, 275, 296, 303
Osten, Anton Prokesch von, 199
Osterman, Ivan Andreevich, 220
Otto, Prince, 107
Ouroussow, A. M.: see Urusov

Pacta sunt servanda, 307, 328
Padelletti, Guido, xii, 115, 117, 136, 281
Palma, Luigi, xii, 116, 135
Palmerston, Henry John Temple, 3d Viscount, xix, 261, 266

Panin, Nikita Ivanovich, 86
Pardessus, Jean-Marie, 36, 64, 146
Parieu, Felix Marie Louis Pierre Esquinou de, 173
Parker, Courtland, 223
Paris Conference (1858), 209
Paris Conference (1860), 205, 206
Paris Conference (1869), 179
Paris Declaration (1856), 5, 108, 109, 147, 149, 320-322
Paris Peace Treaty (1763), 234
Paris Peace Treaty (1814), 95, 99, 188, 260
Paris Peace Treaty (1815), 96, 101, 102, 107, 109, 234
Paris Treaty (1856), 23, 87, 108, 113, 142, 176, 208, 209, 211, 234, 290, 305, 309, 323
Parodo, Augusto, xiii, 150
Partitions of Poland, 85-87
Parton, James, 281, 315
Paul I, Tsar, ix, 91, 97, 241
Peking, Sino-Russian Treaty of (1860), 292
Pellew, Edward, Viscount Exmouth, 258
Perels, Ferdinand, 146, 272, 273, 297, 298, 301-303 305
Peritch, Živojin, 287
Permanent Court of International Arbitration, 168, 176
Perty, Maximilian, 26
Peschel, Oscar, 26
Peter I, Emperor, 160, 214, 229, 248, 325, 329, 330
Peter III, Tsar, ix, 84, 85,317
Petersburg Protocol (1826), 106
Philip II of Macedon, 39
Philip IV of France, 62, 72
Philip V, of Spain, 83
Philip, Duke of Anjou, 74, 75
Philippe, King Louis, 107
Phillimore, Robert Joseph, xi, xvi, xix, 1-3, 13, 48, 75, 89, 98, 132, 133, 145, 148, 149, 183, 186, 188, 191, 197, 205, 210, 214-217, 219, 231, 233, 236, 238, 239, 241, 243, 244, 246, 248-251, 254, 258, 266, 270, 275-277, 279, 289, 290, 296-298, 301, 303-305, 307, 312, 329-331, 334
Pic, Paul, 198
Pictet, Jacques, l, li
Piédélièvre, Robert,136
Pierantoni, Augusto, xii, 116, 135, 136
Pilenko, Aleksandr Aleksandrovich, lvii
Pinheiro-Ferreira, Silvestre, 130, 328
Pitt, William, 85, 259
Pius IX, Pope, 107, 337
Plauchut, Edmond, 200
Playfair, Robert Lambert, 204
Poirer, -, xiv
Poletika, Petr Ivanovich, 280
Political equilibrium, principle of, 6, 98
Potemkin, Petr Ivanovich, 81
Pradier-Fodéré, Paul Louis Ernest, 120, 136, 144, 145, 177
Pragmatic Sanction, 82, 192, 321
Prague Congress (1813), 178
Prague, Treaty of (1866), 110, 282
Pressburg Peace (1805), 92
Pretlack, Johann Franz von, 235
Preuss, Hugo, 188
Prida, Joaquin Fernandez, xxiv
Privateers, 300, 320, 321
Prize courts, 149, 211

Prussia-United States treaty (1785), 320
Prutz, Hans, 63
Puchta, Georg Friedrich, 7
Pufendorf, Samuel, xi, 123, 127, 312
Pustogarov, V. V., xxviii-xxx, xxxii, liii
Putin, Vladimir Vladimirovich, xxxvii, lvi
Pütter, Karl Theodor, 25, 58-61
Pypin, Aleksandr Nikolaevich, 269

Quaritsch, Dr., 135

Rachel, Samuel, xi, 127
Rambeau, -, 80
Ranconi, Leone, 116
Ranke, Leopold von, 32, 65, 72, 74, 79, 82, 83, 94, 171, 233
Rashtatt (Rastadt), Congress of (1799), 90, 96
Raumer, Friedrich von, 68
Reeves, John, 59
Renan, Ernest, 116
Renault, Louis, 14, 136, 144, 164
Resch, Peter, 135
Rhine Navigation Commission, 166
Rhine Union, 93
Richard, _, 115
Richelieu, Cardinal Armand Jean du Plessis, 67
Rimskii-Korsakov, Alexander Mikhailovich, 91
Ritter von Poschinger, Heinrich, 188, 189
Rivier, Alphonse Pierre Octave, 120, 137, 193, 214, 216, 219, 236, 248, 275, 278, 287
Rolin-Jaequemyns, Gustave, 281, 291, 336
Rönne, Ludwig von, 190
Rosenkrantz, Karl, 172
Rousseau, Jean-Jacques, xiv, 170
Rousset de Missy, Jean, 128
Rozhdestvenskii, Zinovii Petrovich, lii
Rüdiger, -, 115
Rumiantsev, Nikolai Petrovich, xlix
Russell, Lord John, 215, 222
Russian-American Company, 279
Russian Society of International Law, 153
Russo-German Convention on judicial relations (1879), 329
Rüttimann, Johann Jacob, 196
Rydin, Herman Ludvig, 193
Ryswyck, Peace of (1697), 74

Saint Petersburg Declaration (1868), 6, 324
Saint-Pierre, Abbot, xiv, 171, 172
Salomon, Charles, 277
San Stefano, Treaty of (1878), 113, 114, 200, 201, 209-212, 323
Saripolos, Nikkolaos, 285
Sartorius, Johann Baptiste, xiv, 173
Savigny, Friedrich Carl von, 51, 53, 54, 150
Scala, Rudolf von, 37
Schlief, Eugen, 196, 219, 271
Schmalz, Theodore, 323
Schneidewin, Max Paul Ernst, 32, 35
Schneller, Hans, 287
Schöll, Frédéric, 25
Schömann, Georg Friedrich, 32, 35
Schön, Wilhelm Freiherr von, lv
Schönbrun treaty (1809), 94
Schubert, Friedrich Wilhelm, 172
Schulze, Hermann Johann Friedrich, 135, 190

Schuyler, Eugene, 315
Second Silesian War, 83
Seebohm, Frederic, 162
Selden, John, 296
Sell, -, 50
Serrano, Marshall Francisco, 246
Seven Years War, 84, 85, 88
Shalland, Lev Adamovich, lvii, 270
Shestakov, Lev Nikitich, xxv
Shi Jiuyong, lvi
Shishkin, Nikkolai Pavlovich, xlix
Shneider, Ekaterina Wilhelmina von, xxix
Sidorenko, L., xxx
Simson, Eval'd Karlovich, xlix, lvii, 277
Skobolev, Mikhail Dmitrievich, 259
Slave trade, 102, 103, 176, 257-263, 317, 339
Smith-Stanley, Edward, 14th Earl of Derby, 333
Solov'ev, Vladimir Sergeevich,117
Sorel, Albert, xii, 88, 136, 192, 227, 281
Sovin, Petr G., 77
Spanish succession, war of, 75
Spinoza, Baruch (Benedict de), xi, 123
Stael-Holstein, Anne Louise Germaine, 115
Stein, Heinrich Friedrich Karl vom und zum, x, 100
Stein, Lorenz von, xii, xxxiii, 1, 2, 18, 104, 188, 232
Stern, Alfred, 105, 106
Sternegg, Inama, 275
Stoeckl, Eduard de, 222
Stoerk, Felix, 147, 281
Stoianov, A. N., xii, 137, 139, 326
Stolbovo, Peace of (1617), 77
Story, Joseph, 196
Strathclyde, 301
Strauch, Hermann, 236
Strousberg, Bethel Henry, 227
Suarez, Francisco, xi, 120
Sully, Duke of, 171
Sumner, Charles, 227, 315
Suvorov, Alexander Vasil'evich, 91
Sybel, Heinrich von, 64

Talleyrand-Périgord, Charles Maurice de, x, 98, 100, 101
Taube, K. F. von, 134
Taube, Mikhail Aleksandrovich von, xxxii, xlviii, xlix, lii, lvii, 60
Telesnitskii, -, 309
Teschen Congress (1779), 87, 88, 178, 322
Tevfik-Pasha, 200
Textor, Johann Wolfgang, 127
Thaine, Hippolyte Adolphe, 3, 57, 70, 89
Thierry, Augustin, 52
Thirty Years War, 121
Thomasius, Christian, xi,123
Thon, August, 7
Thucydides, 26
Thurn and Taxis, Princes von, 252, 289
Tianjin, Sino-Russian Treaty of (1858), 292
Tillet, Jean du, 128
Tilsit Peace (1807), 221, 294, 332
Tinsch, Heinrich, 190
Tisdale, Mr., 314
Tocqueville, Alexis de, 70, 196
Tolstoi, Iurii Vasil'evich, 77
Tomsinov, Vladimir Alekseevich, xxv
Treaty (1832) re: Greek independence, 333

Treaty (1856) re: Ottoman inviolability, 333
Treaty (1857) re: Neuchatel, 191
Treitschke, Heinrich von, 93, 100, 103, 106, 158, 188
Trendelenburg, Friedrich Adolf, 232
Troppau, Congress of (1820), 106, 175, 177, 228, 237
Tsvetaev, Dmitrii Vladimirovich, 269
Ture, Catherina, xxviii, xxix
Ture, Nikolai Andreevich, xxviii, xxix
Turin, Convention of (1860), 109, 282
Turkmenchai, Treaty of (1828), 298
Tuyll, Diderick Jacob van, 280
Twiss, Travers, 133, 183, 184, 192, 232, 270, 275

Ubri, Petr Iakovlevich, 317
Ul'ianitskii, V. A., 135
Unger, -, 311, 312
Universal Postal Union, 5, 166
Urusov, Prince A. M., 25
Utrecht, Peace of (1713), 75, 98, 259, 290

Vaçlik, Jean, 211
Valfrey, Jules Joseph, 111, 192
Van Kriecken, -, 157
Vandal, Albert, 94
Vashkevich, Michman, 148
Vasilii Ivanovich, Grand Prince, 80
Vattel, Emer, xi, 13, 125, 126, 216, 223, 254, 276, 278, 311, 312, 326, 329, 334
Vergé, Charles, 130
Verona, Congress of (1822), 106, 107, 175
Versailles Treaty of alliance (1756), 84
Versailles Treaty of peace (1783), 88, 214
Victor Emmanuel II, King, 246
Victor Emmanuel III, King, lv
Victoria, Queen, l, 191, 229, 250
Vienna, Treaty of (1809), 102
Vienna Treaty of (1814), 221
Vienna, Treaty of (1815), 211, 217, 237, 294, 305, 306, 323, 333
Vienna, Treaty of (1864), 110
Villafranca, Treaty of (1859), 109, 314
Virginius, 233, 234
Vixen, 303
Voigt, Moritz, 46, 50, 51
Vorontsov, Mikhail Illarion, 83

Wachsmuth, Wilhelm, 38
Wagner, Adolph, 116
Waitz, Theodor, 26
Walker, Thomas Alfred, 25, 133
Walter, Ferdinand, 42
Ward, Robert Plumer, 25, 43, 49, 59-61
Wehberg, H., xxxi, l, li
Weiss, André, 49
Welzhofer, -, 157
Wenck, Friedrich August Wilhelm, 83, 128, 330
Westlake, John, 252
Westphalia, Peace of, 21, 22, 67-69, 72, 73, 88, 96-98, 128, 176, 214
Wheaton, Henry, xi, 1, 13, 21, 25, 39, 51, 74, 132, 172, 182, 188, 223, 231, 232, 240, 244, 249, 278, 297, 305, 319, 326, 331
Wheeler, James Talboys, 29
Whewell, William, 120, 121
White, Andrew Dickson, lv

Wilberforce, William, 259
Wilhelm II, Emperor, lv
Wilhelm III, Emperor, 93
William I, Elector of Hesse, 218
William of Orange, viii, 73, 217, 246, 247
William the Conqueror, 65
Wolff, Christian von, xi, 123-125
Woolsey, Theodore Dwight, 142, 146, 234, 272, 303
Wurm, Christian Friedrich, 312
Zablotskii-Desiatovskii, Andrei Parfenovich, 208
Zaleski, Witold, 157, 177
Zamiatin, A., xxv
Zorn, Philipp, 1
Zouche, Richard, xi, 14, 126, 127
Zubov, Platon, xiv, 173
Zurich, Treaty of (1859), 109, 224